空手

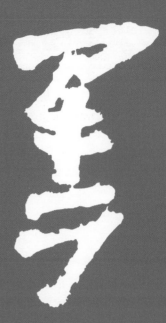

translation and english-language adaptation
YOKO UMEZAWA, JO DUFFY, STUDIO PROTEUS,
and **DARK HORSE COMICS**

graphics adaptation and sound-effects lettering
DAVID SCHMIT *for* **DIGIBOX**
and **ÉDITIONS GLÉNAT**

digital lettering and additional graphics adaptation
DIGITAL CHAMELEON
and **DARK HORSE COMICS**

publisher
MIKE RICHARDSON

original series editor
KOICHI YURI

editor
CHRIS WARNER

consulting editors
TOREN SMITH *and* **DANA LEWIS** *for* **STUDIO PROTEUS**

collection designer
LIA RIBACCHI

art director
MARK COX

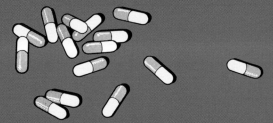

AKIRA BOOK FIVE

The artwork of this volume has been produced as a mirror-image of the original Japanese edition to conform to English-language standards.

Published by Dark Horse Comics, Inc., 10956 S.E. Main Street, Milwaukie, OR 97222 • www.darkhorse.com

To find a comics shop in your area, call the Comic Shop Locator Service toll-free at 1-888-266-4226

First edition: December 2001 • ISBN: 1-56971-527-0

Printed in Canada • 10 9 8 7 6 5 4 3 2 1

AKIRA

KATSUHIRO OTOMO

BOOK FIVE

THE STORY SO FAR

21st century Neo-Tokyo stands on the ashes of Tokyo, destroyed four decades earlier by the mind of a child — the mind of Akira. Subject of a military project gone horribly wrong, Akira was placed in cryogenic hibernation after the holocaust until his infinite powers could be harnessed. The other survivors of "The Project," formidable psychics withering away in children's bodies, know that one day Akira will awaken.

Enter Tetsuo, an angry young member of a motorcycle gang led by his friend Kaneda. A violent accident sets off within Tetsuo dormant psychokinetic abilities that grow rapidly, as do a raging headache and a virulent madness. Tetsuo soon explodes in a psychic killing spree against friend and foe, turning Kaneda from blood-brother to mortal enemy. Tetsuo has not gone unnoticed by The Project's leader, the mysterious Colonel, who uses a super-drug to quell Tetsuo's agony while stimulating his powers and bringing Tetsuo under his thrall. But Tetsuo soon grows beyond the control of the Colonel and his psychics — Takashi, Masaru, and Kiyoko — and Tetsuo's discovery of Akira's existence foments within him the urge to confront the child super-being.

A vengeful Kaneda allies with a resistance group, including the beautiful Kei and her partner Ryu, in an attempt to kill Tetsuo and infiltrate the secret subterranean lab that houses the sleeping Akira. They enter the facility and find Tetsuo in combat with the Colonel's security forces. Tetsuo's psychic vibrations stir Akira, and the child emerges from his frozen prison. Tetsuo helps the bewildered child to the surface, but the frantic Colonel orders the gigantic laser cannon of the military satellite SOL to fire on Tetsuo and Akira. Tetsuo's arm is shredded, and the two become separated in the mayhem. Tetsuo disappears, but Kaneda and Kei find Akira and take him to safety.

A state of emergency blankets Neo-Tokyo as the population heads for shelter, the streets quarantined by military patrols and Caretaker robot sentries. Kaneda and Kei — along with Chiyoko, a powerful woman of the resistance — bring Akira to a yacht for safekeeping, but the duplicitous resistance leader, Nezu, takes Akira to use as a weapon against the government and orders the three killed. Chiyoko fights their way to freedom, and they invade Nezu's home and recapture Akira. The Colonel's forces eventually corner Akira, who for the first time in decades sees Masaru, Kiyoko, and Takashi. The reunion is cut short by Nezu, who in trying to kill Akira rather than let him fall into government hands, shoots Takashi, whose death triggers Akira's power. A titanic psychic wave surges through Neo-Tokyo, and the citizenry struggle desperately to survive the cataclysm. As the destruction subsides, Akira sits alone at ground zero. A lone figure approaches him through the wreckage. It is Tetsuo!

From the flooded ruins rises the Great Tokyo Empire, a small army of crazed zealots focused around Akira's miracles but under the malefic control of Tetsuo. The Empire seals itself off from the world, but undercover agents from the outside arrive to assess the threat. The Empire plans to neutralize its most immediate enemies, the child psychics and Lady Miyako — an enigmatic religious figure and Project survivor — whose temple is a haven for refugees. Tetsuo begins feeding the super-drug to "volunteers." Most die, but a handful develop the Power and become Empire shock troops. The infiltrators are caught and executed by the new psychics, but one operative, Yamada, evades capture.

Kei, Chiyoko, and Ryu have survived along with Masaru and Kiyoko, but Kaneda is nowhere to be found, assumed lost in the holocaust. Deprived of the super-drug, Masaru and Kiyoko are incapacitated, and Chiyoko and Kei set out to enlist the aid of Miyako, who gives them the drug and instructs them to return with Masaru and Kiyoko. Meanwhile, Ryu observes Yamada's escape and leaves to investigate. He finds the agent and offers his assistance to Yamada, who makes a beeline for Akira's stronghold. With Ryu gone, Empire spies kidnap Masaru and Kiyoko. Chiyoko and Kei return to find the children missing, and the two set off after their charges. They catch up to the Empire's soldiers and free Masaru, but Kiyoko's captors escape. Kei sets off for the Temple with Masaru while Chiyoko, wounded in battle, goes after Kiyoko.

Tetsuo also gives the drug to young women for his pleasure and amusement. They die in agony, all but Kaori, who palms the drug. She becomes Tetsuo's companion and Akira's nanny. Tetsuo has a series of confusing visions, and he realizes his thoughts are being manipulated by Akira. Tetsuo confronts the child, who draws Tetsuo into his mind and teleports him back to his chambers. Tetsuo withdraws in terror, having seen too far into the thoughts of the psychic colossus. He eventually comes to his senses and decides that Miyako might be of some use to him. He takes more drugs, kicking his power to new heights, and transports across space to Miyako's chamber. Miyako gives him the history of the Project and the revelation that the drug is designed to inhibit his psychic development. Only by going cold turkey will he become all he can — perhaps even a match for Akira. He leaves to contemplate his future.

Chiyoko recaptures Kiyoko but is trapped and further injured after narrowly escaping one of Tetsuo's newly bred psychics. Facing almost certain capture, the two are rescued by the Colonel, who takes them back to a still-intact facility manned by a scientist stricken with nicotine withdrawal. Kiyoko reveals that Masaru is in Miyako's temple, and the Colonel places her inside a Caretaker robot and begins the arduous journey through the rubble to the temple. He takes with him a special miniature targeting device for the super-laser of SOL.

Tetsuo begins his agonizing withdrawal. Tetsuo's lieutenant, upon discovering that Masaru has reached safety in Miyako's shrine, is unable to get through to his anguished master and takes matters into his own hands by organizing an assault on the temple. Many innocent refugees and monks are killed, but the attack is eventually repelled, partially by the psychic skills of the temple's priests and finally by Kei taking Tetsuo's lieutenant hostage. She eventually lets him go, but he vows to return.

Tetsuo appears to Ryu and Yamada and tells them that he has seen the American fleet not far from shore, ready to attack, but unwilling to get too close due to the power of Akira. Yamada tries to shoot Tetsuo, who easily stops him, and then he disappears as quickly as he appeared.

As the Colonel nears the Temple, a second attack by the Empire begins. Cornered, the Colonel prepares to unleash the power of SOL. Kei, Masaru, Miyako, and her monks retreat to the citadel of the temple as a final stronghold. At that moment, Tetsuo appears, half-mad with pain, demanding drugs from Miyako. As the superlaser of SOL ignites, Tetsuo rises howling into the air, unleashing his power and tossing wrecked skyscrapers about like so many toys. But Tetsuo goes on, transcending time and space, reliving his birth, and eventually arriving at...Akira. Tetsuo falls to his knees before his master.

And in the vast wasteland of ruined Neo-Tokyo, Kaneda suddenly appears...

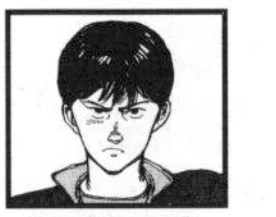
KANEDA

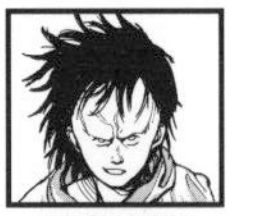
TETSUO

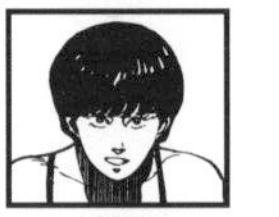
KEI

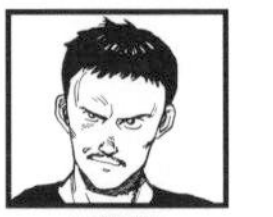
RYU

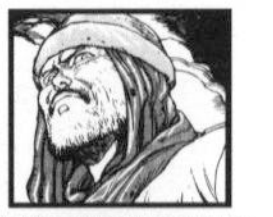
THE COLONEL

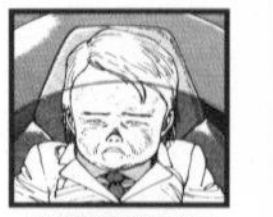
MASARU

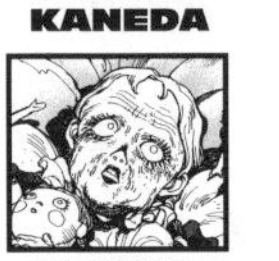
KIYOKO

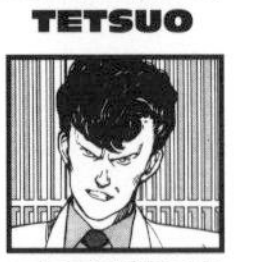
TETSUO'S AIDE

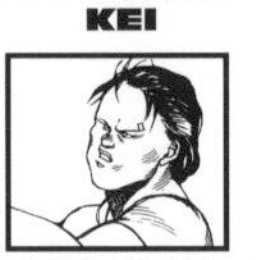
CHIYOKO

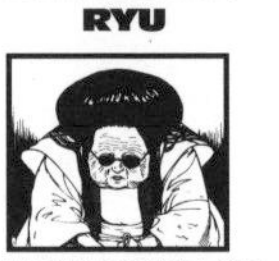
LADY MIYAKO

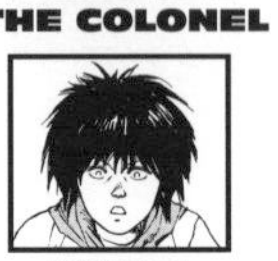
KAORI

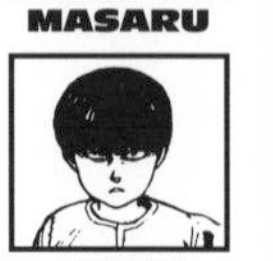
AKIRA

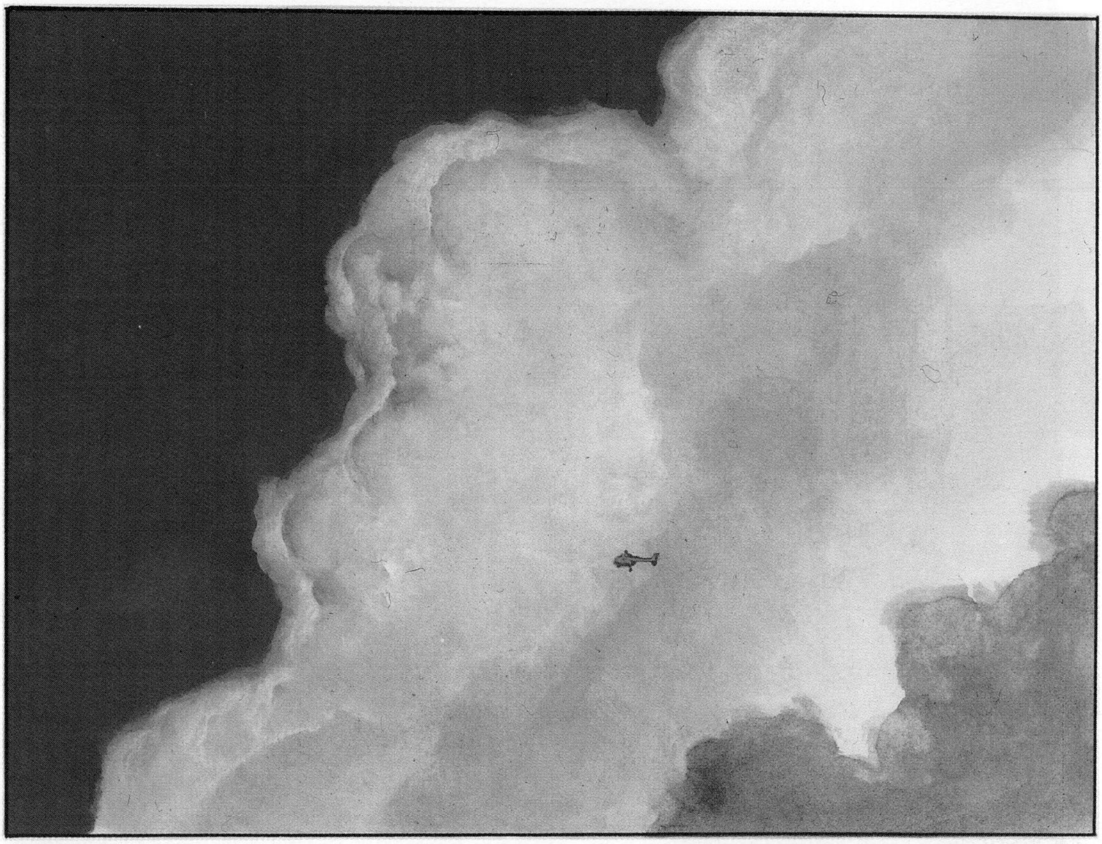

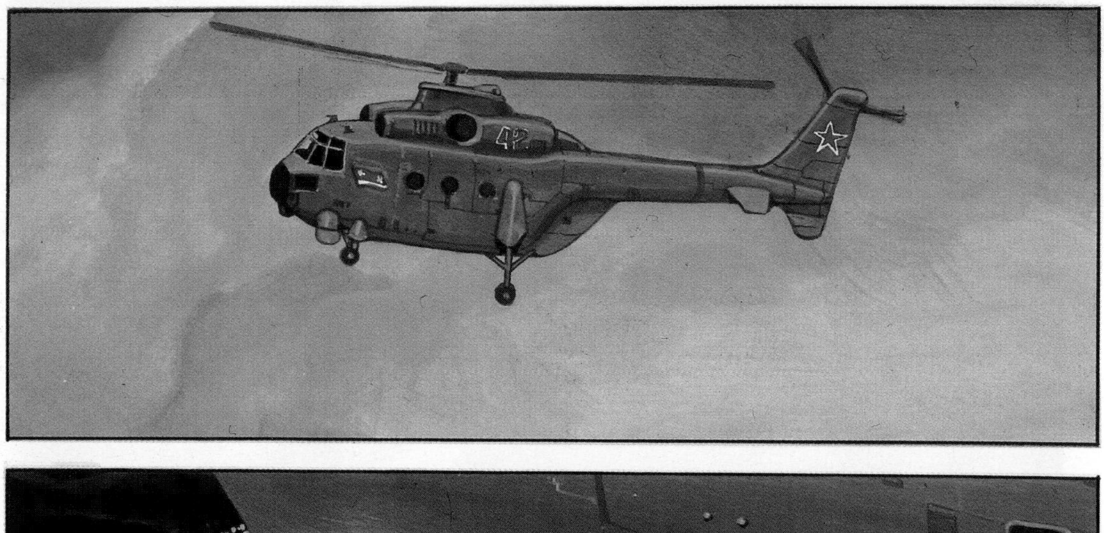

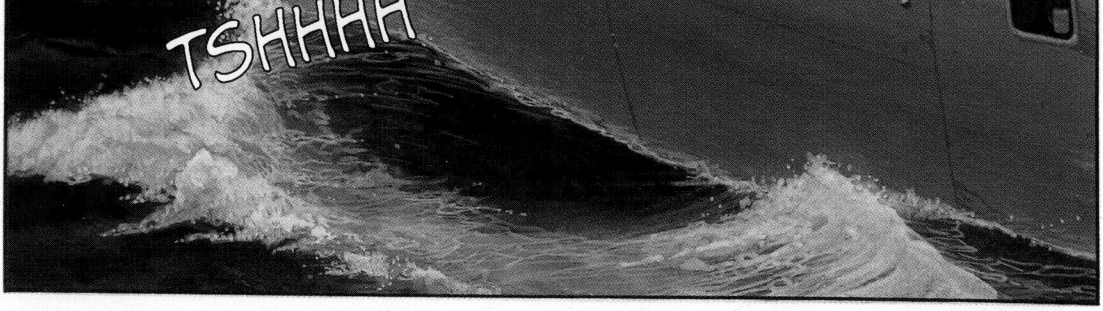
TSHHHH

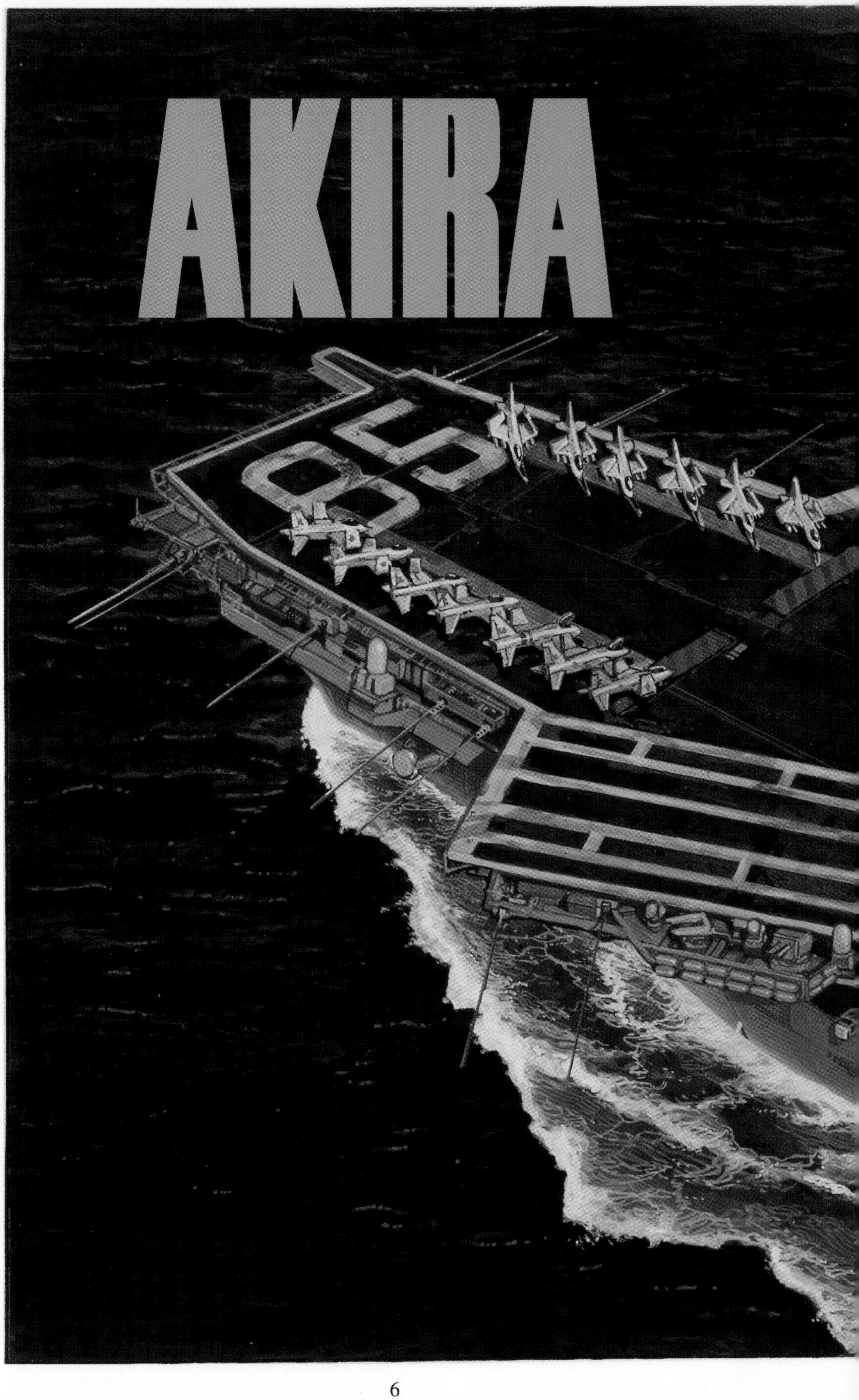
AKIRA

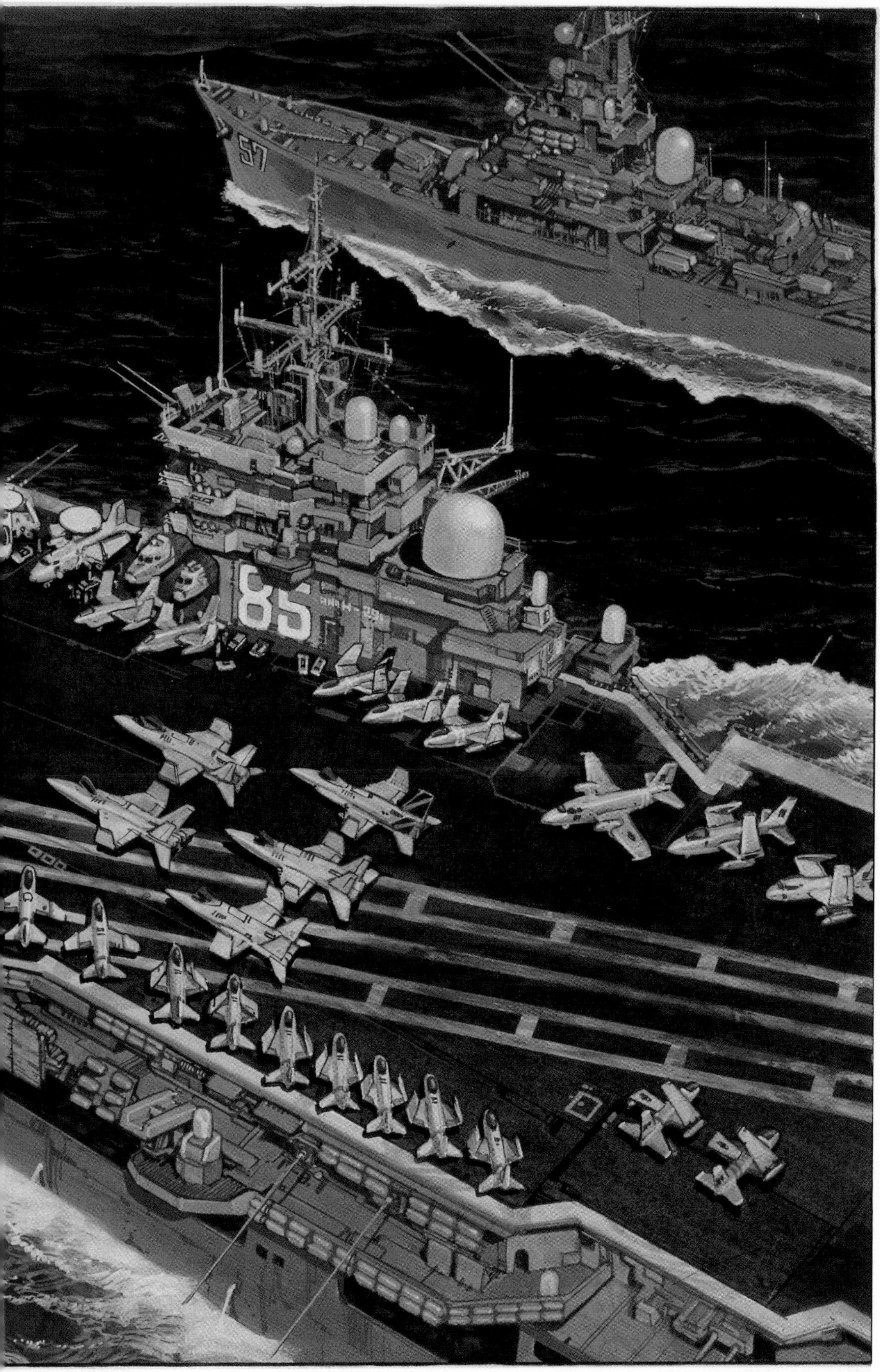
57
85

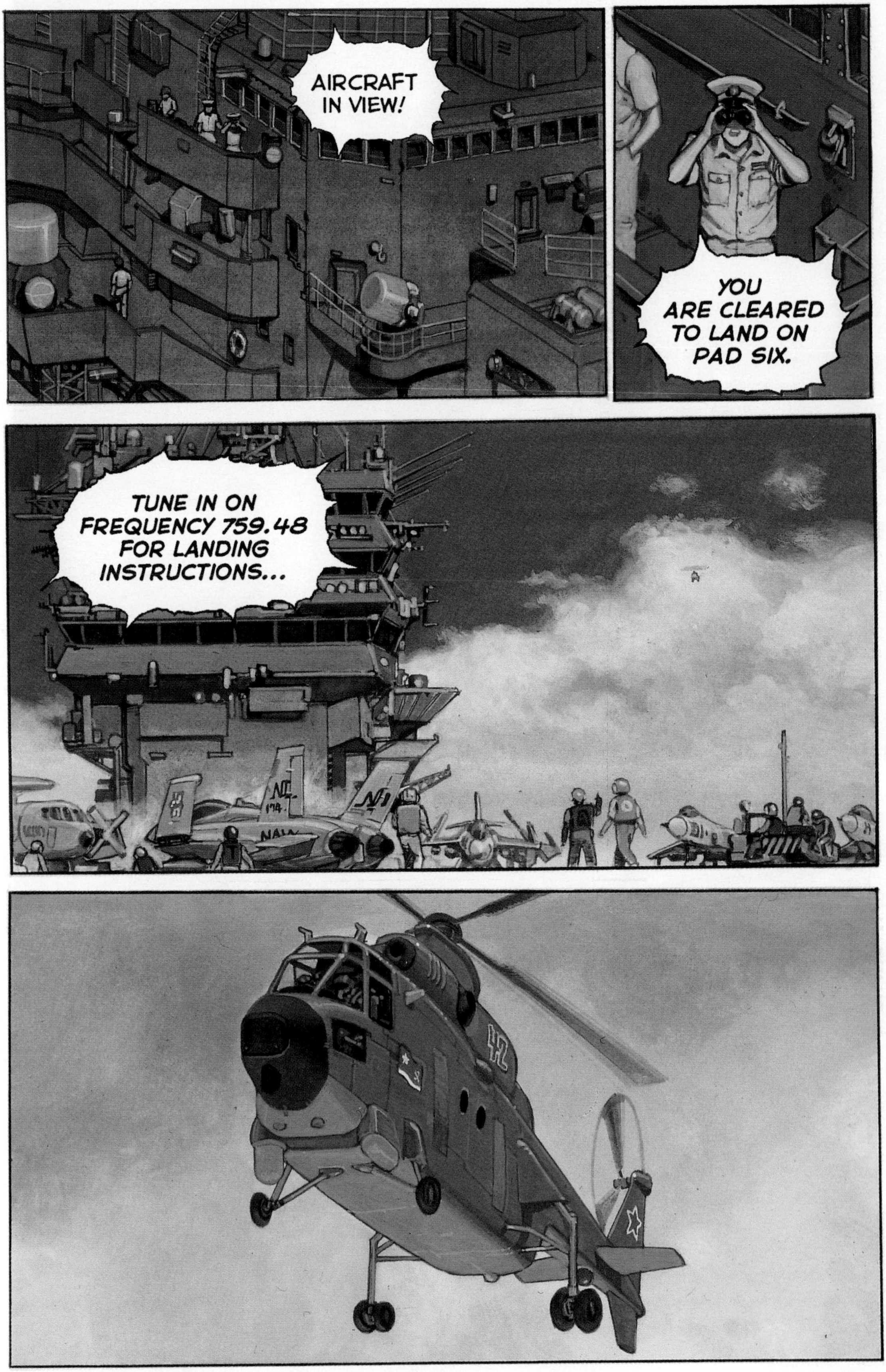
AIRCRAFT IN VIEW!
YOU ARE CLEARED TO LAND ON PAD SIX.
TUNE IN ON FREQUENCY 759.48 FOR LANDING INSTRUCTIONS...

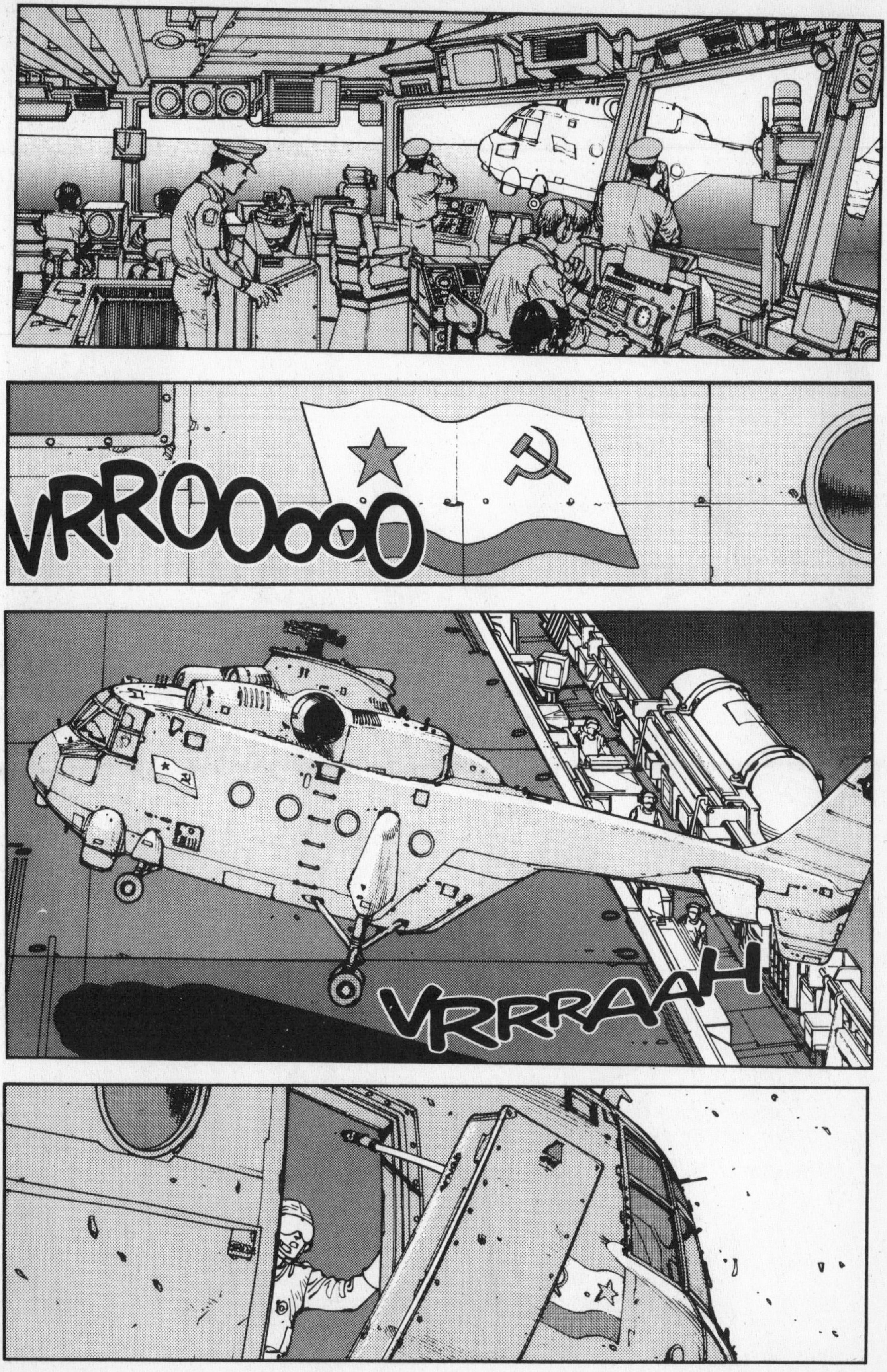
VRROOoooO
VRRRAAH

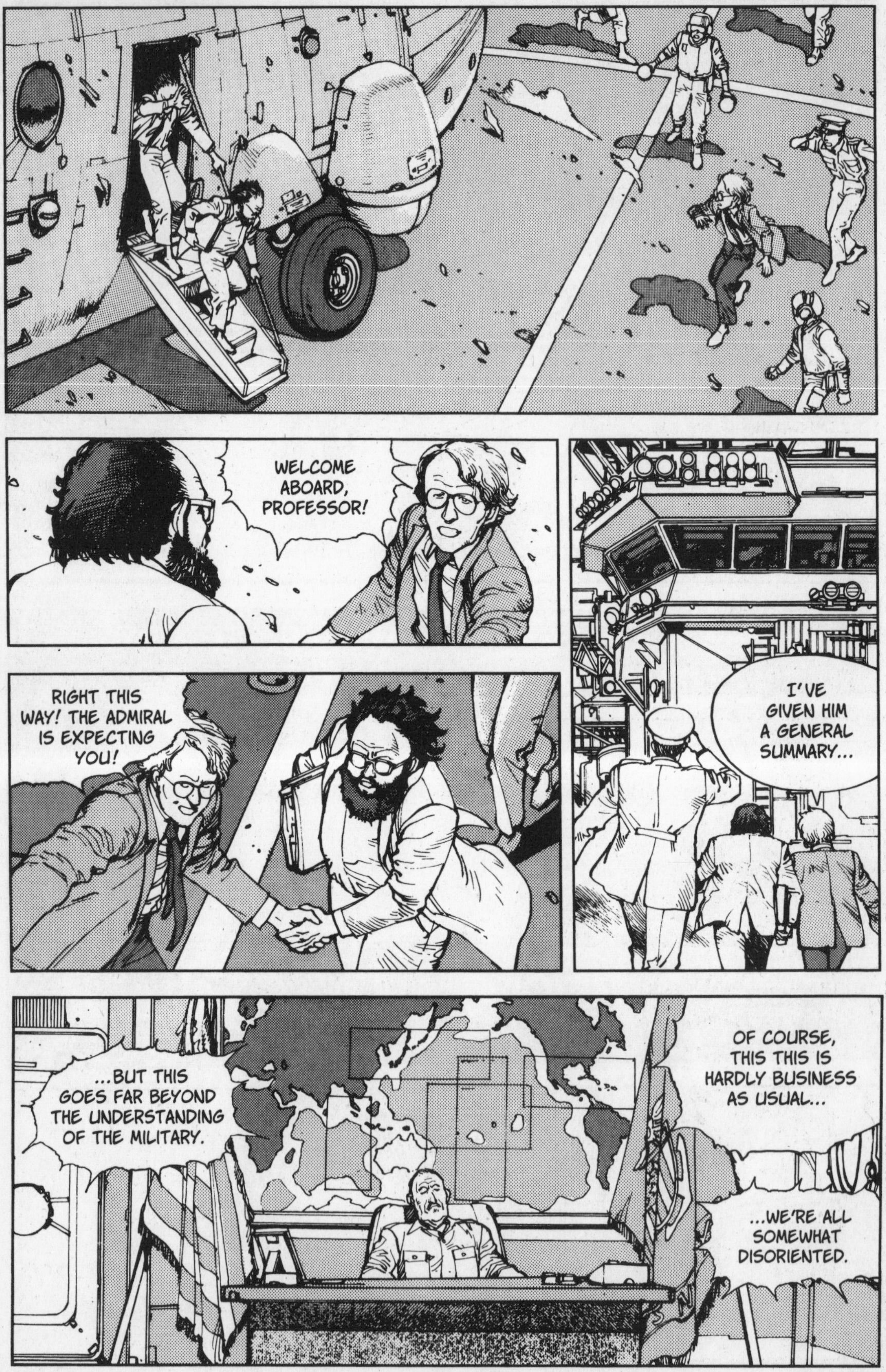
WELCOME ABOARD, PROFESSOR!
RIGHT THIS WAY! THE ADMIRAL IS EXPECTING YOU!
I'VE GIVEN HIM A GENERAL SUMMARY...
...BUT THIS GOES FAR BEYOND THE UNDERSTANDING OF THE MILITARY.
OF COURSE, THIS THIS IS HARDLY BUSINESS AS USUAL...
...WE'RE ALL SOMEWHAT DISORIENTED.

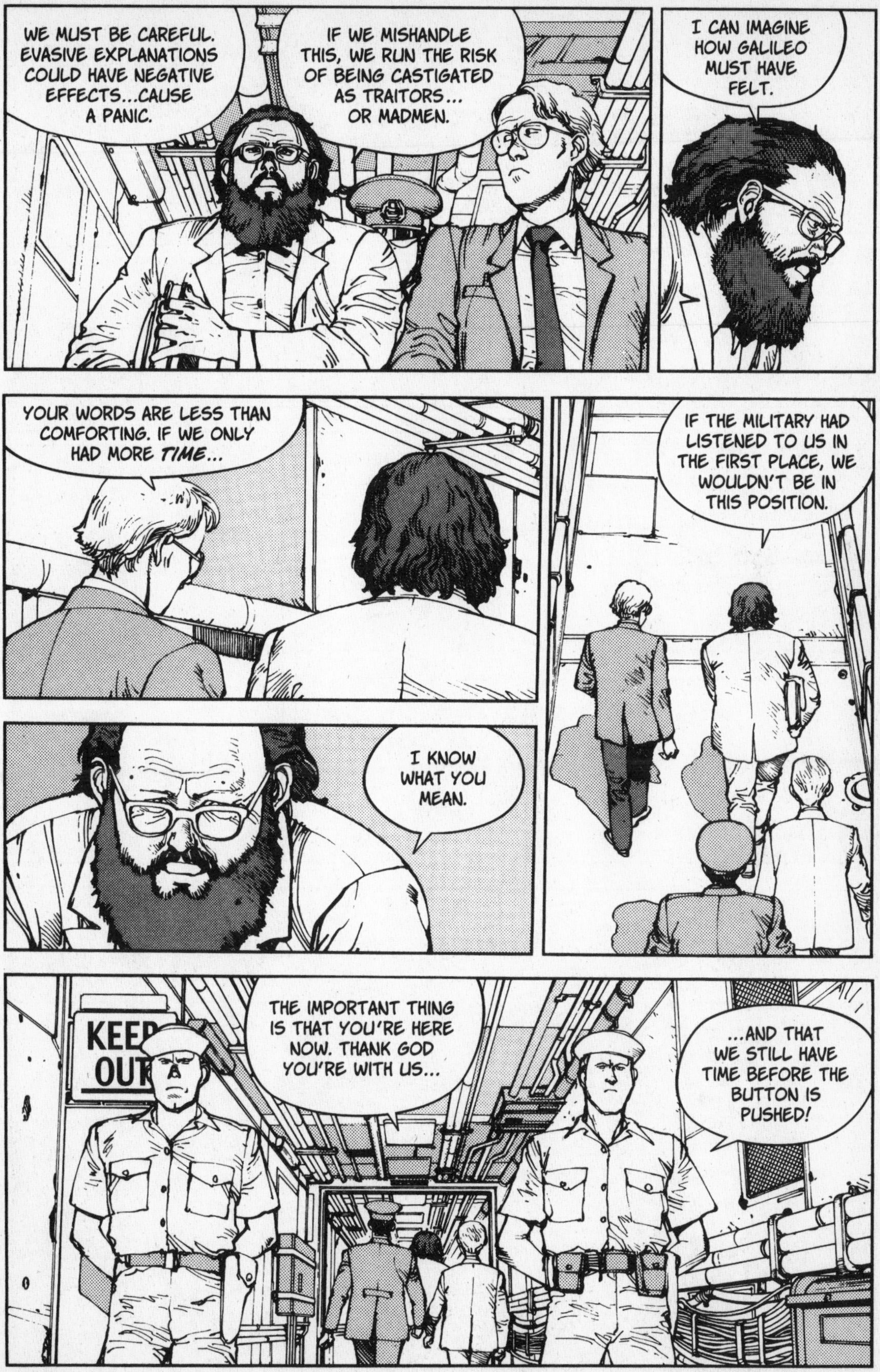
WE MUST BE CAREFUL. EVASIVE EXPLANATIONS COULD HAVE NEGATIVE EFFECTS...CAUSE A PANIC.
IF WE MISHANDLE THIS, WE RUN THE RISK OF BEING CASTIGATED AS TRAITORS... OR MADMEN.
I CAN IMAGINE HOW GALILEO MUST HAVE FELT.
YOUR WORDS ARE LESS THAN COMFORTING. IF WE ONLY HAD MORE *TIME*...
I KNOW WHAT YOU MEAN.
IF THE MILITARY HAD LISTENED TO US IN THE FIRST PLACE, WE WOULDN'T BE IN THIS POSITION.
KEEP OUT
THE IMPORTANT THING IS THAT YOU'RE HERE NOW. THANK GOD YOU'RE WITH US...
...AND THAT WE STILL HAVE TIME BEFORE THE BUTTON IS PUSHED!

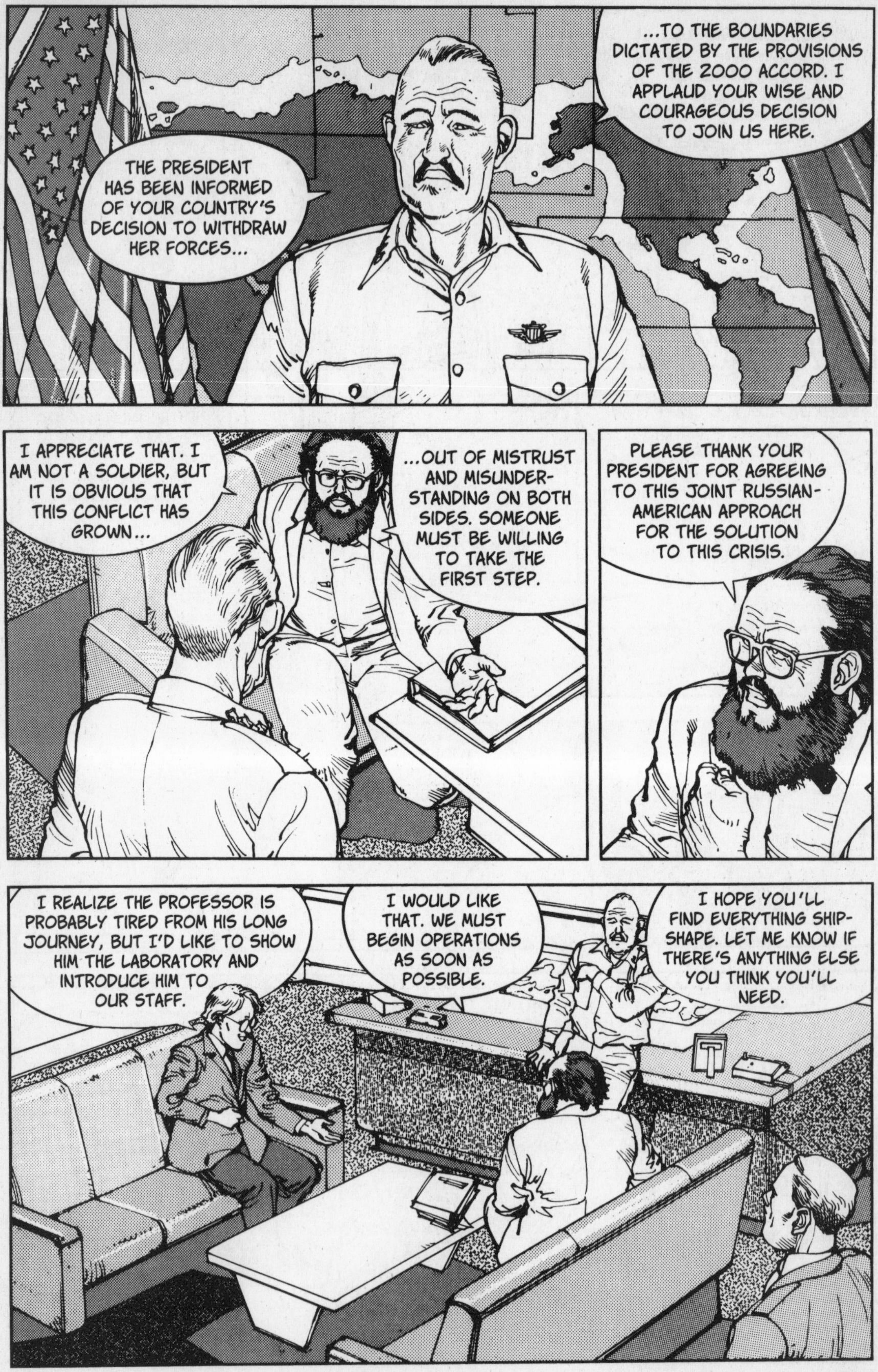
THE PRESIDENT HAS BEEN INFORMED OF YOUR COUNTRY'S DECISION TO WITHDRAW HER FORCES...
...TO THE BOUNDARIES DICTATED BY THE PROVISIONS OF THE 2000 ACCORD. I APPLAUD YOUR WISE AND COURAGEOUS DECISION TO JOIN US HERE.
I APPRECIATE THAT. I AM NOT A SOLDIER, BUT IT IS OBVIOUS THAT THIS CONFLICT HAS GROWN...
...OUT OF MISTRUST AND MISUNDER-STANDING ON BOTH SIDES. SOMEONE MUST BE WILLING TO TAKE THE FIRST STEP.
PLEASE THANK YOUR PRESIDENT FOR AGREEING TO THIS JOINT RUSSIAN-AMERICAN APPROACH FOR THE SOLUTION TO THIS CRISIS.
I REALIZE THE PROFESSOR IS PROBABLY TIRED FROM HIS LONG JOURNEY, BUT I'D LIKE TO SHOW HIM THE LABORATORY AND INTRODUCE HIM TO OUR STAFF.
I WOULD LIKE THAT. WE MUST BEGIN OPERATIONS AS SOON AS POSSIBLE.
I HOPE YOU'LL FIND EVERYTHING SHIP-SHAPE. LET ME KNOW IF THERE'S ANYTHING ELSE YOU THINK YOU'LL NEED.

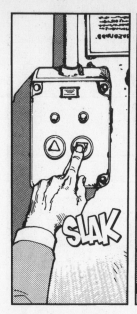

AN ELEVATOR...?

SPACE IS LIMITED, BUT OUR FACILITIES ARE FIRST-RATE.

SLAK

BY THE WAY... CERTAIN PARTS OF THE SHIP ARE POSTED AS BEING OFF-LIMITS. I'M AFRAID THAT APPLIES TO YOU.

OF COURSE. I UNDERSTAND.

PERFECT.

13

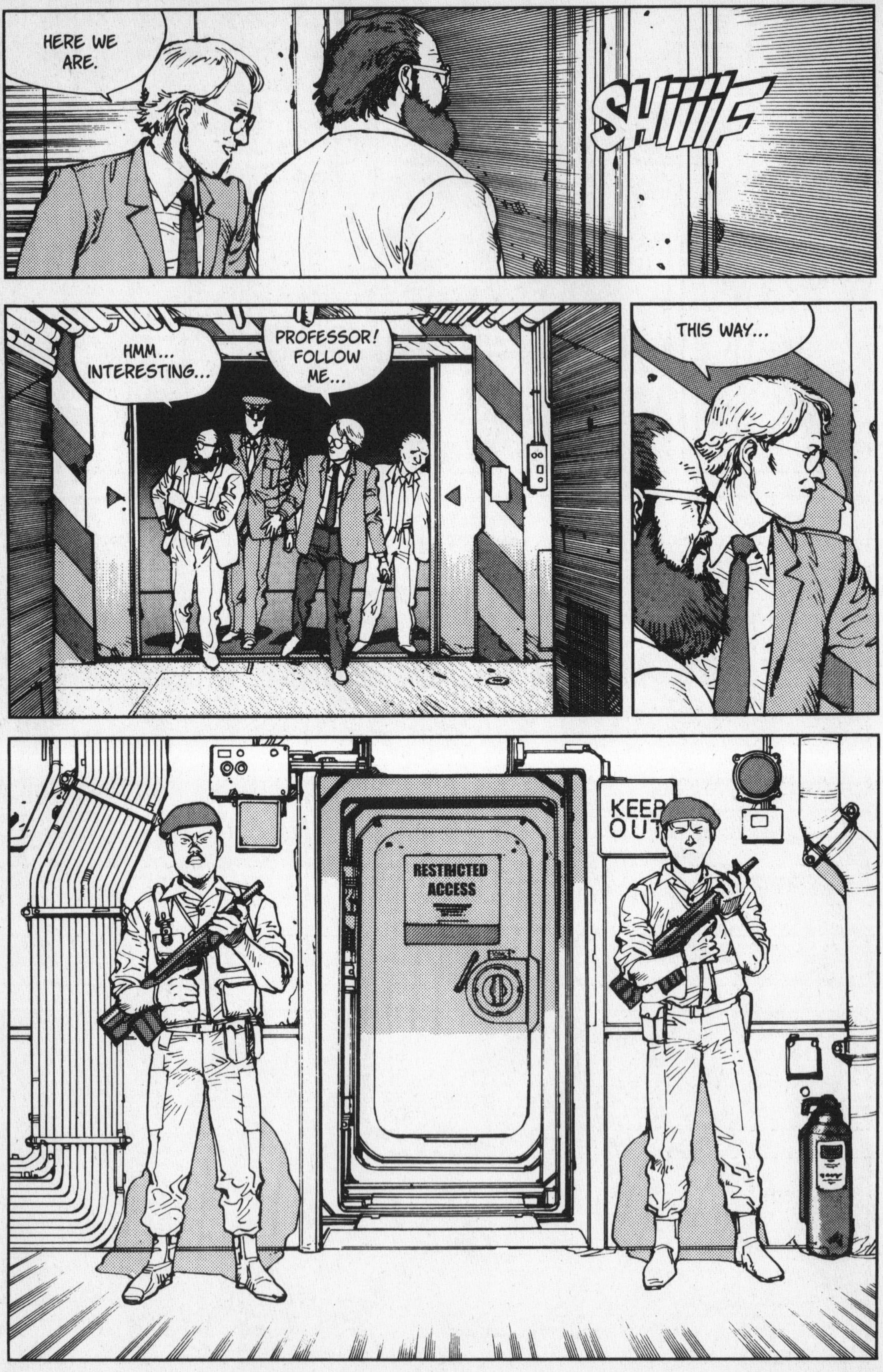
HERE WE ARE.
SHIIIIF
HMM... INTERESTING...
PROFESSOR! FOLLOW ME...
THIS WAY...
KEEP OUT
RESTRICTED ACCESS

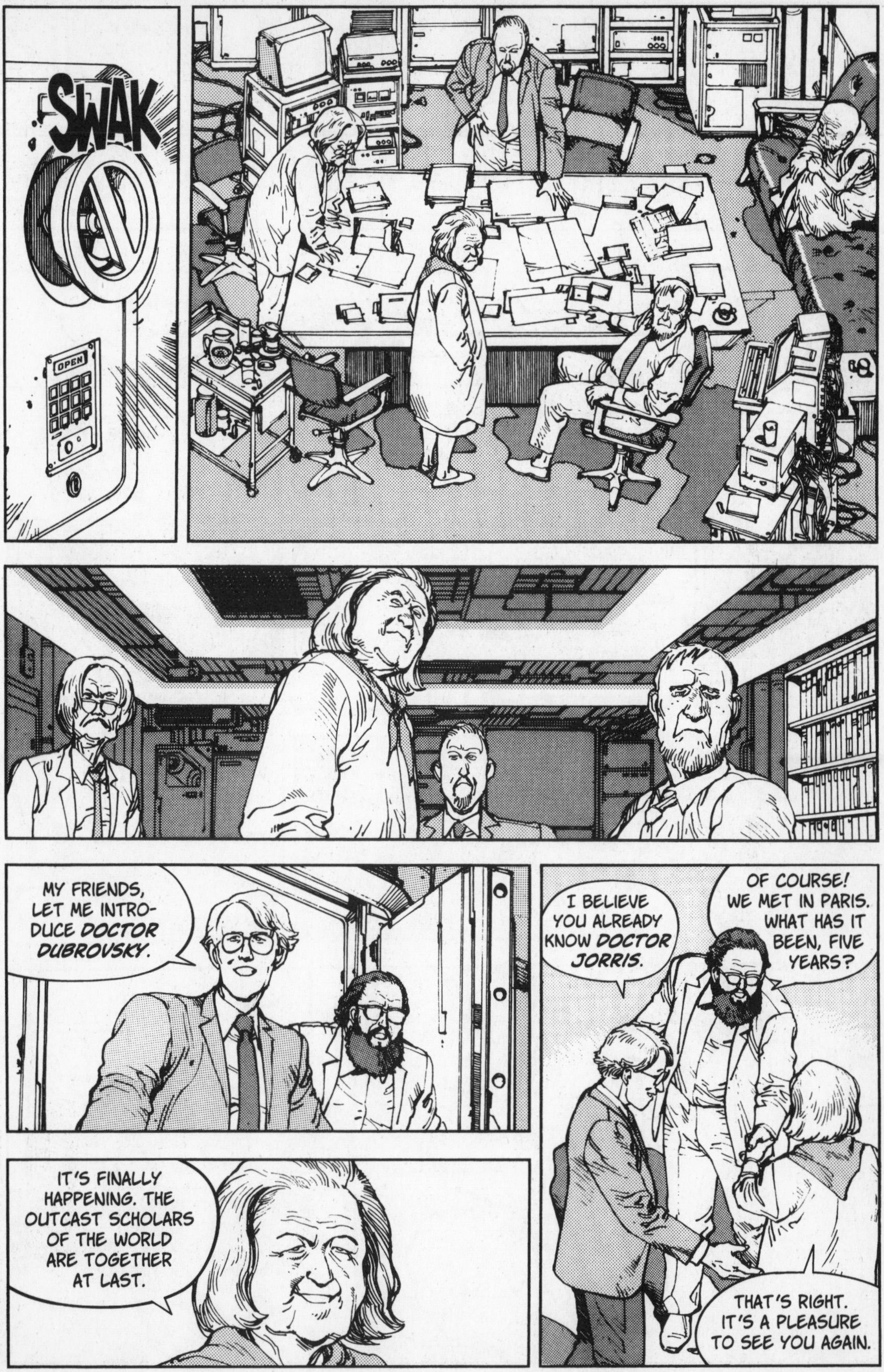
SWAK
OPEN
MY FRIENDS, LET ME INTRODUCE DOCTOR DUBROVSKY.
IT'S FINALLY HAPPENING. THE OUTCAST SCHOLARS OF THE WORLD ARE TOGETHER AT LAST.
I BELIEVE YOU ALREADY KNOW DOCTOR JORRIS.
OF COURSE! WE MET IN PARIS. WHAT HAS IT BEEN, FIVE YEARS?
THAT'S RIGHT. IT'S A PLEASURE TO SEE YOU AGAIN.

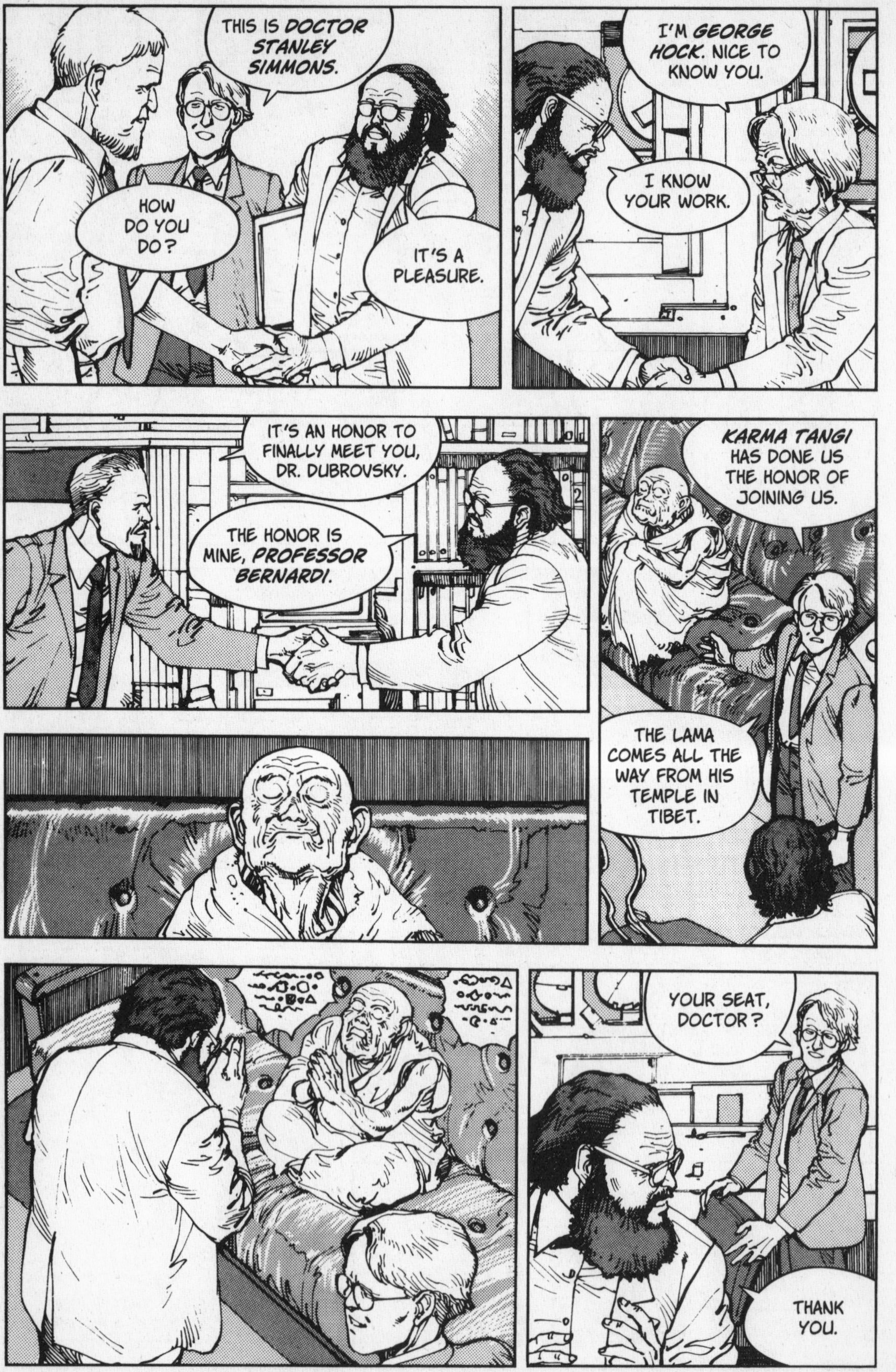
THIS IS *DOCTOR STANLEY SIMMONS*.
HOW DO YOU DO?
IT'S A PLEASURE.
I'M *GEORGE HOCK*. NICE TO KNOW YOU.
I KNOW YOUR WORK.
IT'S AN HONOR TO FINALLY MEET YOU, DR. DUBROVSKY.
THE HONOR IS MINE, *PROFESSOR BERNARDI*.
KARMA TANGI HAS DONE US THE HONOR OF JOINING US.
THE LAMA COMES ALL THE WAY FROM HIS TEMPLE IN TIBET.
YOUR SEAT, DOCTOR?
THANK YOU.

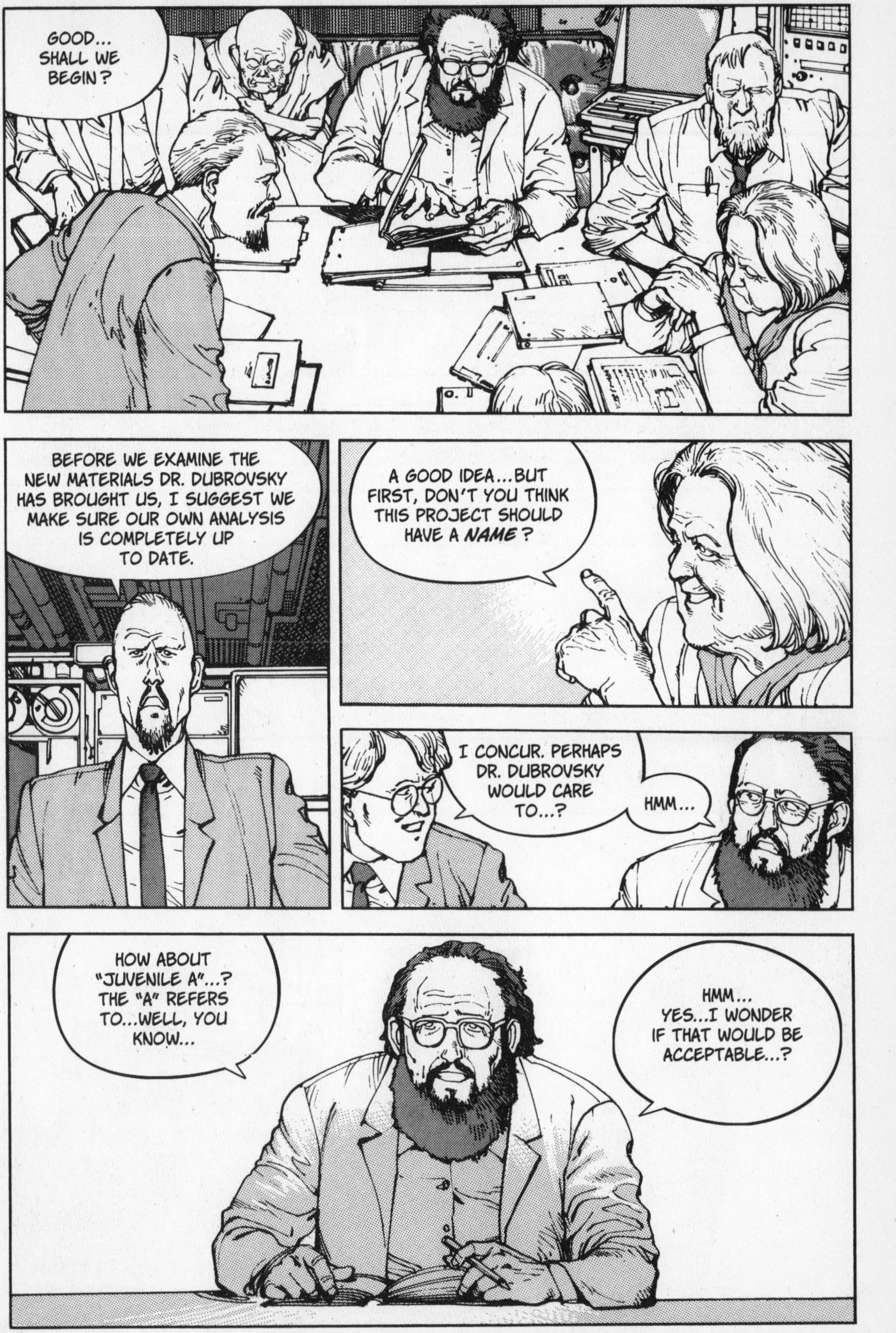
GOOD... SHALL WE BEGIN?
BEFORE WE EXAMINE THE NEW MATERIALS DR. DUBROVSKY HAS BROUGHT US, I SUGGEST WE MAKE SURE OUR OWN ANALYSIS IS COMPLETELY UP TO DATE.
A GOOD IDEA...BUT FIRST, DON'T YOU THINK THIS PROJECT SHOULD HAVE A *NAME*?
I CONCUR. PERHAPS DR. DUBROVSKY WOULD CARE TO...?
HMM...
HOW ABOUT "JUVENILE A"...? THE "A" REFERS TO...WELL, YOU KNOW...
HMM... YES...I WONDER IF THAT WOULD BE ACCEPTABLE...?

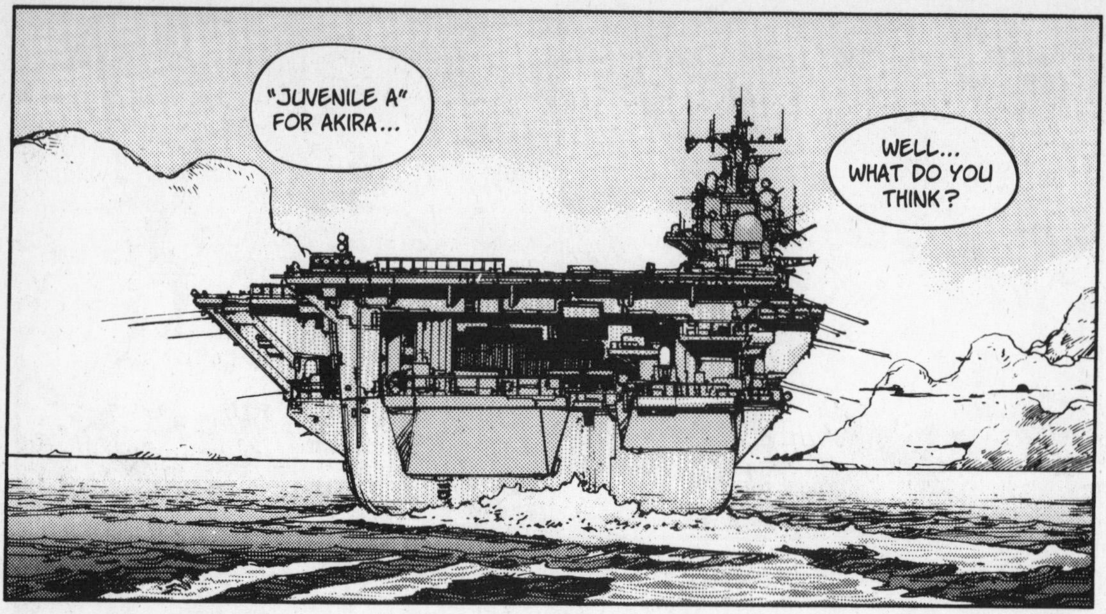
"JUVENILE A" FOR AKIRA...
WELL... WHAT DO YOU THINK?
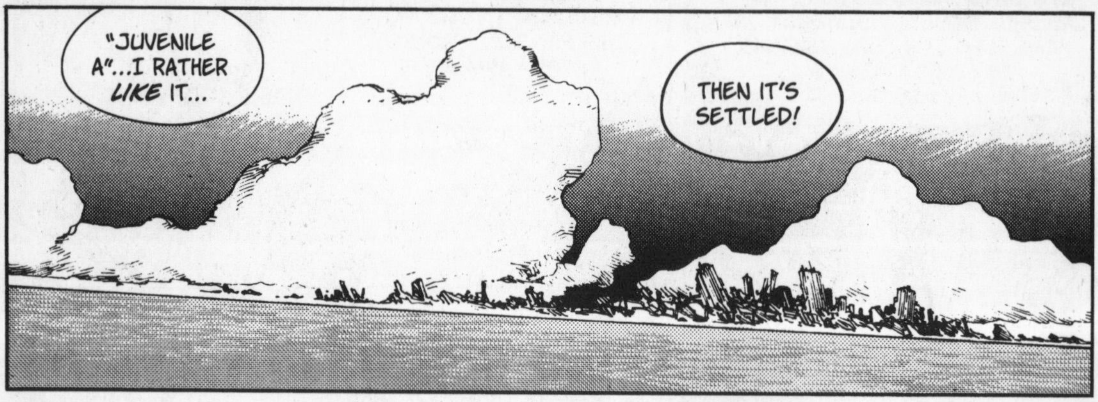
"JUVENILE A"...I RATHER LIKE IT...
THEN IT'S SETTLED!
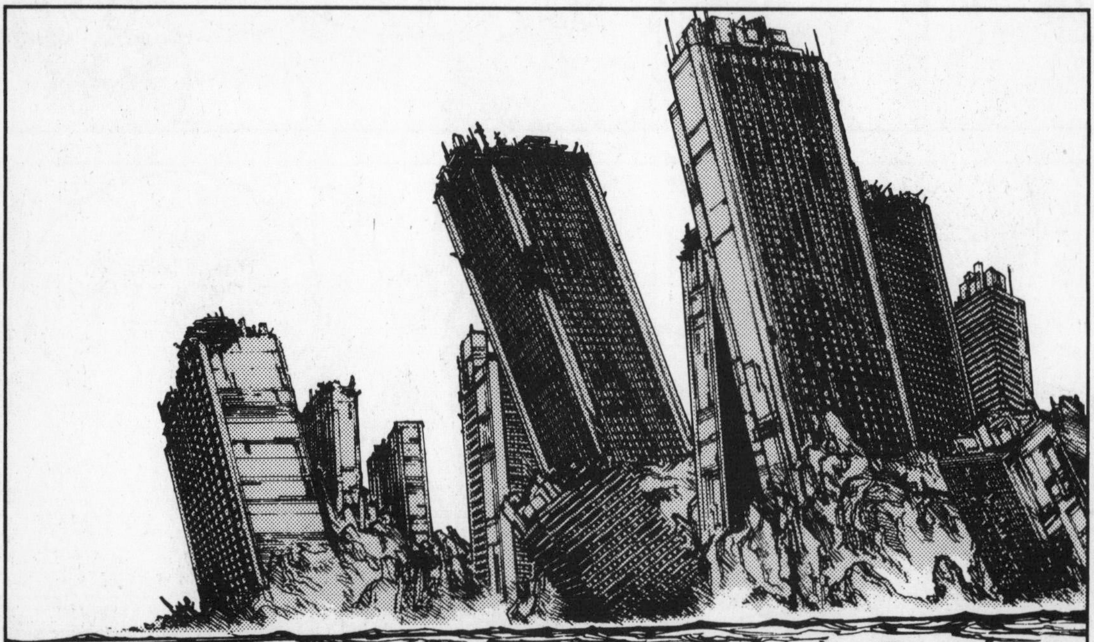

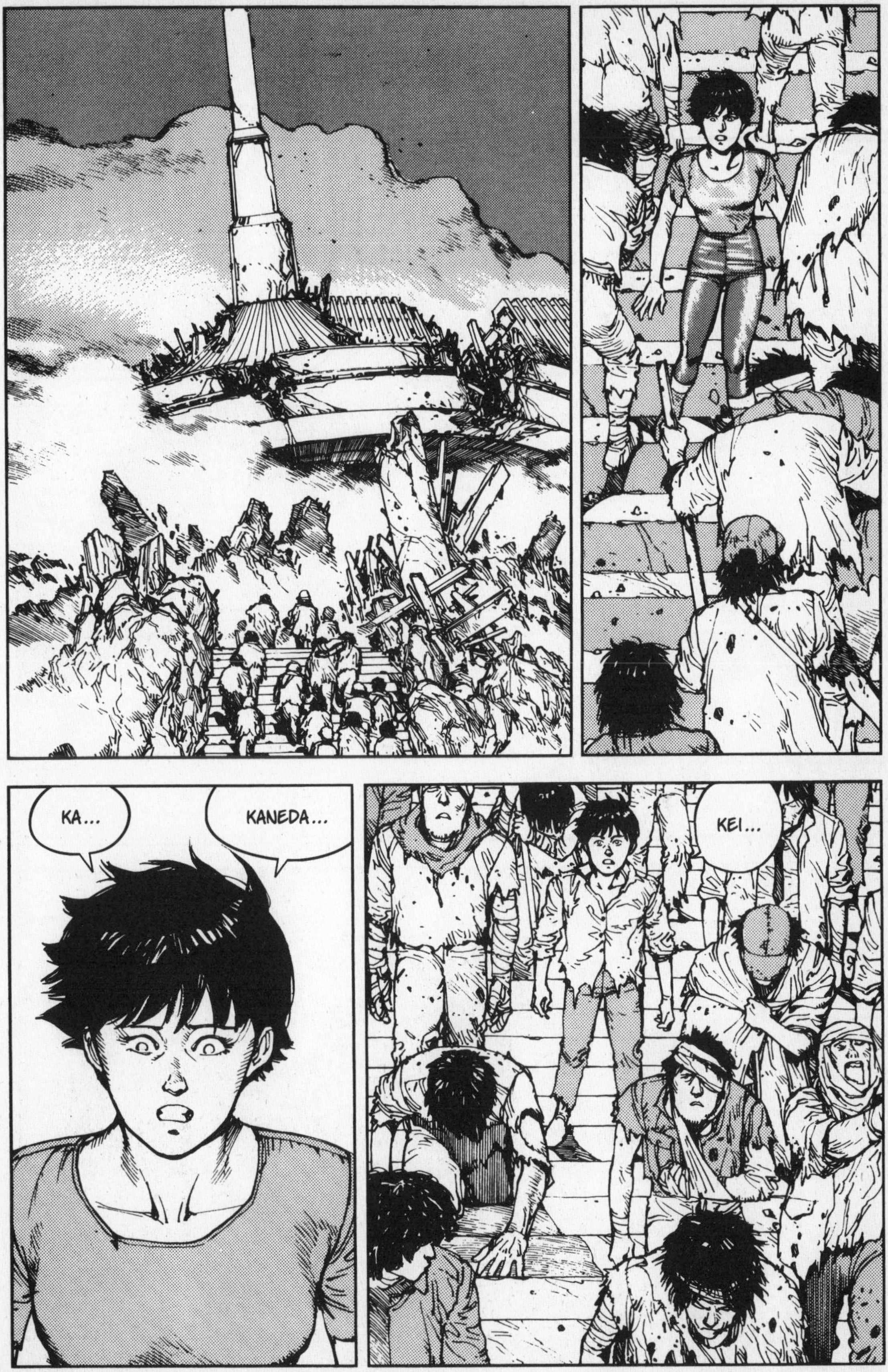
KA...
KANEDA...
KEI...

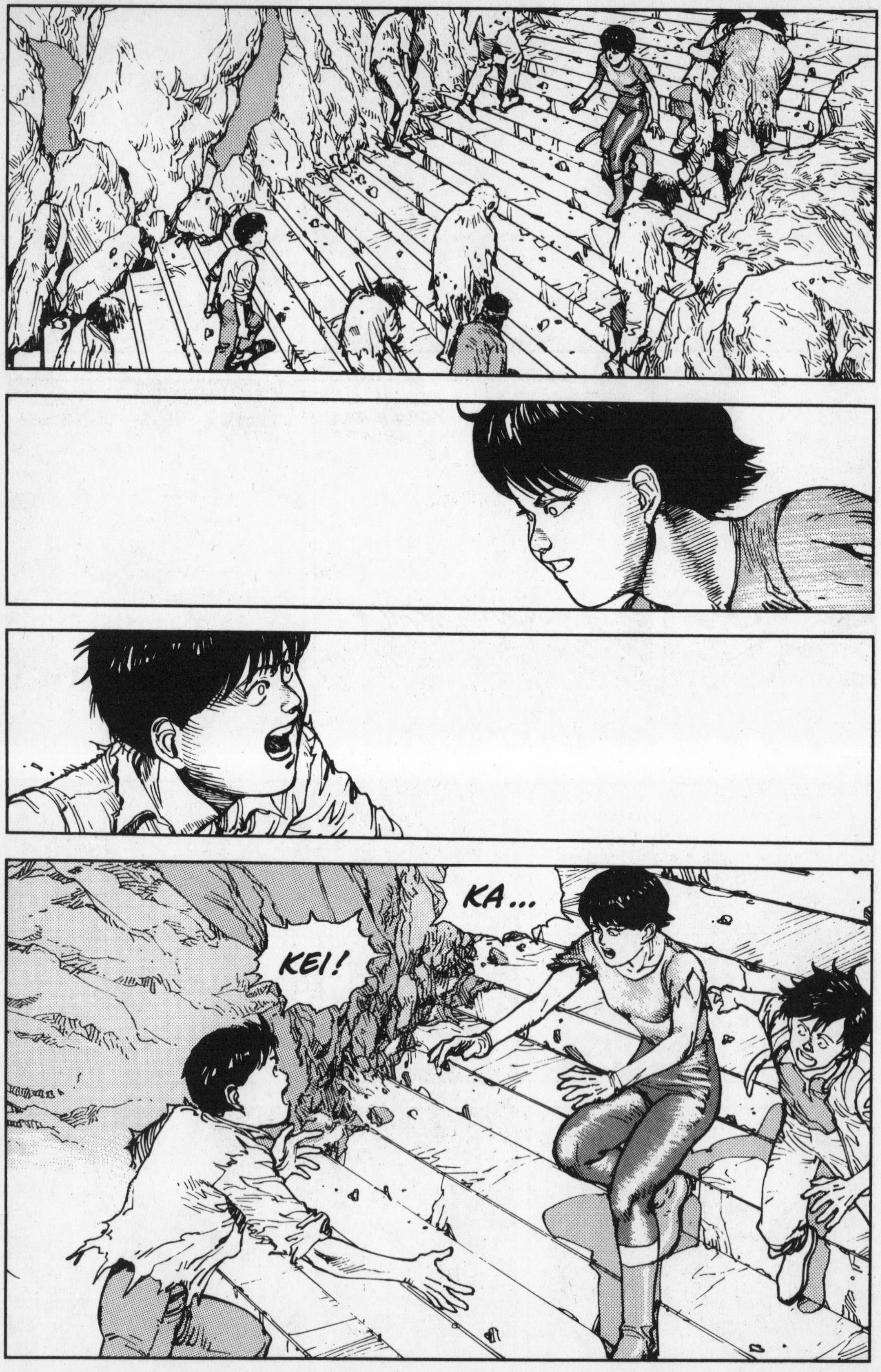
KEI!
KA...

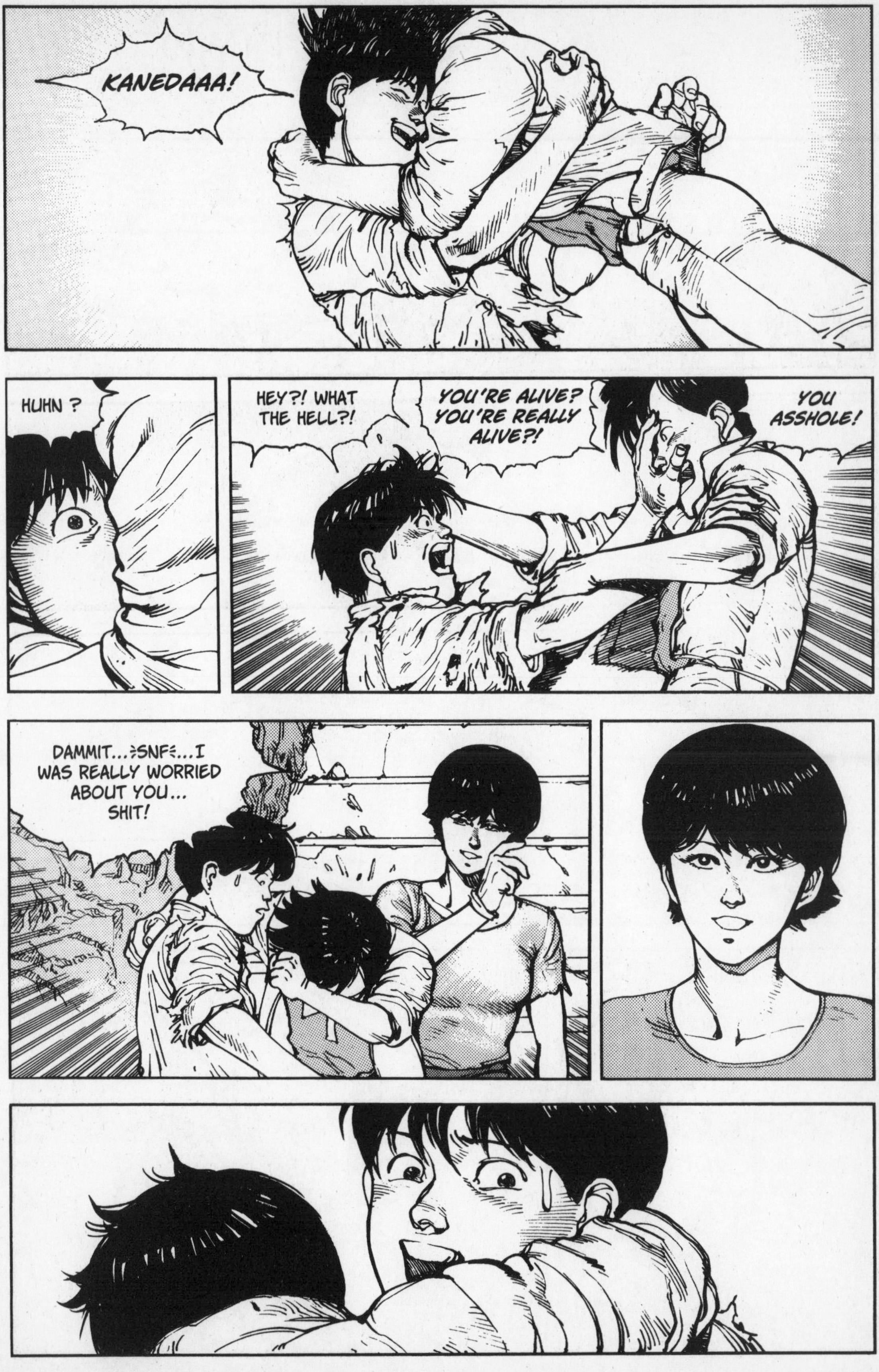
KANEDAAA!
HUHN ?
HEY?! WHAT THE HELL?!
YOU'RE ALIVE? YOU'RE REALLY ALIVE?!
YOU ASSHOLE!
DAMMIT...⋟SNF⋞...I WAS REALLY WORRIED ABOUT YOU... SHIT!

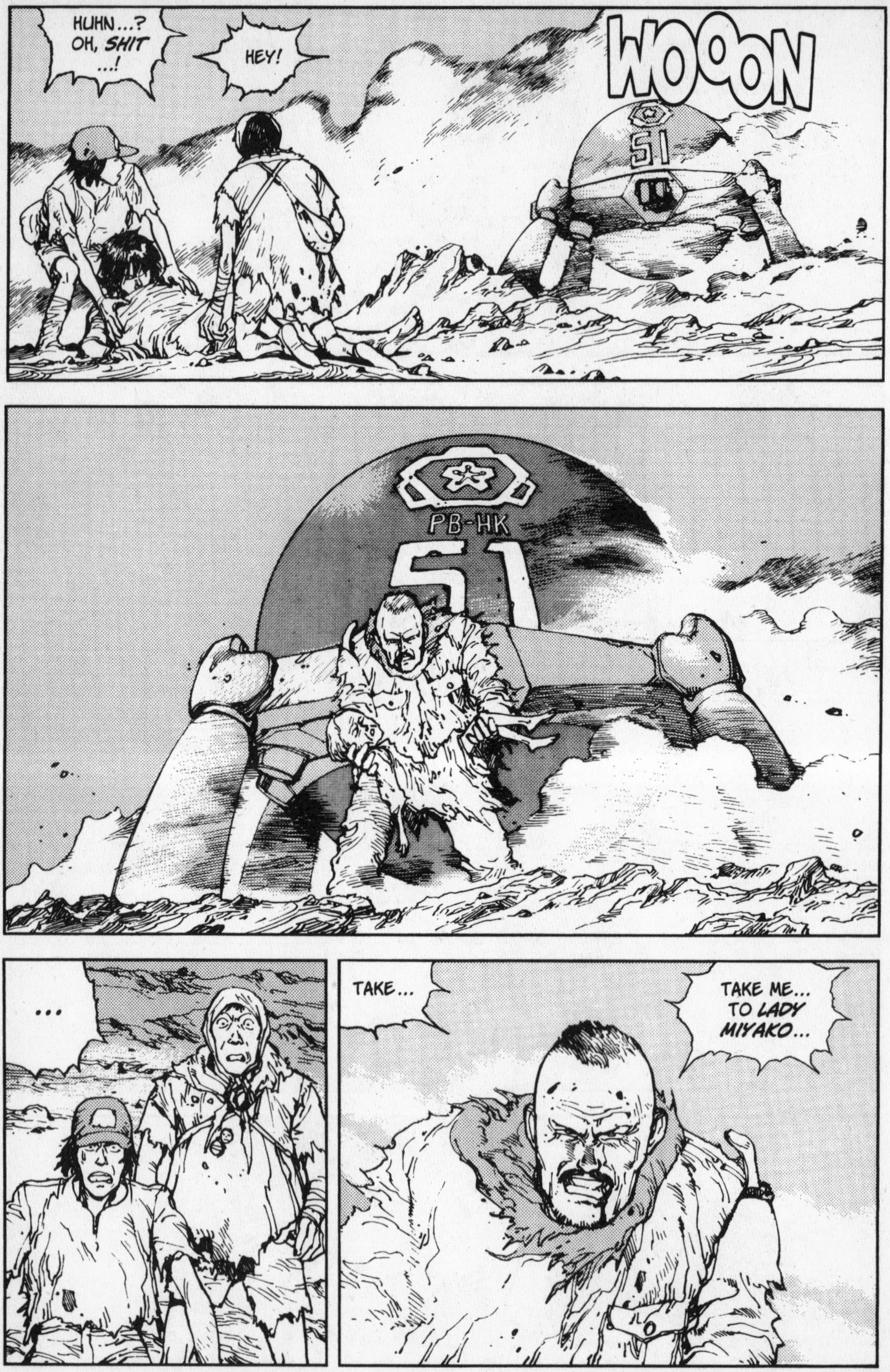

HUHN...? OH, *SHIT* ...!
HEY!
WOOON
51
PB-HK
51
...
TAKE...
TAKE ME... TO *LADY MIYAKO*...

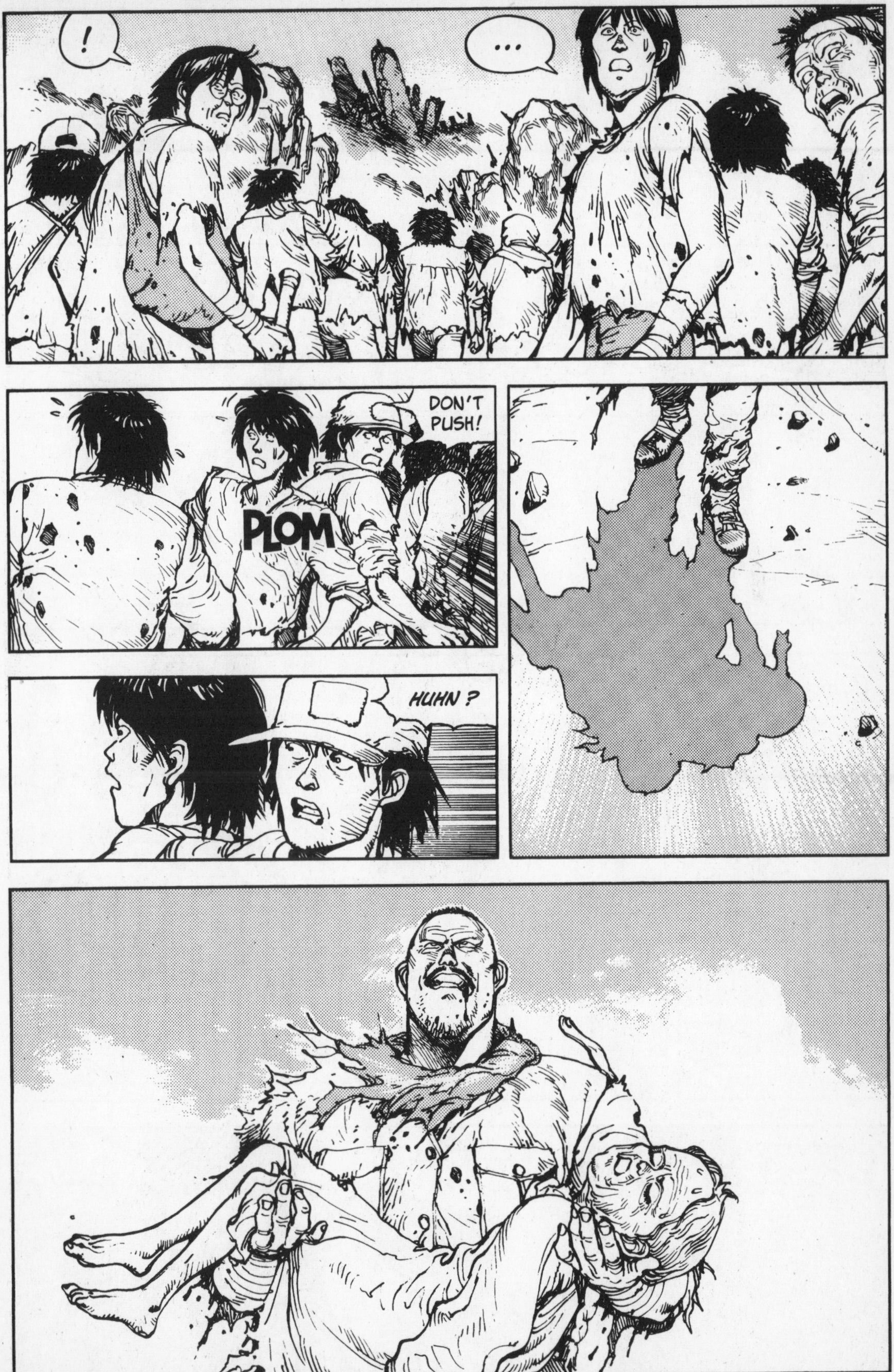
!
...
DON'T PUSH!
PLOM
HUHN ?

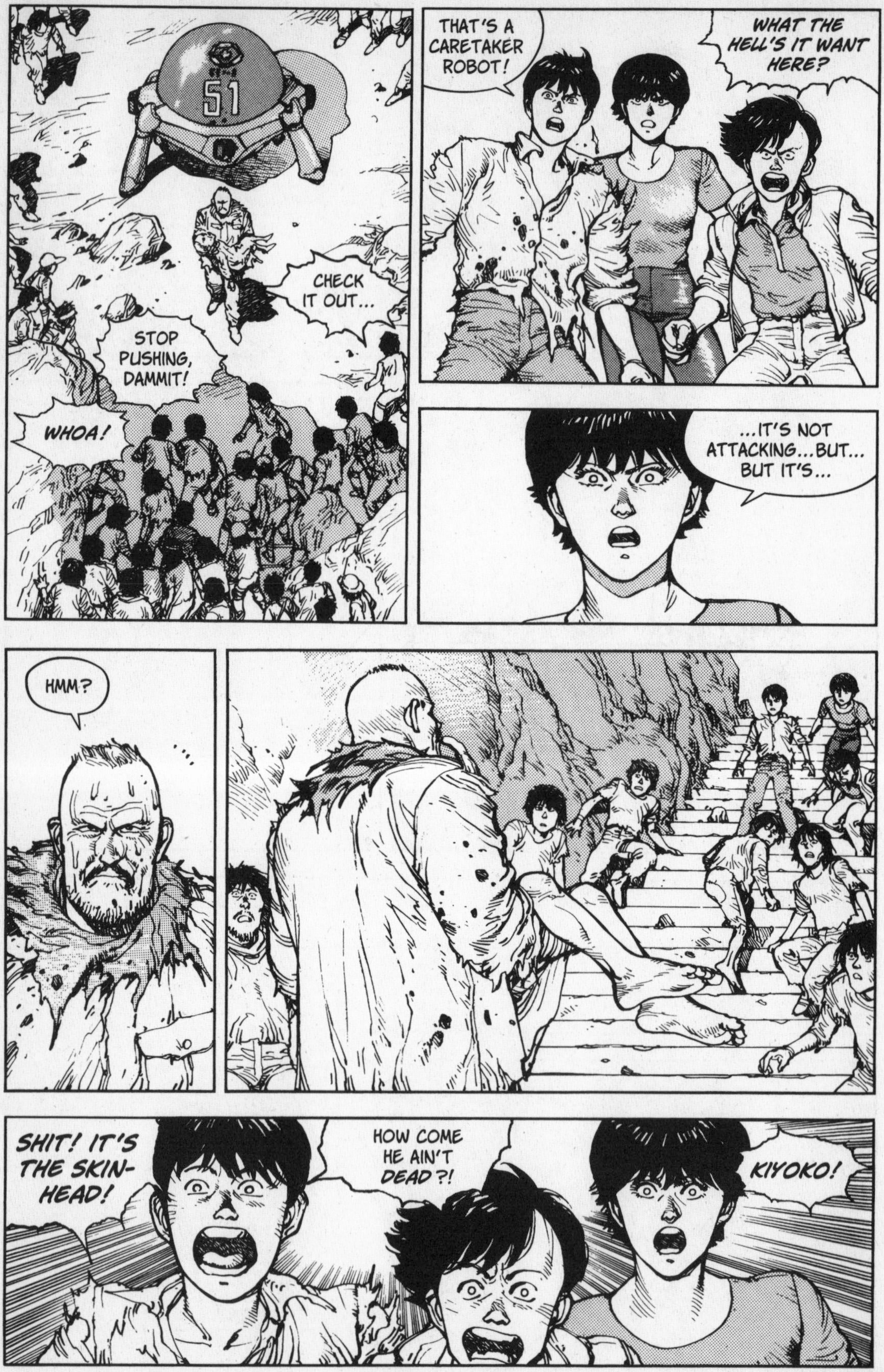
CHECK IT OUT...
STOP PUSHING, DAMMIT!
WHOA!
THAT'S A CARETAKER ROBOT!
WHAT THE HELL'S IT WANT HERE?
...IT'S NOT ATTACKING...BUT... BUT IT'S...
HMM?
SHIT! IT'S THE SKIN-HEAD!
HOW COME HE AIN'T DEAD?!
KIYOKO!

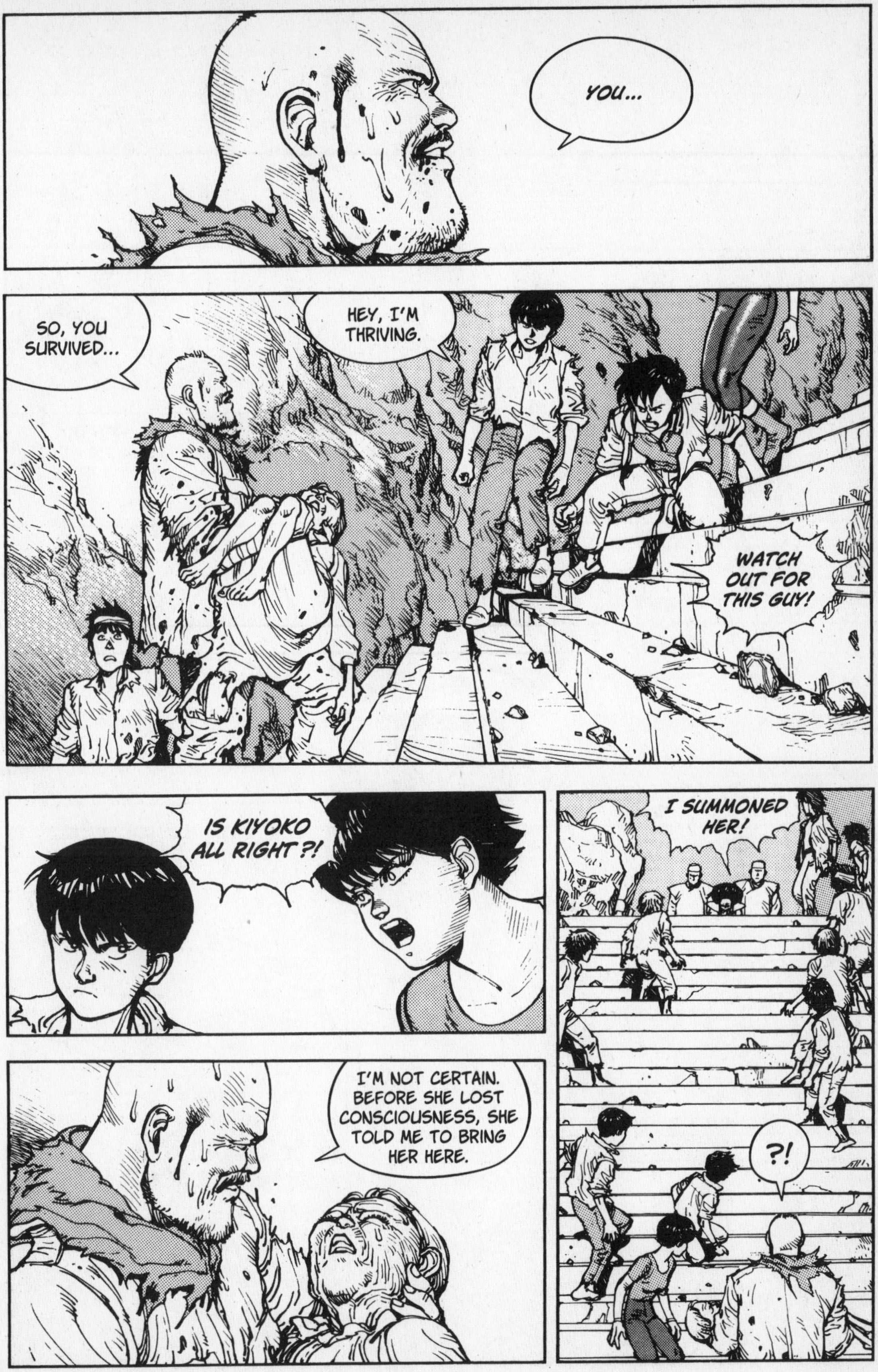
YOU...
SO, YOU SURVIVED...
HEY, I'M THRIVING.
WATCH OUT FOR THIS GUY!
IS KIYOKO ALL RIGHT?!
I SUMMONED HER!
?!
I'M NOT CERTAIN. BEFORE SHE LOST CONSCIOUSNESS, SHE TOLD ME TO BRING HER HERE.

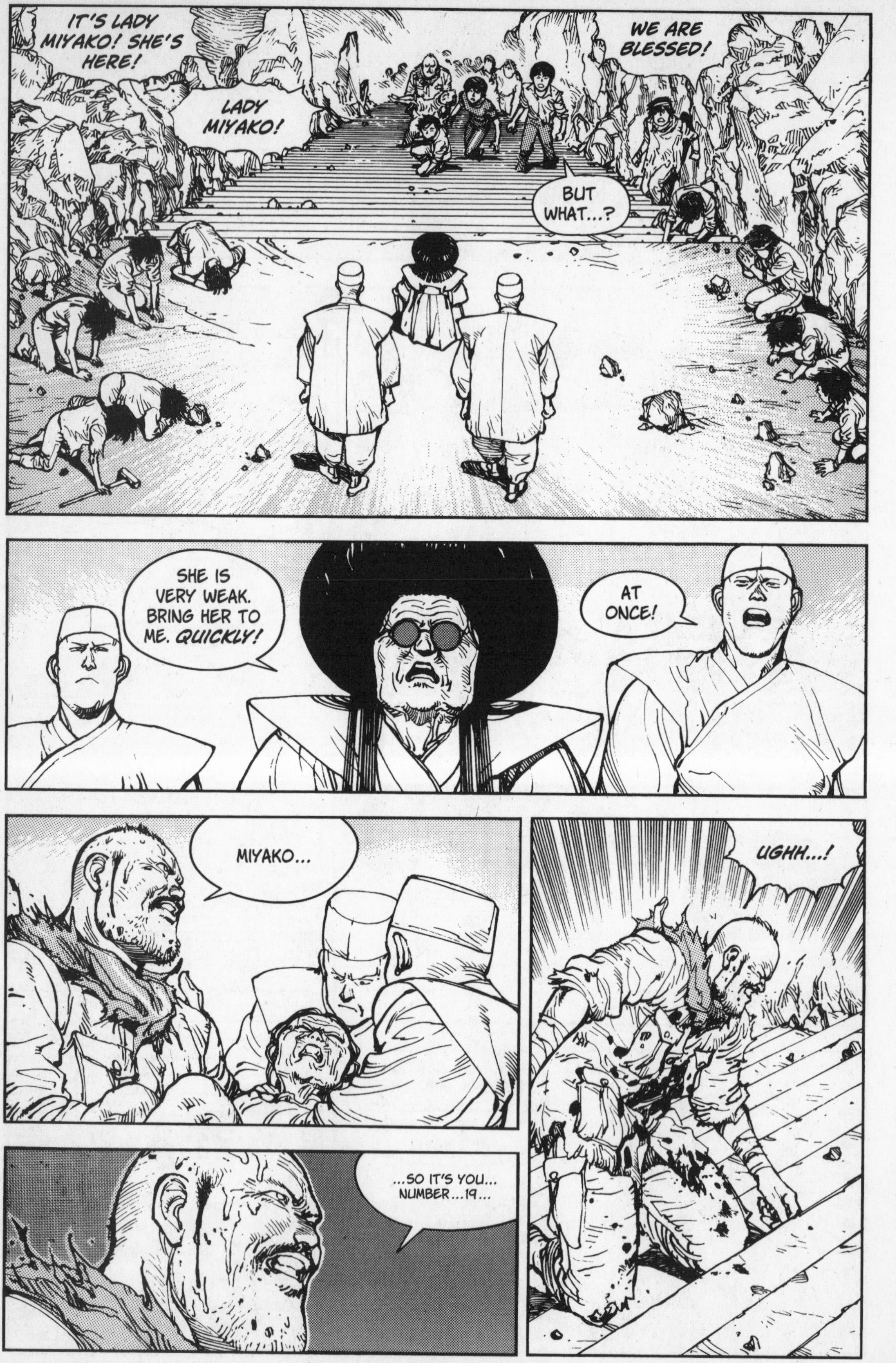
IT'S LADY MIYAKO! SHE'S HERE!
LADY MIYAKO!
WE ARE BLESSED!
BUT WHAT...?
SHE IS VERY WEAK. BRING HER TO ME. QUICKLY!
AT ONCE!
MIYAKO...
...SO IT'S YOU... NUMBER...19...
UGHH...!

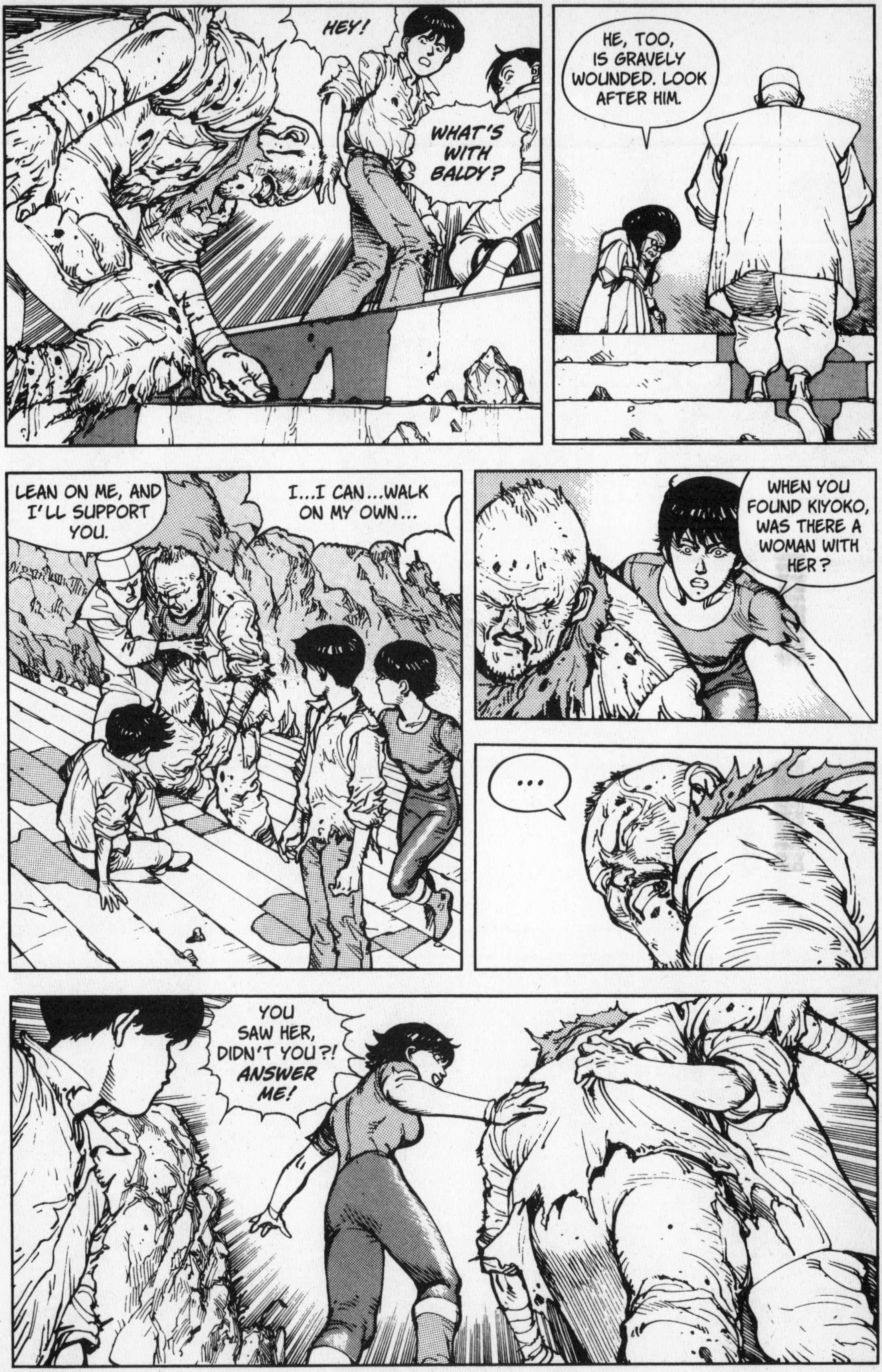
HEY!
WHAT'S WITH BALDY?
HE, TOO, IS GRAVELY WOUNDED. LOOK AFTER HIM.
LEAN ON ME, AND I'LL SUPPORT YOU.
I...I CAN...WALK ON MY OWN...
WHEN YOU FOUND KIYOKO, WAS THERE A WOMAN WITH HER?
...
YOU SAW HER, DIDN'T YOU?! ANSWER ME!

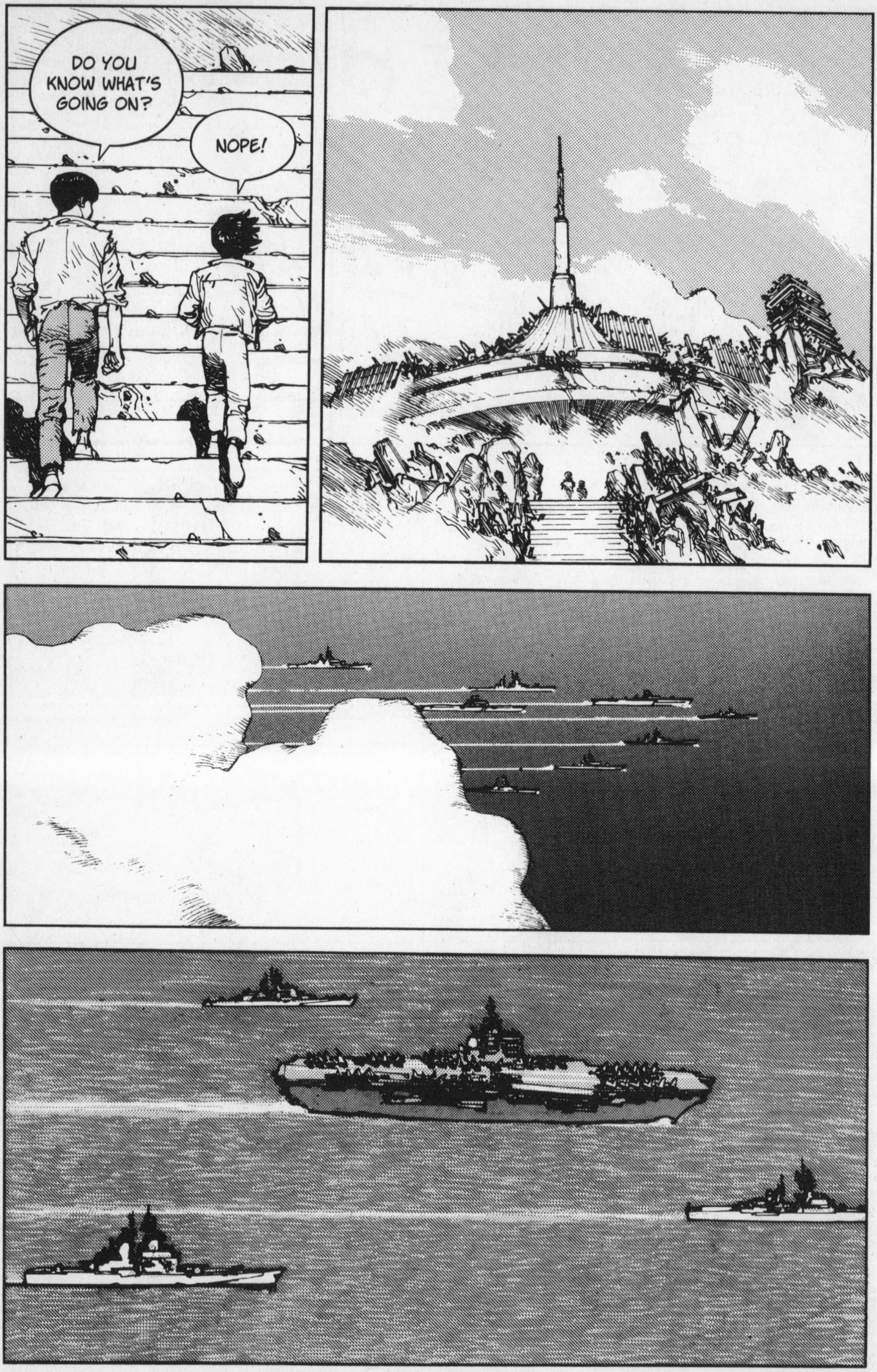
DO YOU KNOW WHAT'S GOING ON?
NOPE!

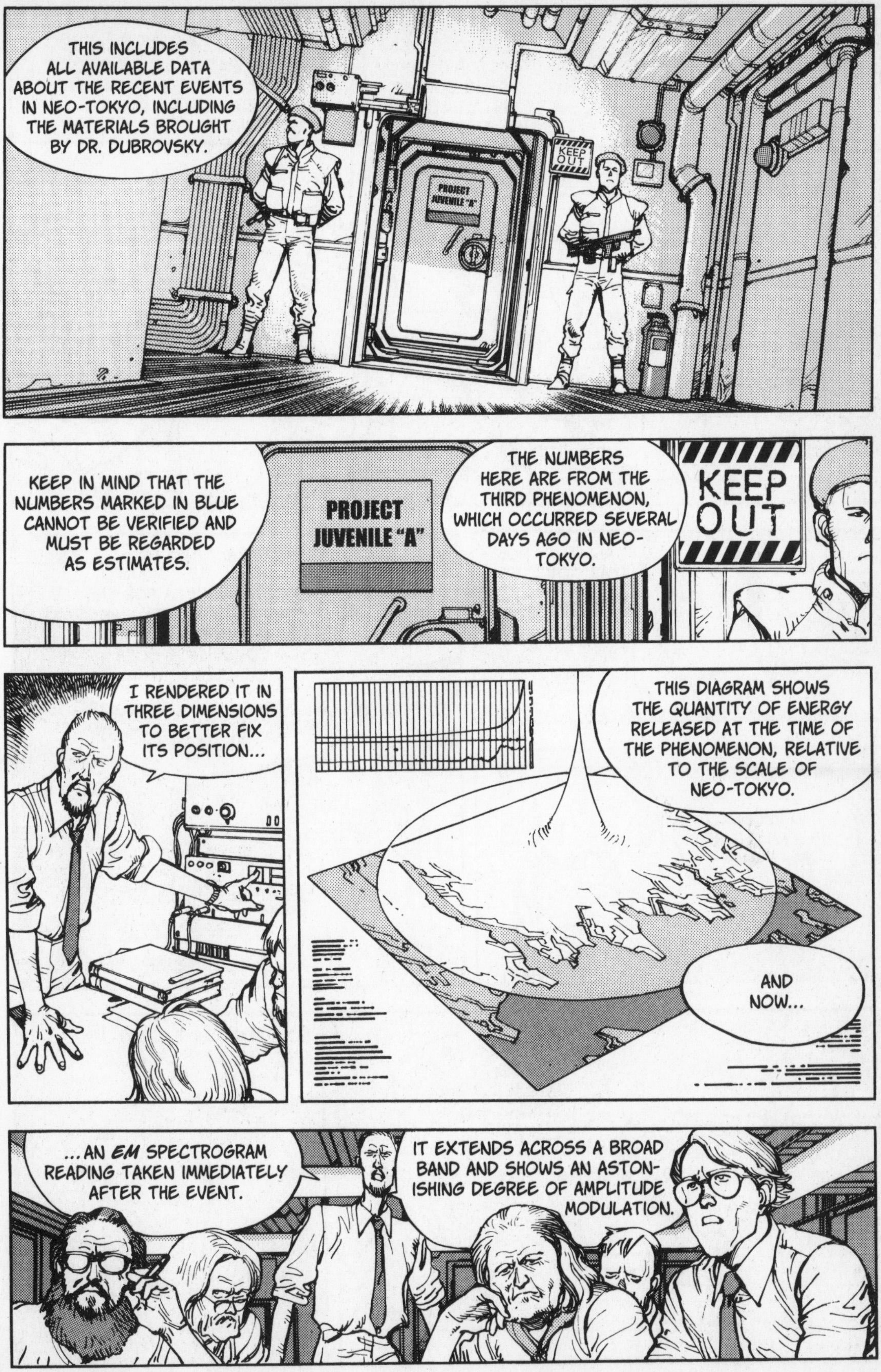
THIS INCLUDES ALL AVAILABLE DATA ABOUT THE RECENT EVENTS IN NEO-TOKYO, INCLUDING THE MATERIALS BROUGHT BY DR. DUBROVSKY.
KEEP OUT
PROJECT JUVENILE "A"
KEEP IN MIND THAT THE NUMBERS MARKED IN BLUE CANNOT BE VERIFIED AND MUST BE REGARDED AS ESTIMATES.
PROJECT JUVENILE "A"
THE NUMBERS HERE ARE FROM THE THIRD PHENOMENON, WHICH OCCURRED SEVERAL DAYS AGO IN NEO-TOKYO.
KEEP OUT
I RENDERED IT IN THREE DIMENSIONS TO BETTER FIX ITS POSITION...
THIS DIAGRAM SHOWS THE QUANTITY OF ENERGY RELEASED AT THE TIME OF THE PHENOMENON, RELATIVE TO THE SCALE OF NEO-TOKYO.
AND NOW...
...AN *EM* SPECTROGRAM READING TAKEN IMMEDIATELY AFTER THE EVENT.
IT EXTENDS ACROSS A BROAD BAND AND SHOWS AN ASTONISHING DEGREE OF AMPLITUDE MODULATION.

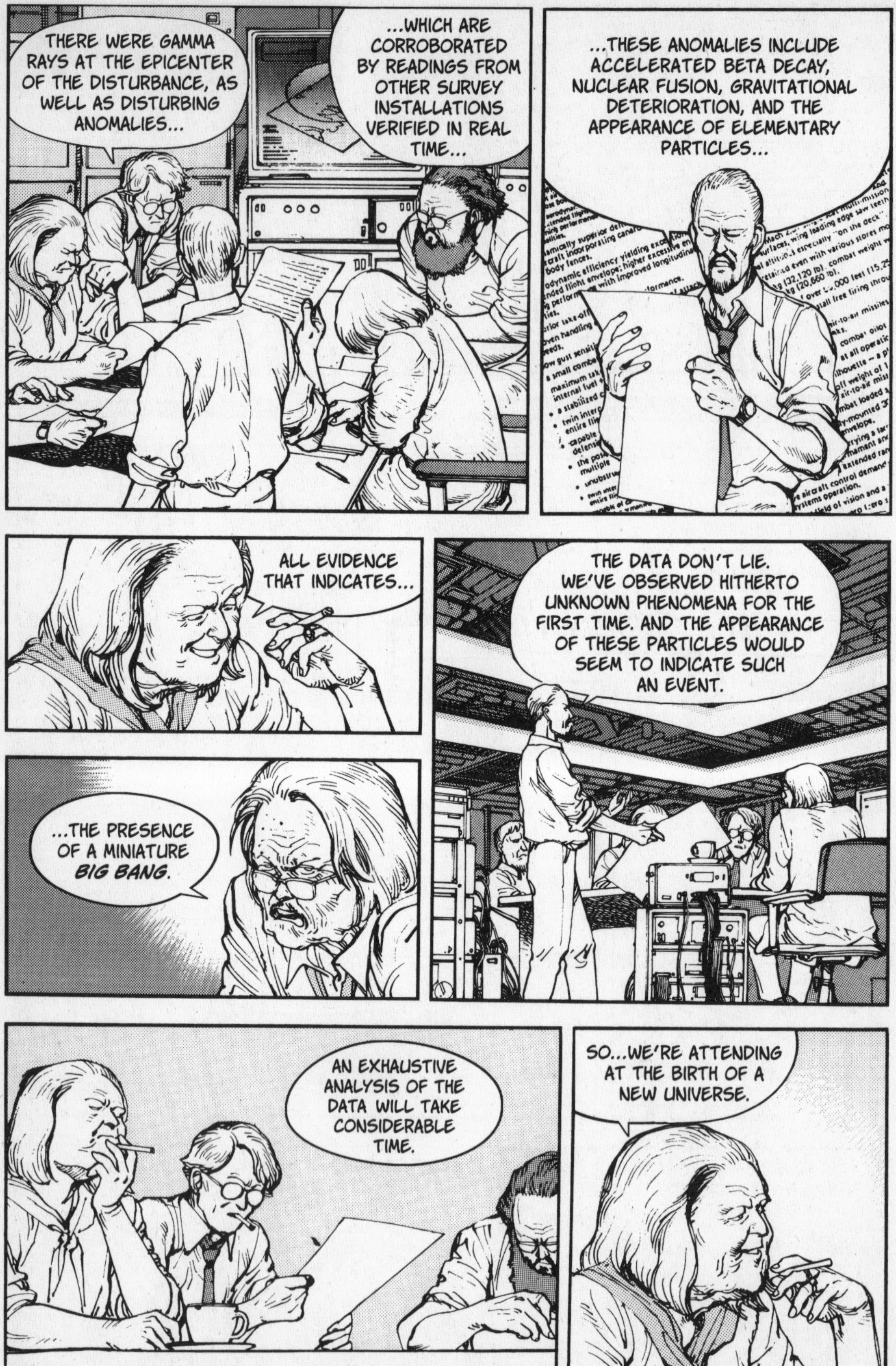
THERE WERE GAMMA RAYS AT THE EPICENTER OF THE DISTURBANCE, AS WELL AS DISTURBING ANOMALIES...
...WHICH ARE CORROBORATED BY READINGS FROM OTHER SURVEY INSTALLATIONS VERIFIED IN REAL TIME...
...THESE ANOMALIES INCLUDE ACCELERATED BETA DECAY, NUCLEAR FUSION, GRAVITATIONAL DETERIORATION, AND THE APPEARANCE OF ELEMENTARY PARTICLES...
ALL EVIDENCE THAT INDICATES...
...THE PRESENCE OF A MINIATURE *BIG BANG*.
THE DATA DON'T LIE. WE'VE OBSERVED HITHERTO UNKNOWN PHENOMENA FOR THE FIRST TIME. AND THE APPEARANCE OF THESE PARTICLES WOULD SEEM TO INDICATE SUCH AN EVENT.
AN EXHAUSTIVE ANALYSIS OF THE DATA WILL TAKE CONSIDERABLE TIME.
SO...WE'RE ATTENDING AT THE BIRTH OF A NEW UNIVERSE.

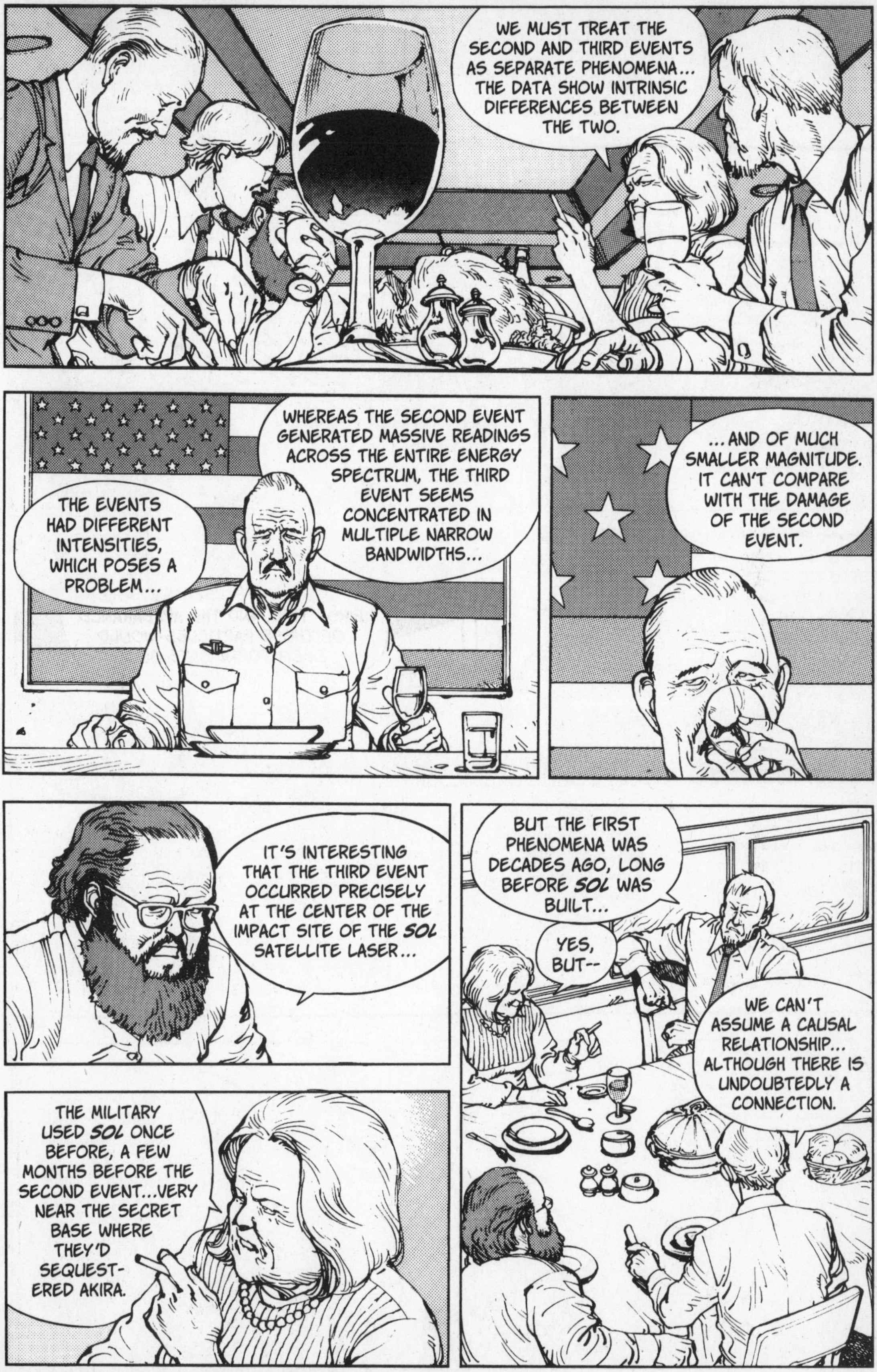
WE MUST TREAT THE SECOND AND THIRD EVENTS AS SEPARATE PHENOMENA... THE DATA SHOW INTRINSIC DIFFERENCES BETWEEN THE TWO.
THE EVENTS HAD DIFFERENT INTENSITIES, WHICH POSES A PROBLEM...
WHEREAS THE SECOND EVENT GENERATED MASSIVE READINGS ACROSS THE ENTIRE ENERGY SPECTRUM, THE THIRD EVENT SEEMS CONCENTRATED IN MULTIPLE NARROW BANDWIDTHS...
...AND OF MUCH SMALLER MAGNITUDE. IT CAN'T COMPARE WITH THE DAMAGE OF THE SECOND EVENT.
IT'S INTERESTING THAT THE THIRD EVENT OCCURRED PRECISELY AT THE CENTER OF THE IMPACT SITE OF THE SOL SATELLITE LASER...
THE MILITARY USED SOL ONCE BEFORE, A FEW MONTHS BEFORE THE SECOND EVENT...VERY NEAR THE SECRET BASE WHERE THEY'D SEQUEST-ERED AKIRA.
BUT THE FIRST PHENOMENA WAS DECADES AGO, LONG BEFORE SOL WAS BUILT...
YES, BUT--
WE CAN'T ASSUME A CAUSAL RELATIONSHIP... ALTHOUGH THERE IS UNDOUBTEDLY A CONNECTION.

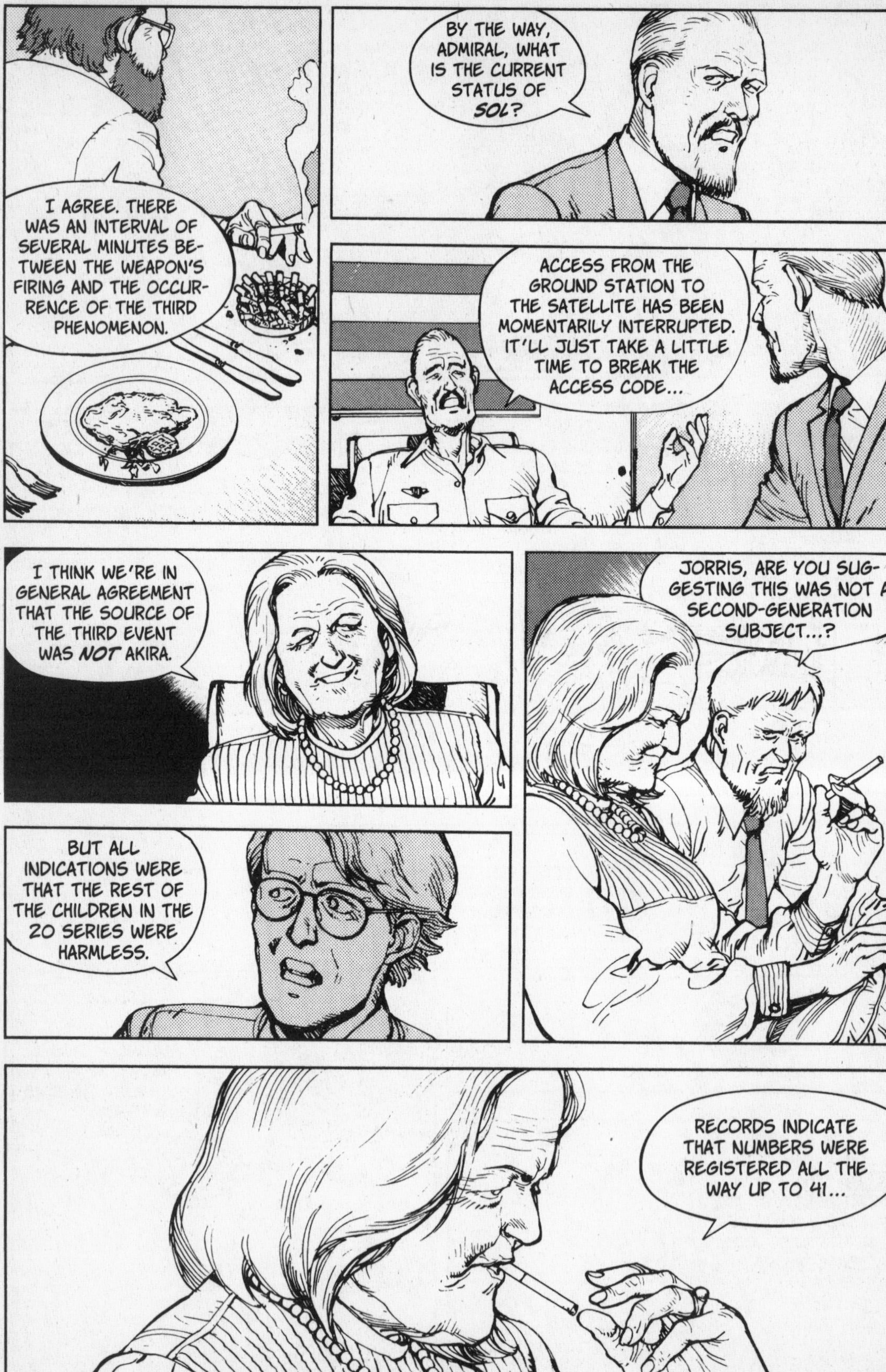
I AGREE. THERE WAS AN INTERVAL OF SEVERAL MINUTES BETWEEN THE WEAPON'S FIRING AND THE OCCURRENCE OF THE THIRD PHENOMENON.
BY THE WAY, ADMIRAL, WHAT IS THE CURRENT STATUS OF *SOL*?
ACCESS FROM THE GROUND STATION TO THE SATELLITE HAS BEEN MOMENTARILY INTERRUPTED. IT'LL JUST TAKE A LITTLE TIME TO BREAK THE ACCESS CODE...
I THINK WE'RE IN GENERAL AGREEMENT THAT THE SOURCE OF THE THIRD EVENT WAS *NOT* AKIRA.
BUT ALL INDICATIONS WERE THAT THE REST OF THE CHILDREN IN THE 20 SERIES WERE HARMLESS.
JORRIS, ARE YOU SUGGESTING THIS WAS NOT A SECOND-GENERATION SUBJECT...?
RECORDS INDICATE THAT NUMBERS WERE REGISTERED ALL THE WAY UP TO 41...

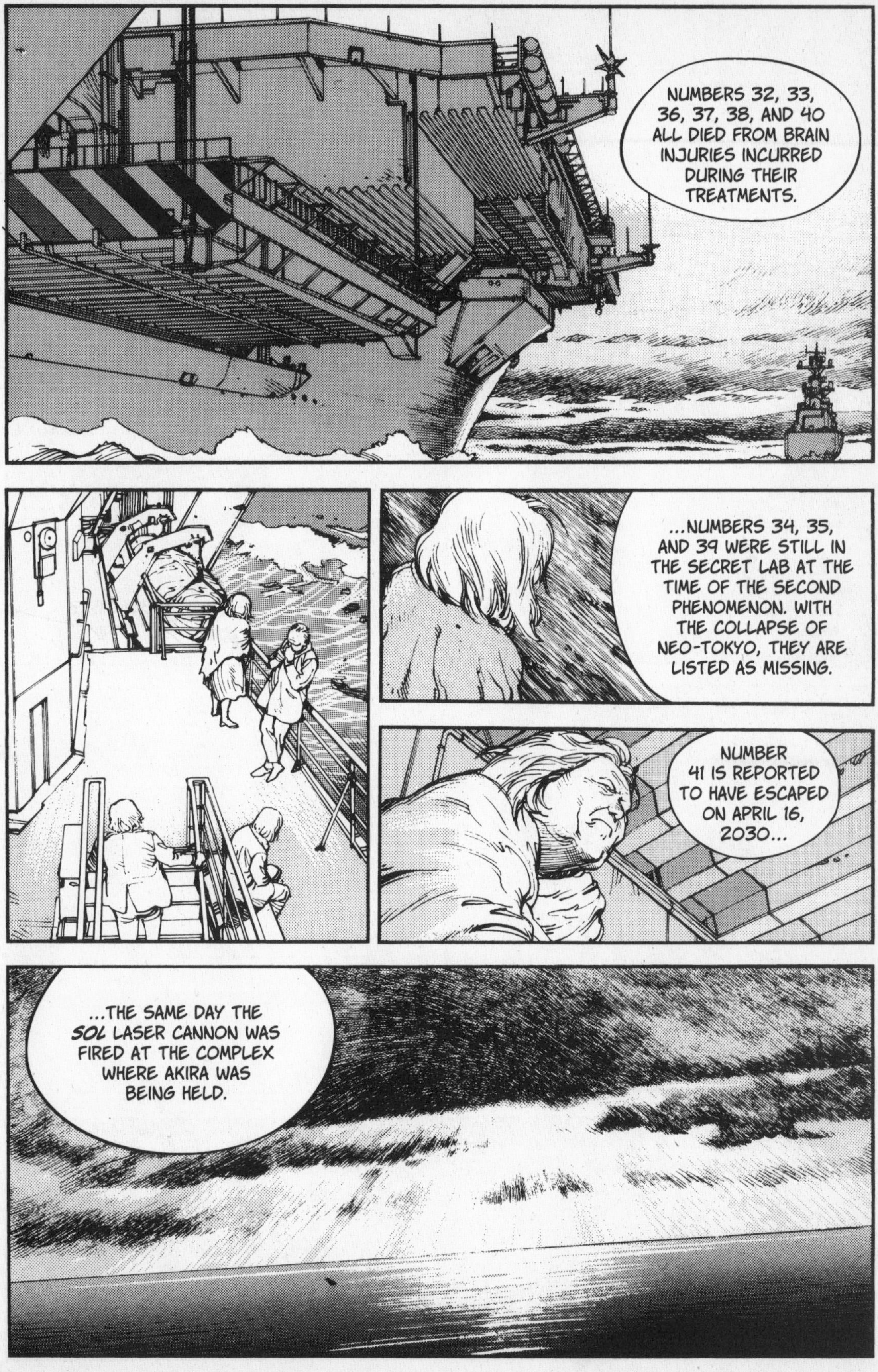
NUMBERS 32, 33, 36, 37, 38, AND 40 ALL DIED FROM BRAIN INJURIES INCURRED DURING THEIR TREATMENTS.
...NUMBERS 34, 35, AND 39 WERE STILL IN THE SECRET LAB AT THE TIME OF THE SECOND PHENOMENON. WITH THE COLLAPSE OF NEO-TOKYO, THEY ARE LISTED AS MISSING.
NUMBER 41 IS REPORTED TO HAVE ESCAPED ON APRIL 16, 2030...
...THE SAME DAY THE *SOL* LASER CANNON WAS FIRED AT THE COMPLEX WHERE AKIRA WAS BEING HELD.

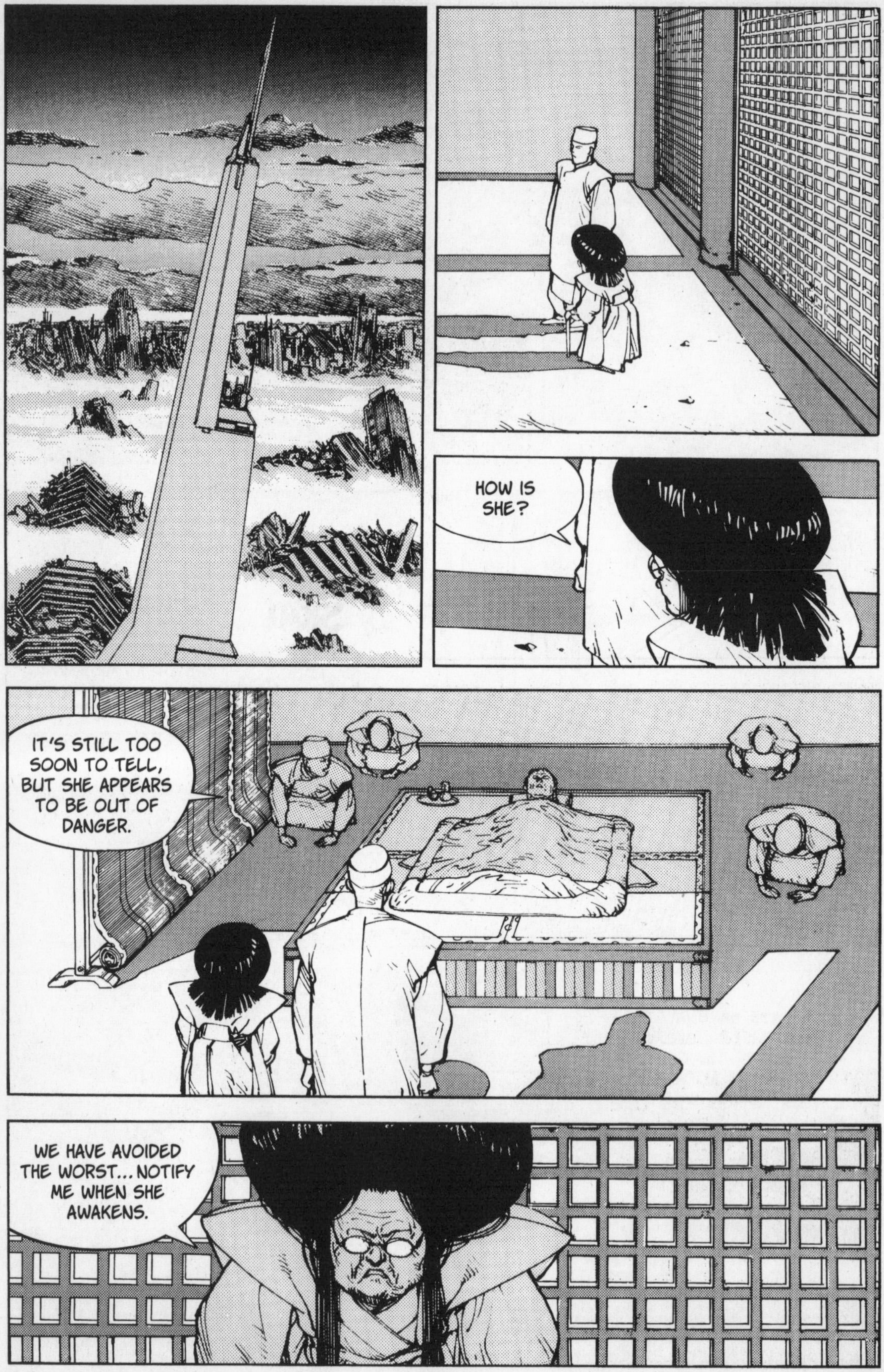
HOW IS SHE?
IT'S STILL TOO SOON TO TELL, BUT SHE APPEARS TO BE OUT OF DANGER.
WE HAVE AVOIDED THE WORST... NOTIFY ME WHEN SHE AWAKENS.

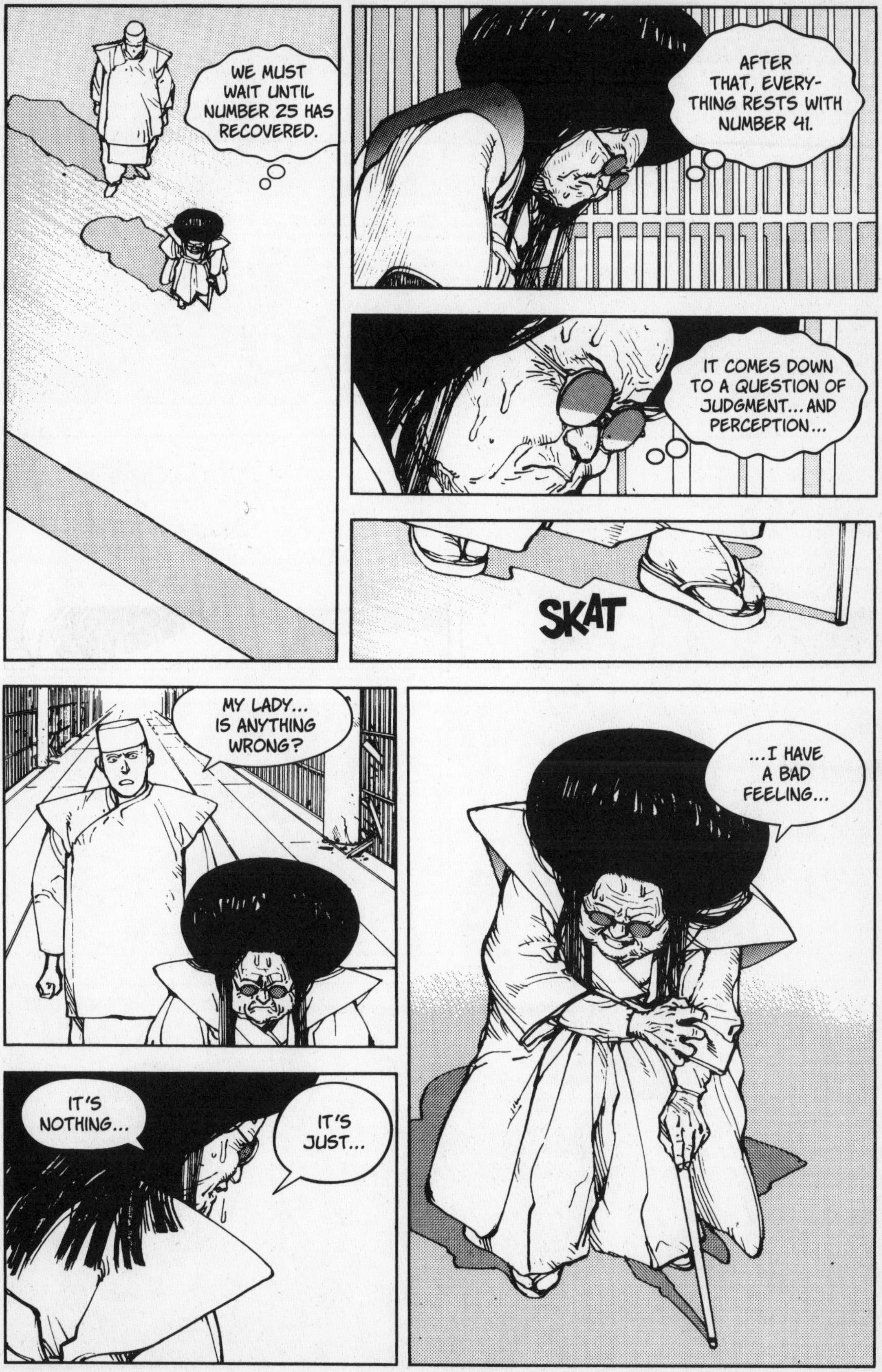
WE MUST WAIT UNTIL NUMBER 25 HAS RECOVERED.
AFTER THAT, EVERY-THING RESTS WITH NUMBER 41.
IT COMES DOWN TO A QUESTION OF JUDGMENT... AND PERCEPTION...
SKAT
MY LADY... IS ANYTHING WRONG?
IT'S NOTHING...
IT'S JUST...
...I HAVE A BAD FEELING...

PLEASE... REST HERE.

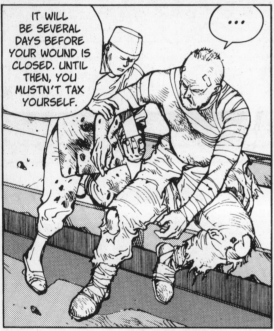

IT WILL BE SEVERAL DAYS BEFORE YOUR WOUND IS CLOSED. UNTIL THEN, YOU MUSTN'T TAX YOURSELF.

...

DID YOU HEAR WHAT HE SAID? IT MEANS I'M STUCK HERE FOR SEVERAL DAYS.

I DON'T KNOW ABOUT THAT...

...BUT I KNOW THAT CHIYOKO IS ALIVE, AND YOU REFUSE TO TELL ME WHERE YOU'VE SEEN HER.

THAT'S RIGHT.

THEN YOU'RE IN FOR A FIGHT.

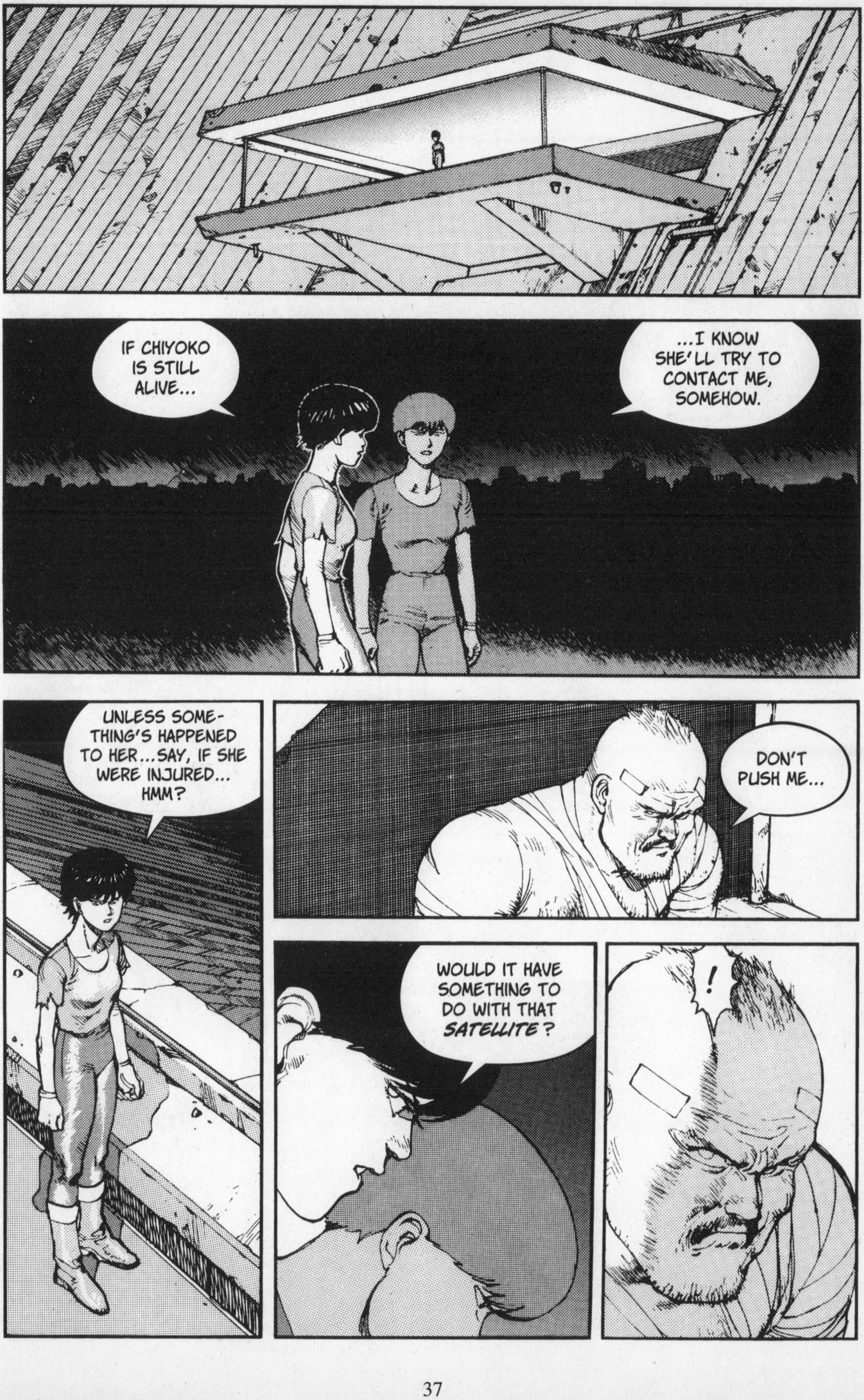
IF CHIYOKO IS STILL ALIVE...
...I KNOW SHE'LL TRY TO CONTACT ME, SOMEHOW.
UNLESS SOME-THING'S HAPPENED TO HER...SAY, IF SHE WERE INJURED... HMM?
DON'T PUSH ME...
WOULD IT HAVE SOMETHING TO DO WITH THAT *SATELLITE* ?
!

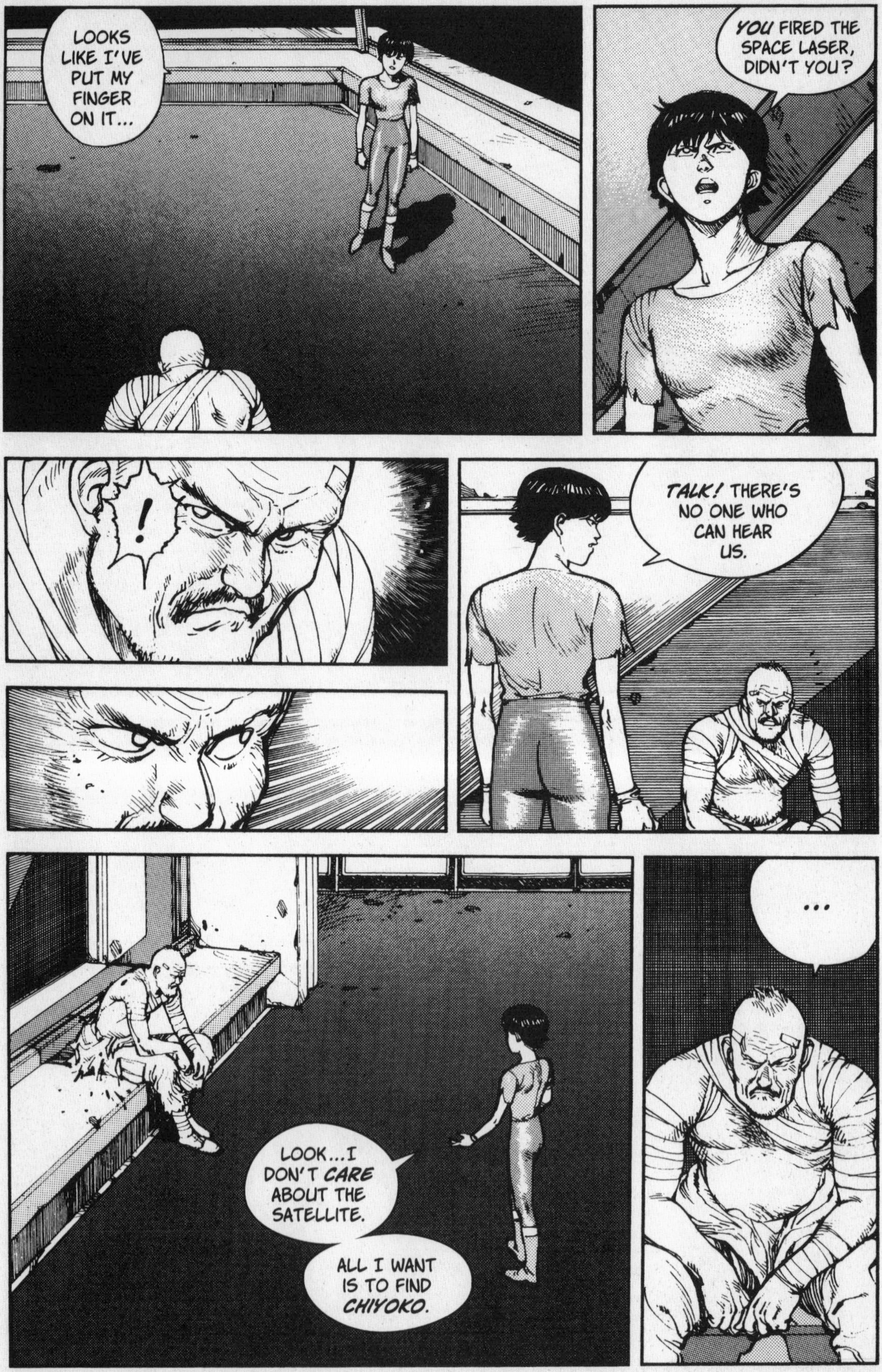
LOOKS LIKE I'VE PUT MY FINGER ON IT...
YOU FIRED THE SPACE LASER, DIDN'T YOU?
!
TALK! THERE'S NO ONE WHO CAN HEAR US.
LOOK...I DON'T CARE ABOUT THE SATELLITE.
ALL I WANT IS TO FIND CHIYOKO.
...

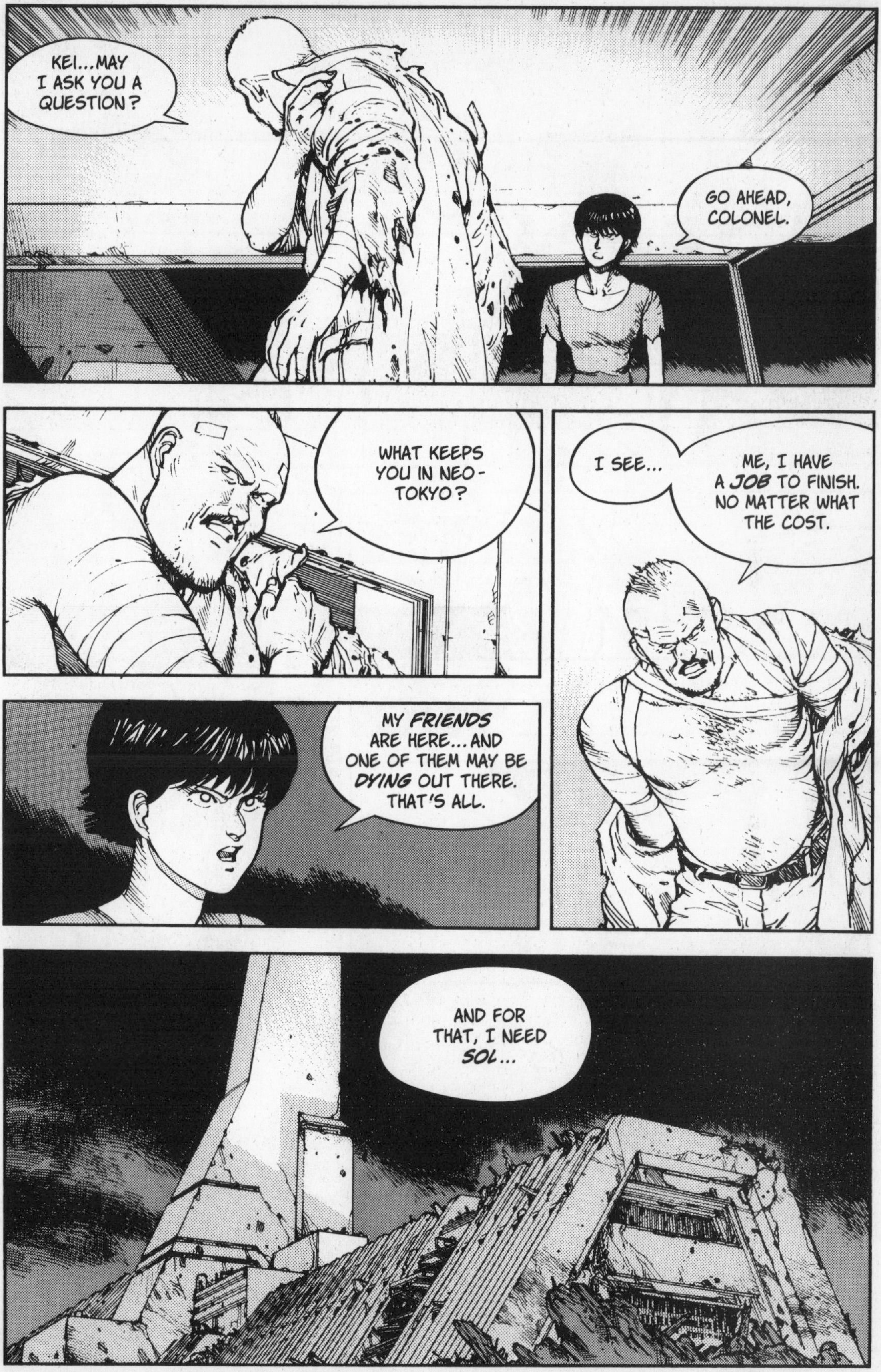
KEI...MAY I ASK YOU A QUESTION?
GO AHEAD, COLONEL.
WHAT KEEPS YOU IN NEO-TOKYO?
MY FRIENDS ARE HERE...AND ONE OF THEM MAY BE DYING OUT THERE. THAT'S ALL.
I SEE...
ME, I HAVE A JOB TO FINISH. NO MATTER WHAT THE COST.
AND FOR THAT, I NEED SOL...

SOL...?

THE SPACE LASER.

YOU PLAN TO USE IT TO--

I HAVE TO *REAP* WHAT I'VE SOWN...

...BEFORE HE GROWS INTO ANOTHER *AKIRA.*

YOU MEAN *TETSUO!*

I LEAVE BEFORE DAWN. IF YOU WANT TO COME WITH ME, BE WAITING AT THE FRONT GATES.

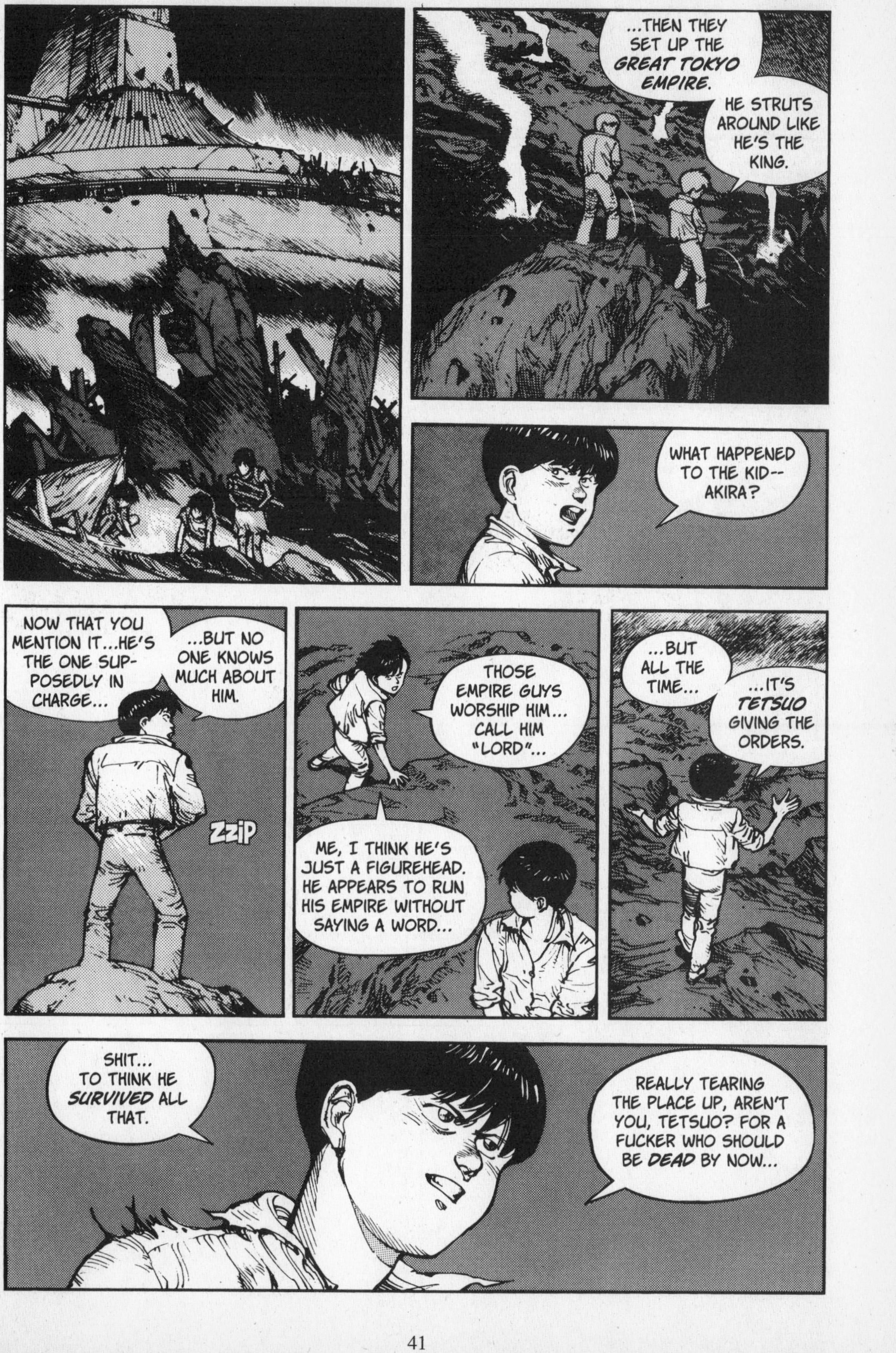
...THEN THEY SET UP THE GREAT TOKYO EMPIRE.
HE STRUTS AROUND LIKE HE'S THE KING.
WHAT HAPPENED TO THE KID--AKIRA?
NOW THAT YOU MENTION IT...HE'S THE ONE SUPPOSEDLY IN CHARGE...
...BUT NO ONE KNOWS MUCH ABOUT HIM.
ZZIP
THOSE EMPIRE GUYS WORSHIP HIM... CALL HIM "LORD"...
ME, I THINK HE'S JUST A FIGUREHEAD. HE APPEARS TO RUN HIS EMPIRE WITHOUT SAYING A WORD...
...BUT ALL THE TIME...
...IT'S TETSUO GIVING THE ORDERS.
SHIT... TO THINK HE SURVIVED ALL THAT.
REALLY TEARING THE PLACE UP, AREN'T YOU, TETSUO? FOR A FUCKER WHO SHOULD BE DEAD BY NOW...

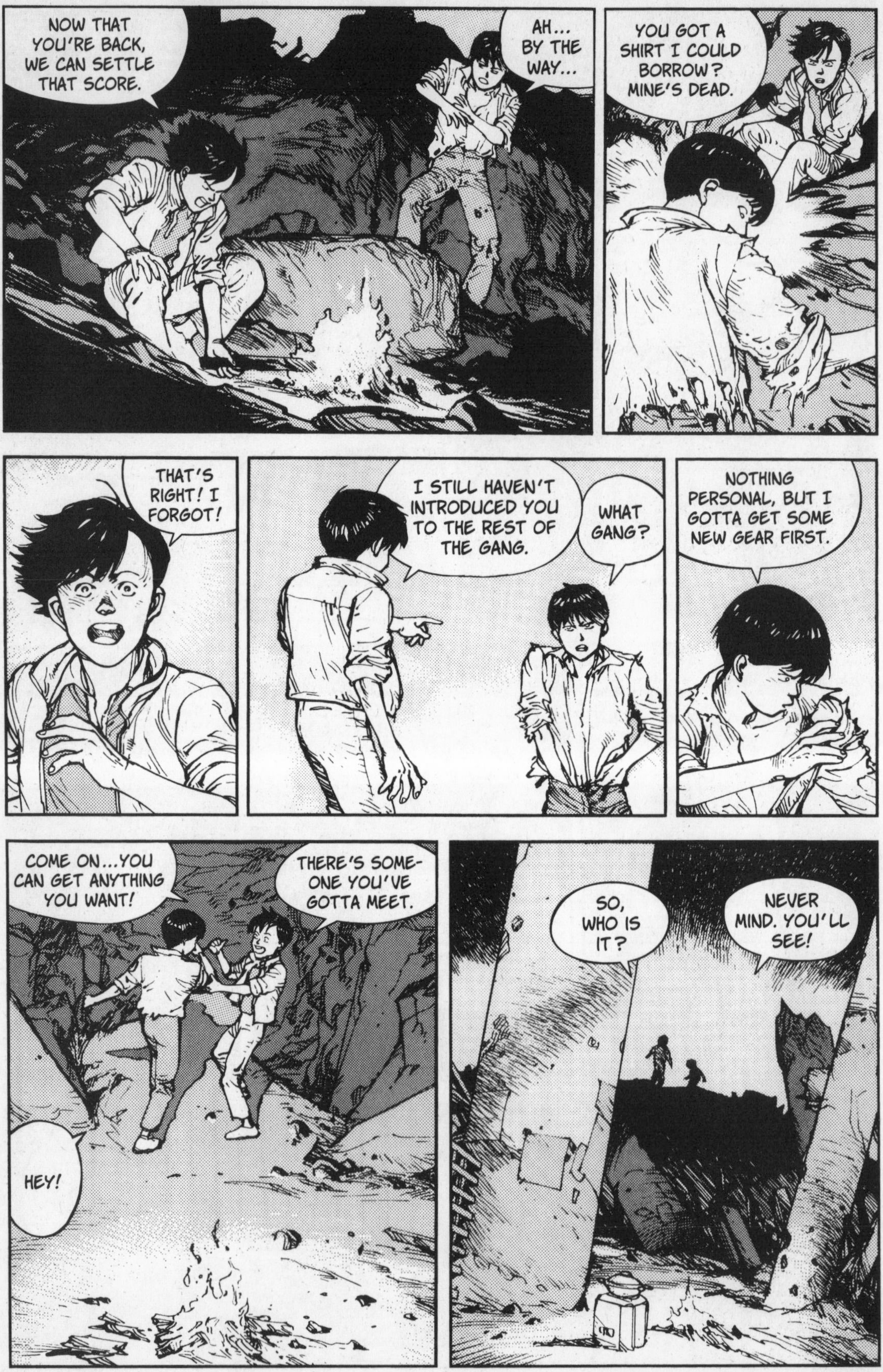
NOW THAT YOU'RE BACK, WE CAN SETTLE THAT SCORE.
AH... BY THE WAY...
YOU GOT A SHIRT I COULD BORROW? MINE'S DEAD.
THAT'S RIGHT! I FORGOT!
I STILL HAVEN'T INTRODUCED YOU TO THE REST OF THE GANG.
WHAT GANG?
NOTHING PERSONAL, BUT I GOTTA GET SOME NEW GEAR FIRST.
COME ON...YOU CAN GET ANYTHING YOU WANT!
THERE'S SOME-ONE YOU'VE GOTTA MEET.
HEY!
SO, WHO IS IT?
NEVER MIND. YOU'LL SEE!

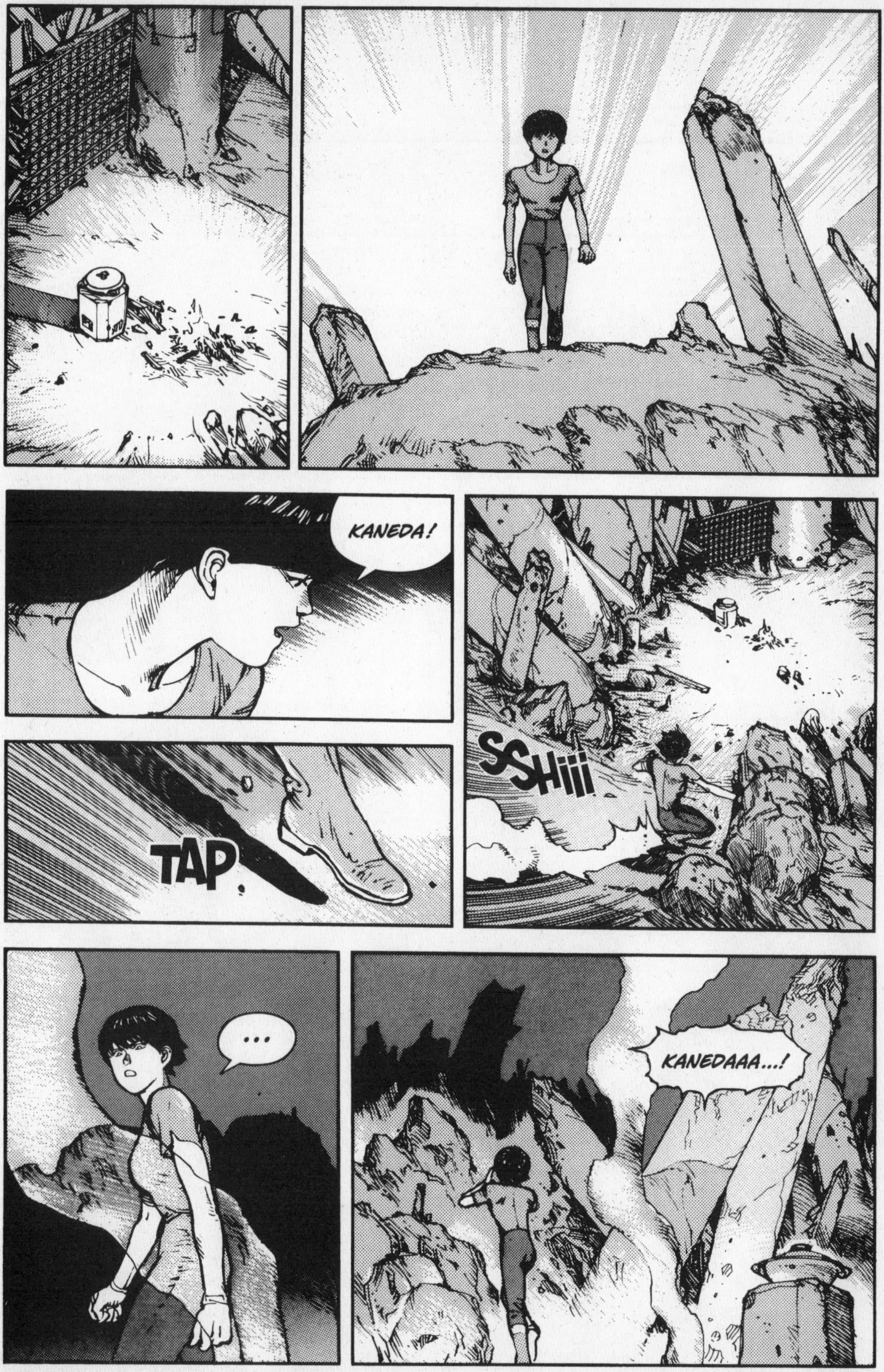
KANEDA!
TAP
SSHiii
...
KANEDAAA...!

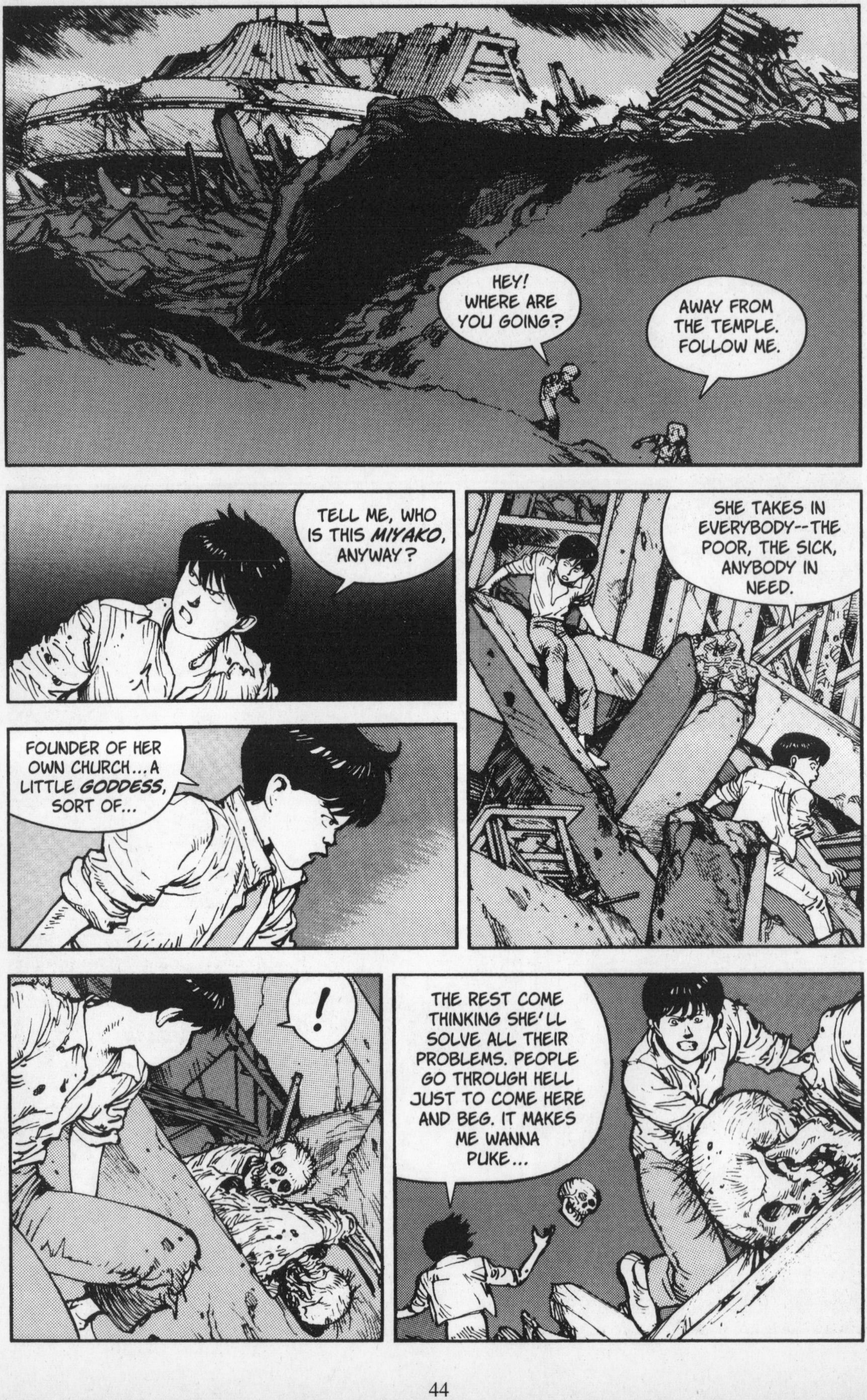
HEY! WHERE ARE YOU GOING?
AWAY FROM THE TEMPLE. FOLLOW ME.
TELL ME, WHO IS THIS *MIYAKO*, ANYWAY?
FOUNDER OF HER OWN CHURCH... A LITTLE *GODDESS*, SORT OF...
SHE TAKES IN EVERYBODY--THE POOR, THE SICK, ANYBODY IN NEED.
!
THE REST COME THINKING SHE'LL SOLVE ALL THEIR PROBLEMS. PEOPLE GO THROUGH HELL JUST TO COME HERE AND BEG. IT MAKES ME WANNA PUKE...

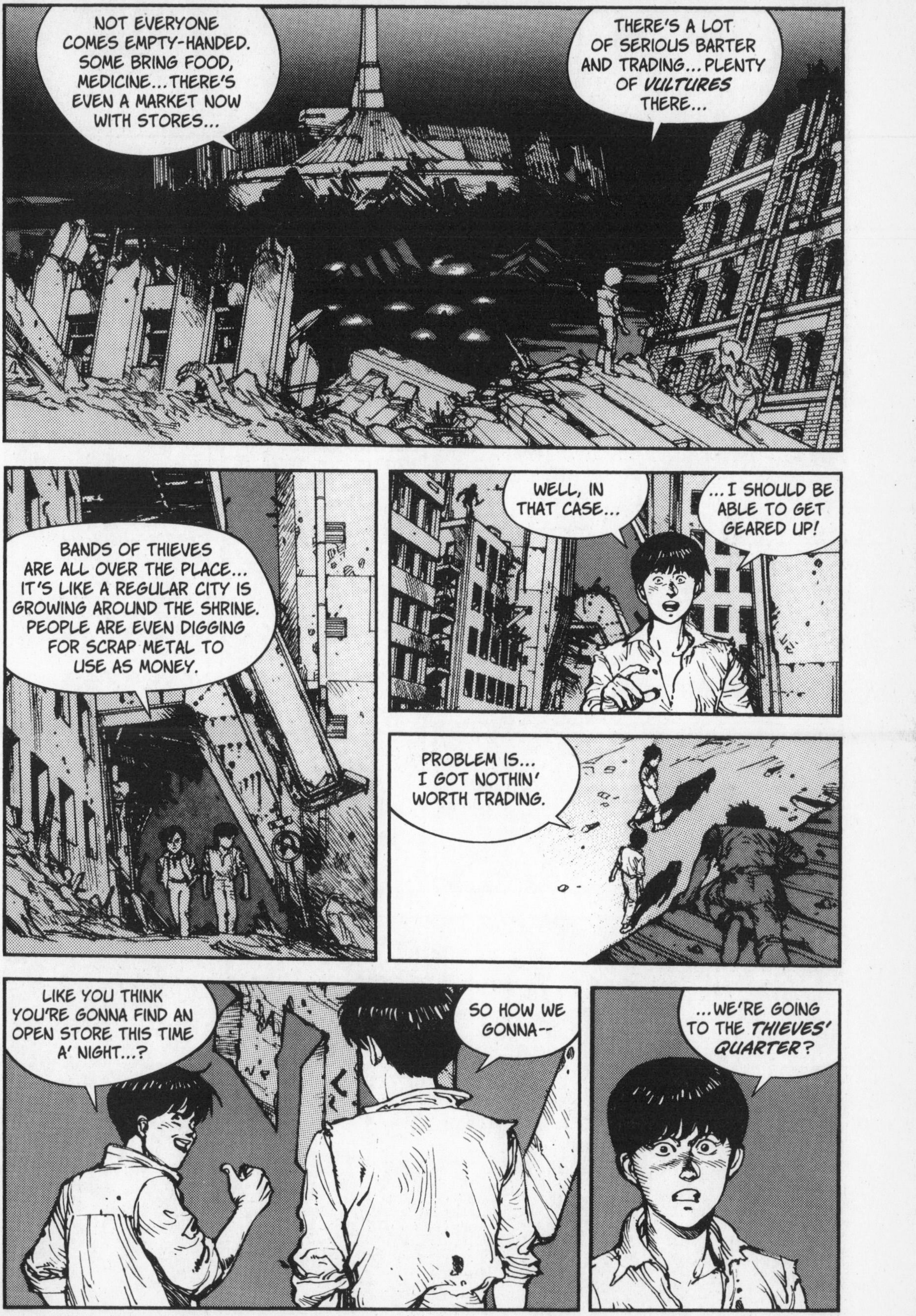
NOT EVERYONE COMES EMPTY-HANDED. SOME BRING FOOD, MEDICINE...THERE'S EVEN A MARKET NOW WITH STORES...
THERE'S A LOT OF SERIOUS BARTER AND TRADING...PLENTY OF *VULTURES* THERE...
BANDS OF THIEVES ARE ALL OVER THE PLACE... IT'S LIKE A REGULAR CITY IS GROWING AROUND THE SHRINE. PEOPLE ARE EVEN DIGGING FOR SCRAP METAL TO USE AS MONEY.
WELL, IN THAT CASE...
...I SHOULD BE ABLE TO GET GEARED UP!
PROBLEM IS... I GOT NOTHIN' WORTH TRADING.
LIKE YOU THINK YOU'RE GONNA FIND AN OPEN STORE THIS TIME A' NIGHT...?
SO HOW WE GONNA--
...WE'RE GOING TO THE *THIEVES' QUARTER*?

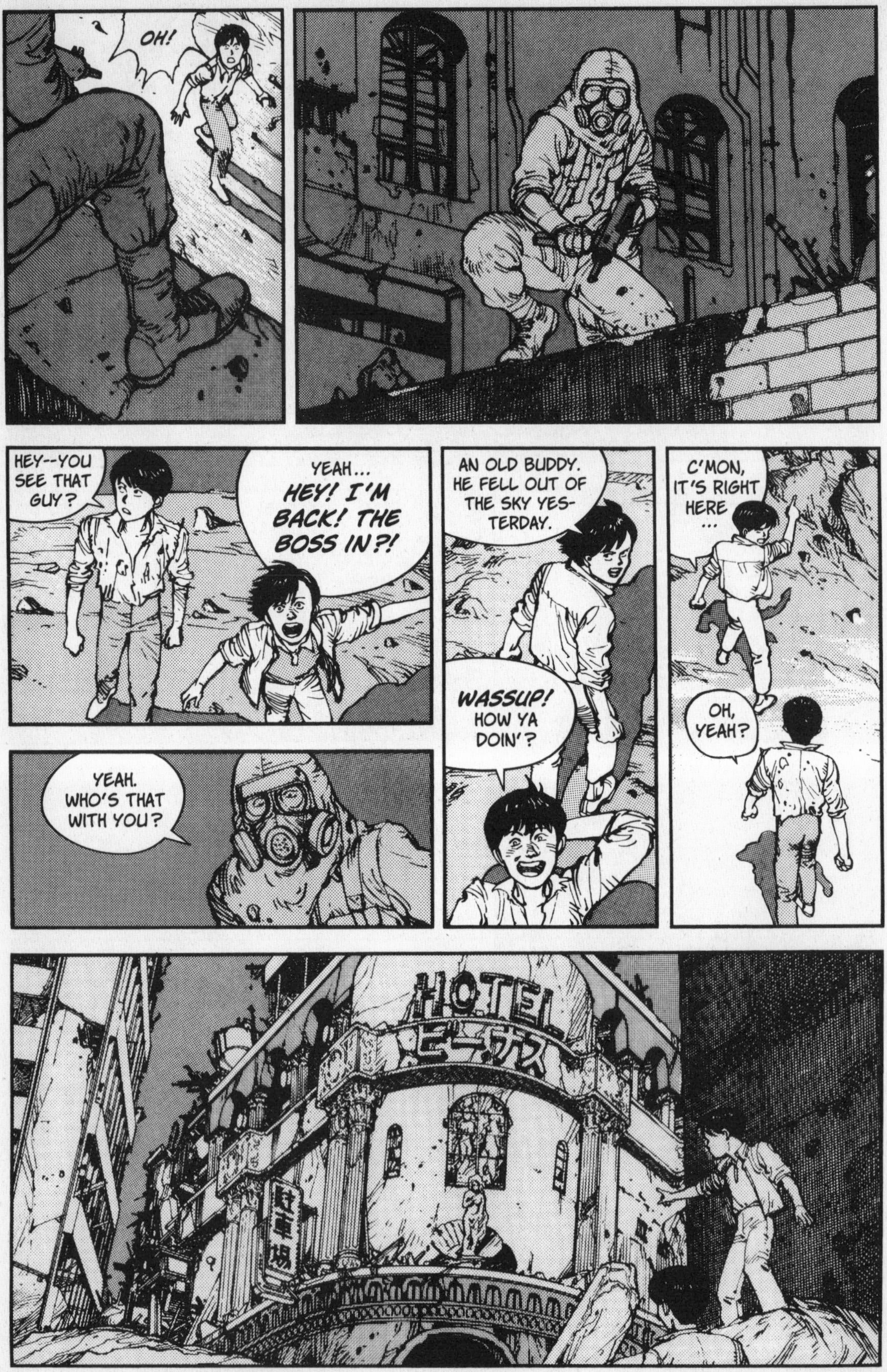
OH!
HEY--YOU SEE THAT GUY?
YEAH... HEY! I'M BACK! THE BOSS IN?!
YEAH. WHO'S THAT WITH YOU?
AN OLD BUDDY. HE FELL OUT OF THE SKY YES-TERDAY.
WASSUP! HOW YA DOIN'?
C'MON, IT'S RIGHT HERE ...
OH, YEAH?
HOTEL
ビーナス
駐車場

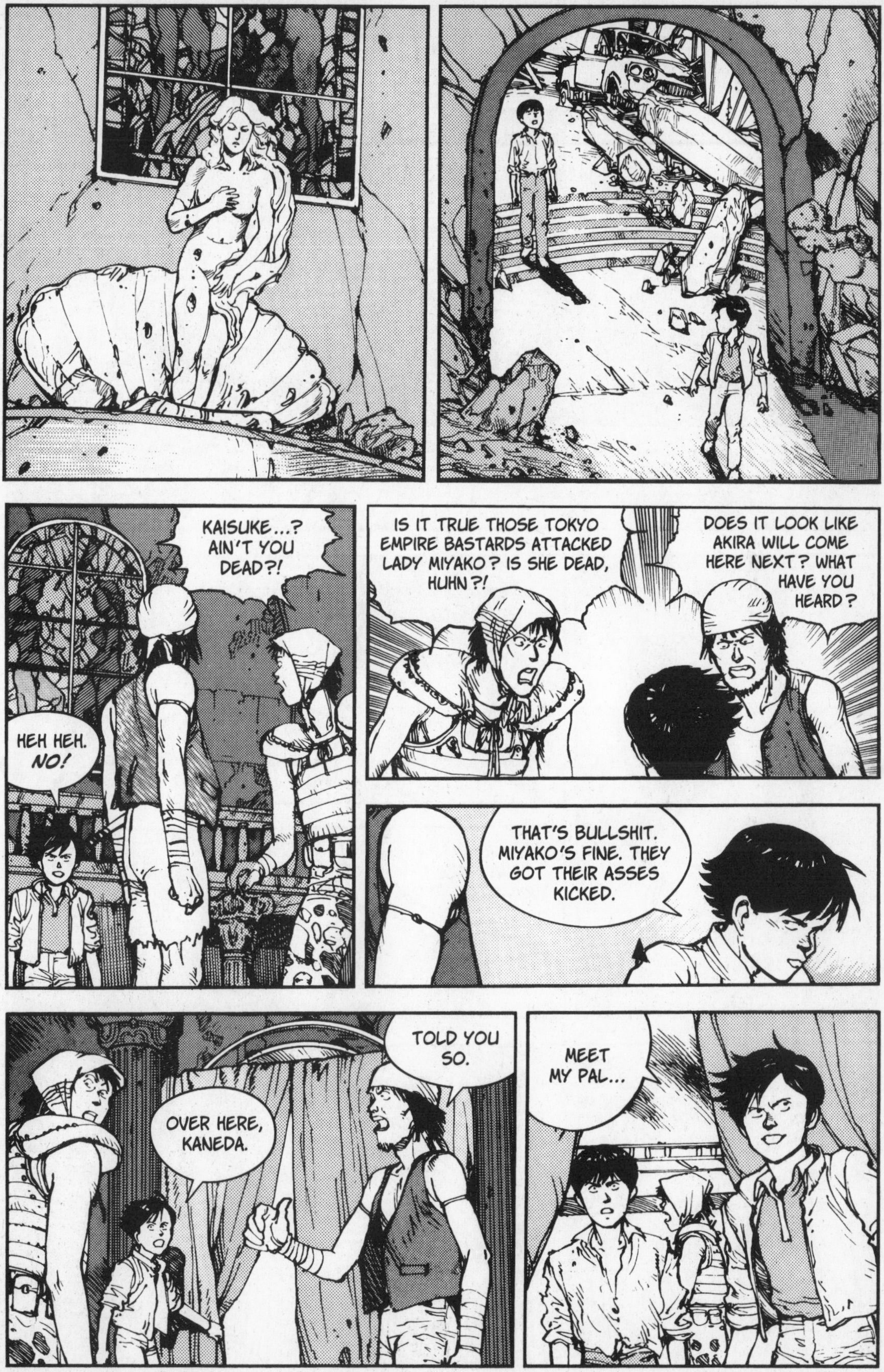
KAISUKE...? AIN'T YOU DEAD?!
HEH HEH. NO!
IS IT TRUE THOSE TOKYO EMPIRE BASTARDS ATTACKED LADY MIYAKO? IS SHE DEAD, HUHN?!
DOES IT LOOK LIKE AKIRA WILL COME HERE NEXT? WHAT HAVE YOU HEARD?
THAT'S BULLSHIT. MIYAKO'S FINE. THEY GOT THEIR ASSES KICKED.
OVER HERE, KANEDA.
TOLD YOU SO.
MEET MY PAL...

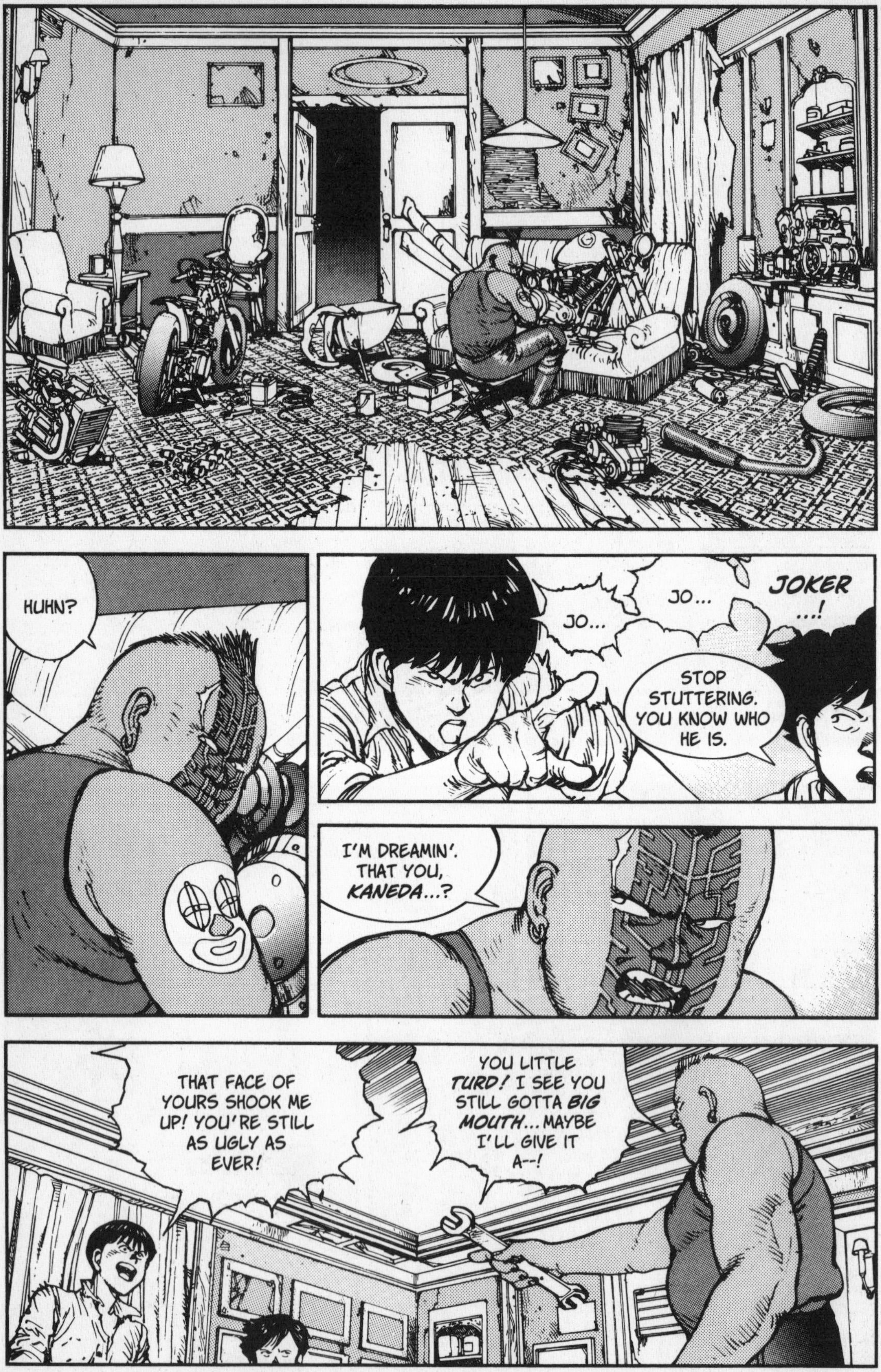
HUHN?
JO...
JO...
JOKER ...!
STOP STUTTERING. YOU KNOW WHO HE IS.
I'M DREAMIN'. THAT YOU, *KANEDA*...?
THAT FACE OF YOURS SHOOK ME UP! YOU'RE STILL AS UGLY AS EVER!
YOU LITTLE *TURD!* I SEE YOU STILL GOTTA *BIG MOUTH*... MAYBE I'LL GIVE IT A--!

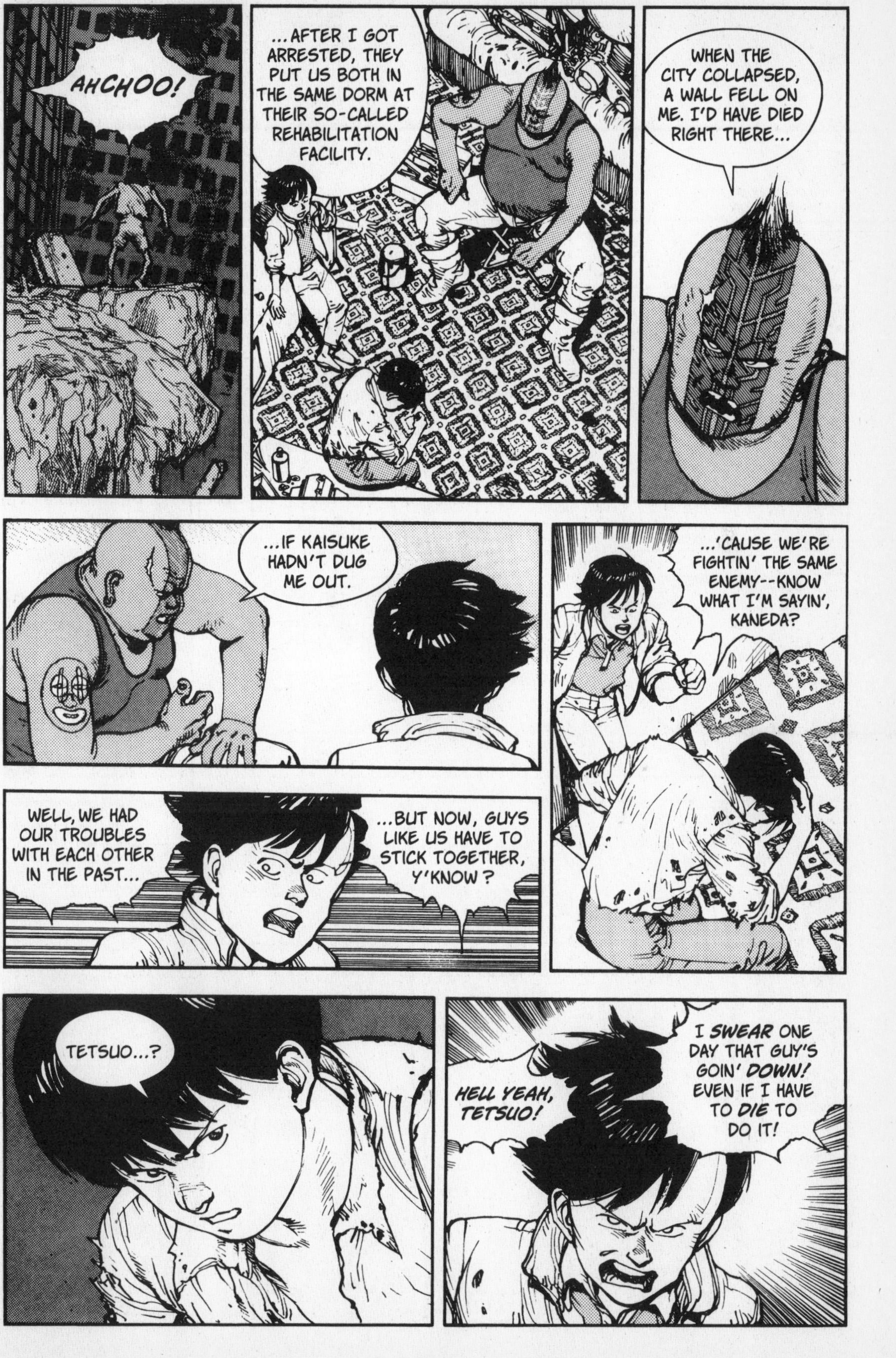
AHCHOO!
...AFTER I GOT ARRESTED, THEY PUT US BOTH IN THE SAME DORM AT THEIR SO-CALLED REHABILITATION FACILITY.
WHEN THE CITY COLLAPSED, A WALL FELL ON ME. I'D HAVE DIED RIGHT THERE...
...IF KAISUKE HADN'T DUG ME OUT.
WELL, WE HAD OUR TROUBLES WITH EACH OTHER IN THE PAST...
...BUT NOW, GUYS LIKE US HAVE TO STICK TOGETHER, Y'KNOW ?
...'CAUSE WE'RE FIGHTIN' THE SAME ENEMY--KNOW WHAT I'M SAYIN', KANEDA?
TETSUO...?
HELL YEAH, TETSUO!
I SWEAR ONE DAY THAT GUY'S GOIN' DOWN! EVEN IF I HAVE TO DIE TO DO IT!

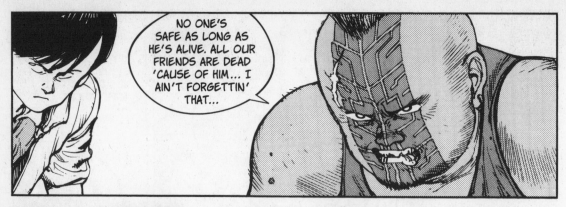

NO ONE'S SAFE AS LONG AS HE'S ALIVE. ALL OUR FRIENDS ARE DEAD 'CAUSE OF HIM... I AIN'T FORGETTIN' THAT...

ALL RIGHT! I'M WITH YOU!

I KNEW IT!

...YOU WANT CLOTHES?

BUT FIRST...

THAT'S IT, ISN'T IT? NEW CLOTHES?

WHAT THE F--?!

WELL, UH...YEAH.

HAH! I KNEW IT!

50

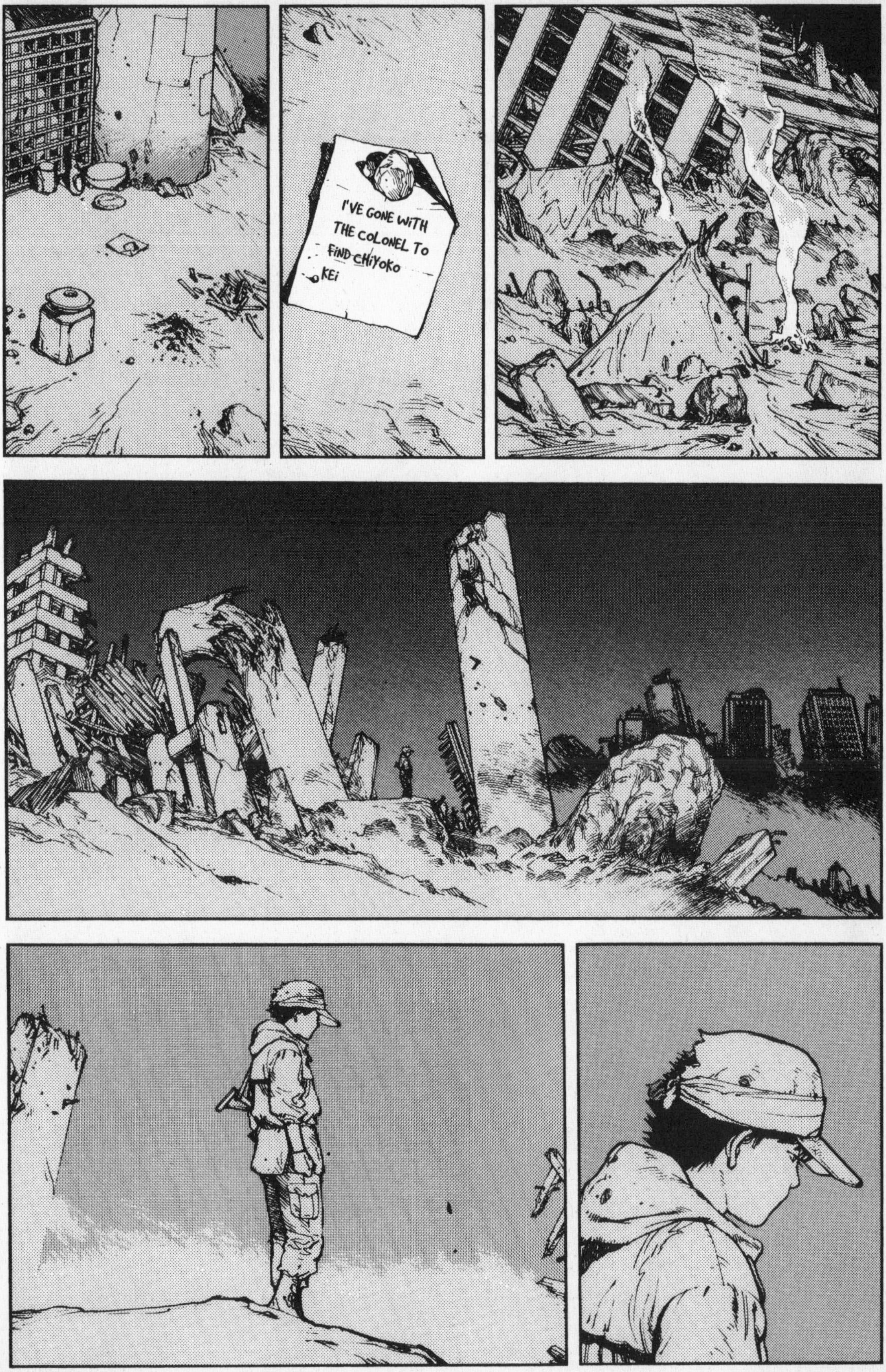
I'VE GONE WITH
THE COLONEL TO
FIND CHIYOKO
KEI

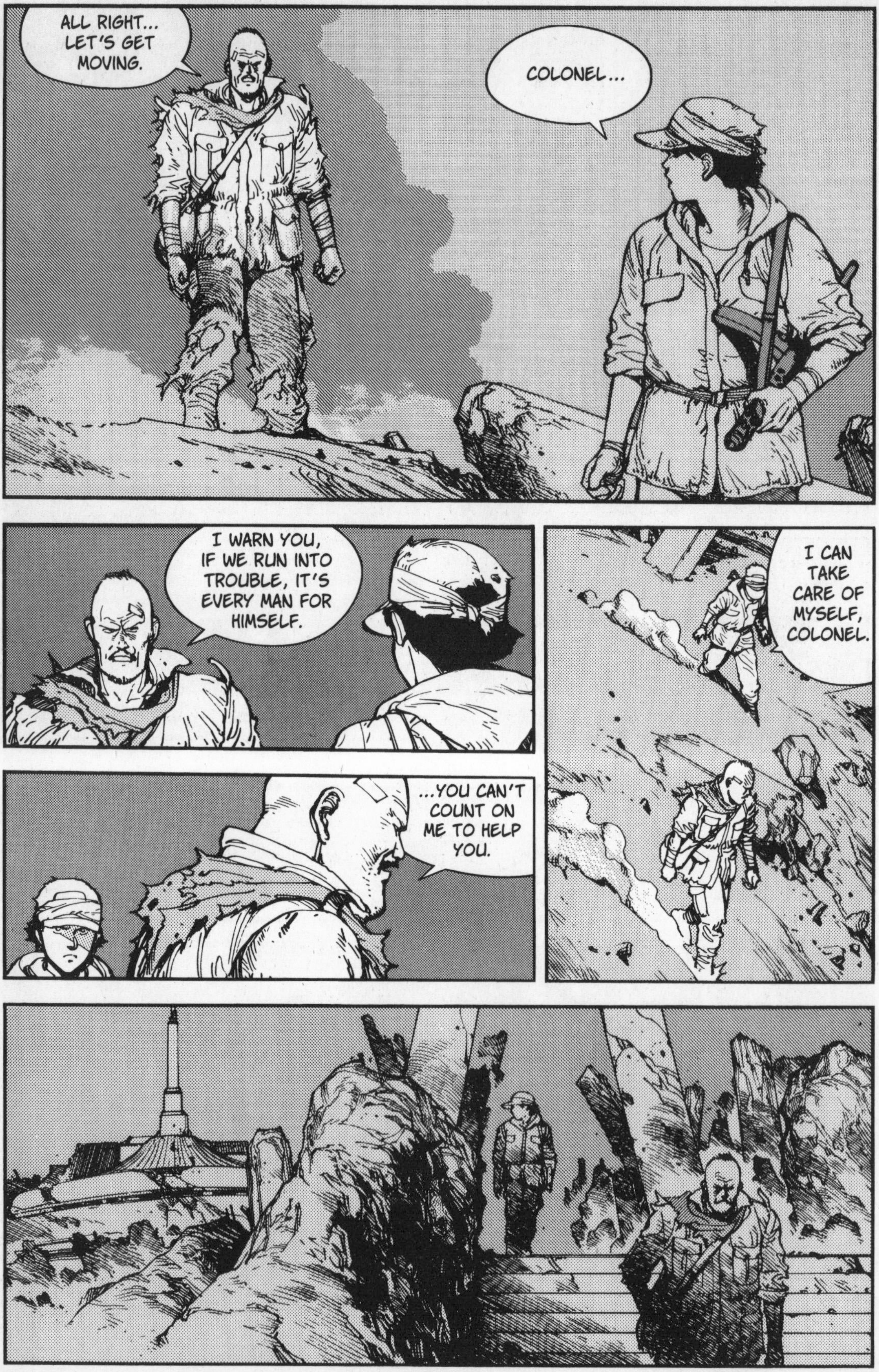
ALL RIGHT... LET'S GET MOVING.
COLONEL...
I WARN YOU, IF WE RUN INTO TROUBLE, IT'S EVERY MAN FOR HIMSELF.
...YOU CAN'T COUNT ON ME TO HELP YOU.
I CAN TAKE CARE OF MYSELF, COLONEL.

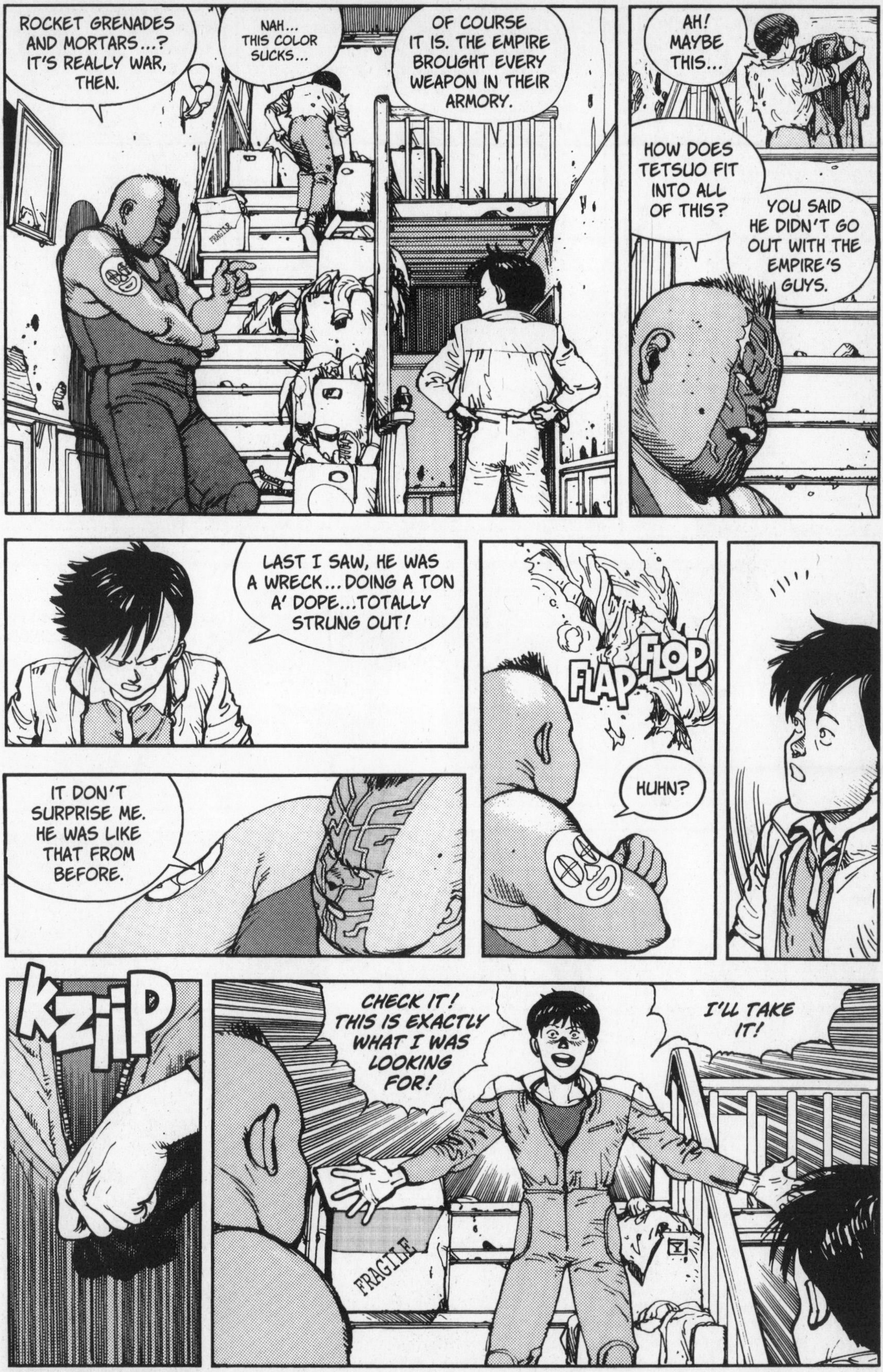
ROCKET GRENADES AND MORTARS...? IT'S REALLY WAR, THEN.
NAH... THIS COLOR SUCKS...
OF COURSE IT IS. THE EMPIRE BROUGHT EVERY WEAPON IN THEIR ARMORY.
FRAGILE
AH! MAYBE THIS...
HOW DOES TETSUO FIT INTO ALL OF THIS?
YOU SAID HE DIDN'T GO OUT WITH THE EMPIRE'S GUYS.
LAST I SAW, HE WAS A WRECK...DOING A TON A' DOPE...TOTALLY STRUNG OUT!
FLAP
FLOP
HUHN?
IT DON'T SURPRISE ME. HE WAS LIKE THAT FROM BEFORE.
KZIIP
CHECK IT! THIS IS EXACTLY WHAT I WAS LOOKING FOR!
I'LL TAKE IT!
FRAGILE

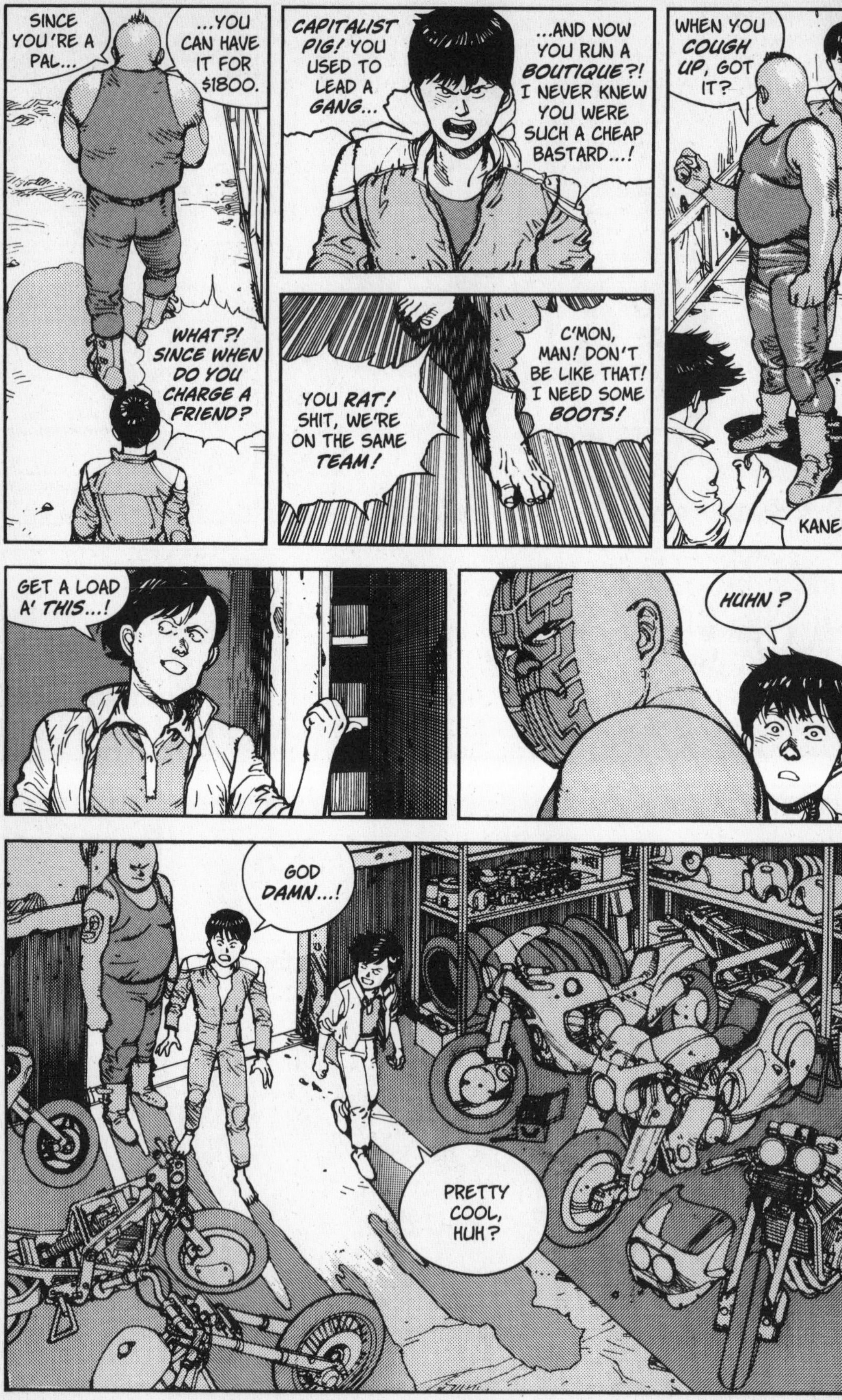
SINCE YOU'RE A PAL...
...YOU CAN HAVE IT FOR $1800.
WHAT?! SINCE WHEN DO YOU CHARGE A FRIEND?
CAPITALIST PIG! YOU USED TO LEAD A GANG...
...AND NOW YOU RUN A BOUTIQUE?! I NEVER KNEW YOU WERE SUCH A CHEAP BASTARD...!
YOU RAT! SHIT, WE'RE ON THE SAME TEAM!
C'MON, MAN! DON'T BE LIKE THAT! I NEED SOME BOOTS!
WHEN YOU COUGH UP, GOT IT?
KANEDA...
GET A LOAD A' THIS...!
HUHN?
GOD DAMN...!
PRETTY COOL, HUH?

DO THESE THINGS RUN?

JUST GAS 'EM UP.

THIS ONE'S PURE DEATH...DOUBLE ITS ORIGINAL HORSEPOWER!

...

IT'S LIKE A DREAM!!

I CANNIBALIZE JUNKERS TO PUT 'EM TOGETHER... ONE'S GOT PARTS FROM TWENTY DIFFERENT BIKES.

I'M HALLUCINATING...THIS TOTALLY KILLS...!

OH, YEAH? WAIT'LL YOU SEE WHAT'S BEHIND THE CURTAIN...

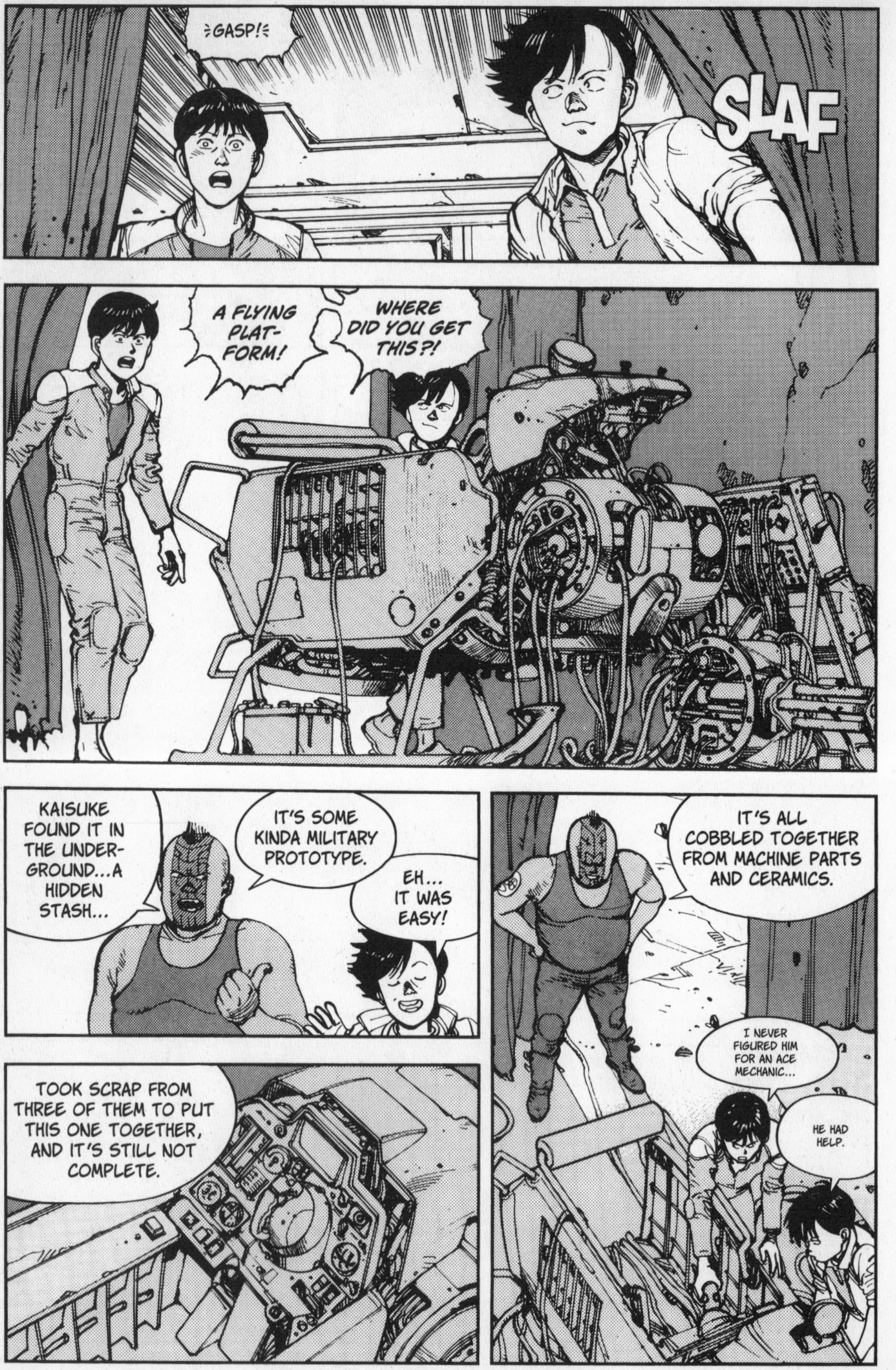
GASP!
SLAF
A FLYING PLAT-FORM!
WHERE DID YOU GET THIS?!
KAISUKE FOUND IT IN THE UNDER-GROUND...A HIDDEN STASH...
IT'S SOME KINDA MILITARY PROTOTYPE.
EH... IT WAS EASY!
IT'S ALL COBBLED TOGETHER FROM MACHINE PARTS AND CERAMICS.
TOOK SCRAP FROM THREE OF THEM TO PUT THIS ONE TOGETHER, AND IT'S STILL NOT COMPLETE.
I NEVER FIGURED HIM FOR AN ACE MECHANIC...
HE HAD HELP.

ARE YOU TELLING ME THAT KEI HAS LEFT THE SHRINE?!

UH...

...YES. SHE WAS GONE THIS MORNING, EMMINENCE.

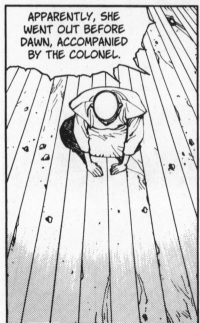

APPARENTLY, SHE WENT OUT BEFORE DAWN, ACCOMPANIED BY THE COLONEL.

HOW FOOLISH! SHE THINKS ONLY OF *HERSELF!* WE NEED HER *HELP!*

THE COLONEL ALSO TOOK ANTIBIOTICS FROM OUR MEDICAL SUPPLIES.

ENOUGH! BRING THEM BACK AT ONCE!

YES, EMMINENCE!

THERE'S TROUBLE AT THE SHRINE...

WHAT'S GOIN' DOWN?

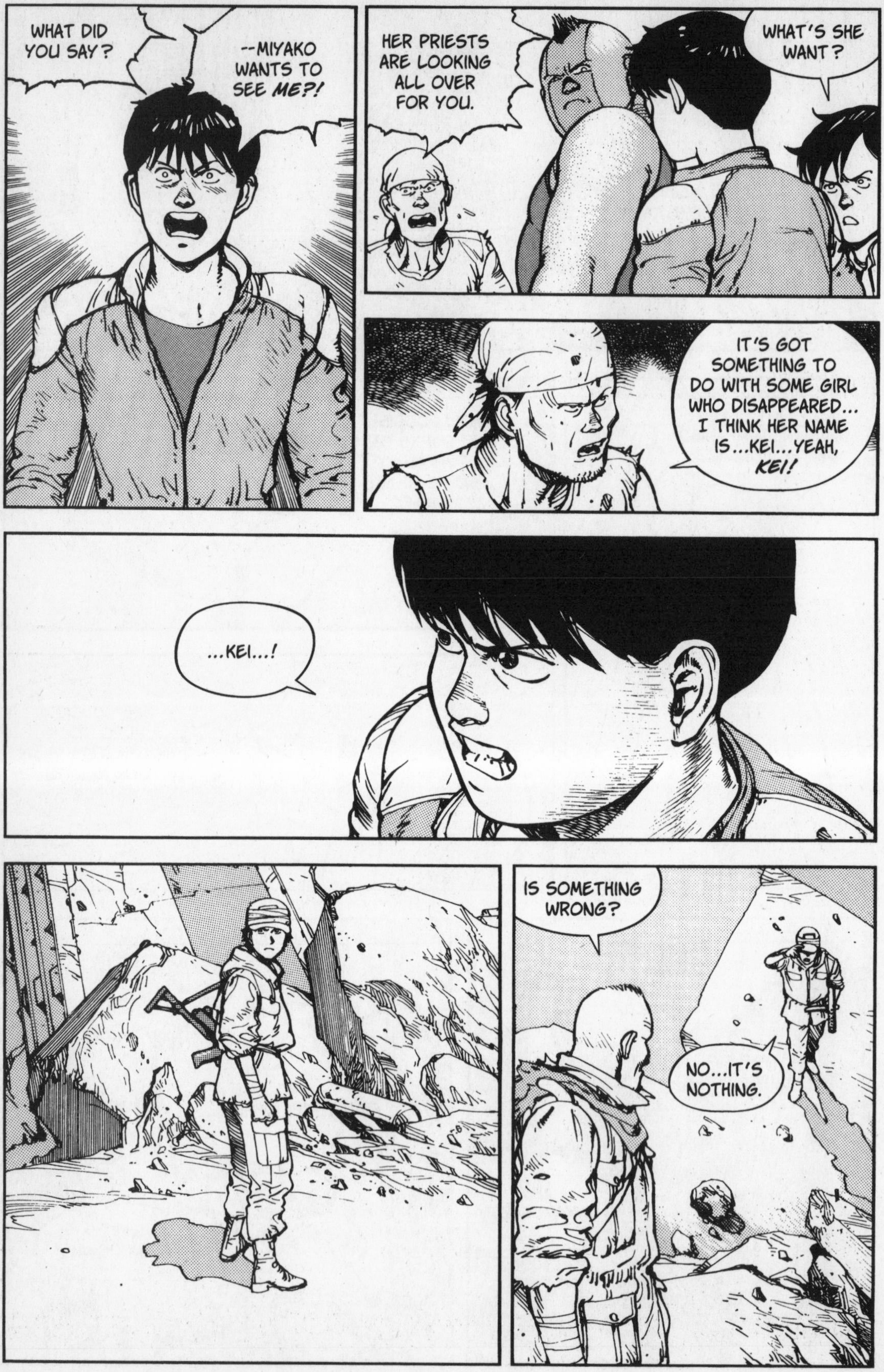
WHAT DID YOU SAY?
--MIYAKO WANTS TO SEE ME?!
HER PRIESTS ARE LOOKING ALL OVER FOR YOU.
WHAT'S SHE WANT?
IT'S GOT SOMETHING TO DO WITH SOME GIRL WHO DISAPPEARED... I THINK HER NAME IS...KEI...YEAH, KEI!
...KEI...!
IS SOMETHING WRONG?
NO...IT'S NOTHING.

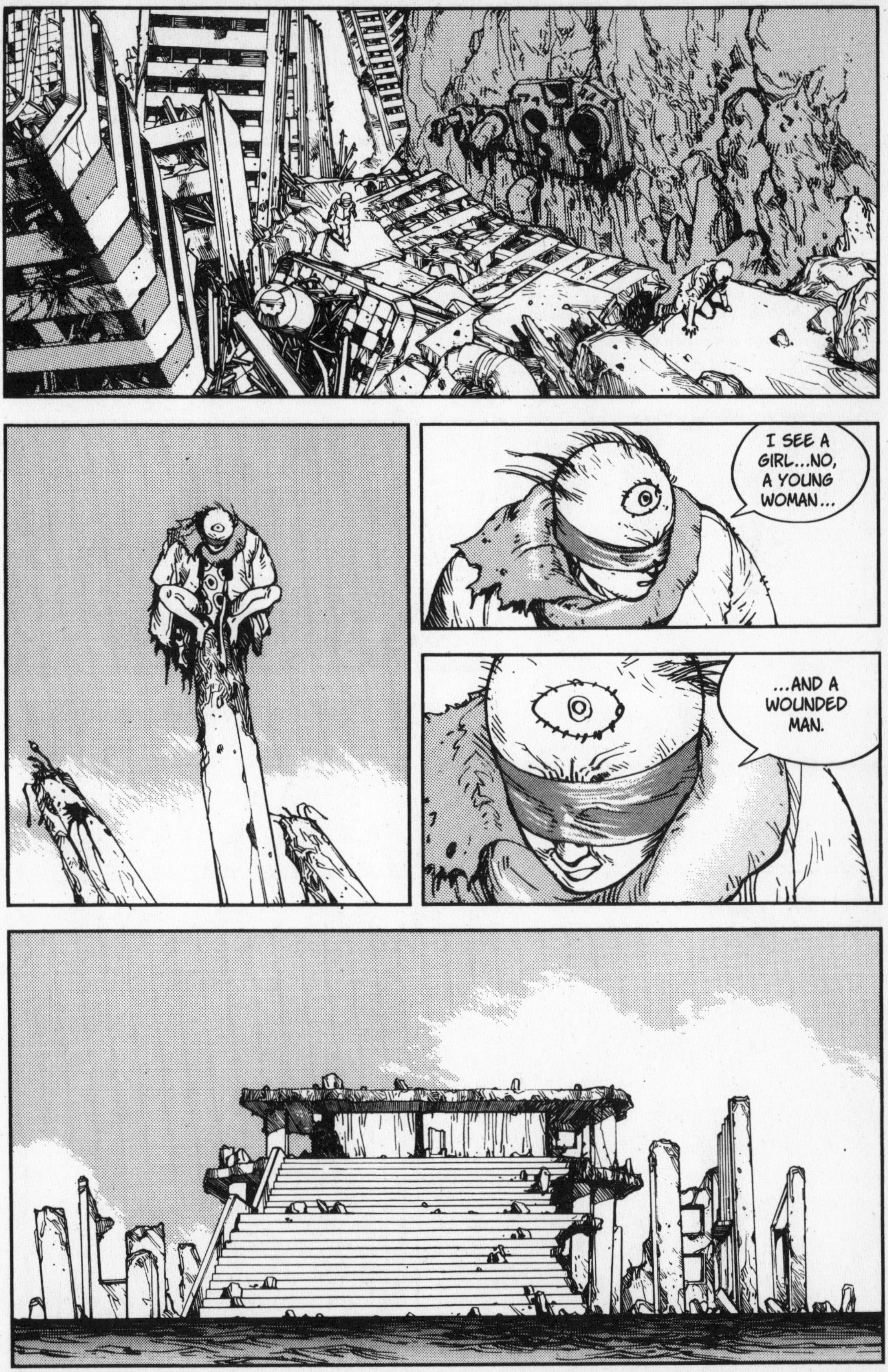
I SEE A GIRL...NO, A YOUNG WOMAN...
...AND A WOUNDED MAN.

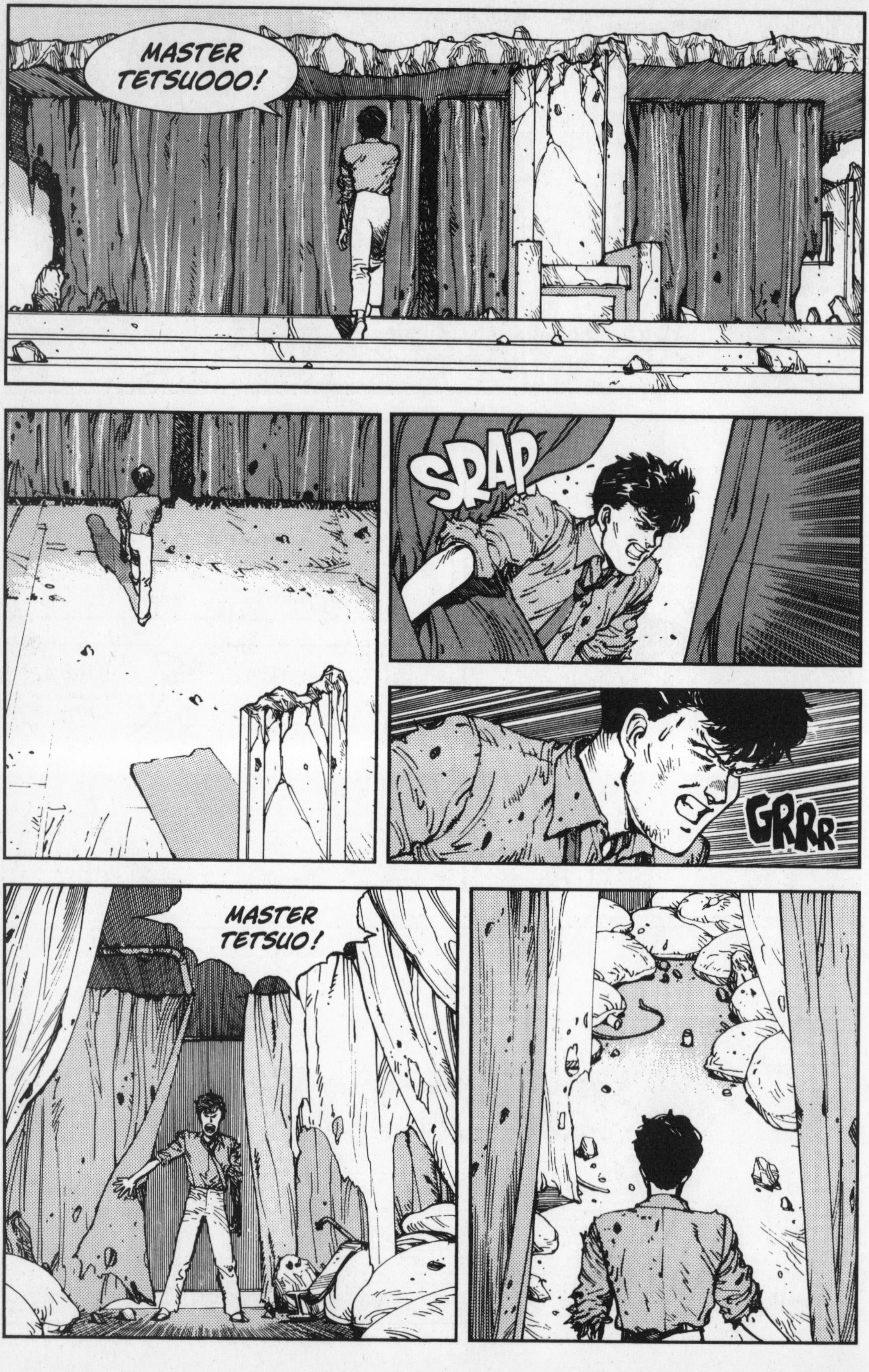
MASTER TETSUOOO!
SRAP
GRRR
MASTER TETSUO!

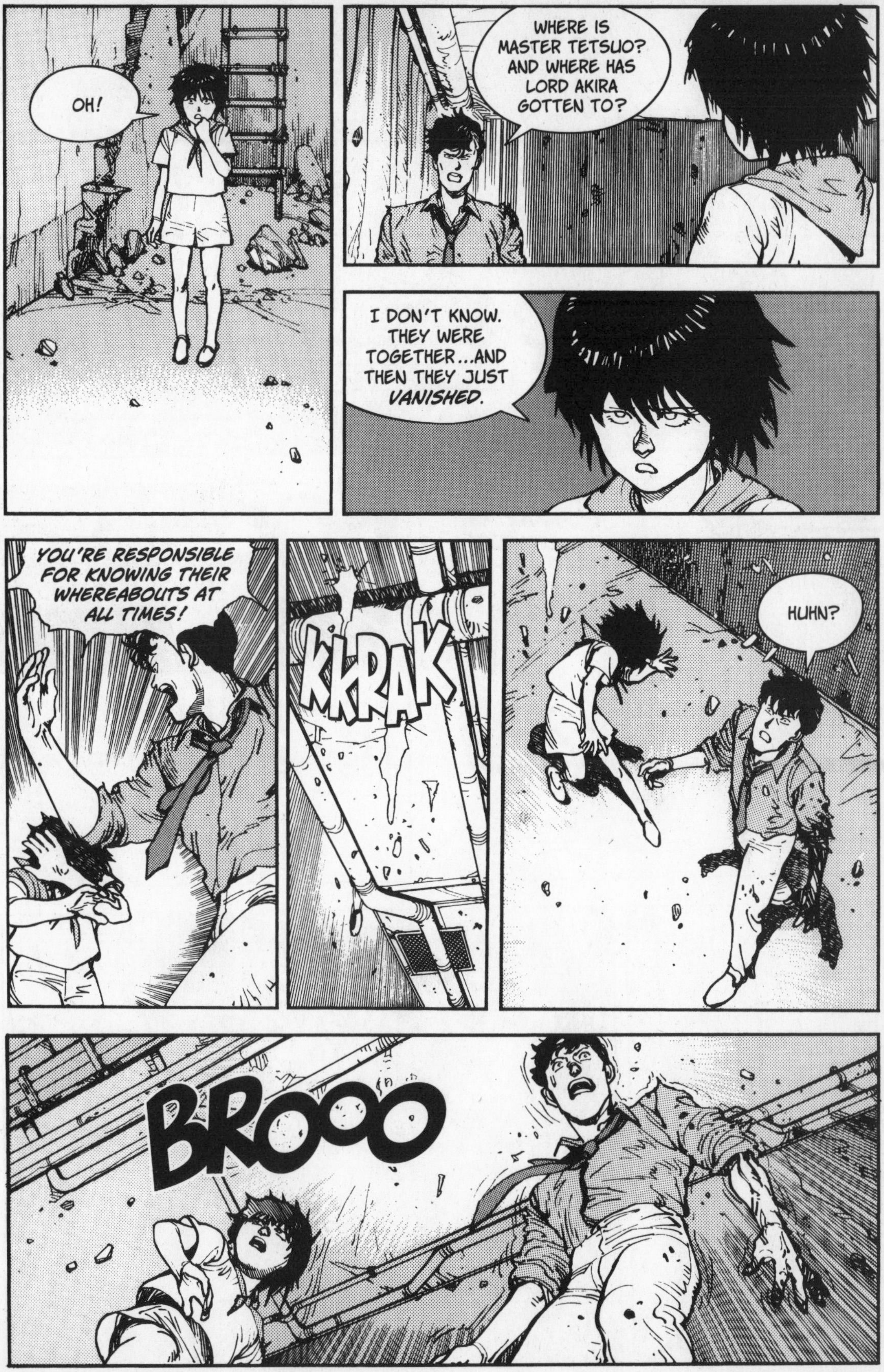
OH!
WHERE IS MASTER TETSUO? AND WHERE HAS LORD AKIRA GOTTEN TO?
I DON'T KNOW. THEY WERE TOGETHER...AND THEN THEY JUST VANISHED.
YOU'RE RESPONSIBLE FOR KNOWING THEIR WHEREABOUTS AT ALL TIMES!
KKRAK
HUHN?
BROOO

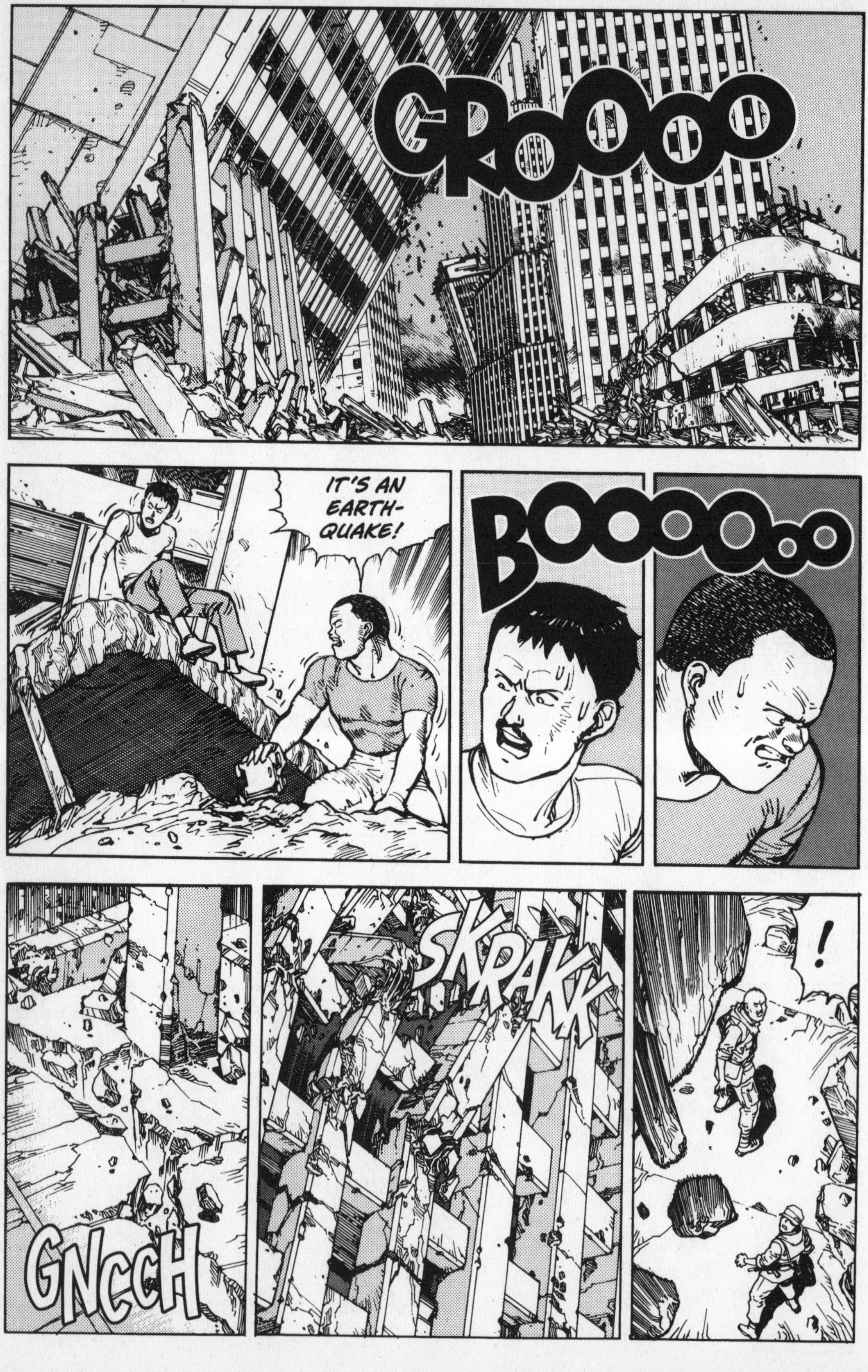
GROOOOO
IT'S AN EARTH-QUAKE!
BOOOOOO
SKRAKK
!
GNCCH

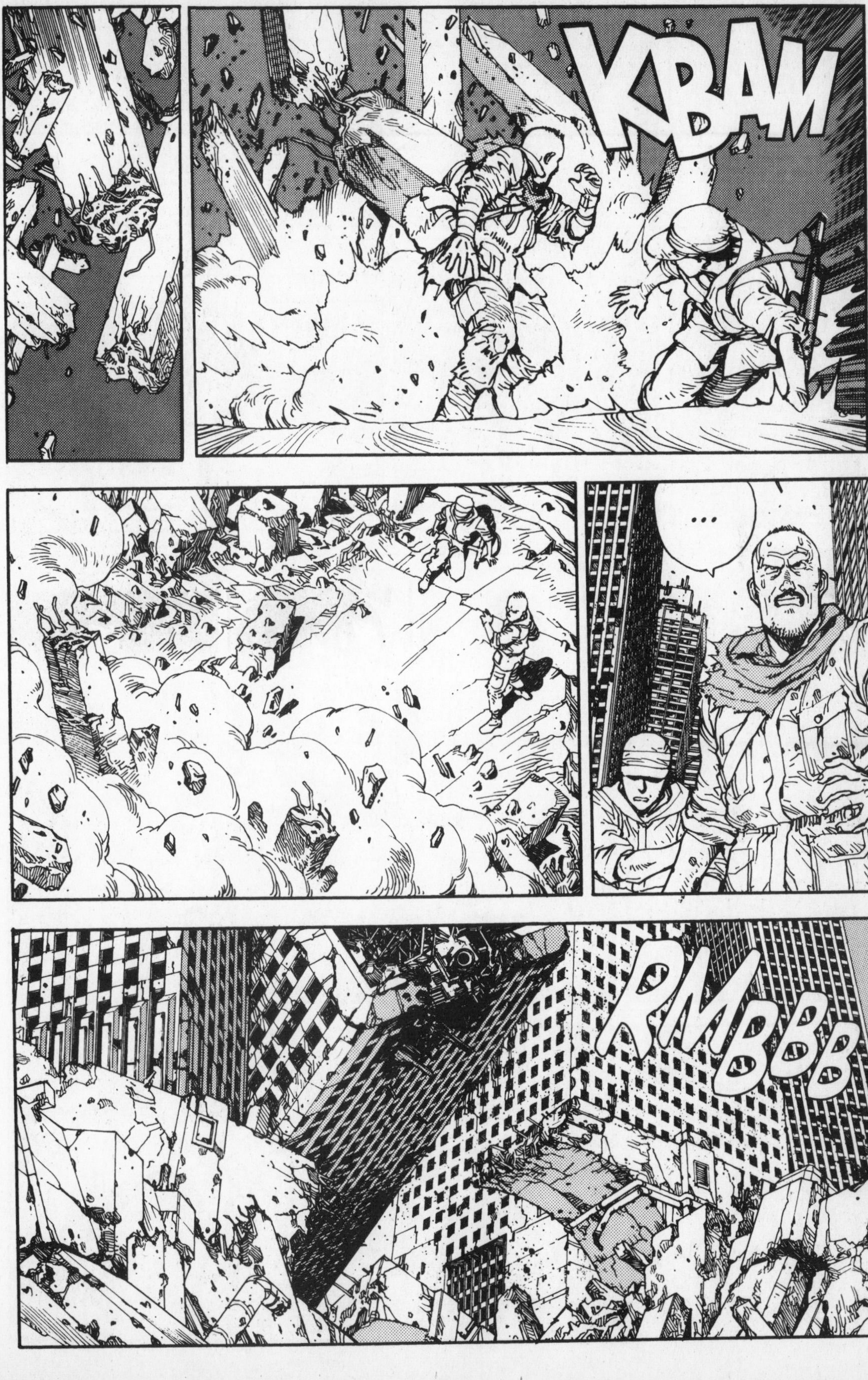
KBAM
...
RMBBB

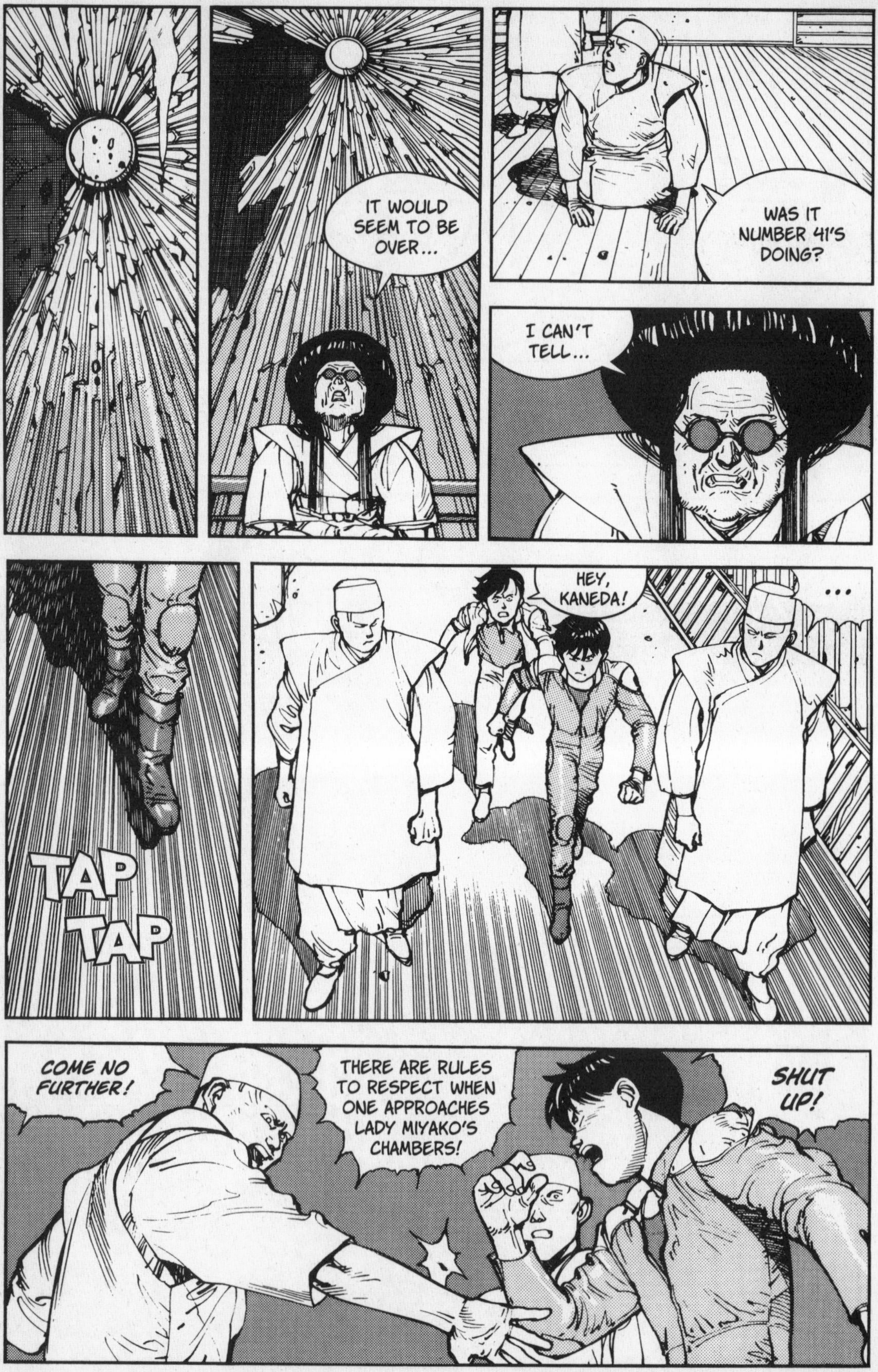
IT WOULD SEEM TO BE OVER...
WAS IT NUMBER 41'S DOING?
I CAN'T TELL...
TAP
TAP
HEY, KANEDA!
...
COME NO FURTHER!
THERE ARE RULES TO RESPECT WHEN ONE APPROACHES LADY MIYAKO'S CHAMBERS!
SHUT UP!

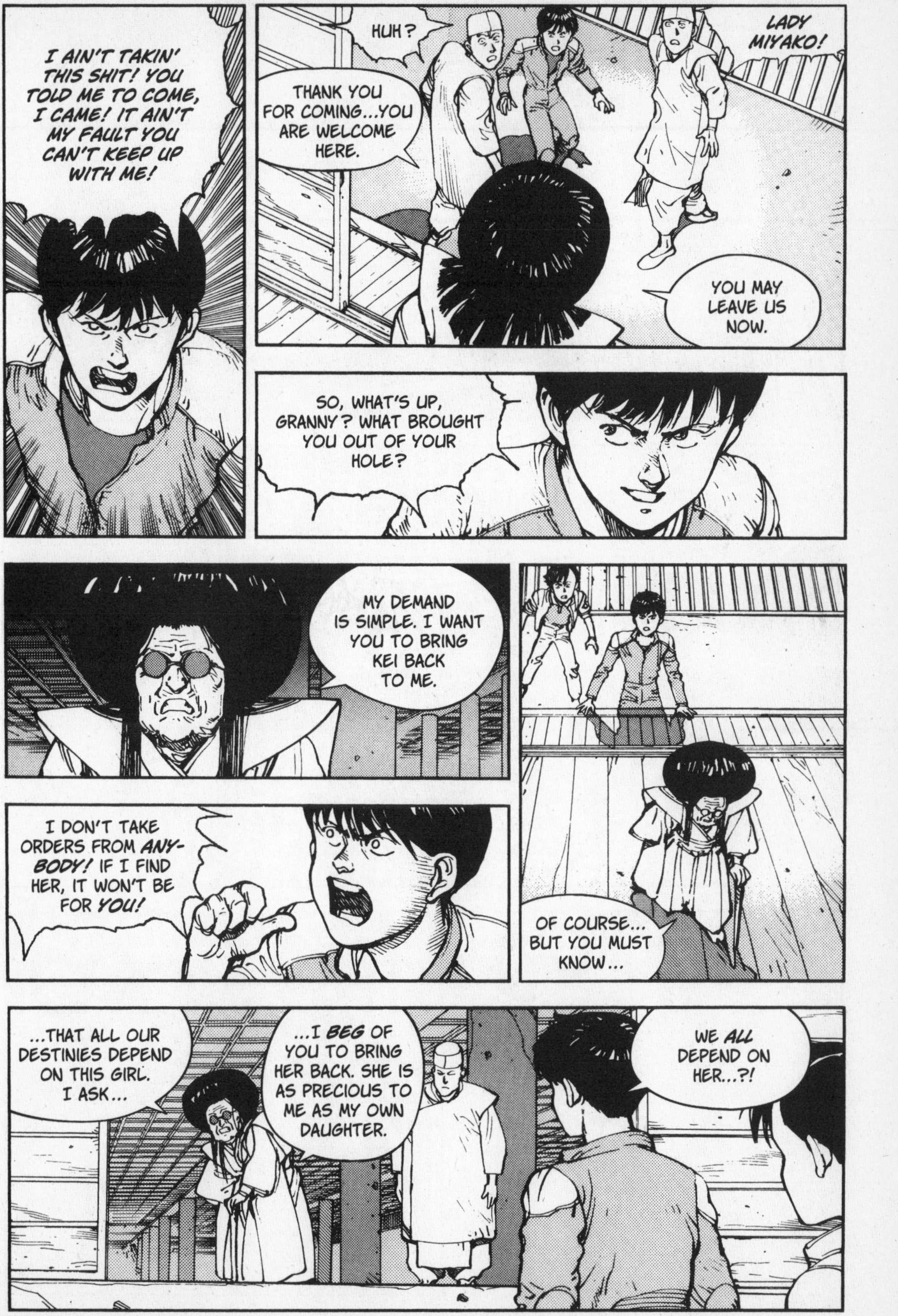
I AIN'T TAKIN' THIS SHIT! YOU TOLD ME TO COME, I CAME! IT AIN'T MY FAULT YOU CAN'T KEEP UP WITH ME!
HUH?
THANK YOU FOR COMING...YOU ARE WELCOME HERE.
LADY MIYAKO!
YOU MAY LEAVE US NOW.
SO, WHAT'S UP, GRANNY? WHAT BROUGHT YOU OUT OF YOUR HOLE?
MY DEMAND IS SIMPLE. I WANT YOU TO BRING KEI BACK TO ME.
I DON'T TAKE ORDERS FROM ANY-BODY! IF I FIND HER, IT WON'T BE FOR YOU!
OF COURSE... BUT YOU MUST KNOW...
...THAT ALL OUR DESTINIES DEPEND ON THIS GIRL. I ASK...
...I BEG OF YOU TO BRING HER BACK. SHE IS AS PRECIOUS TO ME AS MY OWN DAUGHTER.
WE ALL DEPEND ON HER...?!

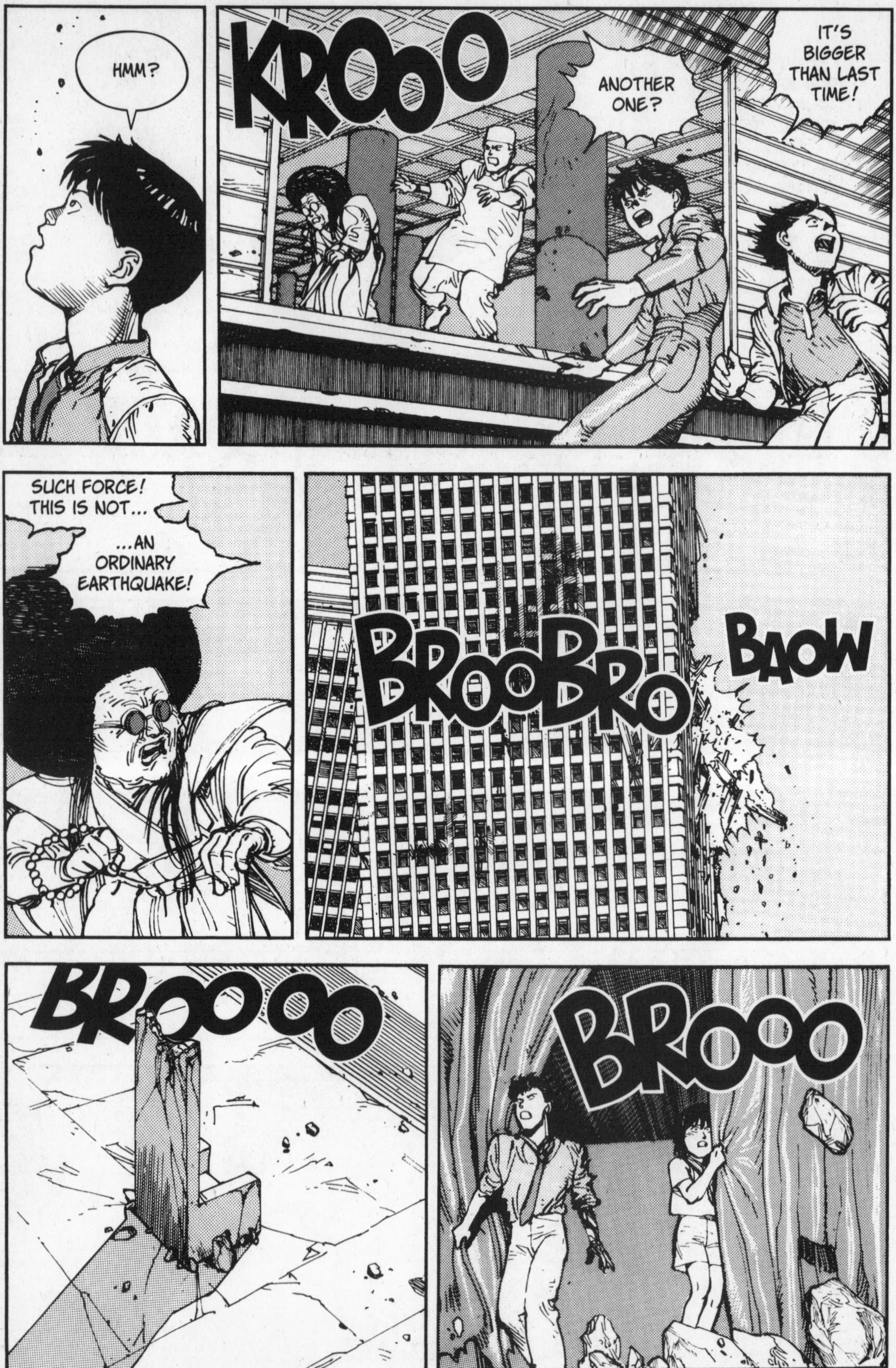

HMM?
KROOO
ANOTHER ONE?
IT'S BIGGER THAN LAST TIME!
SUCH FORCE! THIS IS NOT...
...AN ORDINARY EARTHQUAKE!
BROOBRO
BAOW
BROOOO
BROOO

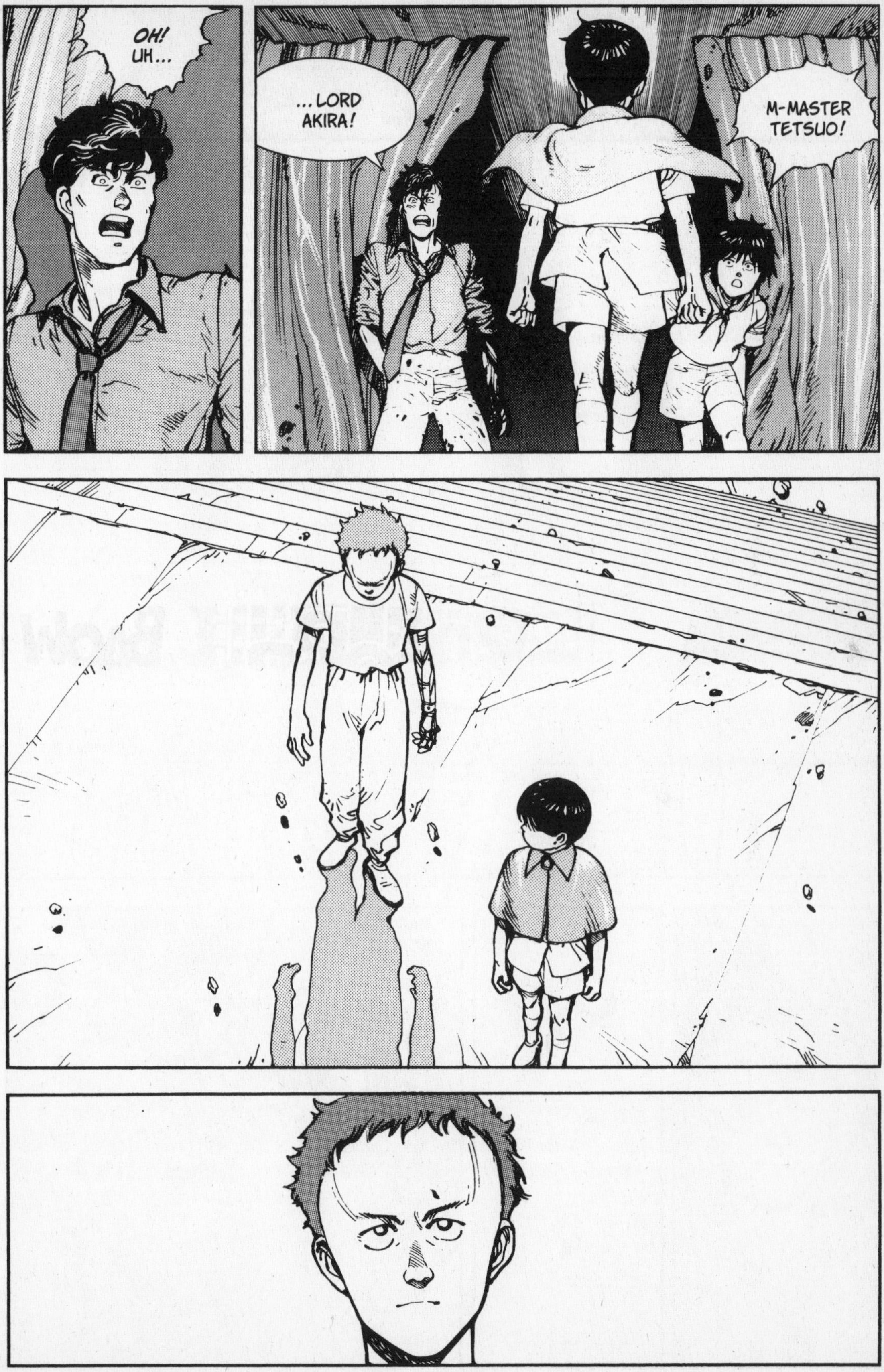
OH!
UH...
...LORD
AKIRA!
M-MASTER
TETSUO!

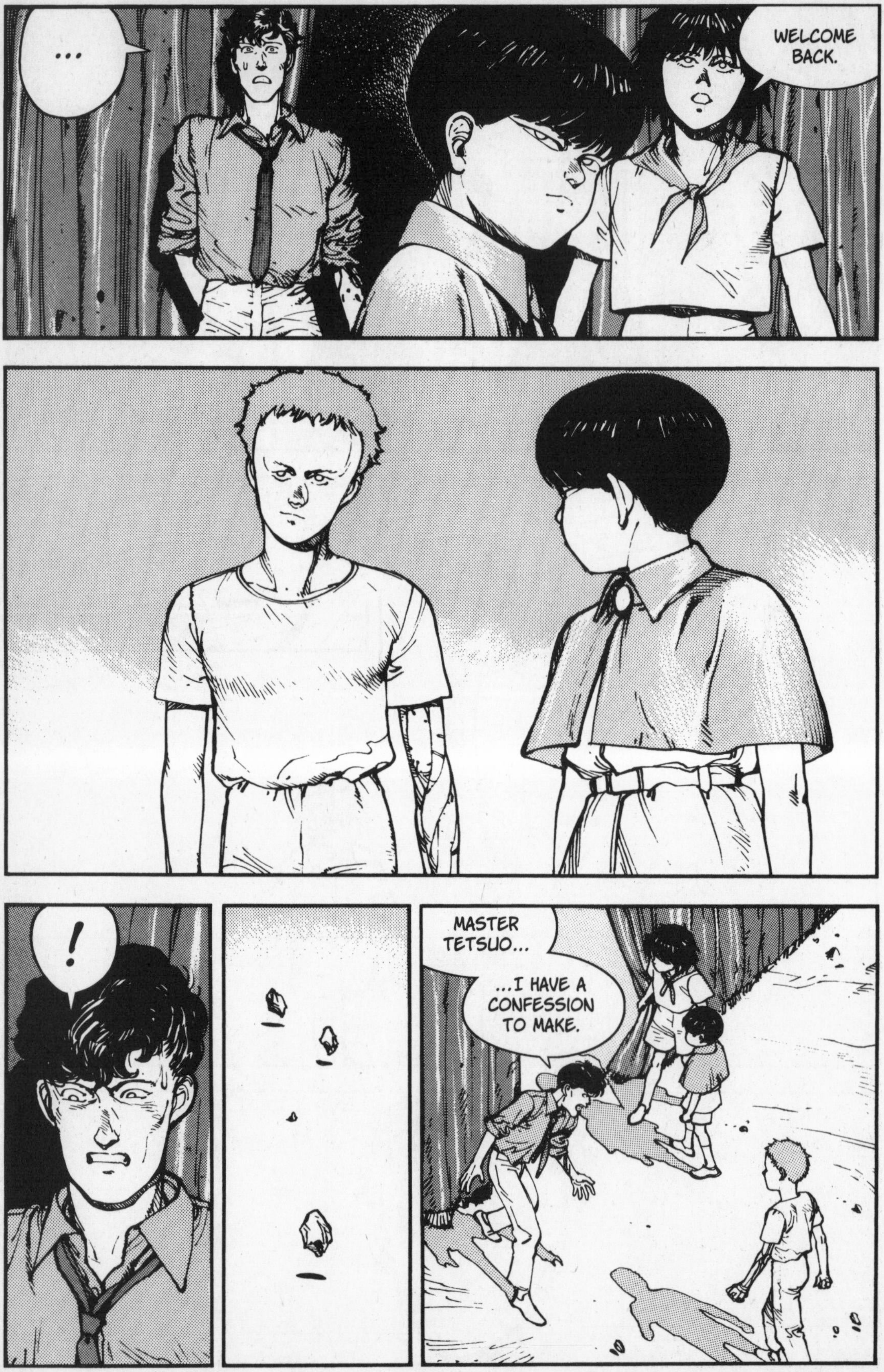
...
WELCOME BACK.
!
MASTER TETSUO...
...I HAVE A CONFESSION TO MAKE.

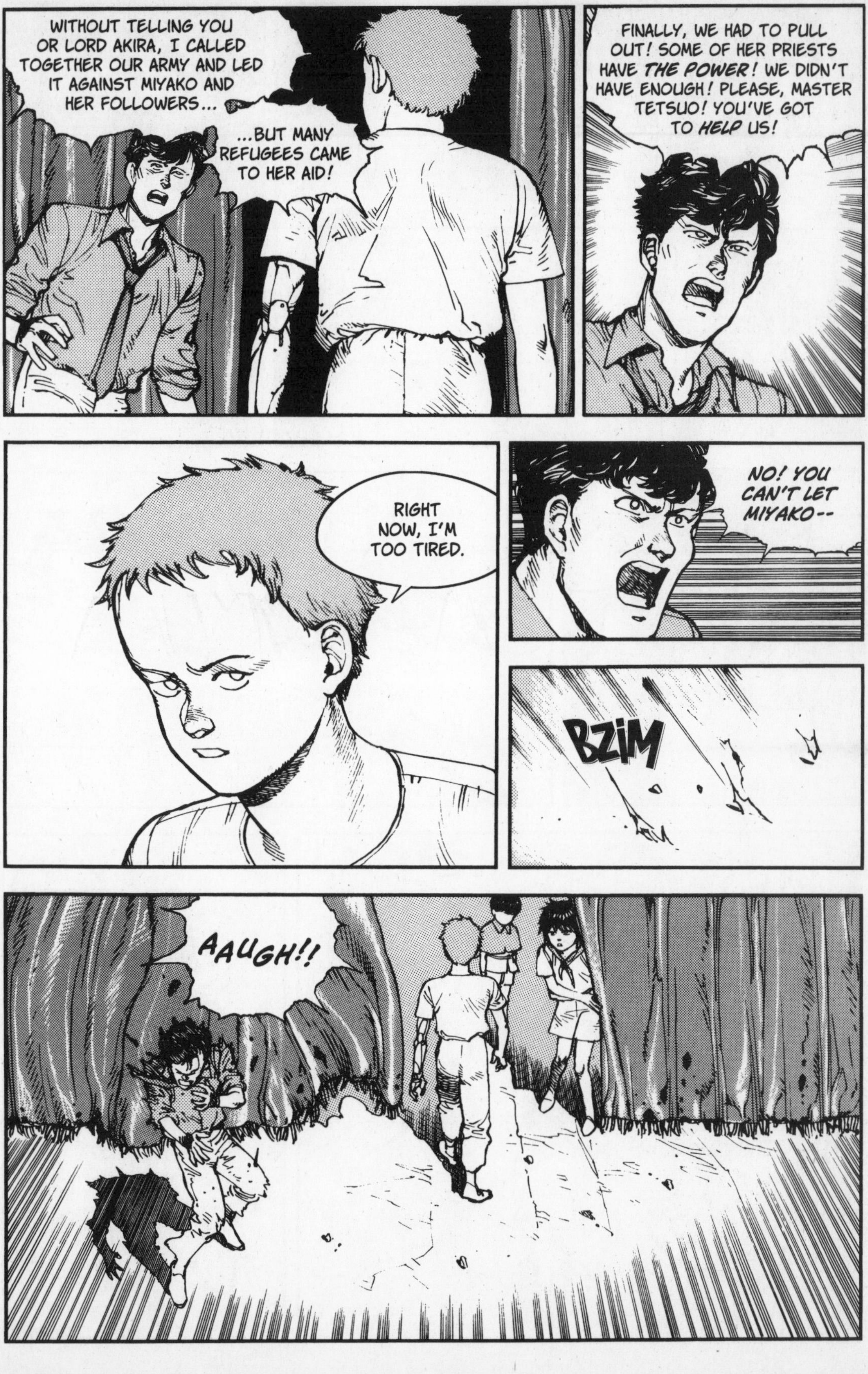
WITHOUT TELLING YOU OR LORD AKIRA, I CALLED TOGETHER OUR ARMY AND LED IT AGAINST MIYAKO AND HER FOLLOWERS...
...BUT MANY REFUGEES CAME TO HER AID!
FINALLY, WE HAD TO PULL OUT! SOME OF HER PRIESTS HAVE THE POWER! WE DIDN'T HAVE ENOUGH! PLEASE, MASTER TETSUO! YOU'VE GOT TO HELP US!
RIGHT NOW, I'M TOO TIRED.
NO! YOU CAN'T LET MIYAKO--
BZIM
AAUGH!!

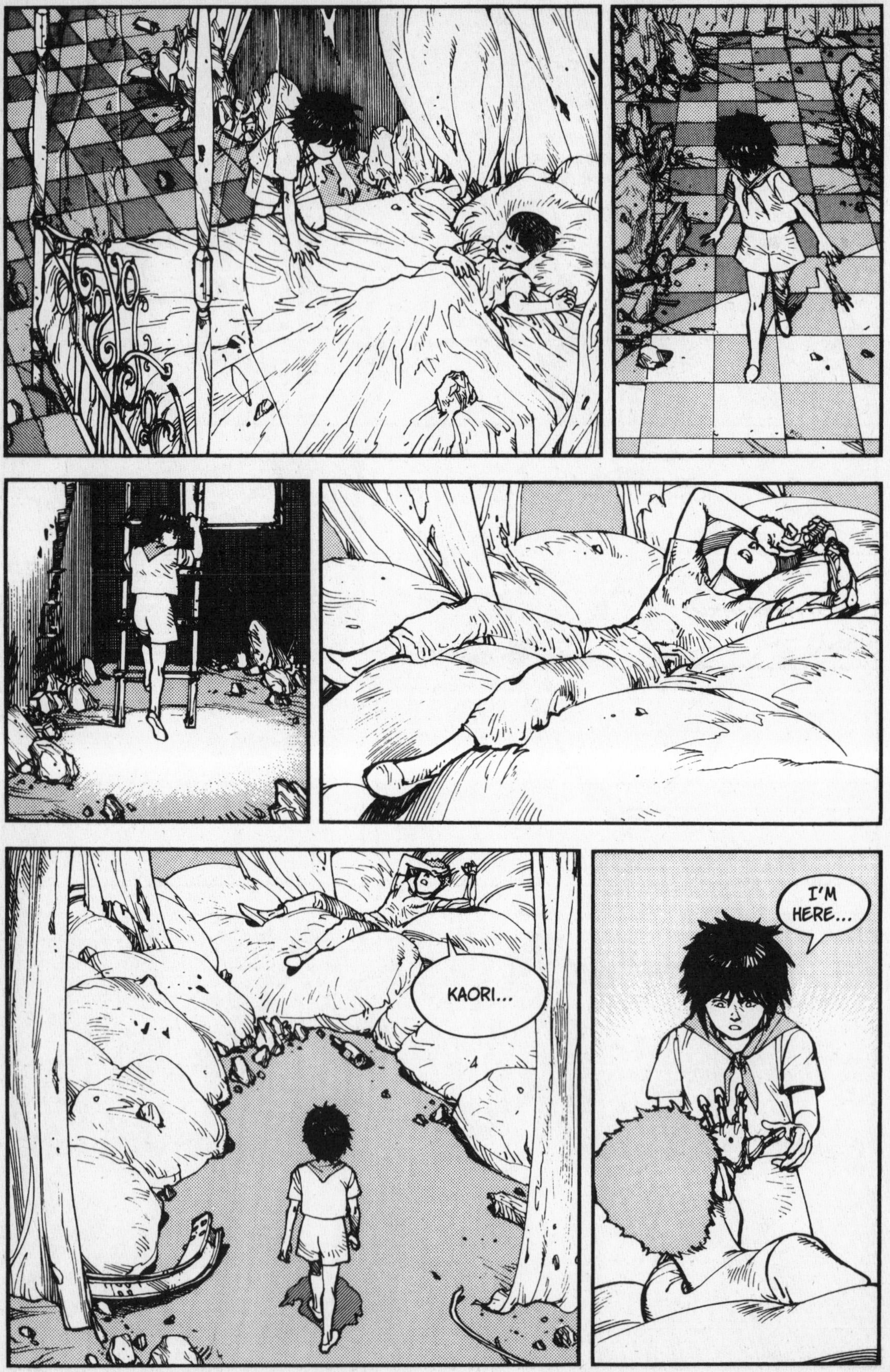
KAORI...
I'M HERE...

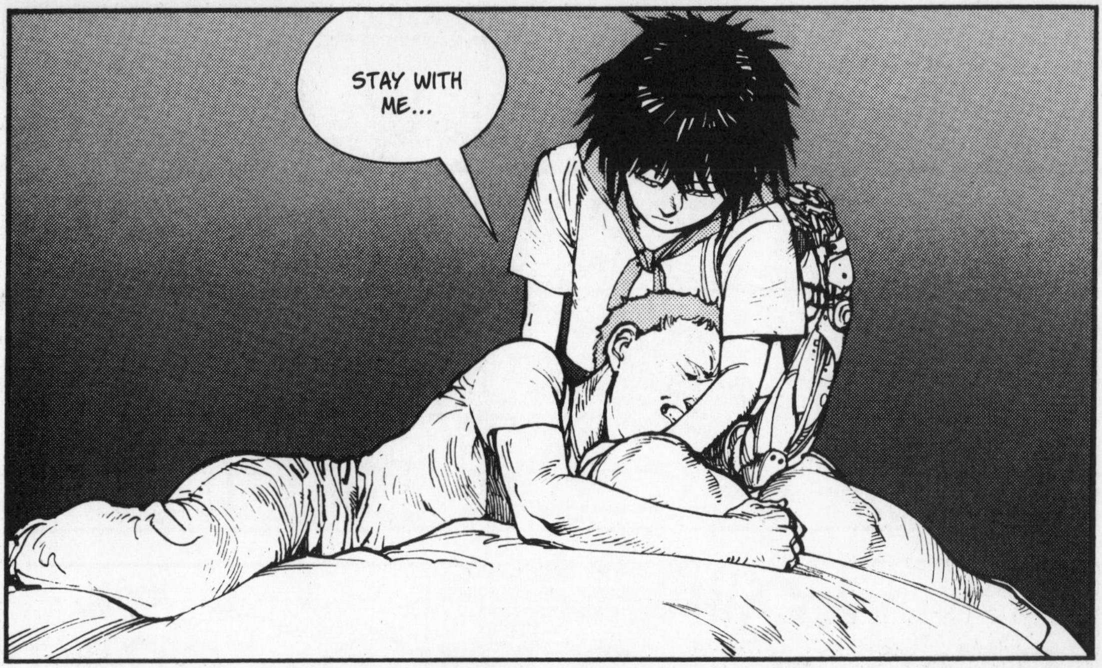
STAY WITH ME...

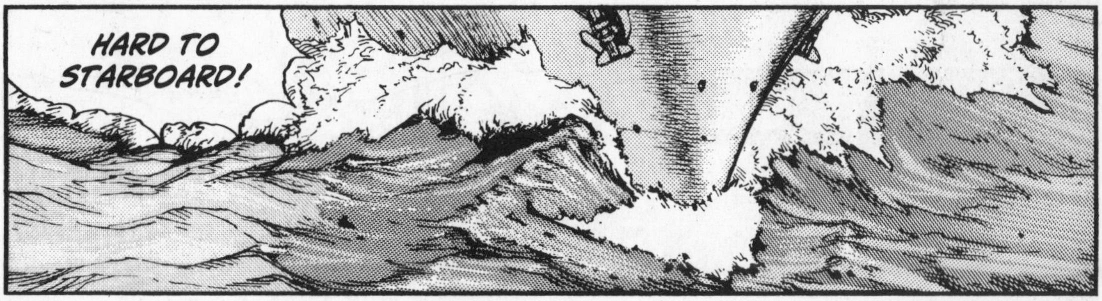
HARD TO STARBOARD!

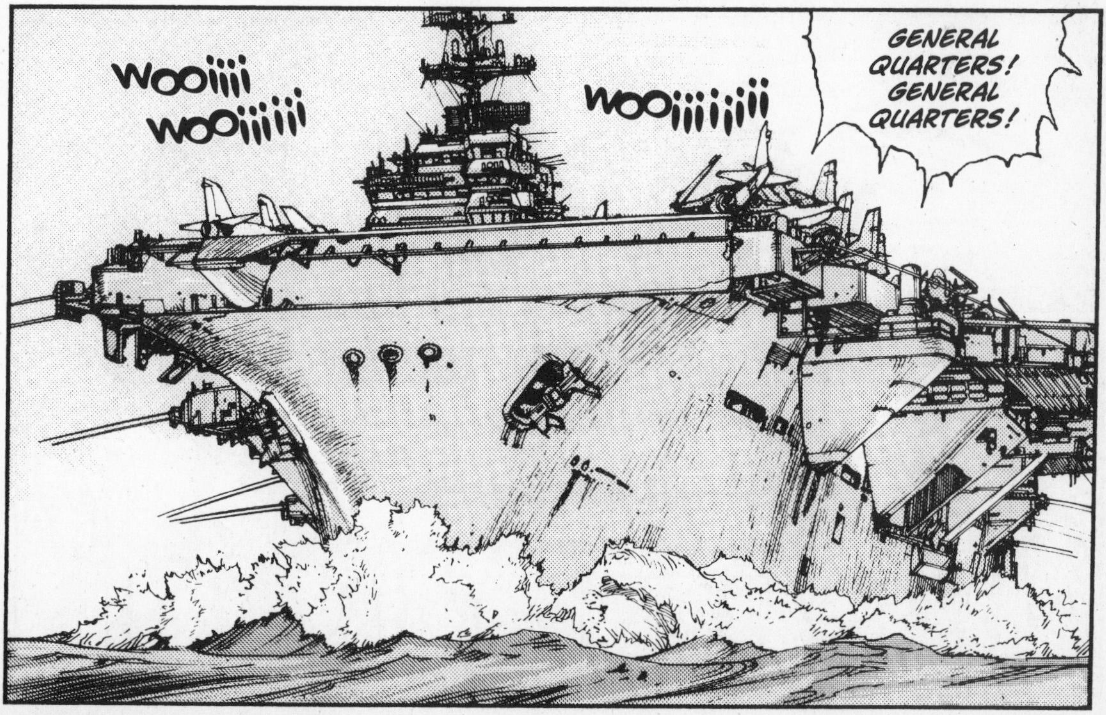
WOOiiii
WOOiiiiii
WOOiiiiiiii
GENERAL QUARTERS! GENERAL QUARTERS!

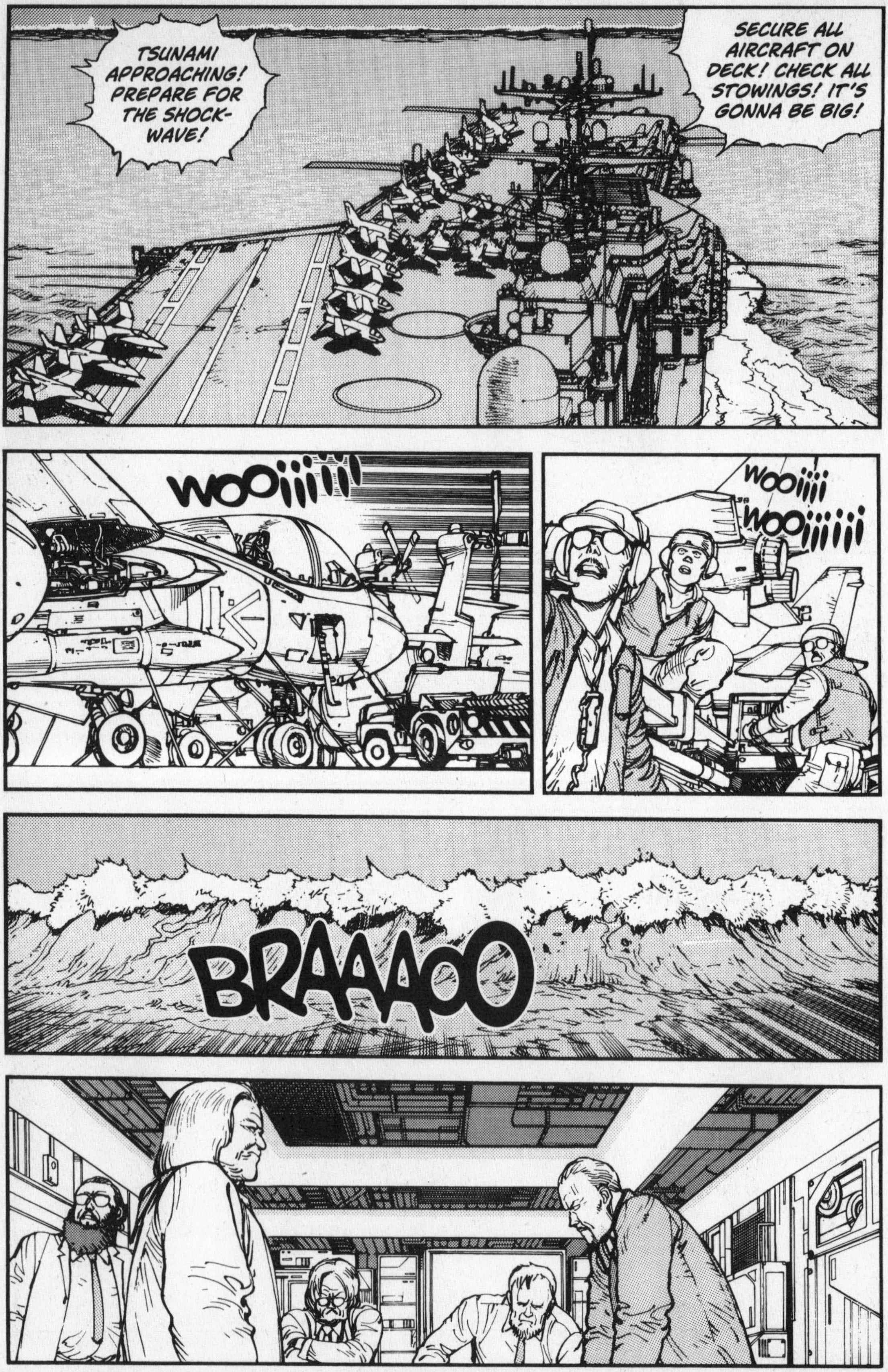
TSUNAMI APPROACHING! PREPARE FOR THE SHOCK-WAVE!
SECURE ALL AIRCRAFT ON DECK! CHECK ALL STOWINGS! IT'S GONNA BE BIG!
WOOiiii
WOOiiii
WOOiiiii
BRAAAOO

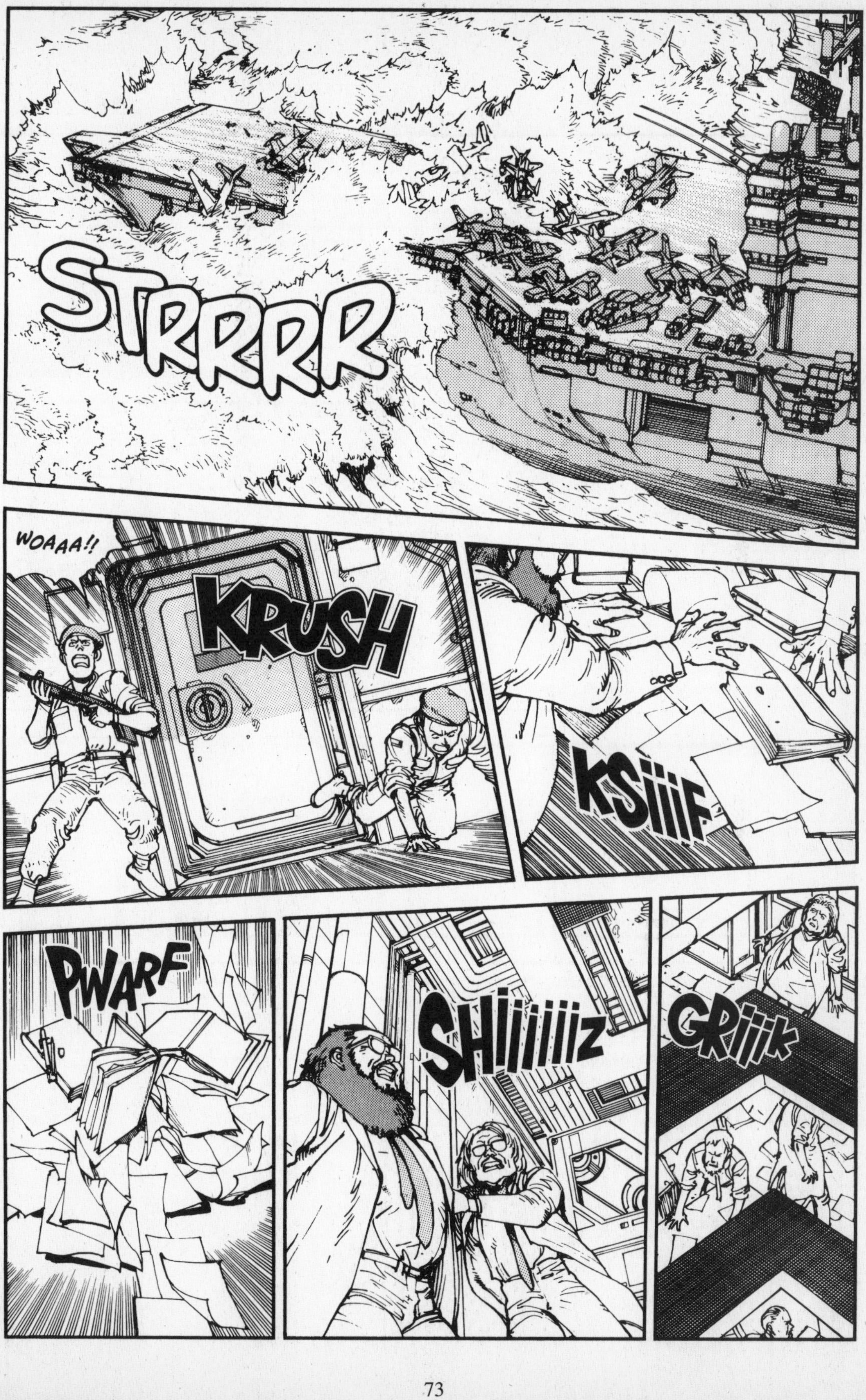
STRRRR
WOAAA!!
KRUSH
KSIIIF
PWARF
SHIIIIIZ
GRIIIK

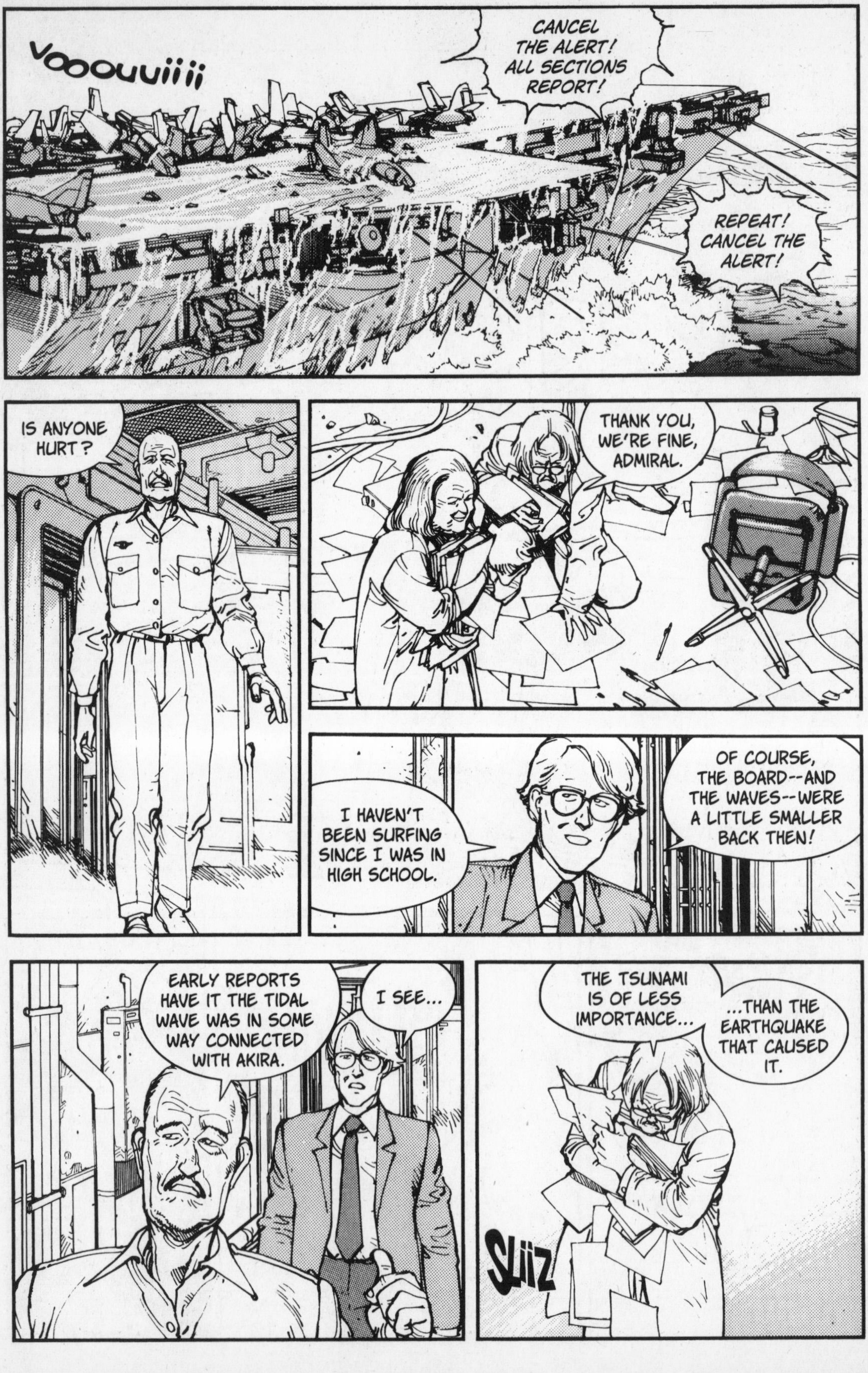
VOOOUUIIII
CANCEL THE ALERT! ALL SECTIONS REPORT!
REPEAT! CANCEL THE ALERT!
IS ANYONE HURT?
THANK YOU, WE'RE FINE, ADMIRAL.
I HAVEN'T BEEN SURFING SINCE I WAS IN HIGH SCHOOL.
OF COURSE, THE BOARD--AND THE WAVES--WERE A LITTLE SMALLER BACK THEN!
EARLY REPORTS HAVE IT THE TIDAL WAVE WAS IN SOME WAY CONNECTED WITH AKIRA.
I SEE...
THE TSUNAMI IS OF LESS IMPORTANCE...
...THAN THE EARTHQUAKE THAT CAUSED IT.
SLIIZ

THE EPICENTER WAS 300 KILOMETERS BELOW NEO-TOKYO'S SURFACE. SHOCKWAVES MEASURE 8.5 ON THE RICHTER SCALE-- A *MAMMOTH* QUAKE!

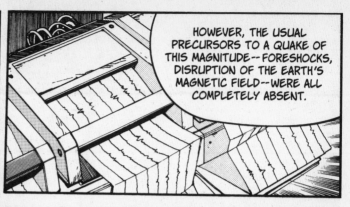

HOWEVER, THE USUAL PRECURSORS TO A QUAKE OF THIS MAGNITUDE-- FORESHOCKS, DISRUPTION OF THE EARTH'S MAGNETIC FIELD-- WERE ALL COMPLETELY ABSENT.

IN FACT, THERE WAS NO TRACE OF INCREASED SEISMO-GRAPHIC READINGS AT ANY OF OUR TRACKING STATIONS. THIS WAS NOT THE RESULT OF NAT-URAL STRESSES DUE TO PLATE TECTONICS, BUT THE RESULT OF HUMAN INTERVENTION OR... AN EXTERNAL POWER...

JAPAN IS A NATURAL EARTH-QUAKE CENTER. YOU'LL NEED IRREFUTABLE EVIDENCE TO LINK THIS PHENOMENON TO AKIRA. OTHERWISE, NO ONE WILL LISTEN...

WHAT'S YOUR OPINION, KARMA TANGI?

THEY ARE SLEEPING, BOTH OF THEM.

THEY PLAYED HARD, AND NOW THEY ARE ASLEEP.

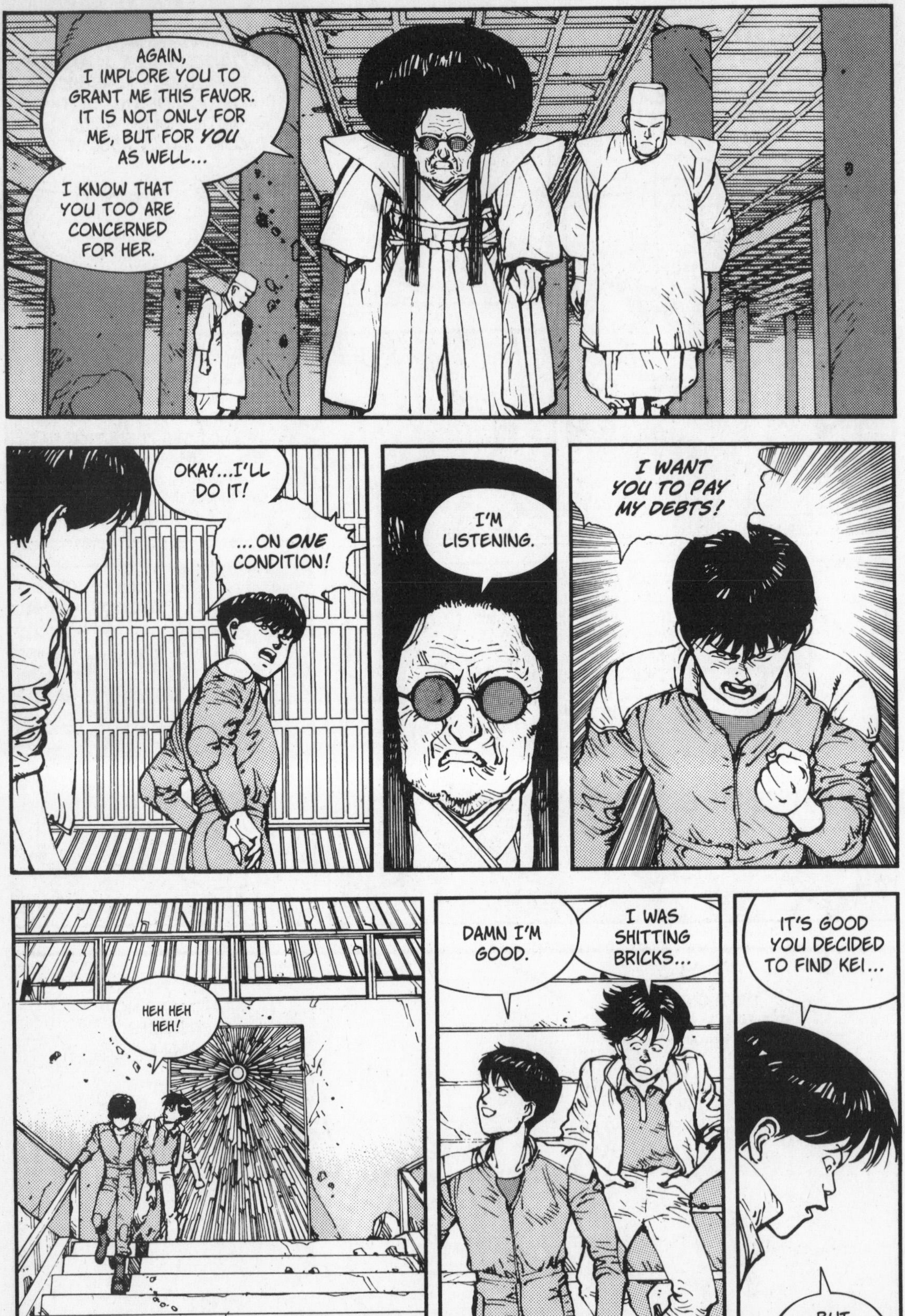
AGAIN, I IMPLORE YOU TO GRANT ME THIS FAVOR. IT IS NOT ONLY FOR ME, BUT FOR *YOU* AS WELL...
I KNOW THAT YOU TOO ARE CONCERNED FOR HER.
OKAY...I'LL DO IT!
...ON *ONE* CONDITION!
I'M LISTENING.
I WANT YOU TO PAY MY DEBTS!
HEH HEH HEH!
DAMN I'M GOOD.
I WAS SHITTING BRICKS...
IT'S GOOD YOU DECIDED TO FIND KEI...
...BUT WHERE WILL YOU LOOK?

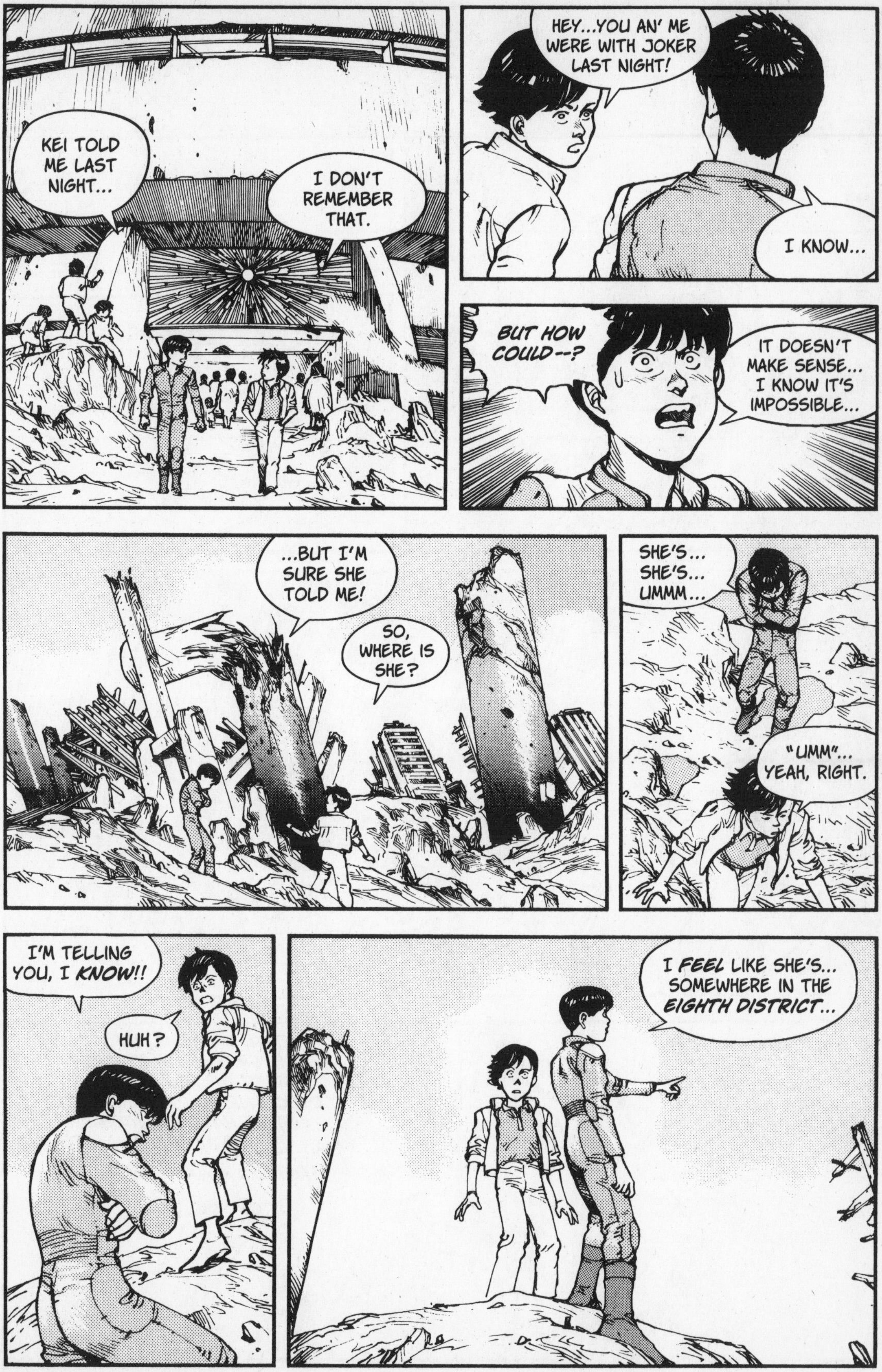
KEI TOLD ME LAST NIGHT...
I DON'T REMEMBER THAT.
HEY...YOU AN' ME WERE WITH JOKER LAST NIGHT!
I KNOW...
BUT HOW COULD--?
IT DOESN'T MAKE SENSE... I KNOW IT'S IMPOSSIBLE...
...BUT I'M SURE SHE TOLD ME!
SO, WHERE IS SHE?
SHE'S... SHE'S... UMMM...
"UMM"... YEAH, RIGHT.
I'M TELLING YOU, I *KNOW*!!
HUH?
I *FEEL* LIKE SHE'S... SOMEWHERE IN THE *EIGHTH DISTRICT*...

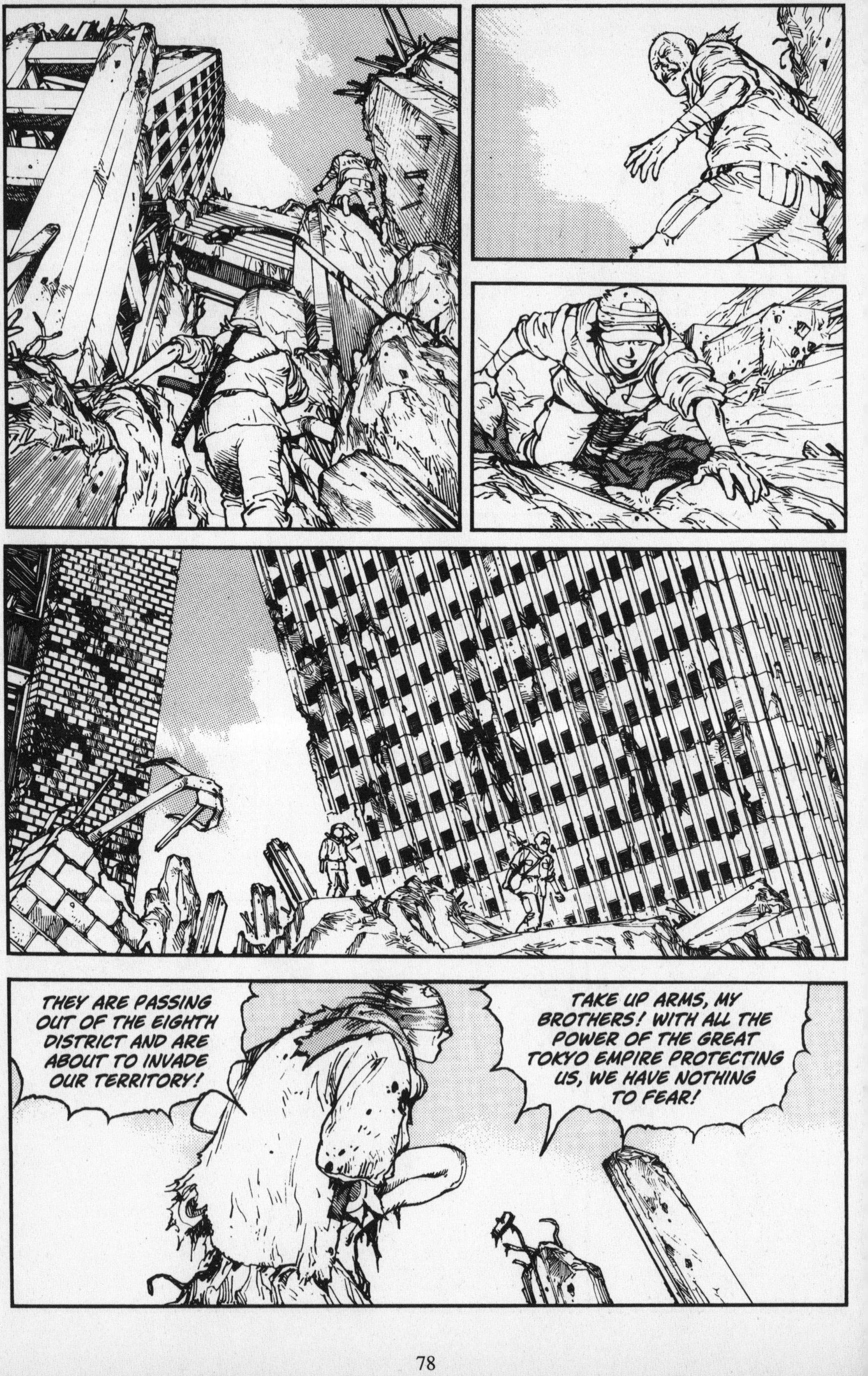
THEY ARE PASSING OUT OF THE EIGHTH DISTRICT AND ARE ABOUT TO INVADE OUR TERRITORY!
TAKE UP ARMS, MY BROTHERS! WITH ALL THE POWER OF THE GREAT TOKYO EMPIRE PROTECTING US, WE HAVE NOTHING TO FEAR!

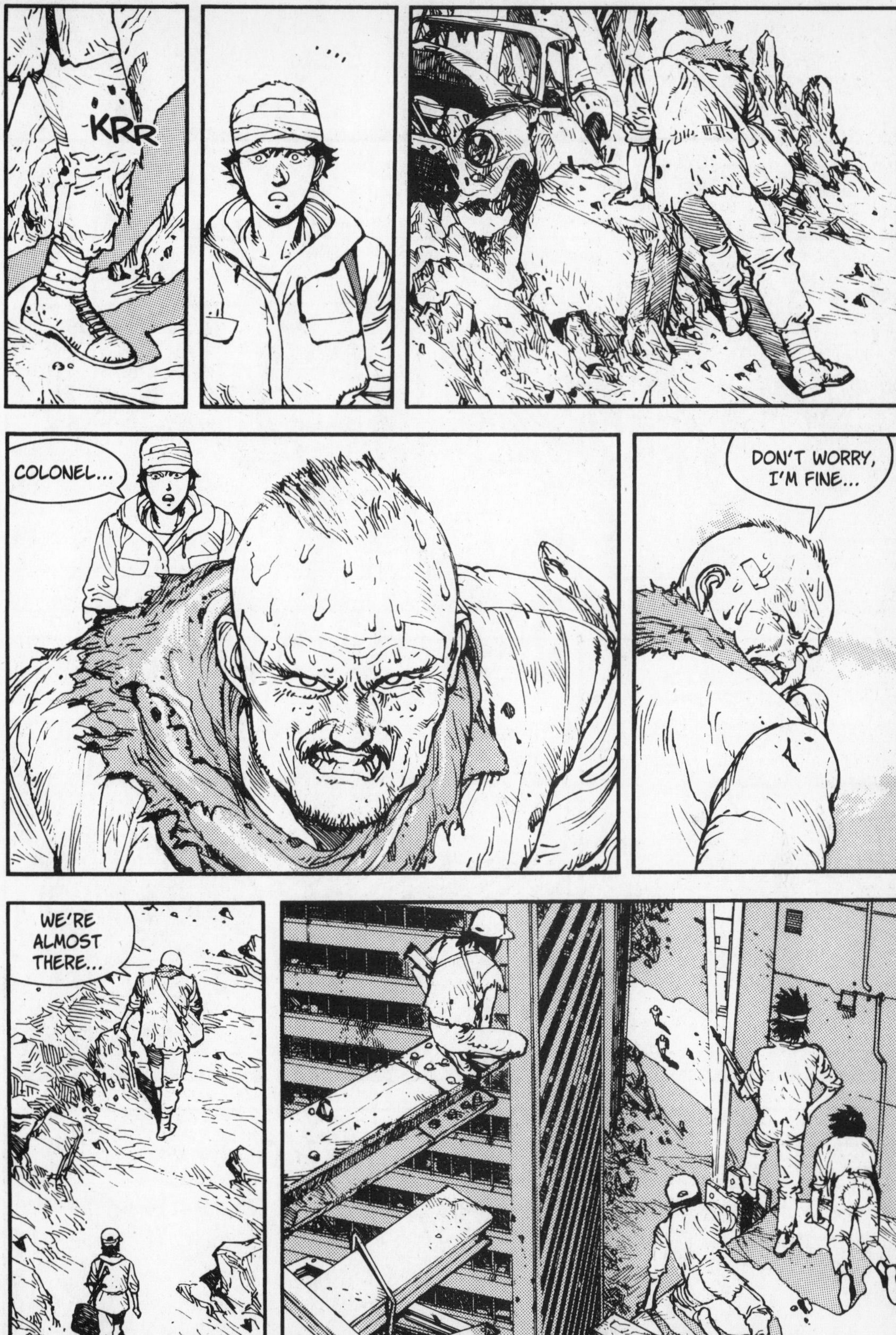
KRR
...
COLONEL...
DON'T WORRY, I'M FINE...
WE'RE ALMOST THERE...

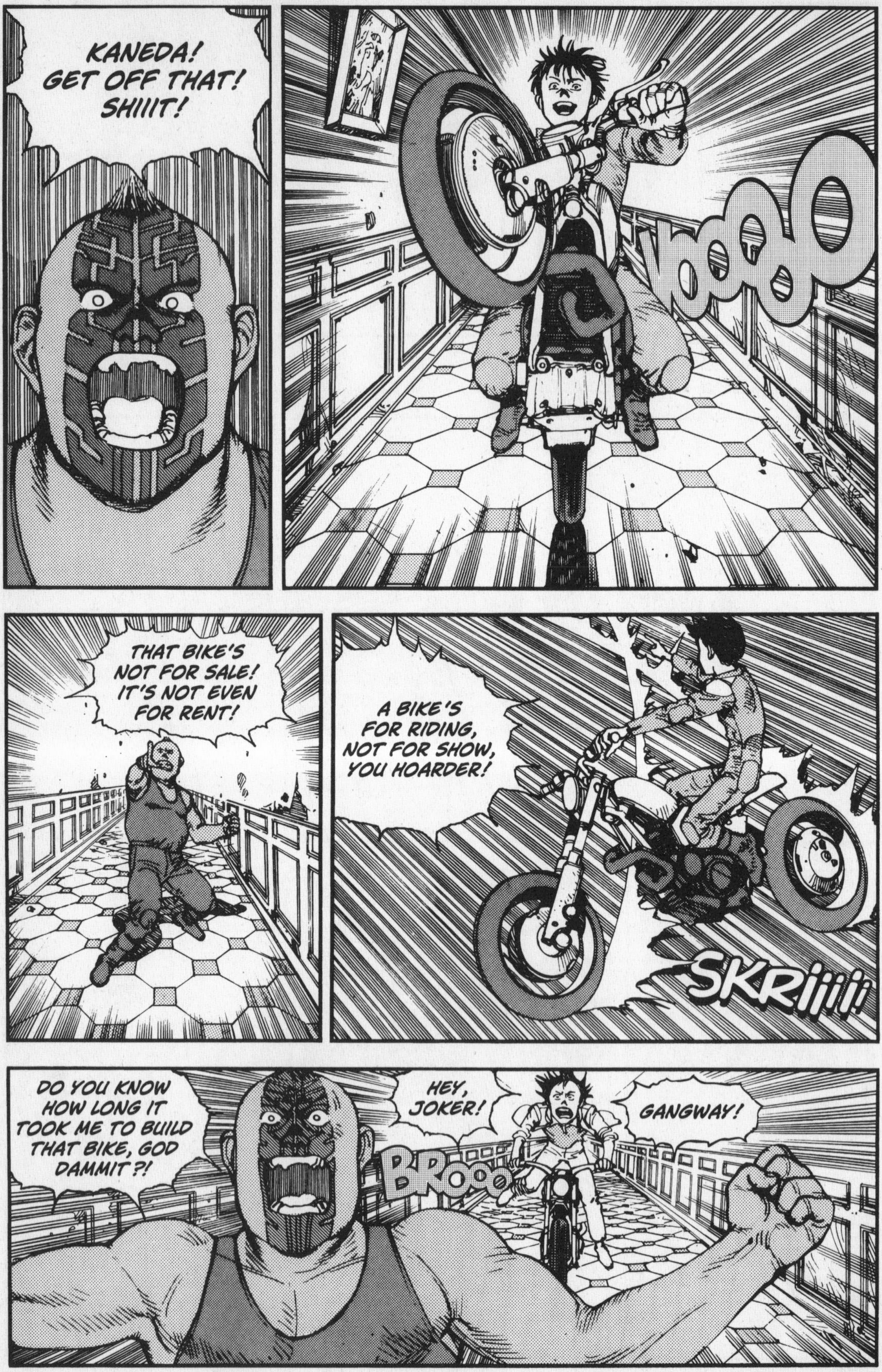
KANEDA! GET OFF THAT! SHIIIT!
VOOOOO
THAT BIKE'S NOT FOR SALE! IT'S NOT EVEN FOR RENT!
A BIKE'S FOR RIDING, NOT FOR SHOW, YOU HOARDER!
SKRIIIII
DO YOU KNOW HOW LONG IT TOOK ME TO BUILD THAT BIKE, GOD DAMMIT?!
HEY, JOKER!
GANGWAY!
BROOOO

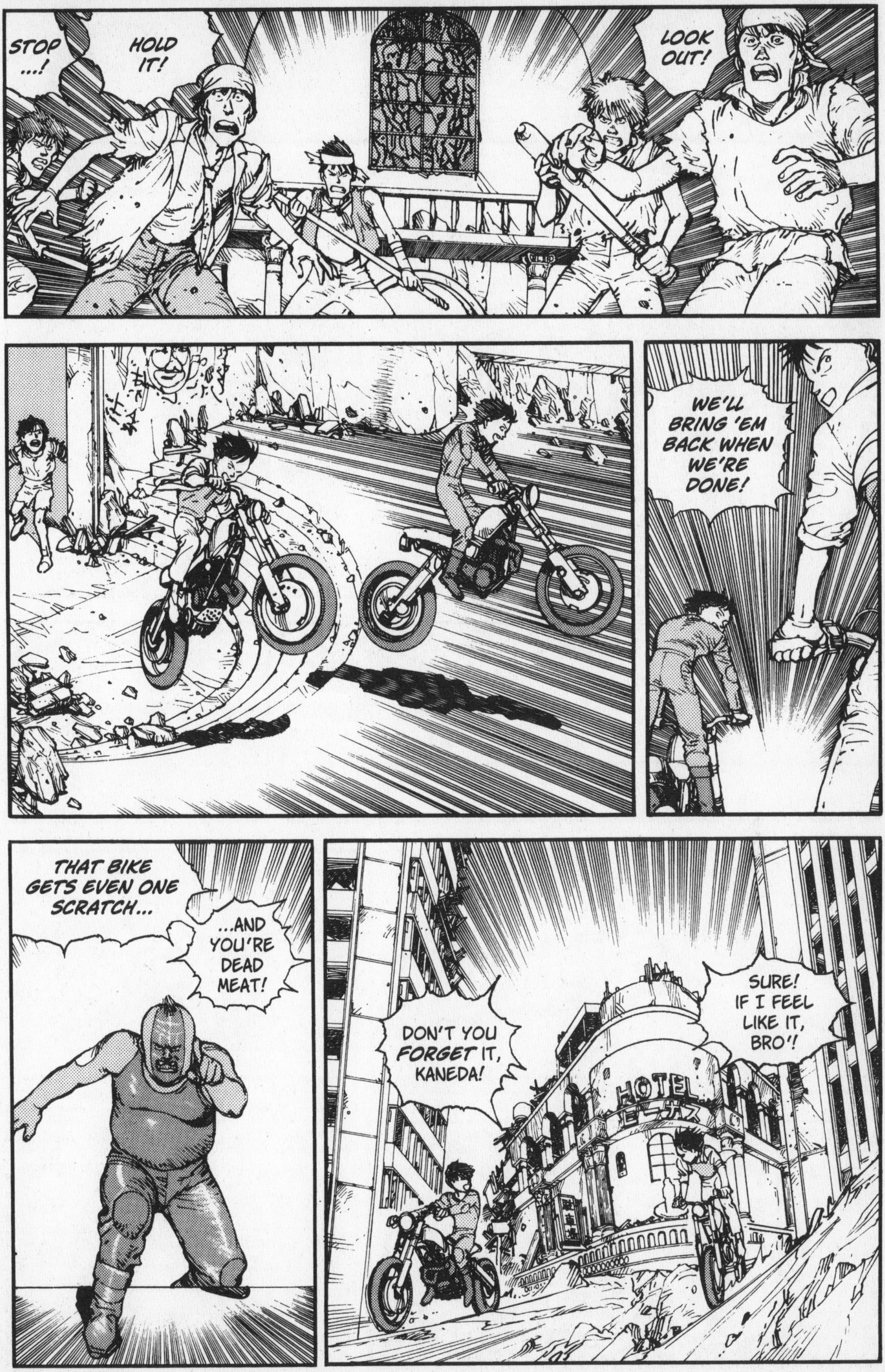
STOP ...!
HOLD IT!
LOOK OUT!
WE'LL BRING 'EM BACK WHEN WE'RE DONE!
THAT BIKE GETS EVEN ONE SCRATCH...
...AND YOU'RE DEAD MEAT!
DON'T YOU FORGET IT, KANEDA!
SURE! IF I FEEL LIKE IT, BRO'!

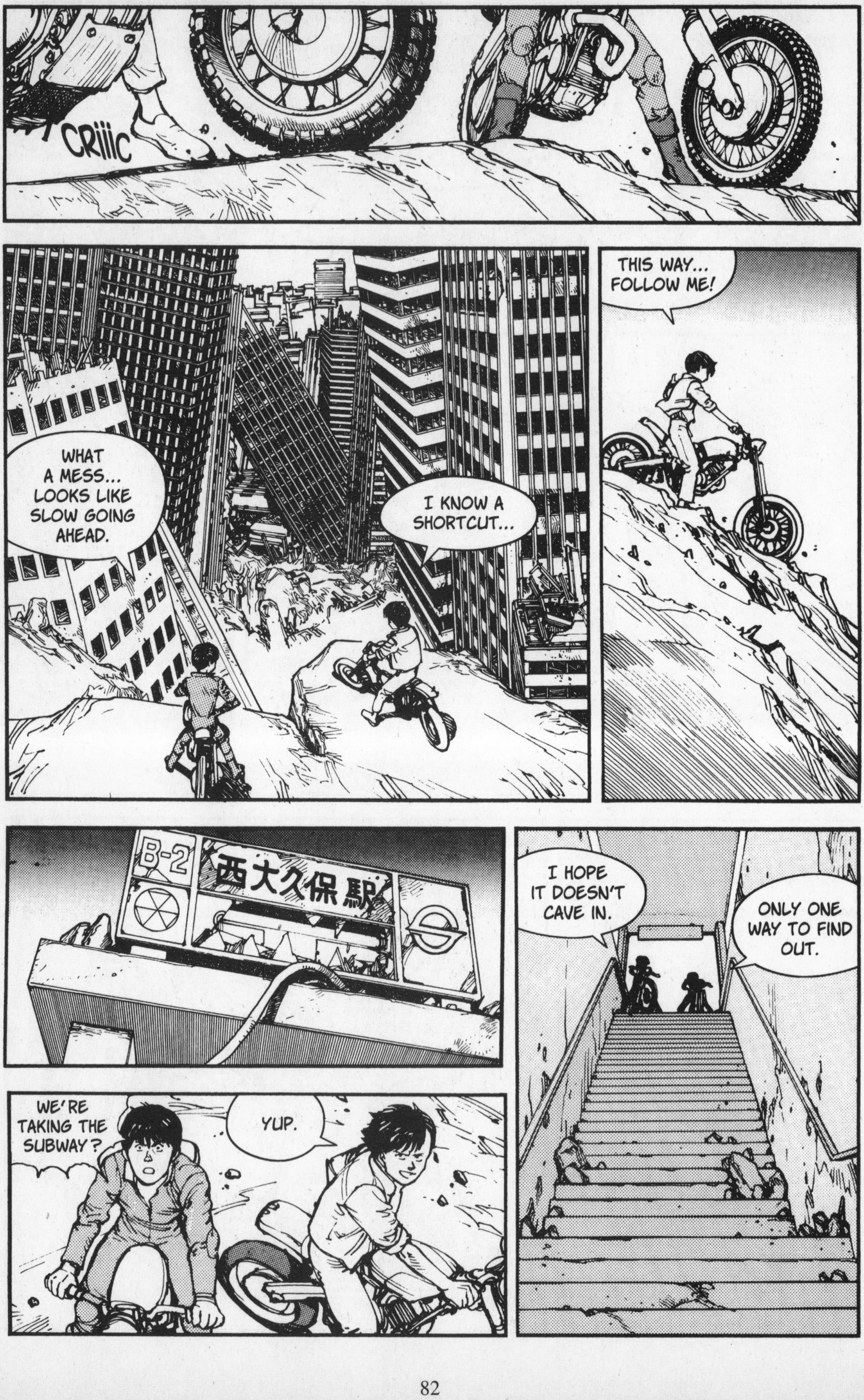
CRiiic
WHAT A MESS... LOOKS LIKE SLOW GOING AHEAD.
I KNOW A SHORTCUT...
THIS WAY... FOLLOW ME!
B-2
西大久保駅
WE'RE TAKING THE SUBWAY?
YUP.
I HOPE IT DOESN'T CAVE IN.
ONLY ONE WAY TO FIND OUT.

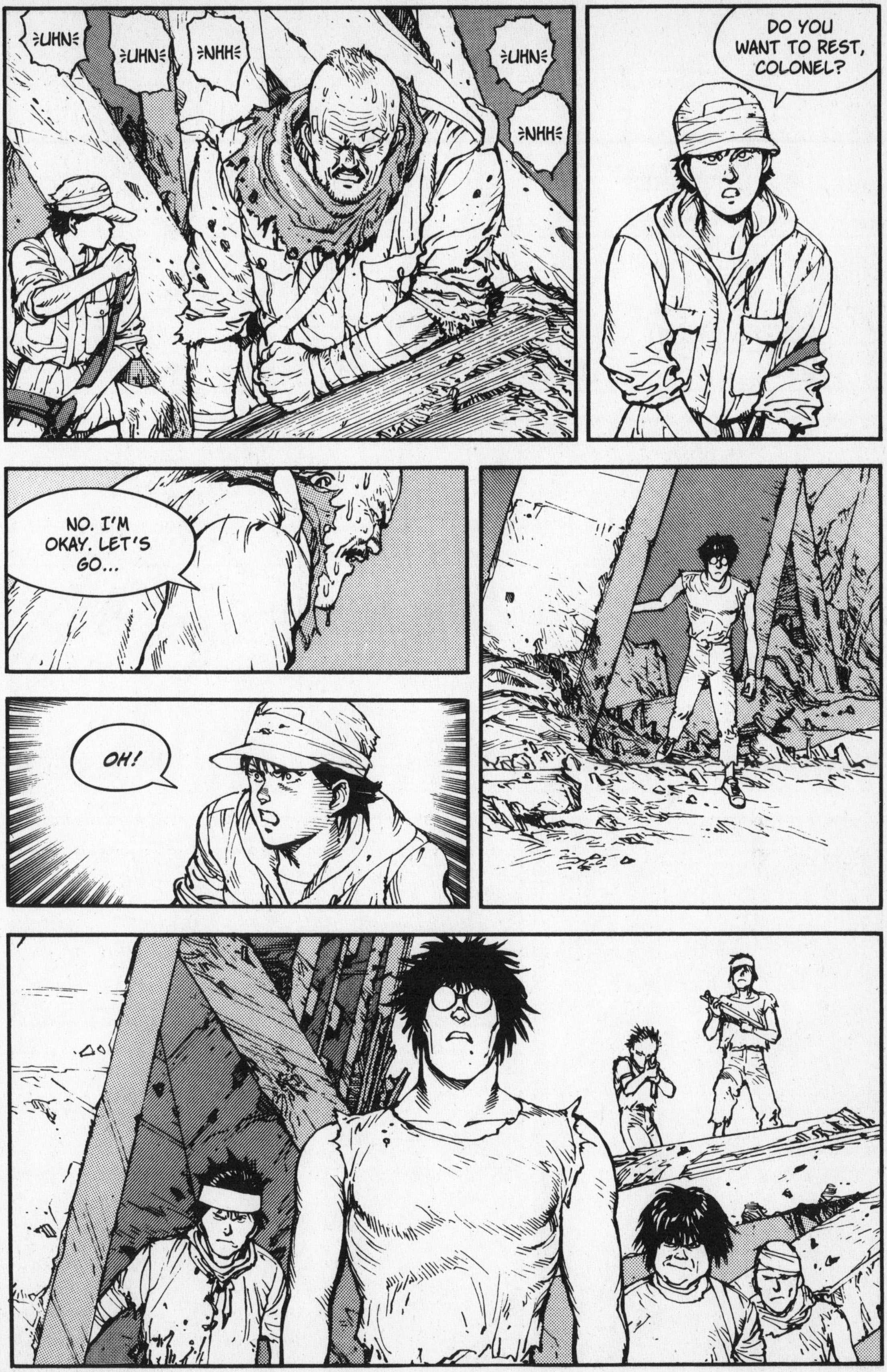
UHN
UHN
NHH
UHN
NHH
DO YOU WANT TO REST, COLONEL?
NO. I'M OKAY. LET'S GO...
OH!

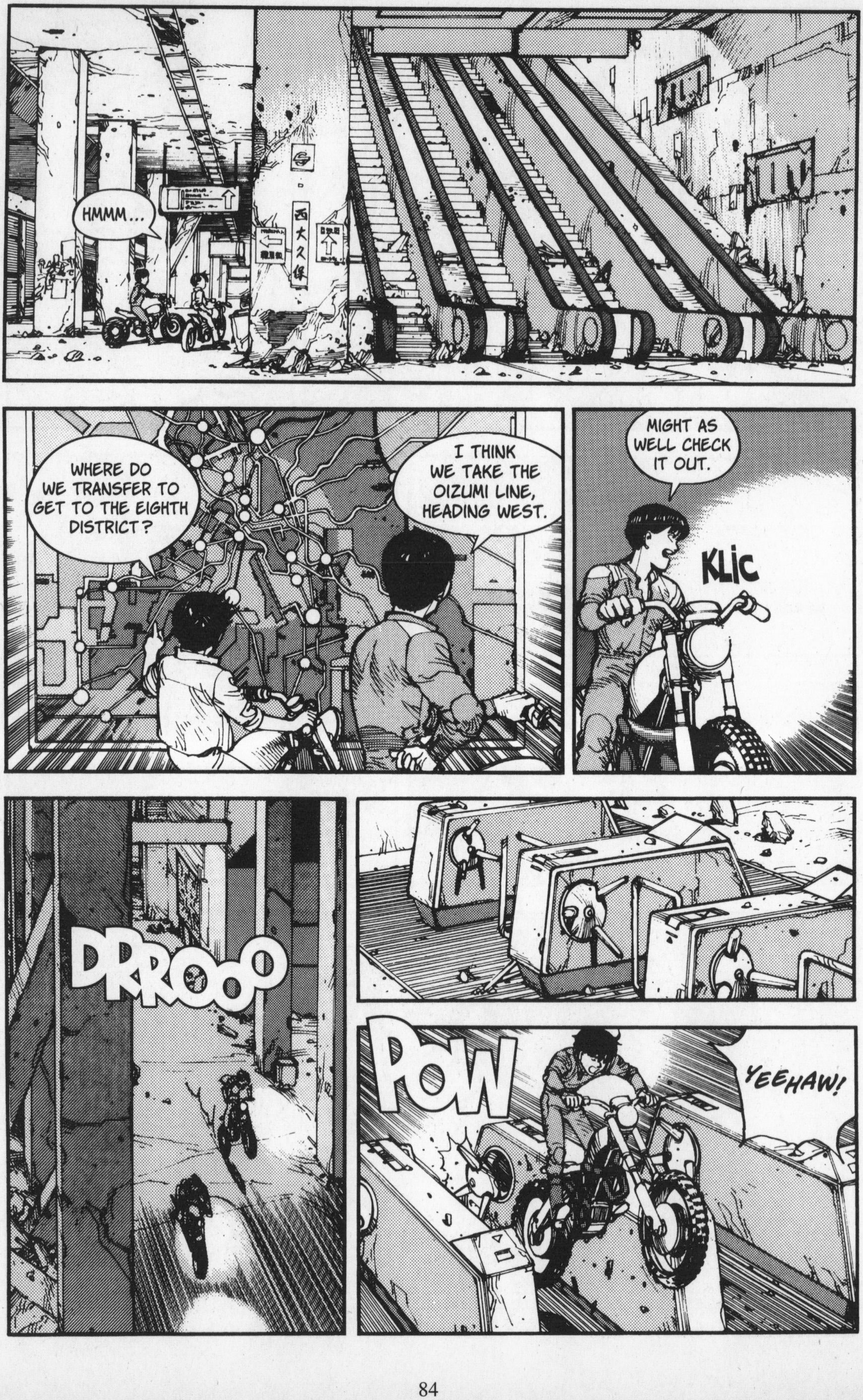
HMMM...
西大久保
WHERE DO WE TRANSFER TO GET TO THE EIGHTH DISTRICT?
I THINK WE TAKE THE OIZUMI LINE, HEADING WEST.
MIGHT AS WELL CHECK IT OUT.
KLIC
DRROOO
POW
YEEHAW!

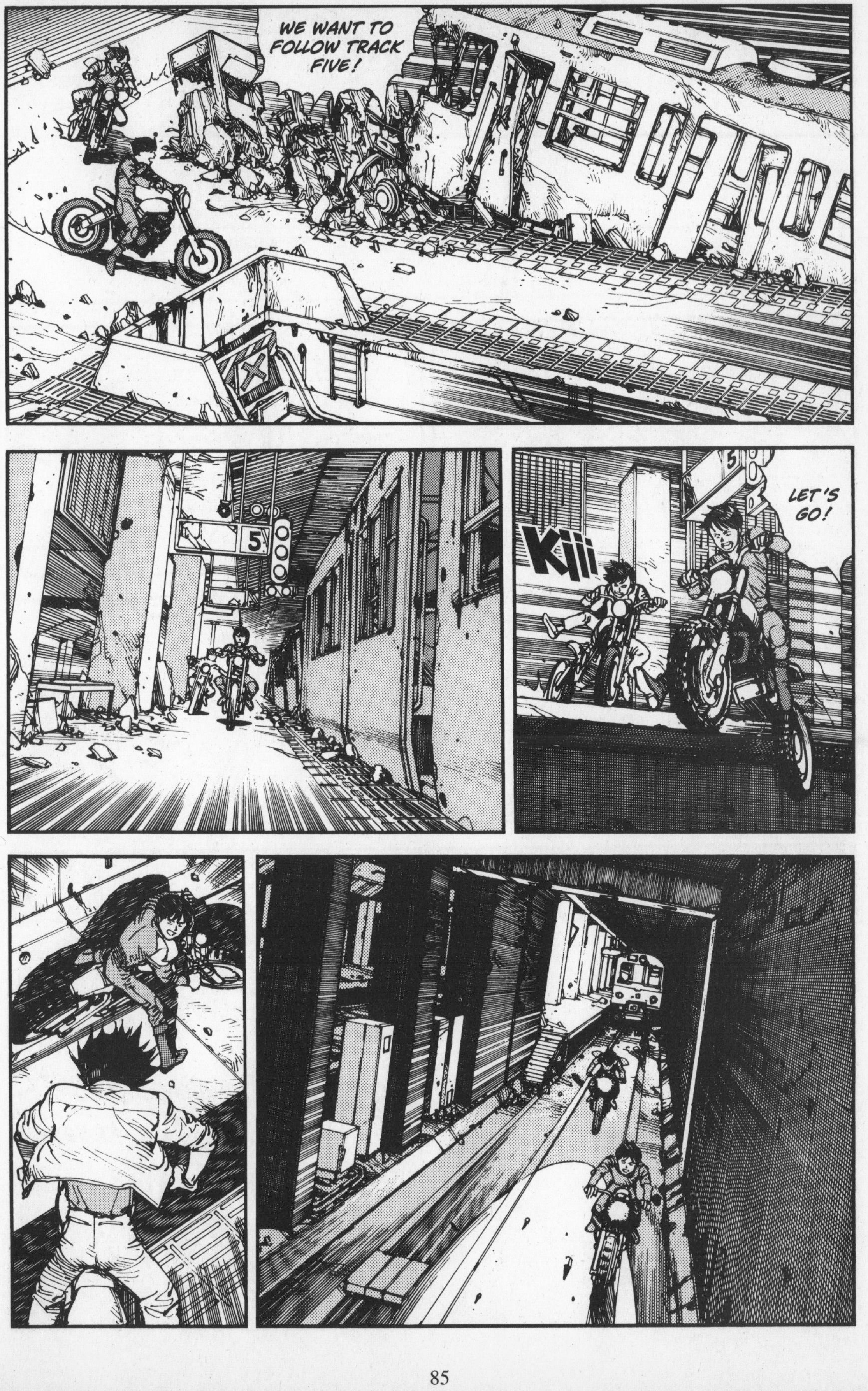
WE WANT TO FOLLOW TRACK FIVE!
5
5
Kiii
LET'S GO!

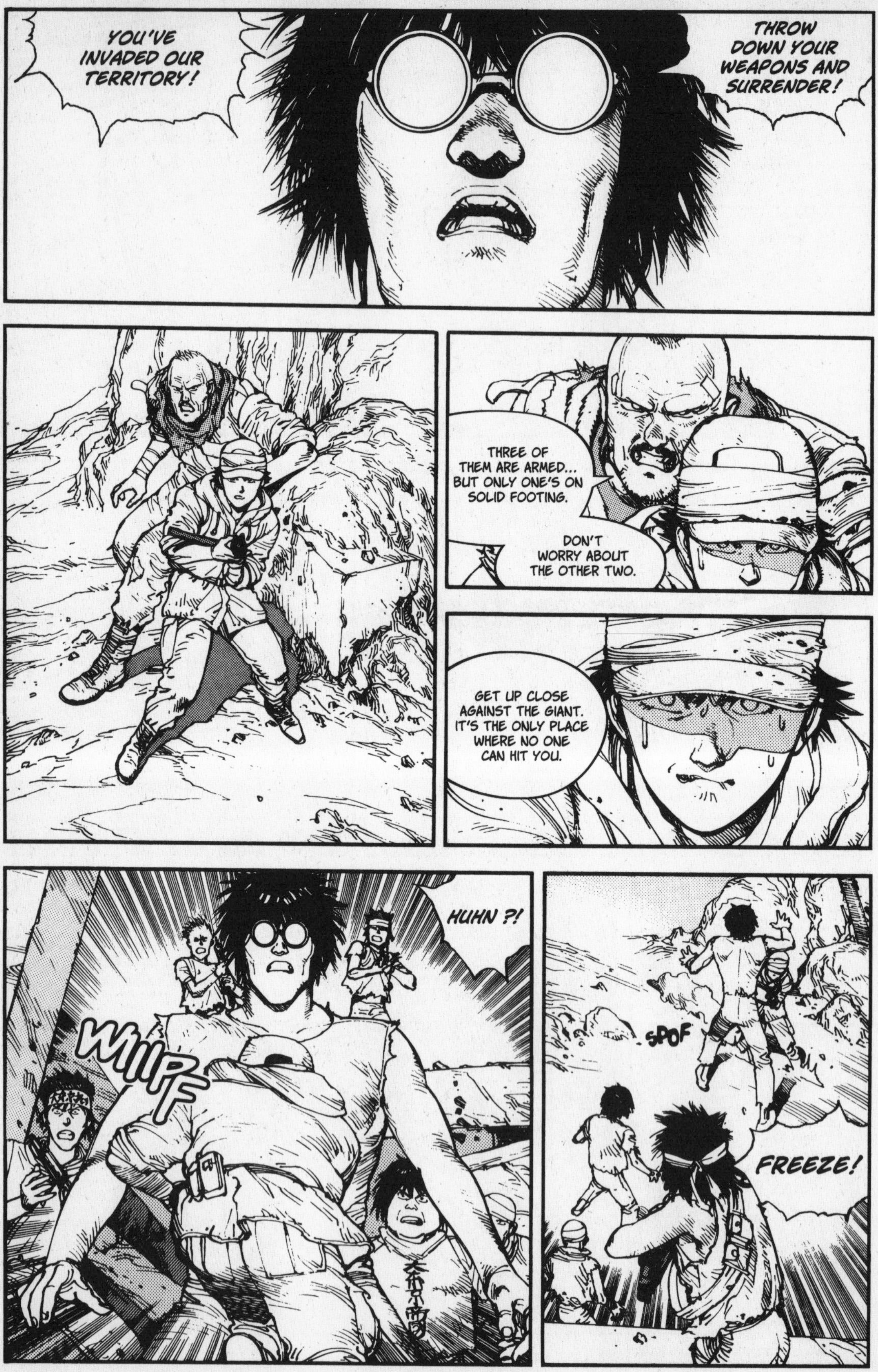
YOU'VE INVADED OUR TERRITORY!
THROW DOWN YOUR WEAPONS AND SURRENDER!
THREE OF THEM ARE ARMED... BUT ONLY ONE'S ON SOLID FOOTING.
DON'T WORRY ABOUT THE OTHER TWO.
GET UP CLOSE AGAINST THE GIANT. IT'S THE ONLY PLACE WHERE NO ONE CAN HIT YOU.
HUHN ?!
WIIIPF
SPOF
FREEZE!

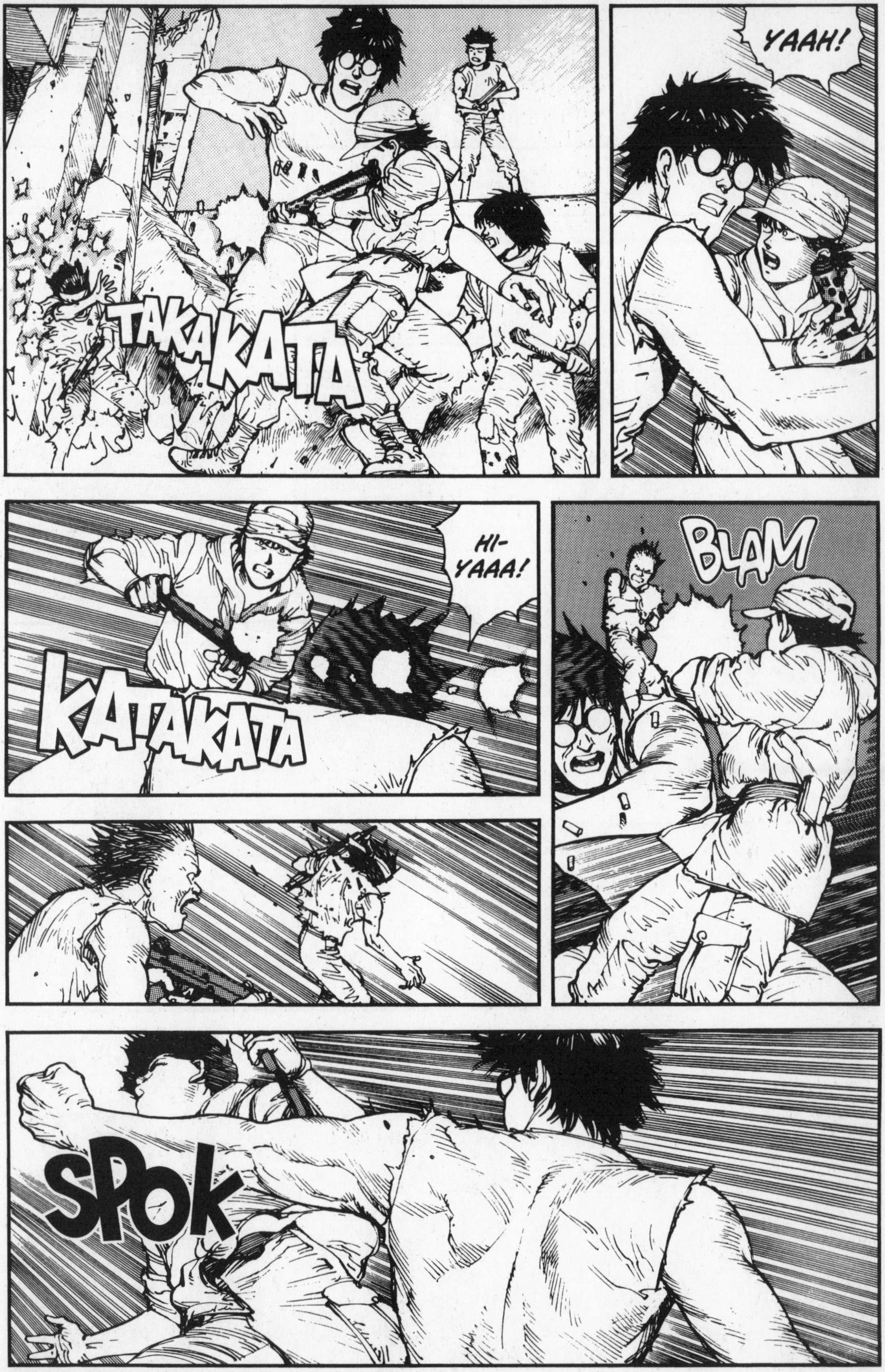
TAKAKATA
YAAH!
HI-YAAA!
KATAKATA
BLAM
SPOK

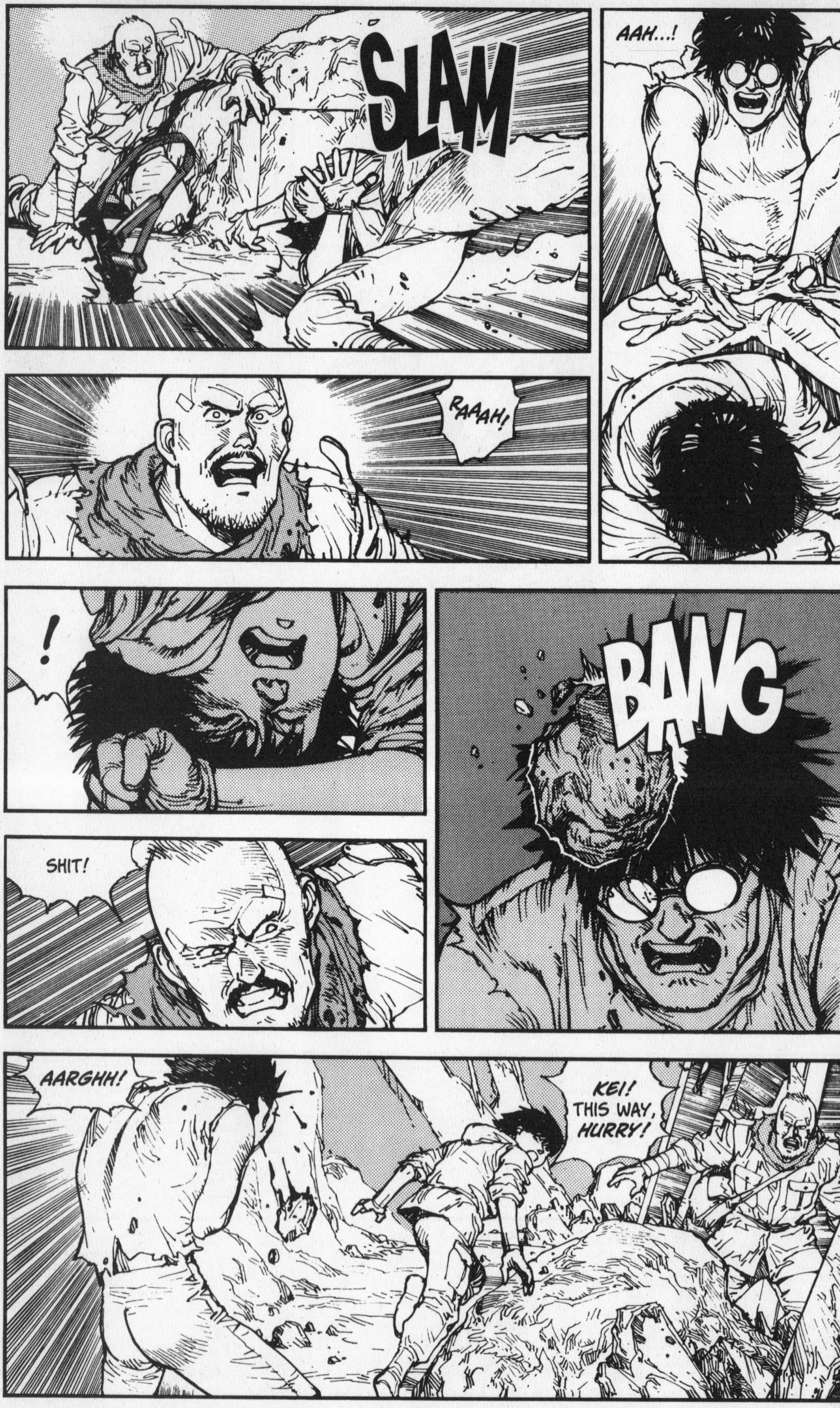
SLAM
AAH...!
RAAAH!
!
BANG
SHIT!
AARGHH!
KEI! THIS WAY, HURRY!

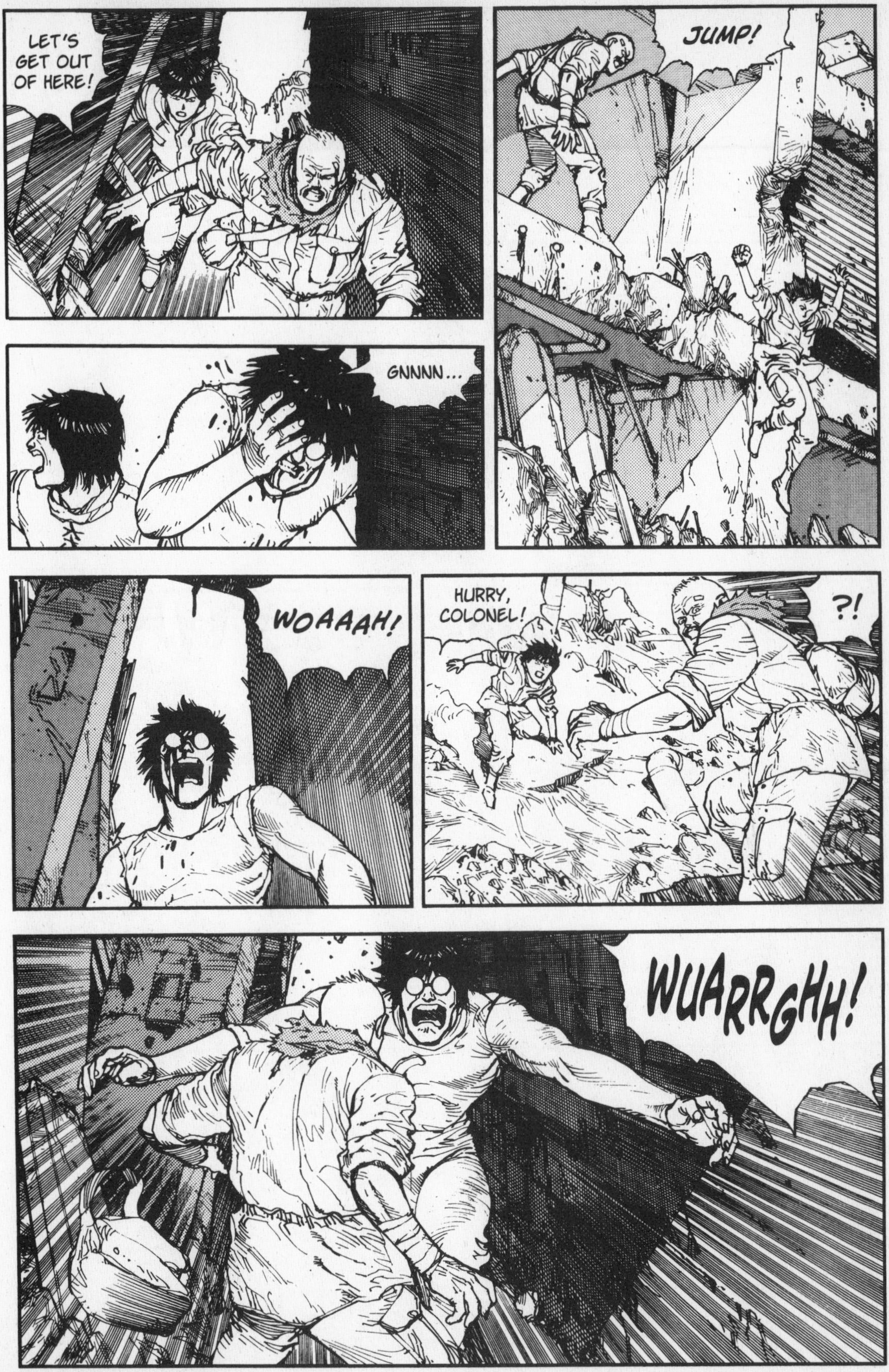
LET'S GET OUT OF HERE!
JUMP!
GNNNN...
WOAAAH!
HURRY, COLONEL!
?!
WUARRGHH!

RAUGHH!

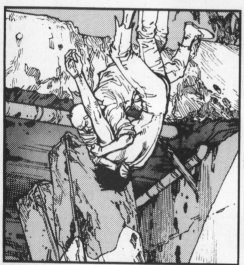

COLONEL!

SMAK

≋UHNN≋

≋NHH≋

ARE YOU HURT? WHAT ABOUT YOUR WOUND?

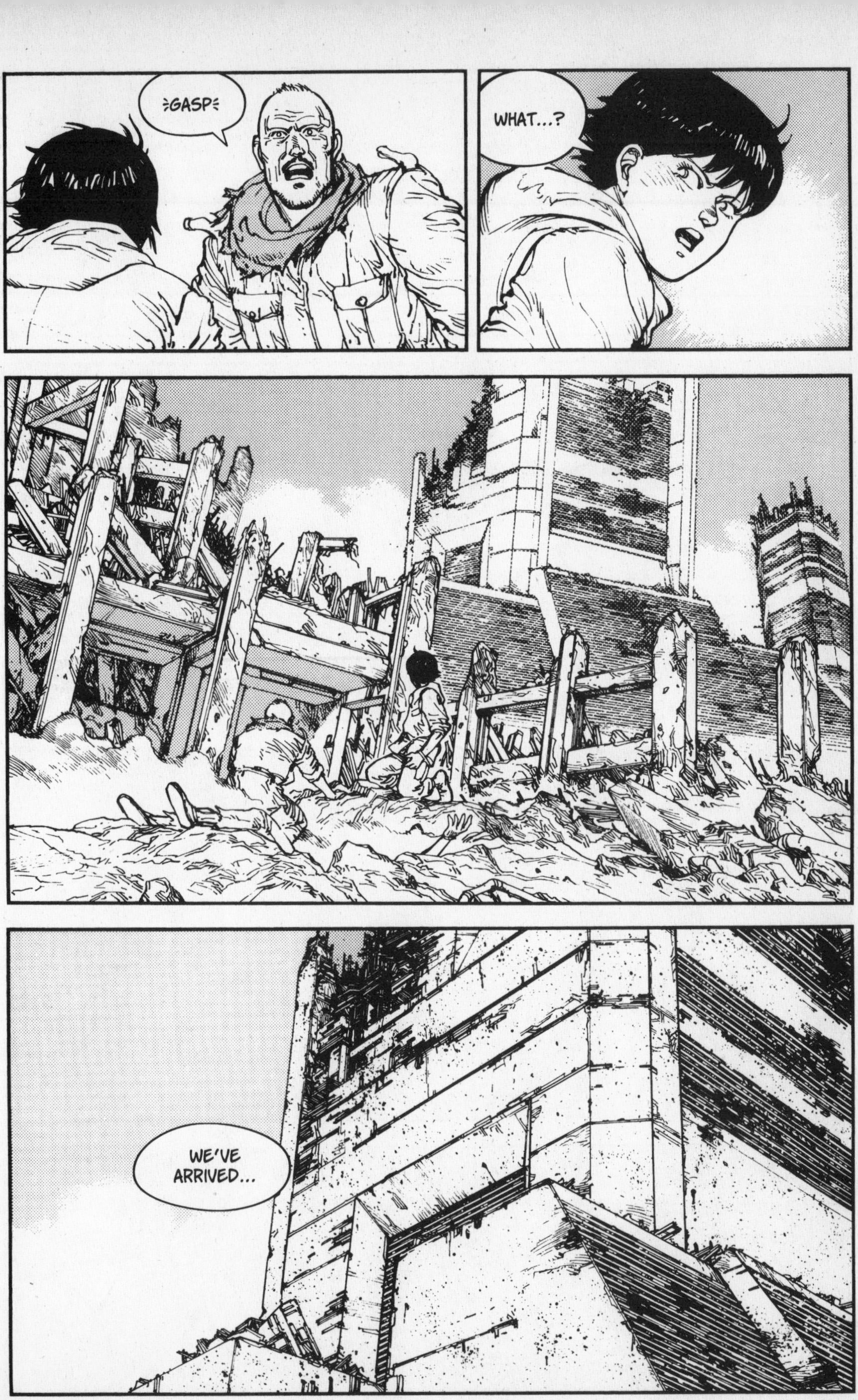
GASP
WHAT...?
WE'VE ARRIVED...

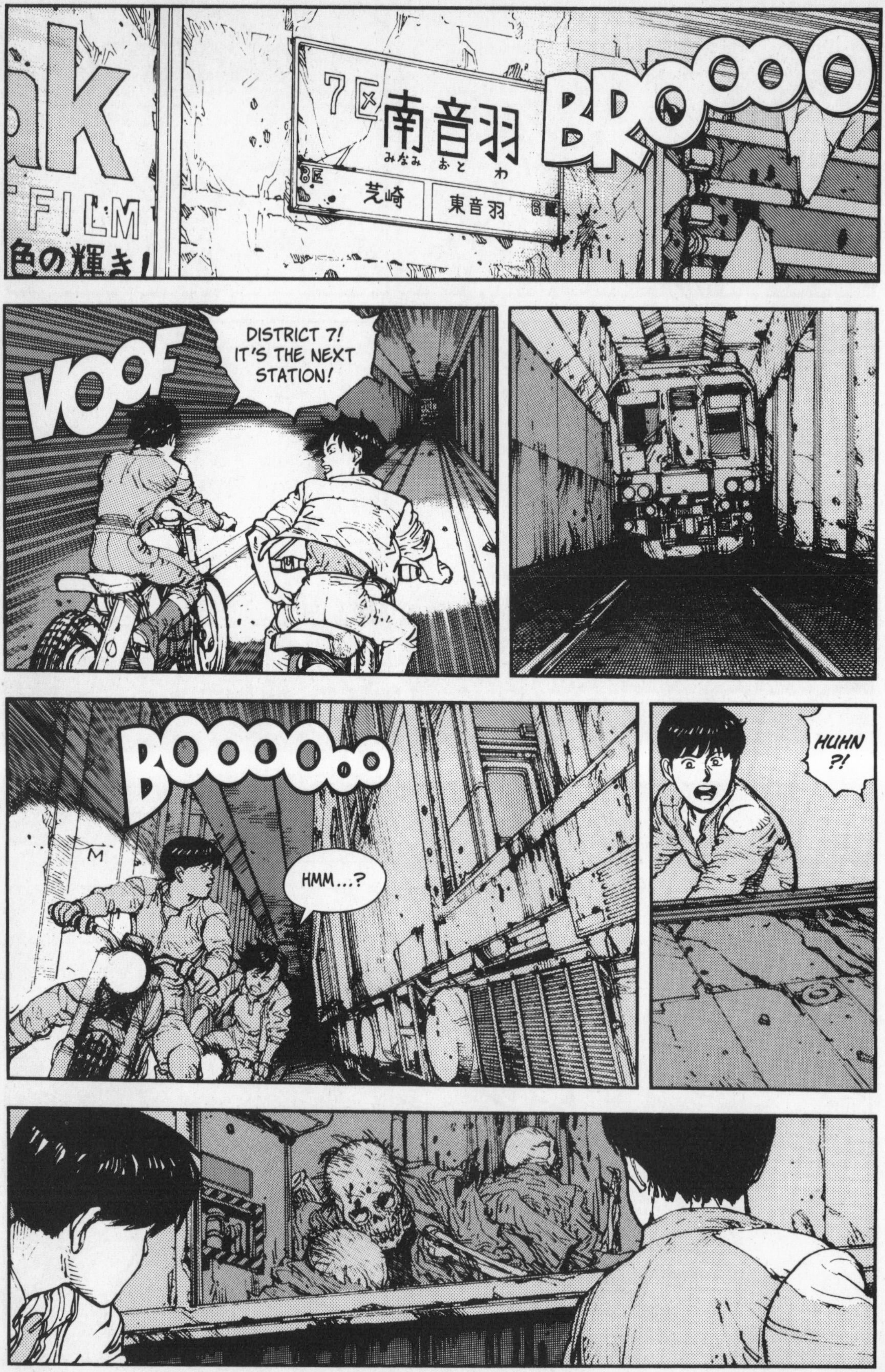
南音羽
みなみ おと わ
芝崎
東音羽
FILM
色の輝き!
BROOOOO
VOOF
DISTRICT 7! IT'S THE NEXT STATION!
BOOOOoo
HMM...?
HUHN ?!

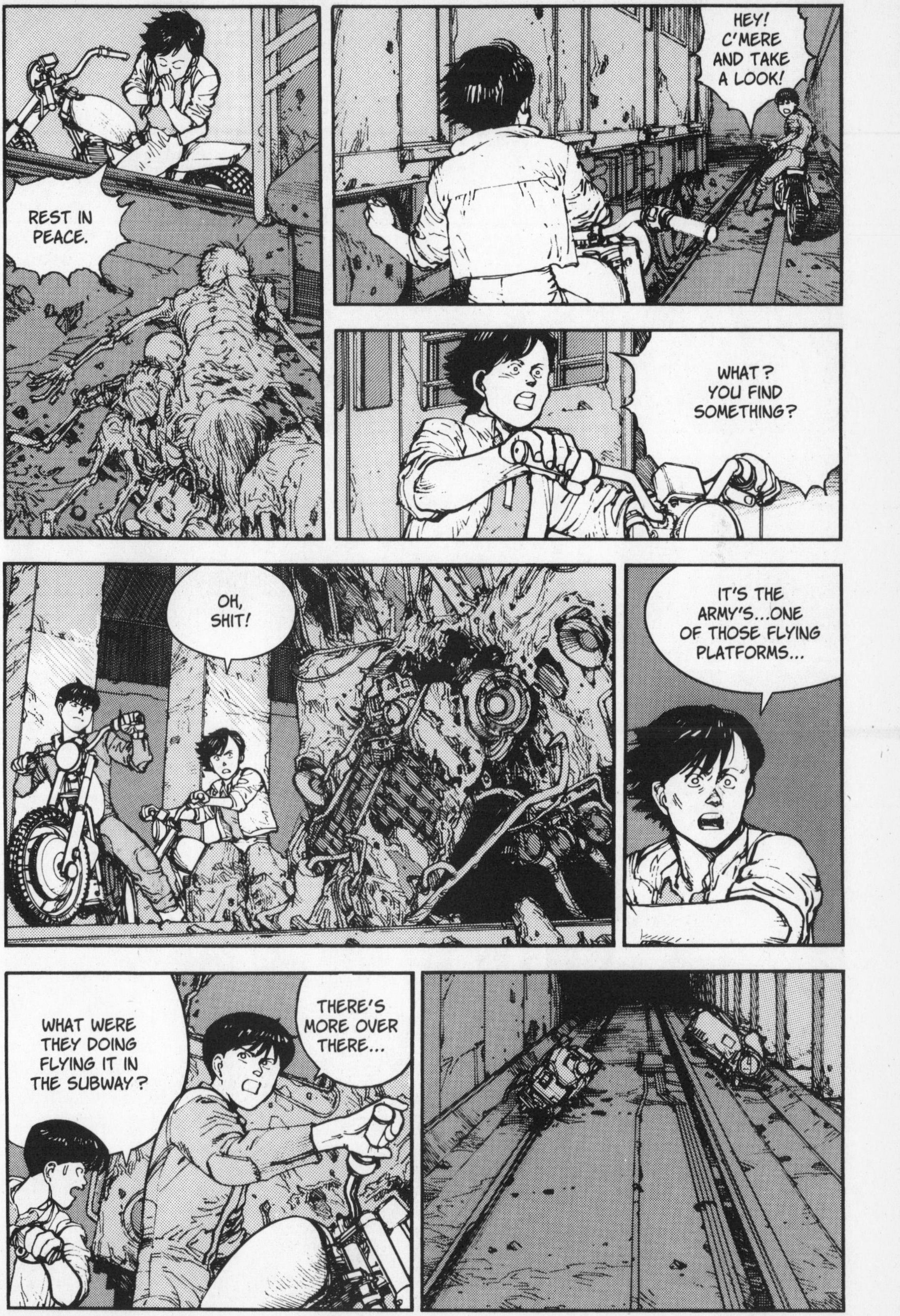
REST IN PEACE.
HEY! C'MERE AND TAKE A LOOK!
WHAT? YOU FIND SOMETHING?
OH, SHIT!
IT'S THE ARMY'S...ONE OF THOSE FLYING PLATFORMS...
WHAT WERE THEY DOING FLYING IT IN THE SUBWAY?
THERE'S MORE OVER THERE...

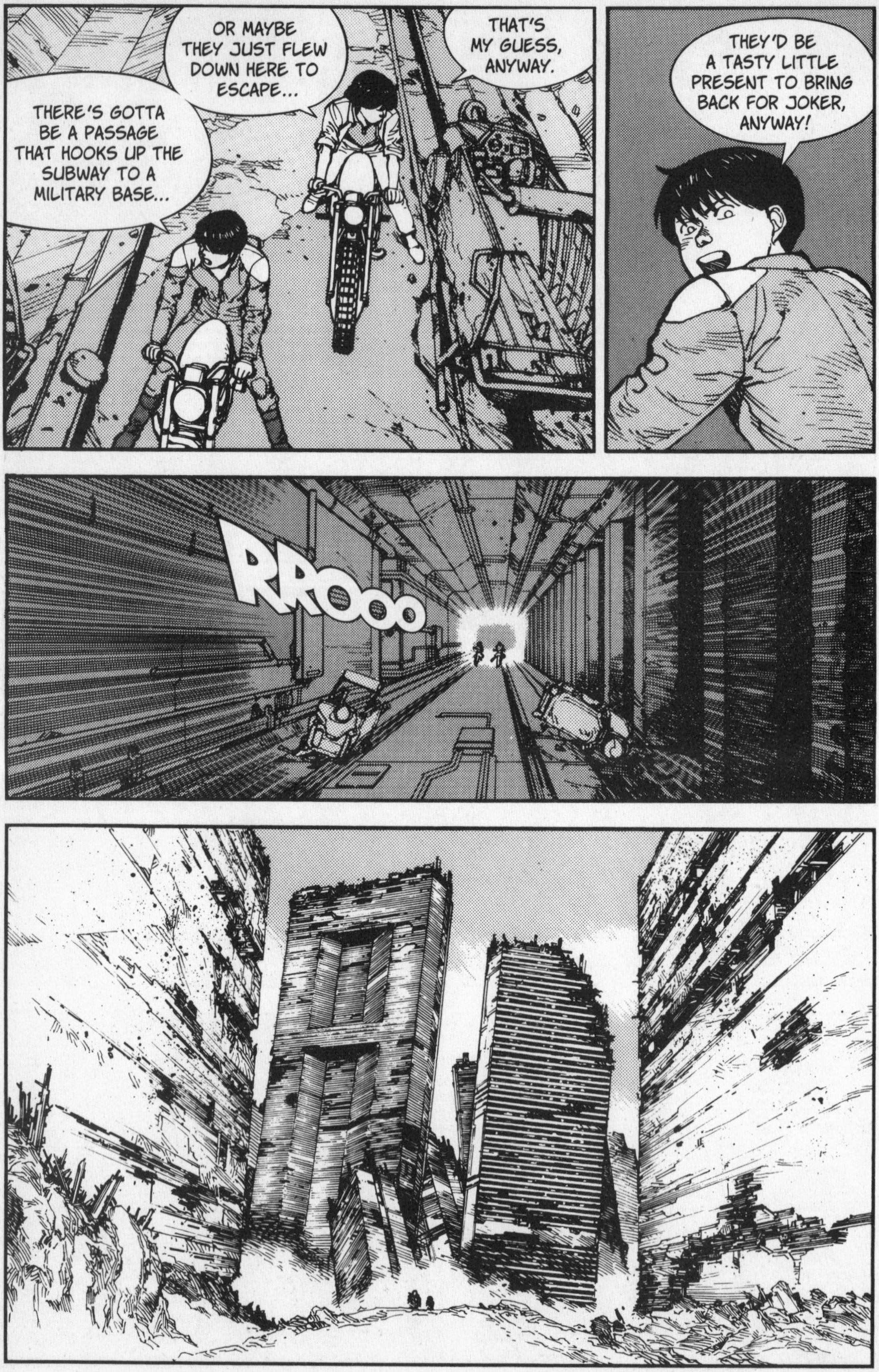
THERE'S GOTTA BE A PASSAGE THAT HOOKS UP THE SUBWAY TO A MILITARY BASE...
OR MAYBE THEY JUST FLEW DOWN HERE TO ESCAPE...
THAT'S MY GUESS, ANYWAY.
THEY'D BE A TASTY LITTLE PRESENT TO BRING BACK FOR JOKER, ANYWAY!
RROOO

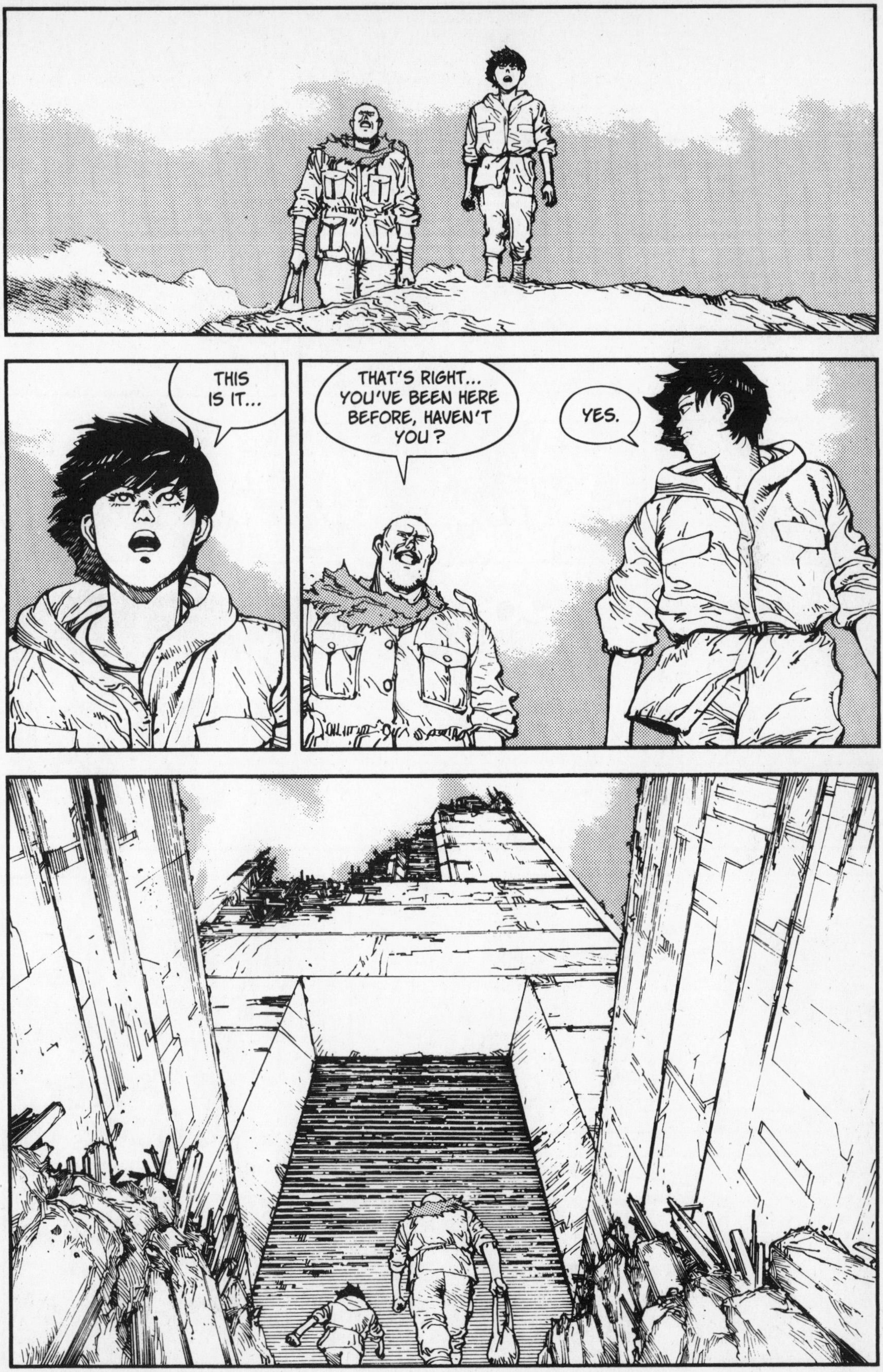
THIS IS IT...
THAT'S RIGHT... YOU'VE BEEN HERE BEFORE, HAVEN'T YOU?
YES.

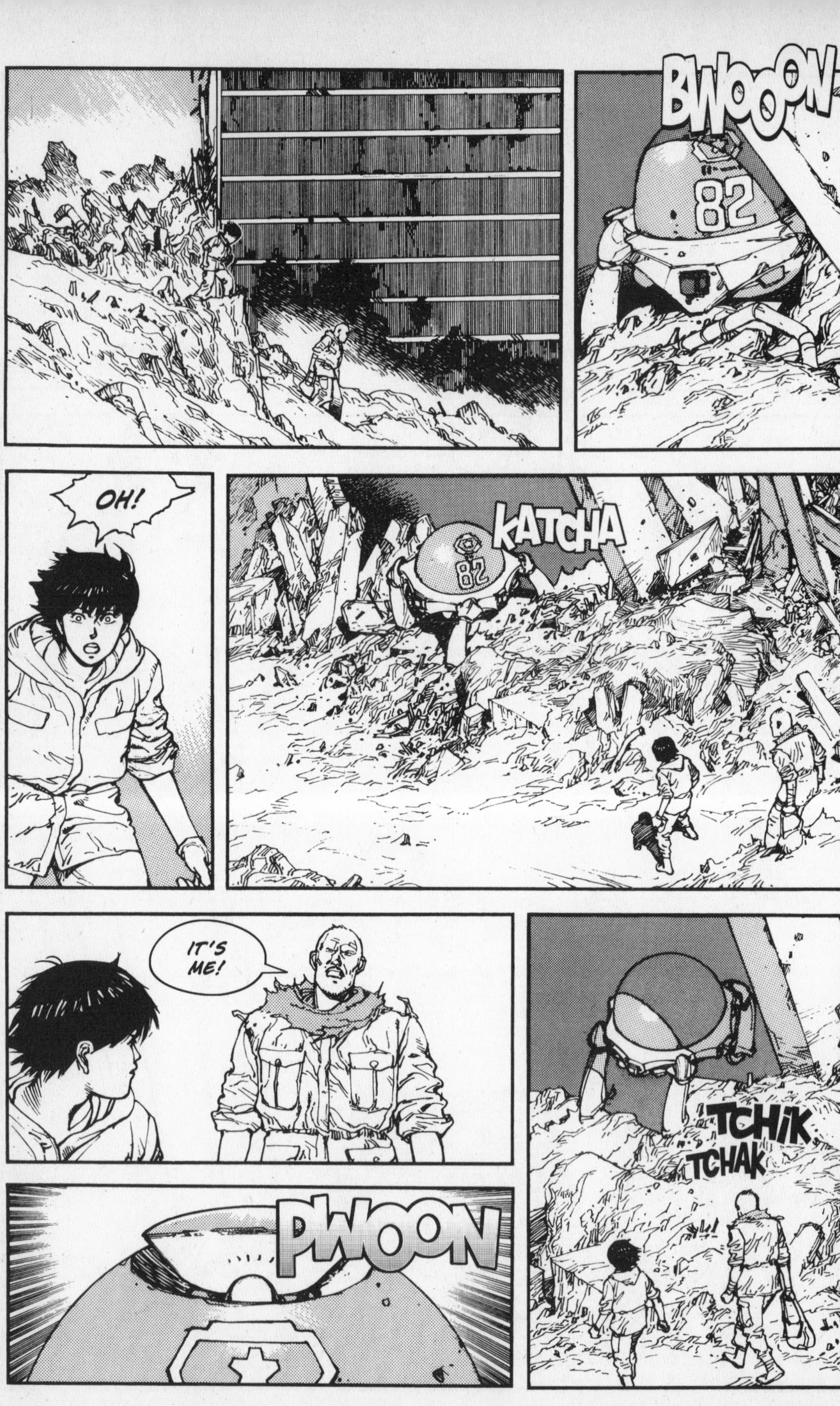
BWOOOON
OH!
KATCHA
IT'S ME!
PWOON
TCHIK
TCHAK

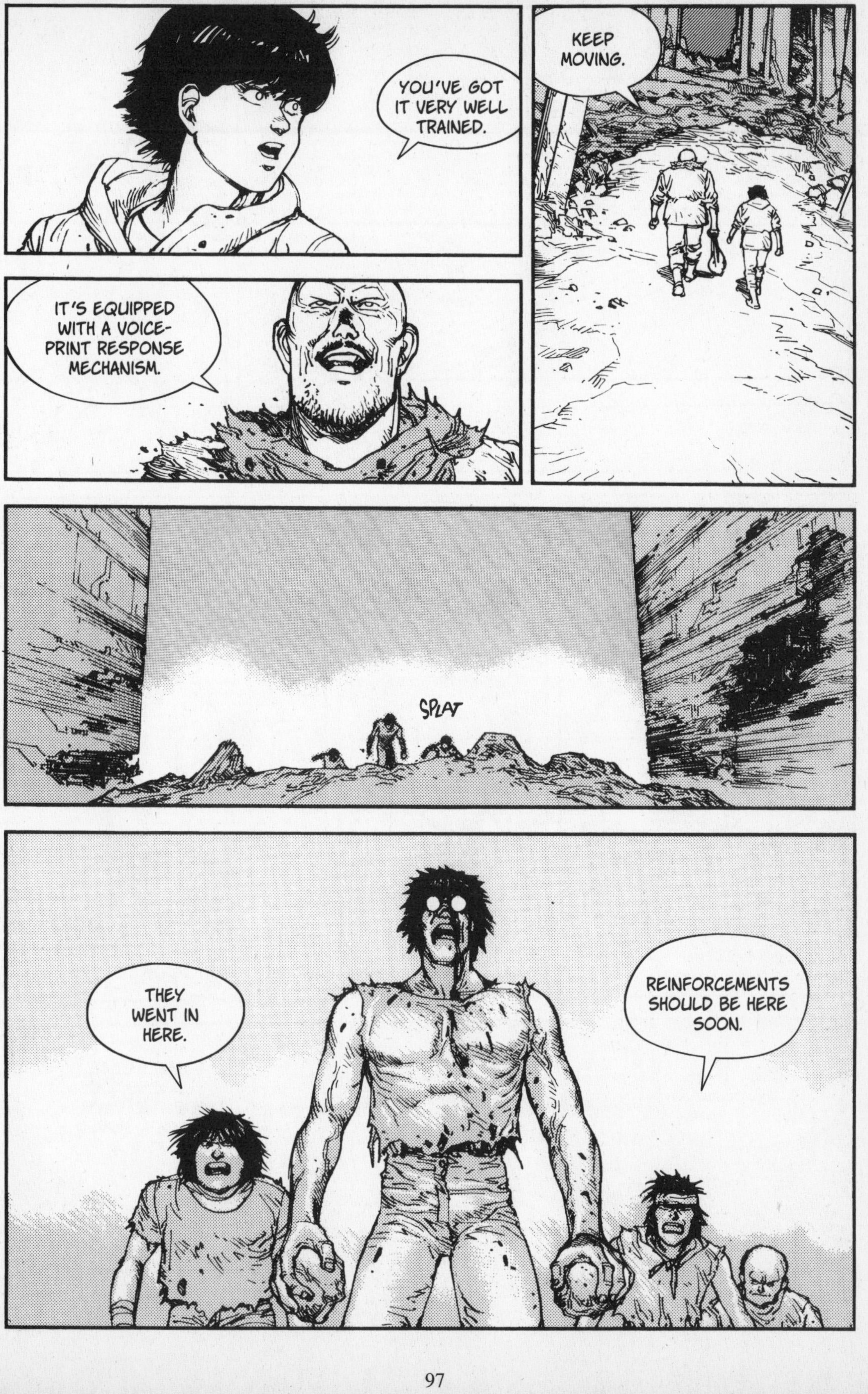
YOU'VE GOT IT VERY WELL TRAINED.
IT'S EQUIPPED WITH A VOICE-PRINT RESPONSE MECHANISM.
KEEP MOVING.
SPLAT
THEY WENT IN HERE.
REINFORCEMENTS SHOULD BE HERE SOON.

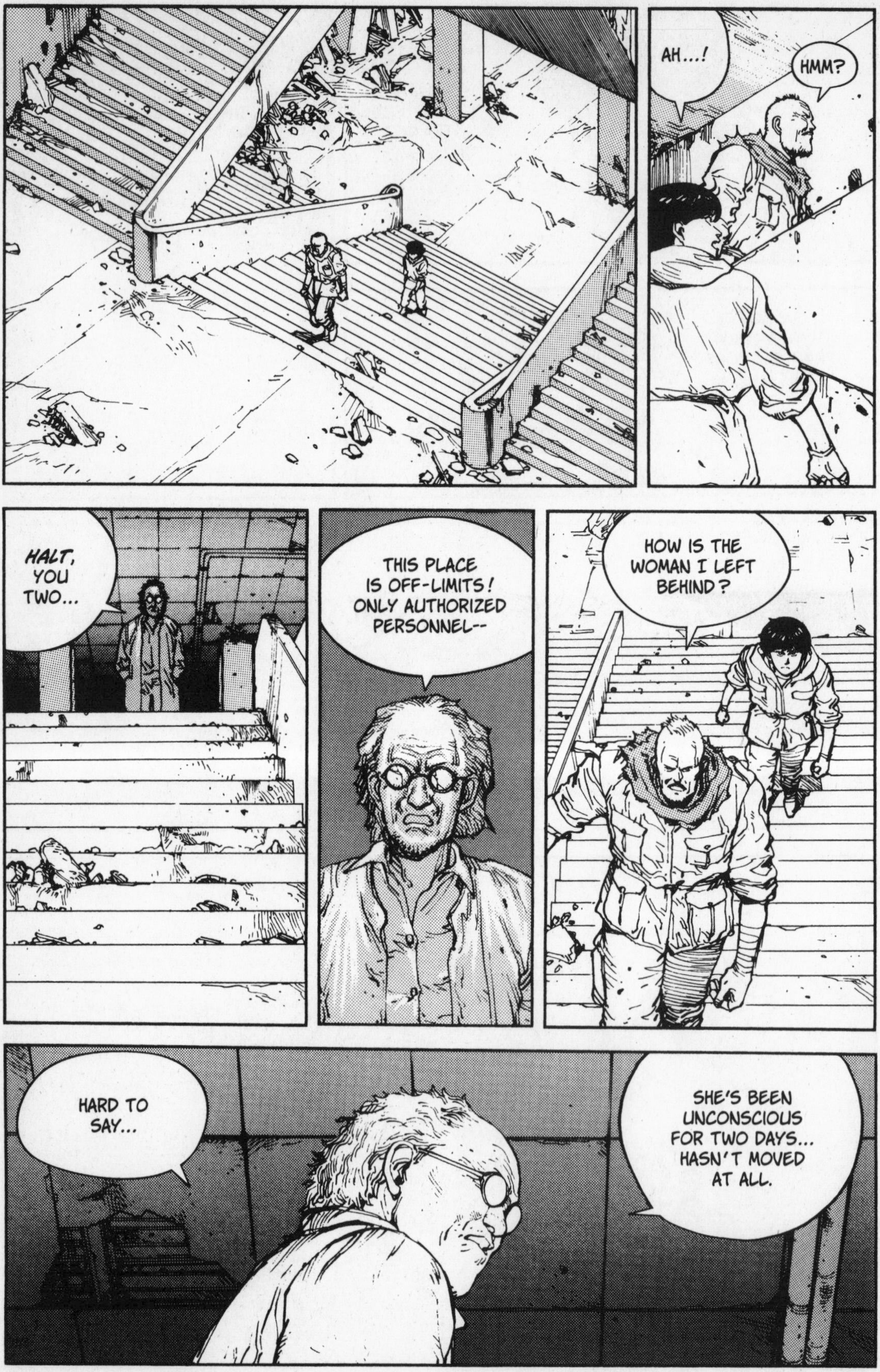
AH...!
HMM?
HALT, YOU TWO...
THIS PLACE IS OFF-LIMITS! ONLY AUTHORIZED PERSONNEL--
HOW IS THE WOMAN I LEFT BEHIND?
HARD TO SAY...
SHE'S BEEN UNCONSCIOUS FOR TWO DAYS... HASN'T MOVED AT ALL.

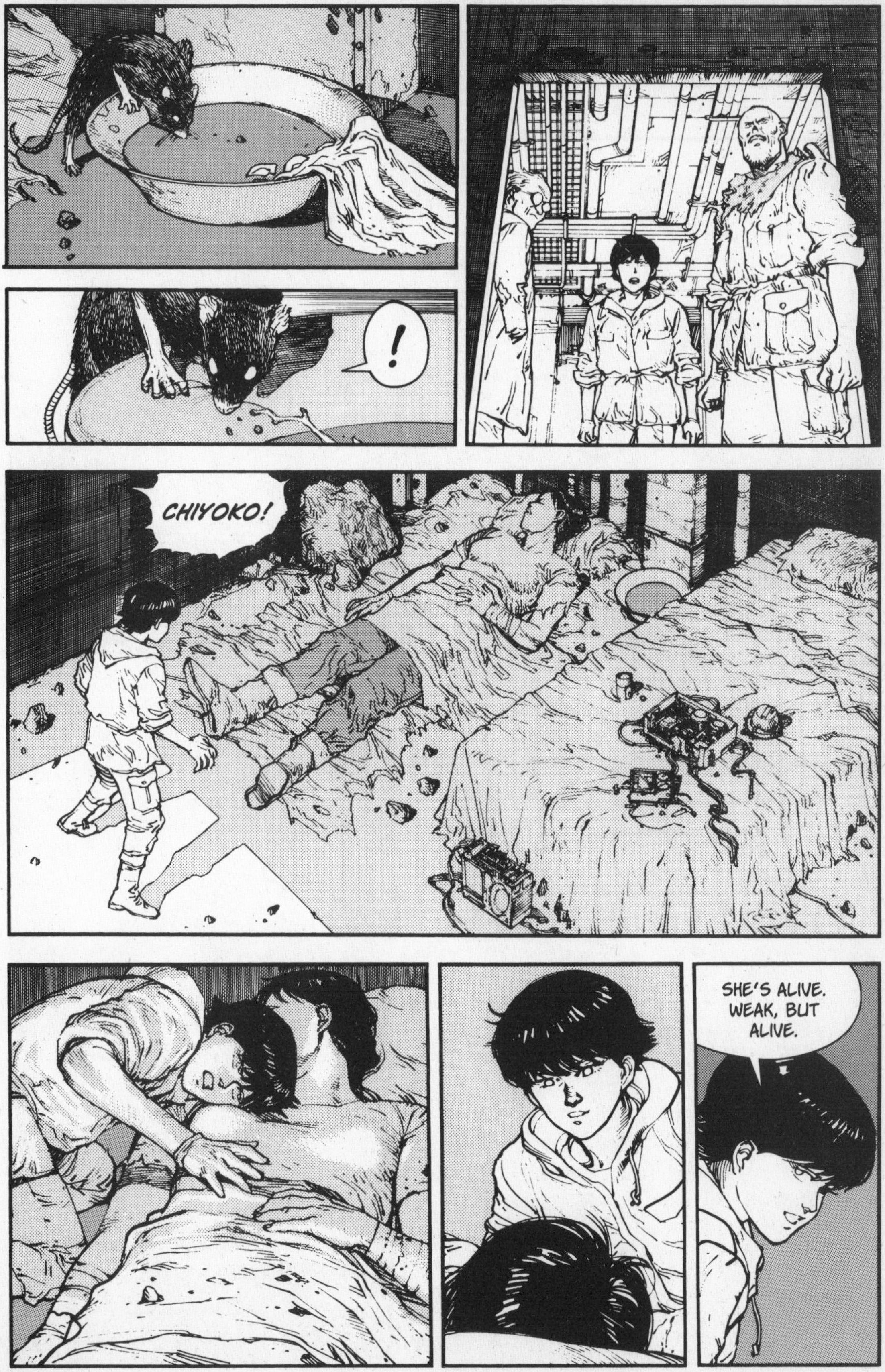
!
CHIYOKO!
SHE'S ALIVE. WEAK, BUT ALIVE.

IF THIS THING'S GUARDING IT, THERE'S GOTTA BE SOME JUICY SHIT INSIDE.

WE'LL DISTRACT IT. THE REST OF YOU HEAD ON IN.

KLAP

EAT THIS!

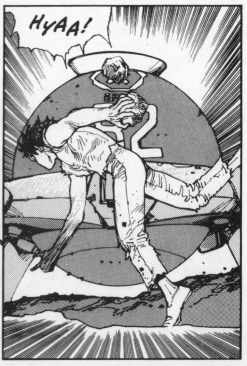

HyAA!

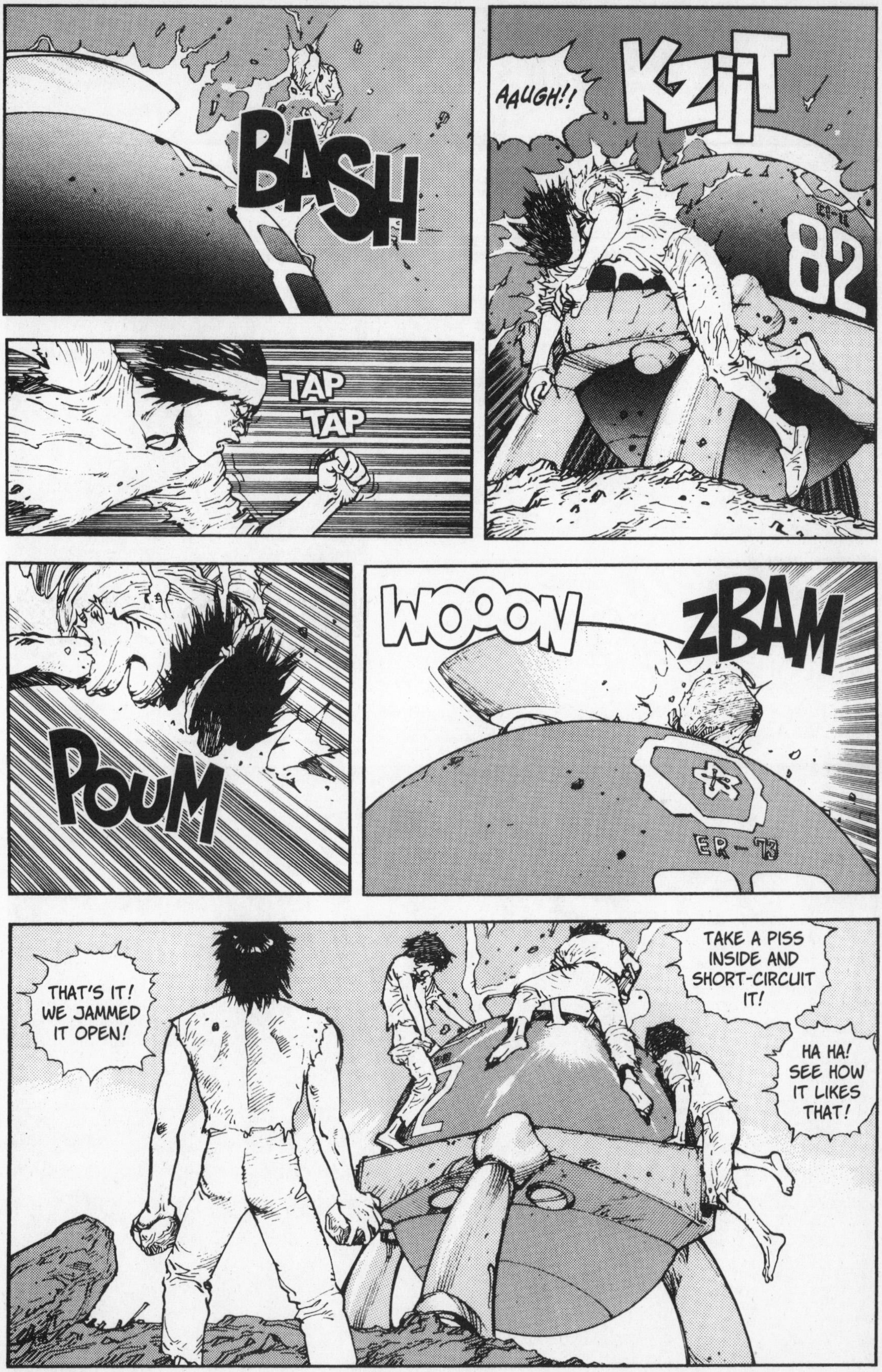
BASH
AAUGH!!
KZIIT
82
TAP
TAP
POUM
WOOON
ZBAM
ER-73
THAT'S IT! WE JAMMED IT OPEN!
TAKE A PISS INSIDE AND SHORT-CIRCUIT IT!
HA HA! SEE HOW IT LIKES THAT!

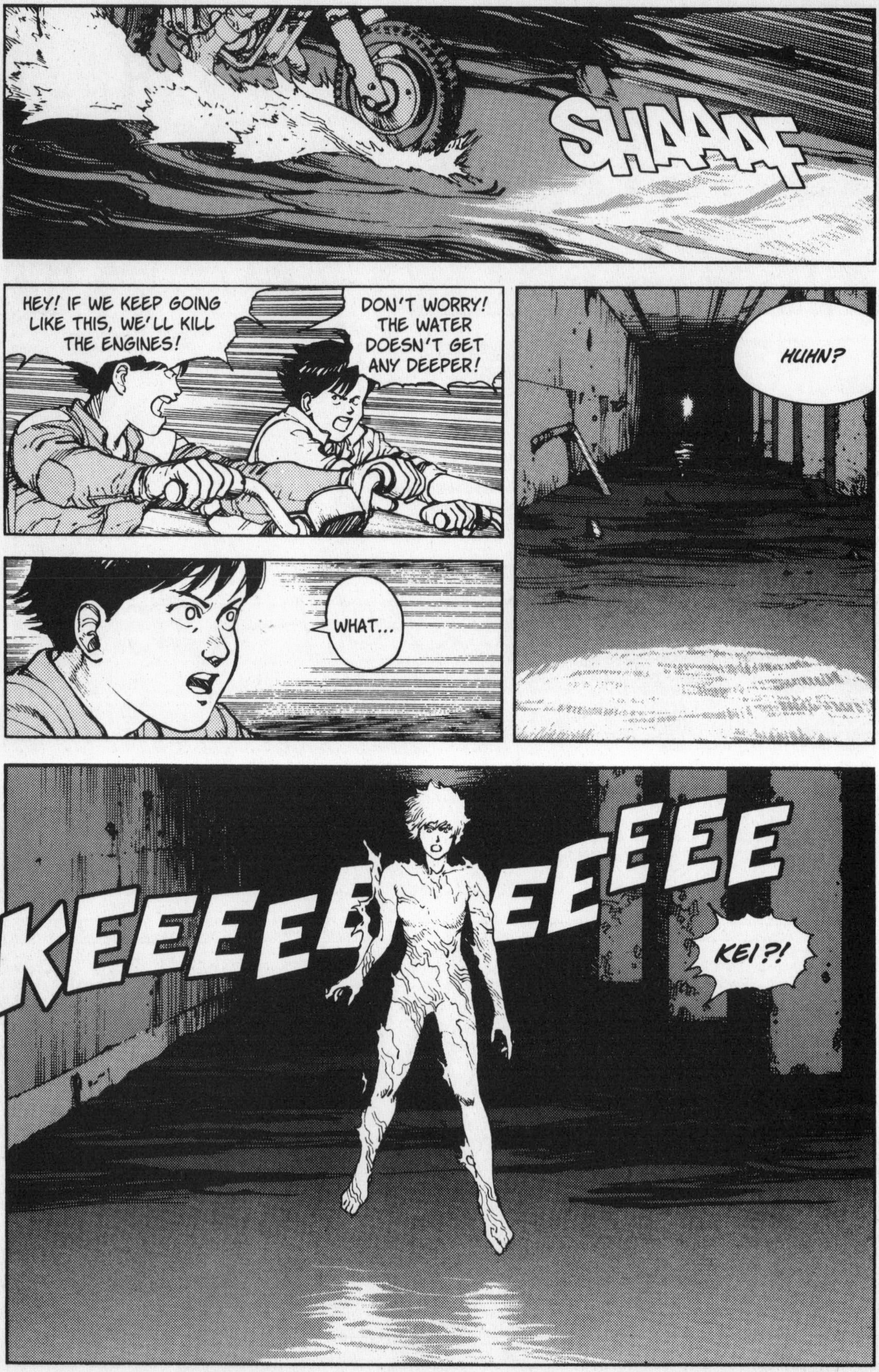
SHAAAF
HEY! IF WE KEEP GOING LIKE THIS, WE'LL KILL THE ENGINES!
DON'T WORRY! THE WATER DOESN'T GET ANY DEEPER!
HUHN?
WHAT...
KEEEEEEEEEEE
KEI?!

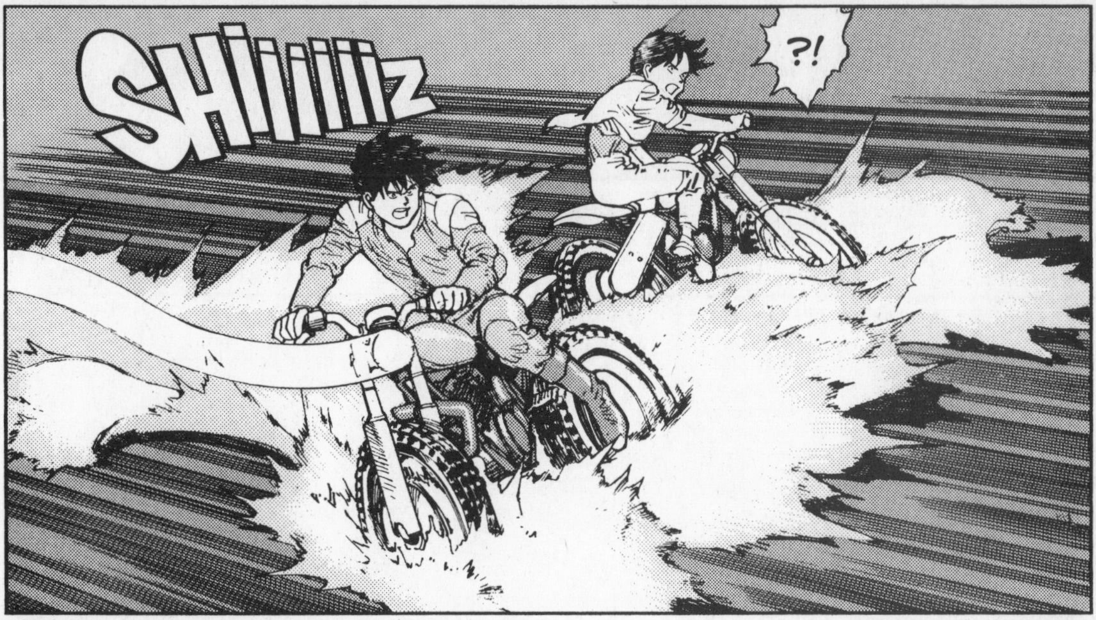
SHIIIIIIZ
?!

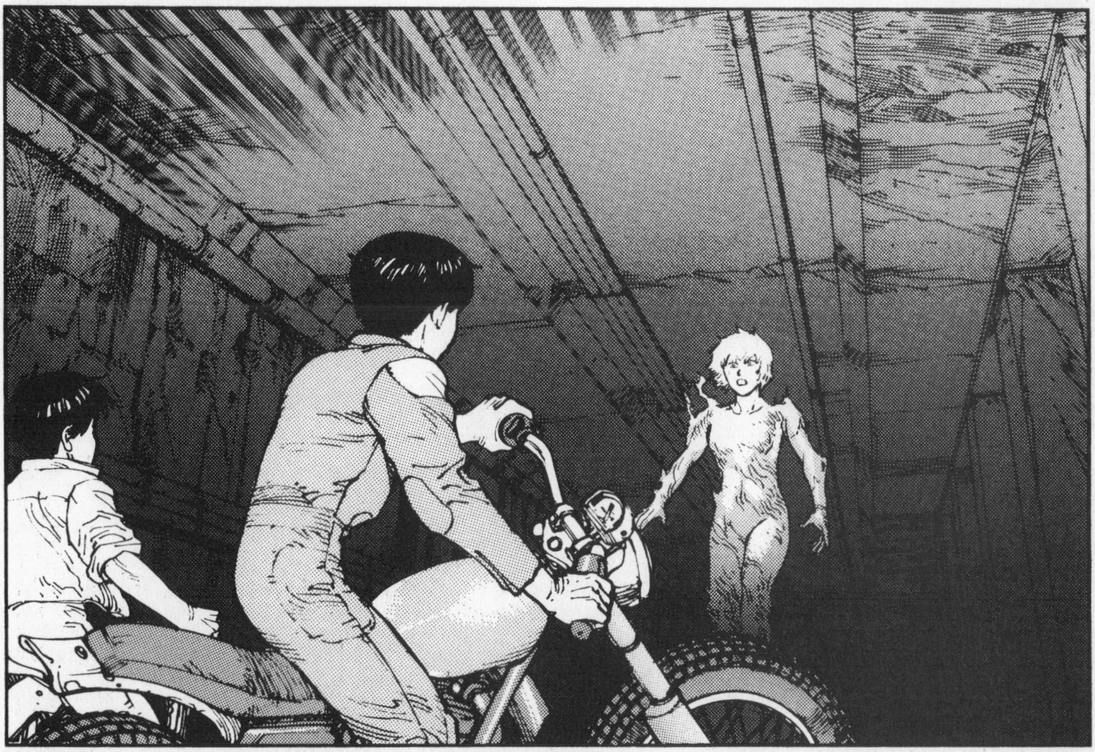

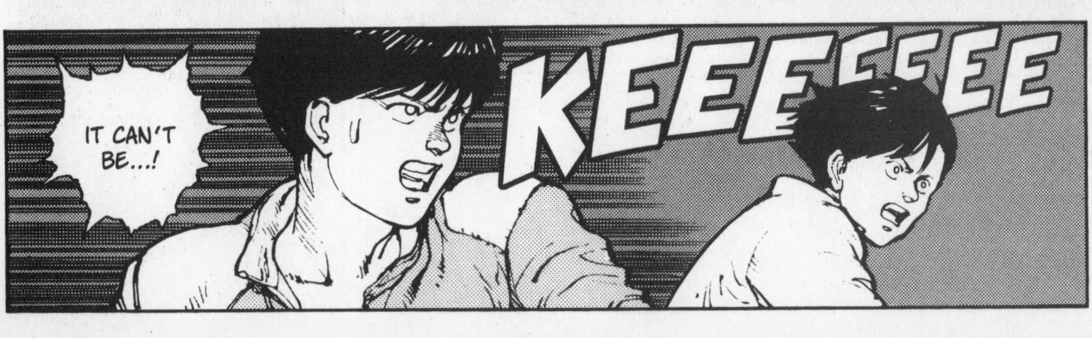
IT CAN'T BE...!
KEEEEEEE

GASP!
KEI...
W-WAIT...!
OOOH!!
KZIIIP
WAAH!!

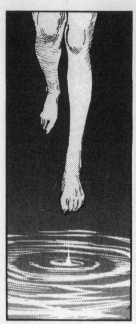

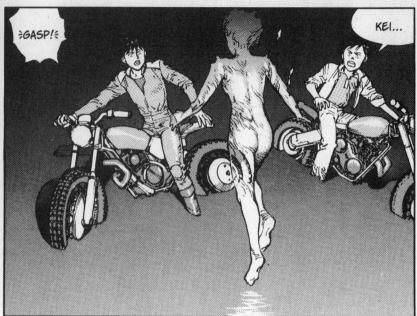

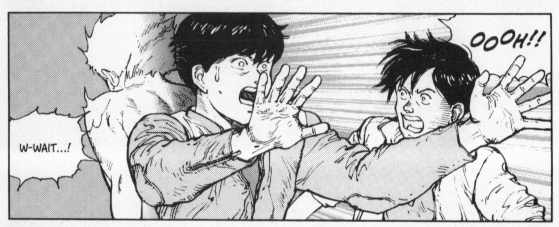

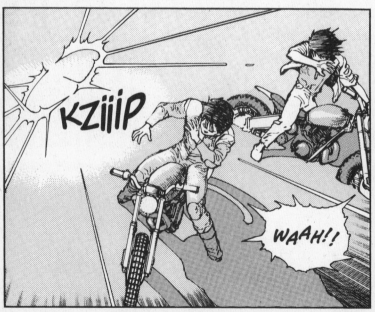

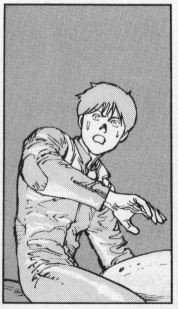

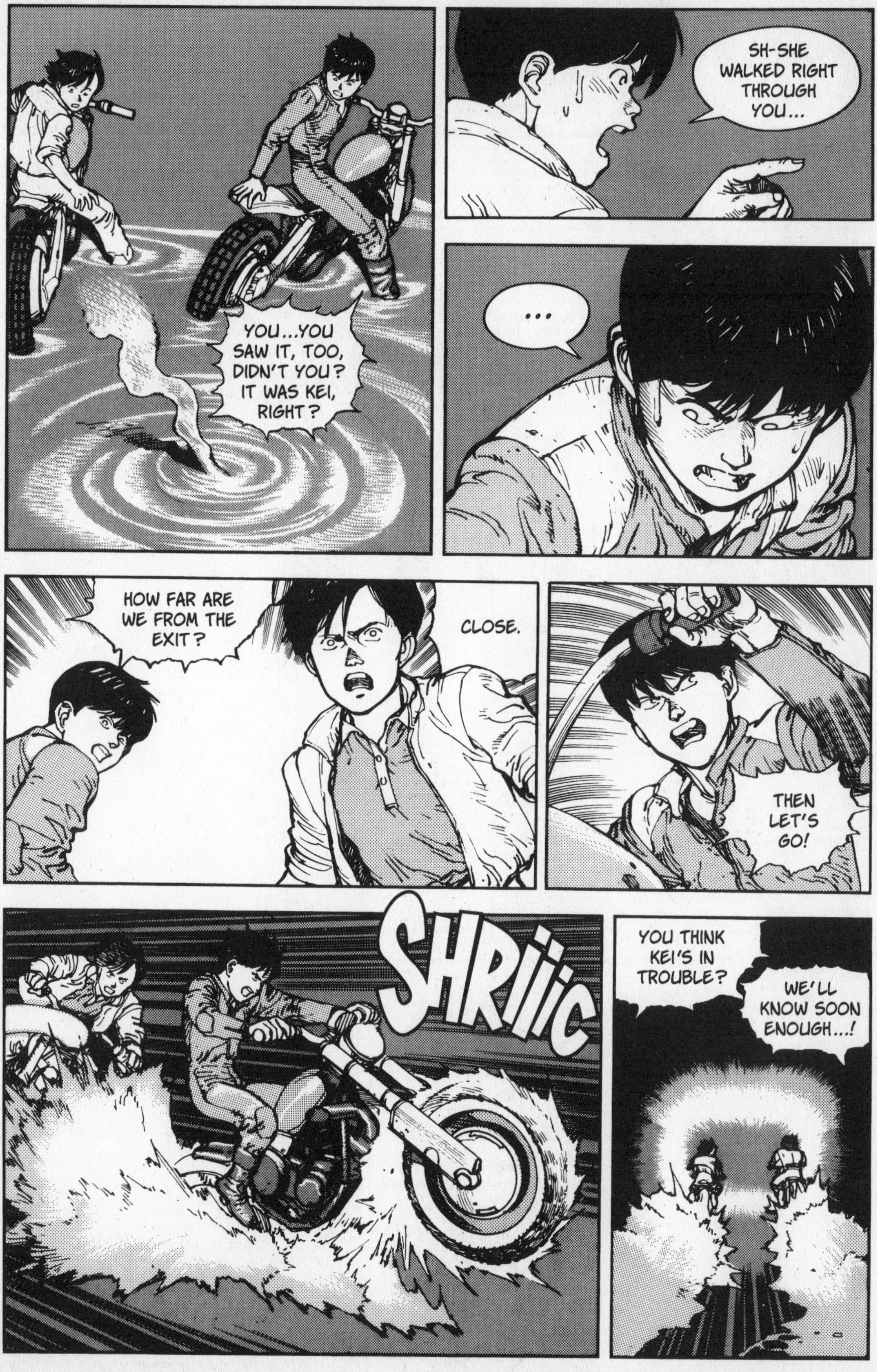
YOU...YOU SAW IT, TOO, DIDN'T YOU? IT WAS KEI, RIGHT?
SH-SHE WALKED RIGHT THROUGH YOU...
...
HOW FAR ARE WE FROM THE EXIT?
CLOSE.
THEN LET'S GO!
SHRIIIC
YOU THINK KEI'S IN TROUBLE?
WE'LL KNOW SOON ENOUGH...!

JUST WHAT DO YOU PLAN TO DO...CARRY HER ON YOUR BACK?

PART OF THE WAY...

I'LL ASK LADY MIYAKO'S PRIESTS TO TAKE HER FROM THERE.

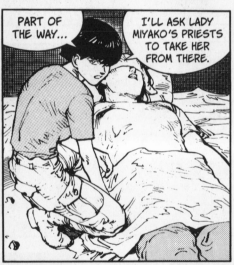

I WONDER IF THEY'LL HAVE TIME FOR YOU...

...

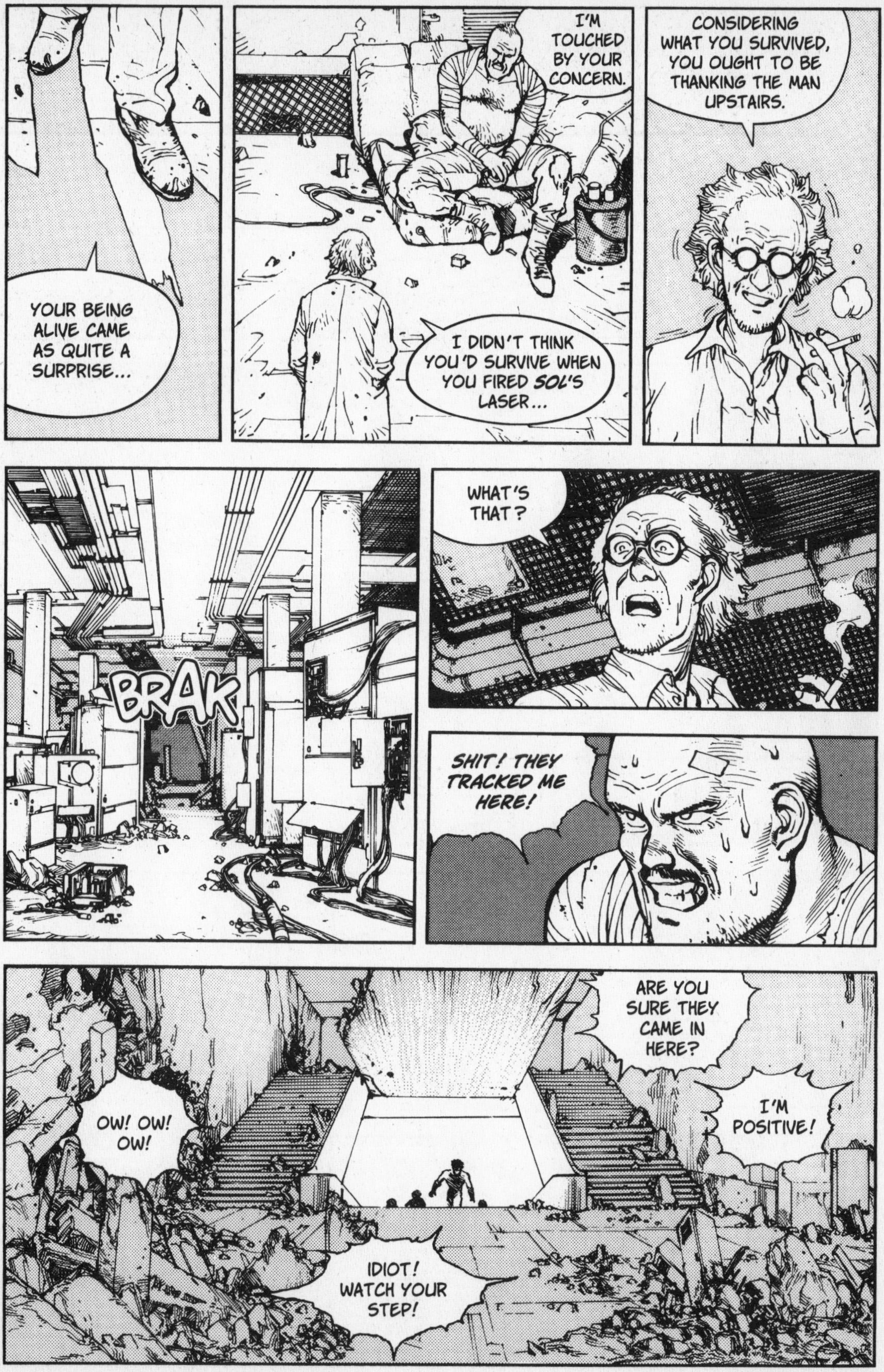
YOUR BEING ALIVE CAME AS QUITE A SURPRISE...
I'M TOUCHED BY YOUR CONCERN.
I DIDN'T THINK YOU'D SURVIVE WHEN YOU FIRED SOL'S LASER...
CONSIDERING WHAT YOU SURVIVED, YOU OUGHT TO BE THANKING THE MAN UPSTAIRS.
BRAK
WHAT'S THAT?
SHIT! THEY TRACKED ME HERE!
OW! OW! OW!
ARE YOU SURE THEY CAME IN HERE?
I'M POSITIVE!
IDIOT! WATCH YOUR STEP!

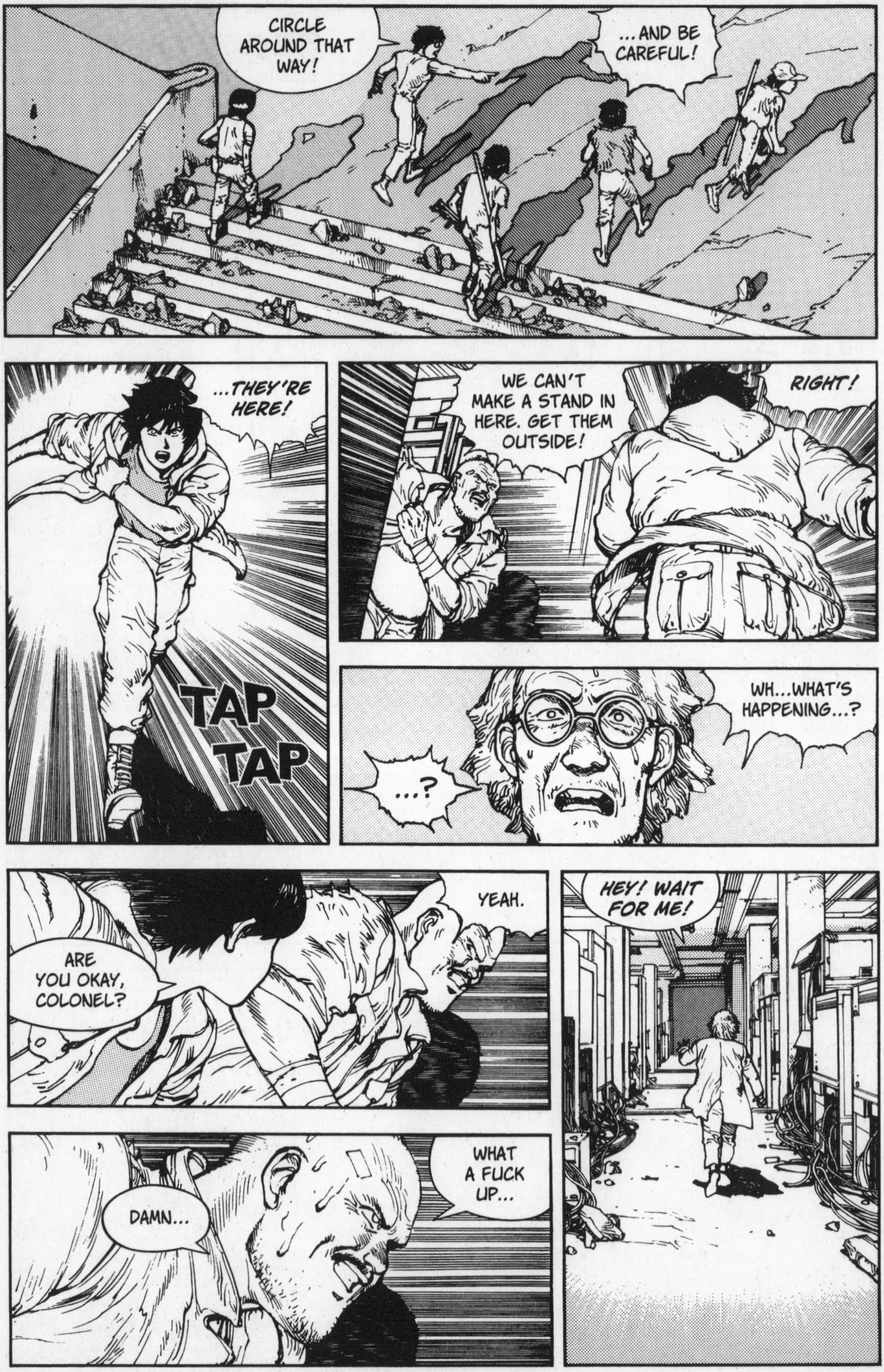
CIRCLE AROUND THAT WAY!
...AND BE CAREFUL!
...THEY'RE HERE!
TAP TAP
WE CAN'T MAKE A STAND IN HERE. GET THEM OUTSIDE!
RIGHT!
WH...WHAT'S HAPPENING...?
...?
ARE YOU OKAY, COLONEL?
YEAH.
DAMN...
WHAT A FUCK UP...
HEY! WAIT FOR ME!

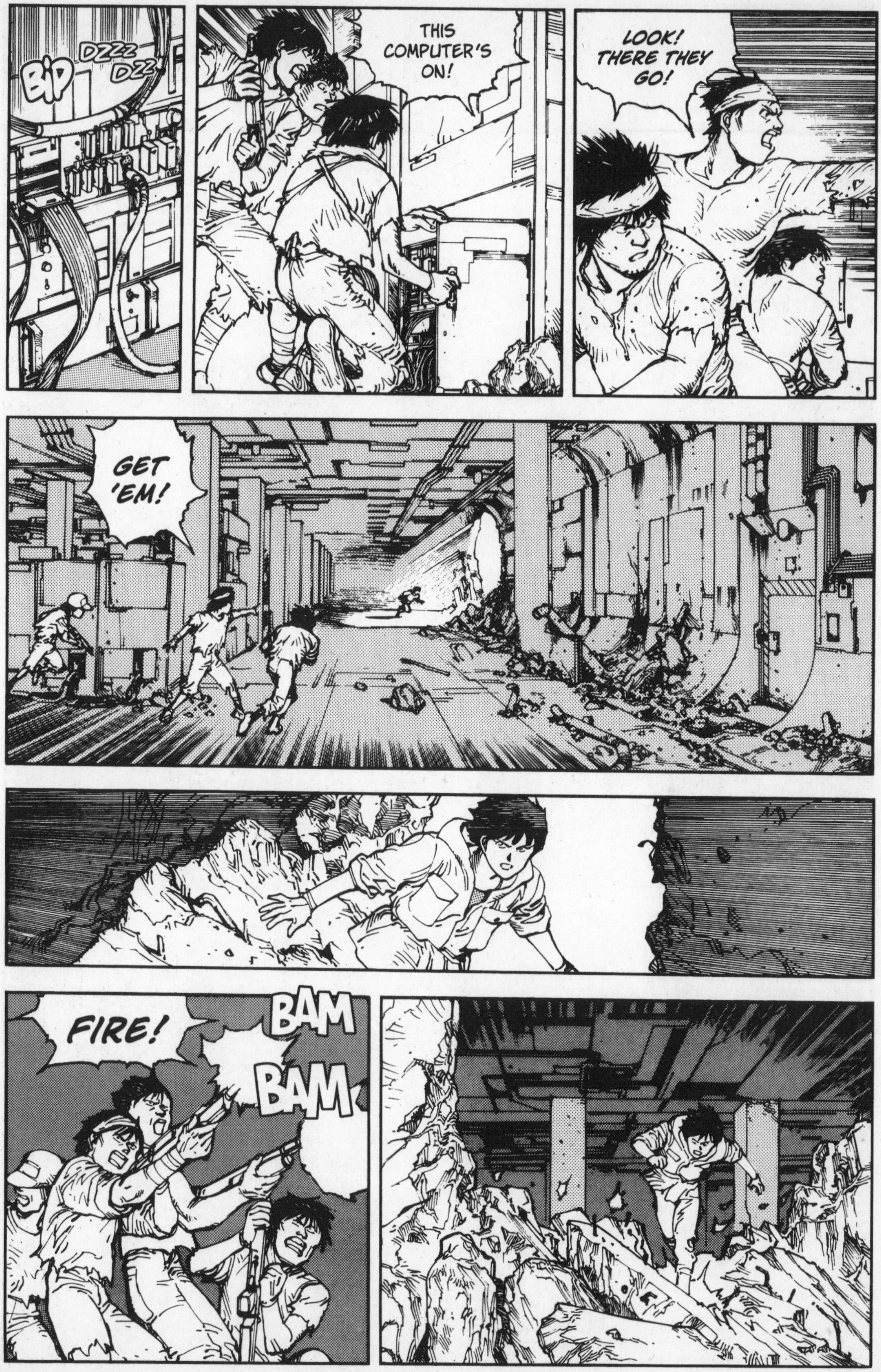
BIP
DZZZ DZZ
THIS COMPUTER'S ON!
LOOK! THERE THEY GO!
GET 'EM!
FIRE!
BAM
BAM

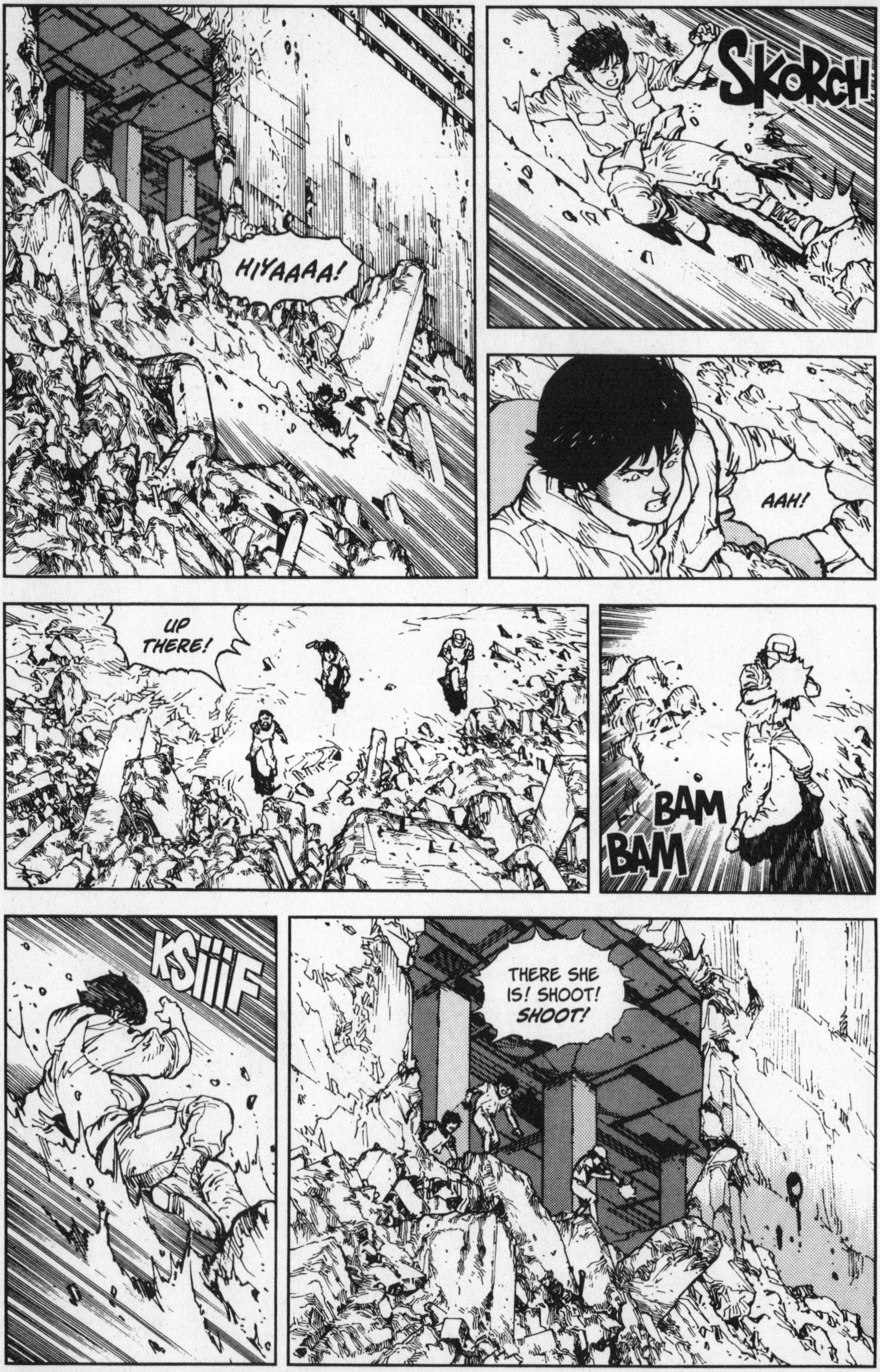
HIYAAAA!
SKORCH
AAH!
UP THERE!
BAM
BAM
KSIIIF
THERE SHE IS! SHOOT! SHOOT!

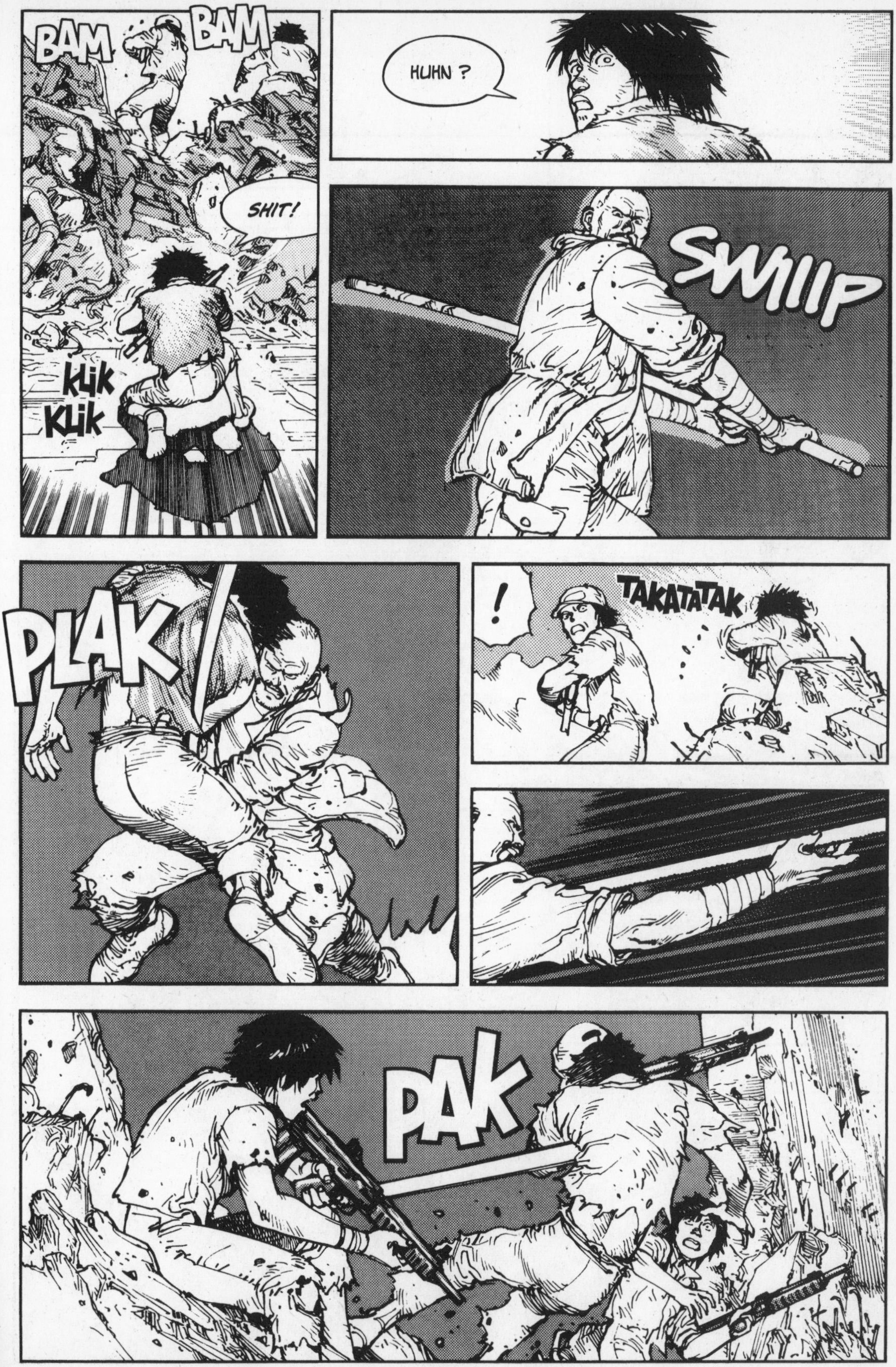
BAM
BAM
SHIT!
KLIK
KLIK
HUHN ?
SWIIIP
PLAK
!
TAKATATAK
PAK

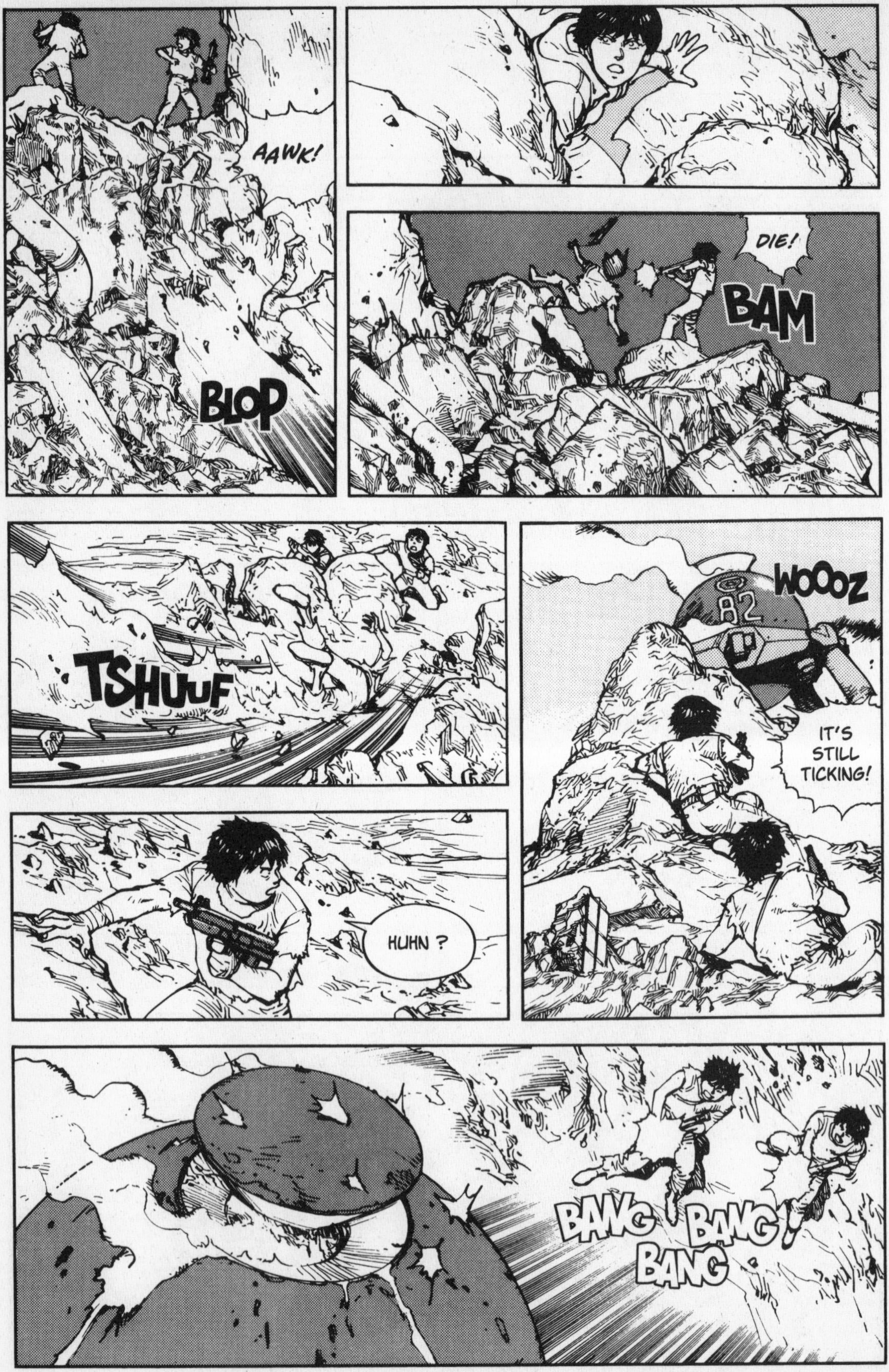
AAWK!
BLOP
DIE!
BAM
TSHUUUF
HUHN ?
WOOOZ
IT'S STILL TICKING!
BANG
BANG
BANG

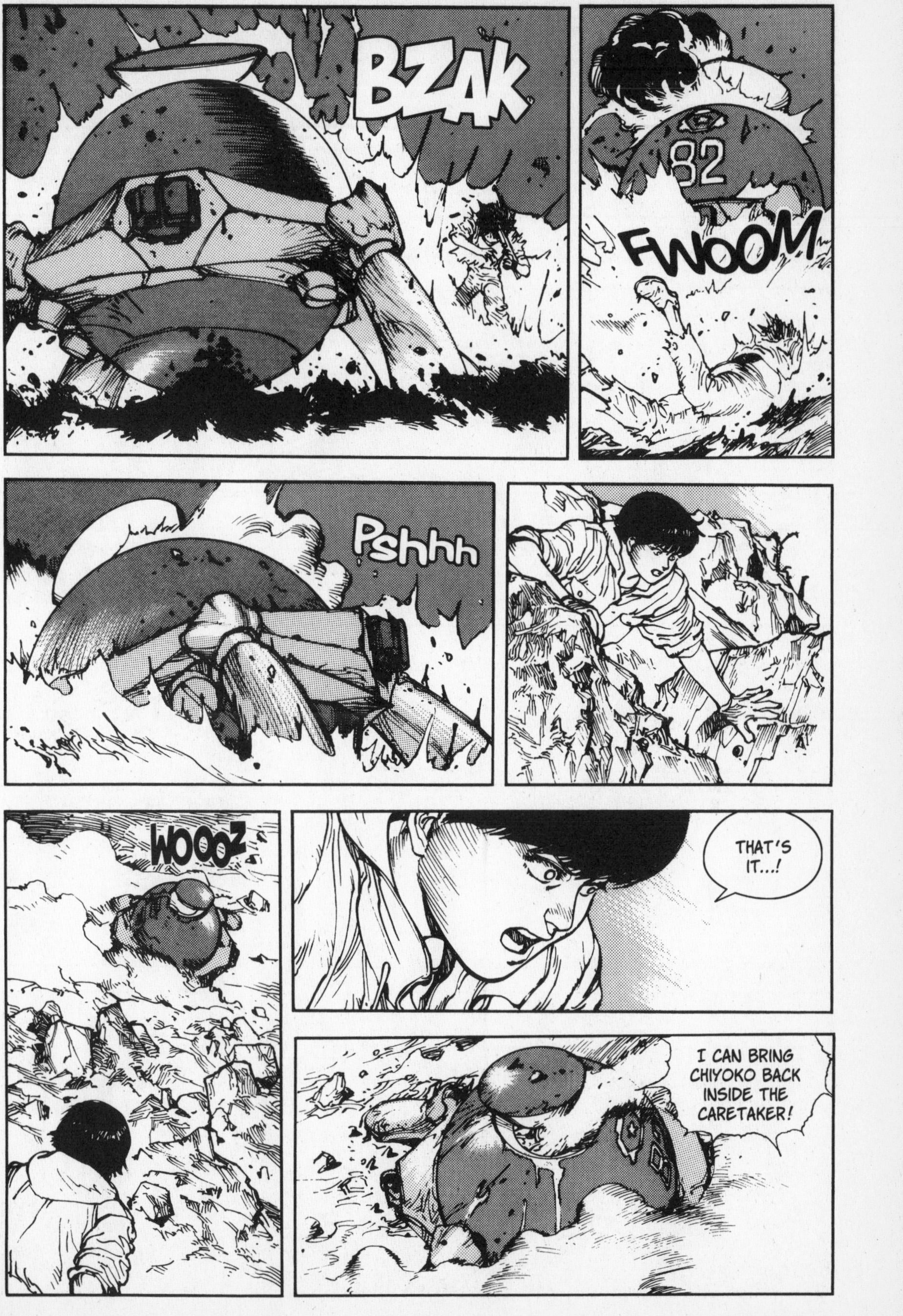
BZAK
82
FWOOM
Pshhh
WOOOZ
THAT'S IT...!
I CAN BRING CHIYOKO BACK INSIDE THE CARETAKER!

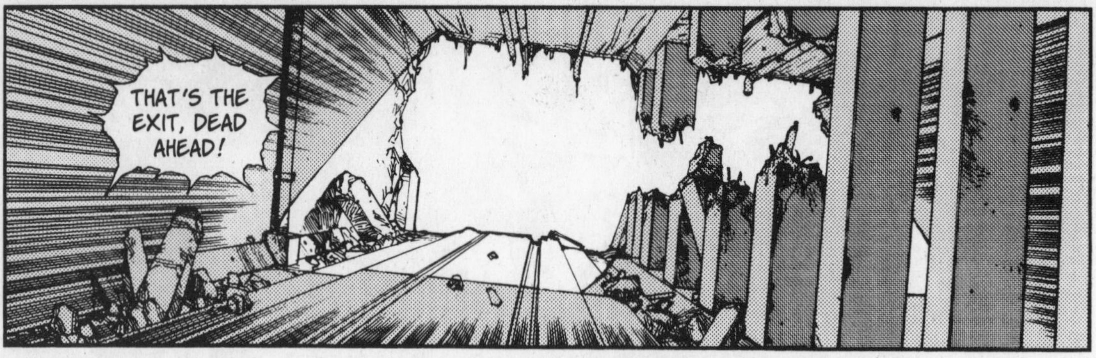
THAT'S THE EXIT, DEAD AHEAD!
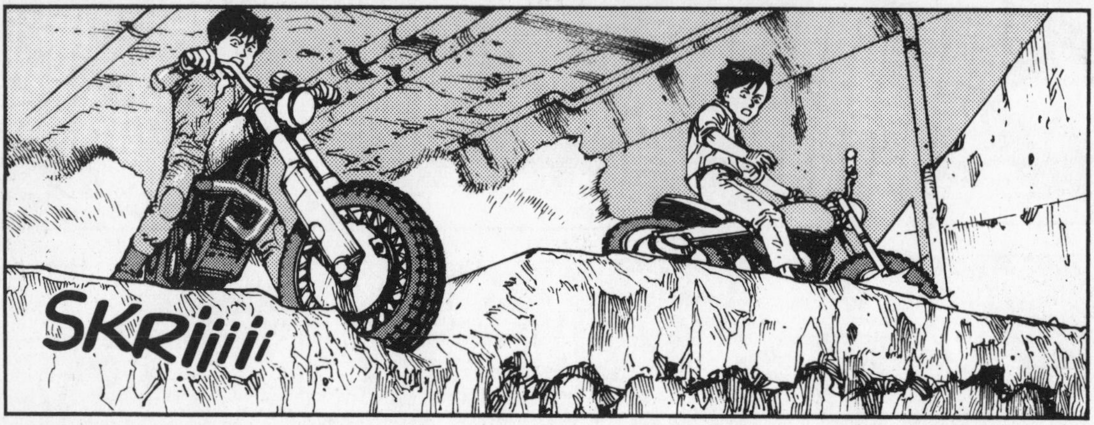
SKRiiiii
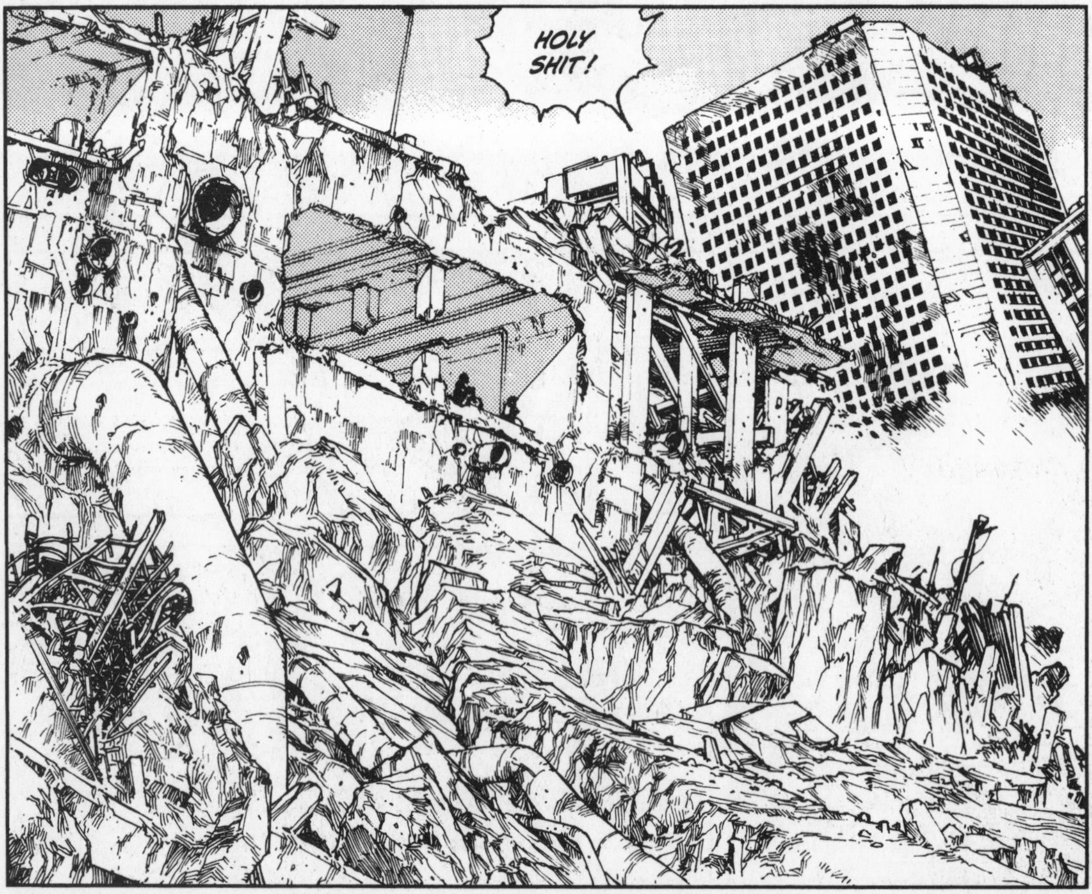
HOLY SHIT!

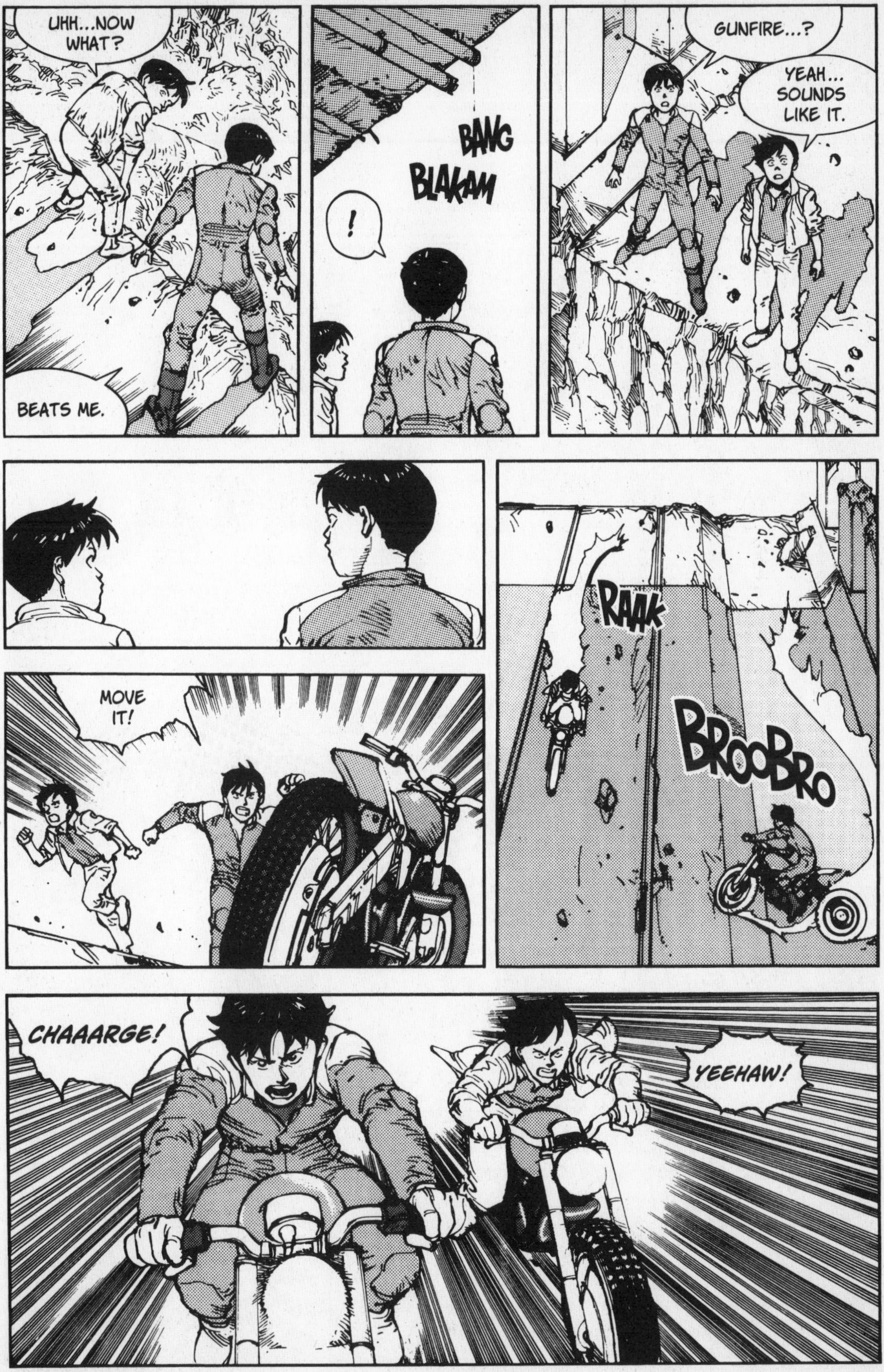
UHH...NOW WHAT?
BEATS ME.
BANG
BLAKAM
!
GUNFIRE...?
YEAH... SOUNDS LIKE IT.
RAAK
BROOBRO
MOVE IT!
CHAAARGE!
YEEHAW!

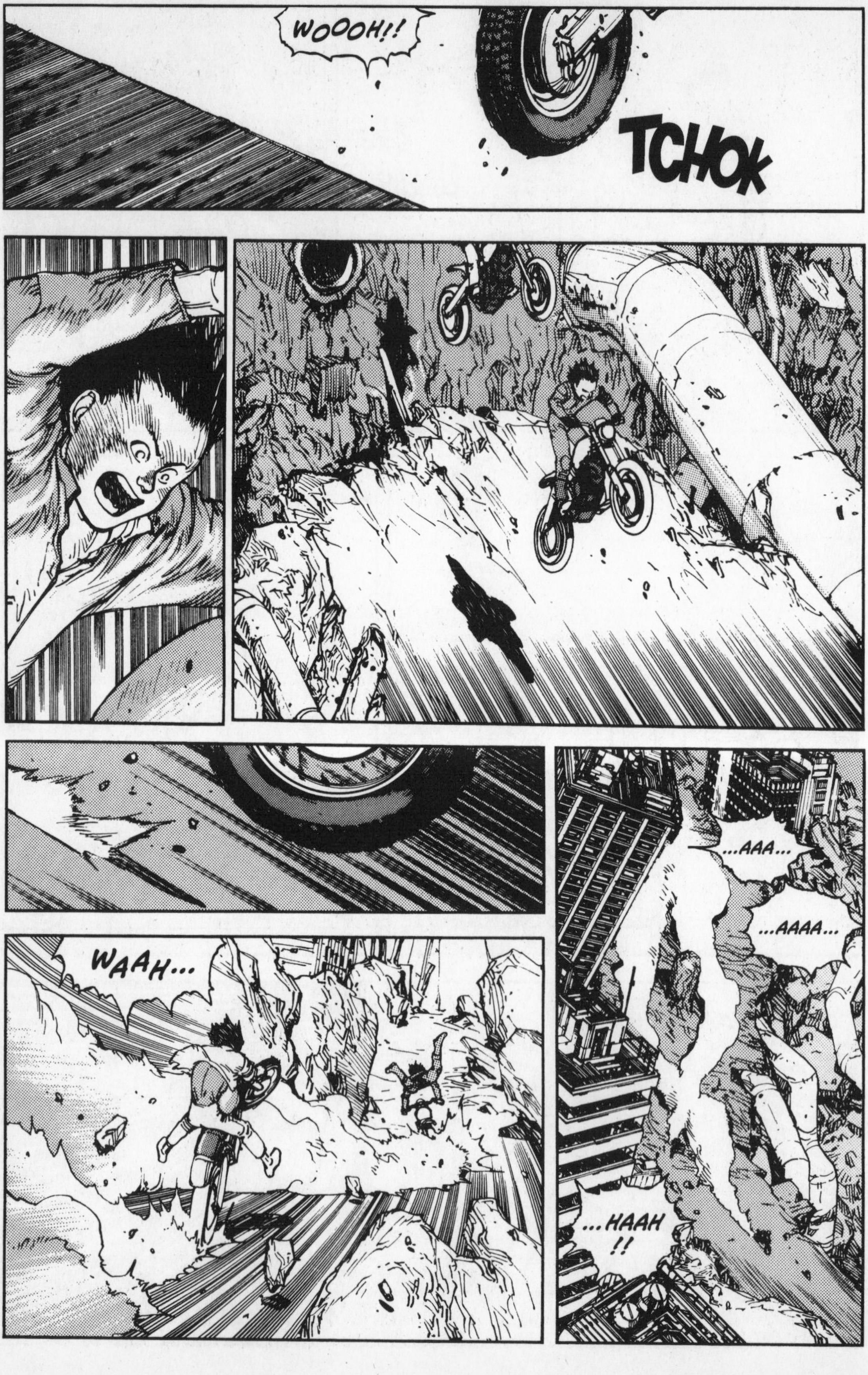
WOOOH!!
TCHOK
WAAH...
...AAA...
...AAAA...
...HAAH !!

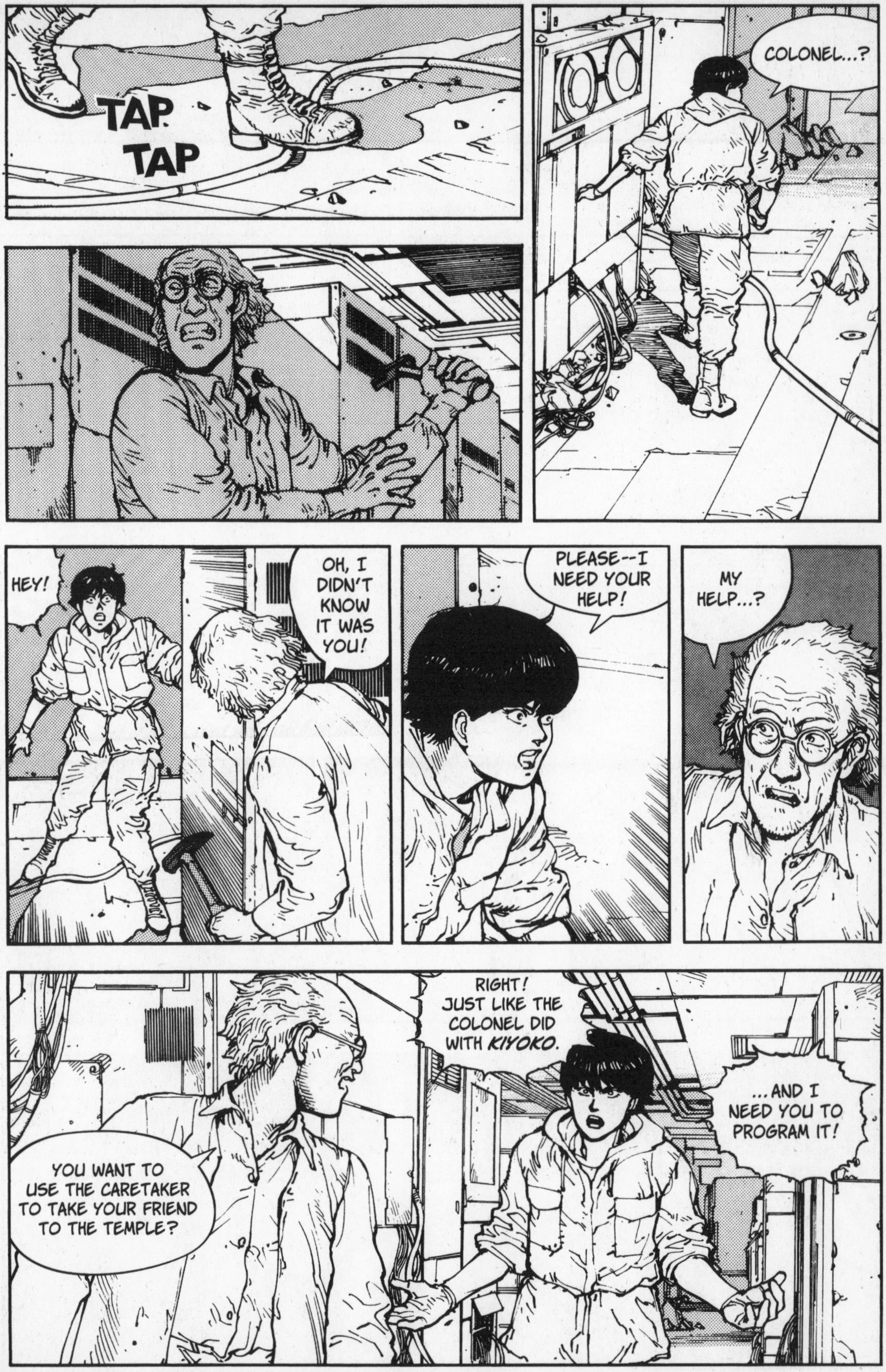
TAP
TAP
COLONEL...?
HEY!
OH, I DIDN'T KNOW IT WAS YOU!
PLEASE--I NEED YOUR HELP!
MY HELP...?
YOU WANT TO USE THE CARETAKER TO TAKE YOUR FRIEND TO THE TEMPLE?
RIGHT! JUST LIKE THE COLONEL DID WITH KIYOKO.
...AND I NEED YOU TO PROGRAM IT!

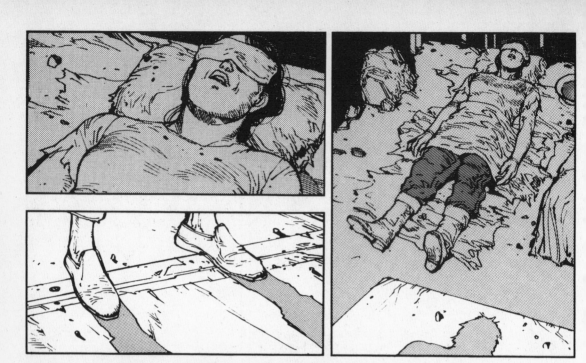

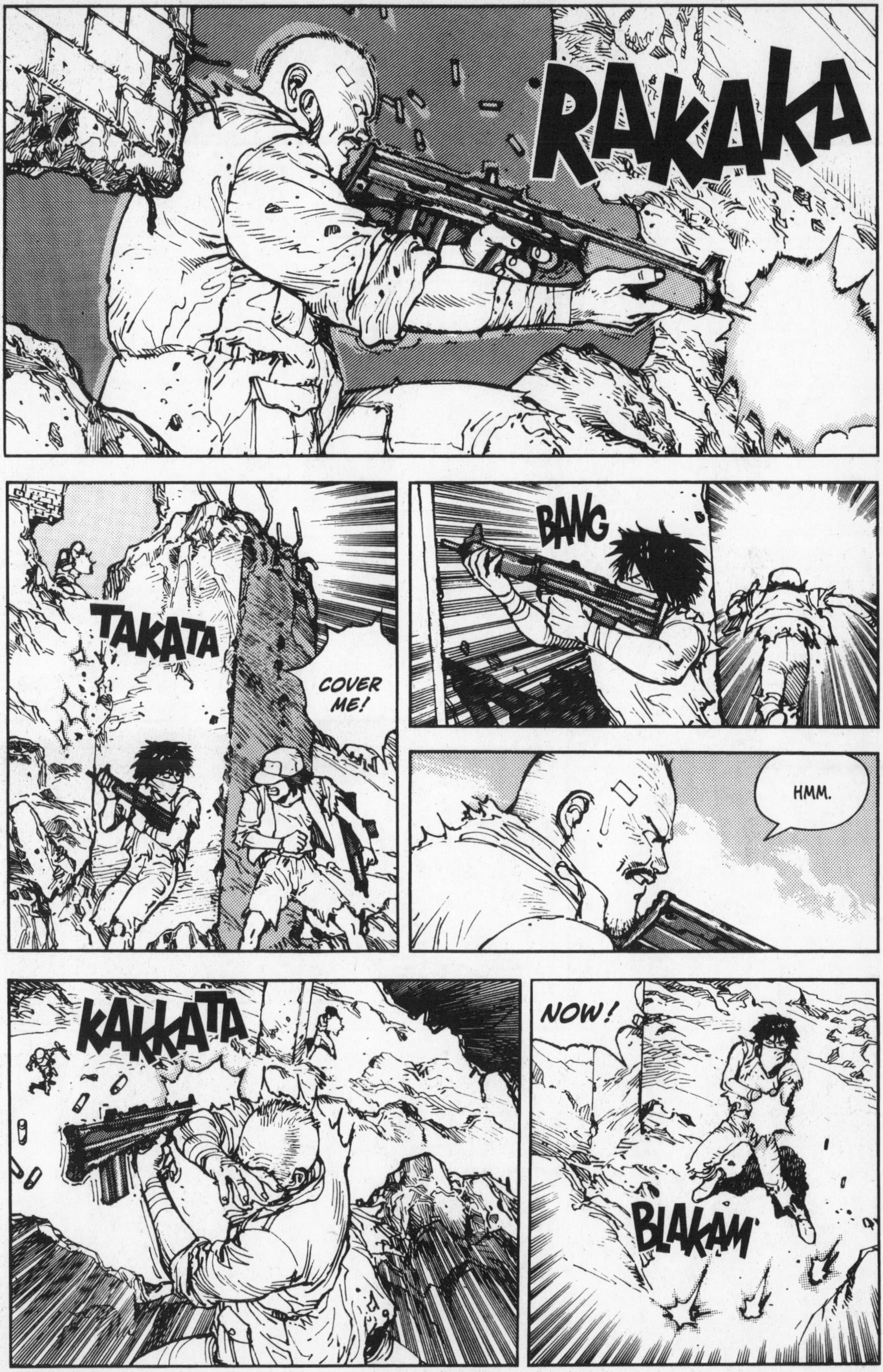
RAKAKA
TAKATA
COVER ME!
BANG
HMM.
KAKKATA
NOW!
BLAKAM

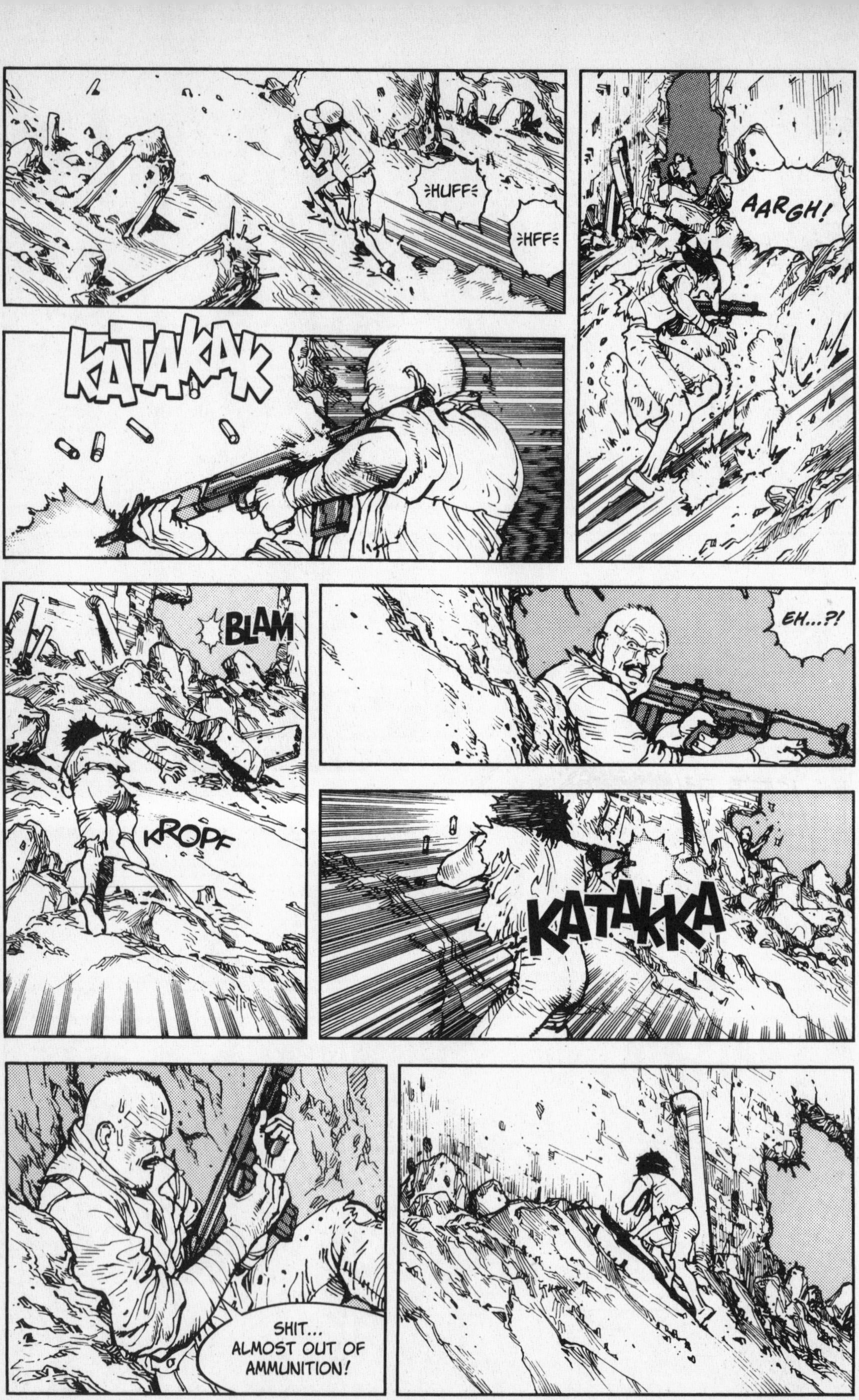
HUFF
HFF
KATAKAK
AARGH!
BLAM
KROPF
EH...?!
KATAKKA
SHIT... ALMOST OUT OF AMMUNITION!

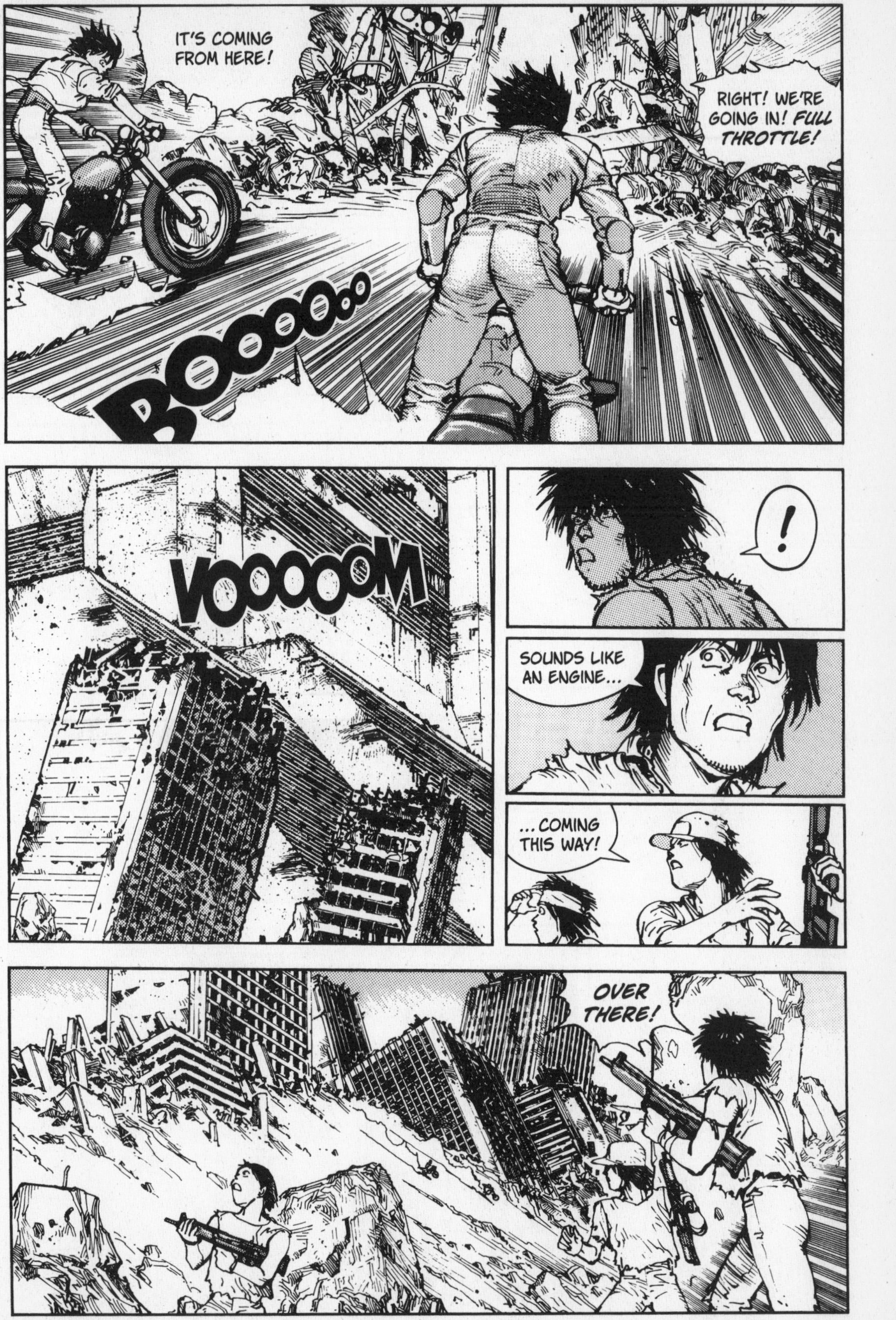
IT'S COMING FROM HERE!
RIGHT! WE'RE GOING IN! FULL THROTTLE!
BOOOOO..O
VOOOOOM
!
SOUNDS LIKE AN ENGINE...
...COMING THIS WAY!
OVER THERE!

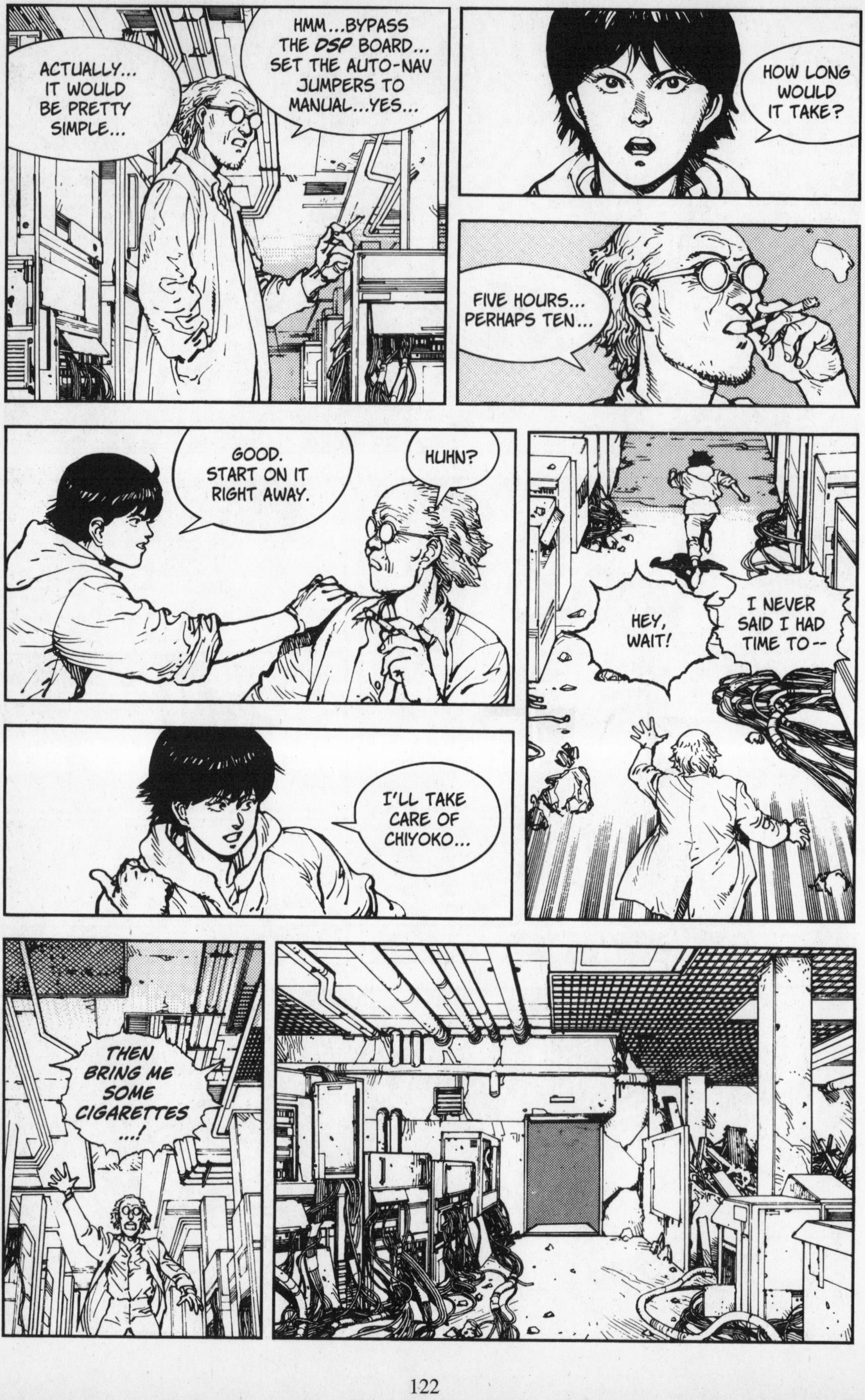

ACTUALLY... IT WOULD BE PRETTY SIMPLE...
HMM...BYPASS THE DSP BOARD... SET THE AUTO-NAV JUMPERS TO MANUAL...YES...
HOW LONG WOULD IT TAKE?
FIVE HOURS... PERHAPS TEN...
GOOD. START ON IT RIGHT AWAY.
HUHN?
I'LL TAKE CARE OF CHIYOKO...
HEY, WAIT!
I NEVER SAID I HAD TIME TO--
THEN BRING ME SOME CIGARETTES ...!

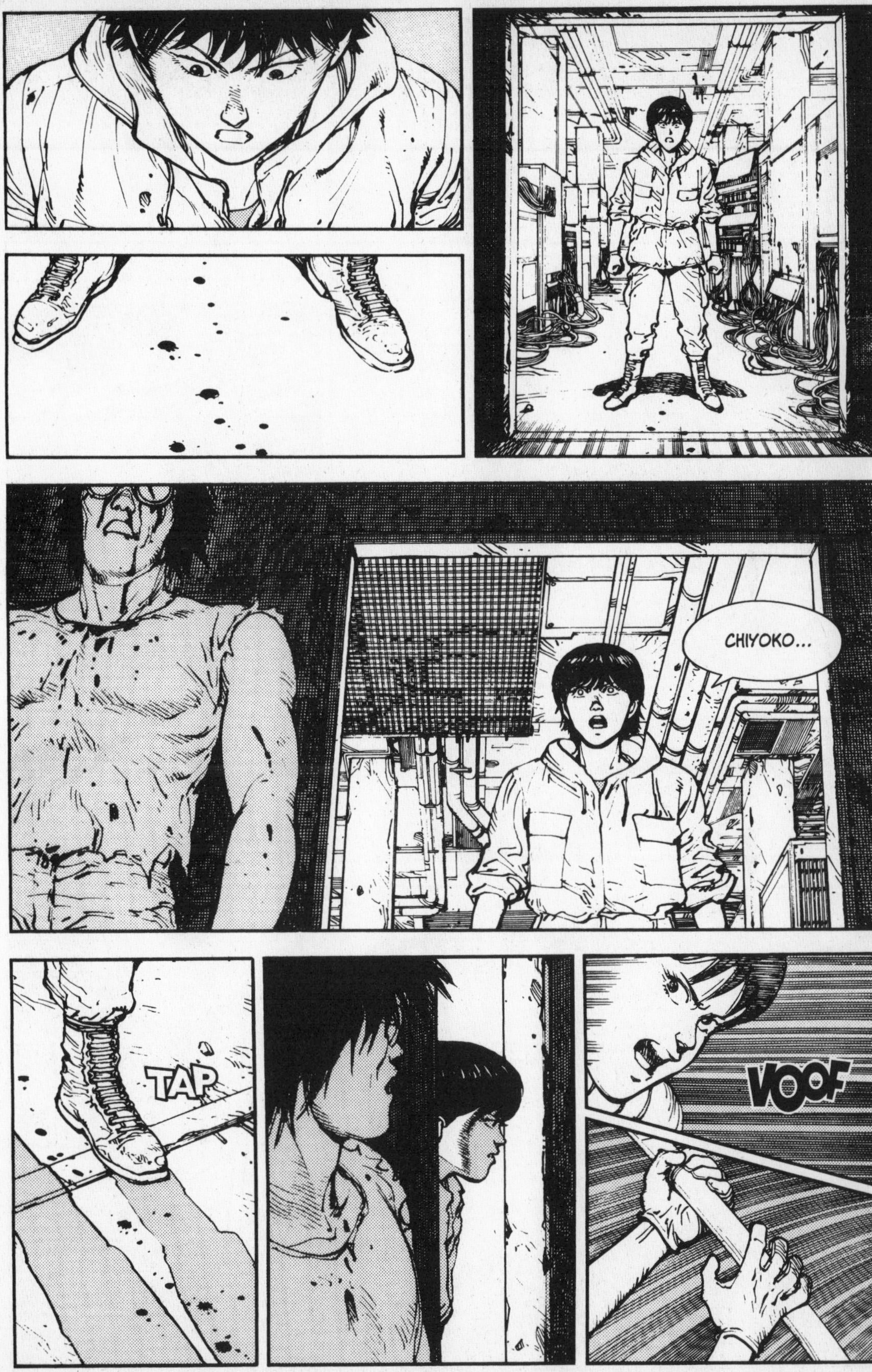
CHIYOKO...
TAP
VOOF

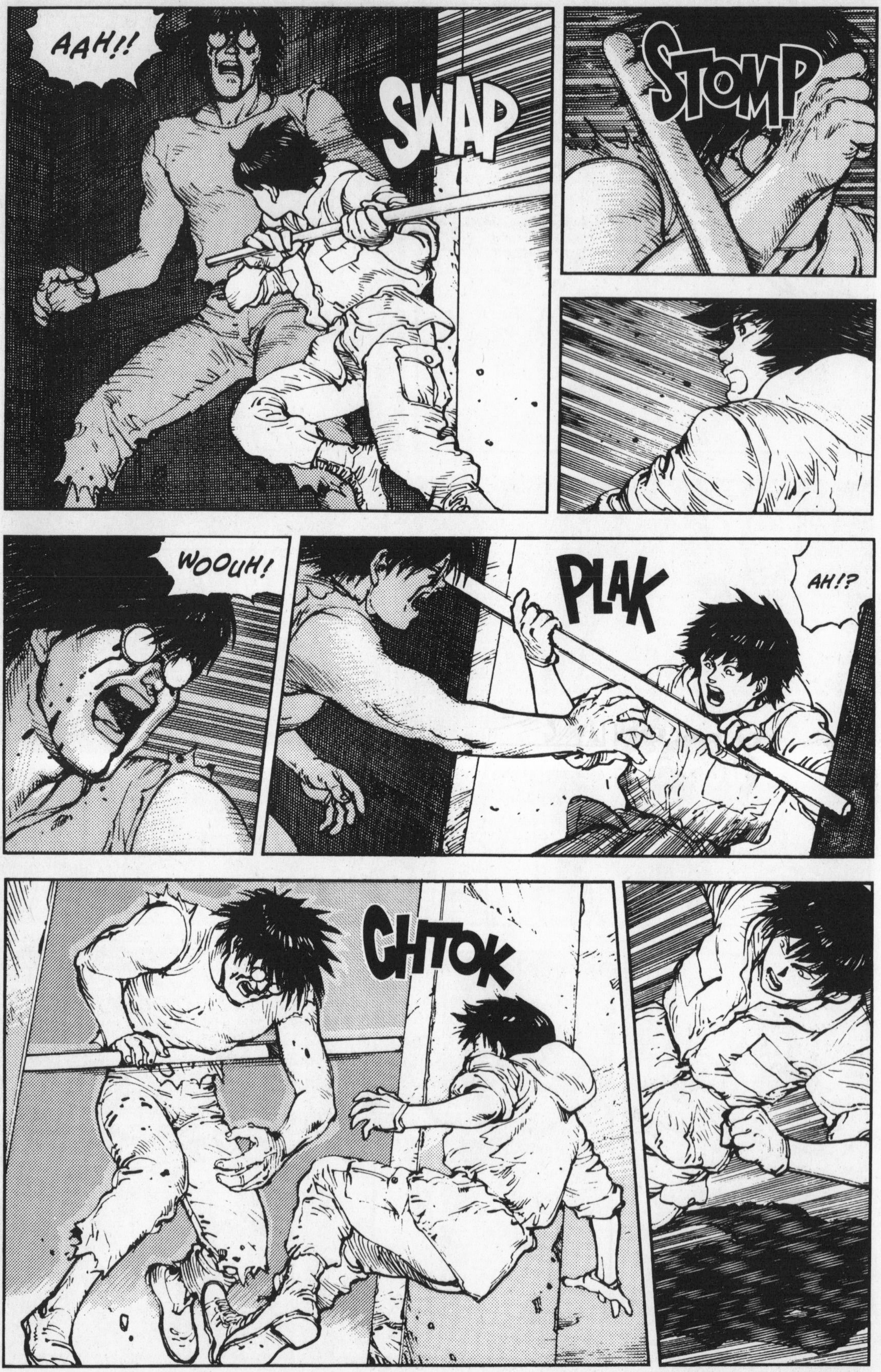
AAH!!
SWAP
STOMP
WOOUH!
PLAK
AH!?
CHTOK

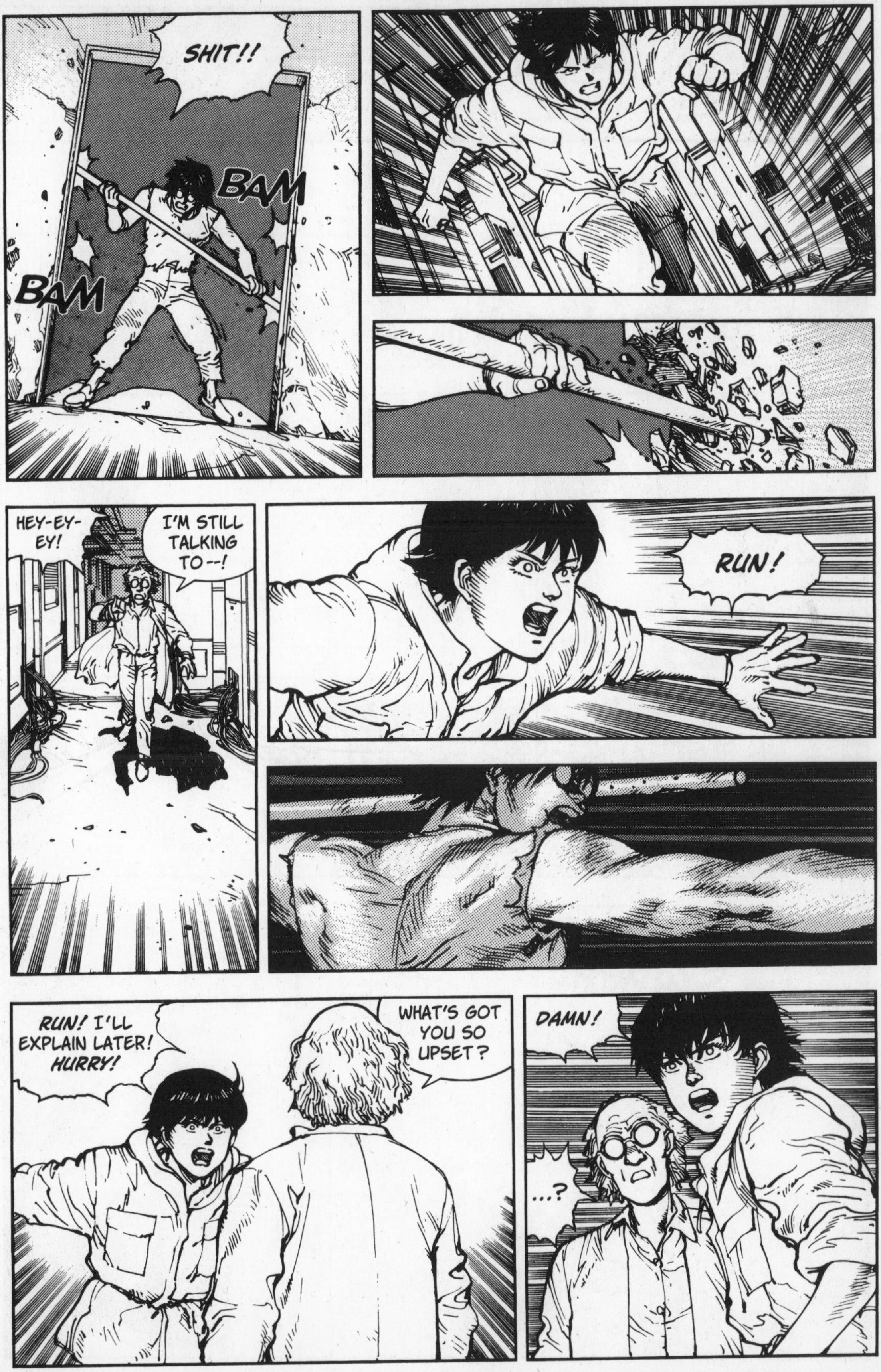
SHIT!!
BAM
BAM
HEY-EY-EY!
I'M STILL TALKING TO--!
RUN!
RUN! I'LL EXPLAIN LATER! HURRY!
WHAT'S GOT YOU SO UPSET?
DAMN!
...?

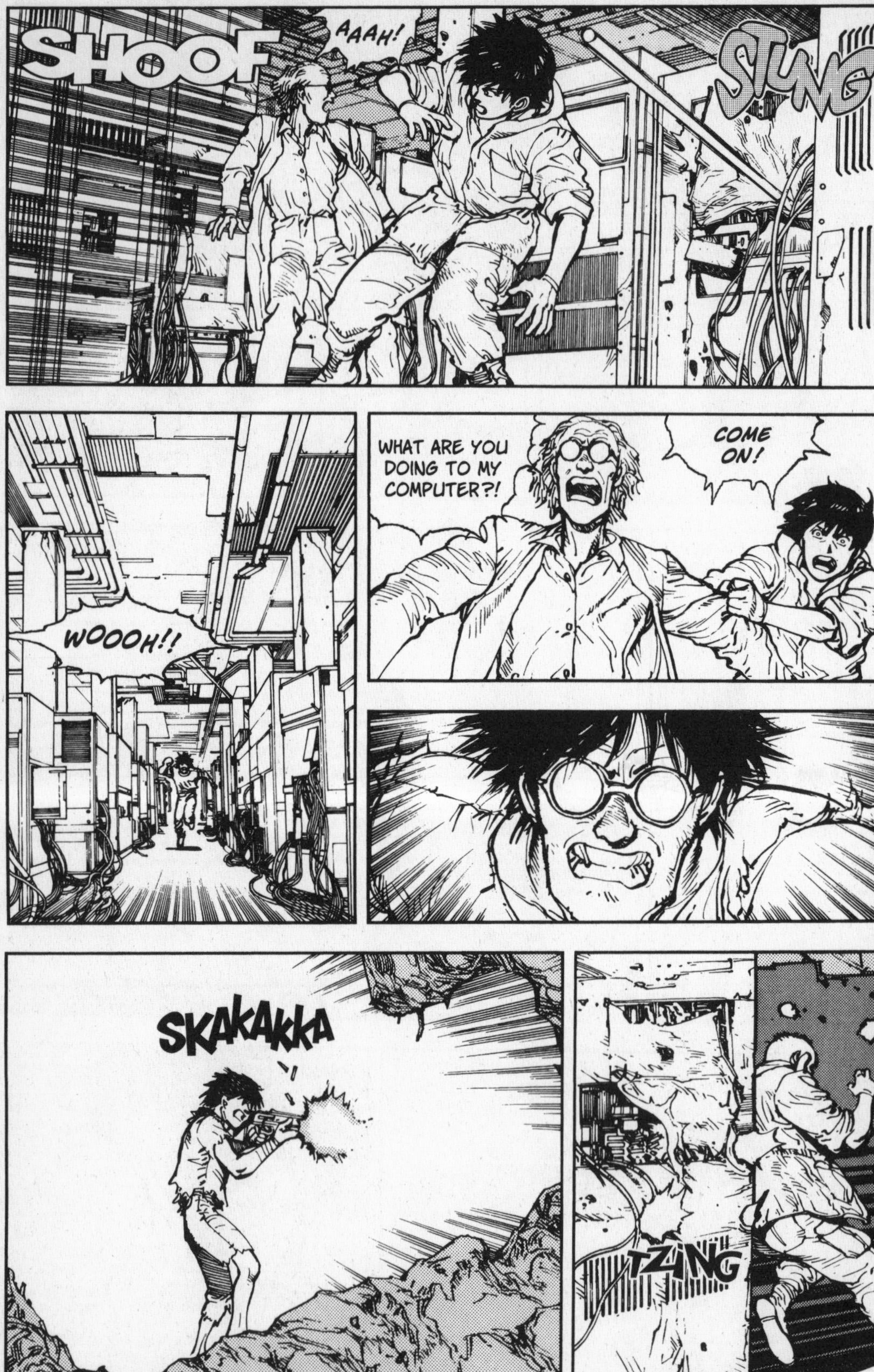
SHOOF
AAAH!
STUNG
WOOOH!!
WHAT ARE YOU DOING TO MY COMPUTER?!
COME ON!
SKAKAKKA
TZING

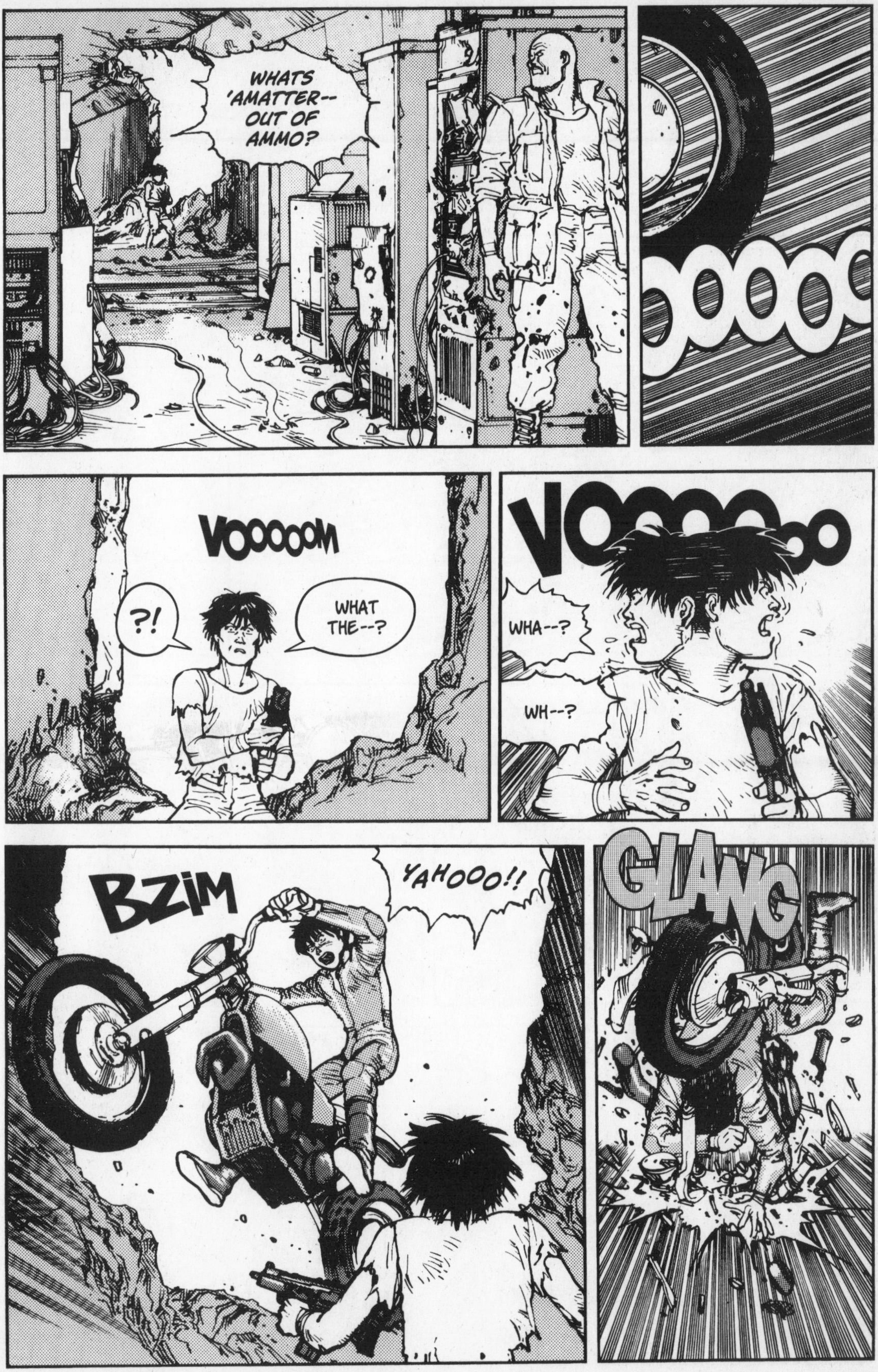
WHATS 'AMATTER-- OUT OF AMMO?
OOOOO
VOOOOOM
?!
WHAT THE--?
VOOOO..O
WHA--?
WH--?
BZIM
YAHOOO!!
GLANG

SHIT!

SHUIIN

BOM

...

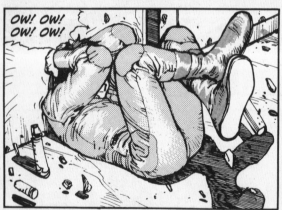

OW! OW!
OW! OW!

LOOKS
LIKE ANOTHER
ENEMY OF THE
EMPIRE!

TSHIK

...

DIE!

VOOOOOM

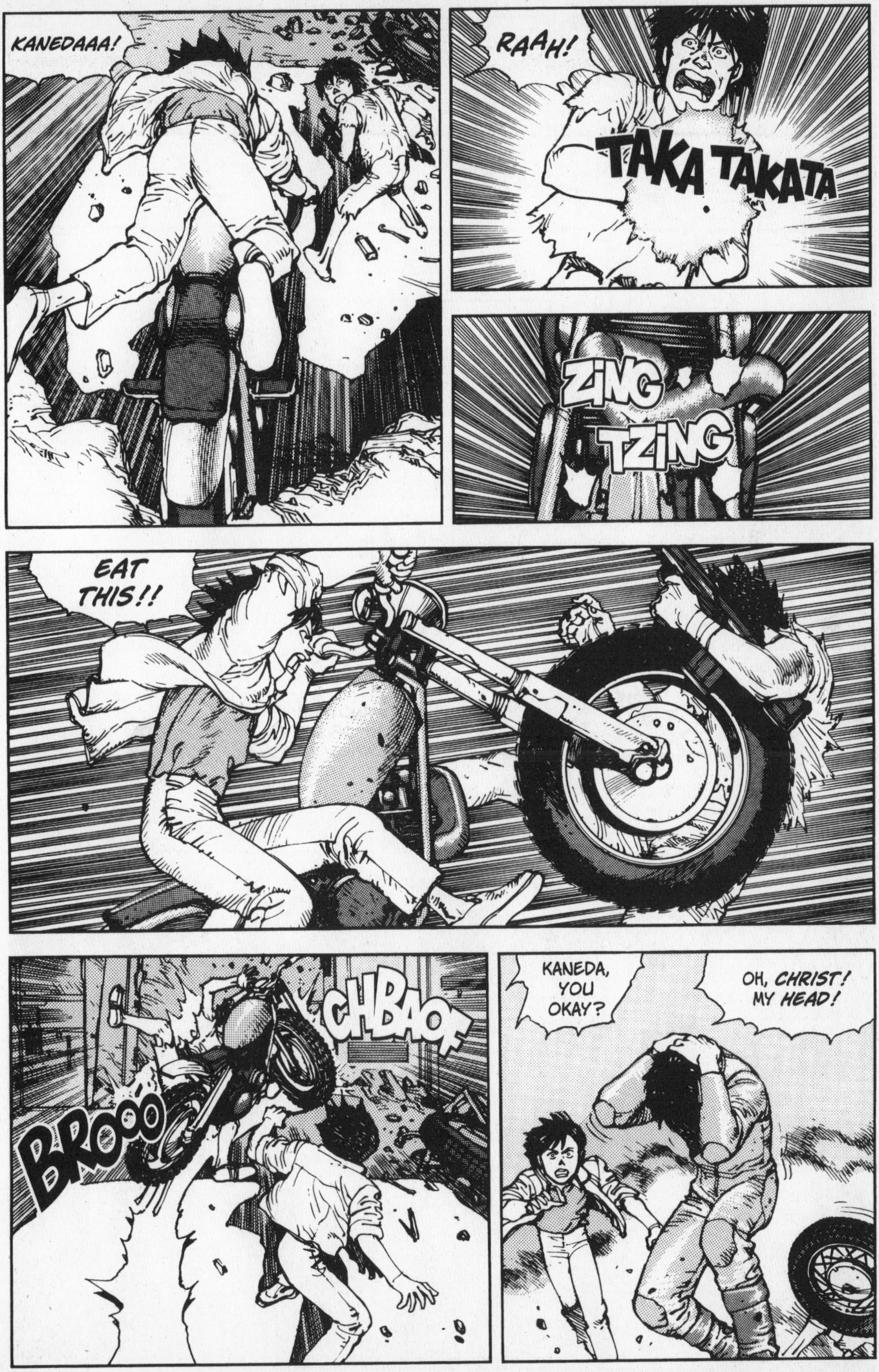
KANEDAAA!
RAAH!
TAKA TAKATA
ZING
TZING
EAT THIS!!
CHBAOF
BROOO
KANEDA, YOU OKAY?
OH, CHRIST! MY HEAD!

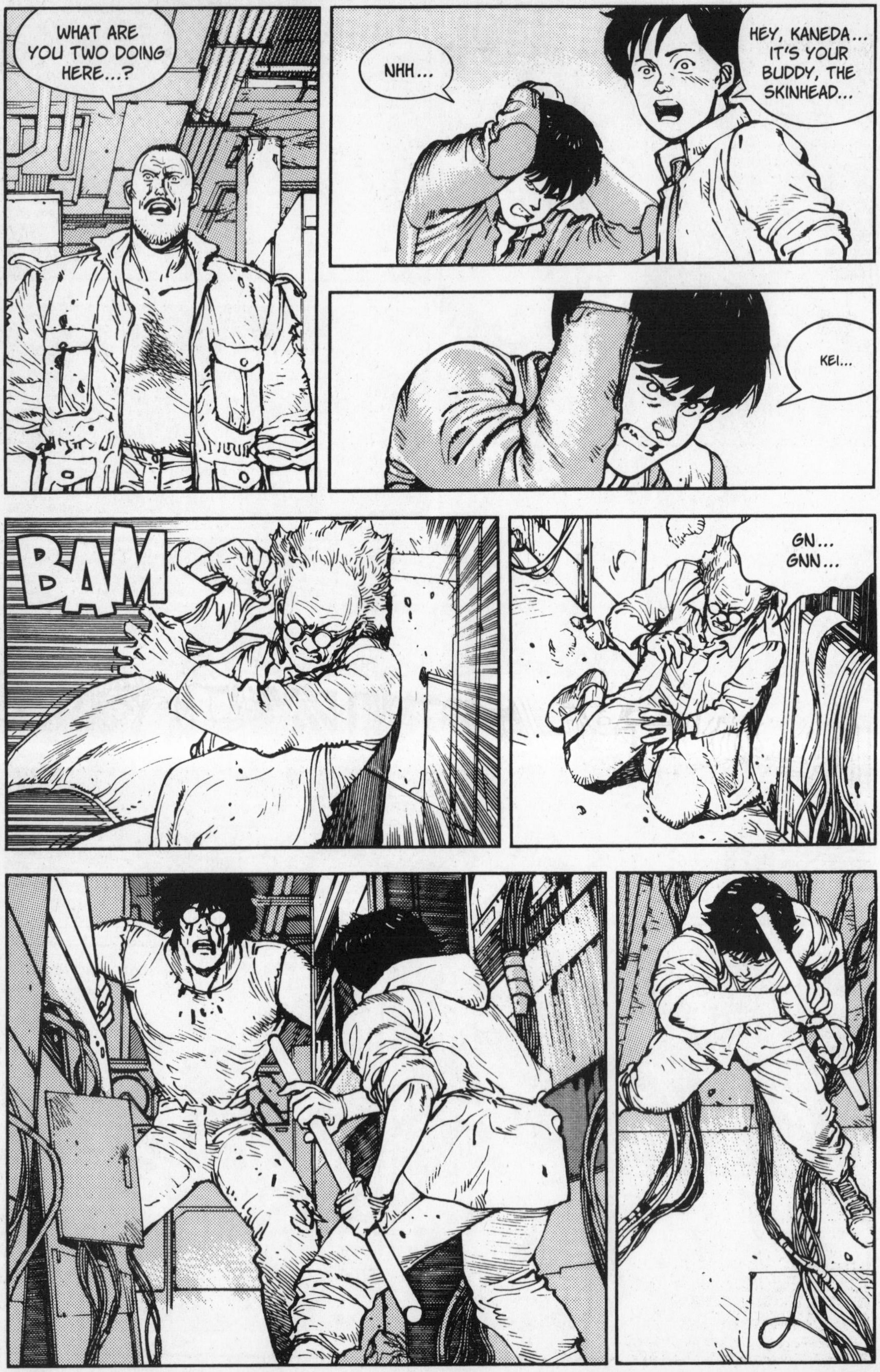
WHAT ARE YOU TWO DOING HERE...?
NHH...
HEY, KANEDA... IT'S YOUR BUDDY, THE SKINHEAD...
KEI...
BAM
GN... GNN...

KSHAK

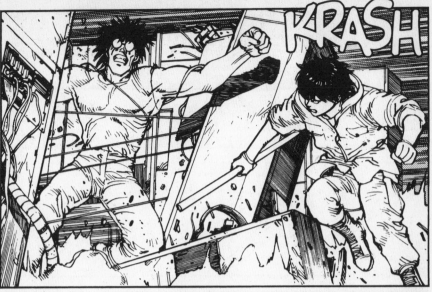

KRASH

HMM ?!

YOU HEAR THAT? SOMEONE'S COMING!

UH--!

SLAP

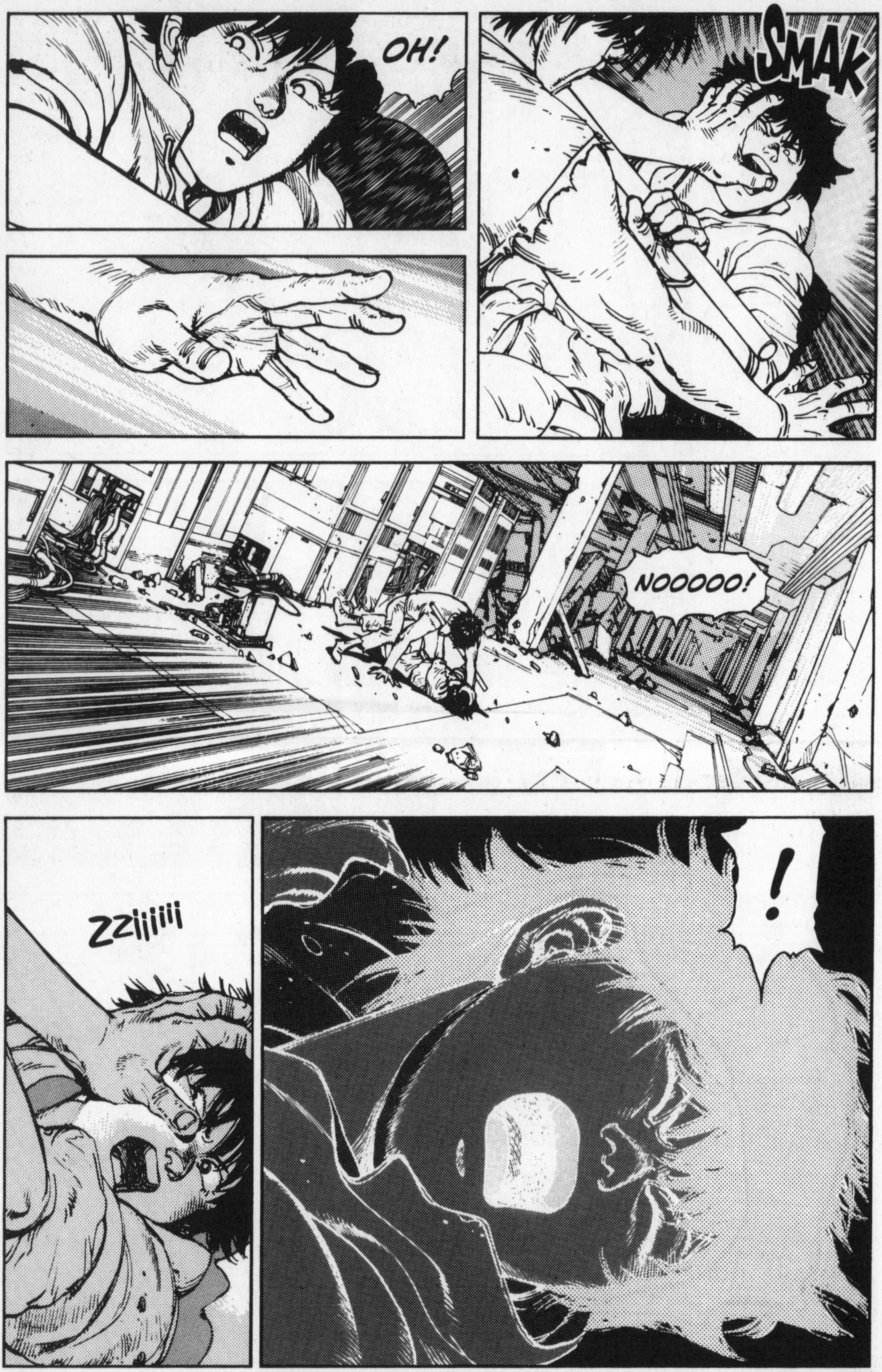
OH!
SMAK
NOOOOO!
ZZiiiiii
!

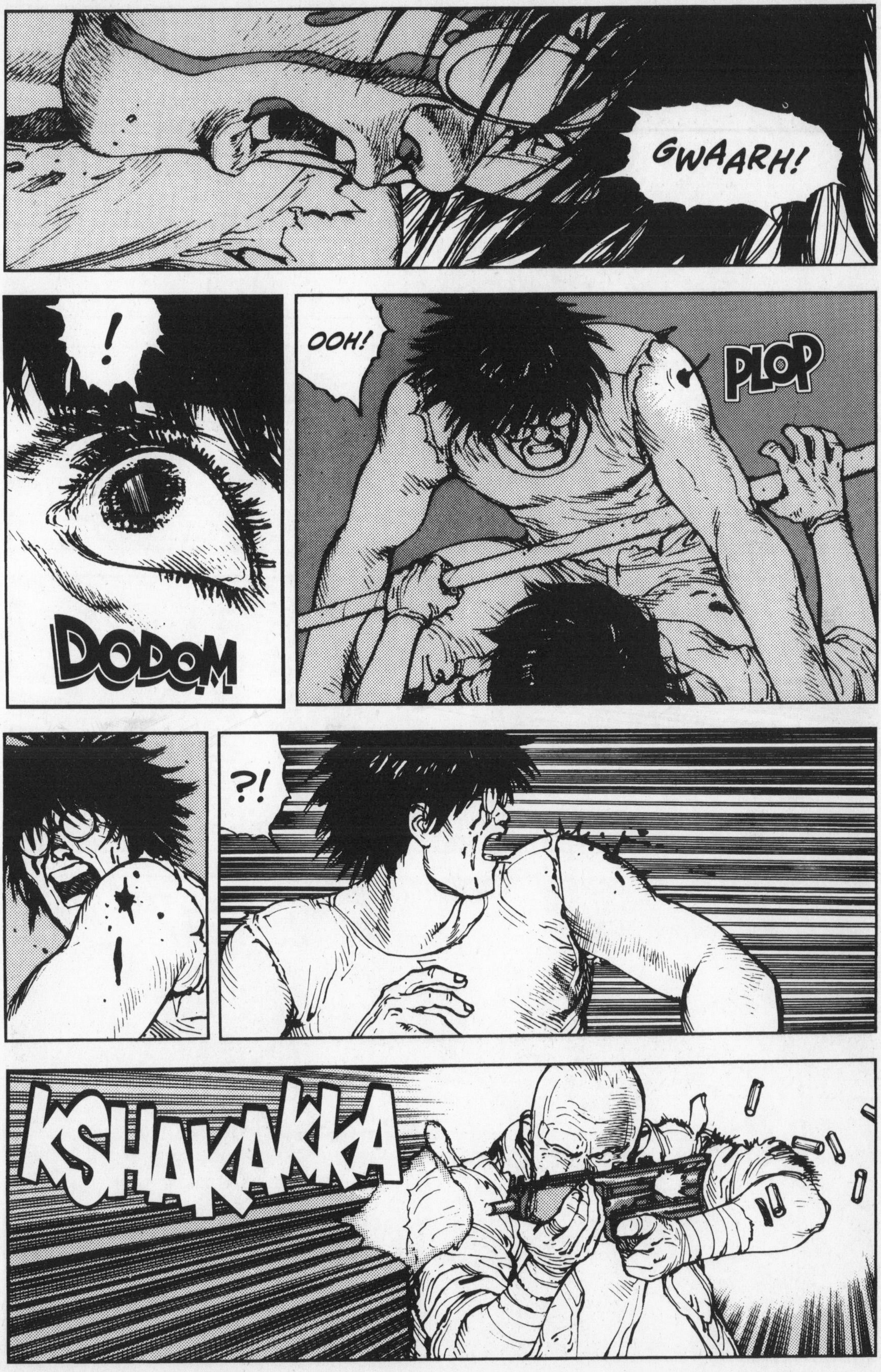
GWAARH!
!
DODOM
OOH!
PLOP
?!
KSHAKAKKA

GRRAH!

KEI! SHE'S DOWN!

KEI!

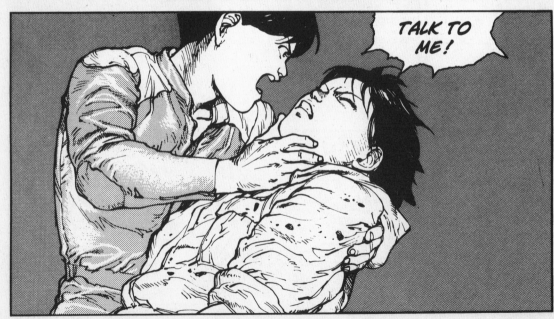

TALK TO ME!

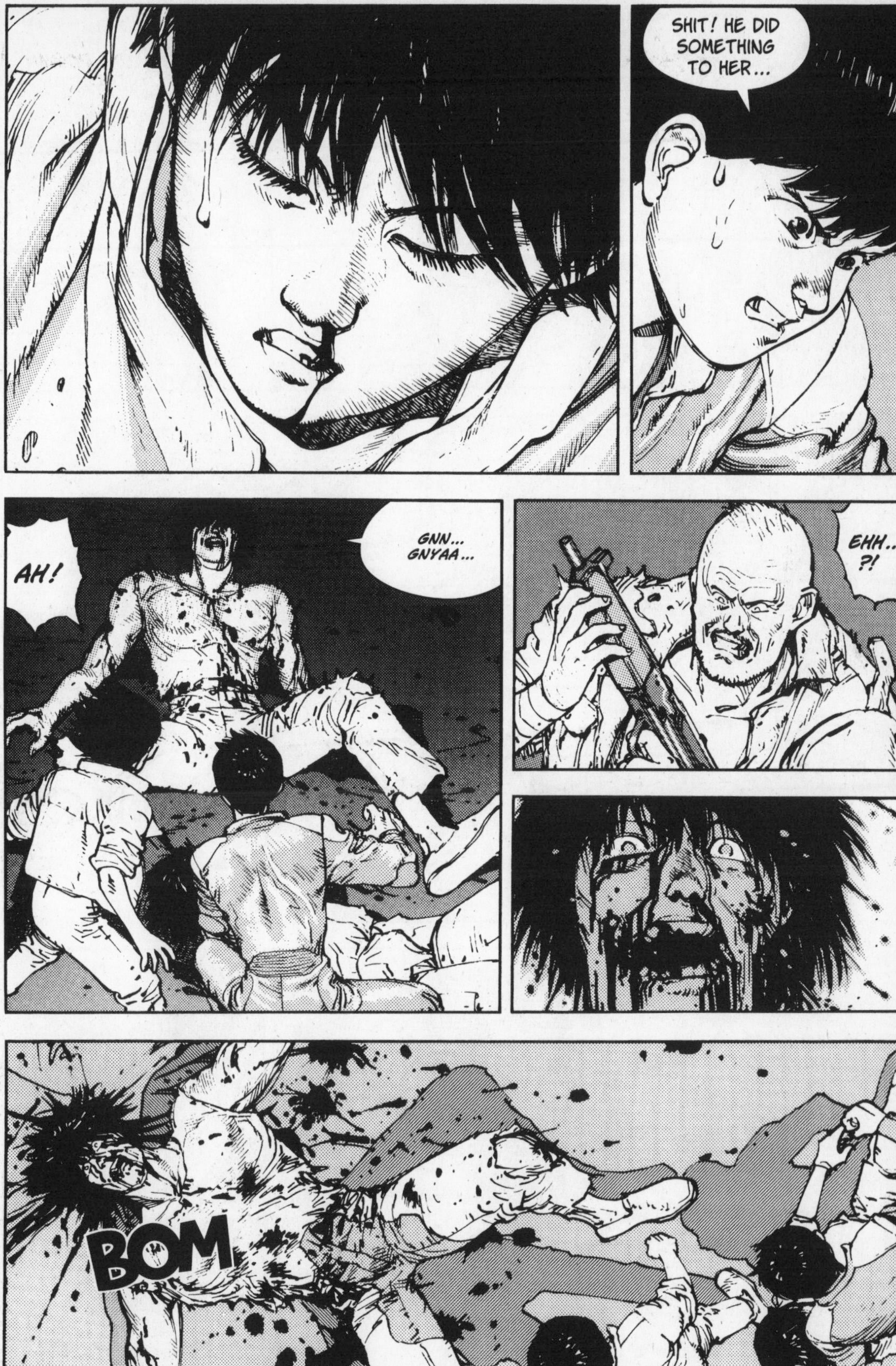
SHIT! HE DID SOMETHING TO HER...
AH!
GNN... GNYAA...
EHH... ?!
BOM

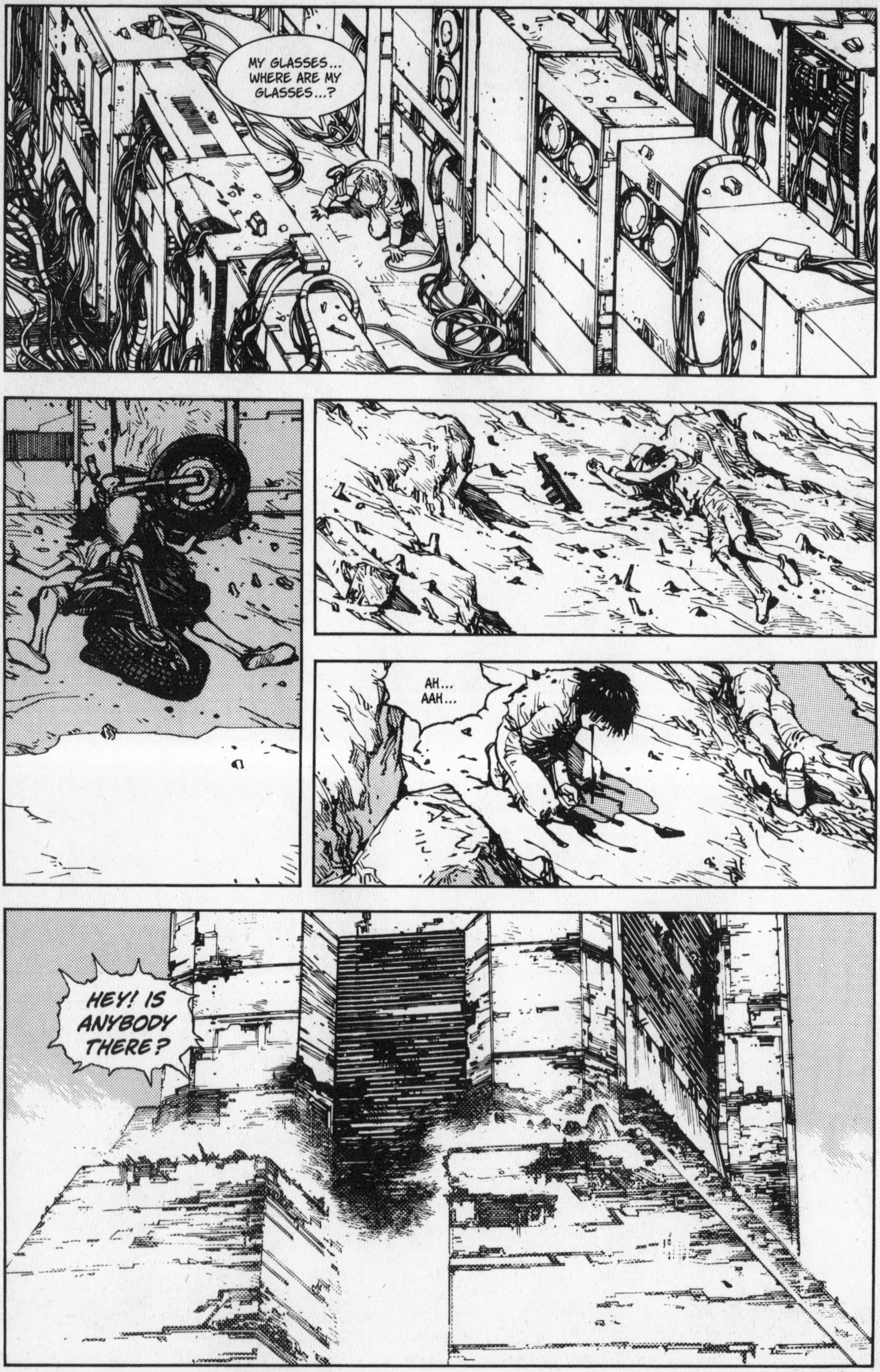
MY GLASSES... WHERE ARE MY GLASSES...?
AH... AAH...
HEY! IS ANYBODY THERE?

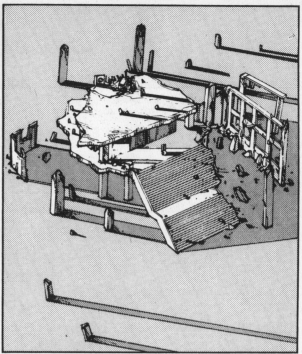

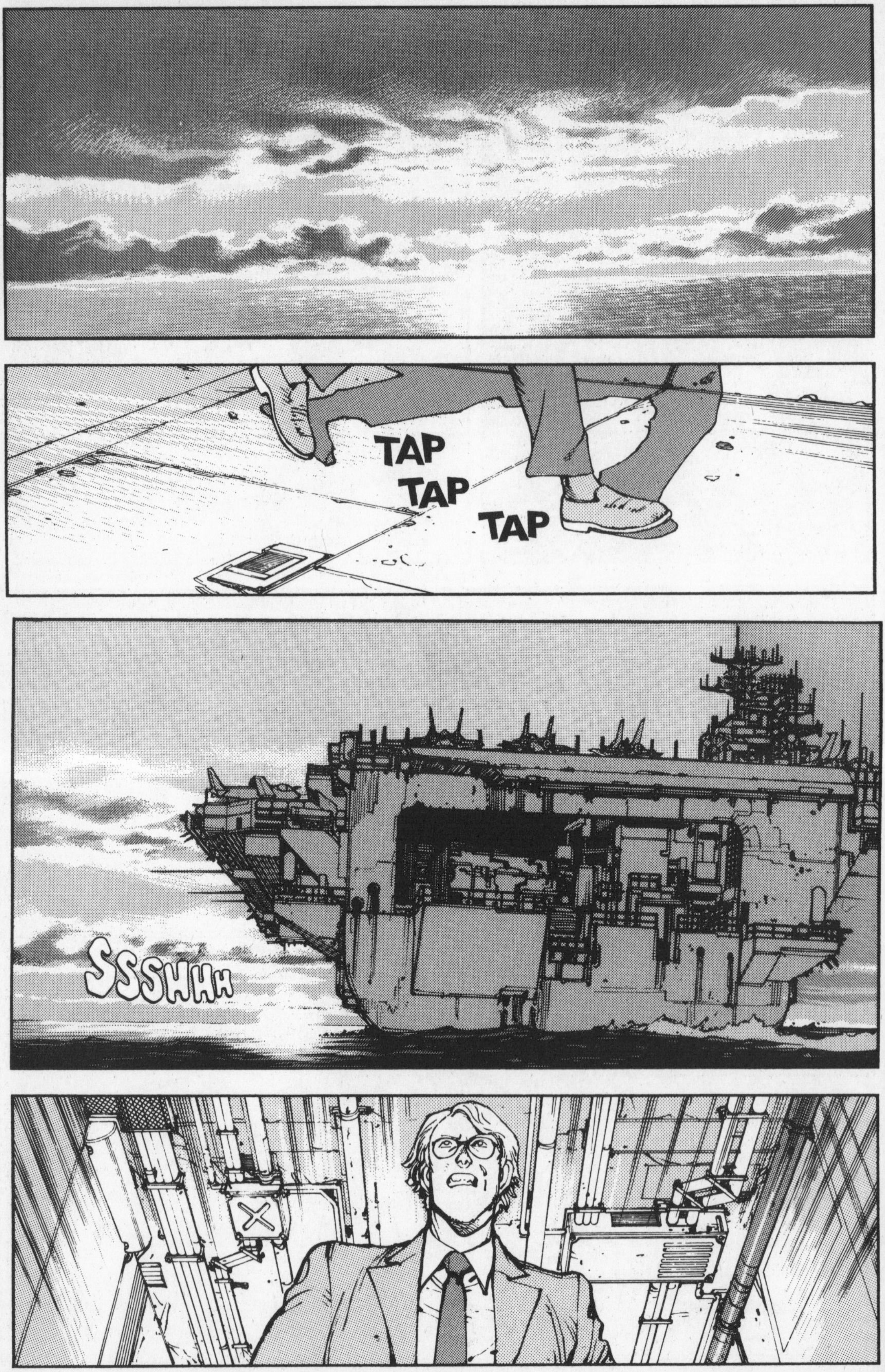
TAP
TAP
TAP
SSSHHH

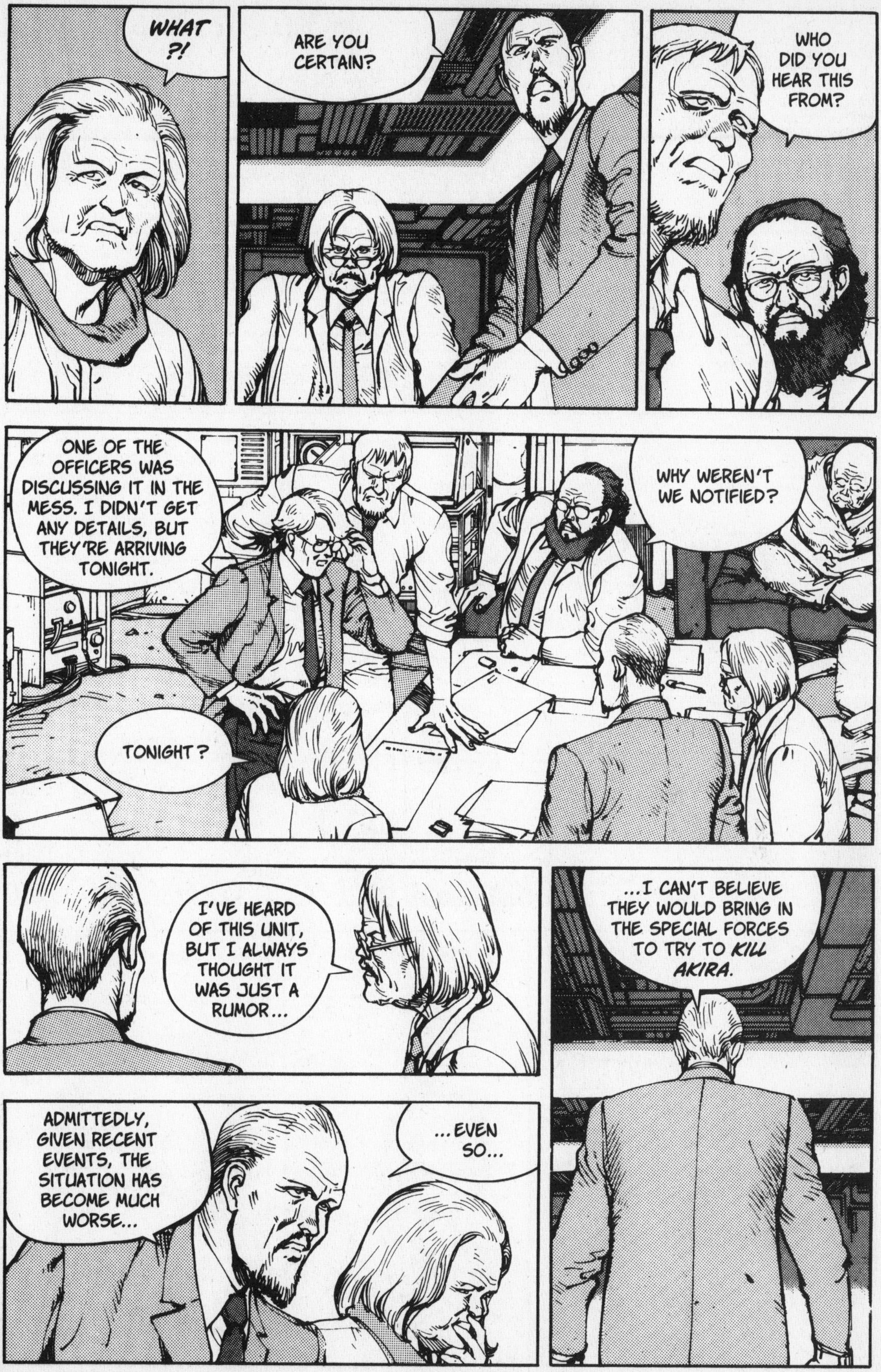
WHAT ?!
ARE YOU CERTAIN?
WHO DID YOU HEAR THIS FROM?
ONE OF THE OFFICERS WAS DISCUSSING IT IN THE MESS. I DIDN'T GET ANY DETAILS, BUT THEY'RE ARRIVING TONIGHT.
WHY WEREN'T WE NOTIFIED?
TONIGHT?
I'VE HEARD OF THIS UNIT, BUT I ALWAYS THOUGHT IT WAS JUST A RUMOR...
ADMITTEDLY, GIVEN RECENT EVENTS, THE SITUATION HAS BECOME MUCH WORSE...
...EVEN SO...
...I CAN'T BELIEVE THEY WOULD BRING IN THE SPECIAL FORCES TO TRY TO *KILL AKIRA*.

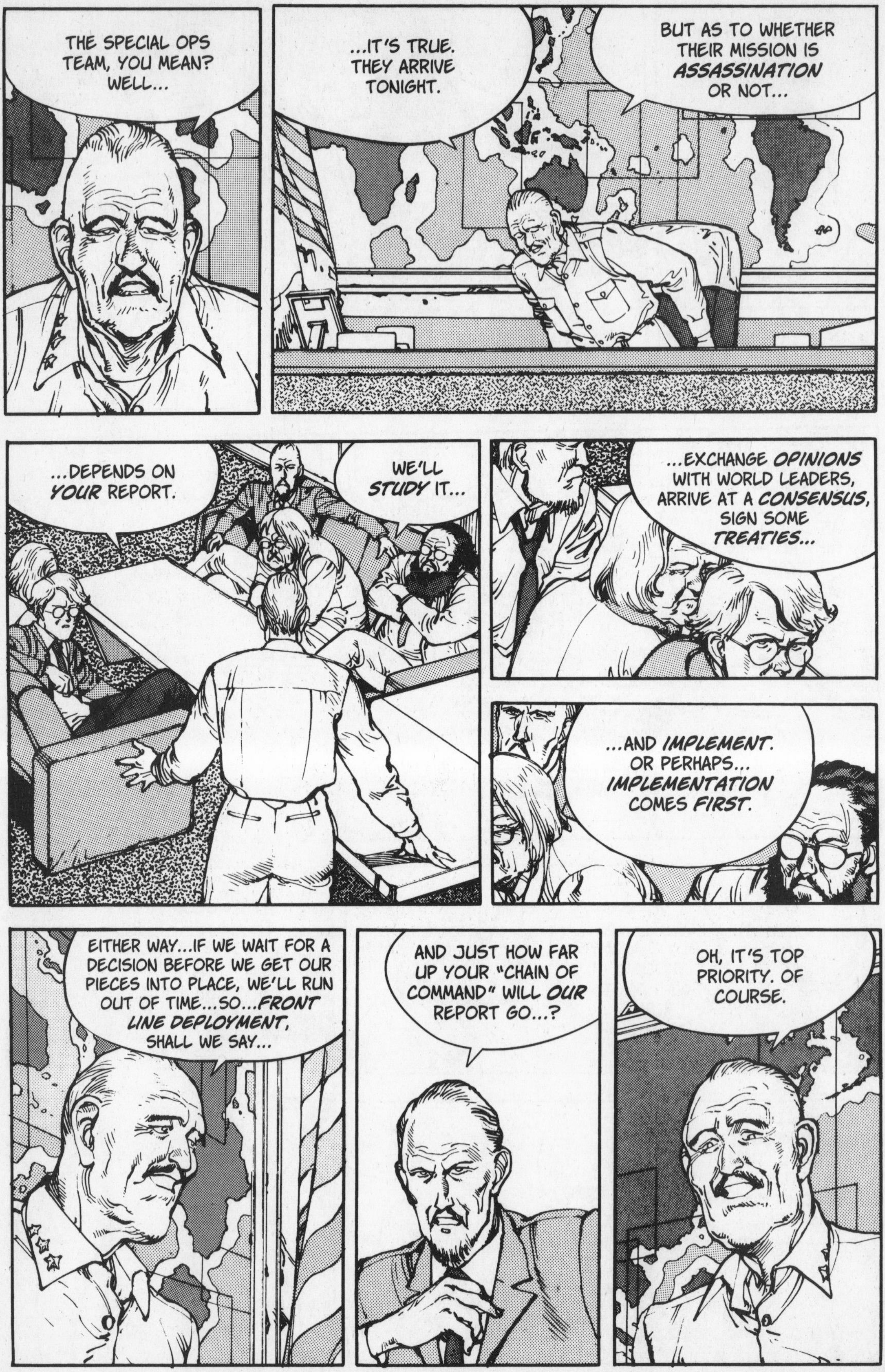
THE SPECIAL OPS TEAM, YOU MEAN? WELL...
...IT'S TRUE. THEY ARRIVE TONIGHT.
BUT AS TO WHETHER THEIR MISSION IS *ASSASSINATION* OR NOT...
...DEPENDS ON *YOUR* REPORT.
WE'LL *STUDY* IT...
...EXCHANGE *OPINIONS* WITH WORLD LEADERS, ARRIVE AT A *CONSENSUS*, SIGN SOME *TREATIES*...
...AND *IMPLEMENT*. OR PERHAPS... *IMPLEMENTATION* COMES *FIRST*.
EITHER WAY...IF WE WAIT FOR A DECISION BEFORE WE GET OUR PIECES INTO PLACE, WE'LL RUN OUT OF TIME...SO...*FRONT LINE DEPLOYMENT*, SHALL WE SAY...
AND JUST HOW FAR UP YOUR "CHAIN OF COMMAND" WILL *OUR* REPORT GO...?
OH, IT'S TOP PRIORITY. OF COURSE.

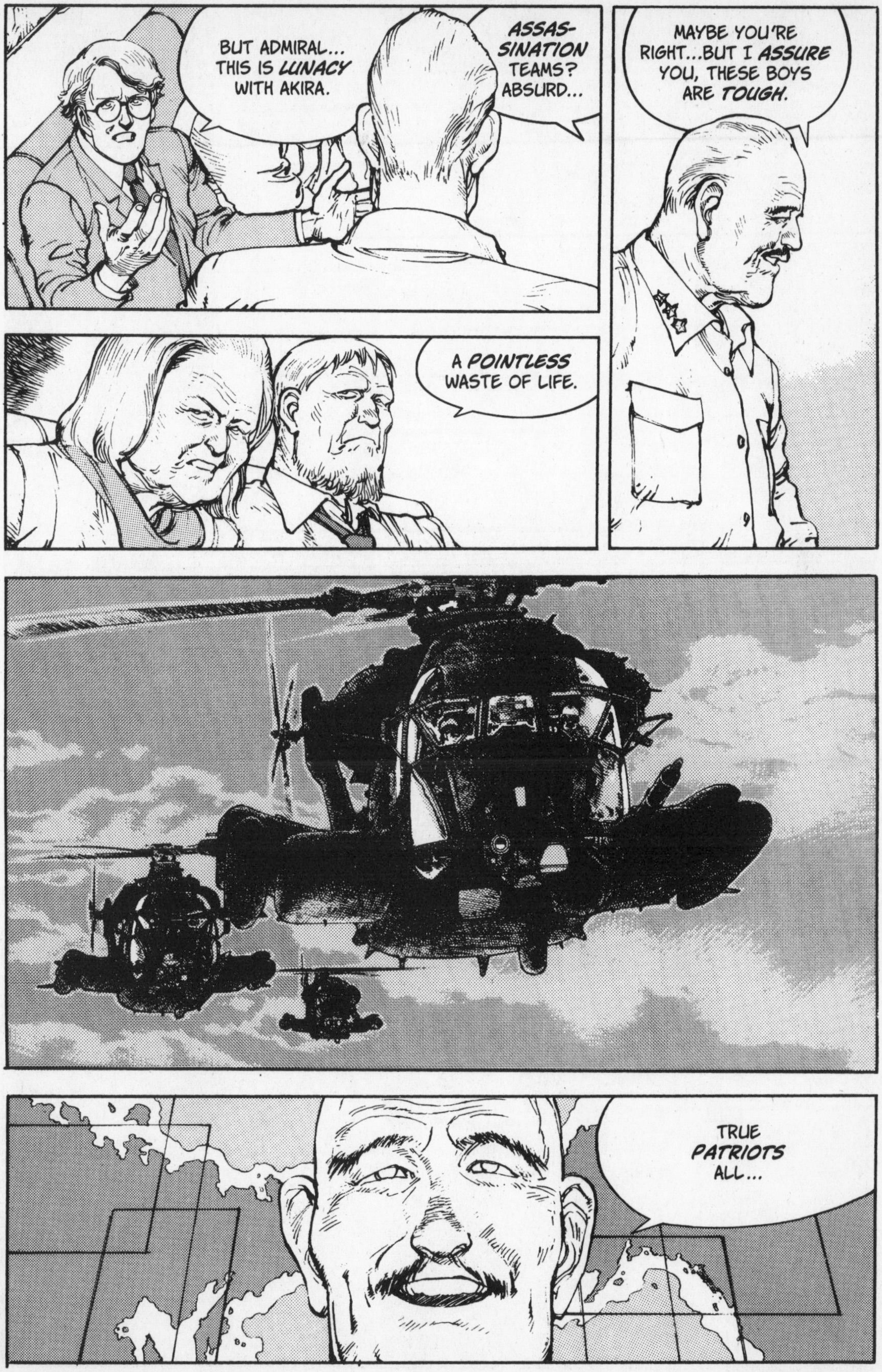
BUT ADMIRAL... THIS IS *LUNACY* WITH AKIRA.
ASSAS-SINATION TEAMS? ABSURD...
MAYBE YOU'RE RIGHT...BUT I *ASSURE* YOU, THESE BOYS ARE *TOUGH*.
A *POINTLESS* WASTE OF LIFE.
TRUE *PATRIOTS* ALL...

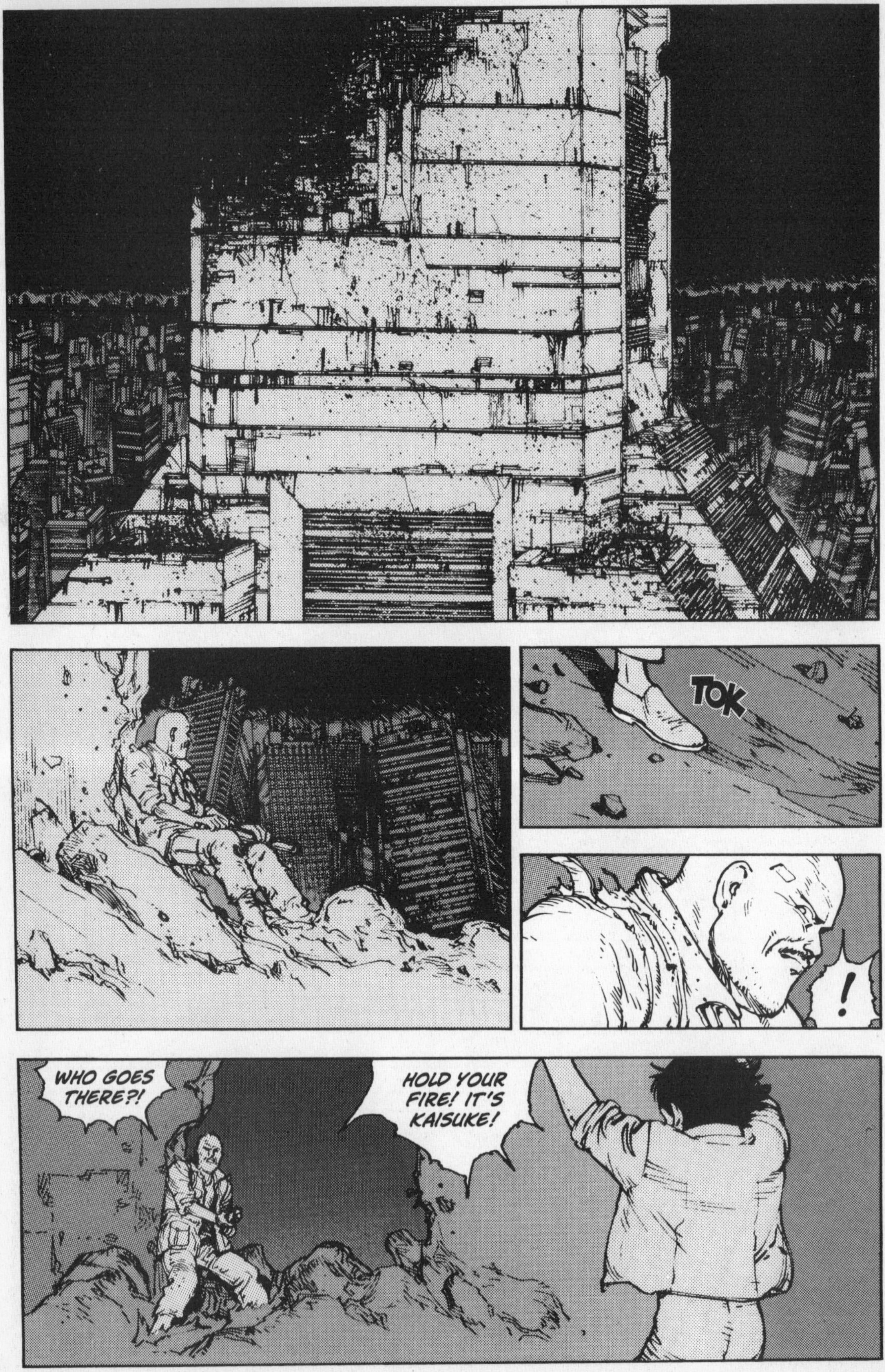
TOK
!
WHO GOES THERE?!
HOLD YOUR FIRE! IT'S KAISUKE!

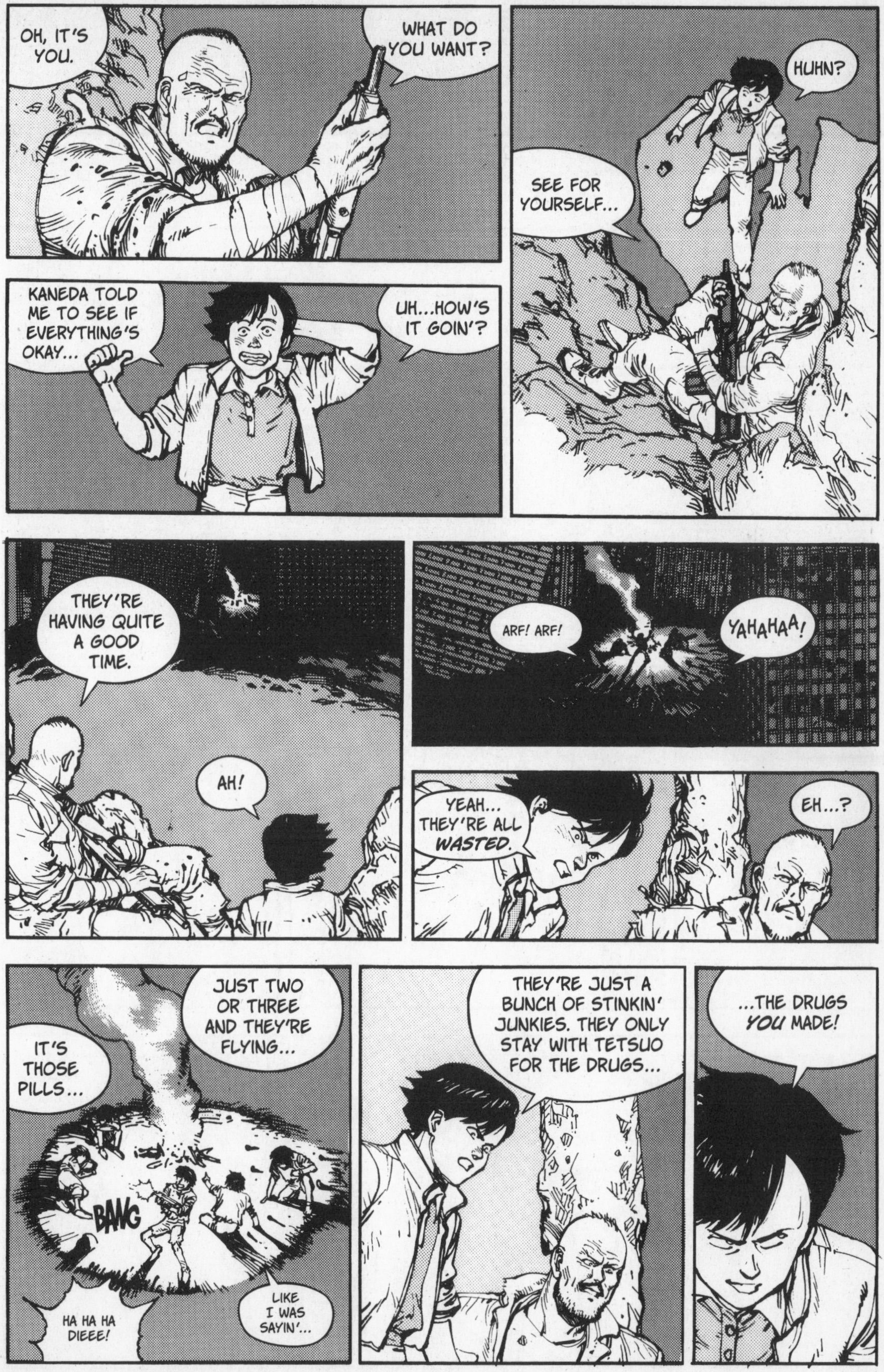
OH, IT'S YOU.
WHAT DO YOU WANT?
KANEDA TOLD ME TO SEE IF EVERYTHING'S OKAY...
UH...HOW'S IT GOIN'?
HUHN?
SEE FOR YOURSELF...
THEY'RE HAVING QUITE A GOOD TIME.
AH!
ARF! ARF!
YAHAHAA!
YEAH... THEY'RE ALL *WASTED*.
EH...?
IT'S THOSE PILLS...
JUST TWO OR THREE AND THEY'RE FLYING...
BANG
HA HA HA DIEEE!
LIKE I WAS SAYIN'...
THEY'RE JUST A BUNCH OF STINKIN' JUNKIES. THEY ONLY STAY WITH TETSUO FOR THE DRUGS...
...THE DRUGS *YOU* MADE!

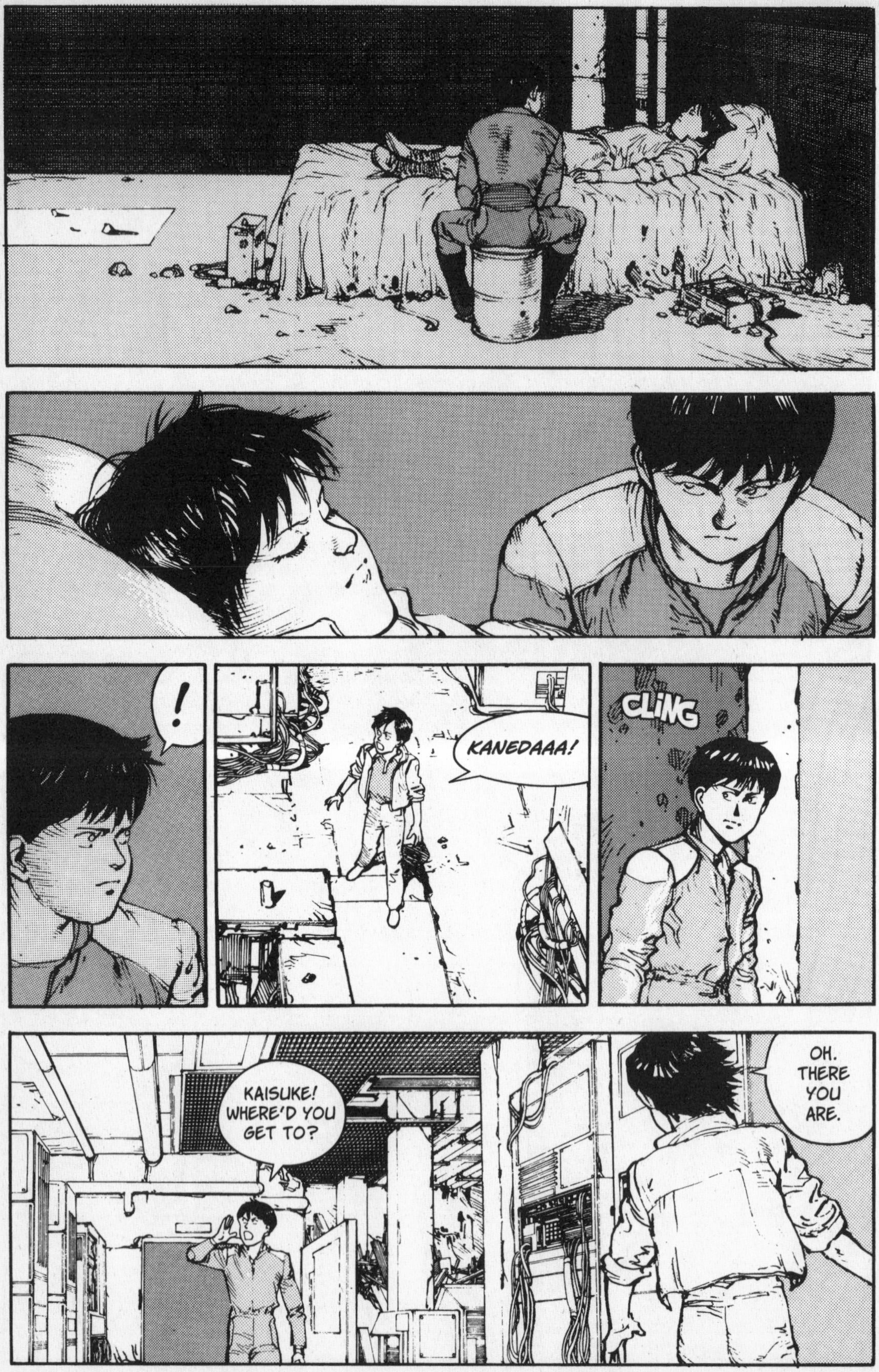
!
KANEDAAA!
CLING
KAISUKE! WHERE'D YOU GET TO?
OH. THERE YOU ARE.

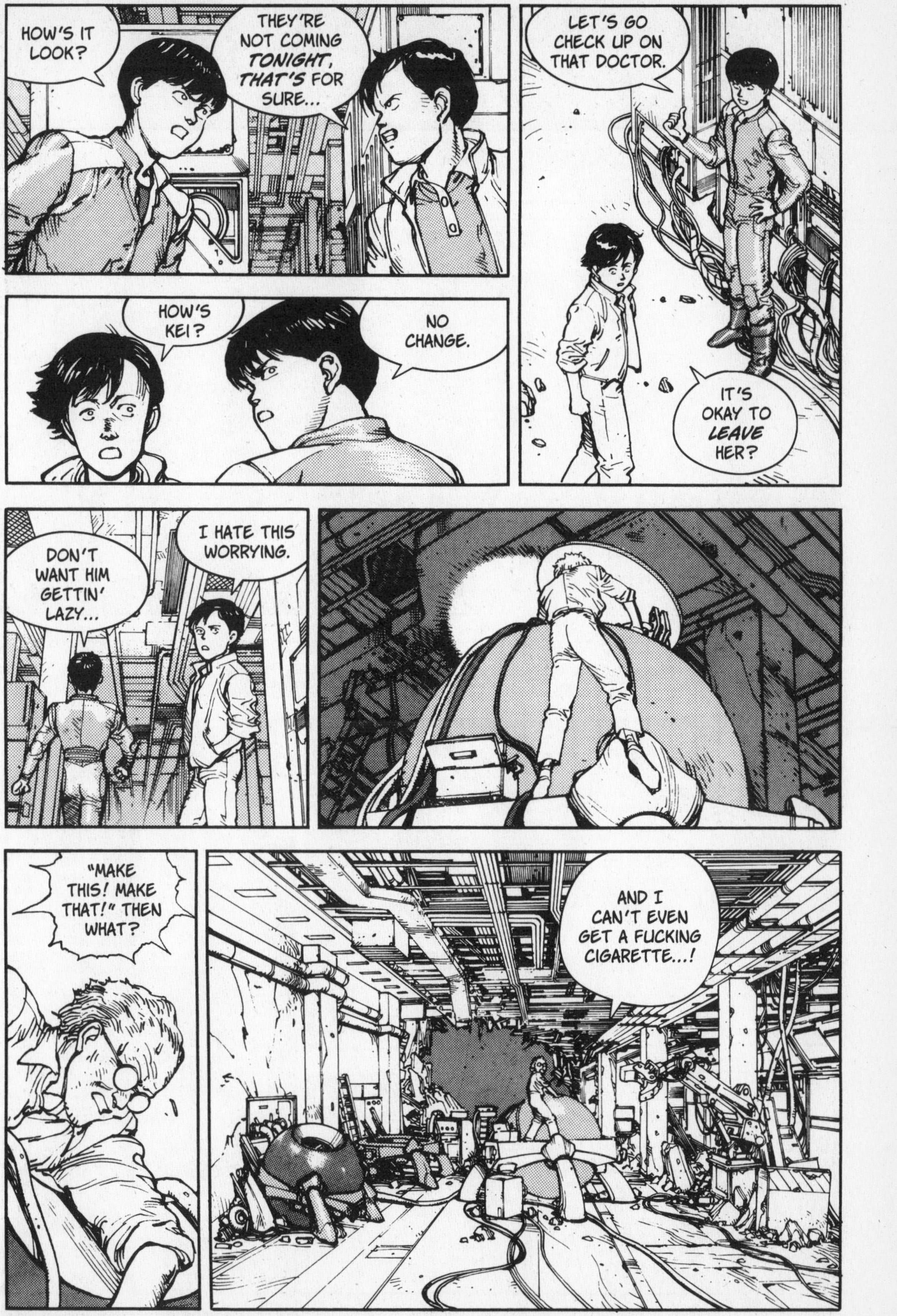
HOW'S IT LOOK?
THEY'RE NOT COMING *TONIGHT*, *THAT'S* FOR SURE...
LET'S GO CHECK UP ON THAT DOCTOR.
HOW'S KEI?
NO CHANGE.
IT'S OKAY TO *LEAVE* HER?
DON'T WANT HIM GETTIN' LAZY...
I HATE THIS WORRYING.
"MAKE THIS! MAKE THAT!" THEN WHAT?
AND I CAN'T EVEN GET A FUCKING CIGARETTE...!

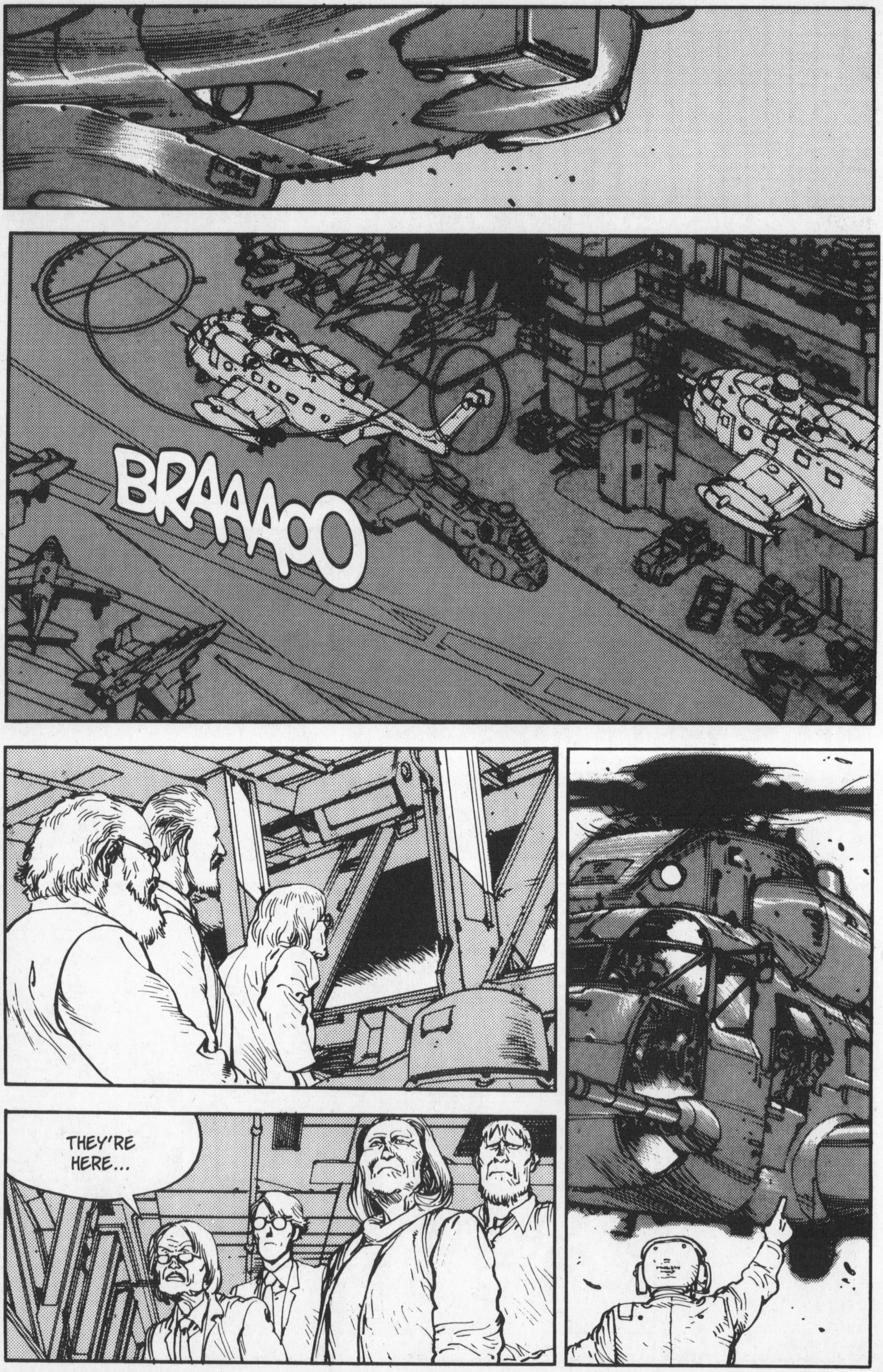
BRAAAOO
THEY'RE HERE...

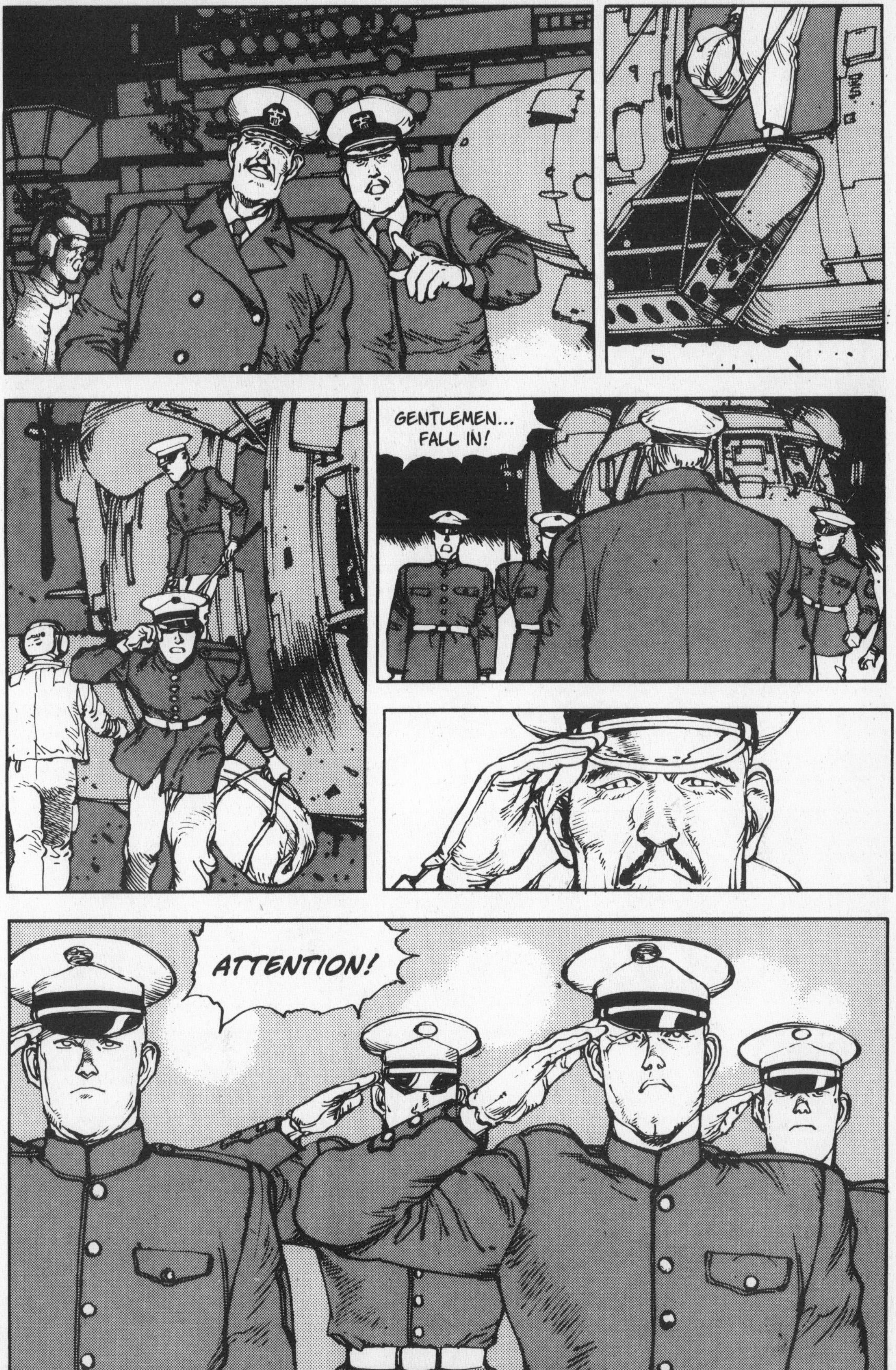
GENTLEMEN... FALL IN!
ATTENTION!

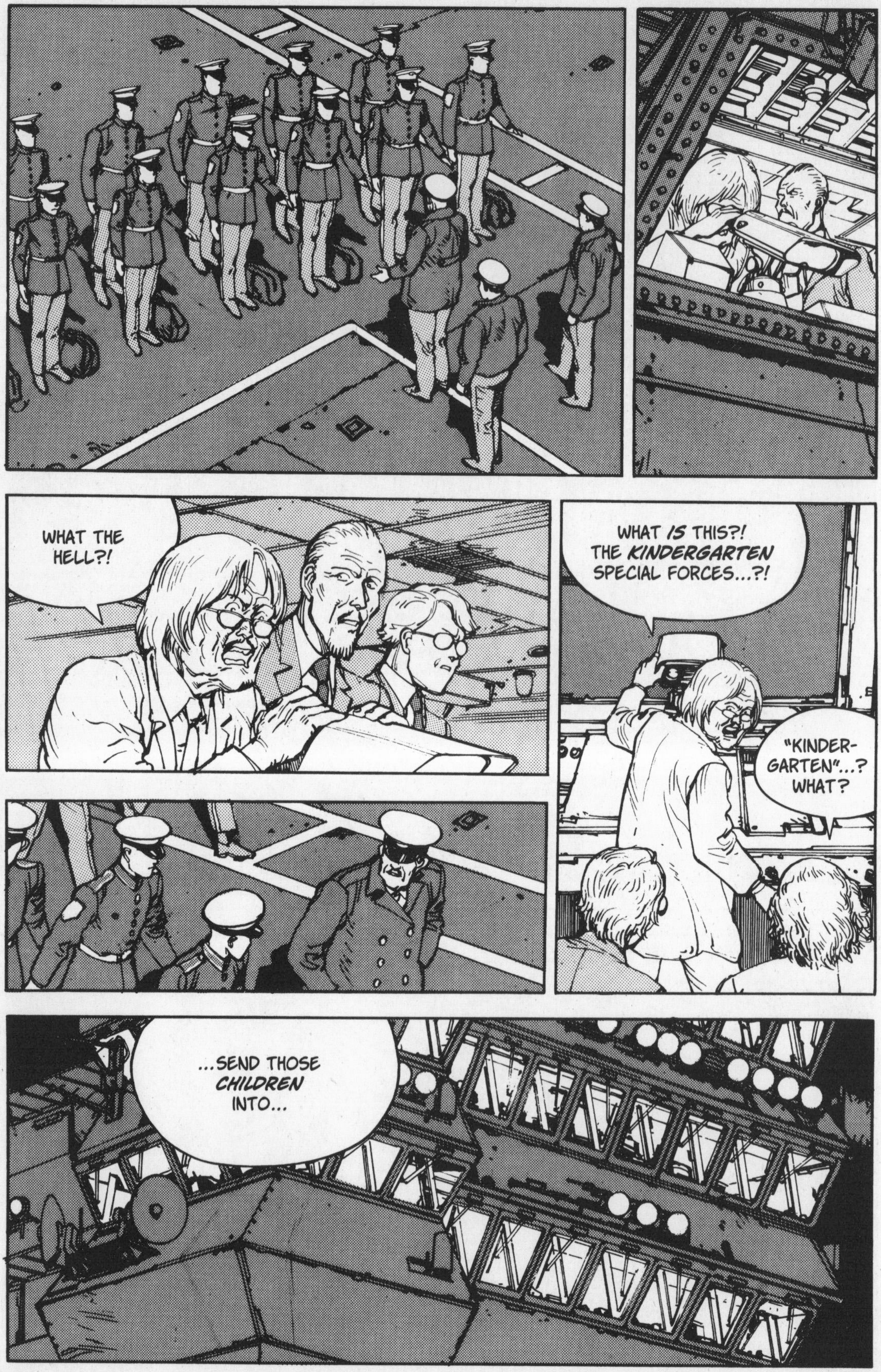
WHAT THE HELL?!
WHAT *IS* THIS?! THE *KINDERGARTEN* SPECIAL FORCES...?!
"KINDER-GARTEN"...? WHAT?
...SEND THOSE *CHILDREN* INTO...

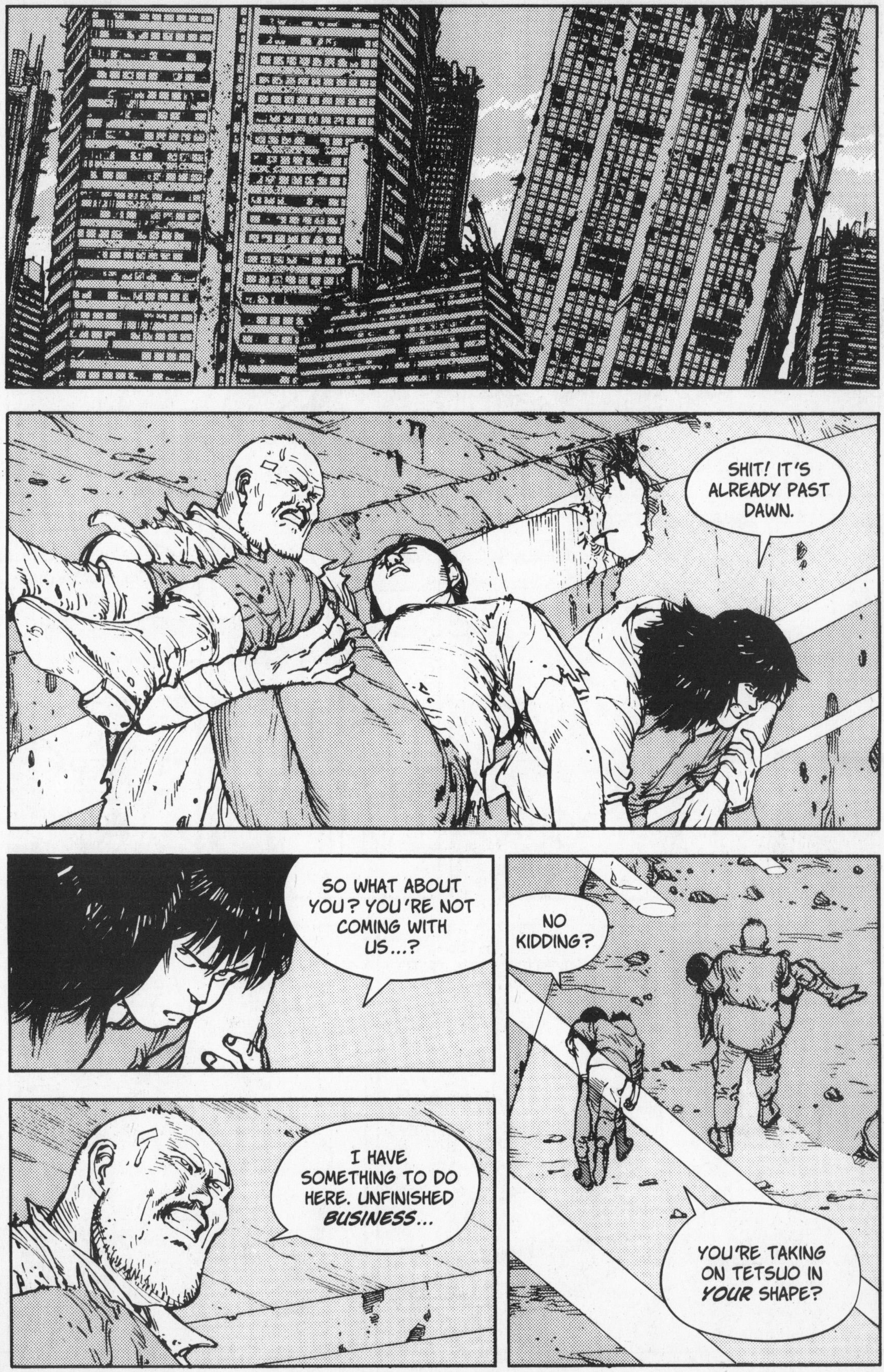
SHIT! IT'S ALREADY PAST DAWN.
SO WHAT ABOUT YOU? YOU'RE NOT COMING WITH US...?
I HAVE SOMETHING TO DO HERE. UNFINISHED *BUSINESS*...
NO KIDDING?
YOU'RE TAKING ON TETSUO IN *YOUR* SHAPE?

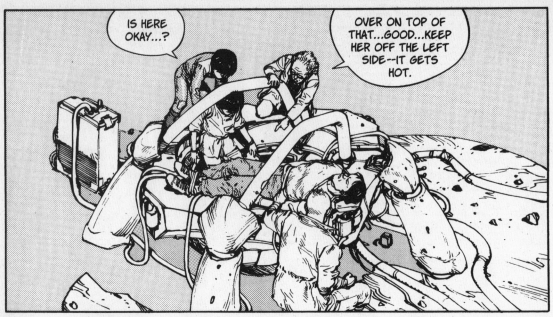

IS HERE OKAY...?

OVER ON TOP OF THAT...GOOD...KEEP HER OFF THE LEFT SIDE--IT GETS HOT.

TELL ME HOW TO RUN IT!

I WAS JUST ABOUT TO.

THIS IS THE CONTROL BOX.

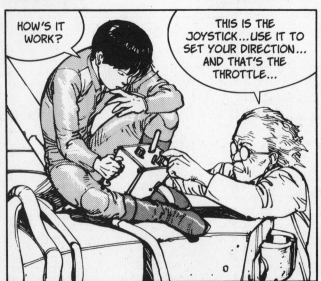

HOW'S IT WORK?

THIS IS THE JOYSTICK...USE IT TO SET YOUR DIRECTION... AND THAT'S THE THROTTLE...

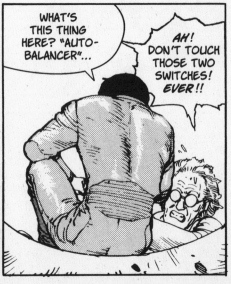

WHAT'S THIS THING HERE? "AUTO-BALANCER"...

AH! DON'T TOUCH THOSE TWO SWITCHES! EVER!!

150

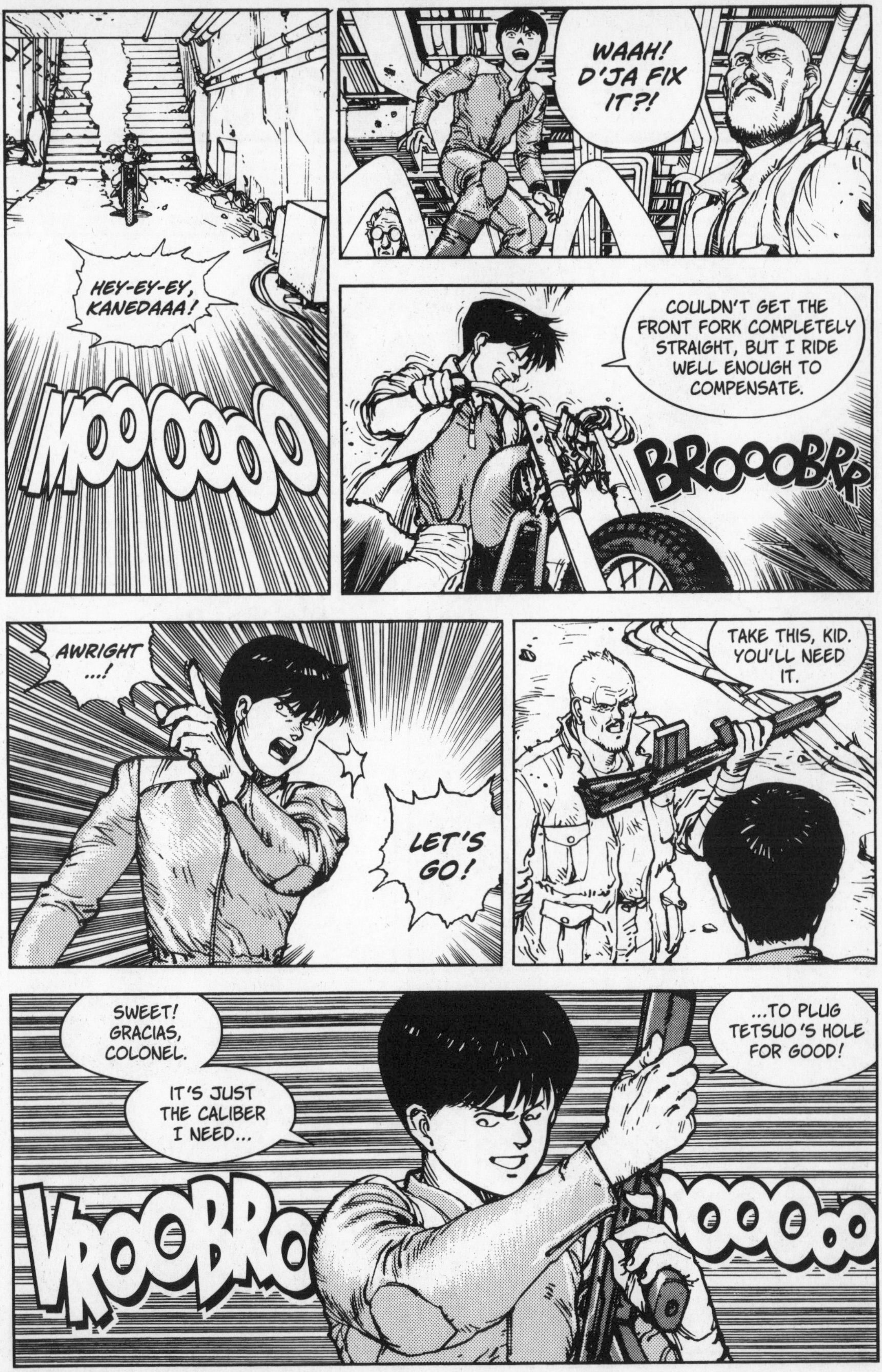
HEY-EY-EY, KANEDAAA!
MOOOOOO
WAAH! D'JA FIX IT?!
COULDN'T GET THE FRONT FORK COMPLETELY STRAIGHT, BUT I RIDE WELL ENOUGH TO COMPENSATE.
BROOOBRR
AWRIGHT ...!
LET'S GO!
TAKE THIS, KID. YOU'LL NEED IT.
SWEET! GRACIAS, COLONEL.
IT'S JUST THE CALIBER I NEED...
...TO PLUG TETSUO'S HOLE FOR GOOD!
VROOBRO
OOOOoo

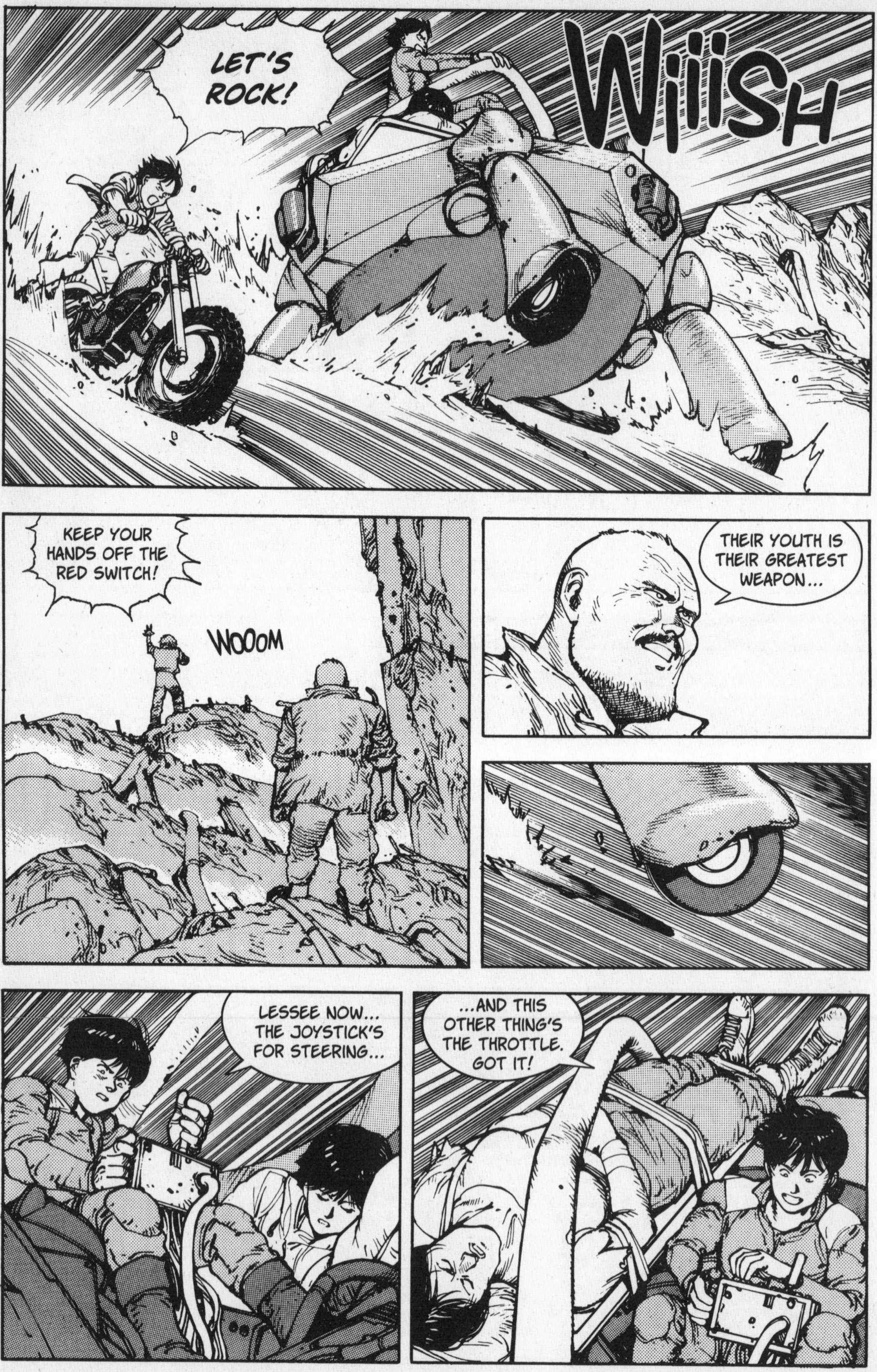
LET'S ROCK!
WIIISH
KEEP YOUR HANDS OFF THE RED SWITCH!
WOOOM
THEIR YOUTH IS THEIR GREATEST WEAPON...
LESSEE NOW... THE JOYSTICK'S FOR STEERING...
...AND THIS OTHER THING'S THE THROTTLE. GOT IT!

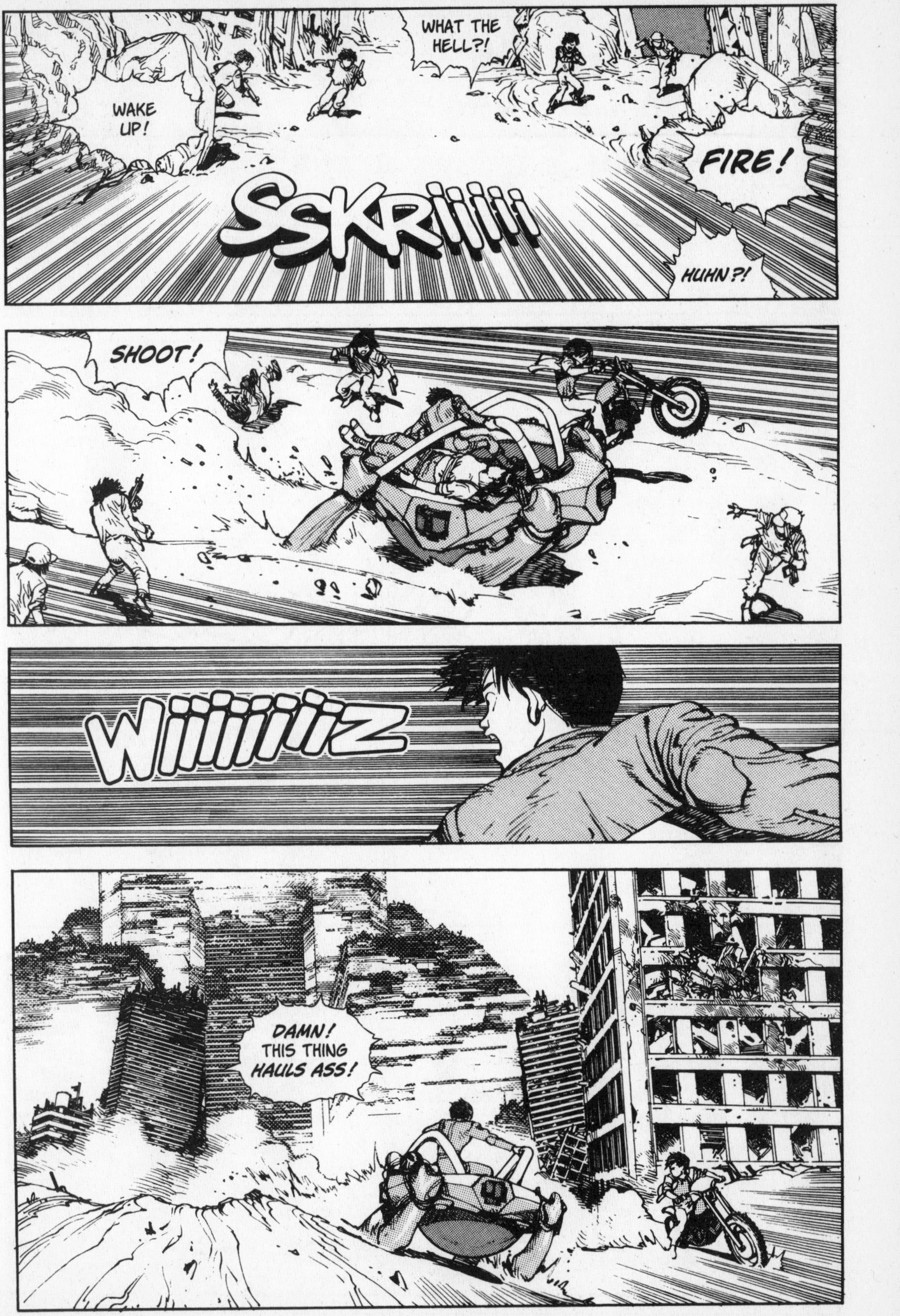
WAKE UP!
WHAT THE HELL?!
FIRE!
SSKRiiiiii
HUHN?!
SHOOT!
Wiiiiiiiz
DAMN! THIS THING HAULS ASS!

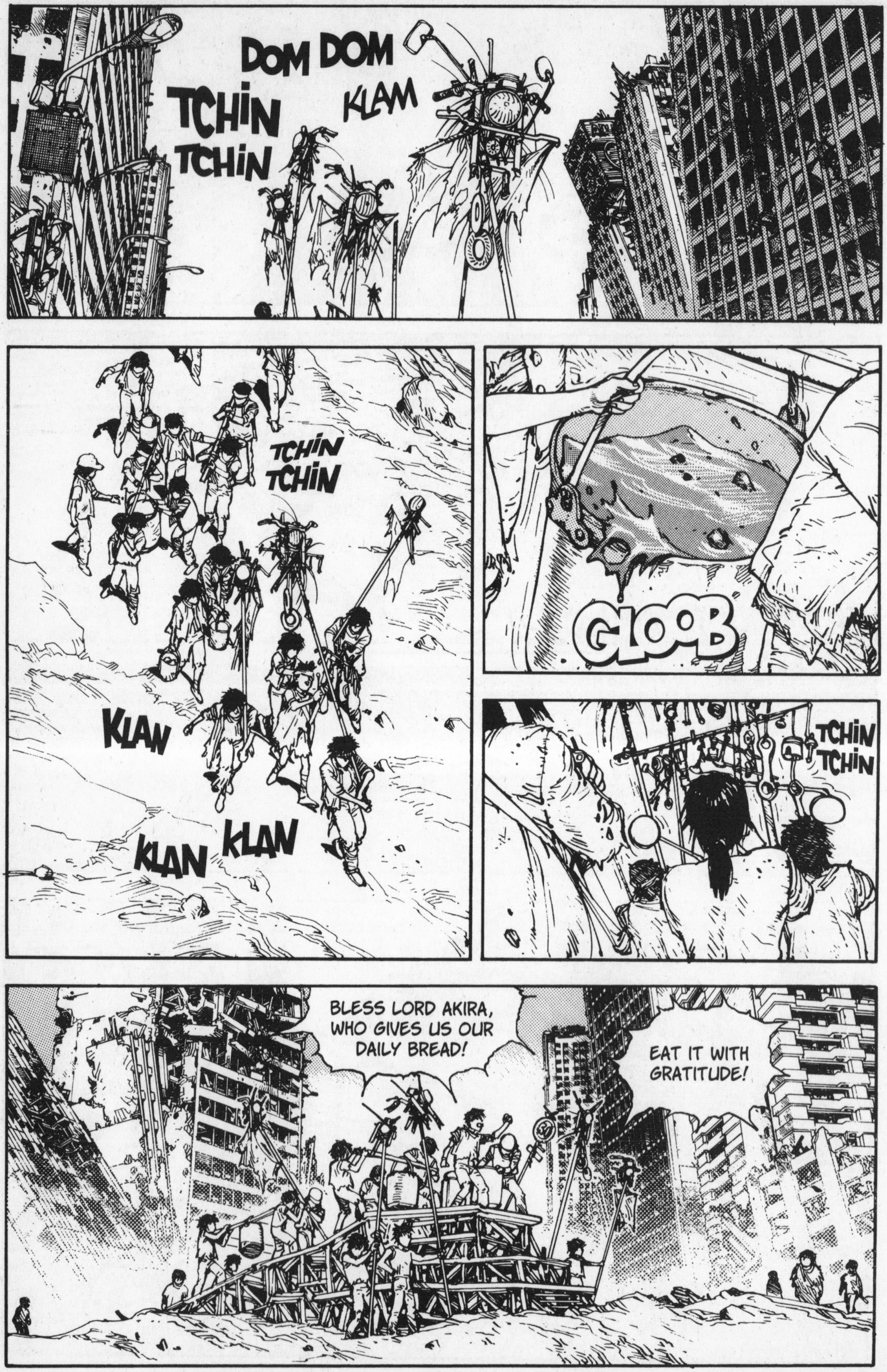
DOM DOM
TCHIN
TCHIN
KLAM
TCHIN
TCHIN
KLAN
KLAN
KLAN
GLOOB
TCHIN
TCHIN
BLESS LORD AKIRA, WHO GIVES US OUR DAILY BREAD!
EAT IT WITH GRATITUDE!

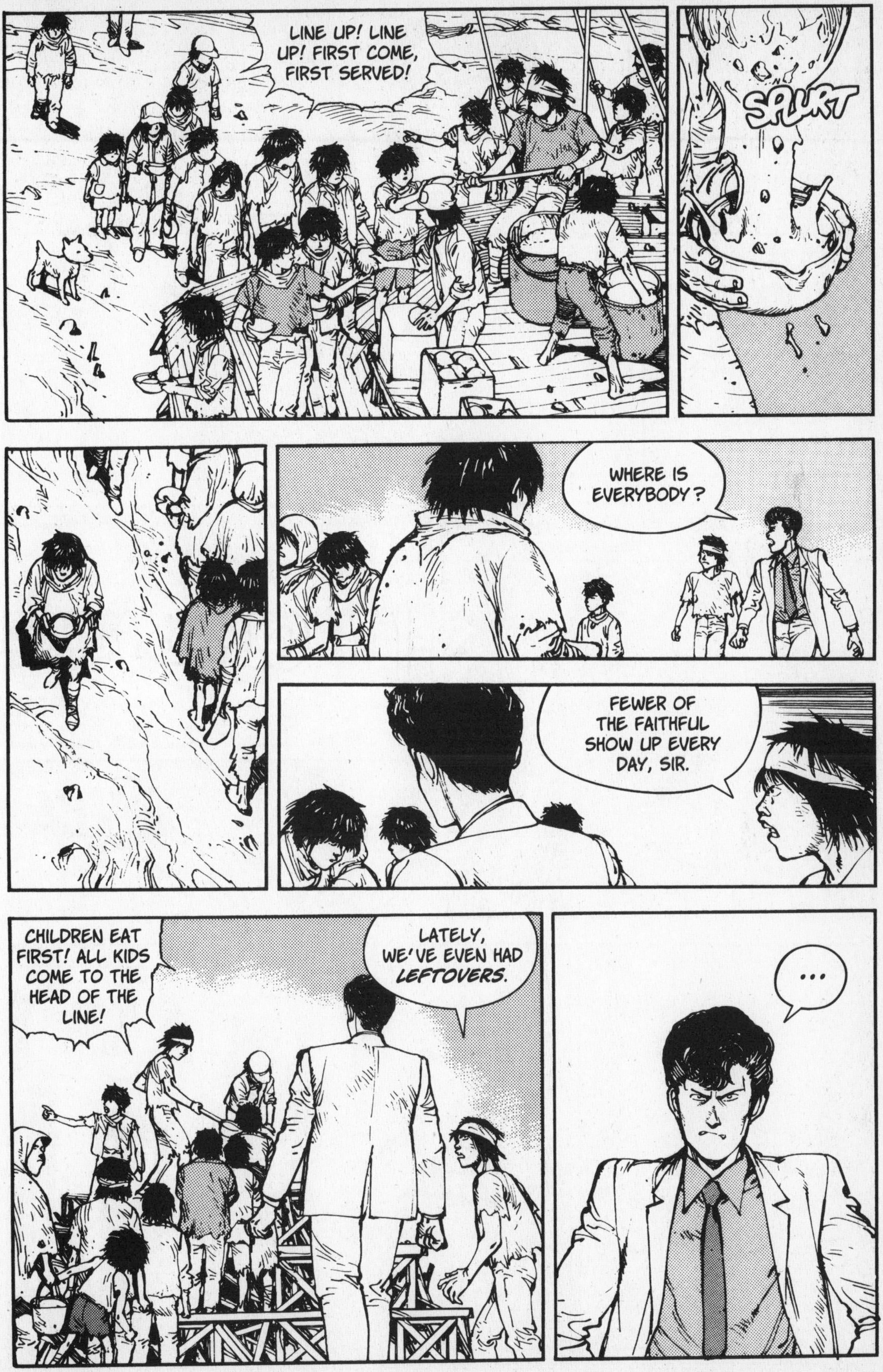

LINE UP! LINE UP! FIRST COME, FIRST SERVED!
SPLURT
WHERE IS EVERYBODY?
FEWER OF THE FAITHFUL SHOW UP EVERY DAY, SIR.
CHILDREN EAT FIRST! ALL KIDS COME TO THE HEAD OF THE LINE!
LATELY, WE'VE EVEN HAD *LEFTOVERS*.
...

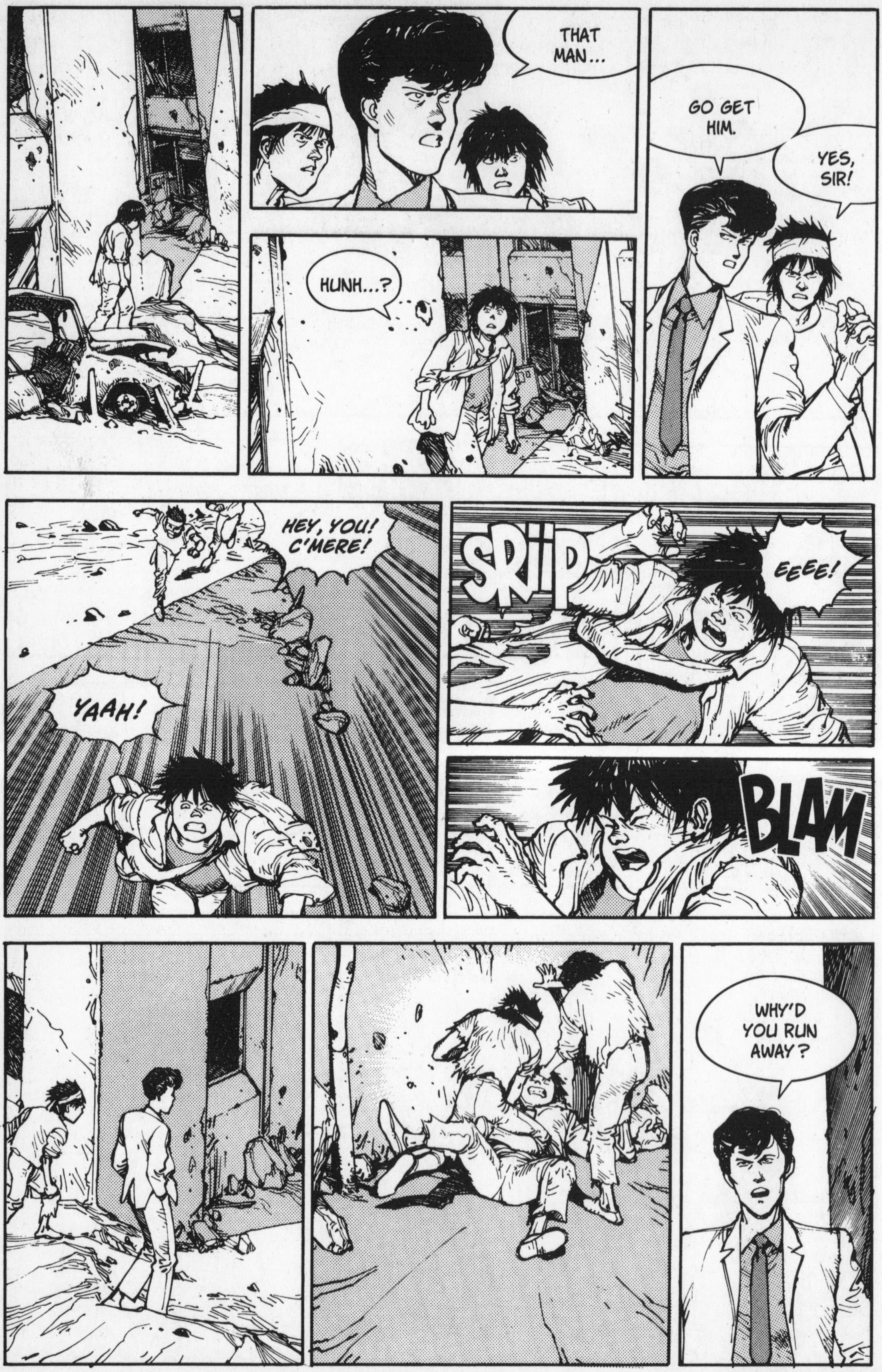
THAT MAN...
HUNH...?
GO GET HIM.
YES, SIR!
HEY, YOU! C'MERE!
YAAH!
SRIIP
EEEE!
BLAM
WHY'D YOU RUN AWAY?

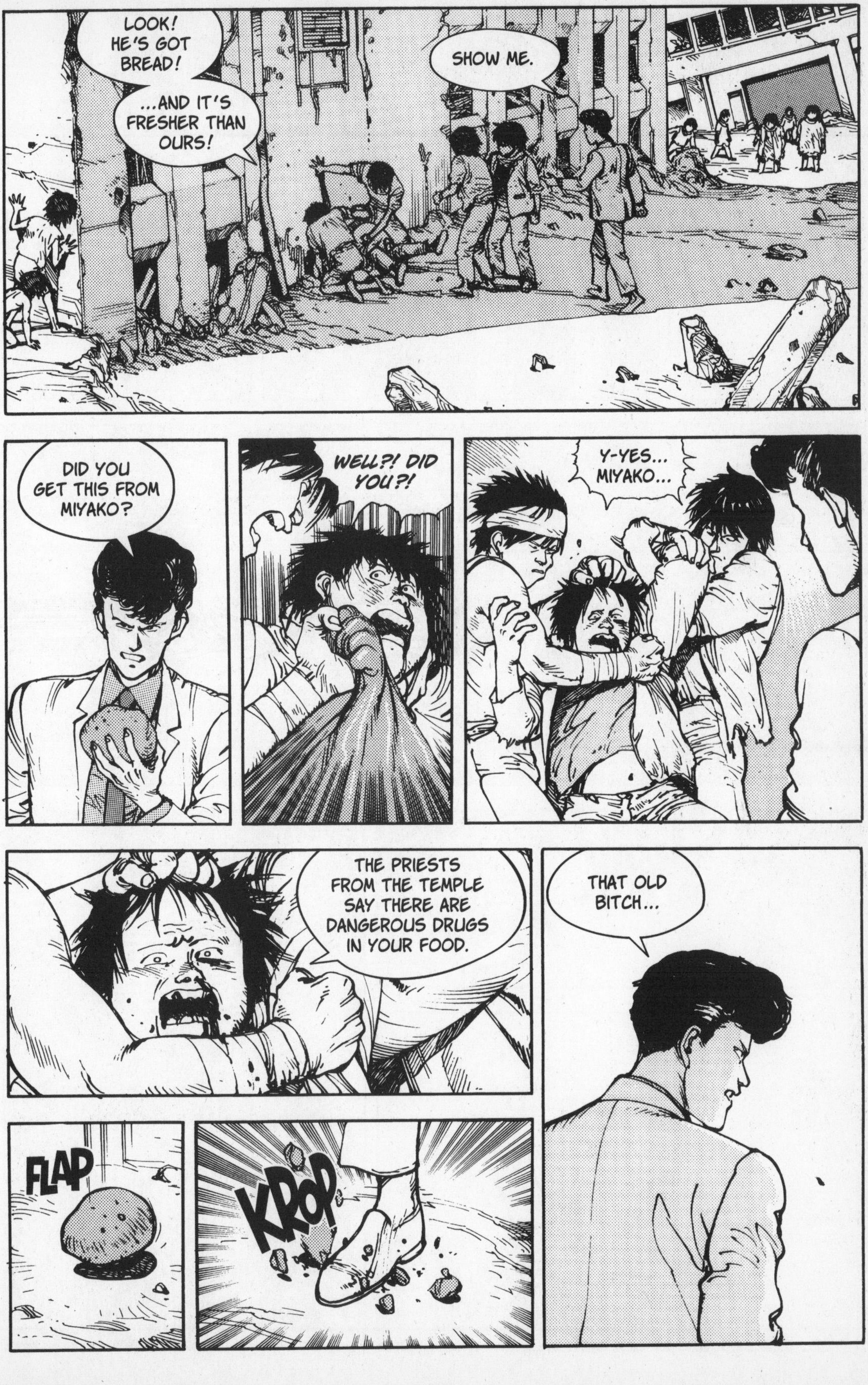

LOOK! HE'S GOT BREAD!
...AND IT'S FRESHER THAN OURS!
SHOW ME.
DID YOU GET THIS FROM MIYAKO?
WELL?! DID YOU?!
Y-YES... MIYAKO...
THE PRIESTS FROM THE TEMPLE SAY THERE ARE DANGEROUS DRUGS IN YOUR FOOD.
THAT OLD BITCH...
FLAP
KROP

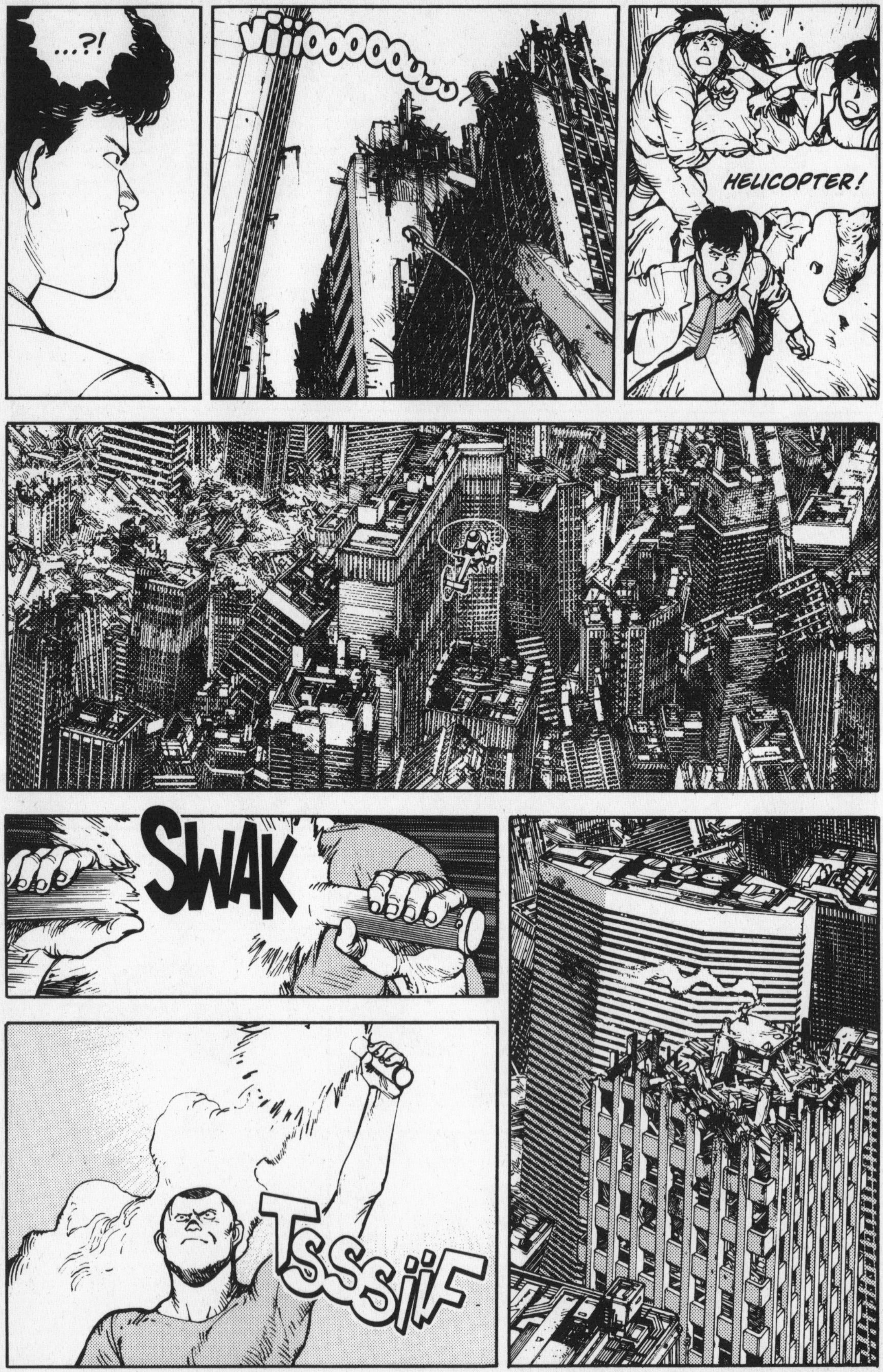
...?!
Viiiooooouuu
HELICOPTER!
SWAK
TSSSIIF

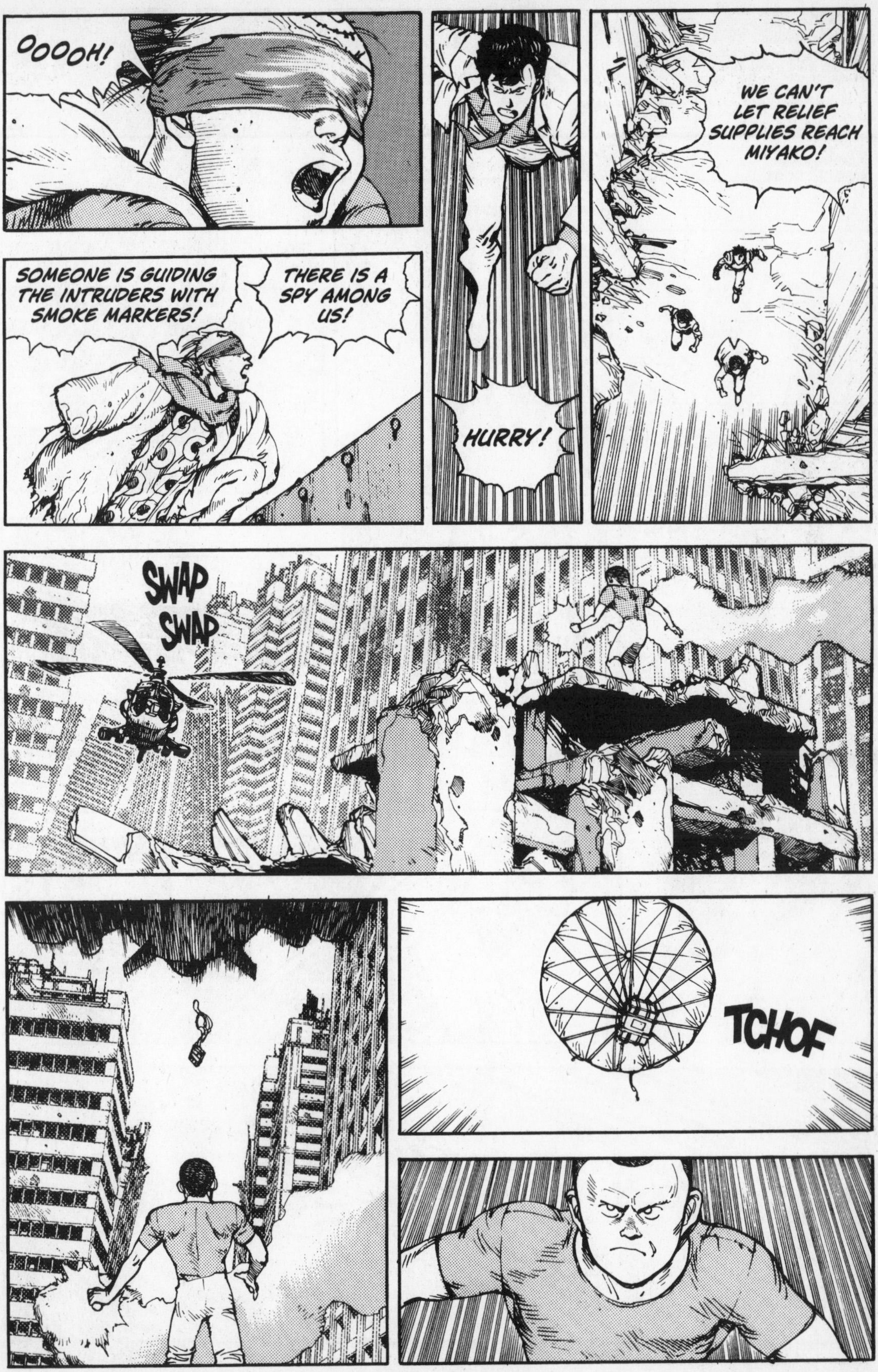
OOOOH!
SOMEONE IS GUIDING THE INTRUDERS WITH SMOKE MARKERS!
THERE IS A SPY AMONG US!
HURRY!
WE CAN'T LET RELIEF SUPPLIES REACH MIYAKO!
SWAP SWAP
TCHOF

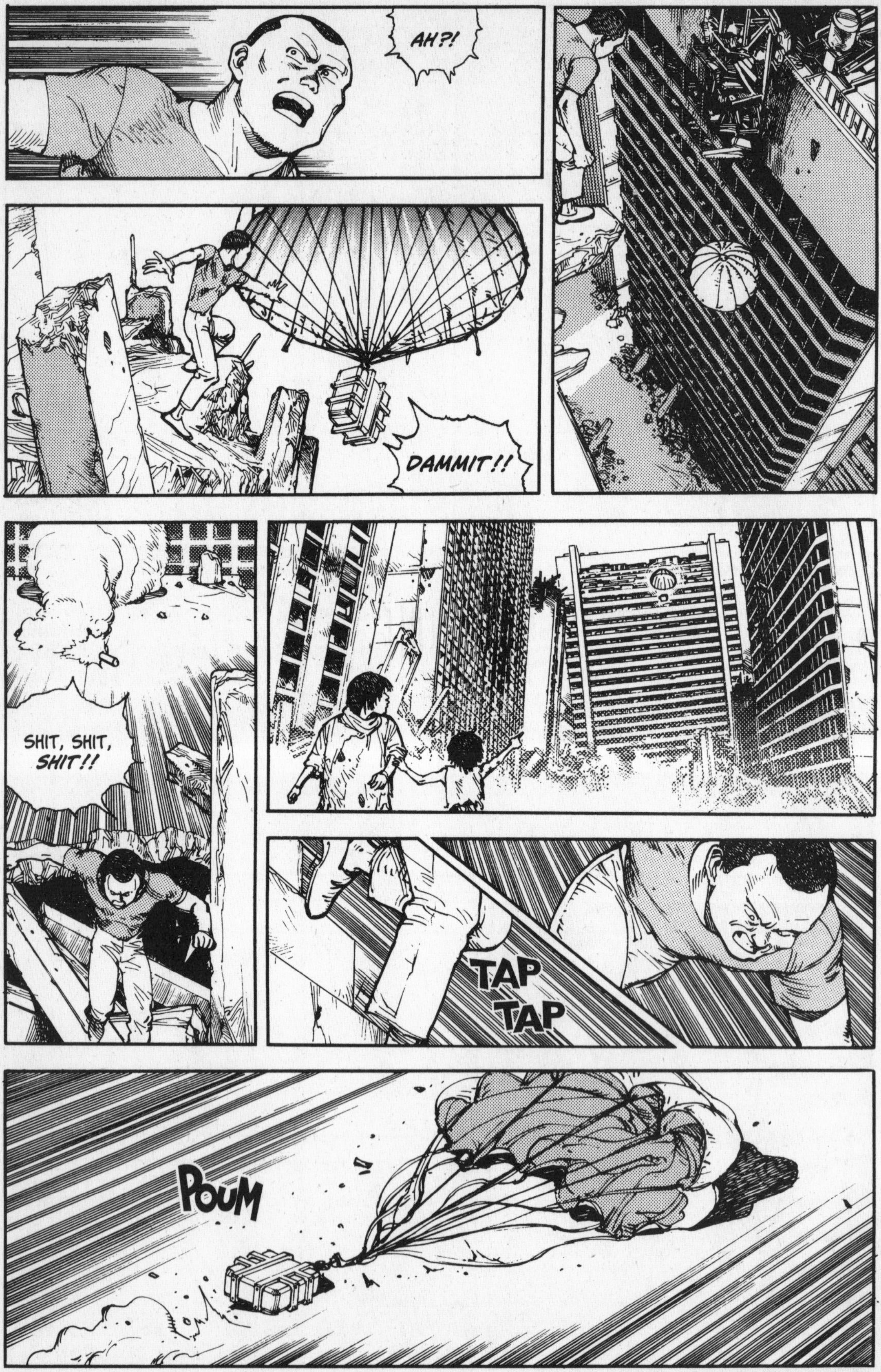
AH?!
DAMMIT!!
SHIT, SHIT, SHIT!!
TAP TAP
POUM

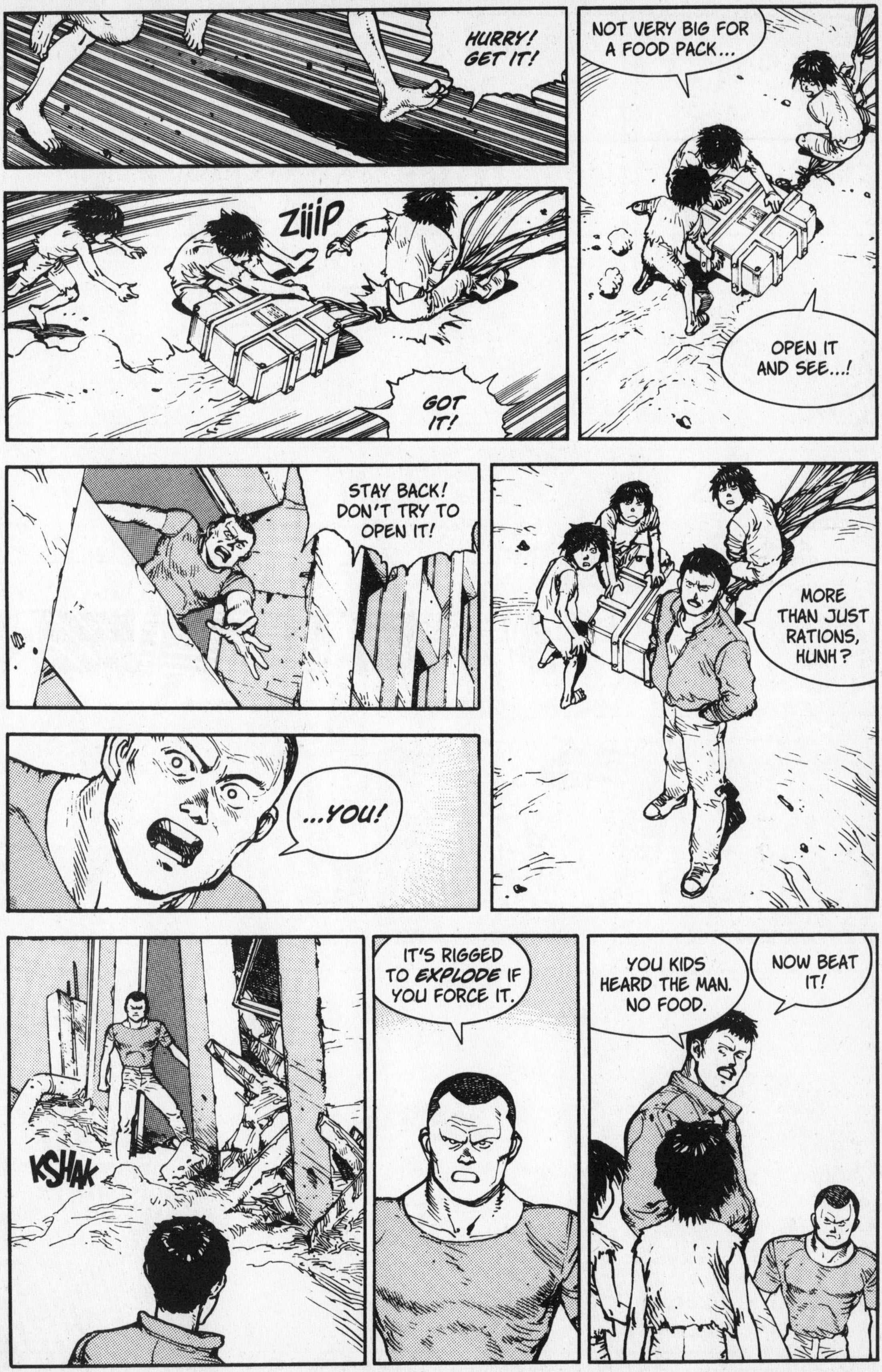
HURRY! GET IT!
ZIIIP
GOT IT!
NOT VERY BIG FOR A FOOD PACK...
OPEN IT AND SEE...!
STAY BACK! DON'T TRY TO OPEN IT!
...YOU!
MORE THAN JUST RATIONS, HUNH?
KSHAK
IT'S RIGGED TO *EXPLODE* IF YOU FORCE IT.
YOU KIDS HEARD THE MAN. NO FOOD.
NOW BEAT IT!

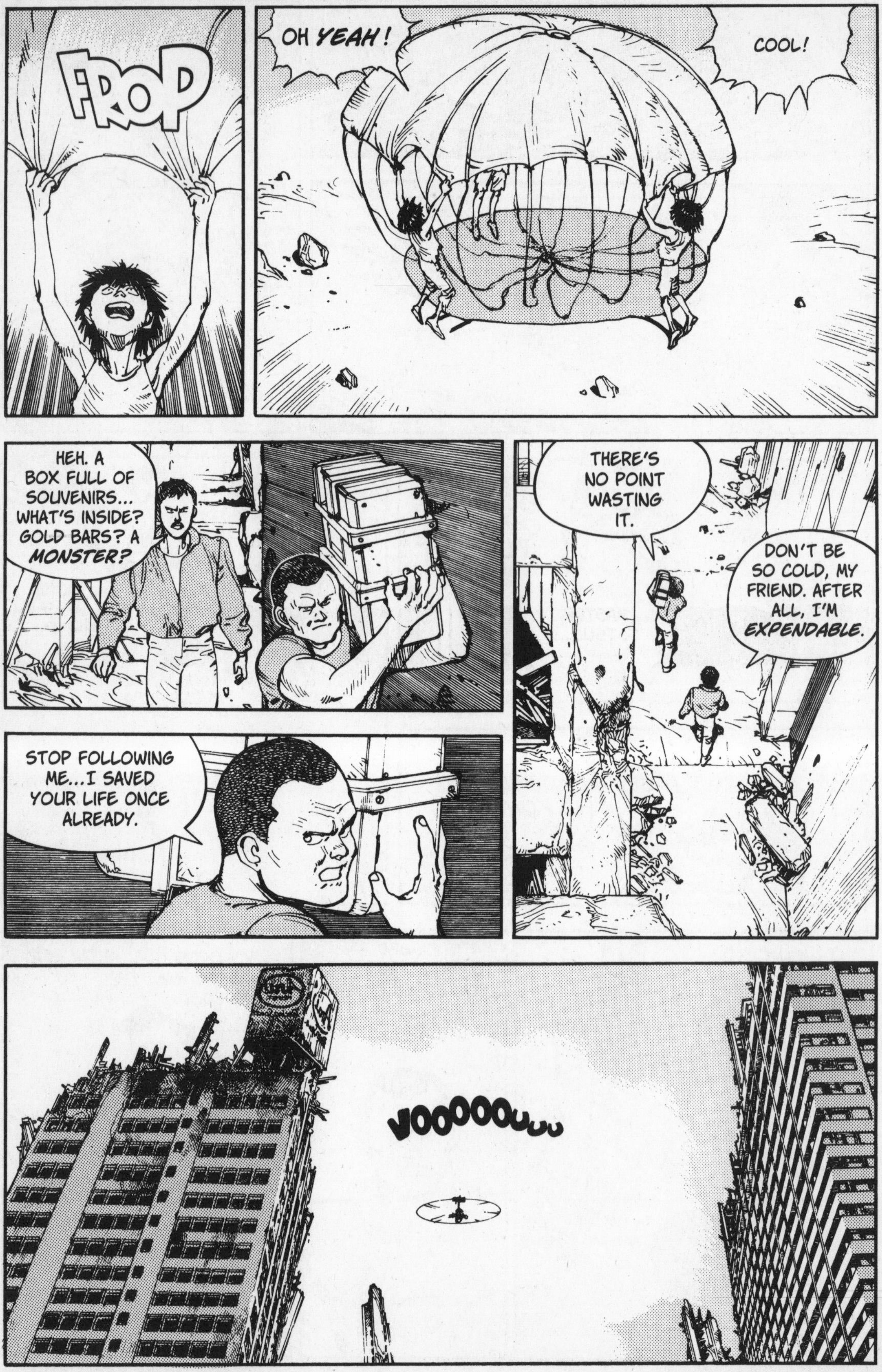
FROP
OH YEAH!
COOL!
HEH. A BOX FULL OF SOUVENIRS... WHAT'S INSIDE? GOLD BARS? A MONSTER?
THERE'S NO POINT WASTING IT.
DON'T BE SO COLD, MY FRIEND. AFTER ALL, I'M EXPENDABLE.
STOP FOLLOWING ME...I SAVED YOUR LIFE ONCE ALREADY.
VOOOOOUUU

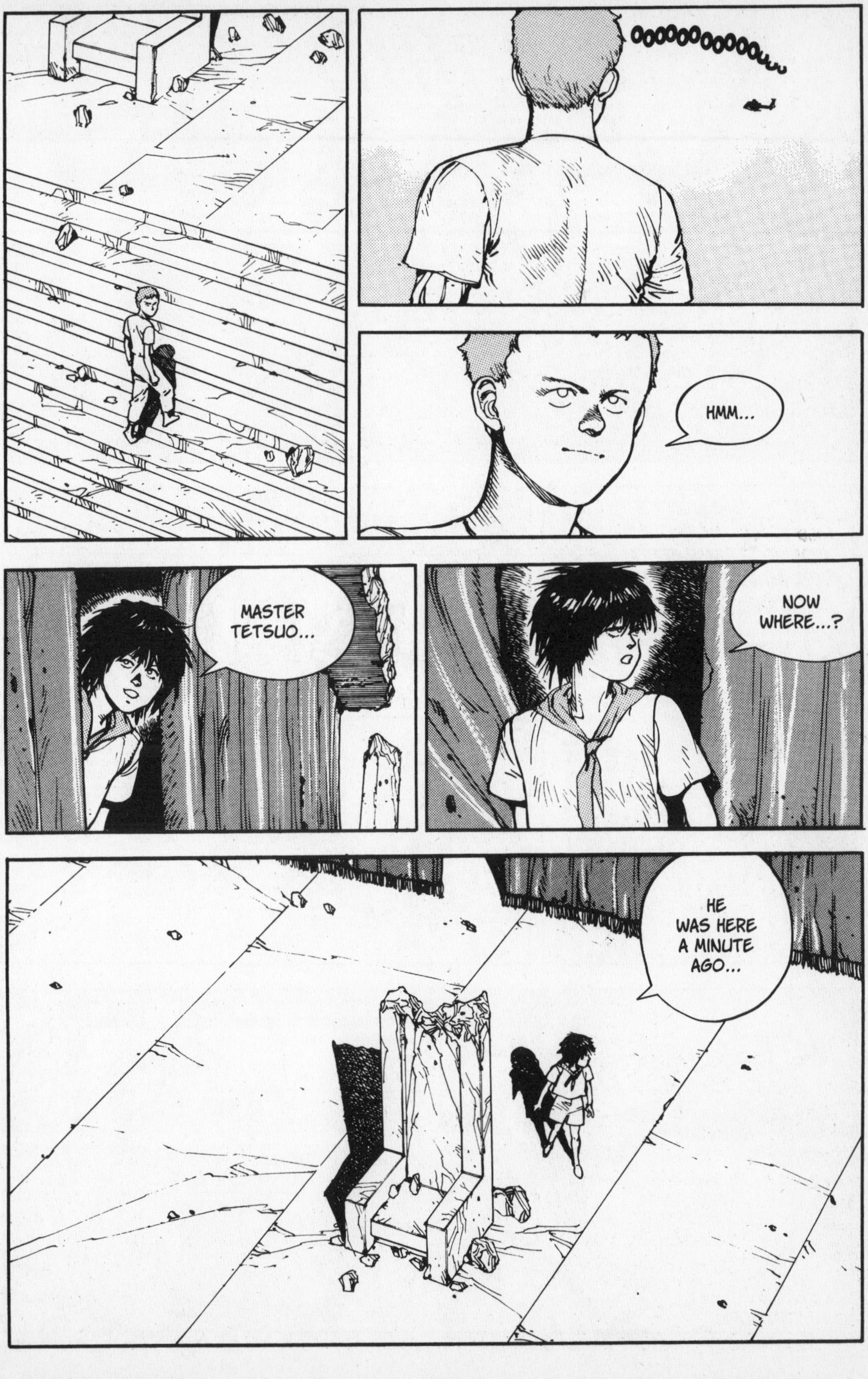
OOOOOOOOOOOOuuu
HMM...
MASTER TETSUO...
NOW WHERE...?
HE WAS HERE A MINUTE AGO...

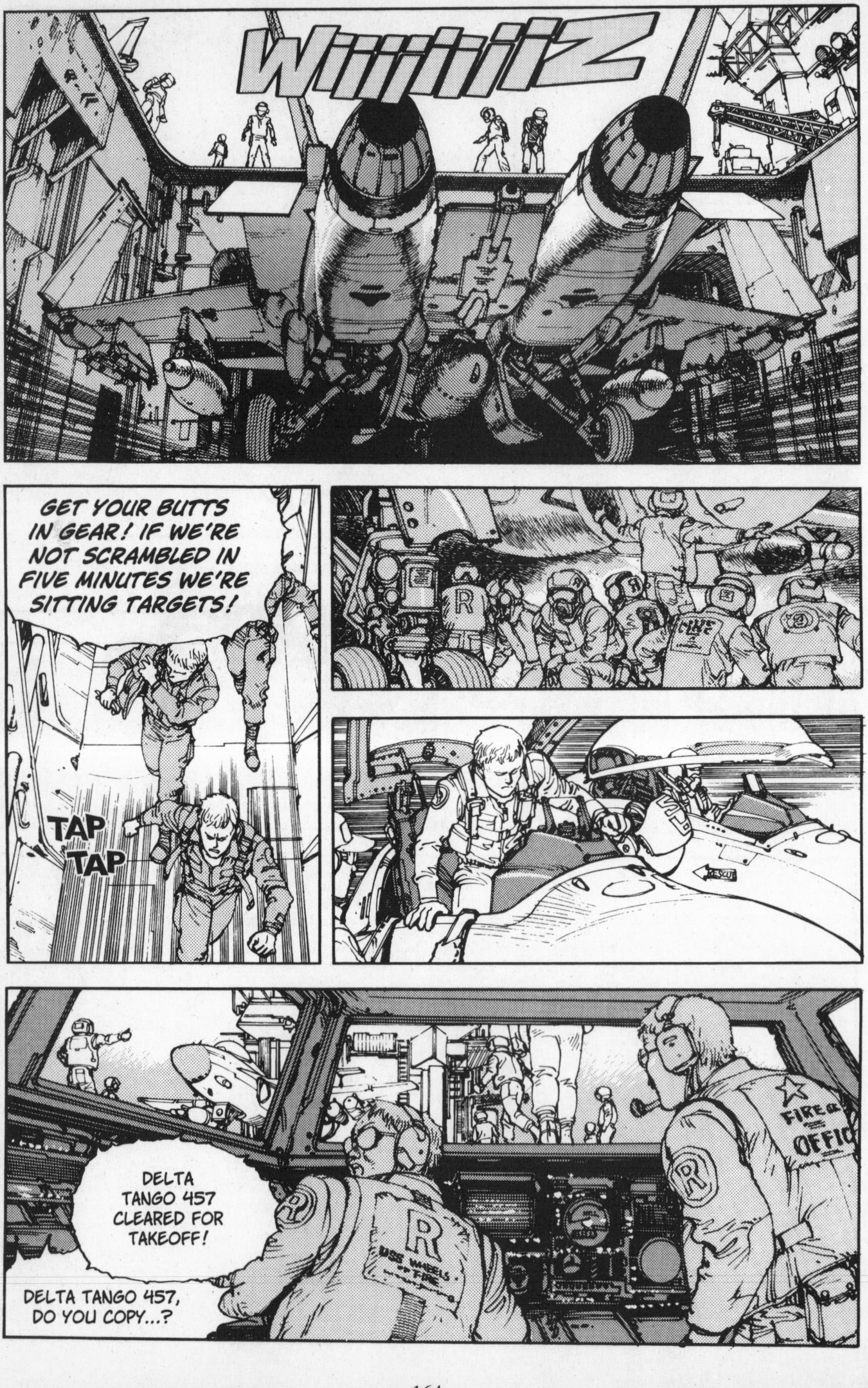
WiiiiiiiZ
GET YOUR BUTTS IN GEAR! IF WE'RE NOT SCRAMBLED IN FIVE MINUTES WE'RE SITTING TARGETS!
TAP
TAP
DELTA TANGO 457 CLEARED FOR TAKEOFF!
DELTA TANGO 457, DO YOU COPY...?

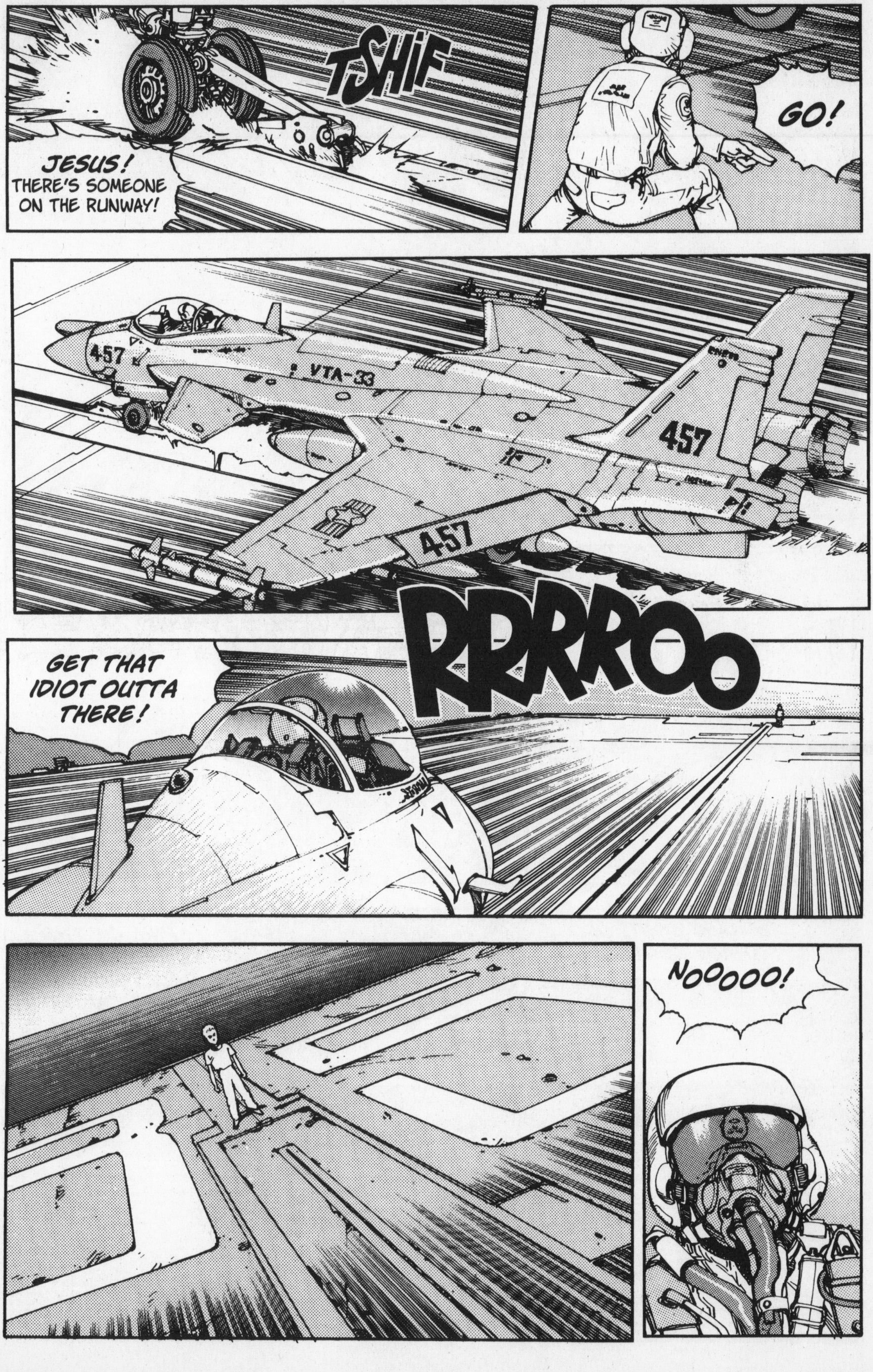
TSHIF
JESUS! THERE'S SOMEONE ON THE RUNWAY!
GO!
RRRROO
GET THAT IDIOT OUTTA THERE!
NOOOOO!

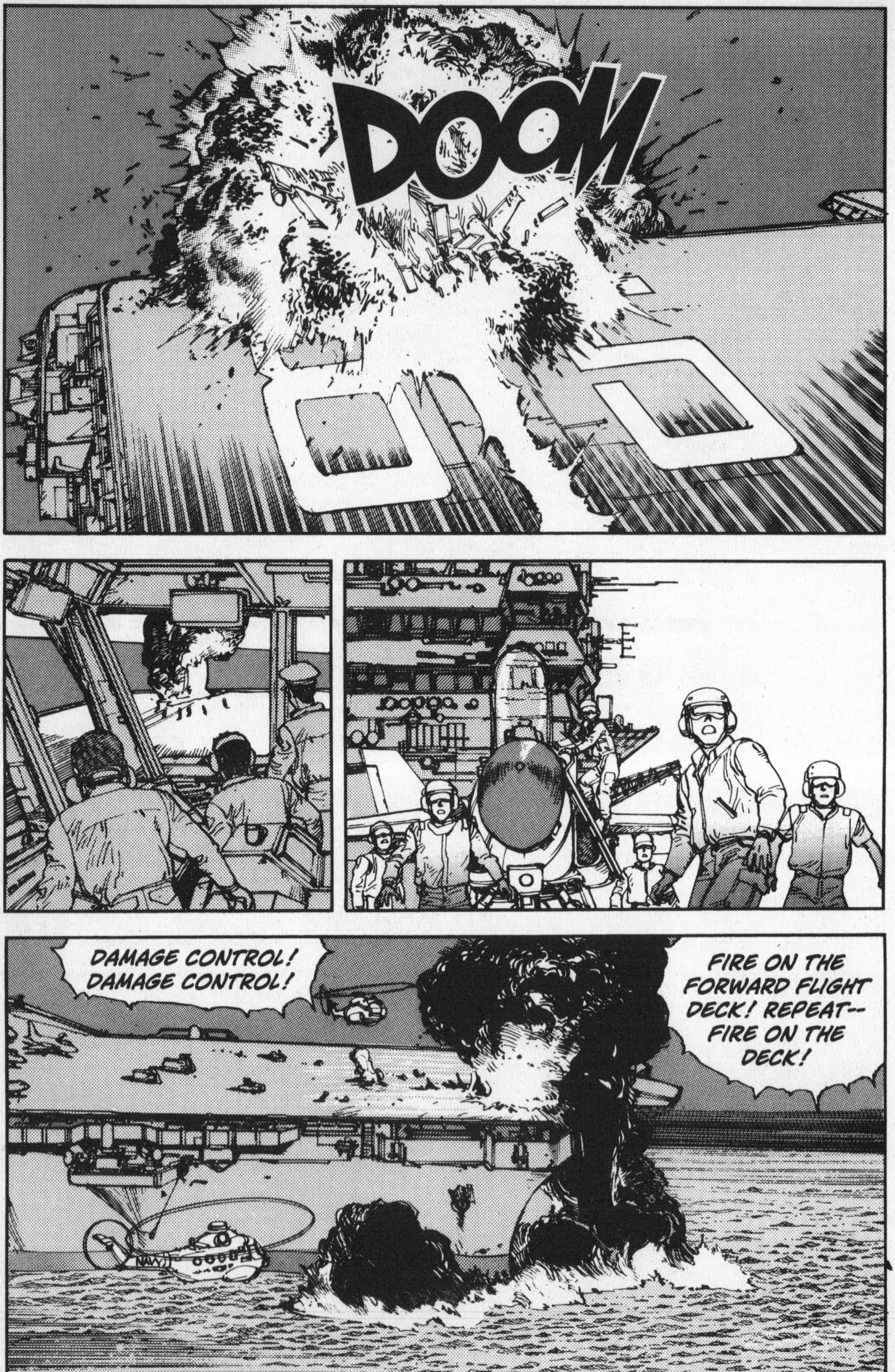
DOOM
DAMAGE CONTROL! DAMAGE CONTROL!
FIRE ON THE FORWARD FLIGHT DECK! REPEAT-- FIRE ON THE DECK!

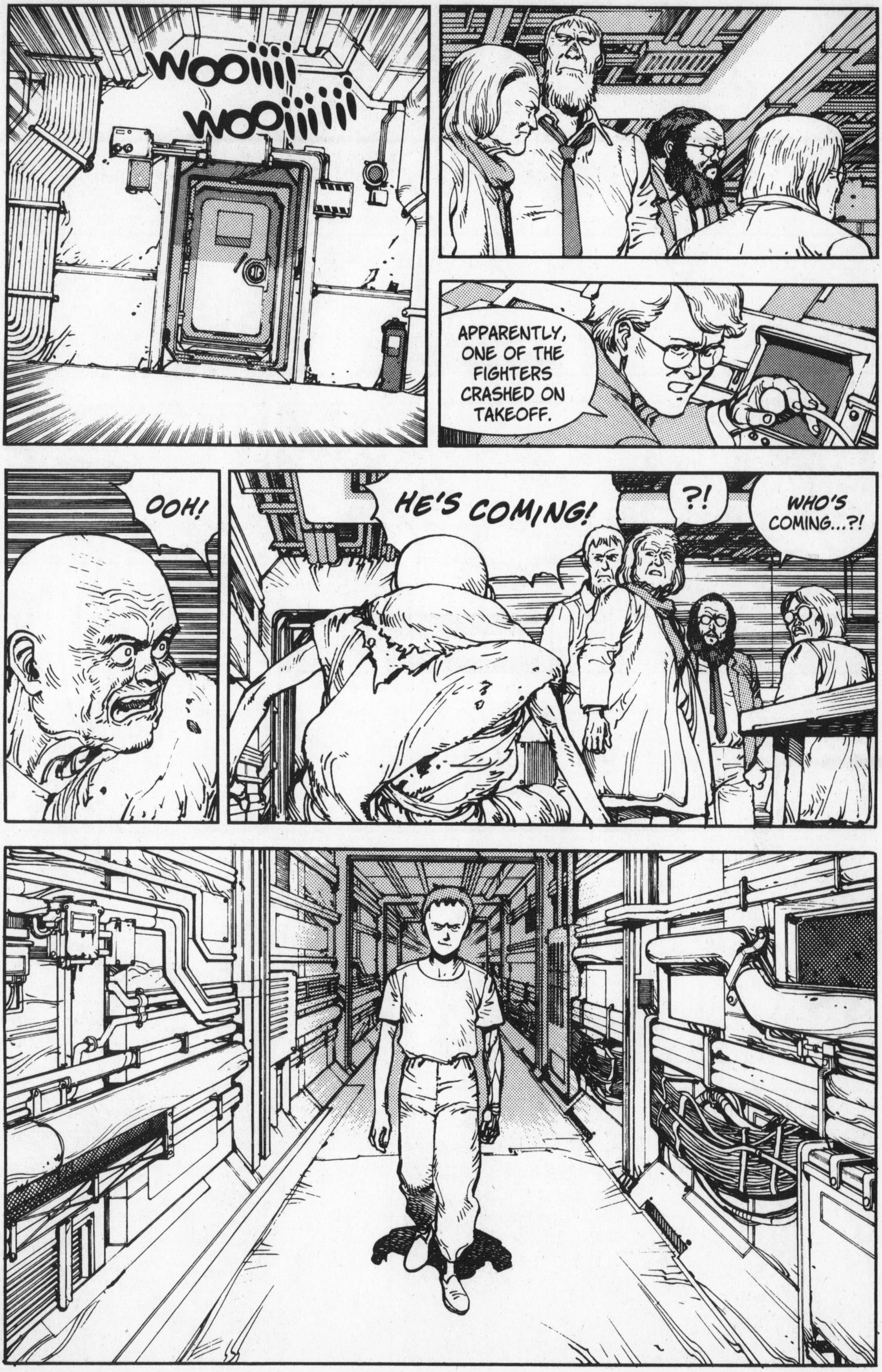
WOOiiii
WOOiiiiii
APPARENTLY, ONE OF THE FIGHTERS CRASHED ON TAKEOFF.
OOH!
HE'S COMING!
?!
WHO'S COMING...?!

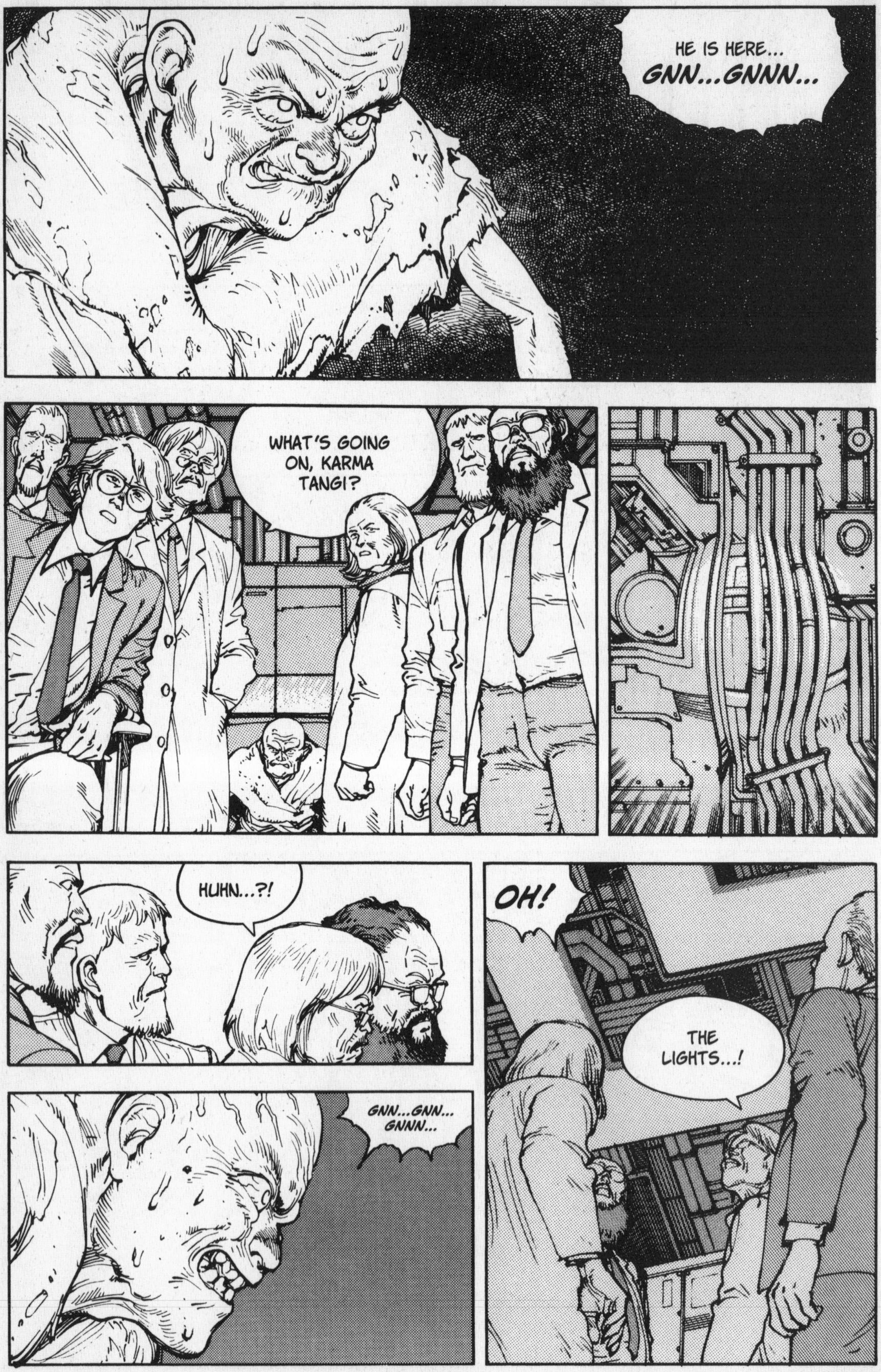
HE IS HERE...
GNN...GNNN...
WHAT'S GOING ON, KARMA TANGI?
HUHN...?!
GNN...GNN... GNNN...
OH!
THE LIGHTS...!

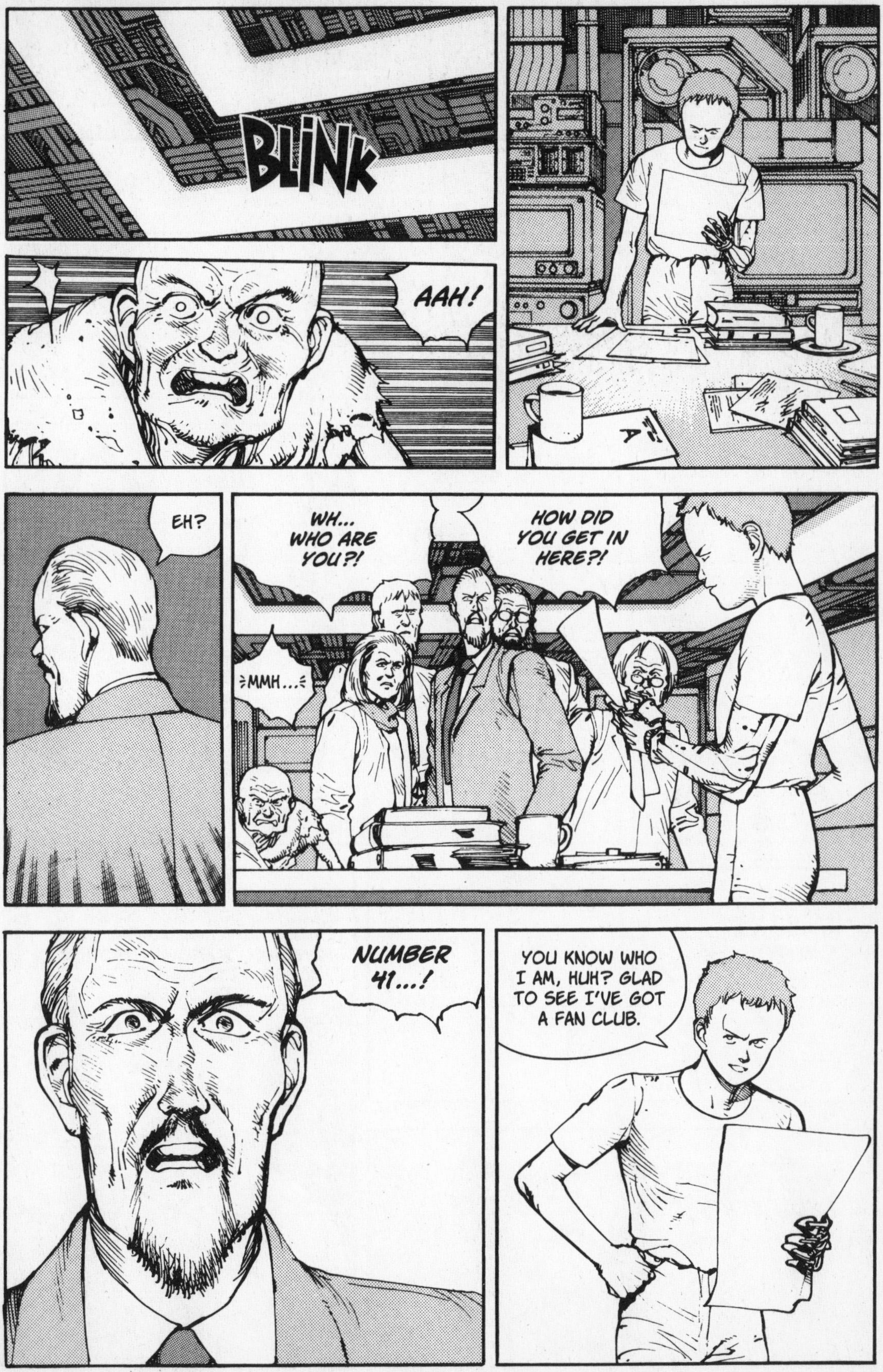
BLINK
AAH!
EH?
WH... WHO ARE YOU?!
HOW DID YOU GET IN HERE?!
MMH...
NUMBER 41...!
YOU KNOW WHO I AM, HUH? GLAD TO SEE I'VE GOT A FAN CLUB.

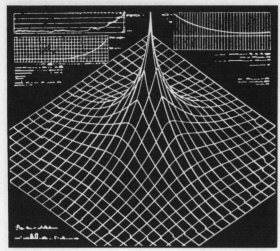

HMM...

THAT'S A 3D GRAPH OF THE THIRD PHENOMENON...

...WHICH WAS OF SMALLER MAGNITUDE THAN THE SECOND.

IT COULD HAVE BEEN CAUSED BY AKIRA...

...BUT IT COULD HAVE BEEN SOME-ONE ELSE... PERHAPS *YOU*, NUMBER 41...

WHAT DO YOU HOPE TO FIND BY STUDYING AKIRA?

MAYBE YOU WANT TO FIND A NON-POLLUTING SOURCE OF POWER TO CONTRIBUTE TO WORLD PEACE? OR MAYBE YOU JUST WANT ANOTHER BOMB TO THREATEN THE REST OF THE WORLD...

HE... HE'S USING TELEPATHY!

170

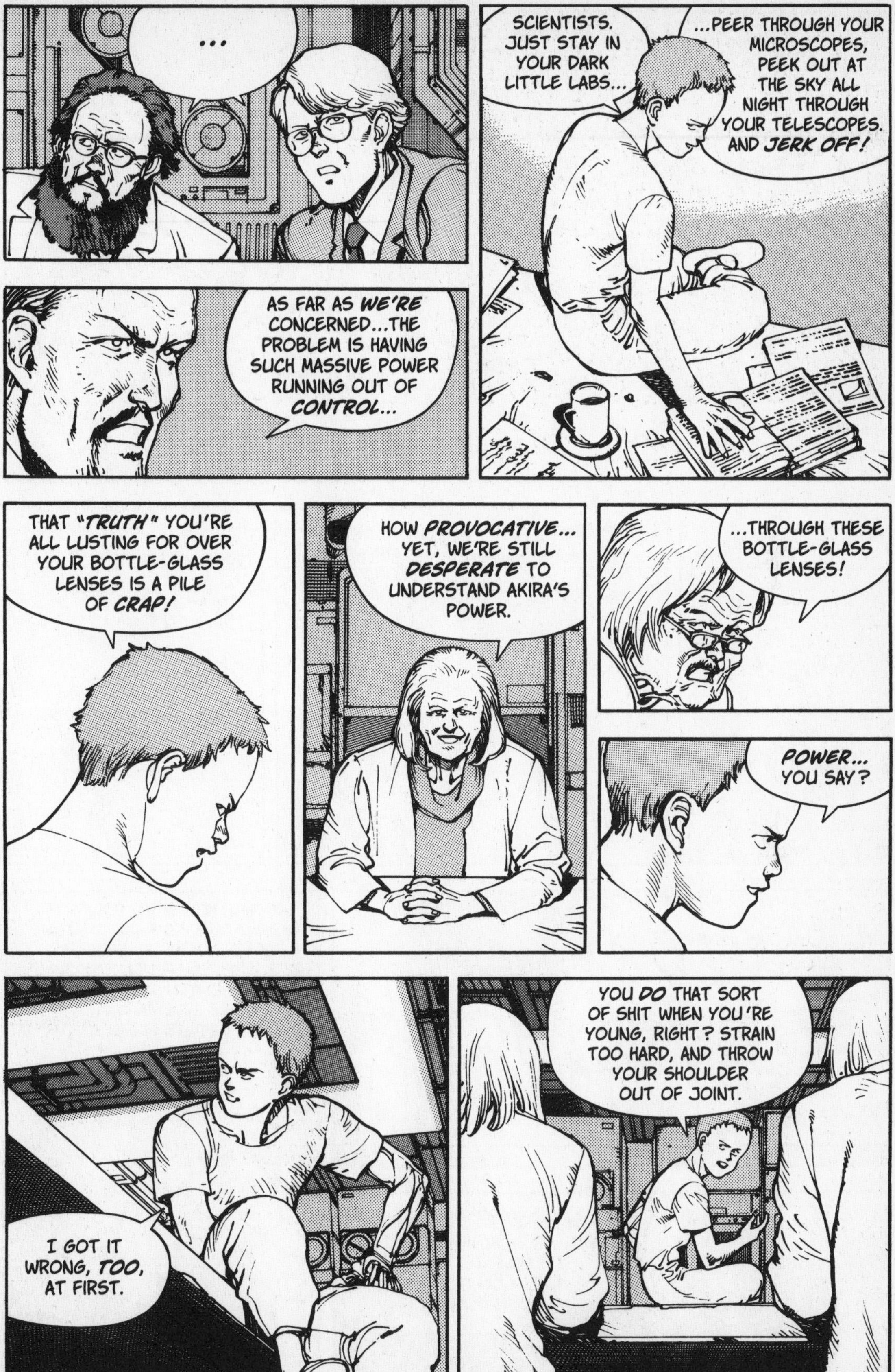
...
AS FAR AS WE'RE CONCERNED...THE PROBLEM IS HAVING SUCH MASSIVE POWER RUNNING OUT OF CONTROL...
SCIENTISTS. JUST STAY IN YOUR DARK LITTLE LABS...
...PEER THROUGH YOUR MICROSCOPES, PEEK OUT AT THE SKY ALL NIGHT THROUGH YOUR TELESCOPES. AND JERK OFF!
THAT "TRUTH" YOU'RE ALL LUSTING FOR OVER YOUR BOTTLE-GLASS LENSES IS A PILE OF CRAP!
HOW PROVOCATIVE... YET, WE'RE STILL DESPERATE TO UNDERSTAND AKIRA'S POWER.
...THROUGH THESE BOTTLE-GLASS LENSES!
POWER... YOU SAY?
I GOT IT WRONG, TOO, AT FIRST.
YOU DO THAT SORT OF SHIT WHEN YOU'RE YOUNG, RIGHT? STRAIN TOO HARD, AND THROW YOUR SHOULDER OUT OF JOINT.

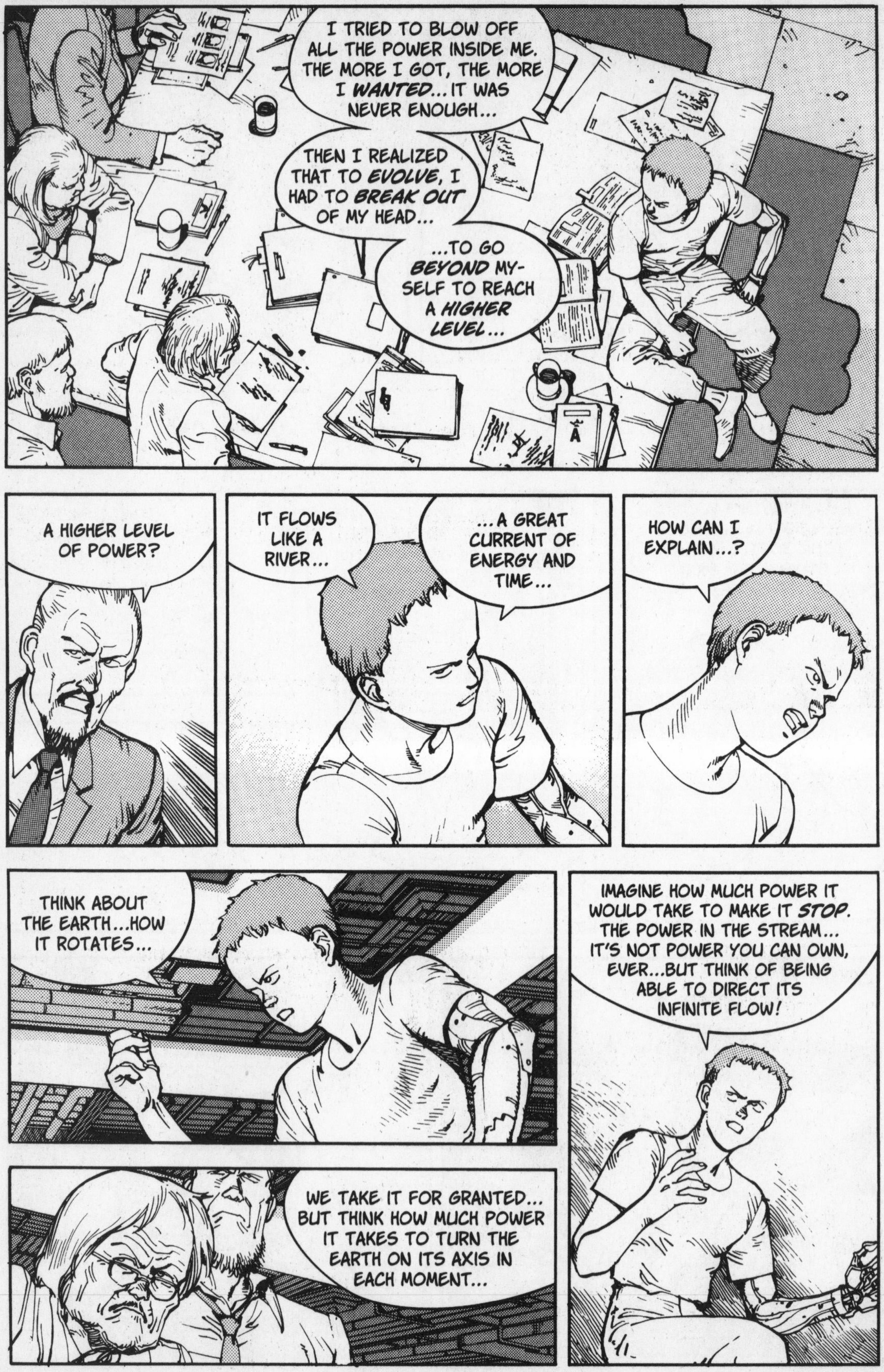
I TRIED TO BLOW OFF ALL THE POWER INSIDE ME. THE MORE I GOT, THE MORE I WANTED... IT WAS NEVER ENOUGH...
THEN I REALIZED THAT TO EVOLVE, I HAD TO BREAK OUT OF MY HEAD...
...TO GO BEYOND MY-SELF TO REACH A HIGHER LEVEL...
A HIGHER LEVEL OF POWER?
IT FLOWS LIKE A RIVER...
...A GREAT CURRENT OF ENERGY AND TIME...
HOW CAN I EXPLAIN...?
THINK ABOUT THE EARTH...HOW IT ROTATES...
WE TAKE IT FOR GRANTED... BUT THINK HOW MUCH POWER IT TAKES TO TURN THE EARTH ON ITS AXIS IN EACH MOMENT...
IMAGINE HOW MUCH POWER IT WOULD TAKE TO MAKE IT STOP. THE POWER IN THE STREAM... IT'S NOT POWER YOU CAN OWN, EVER...BUT THINK OF BEING ABLE TO DIRECT ITS INFINITE FLOW!

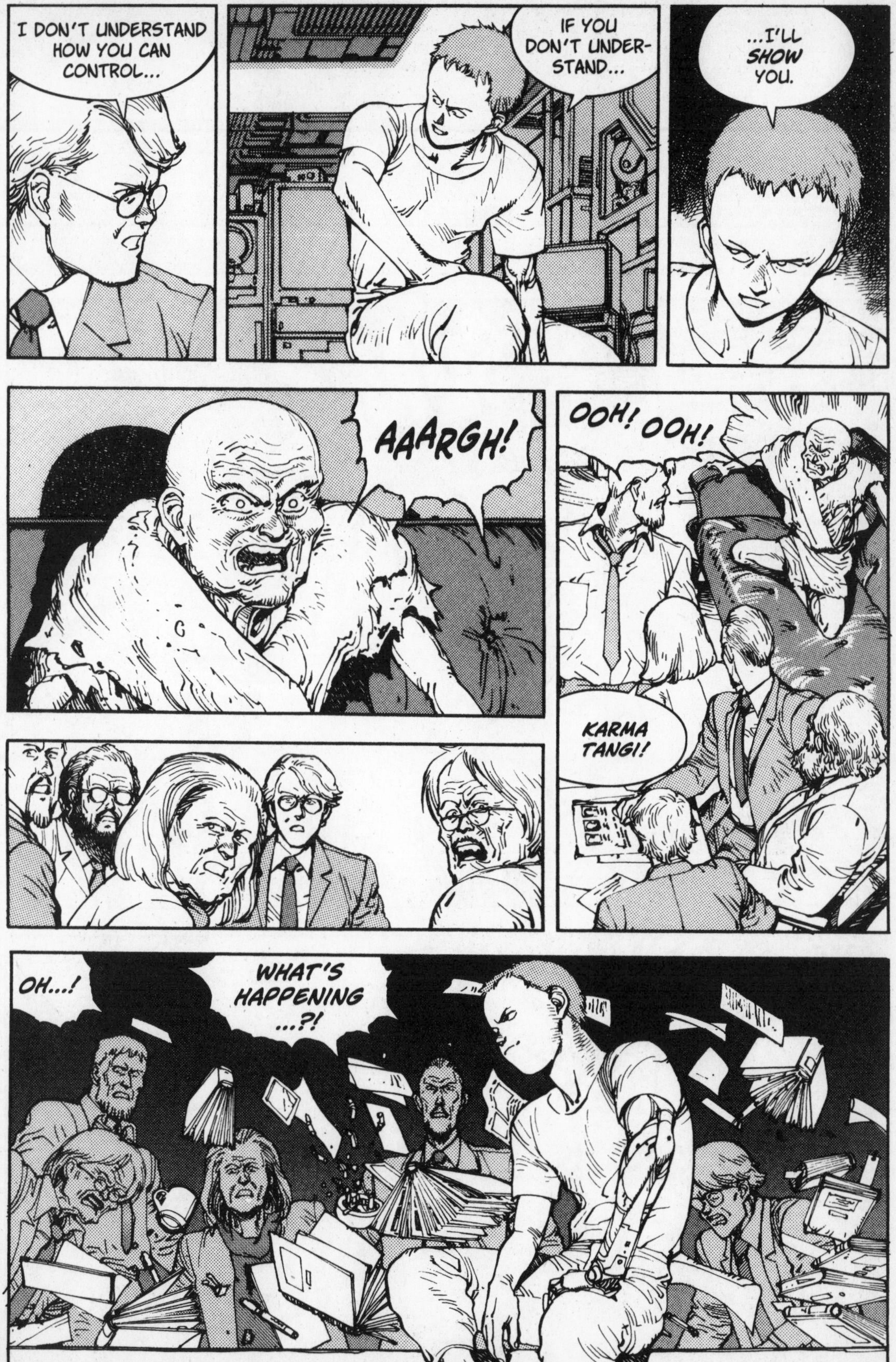
I DON'T UNDERSTAND HOW YOU CAN CONTROL...
IF YOU DON'T UNDER-STAND...
...I'LL SHOW YOU.
AAARGH!
OOH! OOH!
KARMA TANGI!
OH...!
WHAT'S HAPPENING ...?!

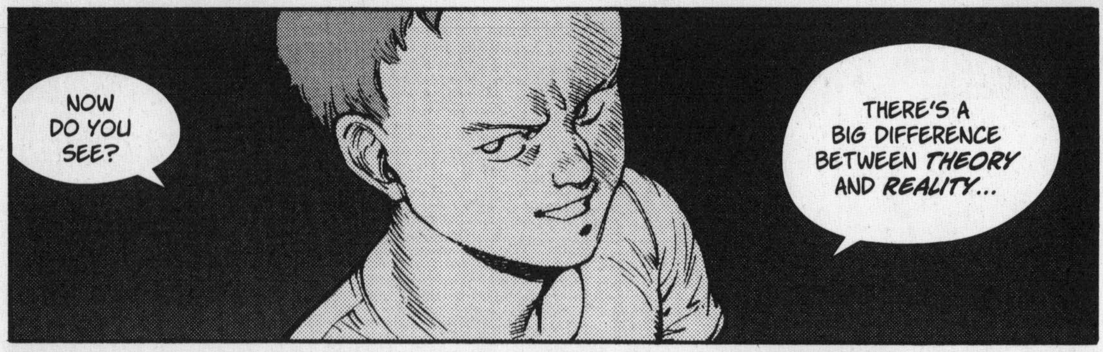
NOW DO YOU SEE?
THERE'S A BIG DIFFERENCE BETWEEN *THEORY* AND *REALITY*...

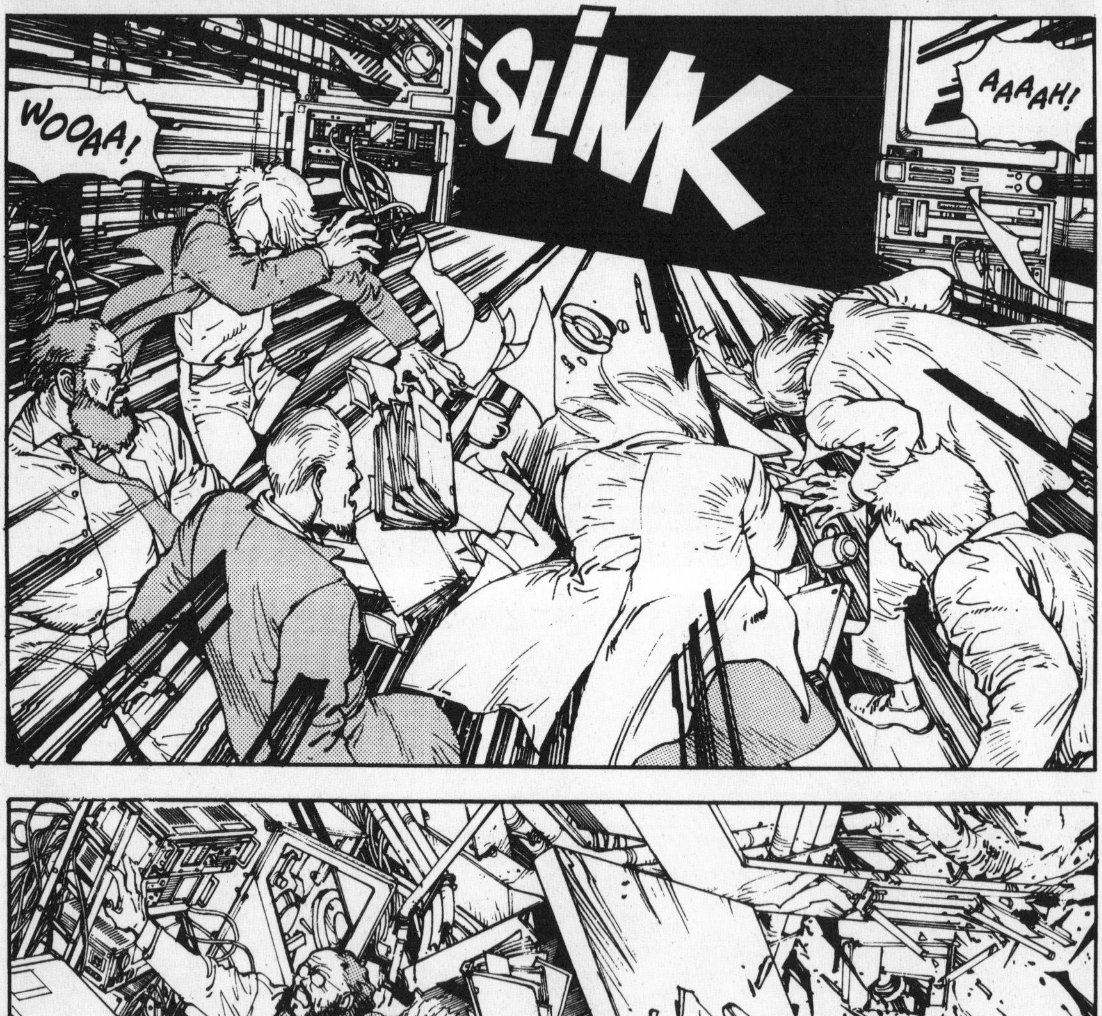
WOOAA!
SLINK
AAAAH!

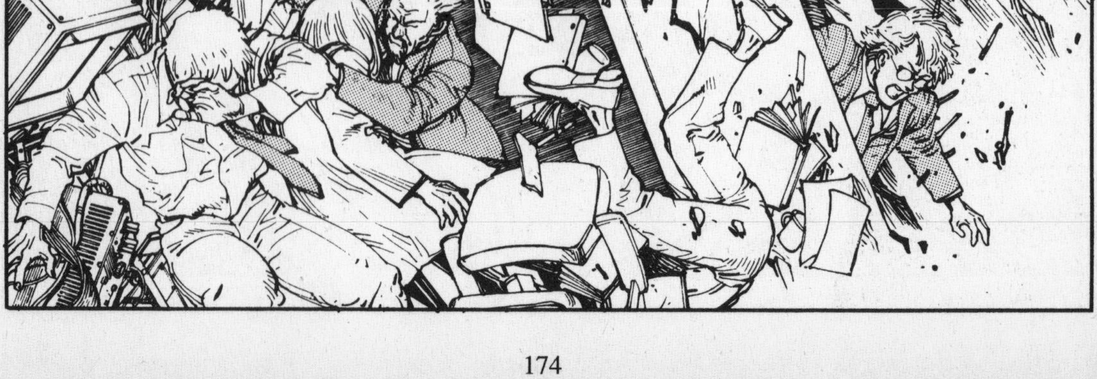

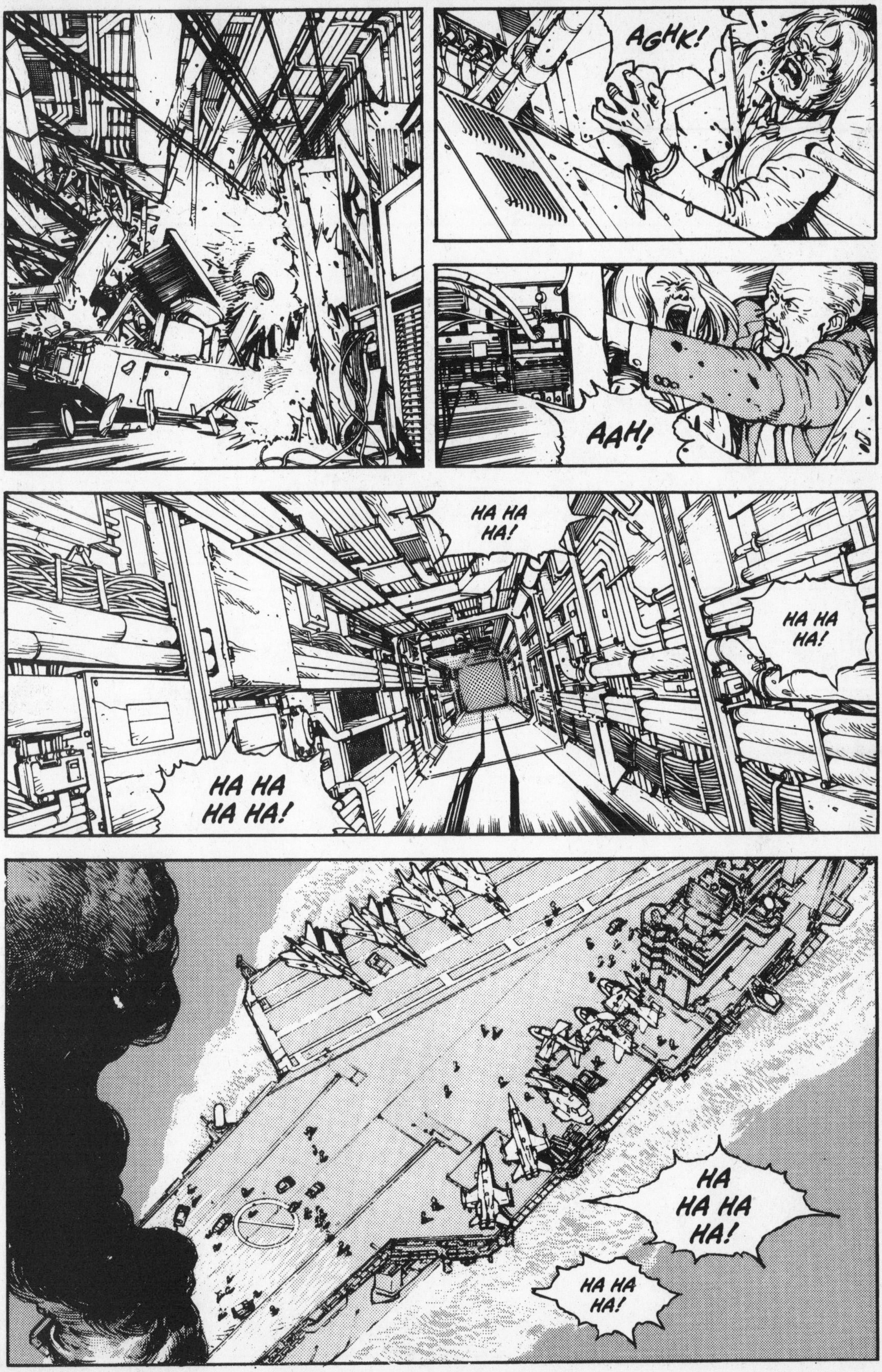
AGHK!
AAH!
HA HA HA!
HA HA HA!
HA HA HA HA!
HA HA HA HA!
HA HA HA!

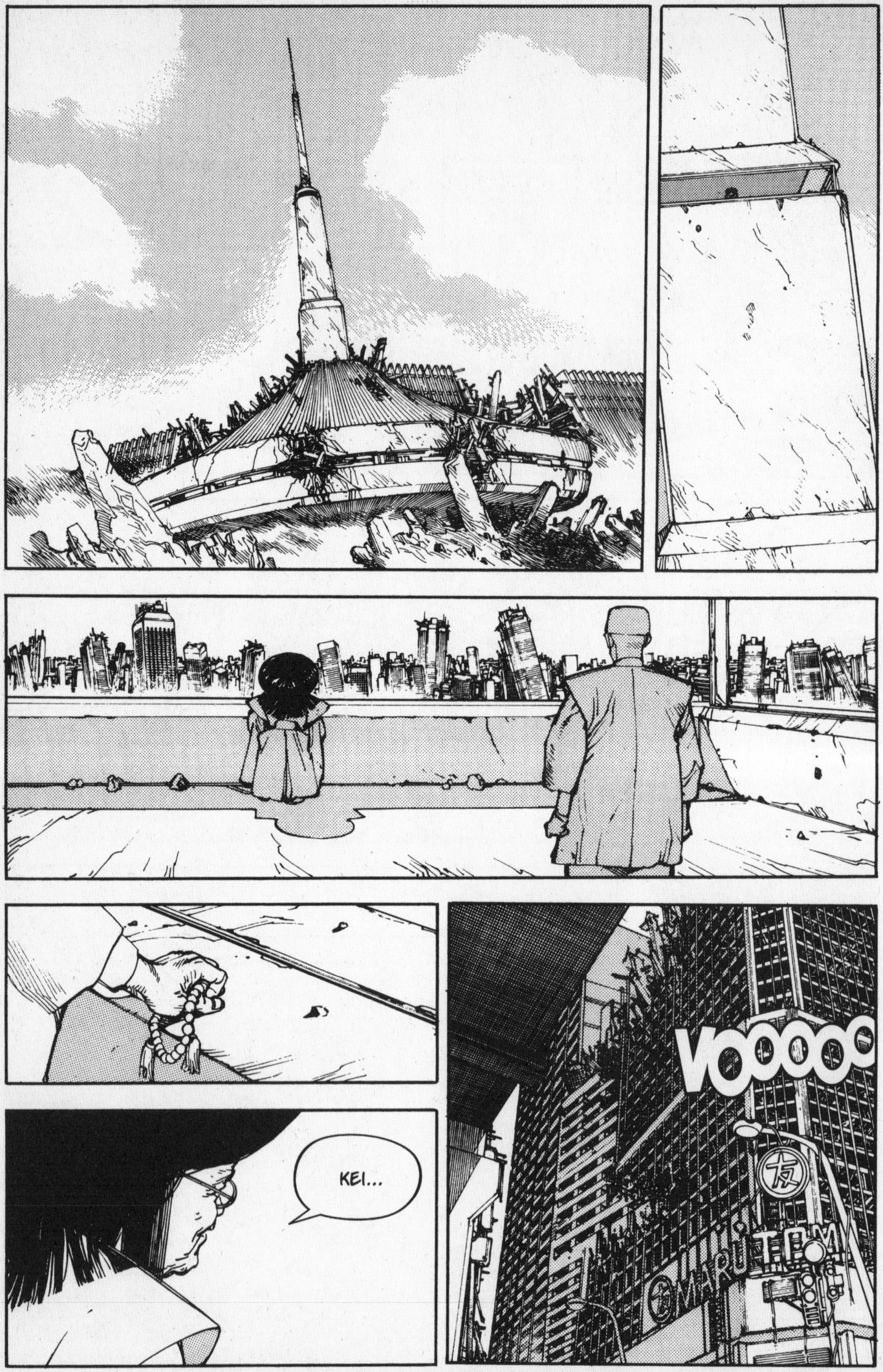
KEI...
VOOOOO

DROOO

KANEDA! I NEED A HAND!

HEY! C'MON!

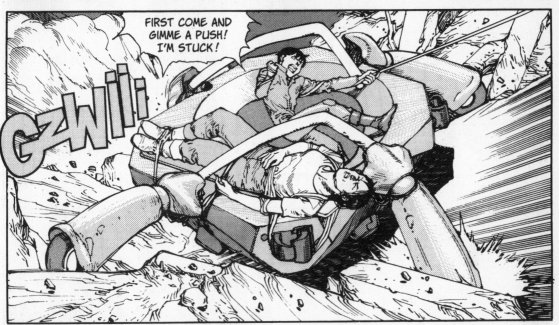

FIRST COME AND GIMME A PUSH! I'M STUCK!

GZWiii

KANEDA!

BROOO

PIECE A'CRAP! SHIT!

THINK THEY'RE FROM THE EMPIRE?

I DUNNO...

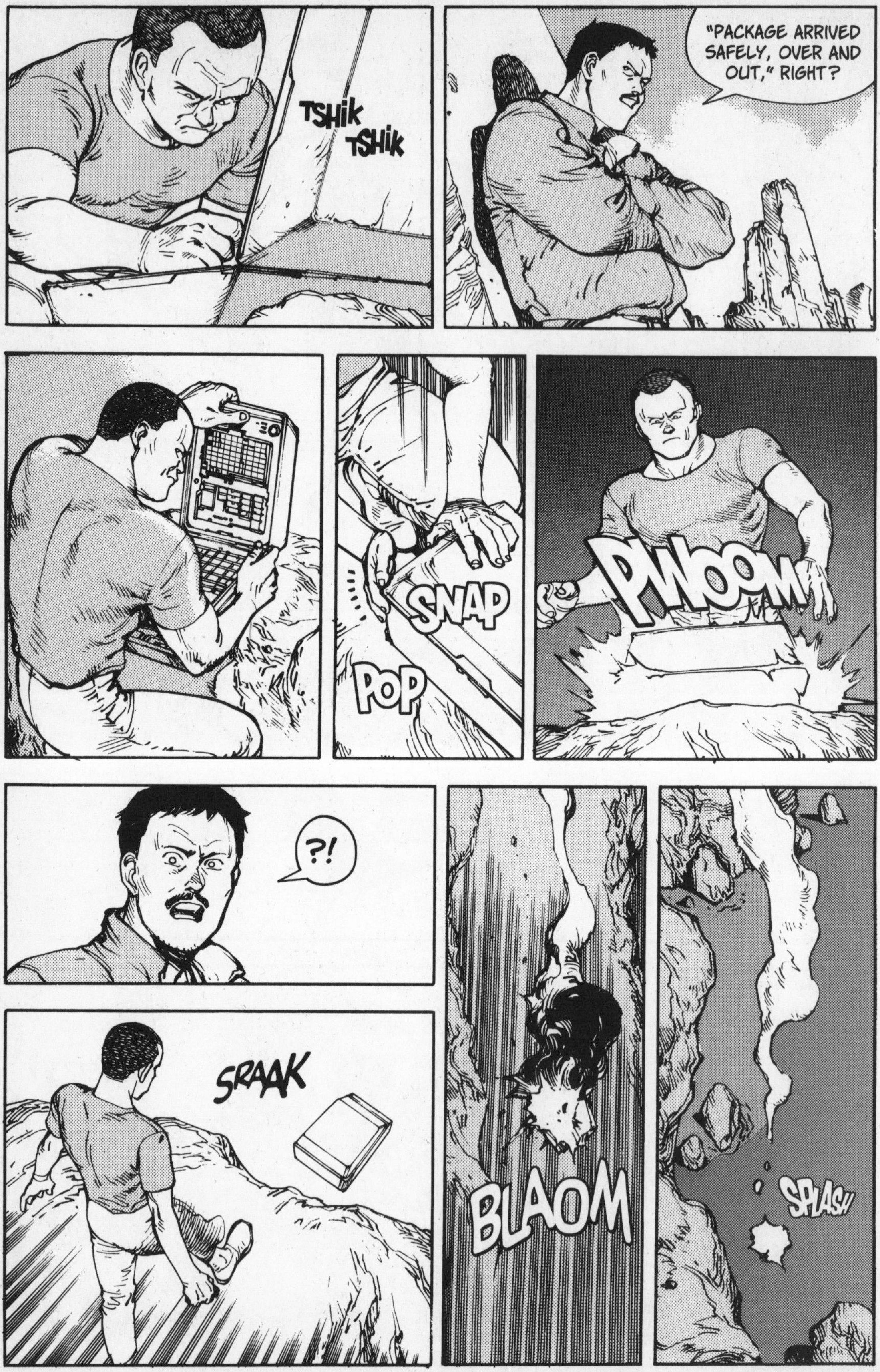
TSHIK
TSHIK
"PACKAGE ARRIVED SAFELY, OVER AND OUT," RIGHT?
SNAP
POP
PWOOM
?!
SRAAK
BLAOM
SPLASH

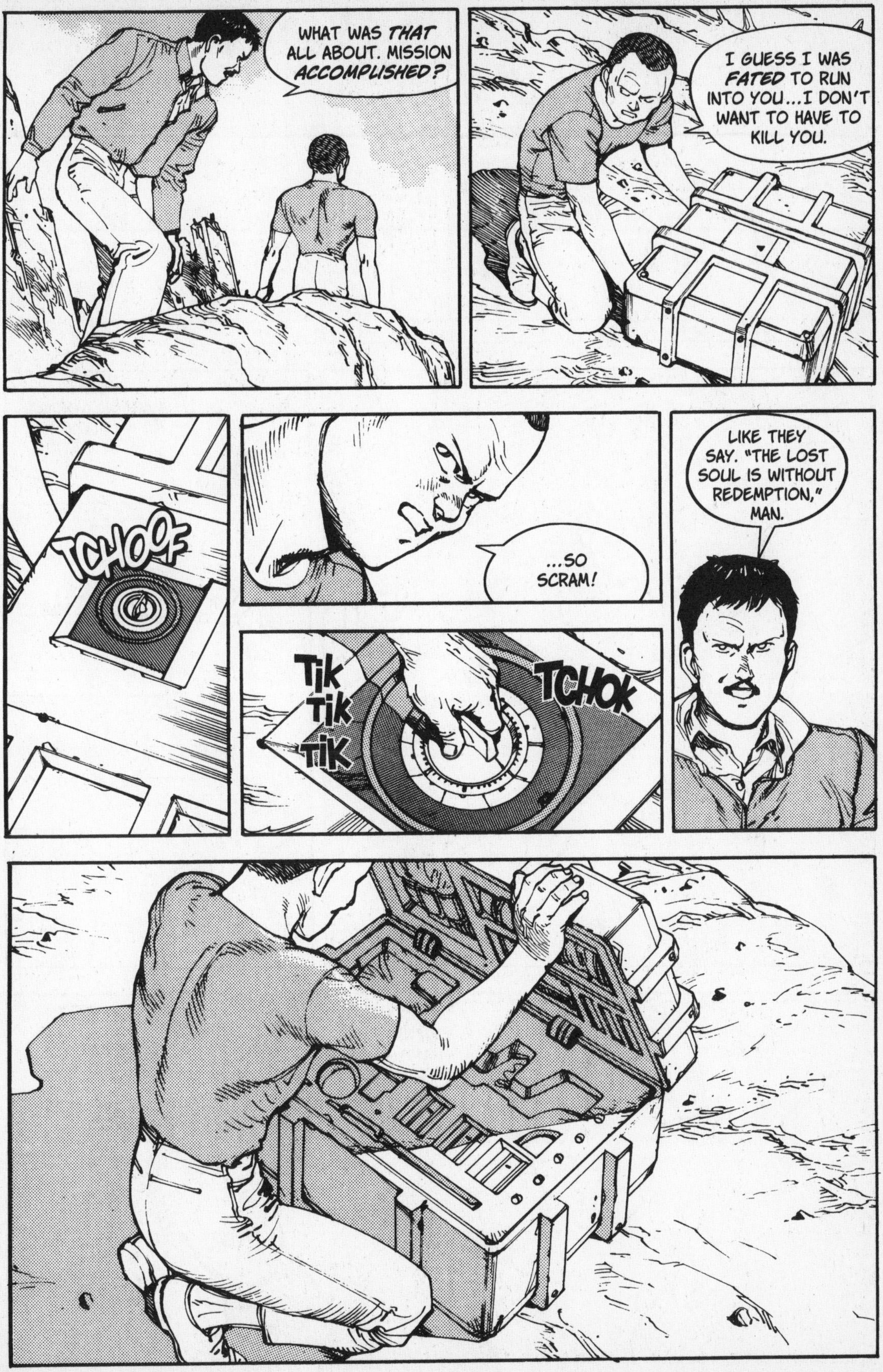
WHAT WAS THAT ALL ABOUT. MISSION ACCOMPLISHED?
I GUESS I WAS FATED TO RUN INTO YOU...I DON'T WANT TO HAVE TO KILL YOU.
TCHOOF
...SO SCRAM!
TIK TIK TIK
TCHOK
LIKE THEY SAY. "THE LOST SOUL IS WITHOUT REDEMPTION," MAN.

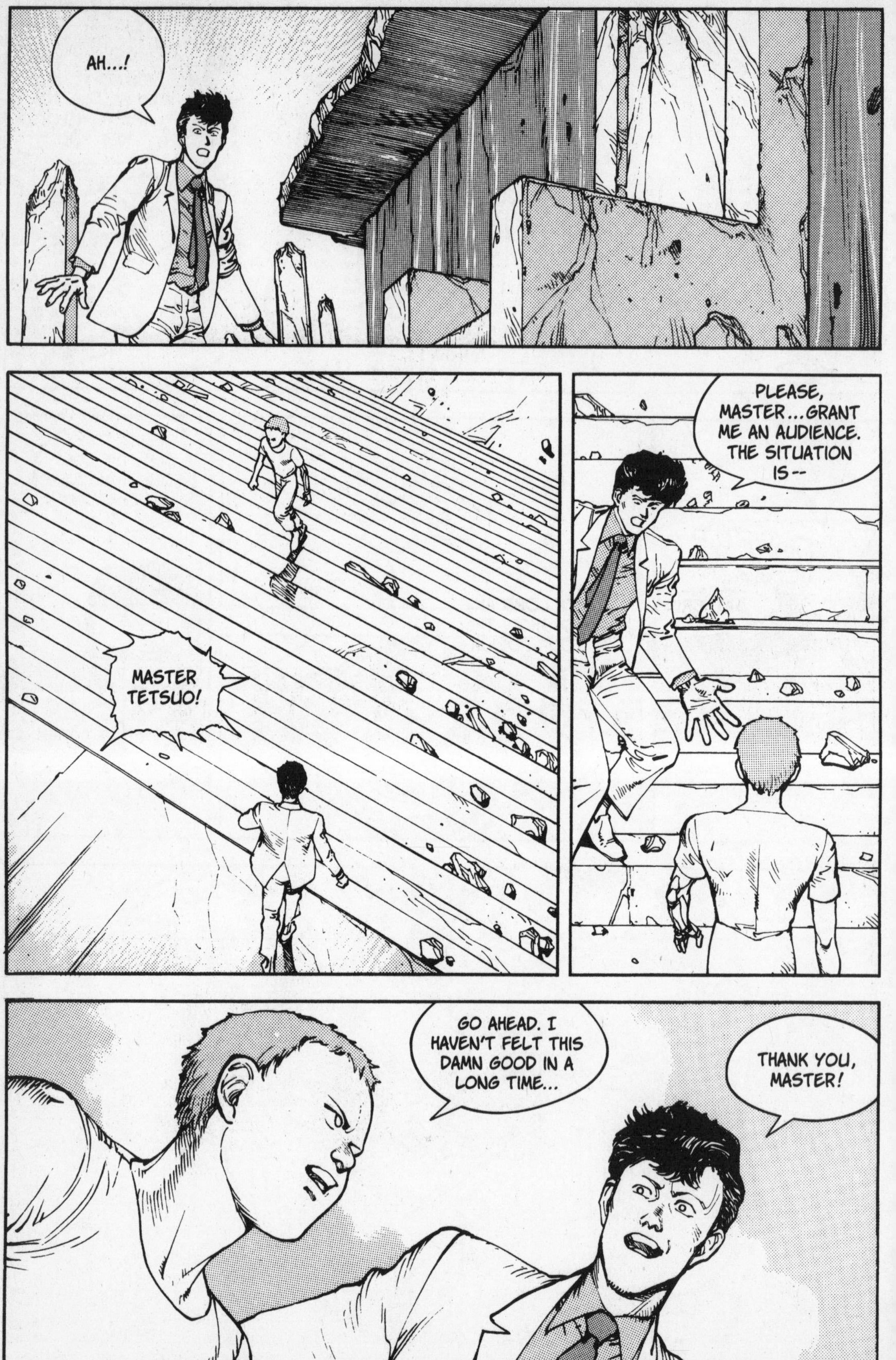
AH...!
MASTER TETSUO!
PLEASE, MASTER...GRANT ME AN AUDIENCE. THE SITUATION IS--
GO AHEAD. I HAVEN'T FELT THIS DAMN GOOD IN A LONG TIME...
THANK YOU, MASTER!

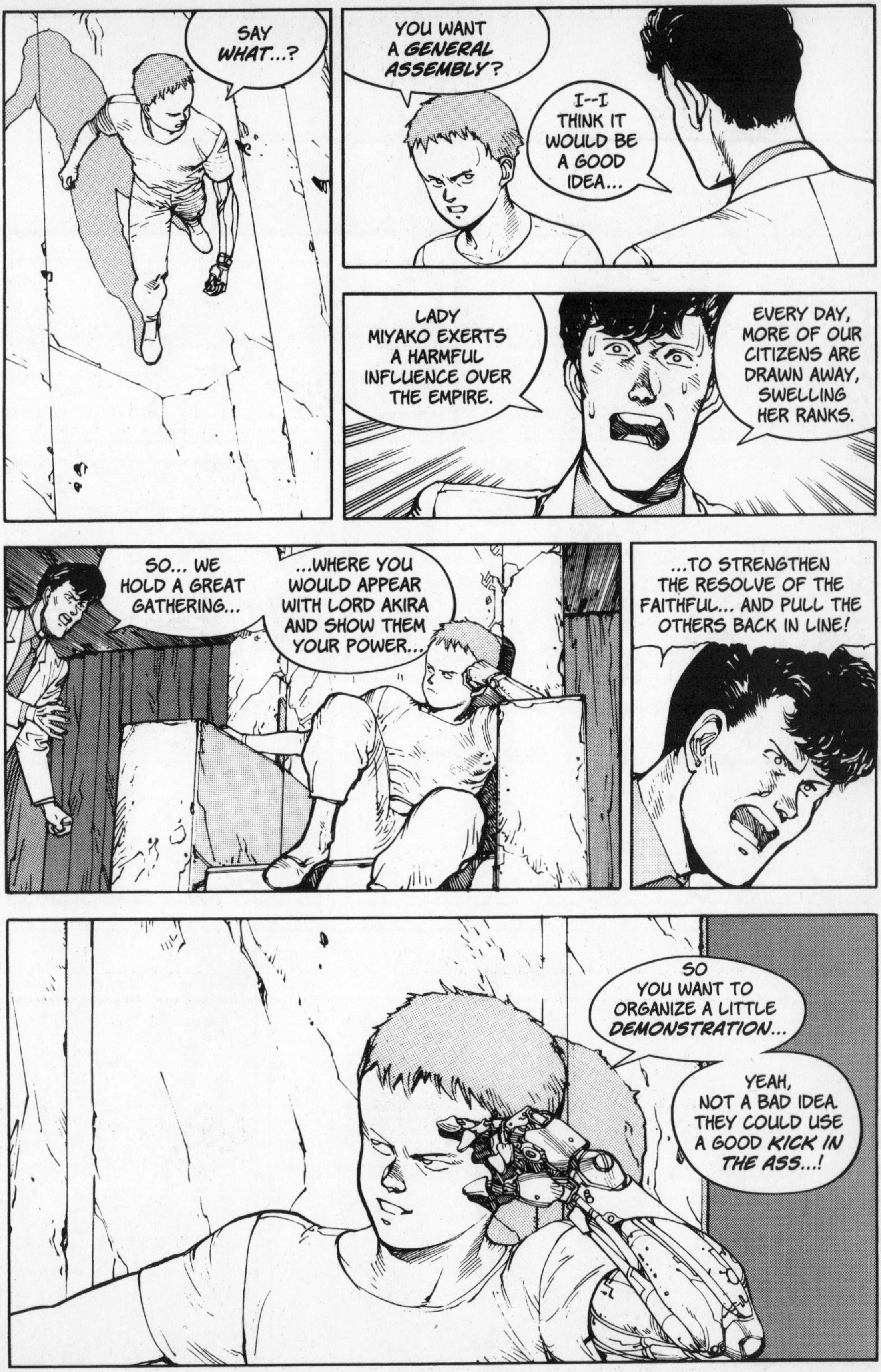
SAY WHAT...?
YOU WANT A GENERAL ASSEMBLY?
I--I THINK IT WOULD BE A GOOD IDEA...
LADY MIYAKO EXERTS A HARMFUL INFLUENCE OVER THE EMPIRE.
EVERY DAY, MORE OF OUR CITIZENS ARE DRAWN AWAY, SWELLING HER RANKS.
SO... WE HOLD A GREAT GATHERING...
...WHERE YOU WOULD APPEAR WITH LORD AKIRA AND SHOW THEM YOUR POWER...
...TO STRENGTHEN THE RESOLVE OF THE FAITHFUL... AND PULL THE OTHERS BACK IN LINE!
SO YOU WANT TO ORGANIZE A LITTLE DEMONSTRATION...
YEAH, NOT A BAD IDEA. THEY COULD USE A GOOD KICK IN THE ASS...!

ZiiiP

STRR

STRRR

? SLAP

YOU'RE MAKING YOURSELF AIR-TIGHT...?

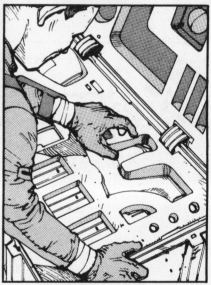

TCHANK

182

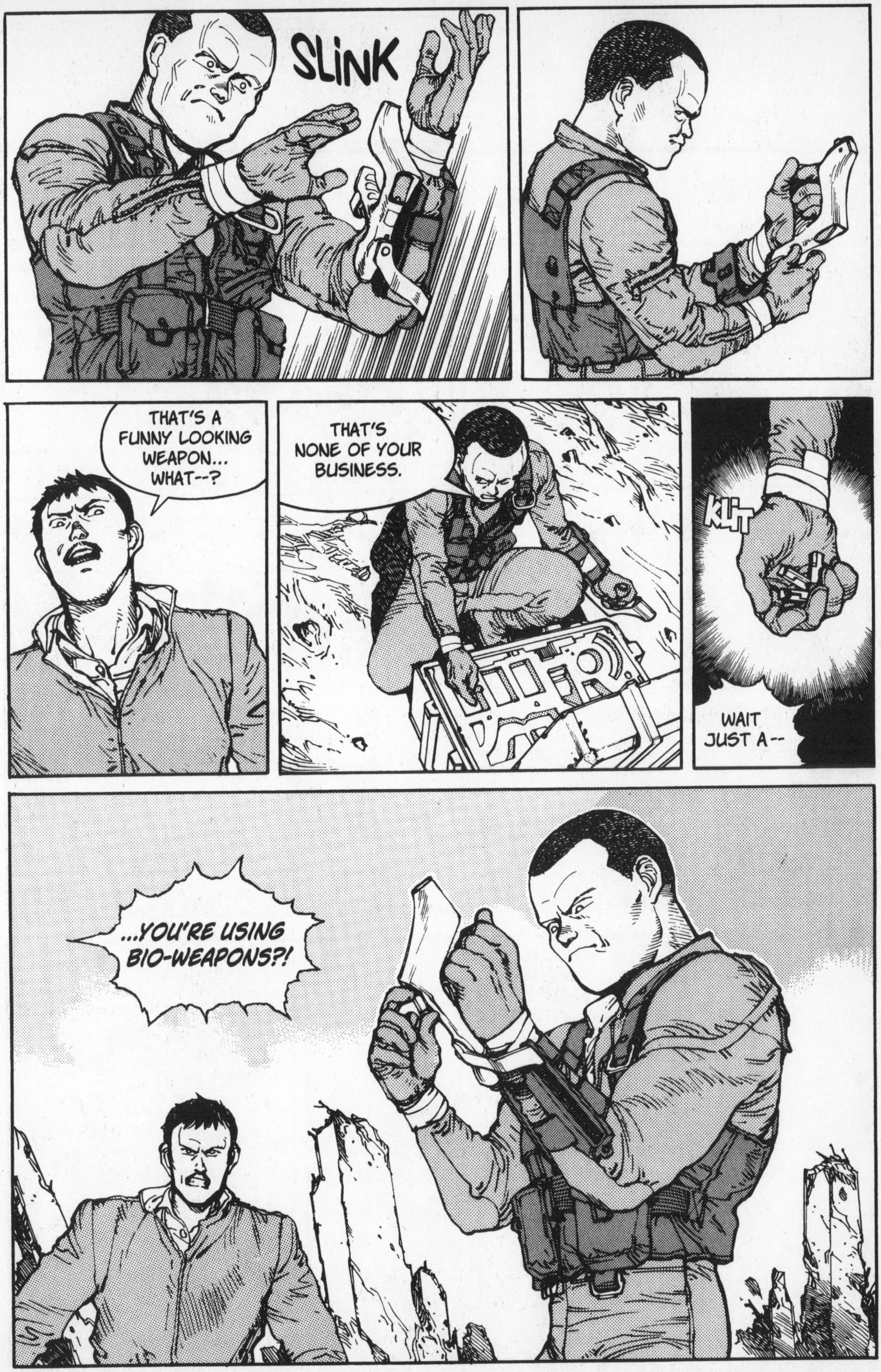
SLINK
THAT'S A FUNNY LOOKING WEAPON... WHAT--?
THAT'S NONE OF YOUR BUSINESS.
KLIT
WAIT JUST A--
...YOU'RE USING BIO-WEAPONS?!

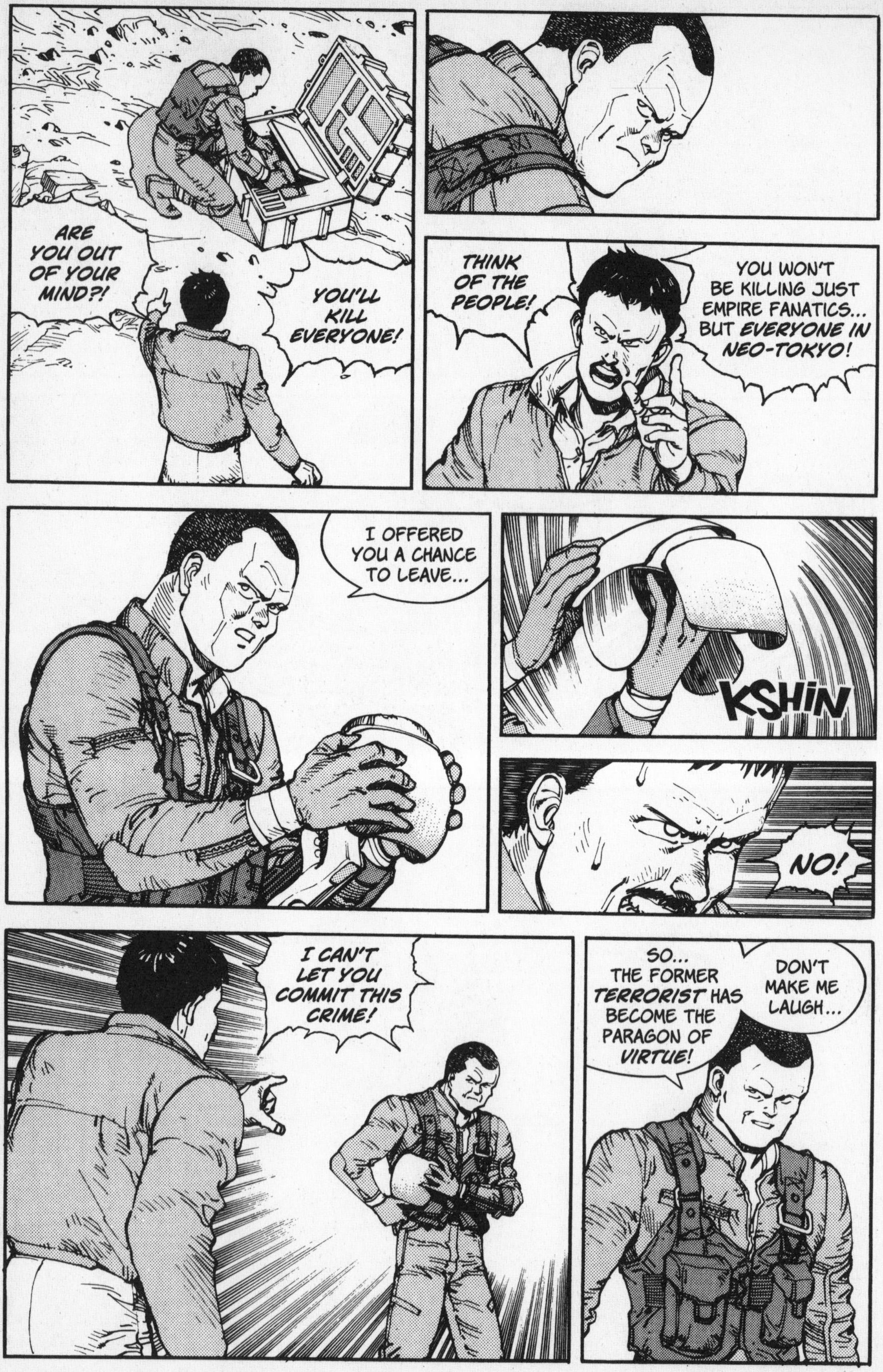
ARE YOU OUT OF YOUR MIND?!
YOU'LL KILL EVERYONE!
THINK OF THE PEOPLE!
YOU WON'T BE KILLING JUST EMPIRE FANATICS... BUT EVERYONE IN NEO-TOKYO!
I OFFERED YOU A CHANCE TO LEAVE...
KSHIN
NO!
I CAN'T LET YOU COMMIT THIS CRIME!
SO... THE FORMER TERRORIST HAS BECOME THE PARAGON OF VIRTUE!
DON'T MAKE ME LAUGH...

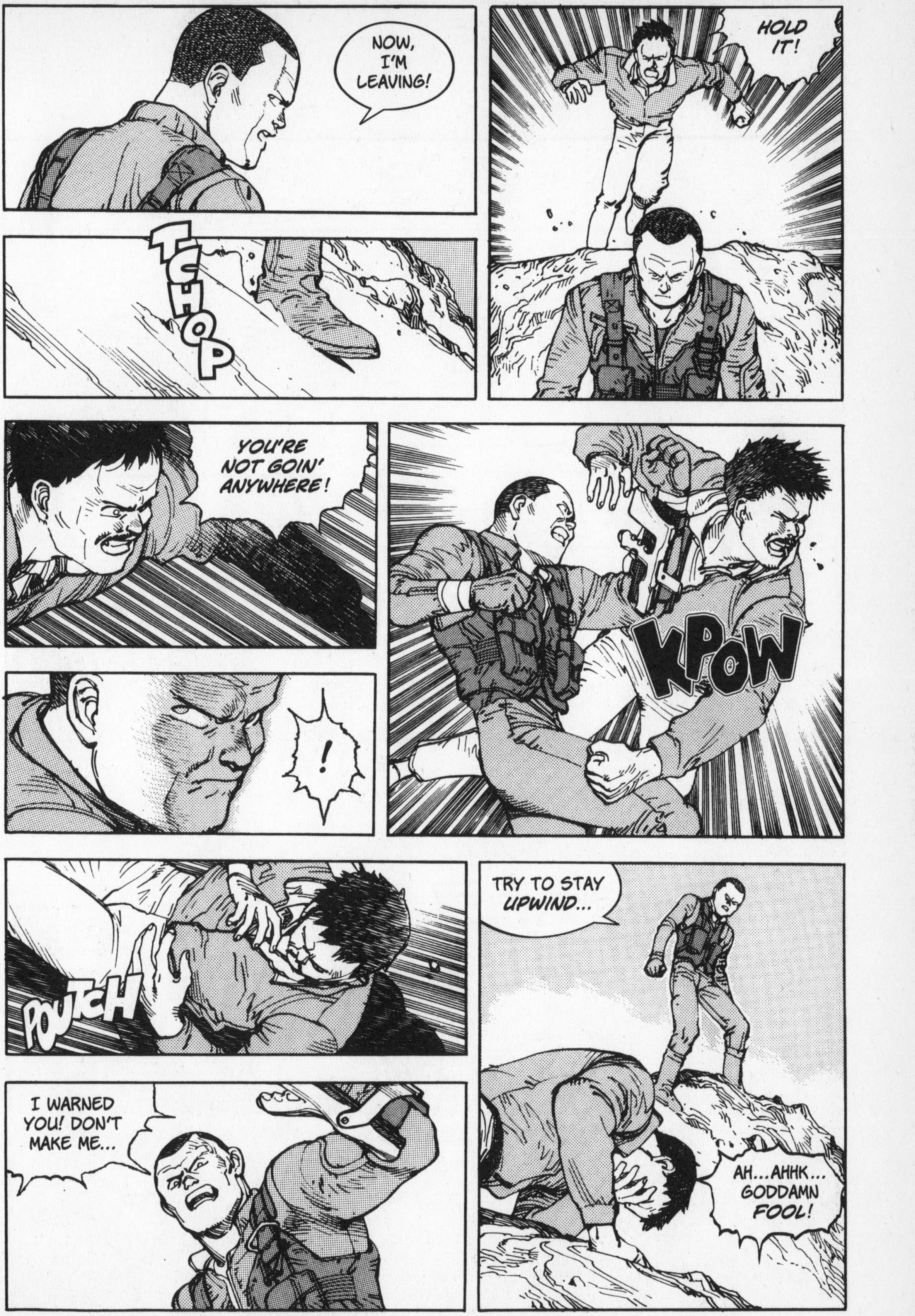
NOW, I'M LEAVING!
TCHOP
HOLD IT!
YOU'RE NOT GOIN' ANYWHERE!
!
KPOW
POUTCH
I WARNED YOU! DON'T MAKE ME...
TRY TO STAY UPWIND...
AH...AHHK... GODDAMN FOOL!

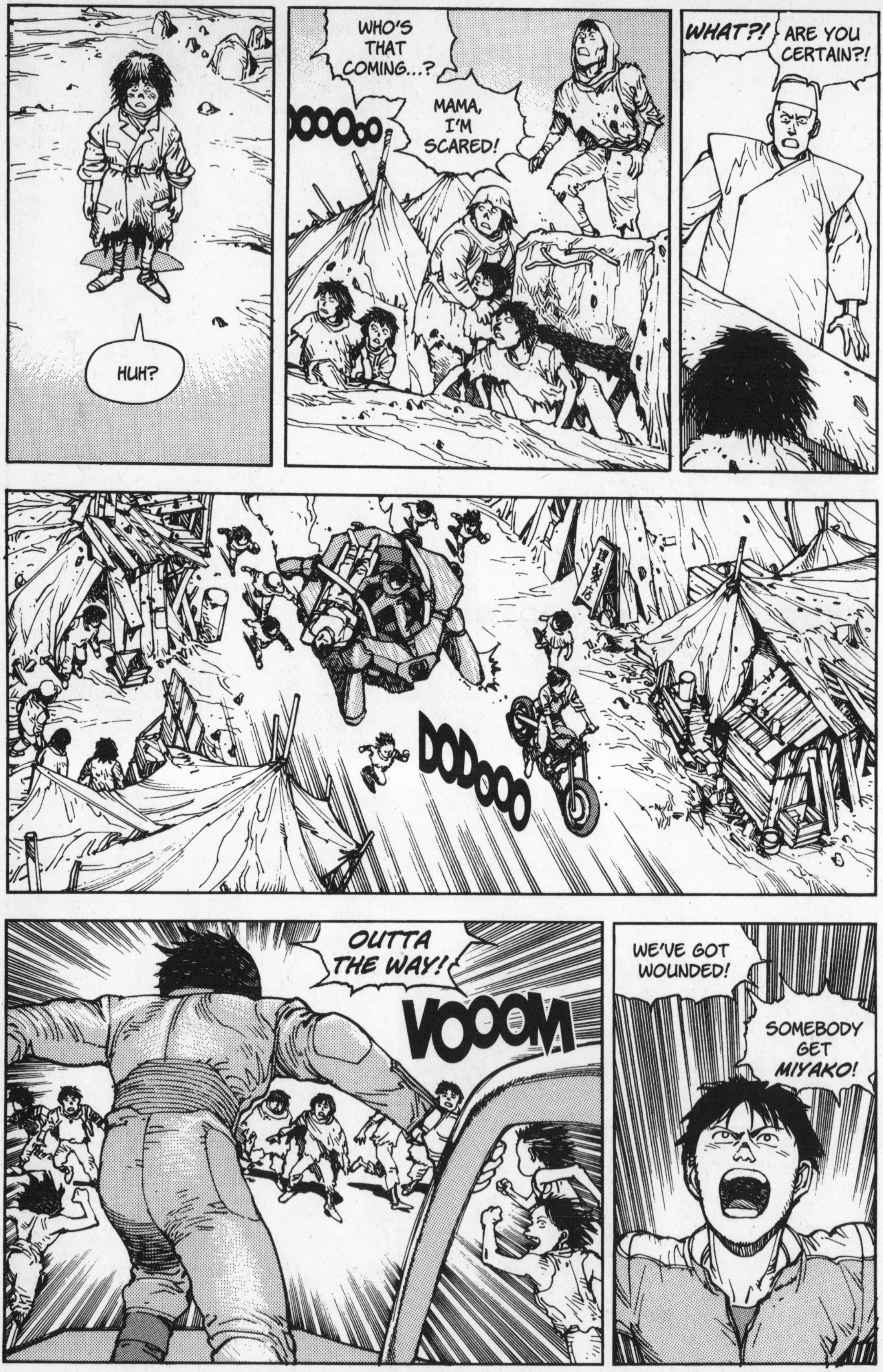
HUH?
WHO'S THAT COMING...?
DOOOOoo
MAMA, I'M SCARED!
WHAT?!
ARE YOU CERTAIN?!
DODOOO
OUTTA THE WAY!
VOOOM
WE'VE GOT WOUNDED!
SOMEBODY GET MIYAKO!

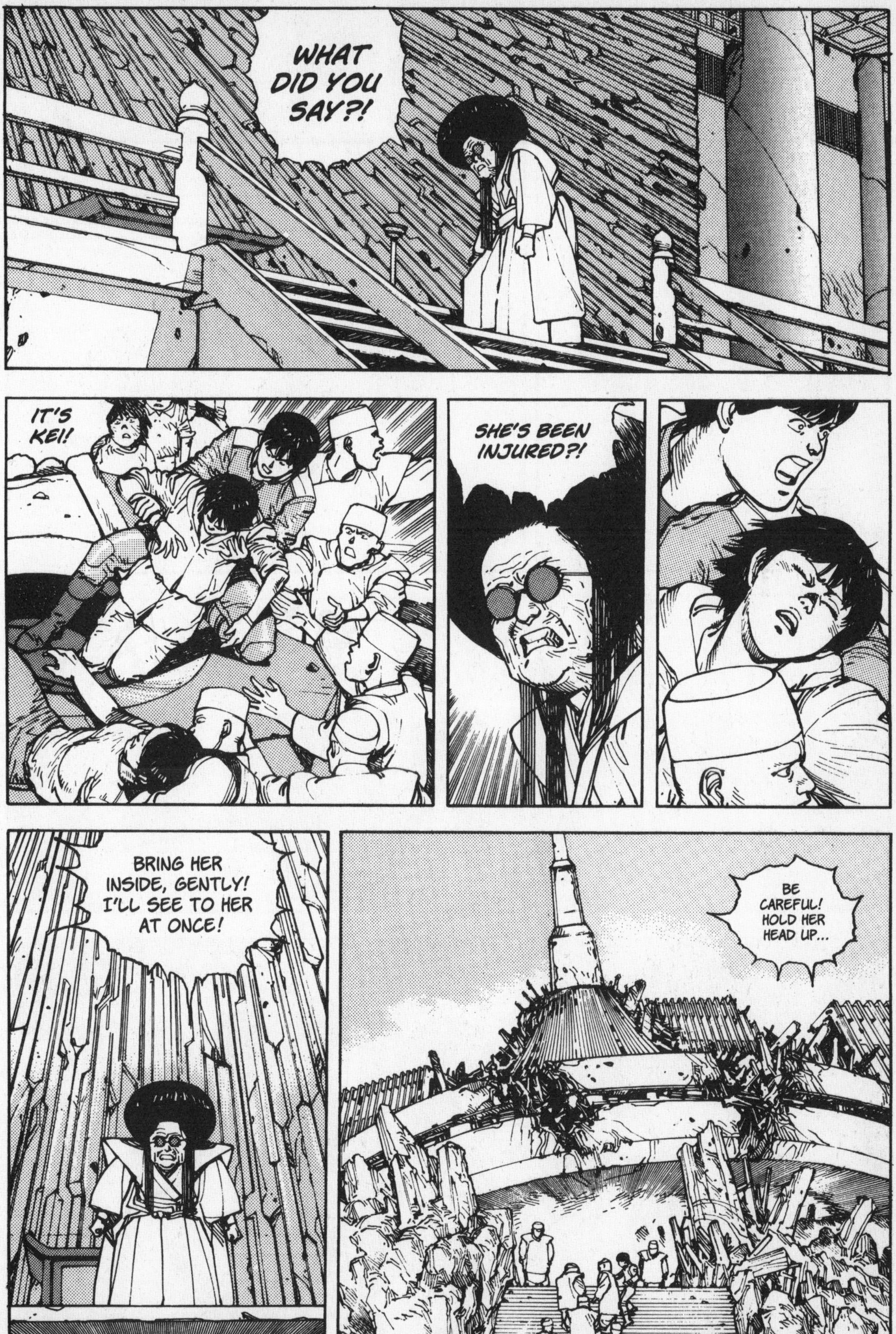
WHAT DID YOU SAY?!
IT'S KEI!
SHE'S BEEN INJURED?!
BRING HER INSIDE, GENTLY! I'LL SEE TO HER AT ONCE!
BE CAREFUL! HOLD HER HEAD UP...

Wiii Wiiii Wiii

TAP
TAP

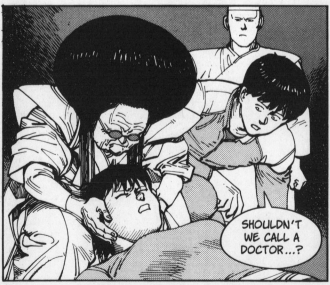

SHOULDN'T
WE CALL A
DOCTOR...?

...

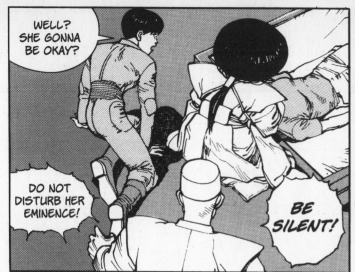

WELL? SHE GONNA BE OKAY?

DO NOT DISTURB HER EMINENCE!

BE SILENT!

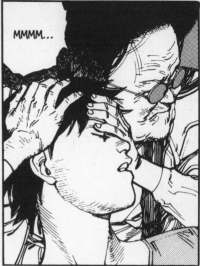

MMMM...

DON'T WORRY. IT IS NOT A SERIOUS HEMORRHAGE.

REALLY?!

SHE'S GONNA COME OUT OF IT!

THE WOUND IS ALREADY CLOSED.

IT WILL TAKE SOME TIME FOR THE BLOOD IN HER BRAIN TO DISSIPATE...

...BUT SHE'LL BE BETTER SOON.

KEI...

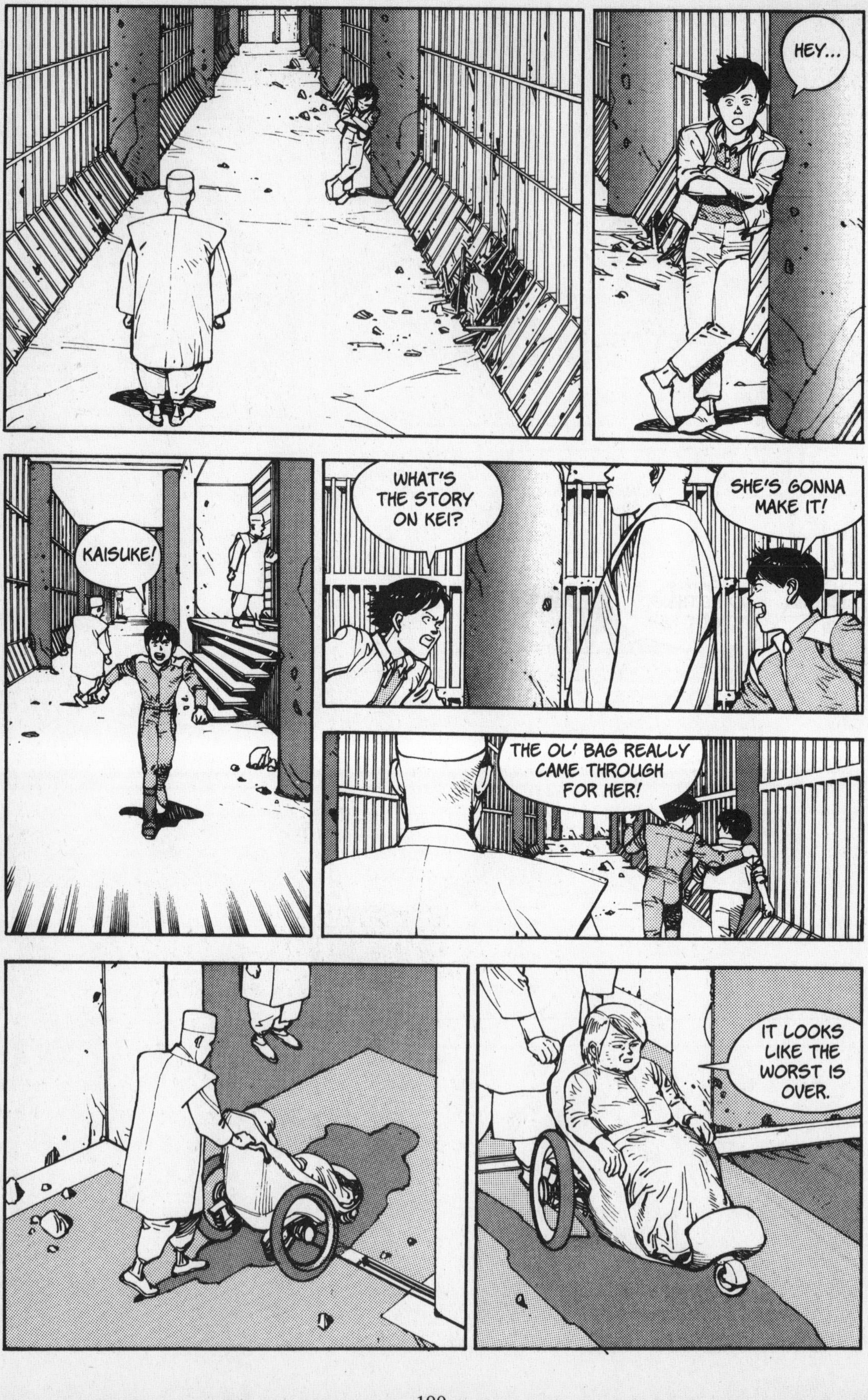
HEY...
KAISUKE!
WHAT'S THE STORY ON KEI?
SHE'S GONNA MAKE IT!
THE OL' BAG REALLY CAME THROUGH FOR HER!
IT LOOKS LIKE THE WORST IS OVER.

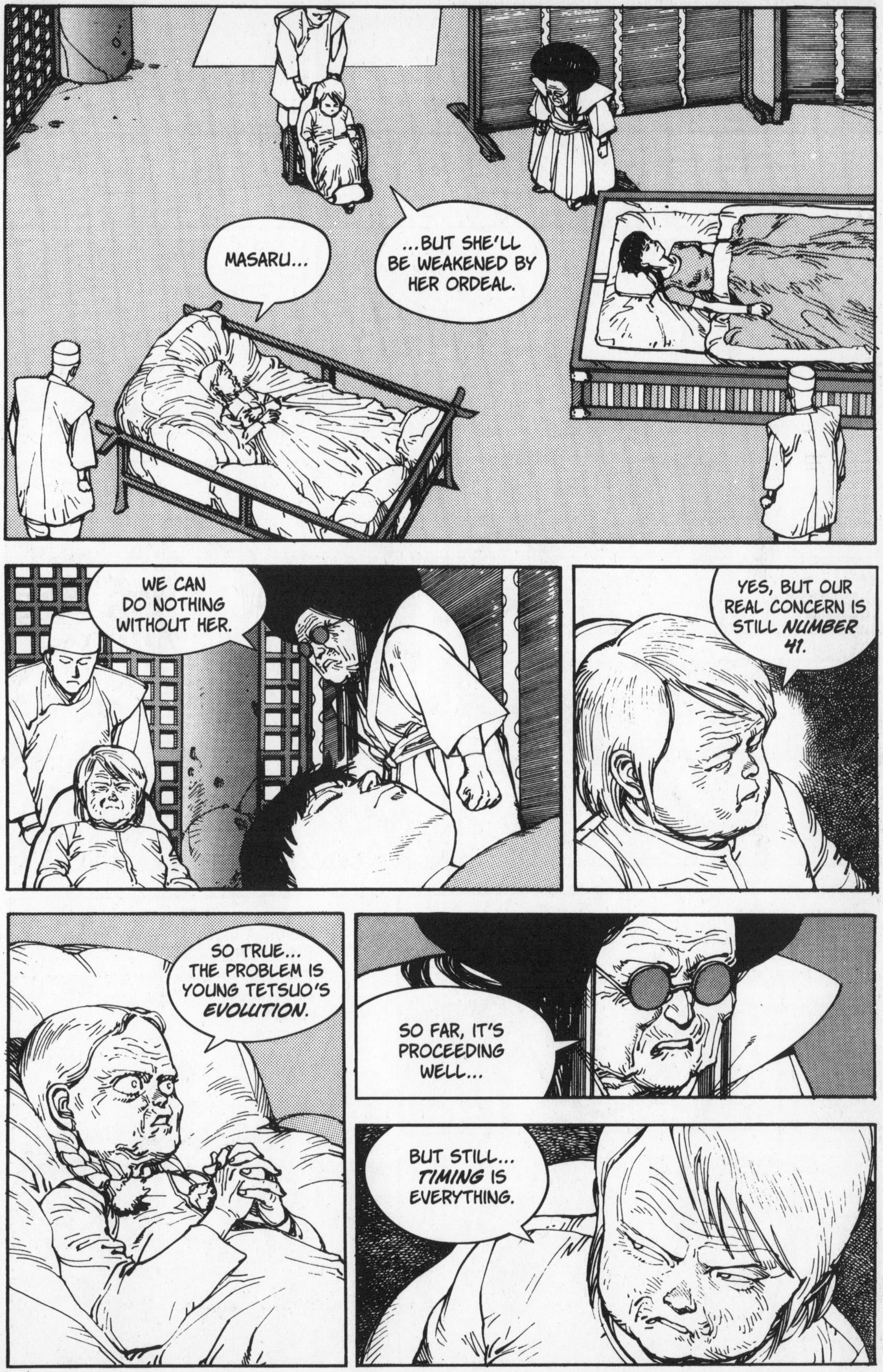
MASARU...
...BUT SHE'LL BE WEAKENED BY HER ORDEAL.
WE CAN DO NOTHING WITHOUT HER.
YES, BUT OUR REAL CONCERN IS STILL NUMBER 41.
SO TRUE... THE PROBLEM IS YOUNG TETSUO'S EVOLUTION.
SO FAR, IT'S PROCEEDING WELL...
BUT STILL... TIMING IS EVERYTHING.

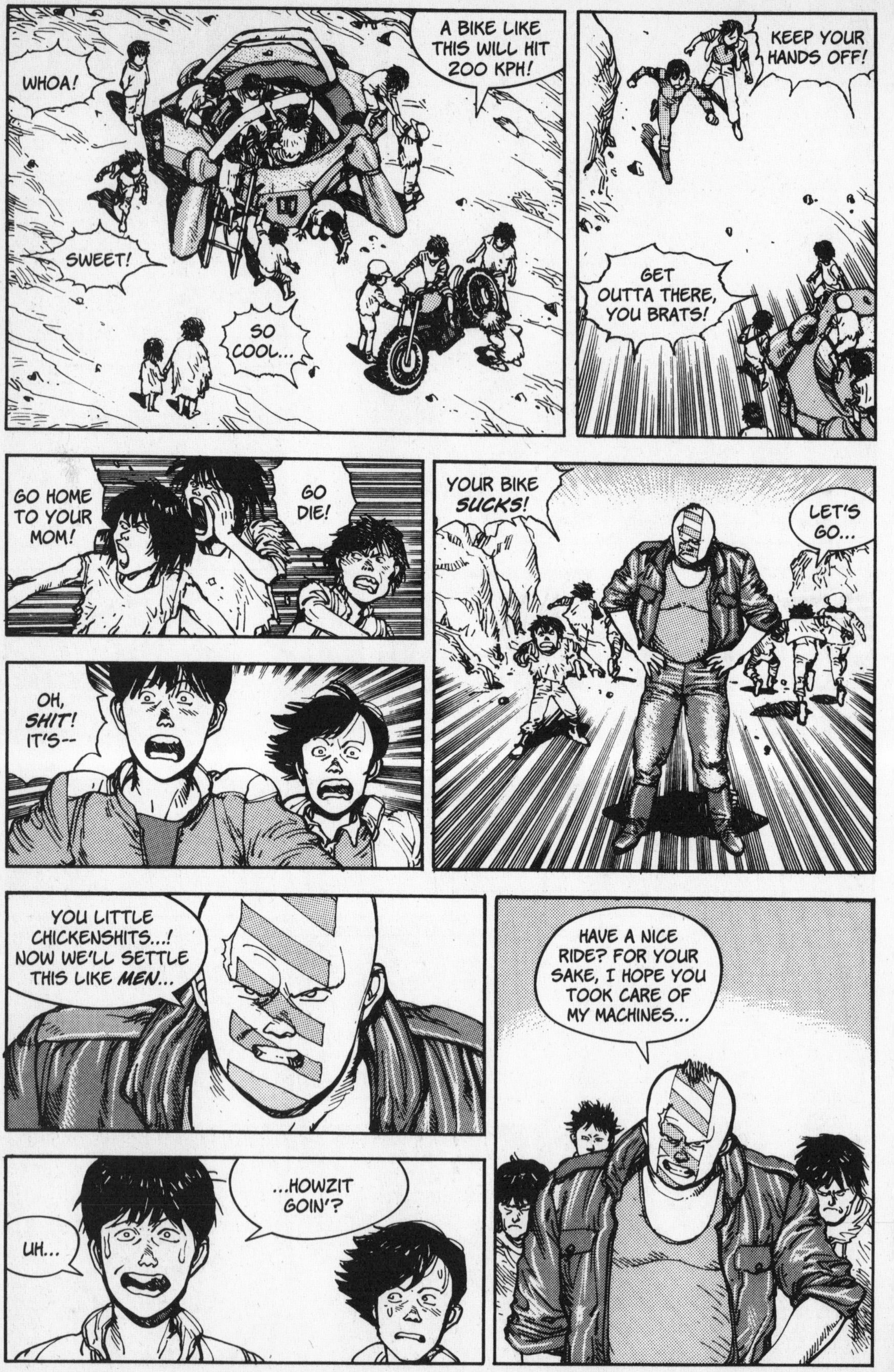
WHOA!
A BIKE LIKE THIS WILL HIT 200 KPH!
SWEET!
SO COOL...
KEEP YOUR HANDS OFF!
GET OUTTA THERE, YOU BRATS!
GO HOME TO YOUR MOM!
GO DIE!
OH, *SHIT*! IT'S--
YOUR BIKE *SUCKS*!
LET'S GO...
YOU LITTLE CHICKENSHITS...! NOW WE'LL SETTLE THIS LIKE *MEN*...
UH...
...HOWZIT GOIN'?
HAVE A NICE RIDE? FOR YOUR SAKE, I HOPE YOU TOOK CARE OF MY MACHINES...

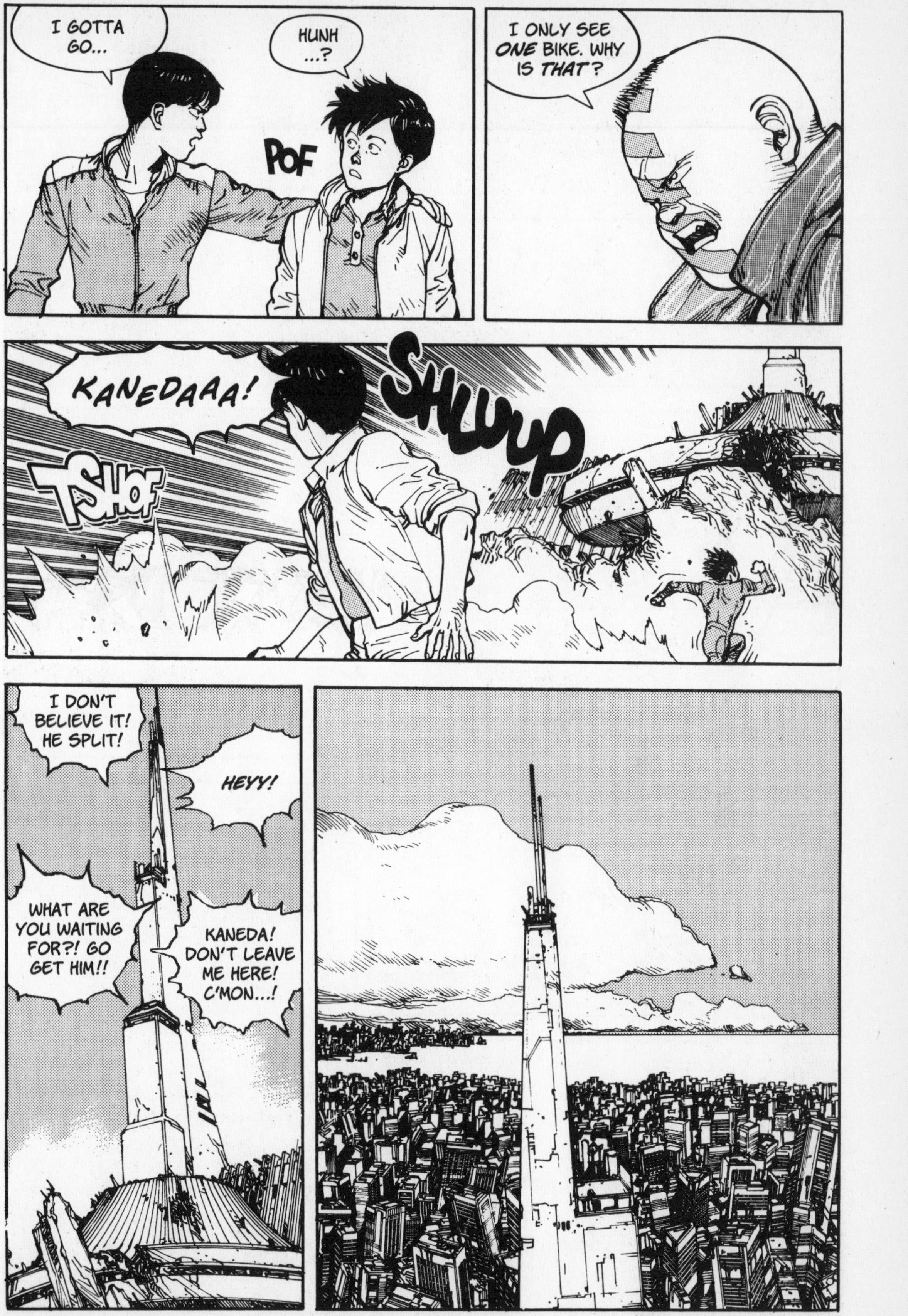
I GOTTA GO...
HUNH ...?
POF
I ONLY SEE *ONE* BIKE. WHY IS *THAT*?
KANEDAAA!
SHUUP
TSHOF
I DON'T BELIEVE IT! HE SPLIT!
HEYY!
WHAT ARE YOU WAITING FOR?! GO GET HIM!!
KANEDA! DON'T LEAVE ME HERE! C'MON...!

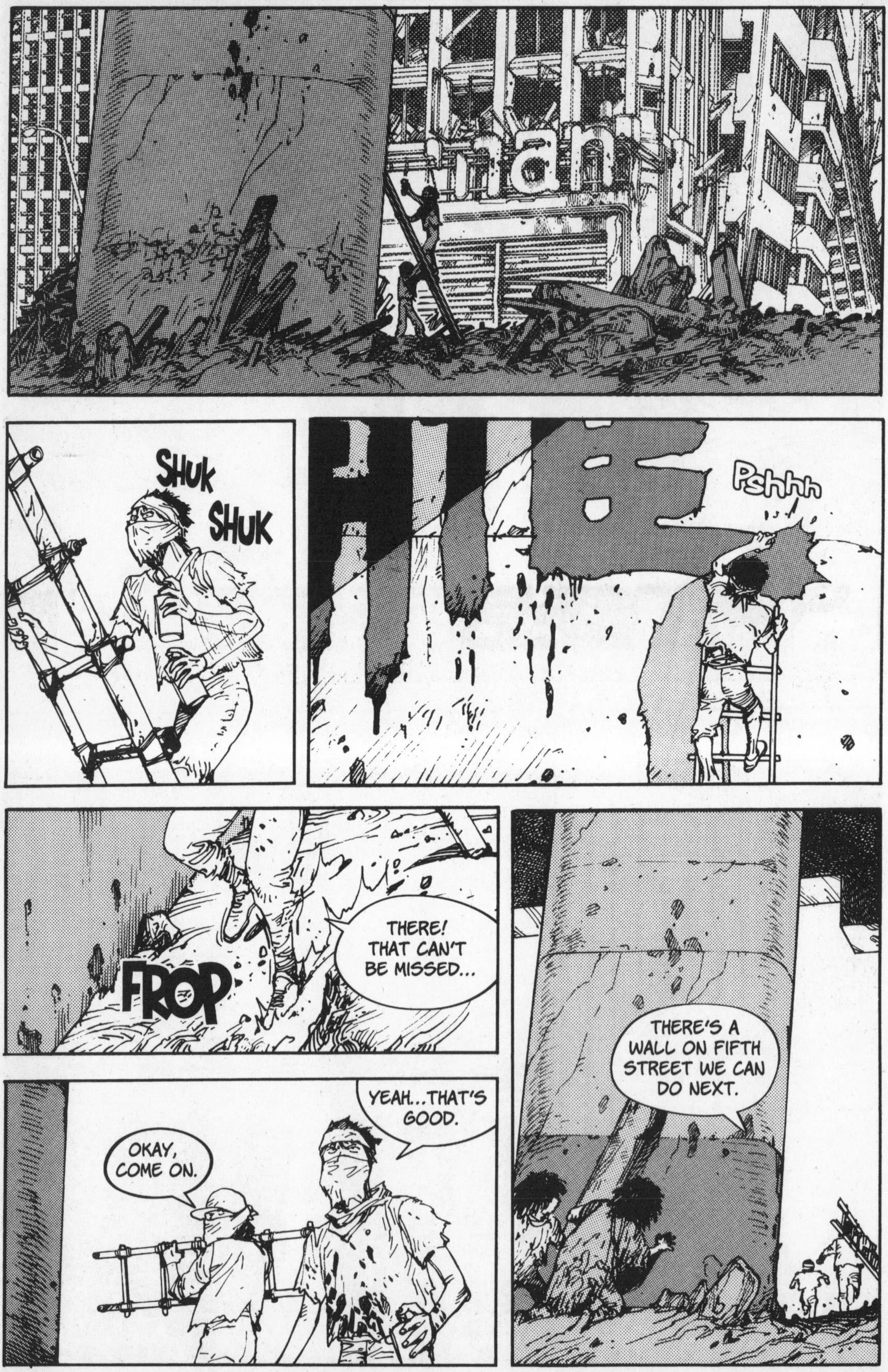
SHUK
SHUK
Pshhh
FROP
THERE! THAT CAN'T BE MISSED...
THERE'S A WALL ON FIFTH STREET WE CAN DO NEXT.
YEAH...THAT'S GOOD.
OKAY, COME ON.

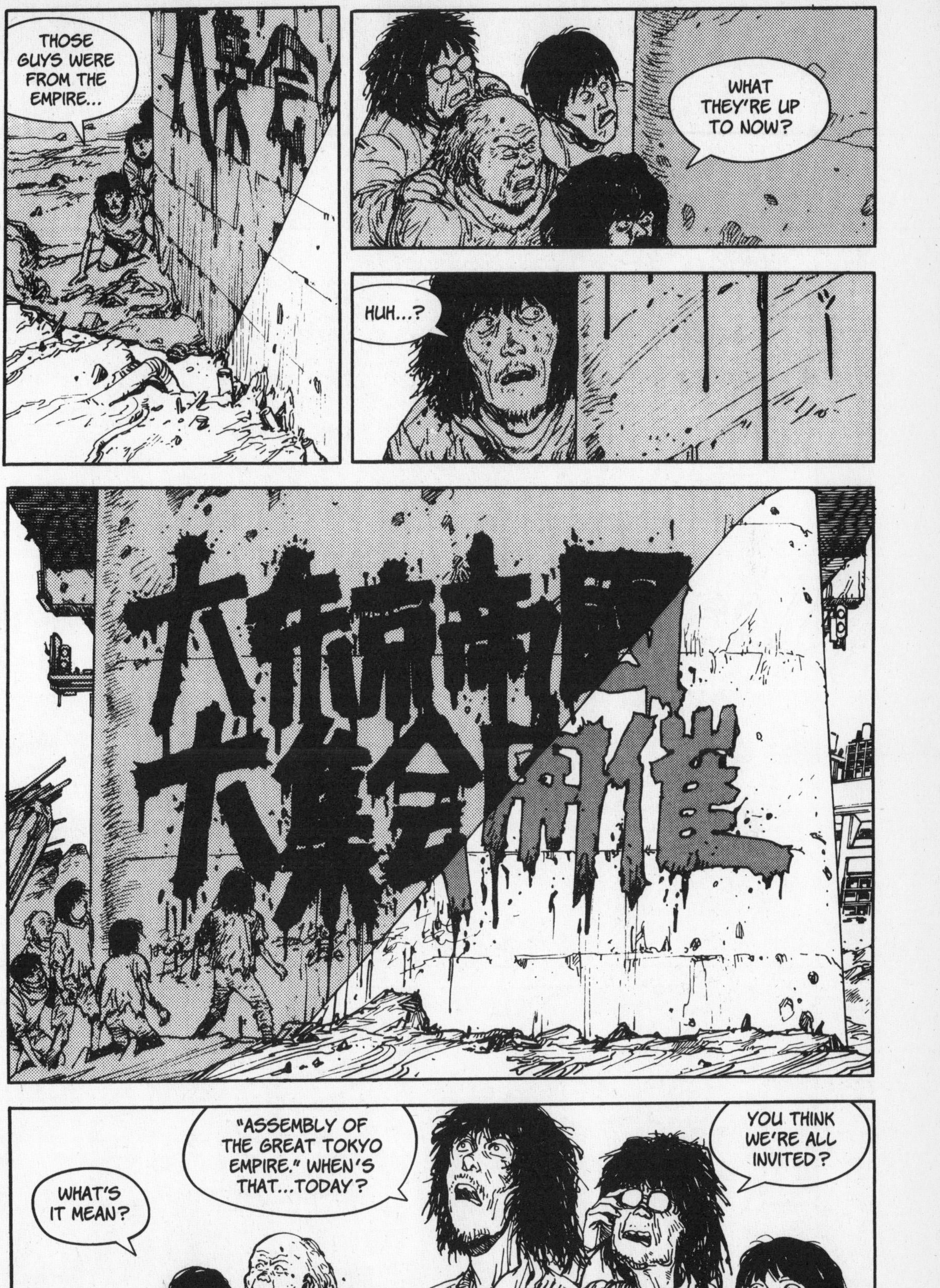
THOSE GUYS WERE FROM THE EMPIRE...
WHAT THEY'RE UP TO NOW?
HUH...?
大東京帝国
大集会開催
WHAT'S IT MEAN?
"ASSEMBLY OF THE GREAT TOKYO EMPIRE." WHEN'S THAT...TODAY?
YOU THINK WE'RE ALL INVITED?

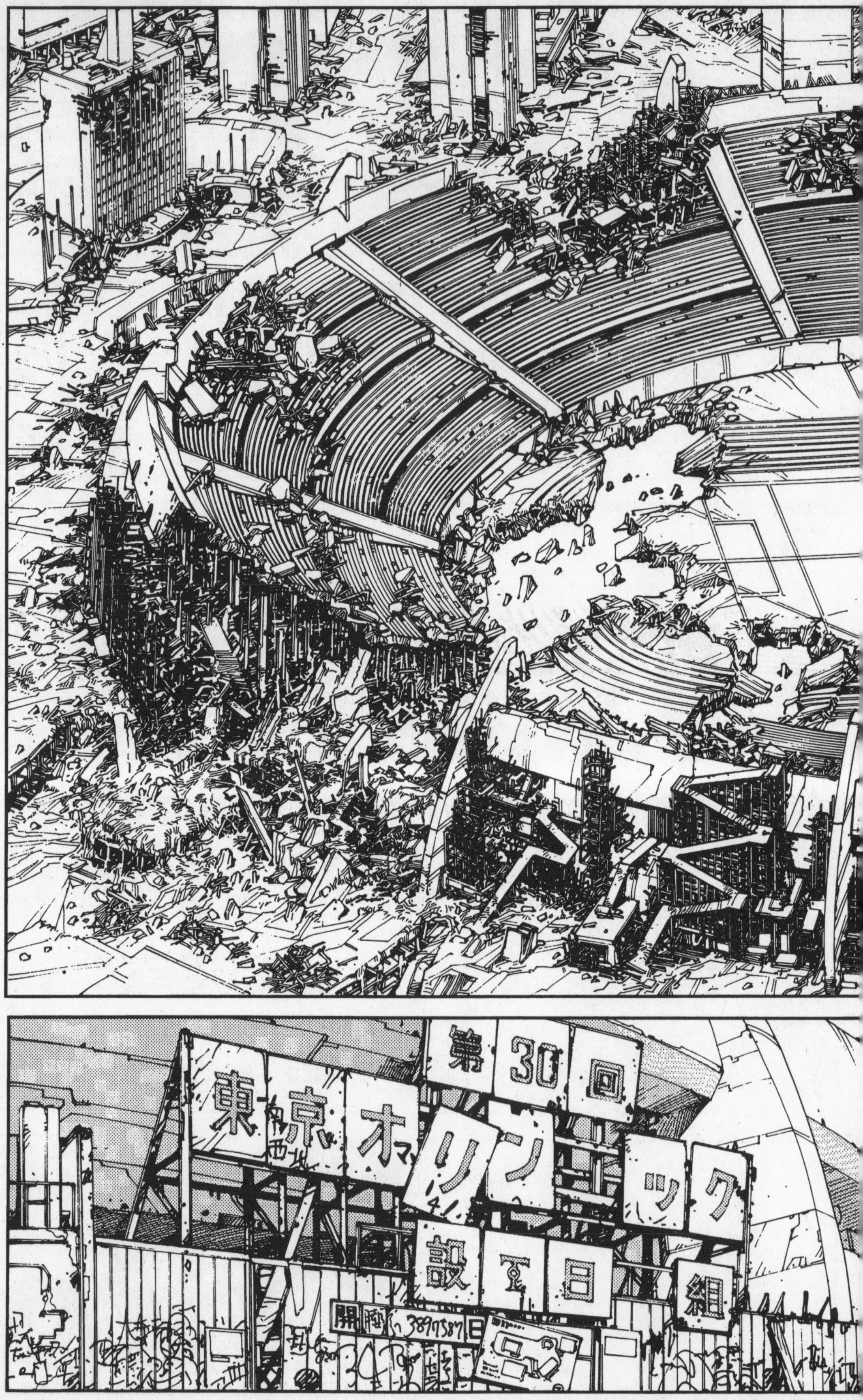
第30回
東京オリン ック

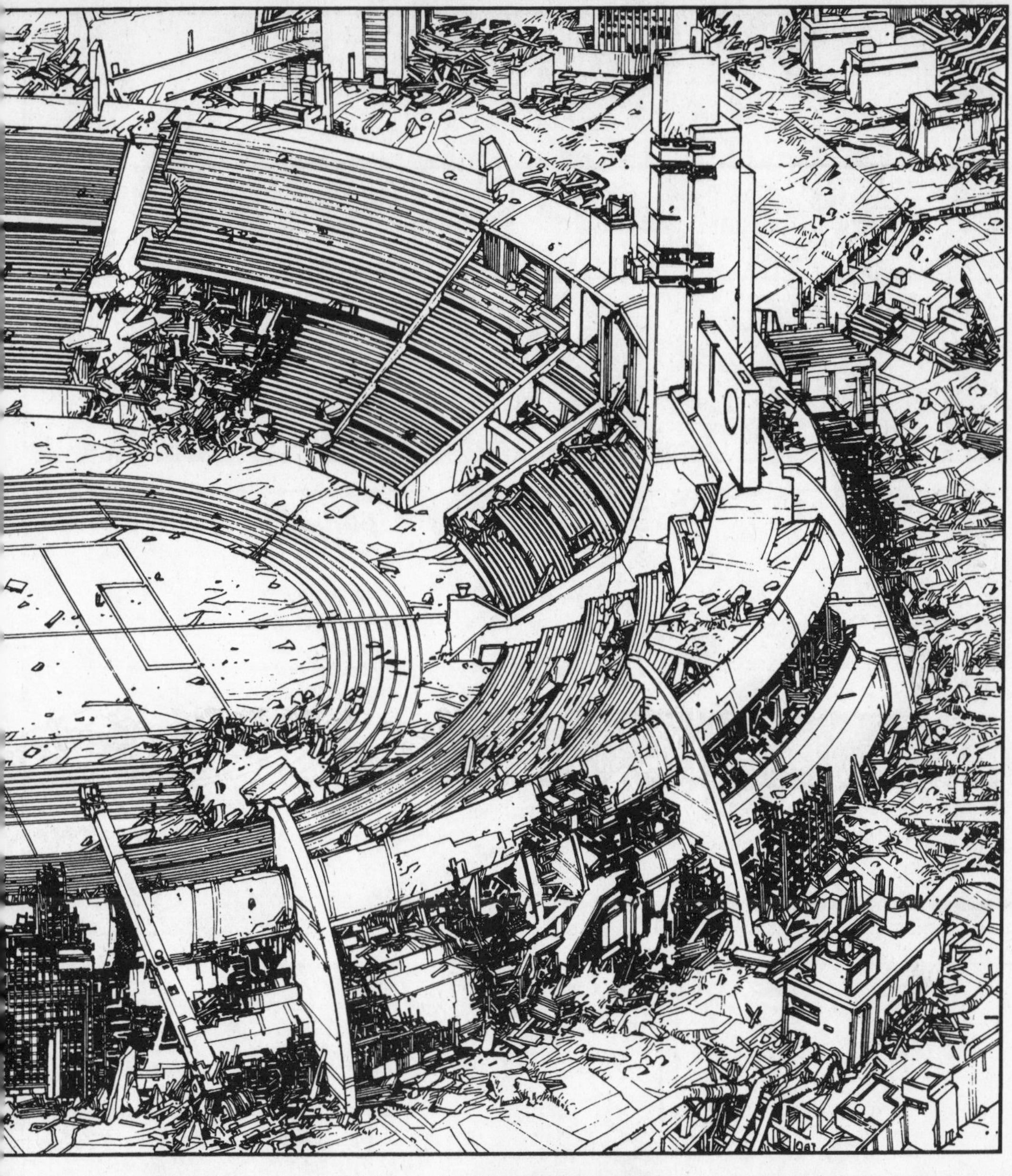

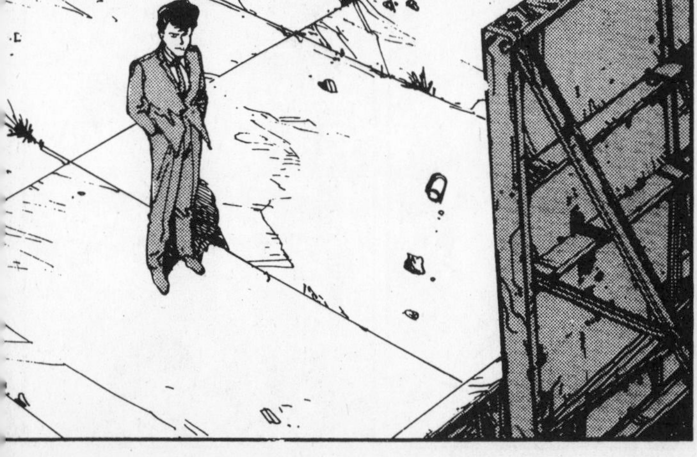

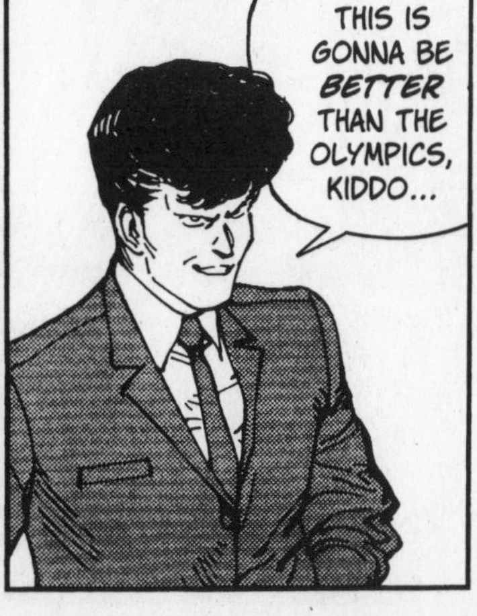
THIS IS GONNA BE BETTER THAN THE OLYMPICS, KIDDO...

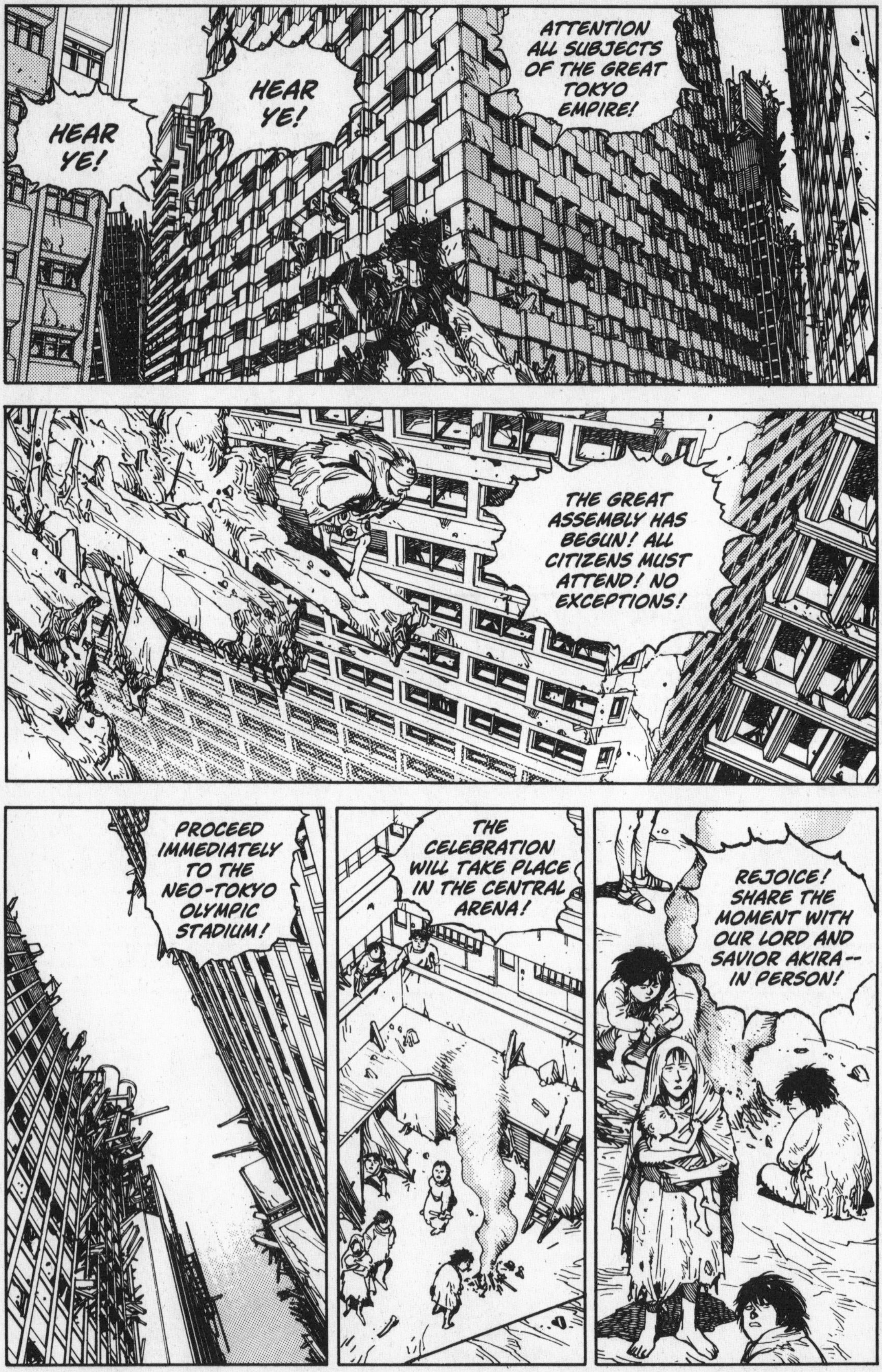
HEAR YE!
HEAR YE!
ATTENTION ALL SUBJECTS OF THE GREAT TOKYO EMPIRE!
THE GREAT ASSEMBLY HAS BEGUN! ALL CITIZENS MUST ATTEND! NO EXCEPTIONS!
PROCEED IMMEDIATELY TO THE NEO-TOKYO OLYMPIC STADIUM!
THE CELEBRATION WILL TAKE PLACE IN THE CENTRAL ARENA!
REJOICE! SHARE THE MOMENT WITH OUR LORD AND SAVIOR AKIRA-- IN PERSON!

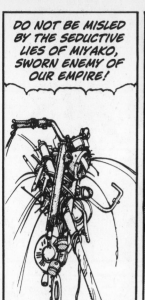

DO NOT BE MISLED BY THE SEDUCTIVE LIES OF MIYAKO, SWORN ENEMY OF OUR EMPIRE!

LET US UNITE UNDER THE SAME BANNER...!

...LET US SHOW OUR LOYALTY TO OUR GREAT LORD AKIRA.

THE FIGHT CONTINUES! WE HAVE NO OTHER CHOICE!

PSSS

PROVE YOUR RESPECT AND YOUR TOTAL DEVOTION -- INCLUDING YOU, YOU *DIRTY LITTLE SHIT!*

THOSE WHO CAN WORK, HELP WITH THE CONSTRUCTION!

THOSE WHO CAN SPEAK, GO OUT AND SPREAD THE WORD!

ALL MUST PARTICIPATE! WITH EVERYONE'S ASSISTANCE, WE CANNOT FAIL!

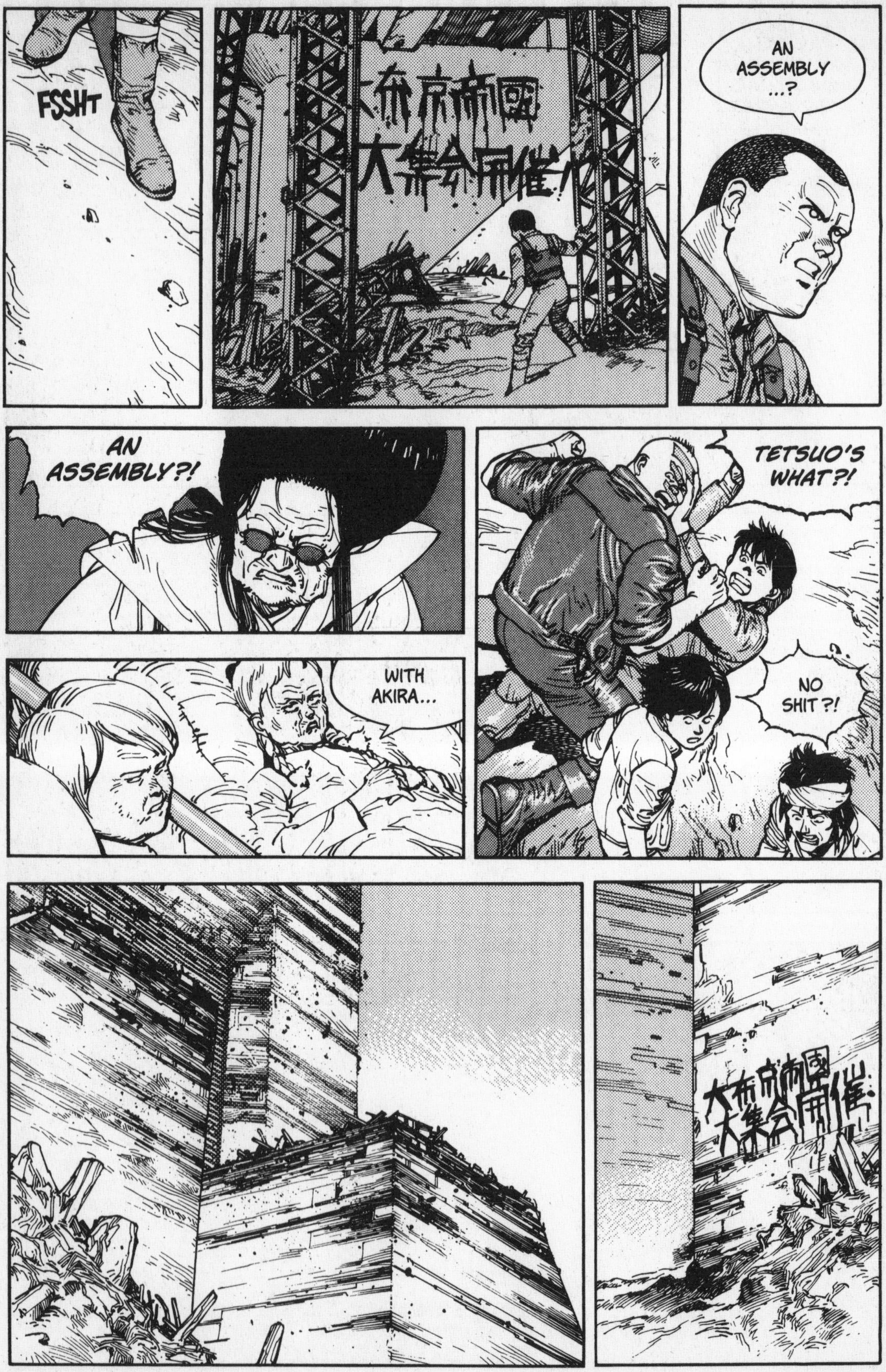
FSSHT
大東京帝國
大集会開催!!
AN ASSEMBLY ...?
AN ASSEMBLY?!
WITH AKIRA...
TETSUO'S WHAT?!
NO SHIT?!
大東京帝國
大集会開催!

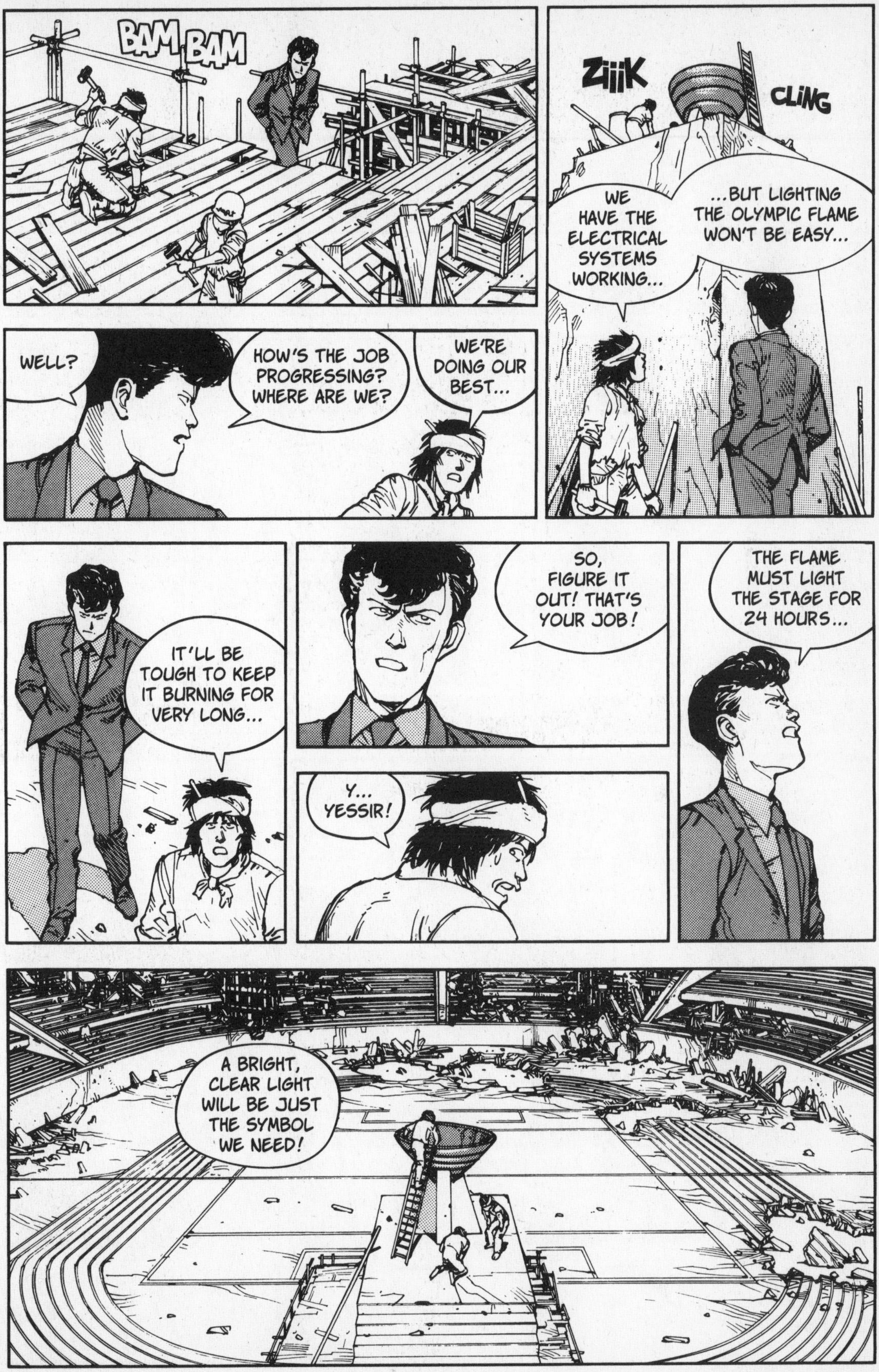
BAM BAM
ZiiiK
CLING
WE HAVE THE ELECTRICAL SYSTEMS WORKING...
...BUT LIGHTING THE OLYMPIC FLAME WON'T BE EASY...
WELL?
HOW'S THE JOB PROGRESSING? WHERE ARE WE?
WE'RE DOING OUR BEST...
IT'LL BE TOUGH TO KEEP IT BURNING FOR VERY LONG...
SO, FIGURE IT OUT! THAT'S YOUR JOB!
Y... YESSIR!
THE FLAME MUST LIGHT THE STAGE FOR 24 HOURS...
A BRIGHT, CLEAR LIGHT WILL BE JUST THE SYMBOL WE NEED!

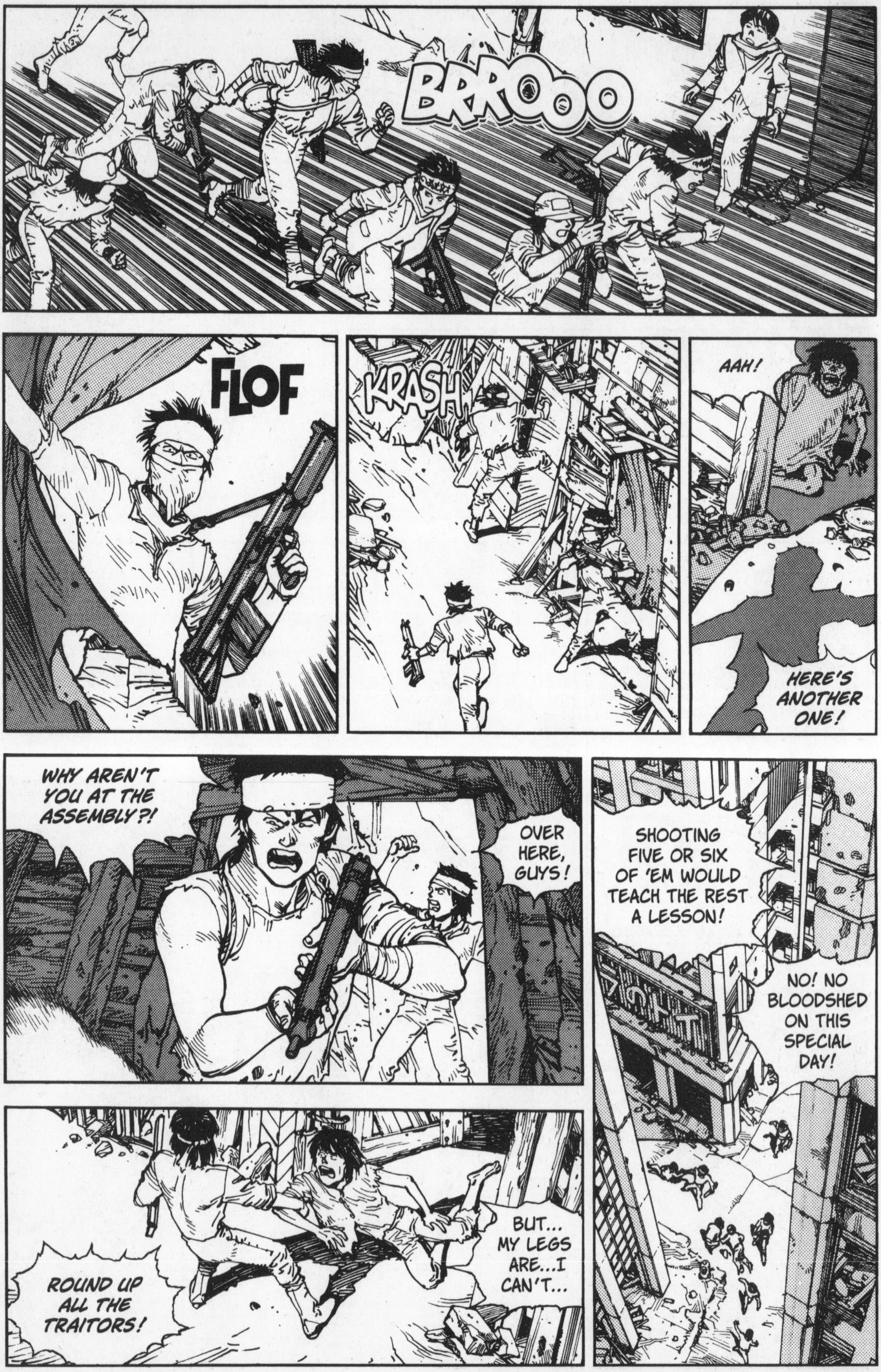
BRROOO
FLOF
KRASH
AAH!
HERE'S ANOTHER ONE!
WHY AREN'T YOU AT THE ASSEMBLY?!
OVER HERE, GUYS!
ROUND UP ALL THE TRAITORS!
BUT... MY LEGS ARE...I CAN'T...
SHOOTING FIVE OR SIX OF 'EM WOULD TEACH THE REST A LESSON!
NO! NO BLOODSHED ON THIS SPECIAL DAY!

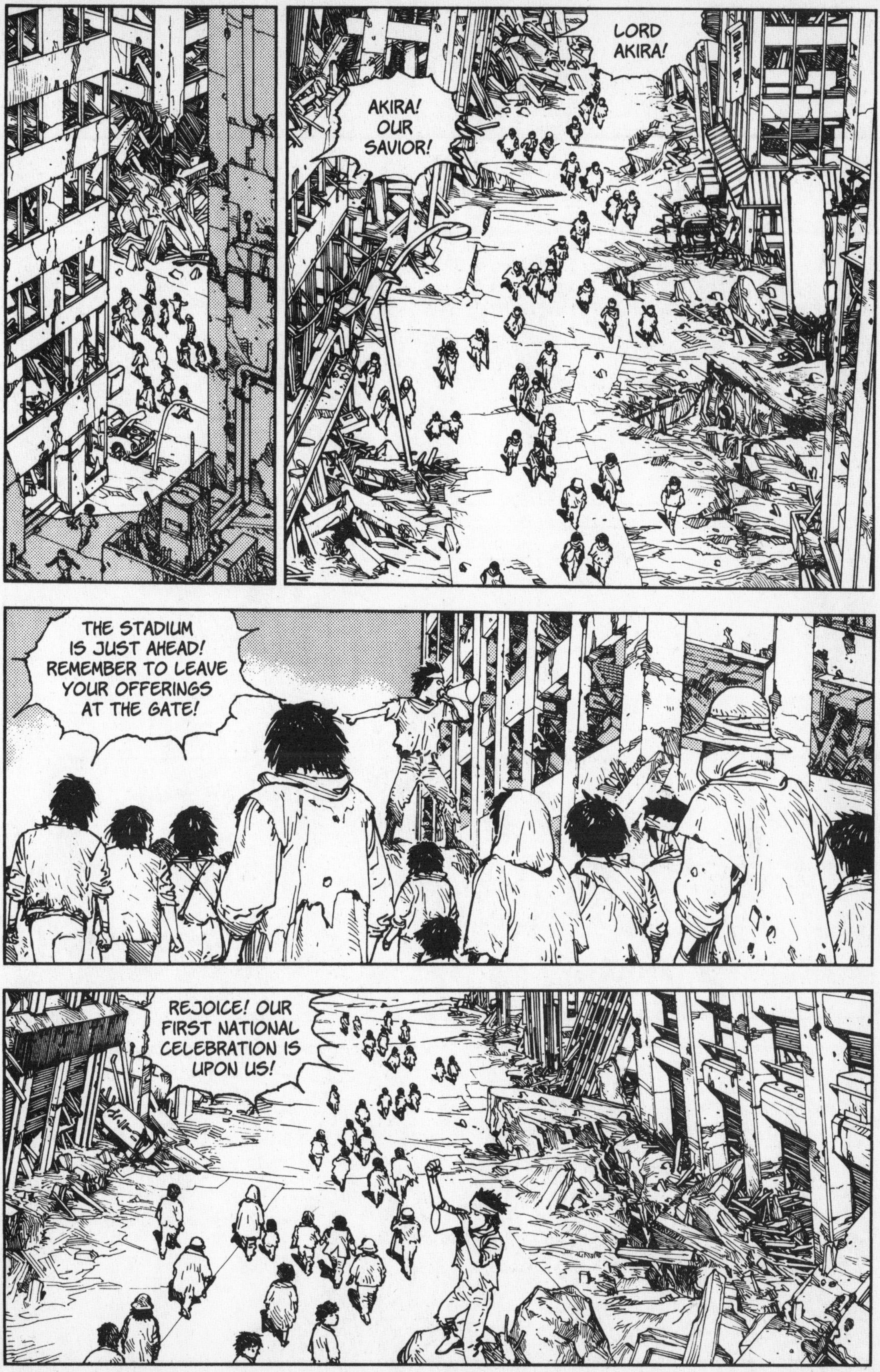
LORD AKIRA!
AKIRA! OUR SAVIOR!
THE STADIUM IS JUST AHEAD! REMEMBER TO LEAVE YOUR OFFERINGS AT THE GATE!
REJOICE! OUR FIRST NATIONAL CELEBRATION IS UPON US!

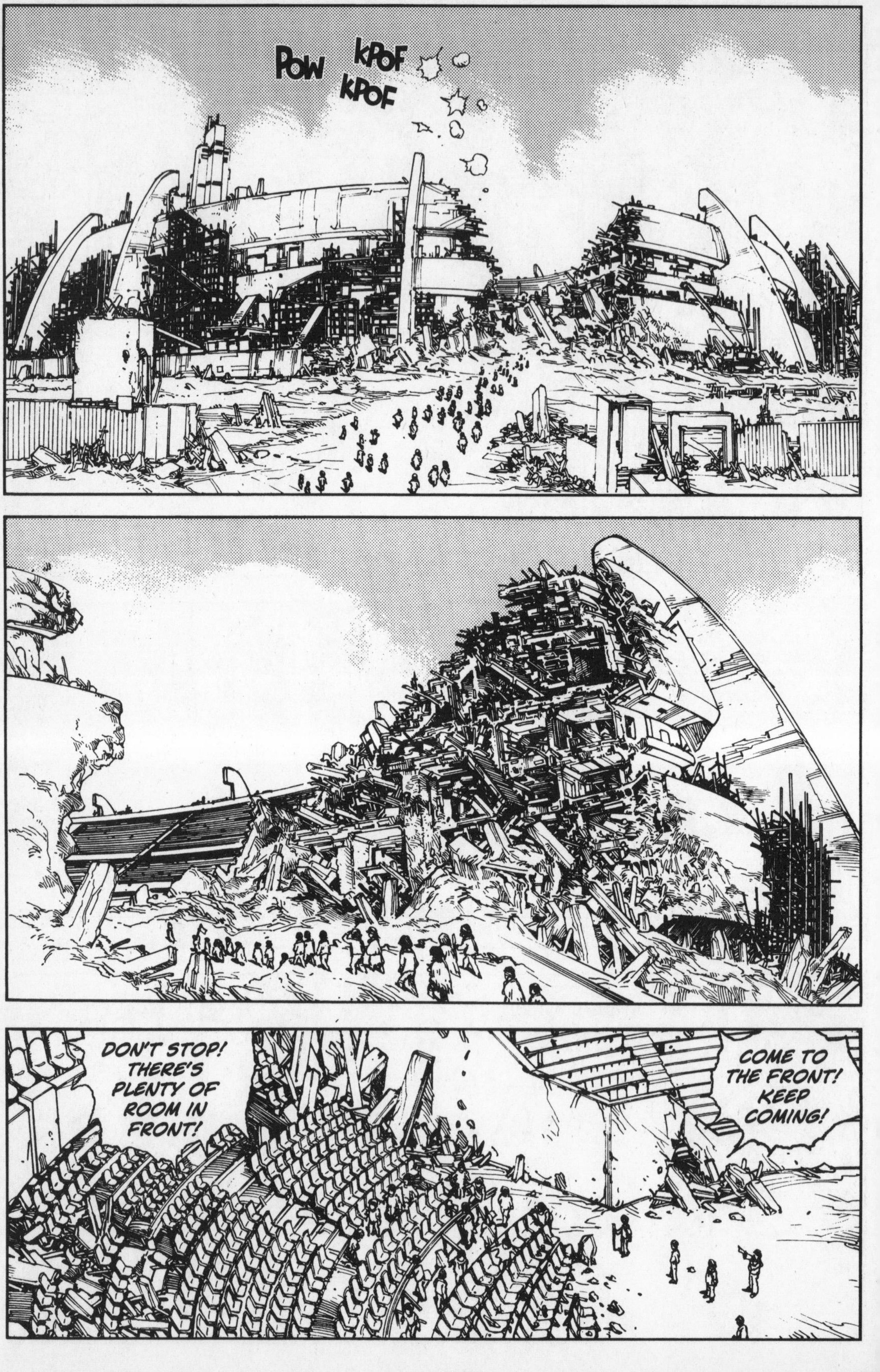
POW
KPOF
KPOF
DON'T STOP! THERE'S PLENTY OF ROOM IN FRONT!
COME TO THE FRONT! KEEP COMING!

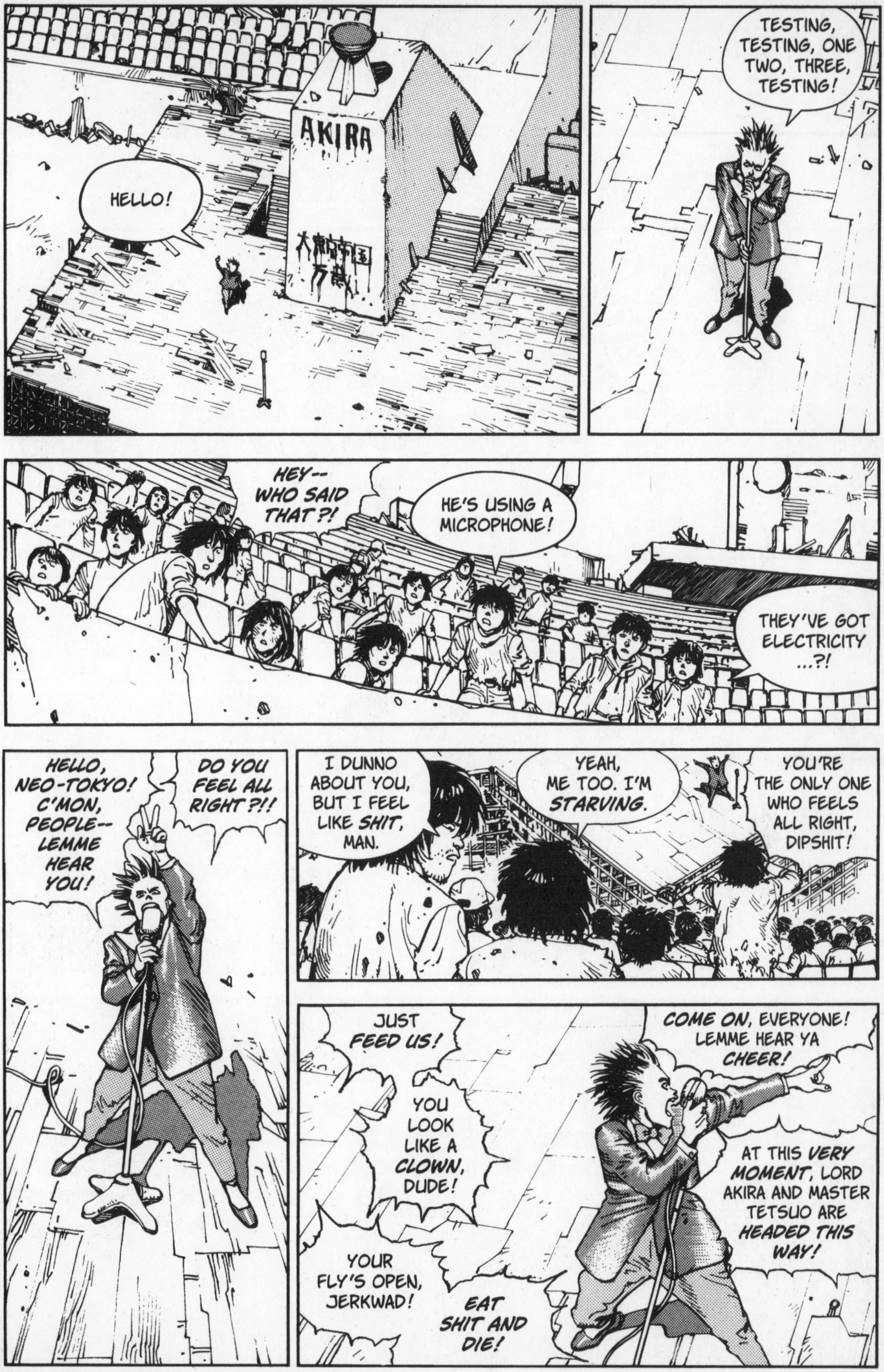
AKIRA
HELLO!
TESTING, TESTING, ONE TWO, THREE, TESTING!
HEY-- WHO SAID THAT?!
HE'S USING A MICROPHONE!
THEY'VE GOT ELECTRICITY ...?!
HELLO, NEO-TOKYO! C'MON, PEOPLE-- LEMME HEAR YOU!
DO YOU FEEL ALL RIGHT?!!
I DUNNO ABOUT YOU, BUT I FEEL LIKE SHIT, MAN.
YEAH, ME TOO. I'M STARVING.
YOU'RE THE ONLY ONE WHO FEELS ALL RIGHT, DIPSHIT!
JUST FEED US!
COME ON, EVERYONE! LEMME HEAR YA CHEER!
YOU LOOK LIKE A CLOWN, DUDE!
AT THIS VERY MOMENT, LORD AKIRA AND MASTER TETSUO ARE HEADED THIS WAY!
YOUR FLY'S OPEN, JERKWAD!
EAT SHIT AND DIE!

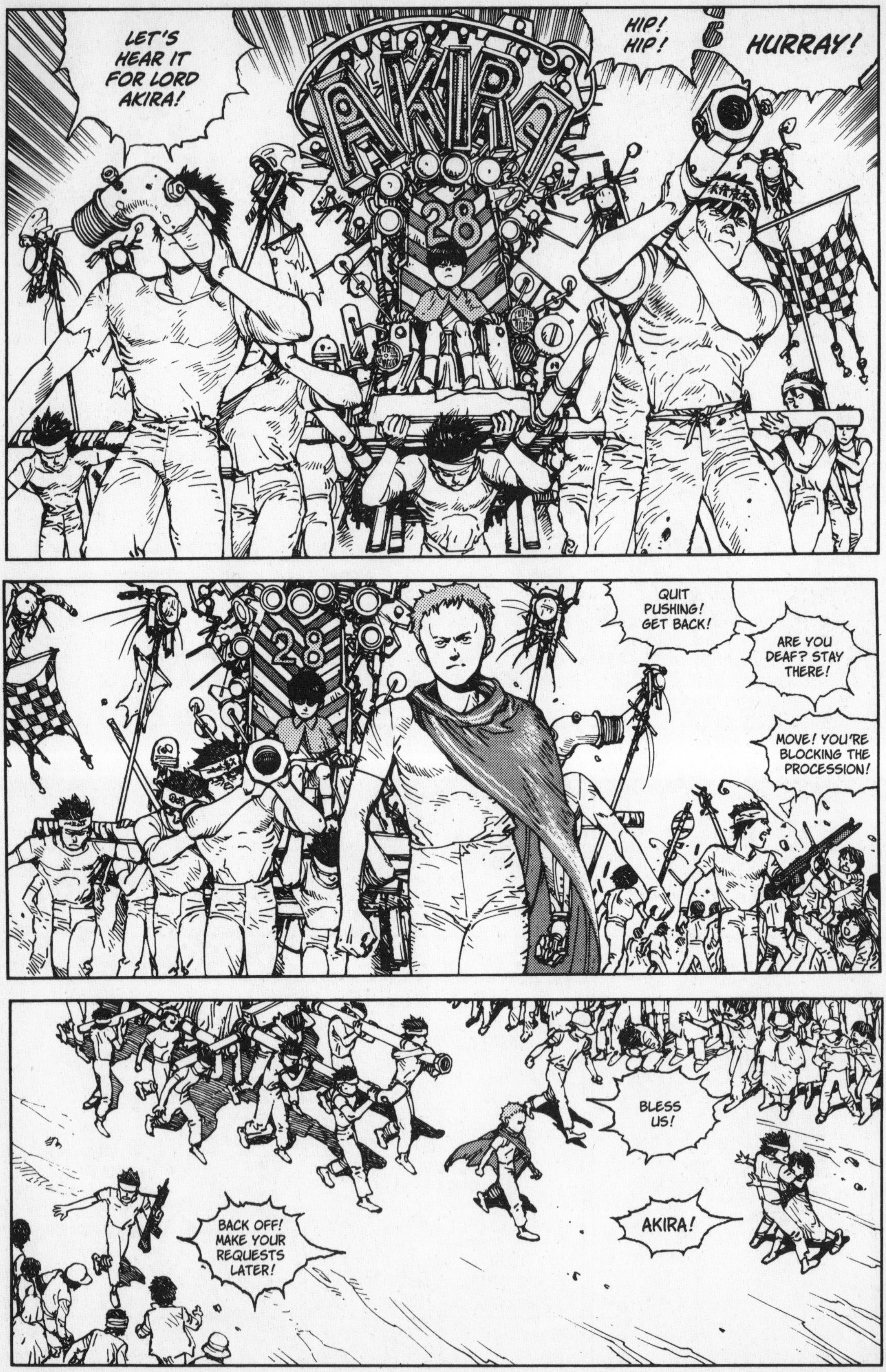
LET'S HEAR IT FOR LORD AKIRA!
HIP! HIP!
HURRAY!
QUIT PUSHING! GET BACK!
ARE YOU DEAF? STAY THERE!
MOVE! YOU'RE BLOCKING THE PROCESSION!
BLESS US!
BACK OFF! MAKE YOUR REQUESTS LATER!
AKIRA!

AKIRA! LONG LIFE TO YOU!

HERE HE COMES!

HOORAY!

DAMN! I CAN'T GET BY THEM!

I'VE GOTTA GET TO THE ARENA BEFORE IT'S TOO LATE...

I CAN'T FIRE IT HERE...

...UNLESS...

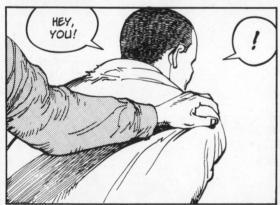

HEY, YOU!

!

I OWE YOU THIS!

THOK

HUHN?

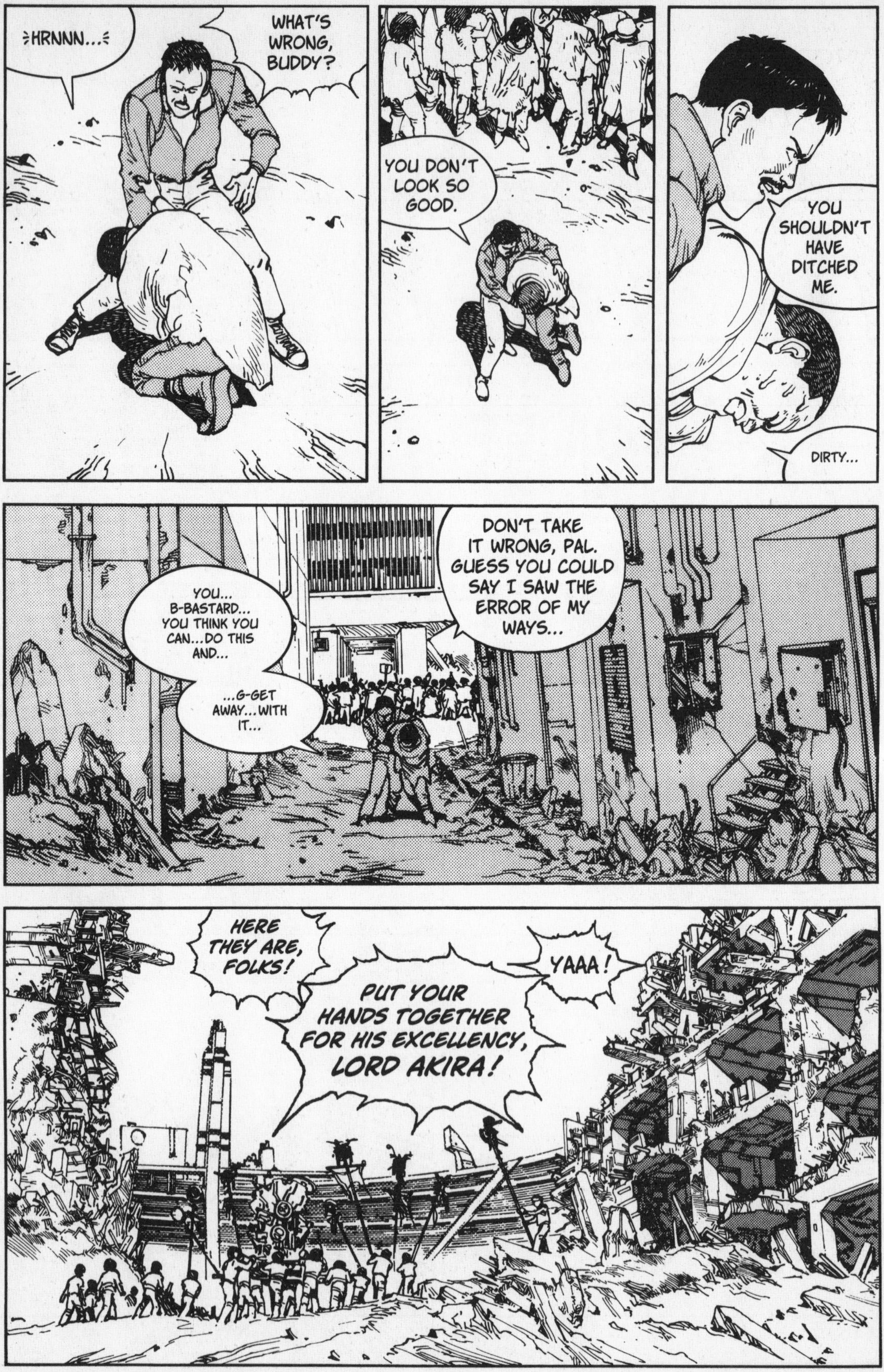
HRNNN...
WHAT'S WRONG, BUDDY?
YOU DON'T LOOK SO GOOD.
YOU SHOULDN'T HAVE DITCHED ME.
DIRTY...
YOU... B-BASTARD... YOU THINK YOU CAN...DO THIS AND...
...G-GET AWAY...WITH IT...
DON'T TAKE IT WRONG, PAL. GUESS YOU COULD SAY I SAW THE ERROR OF MY WAYS...
HERE THEY ARE, FOLKS!
PUT YOUR HANDS TOGETHER FOR HIS EXCELLENCY, LORD AKIRA!
YAAA!

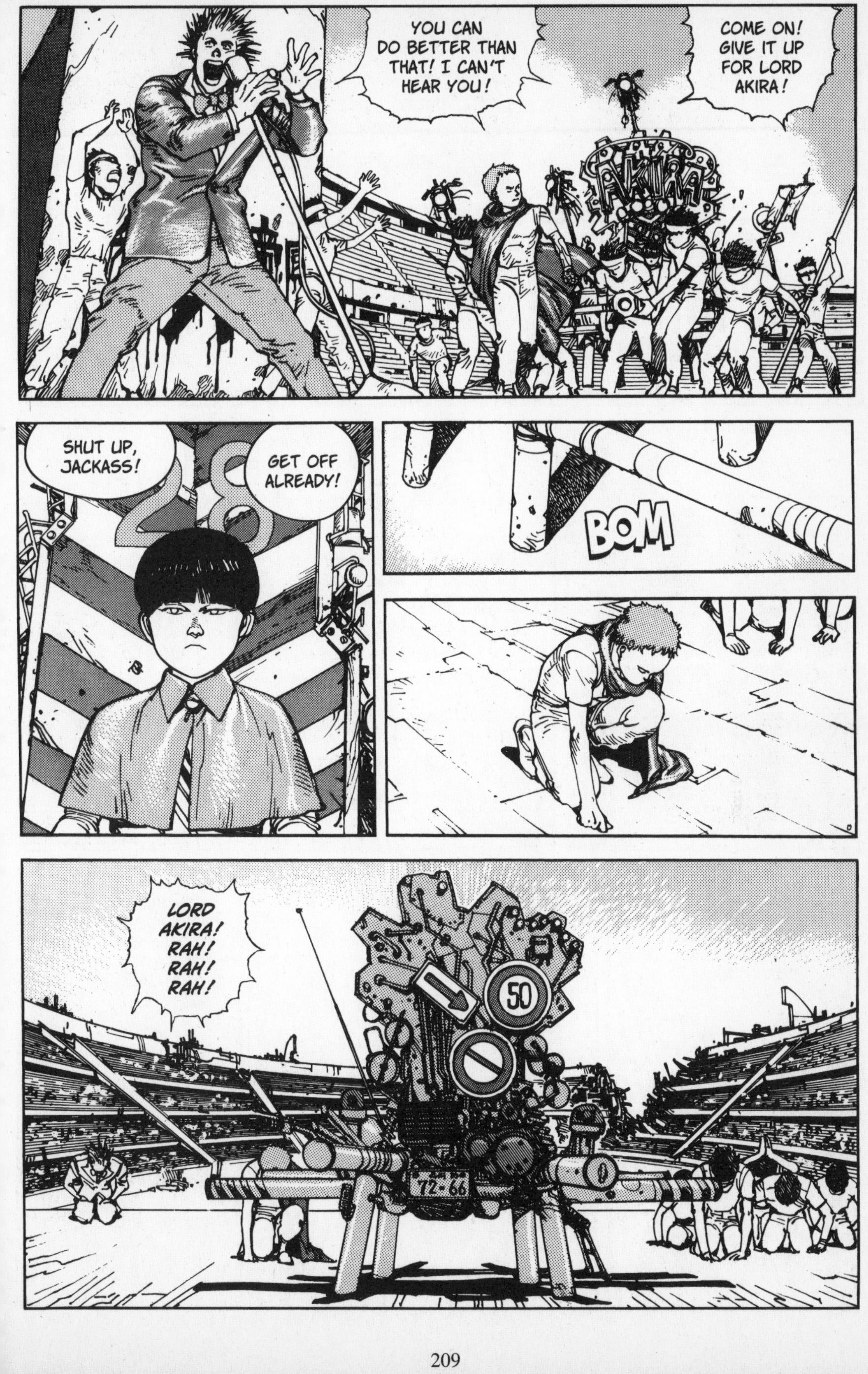
YOU CAN DO BETTER THAN THAT! I CAN'T HEAR YOU!
COME ON! GIVE IT UP FOR LORD AKIRA!
SHUT UP, JACKASS!
GET OFF ALREADY!
BOM
LORD AKIRA! RAH! RAH! RAH!

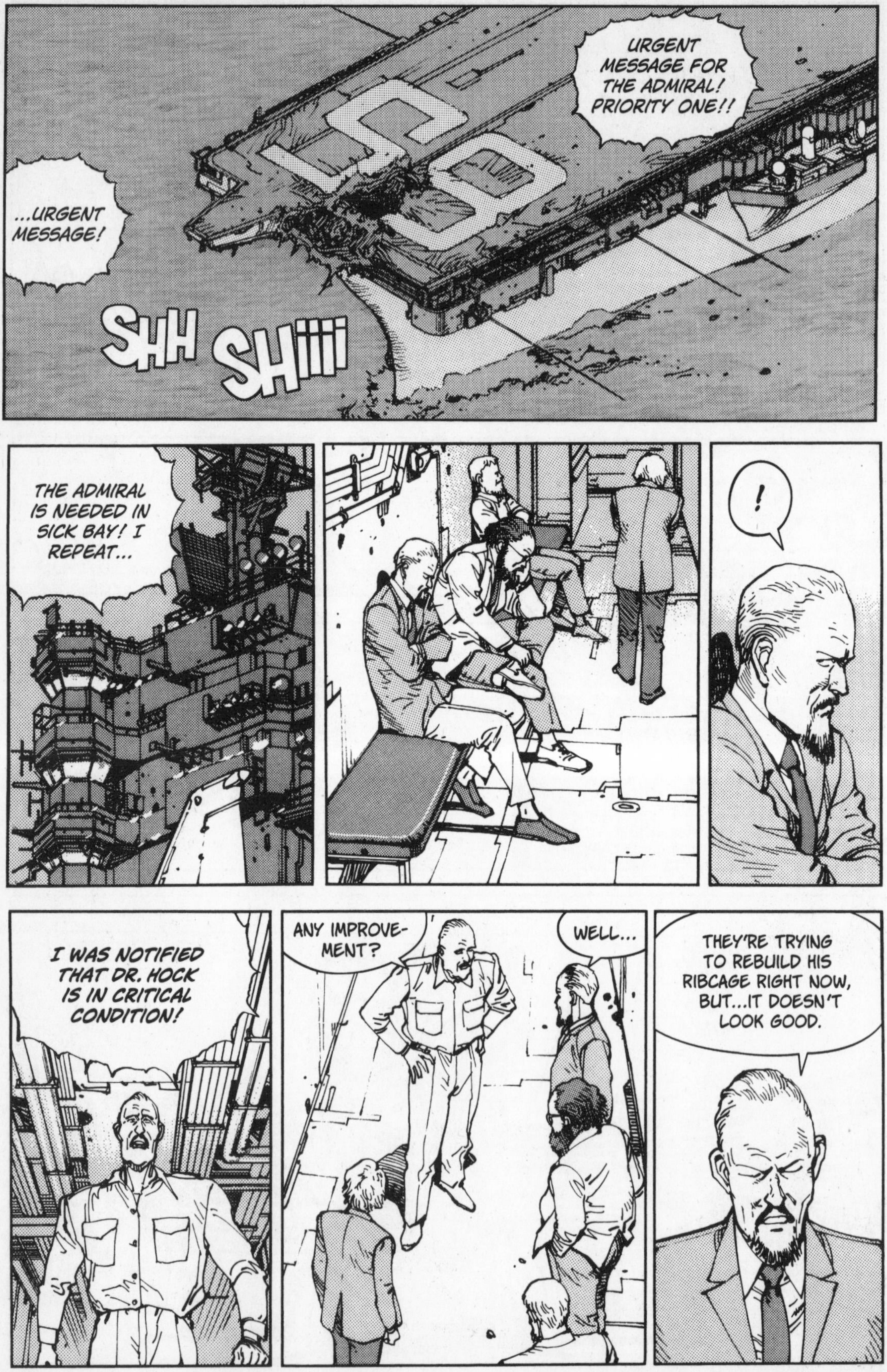

...URGENT MESSAGE!
URGENT MESSAGE FOR THE ADMIRAL! PRIORITY ONE!!
SHH SHiiii
THE ADMIRAL IS NEEDED IN SICK BAY! I REPEAT...
!
I WAS NOTIFIED THAT DR. HOCK IS IN CRITICAL CONDITION!
ANY IMPROVEMENT?
WELL...
THEY'RE TRYING TO REBUILD HIS RIBCAGE RIGHT NOW, BUT...IT DOESN'T LOOK GOOD.

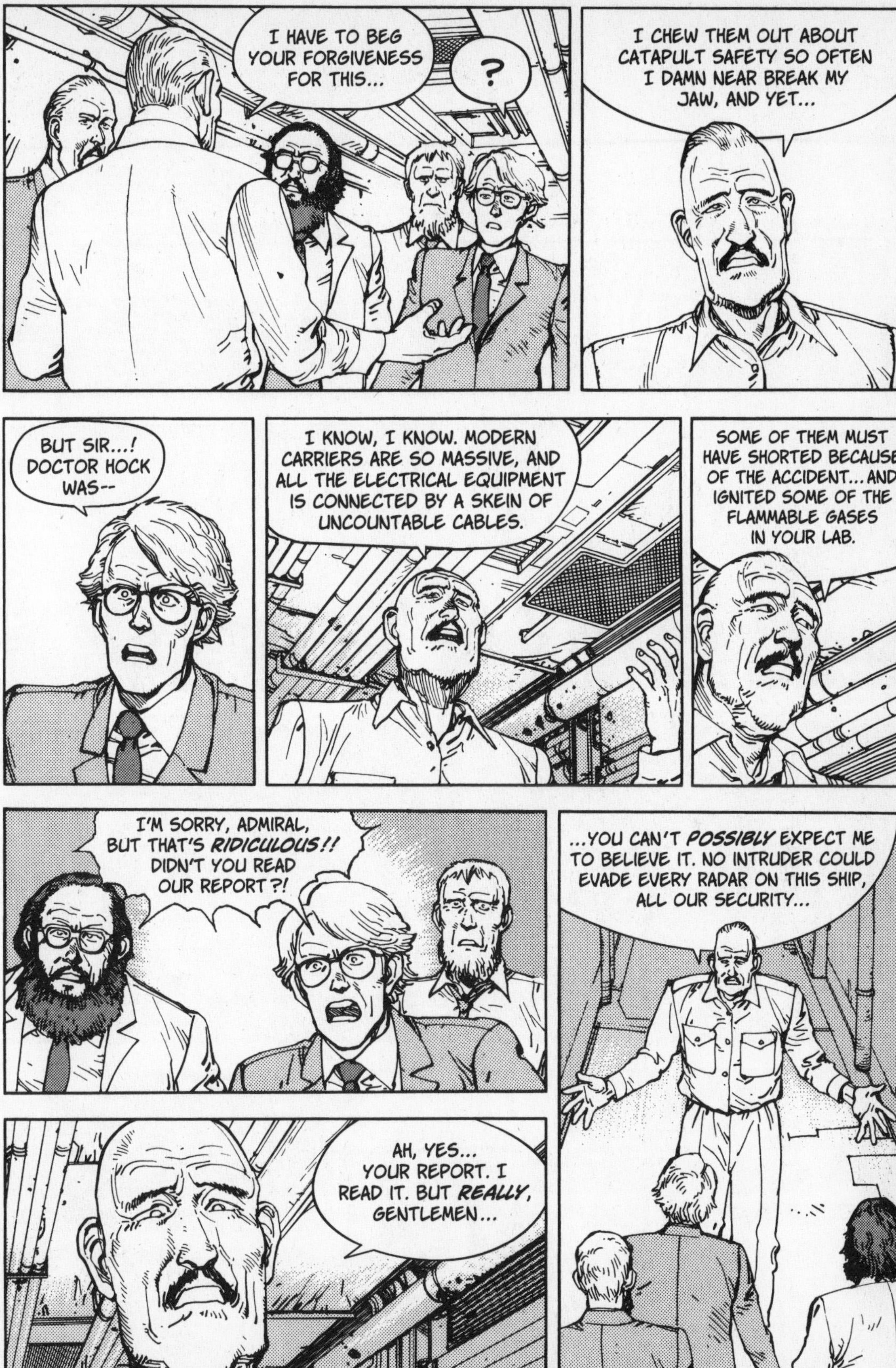
I HAVE TO BEG YOUR FORGIVENESS FOR THIS...
?
I CHEW THEM OUT ABOUT CATAPULT SAFETY SO OFTEN I DAMN NEAR BREAK MY JAW, AND YET...
BUT SIR...! DOCTOR HOCK WAS--
I KNOW, I KNOW. MODERN CARRIERS ARE SO MASSIVE, AND ALL THE ELECTRICAL EQUIPMENT IS CONNECTED BY A SKEIN OF UNCOUNTABLE CABLES.
SOME OF THEM MUST HAVE SHORTED BECAUSE OF THE ACCIDENT...AND IGNITED SOME OF THE FLAMMABLE GASES IN YOUR LAB.
I'M SORRY, ADMIRAL, BUT THAT'S *RIDICULOUS!!* DIDN'T YOU READ OUR REPORT?!
AH, YES... YOUR REPORT. I READ IT. BUT *REALLY*, GENTLEMEN...
...YOU CAN'T *POSSIBLY* EXPECT ME TO BELIEVE IT. NO INTRUDER COULD EVADE EVERY RADAR ON THIS SHIP, ALL OUR SECURITY...

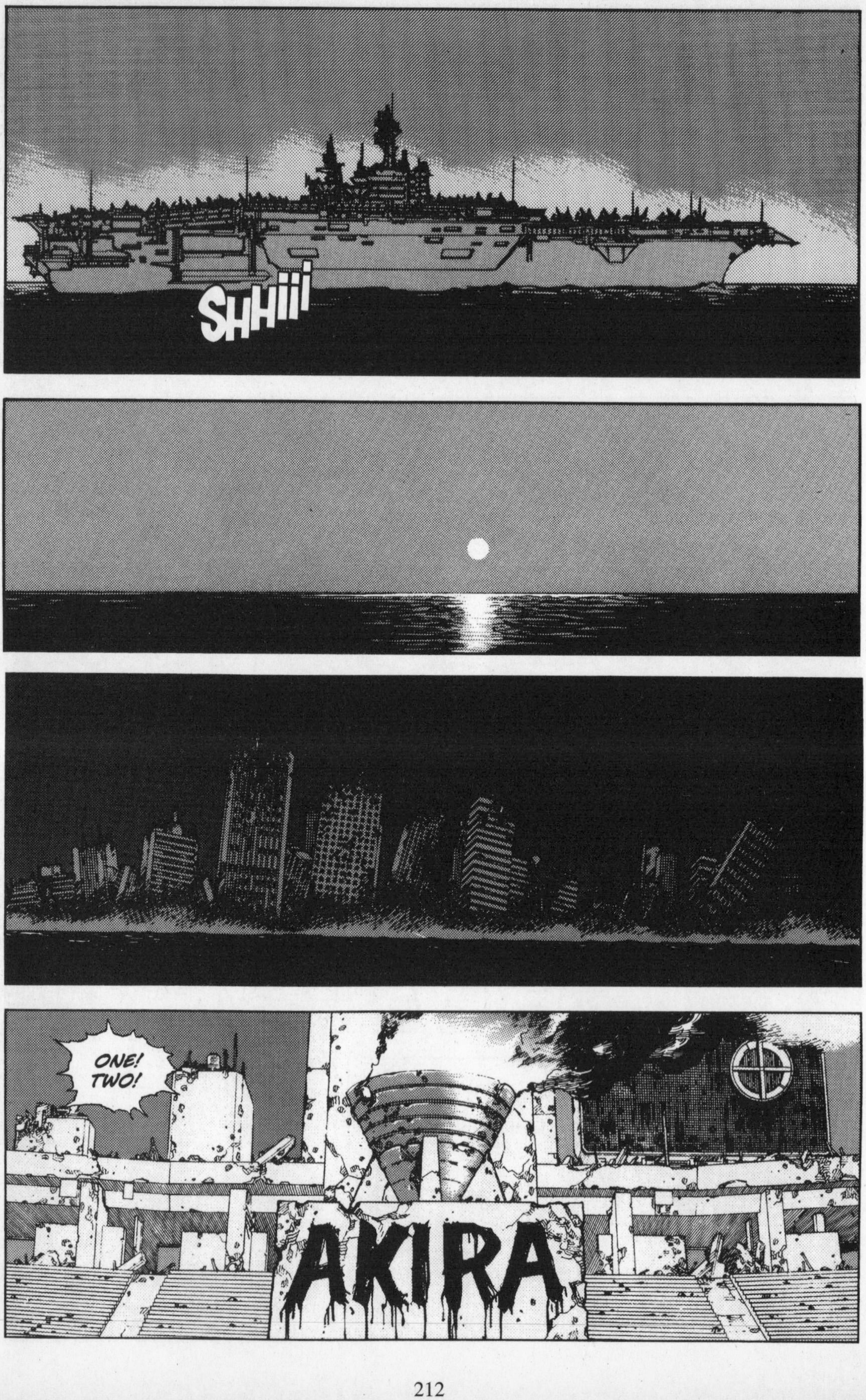
SHHiii
ONE! TWO!
AKIRA

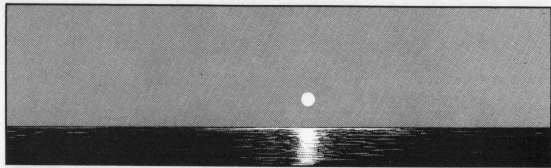

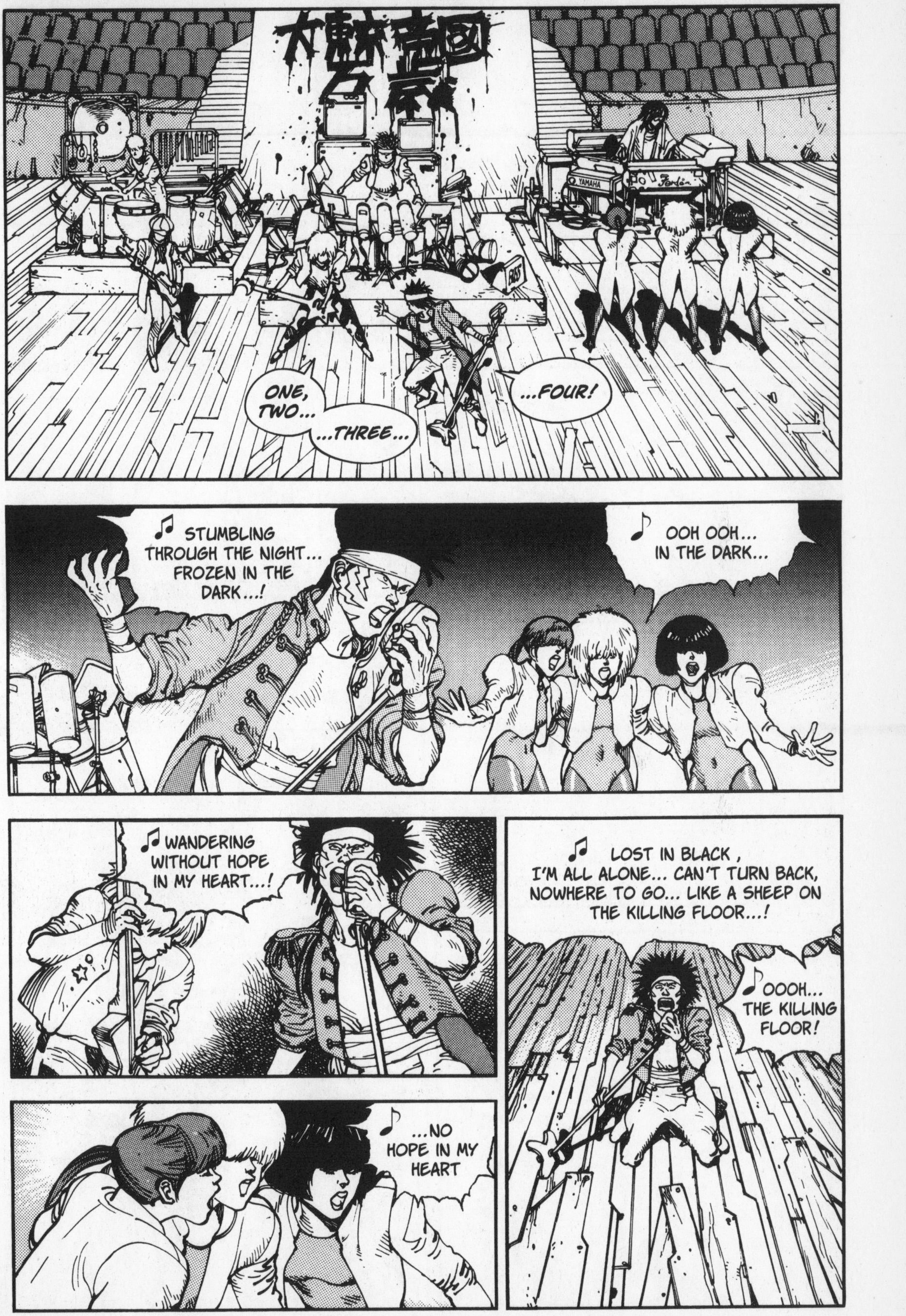

ONE, TWO...
...THREE...
...FOUR!
♫ STUMBLING THROUGH THE NIGHT... FROZEN IN THE DARK...!
♪ OOH OOH... IN THE DARK...
♫ WANDERING WITHOUT HOPE IN MY HEART...!
♪ ...NO HOPE IN MY HEART
♫ LOST IN BLACK , I'M ALL ALONE... CAN'T TURN BACK, NOWHERE TO GO... LIKE A SHEEP ON THE KILLING FLOOR...!
♪ OOOH... THE KILLING FLOOR!

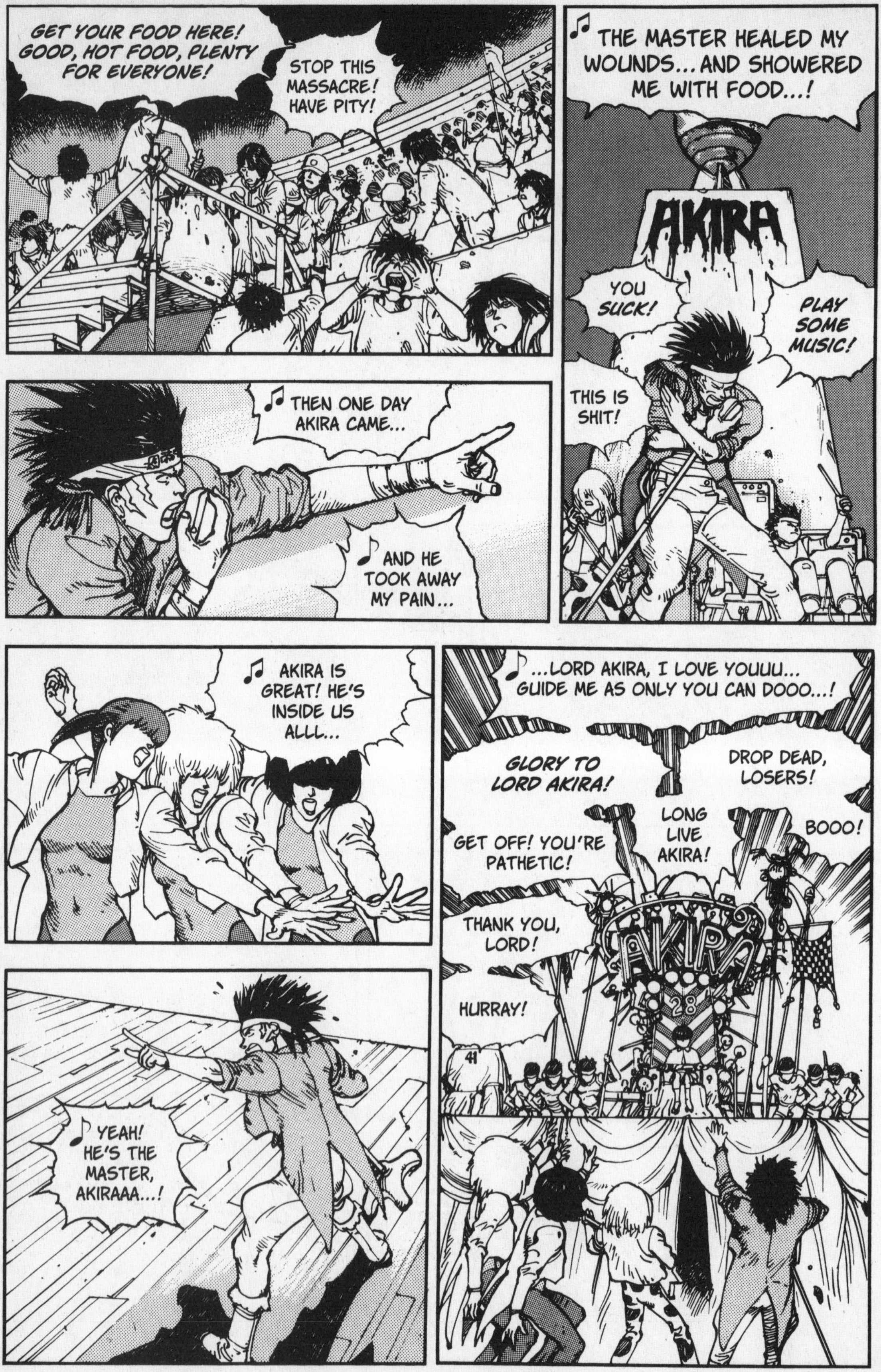
GET YOUR FOOD HERE! GOOD, HOT FOOD, PLENTY FOR EVERYONE!
STOP THIS MASSACRE! HAVE PITY!
THEN ONE DAY AKIRA CAME...
AND HE TOOK AWAY MY PAIN...
THE MASTER HEALED MY WOUNDS... AND SHOWERED ME WITH FOOD...!
AKIRA
YOU SUCK!
PLAY SOME MUSIC!
THIS IS SHIT!
AKIRA IS GREAT! HE'S INSIDE US ALLL...
YEAH! HE'S THE MASTER, AKIRAAA...!
...LORD AKIRA, I LOVE YOUUU... GUIDE ME AS ONLY YOU CAN DOOO...!
GLORY TO LORD AKIRA!
DROP DEAD, LOSERS!
LONG LIVE AKIRA!
BOOO!
GET OFF! YOU'RE PATHETIC!
THANK YOU, LORD!
AKIRA
28
HURRAY!
41

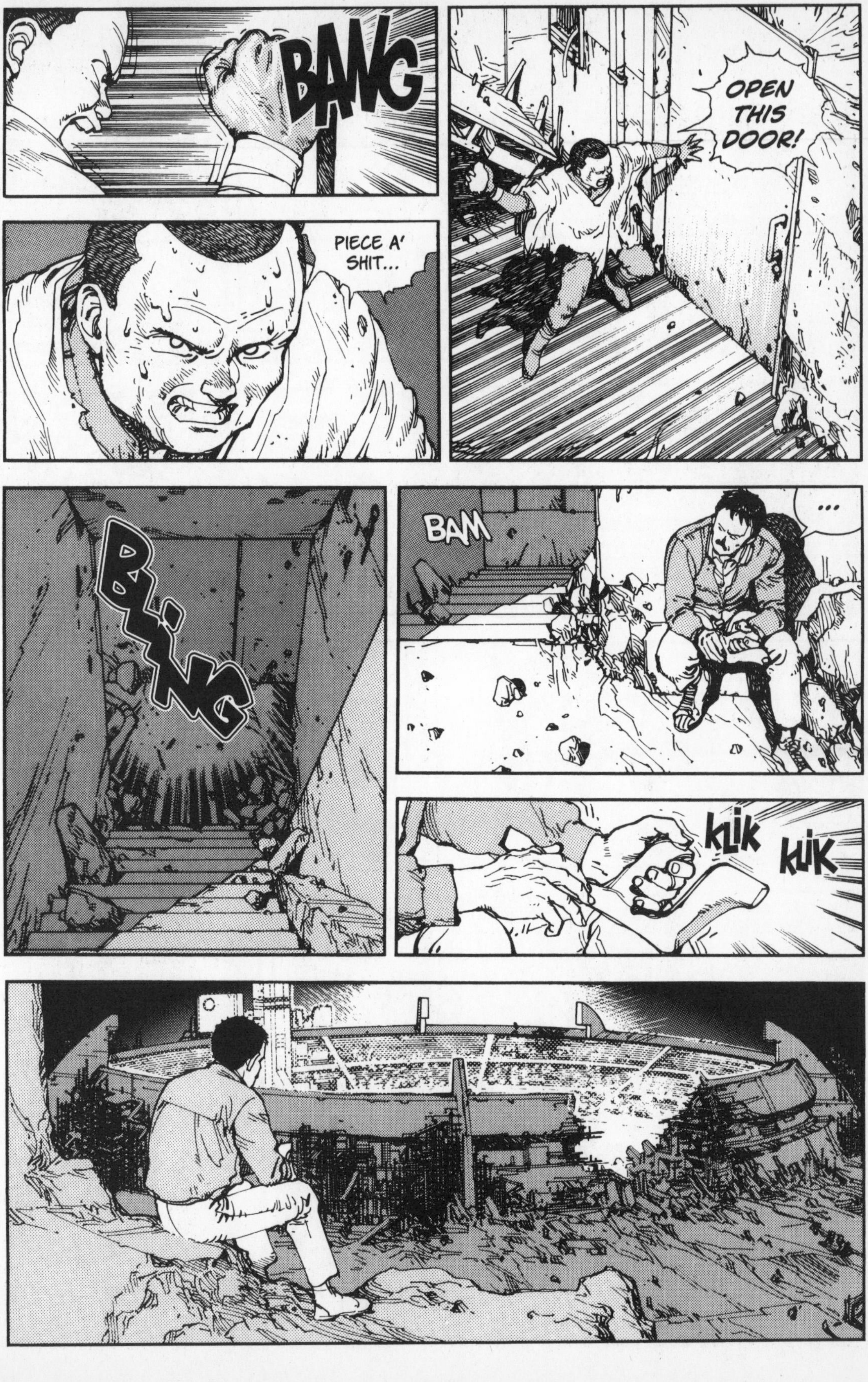
BANG
OPEN THIS DOOR!
PIECE A' SHIT...
BLING
BAM
...
KLIK
KLIK

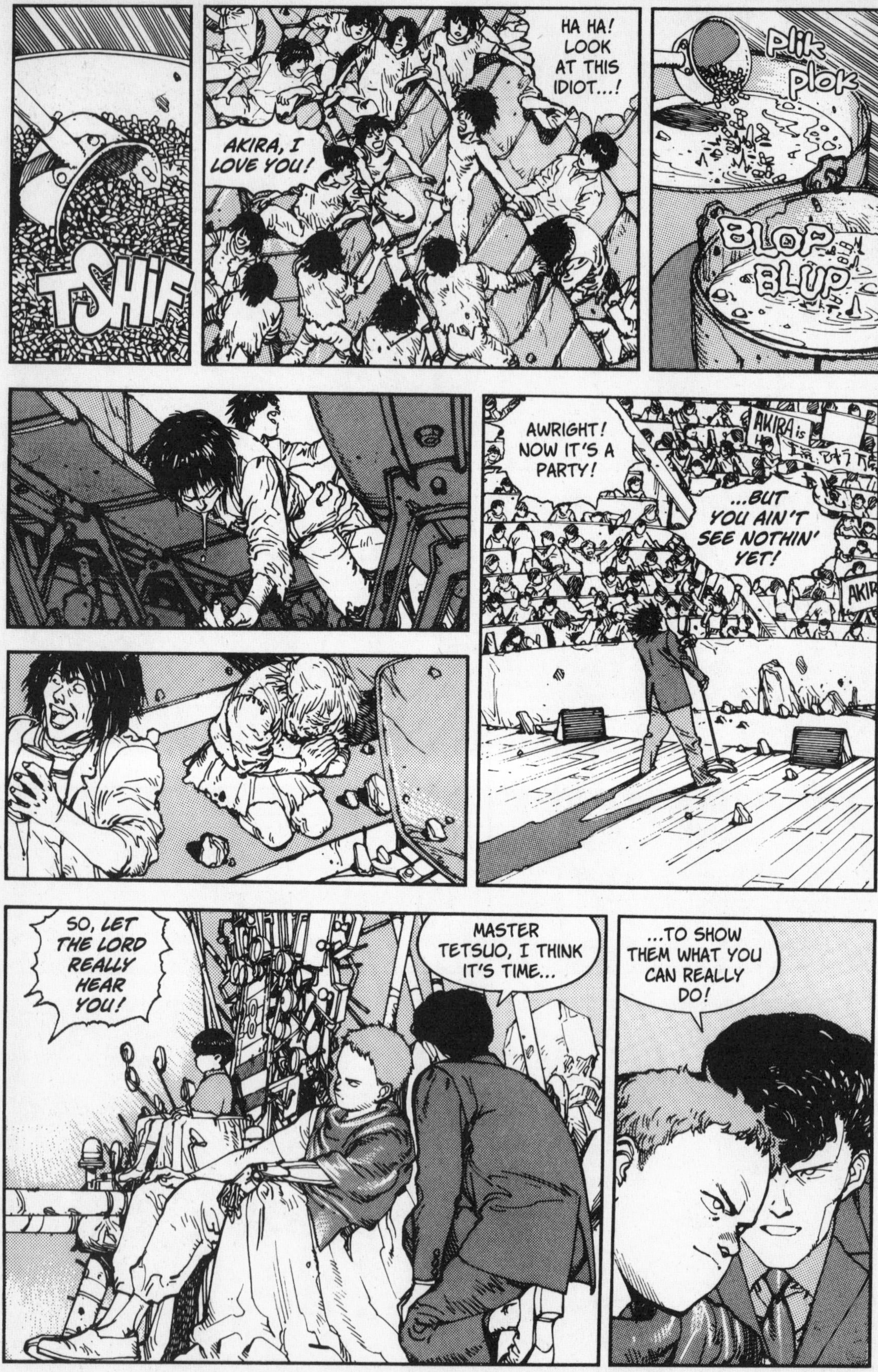
TSHIF
HA HA! LOOK AT THIS IDIOT...!
AKIRA, I LOVE YOU!
Plik plok
BLOP BLUP
AWRIGHT! NOW IT'S A PARTY!
AKIRA is
...BUT YOU AIN'T SEE NOTHIN' YET!
AKIR
SO, LET THE LORD REALLY HEAR YOU!
MASTER TETSUO, I THINK IT'S TIME...
...TO SHOW THEM WHAT YOU CAN REALLY DO!

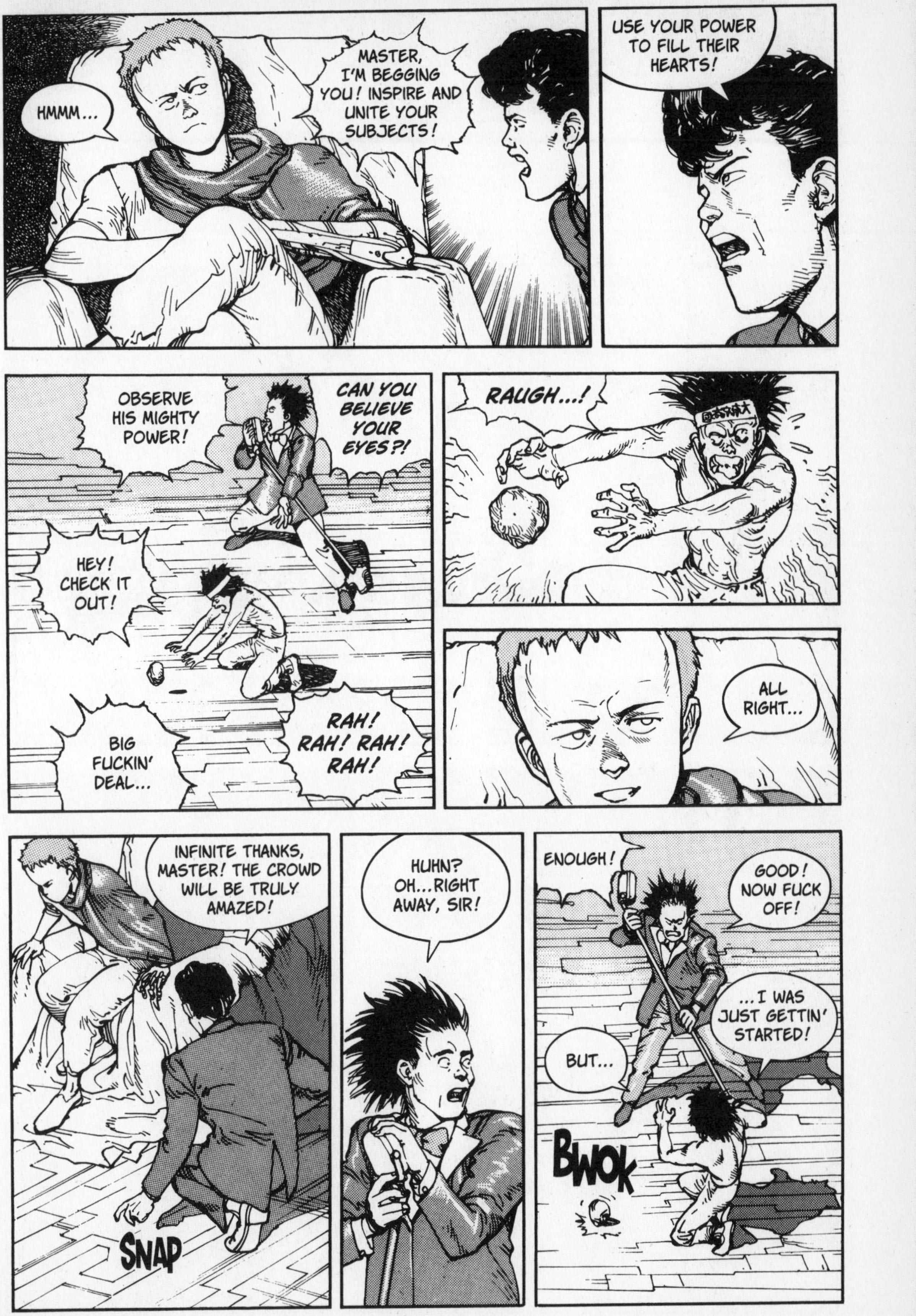
HMMM...
MASTER, I'M BEGGING YOU! INSPIRE AND UNITE YOUR SUBJECTS!
USE YOUR POWER TO FILL THEIR HEARTS!
OBSERVE HIS MIGHTY POWER!
CAN YOU BELIEVE YOUR EYES?!
HEY! CHECK IT OUT!
BIG FUCKIN' DEAL...
RAH! RAH! RAH! RAH!
RAUGH...!
ALL RIGHT...
INFINITE THANKS, MASTER! THE CROWD WILL BE TRULY AMAZED!
SNAP
HUHN? OH...RIGHT AWAY, SIR!
ENOUGH!
GOOD! NOW FUCK OFF!
...I WAS JUST GETTIN' STARTED!
BUT...
BWOK

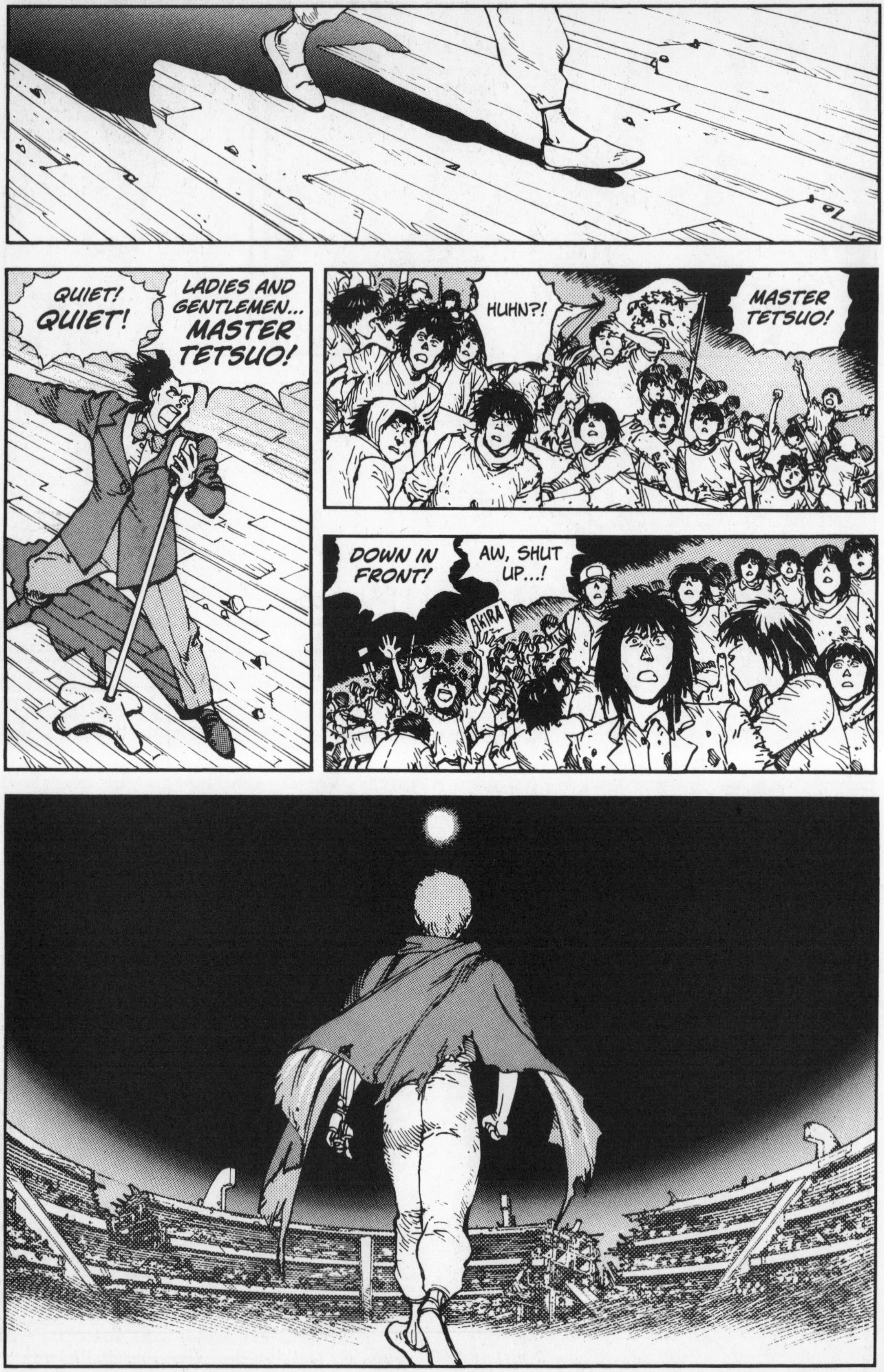
QUIET! QUIET!
LADIES AND GENTLEMEN... MASTER TETSUO!
HUHN?!
MASTER TETSUO!
DOWN IN FRONT!
AW, SHUT UP...!
AKIRA

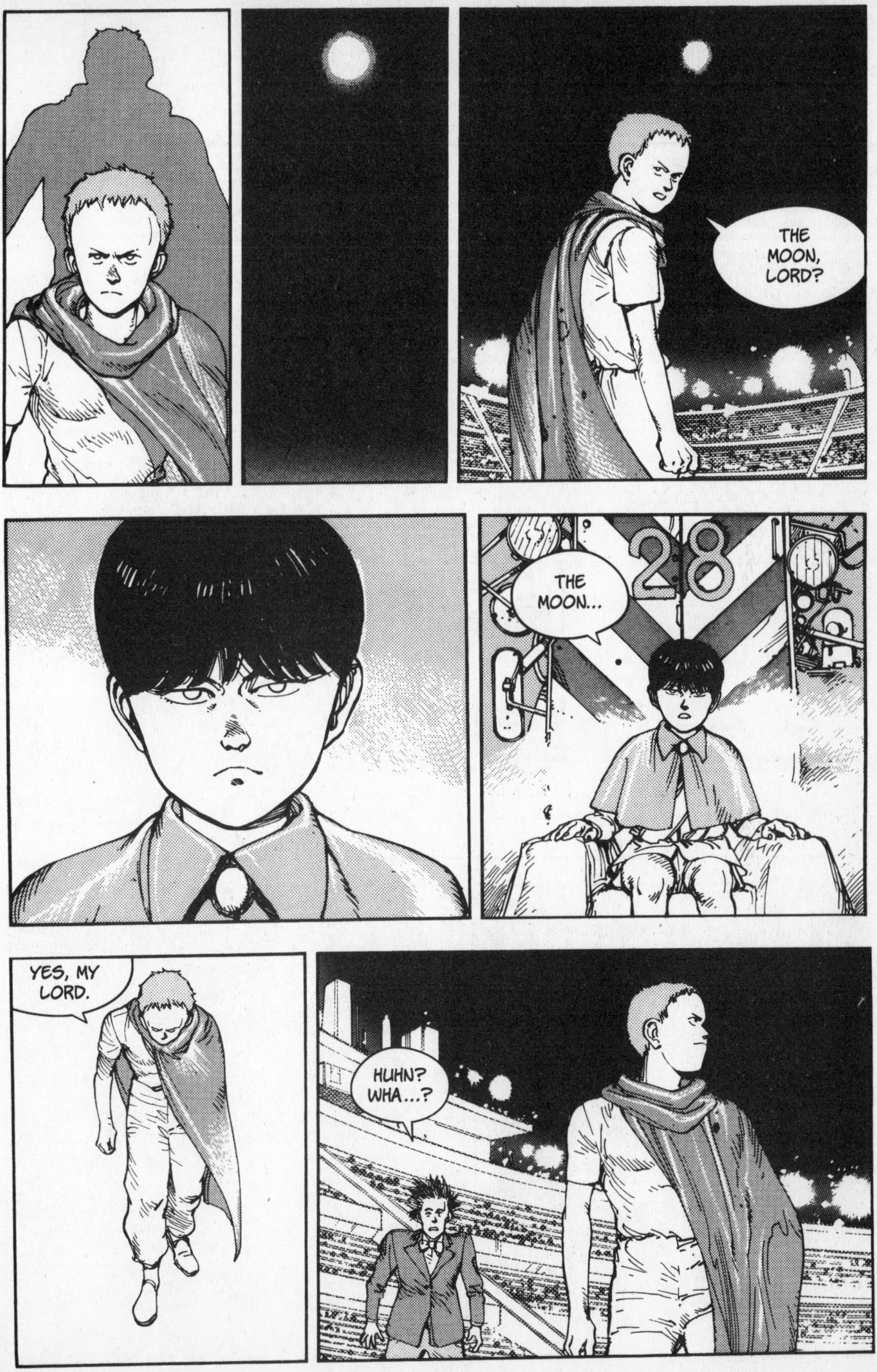
THE MOON, LORD?
THE MOON...
YES, MY LORD.
HUHN? WHA...?

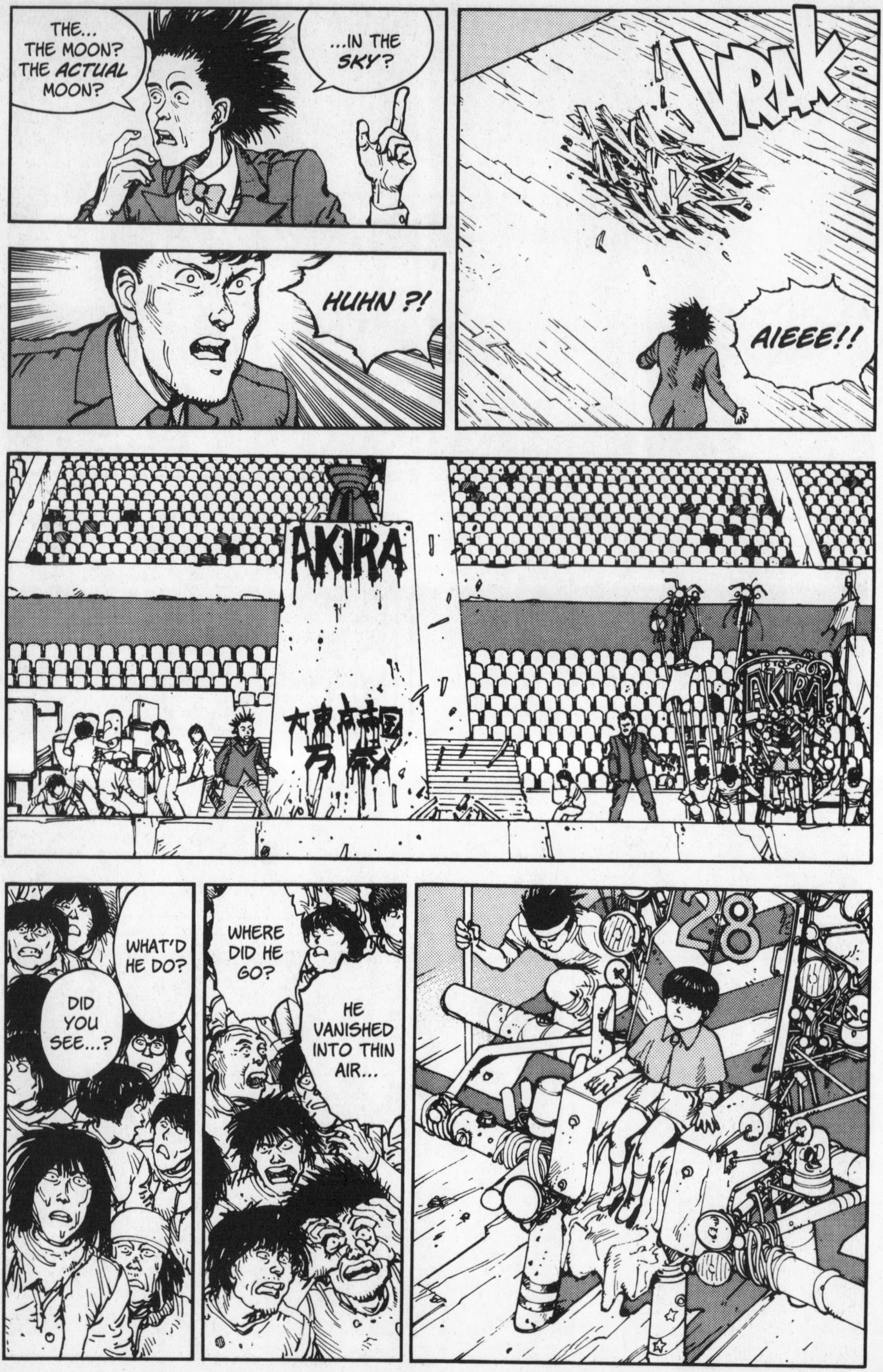
THE... THE MOON? THE ACTUAL MOON?
...IN THE SKY?
HUHN ?!
VRAK
AIEEE!!
AKIRA
大東京帝国
万歳
AKIRA
WHAT'D HE DO?
DID YOU SEE...?
WHERE DID HE GO?
HE VANISHED INTO THIN AIR...
28

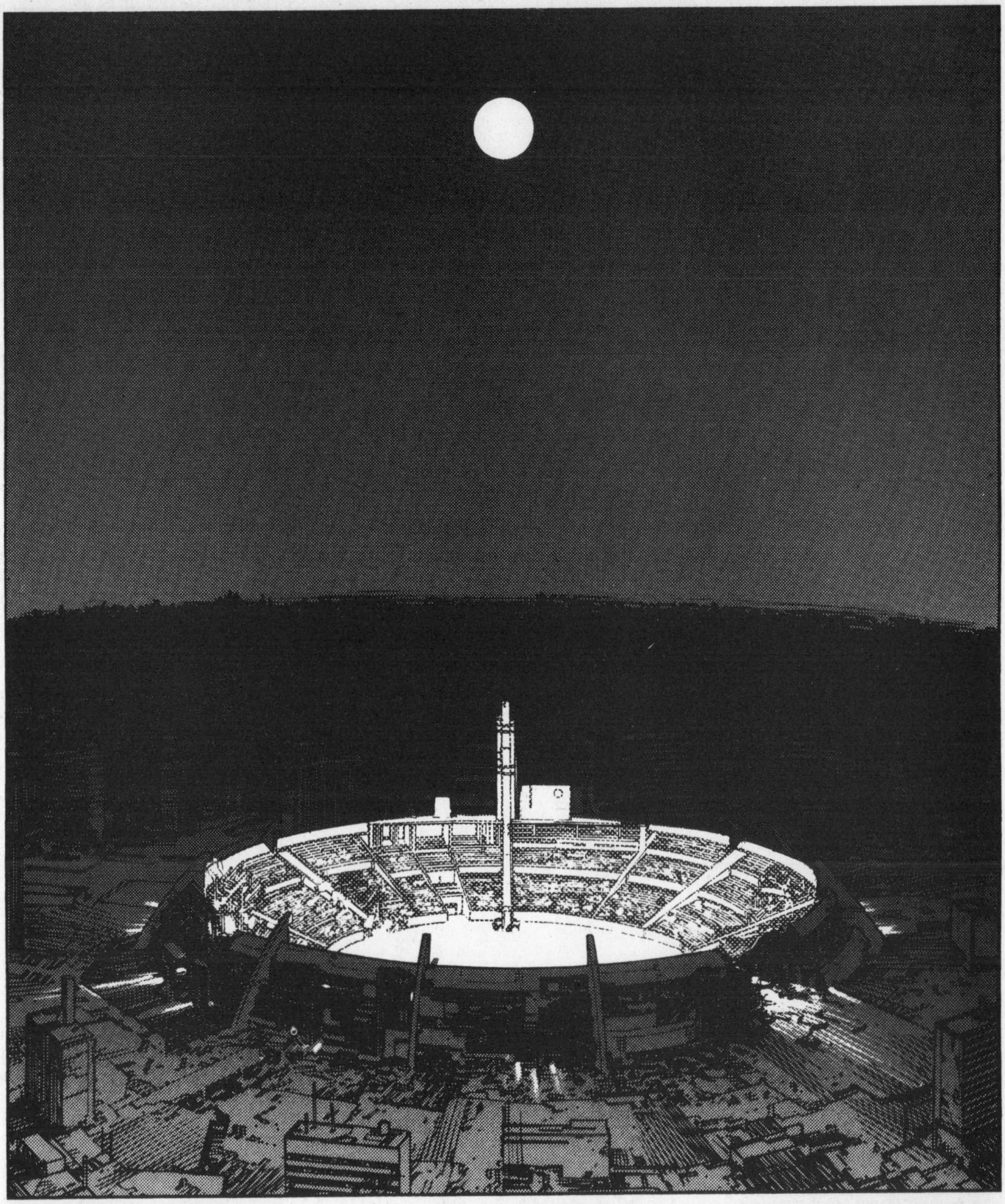

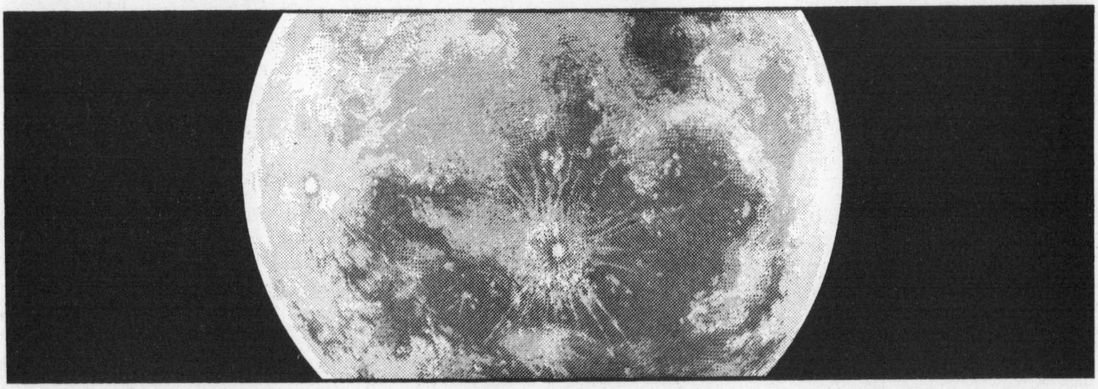

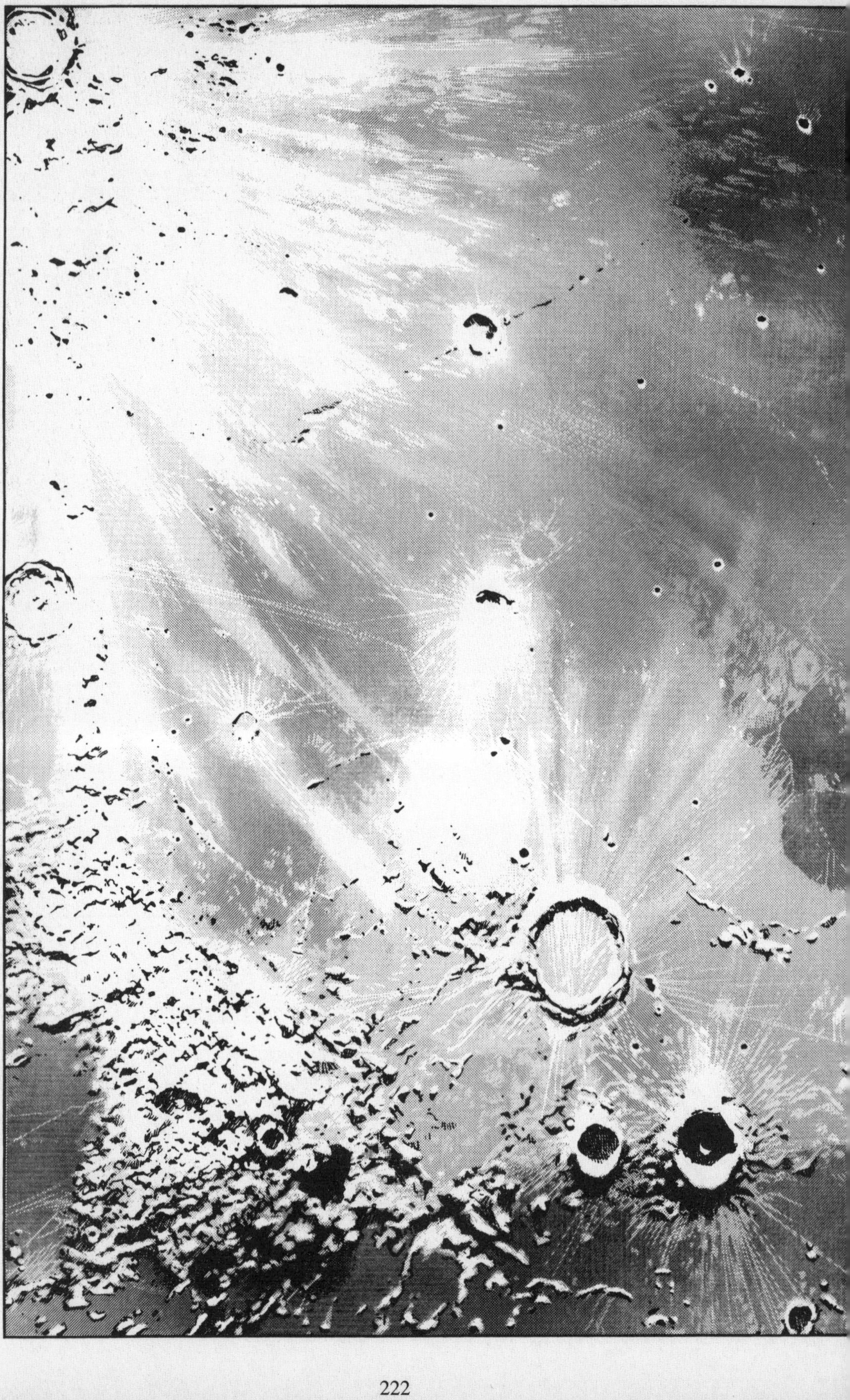

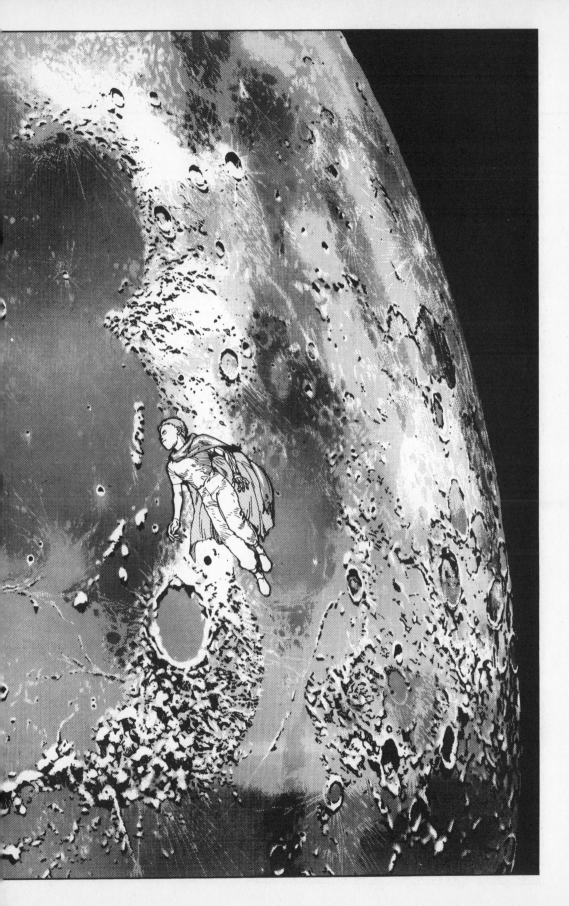

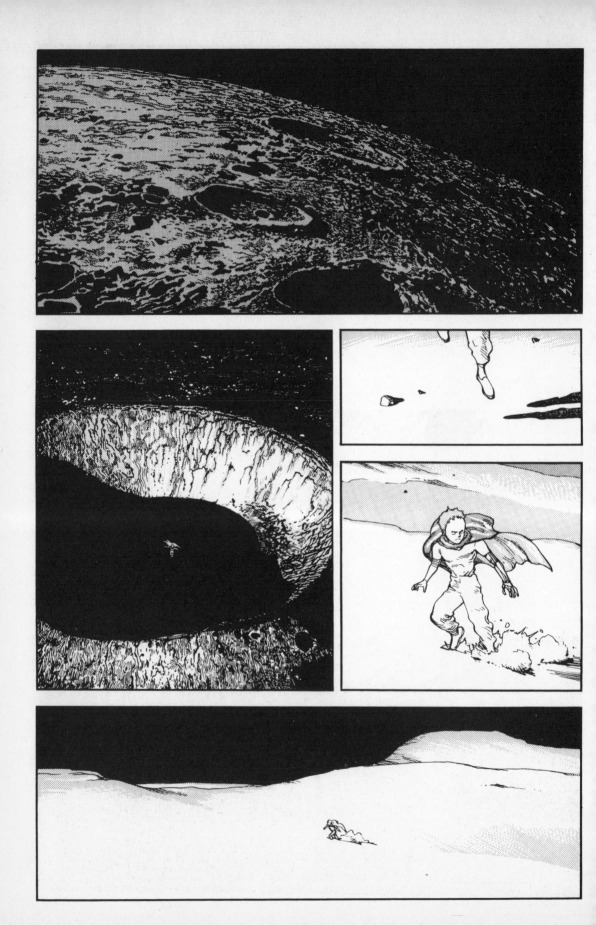

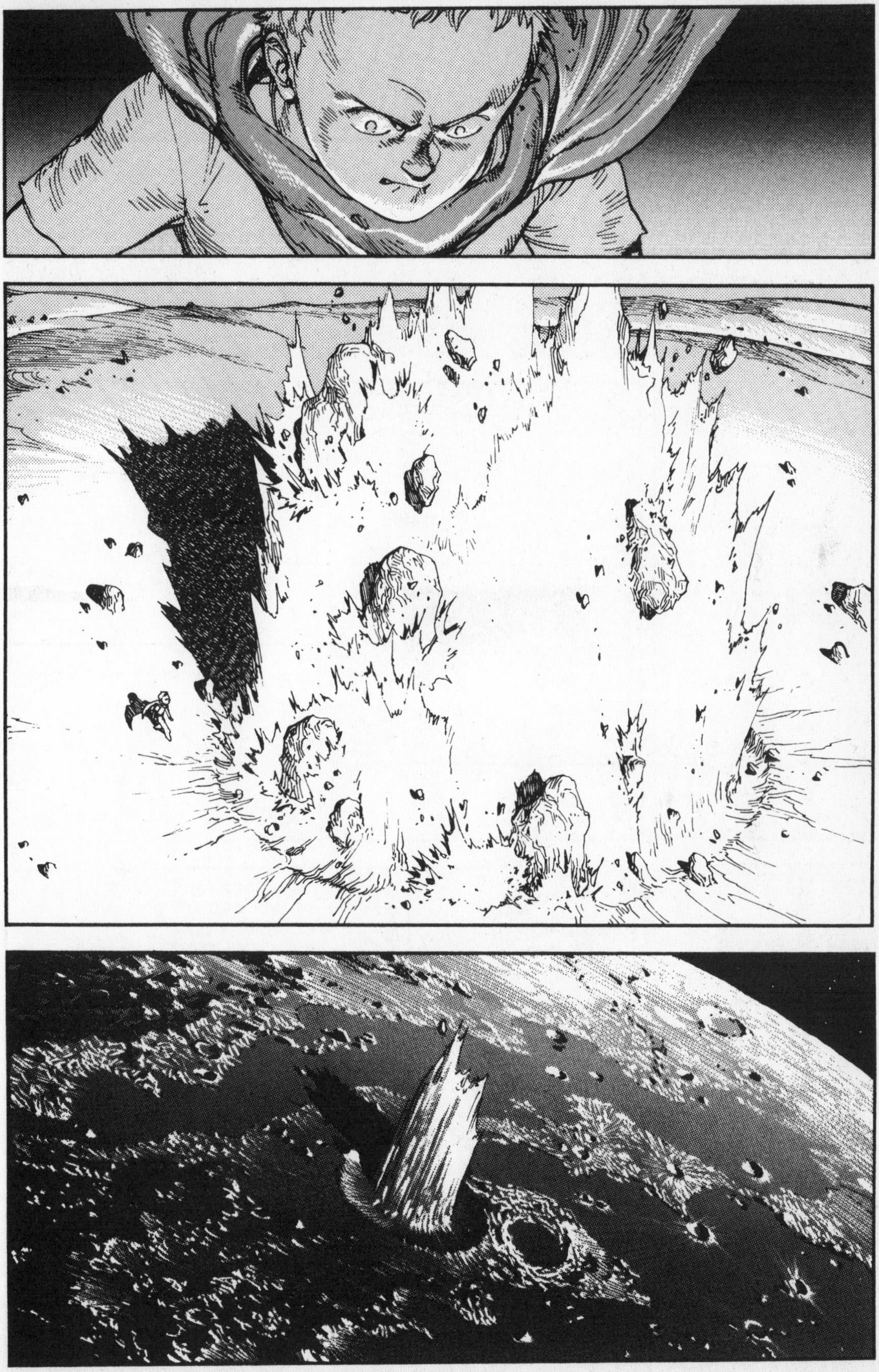

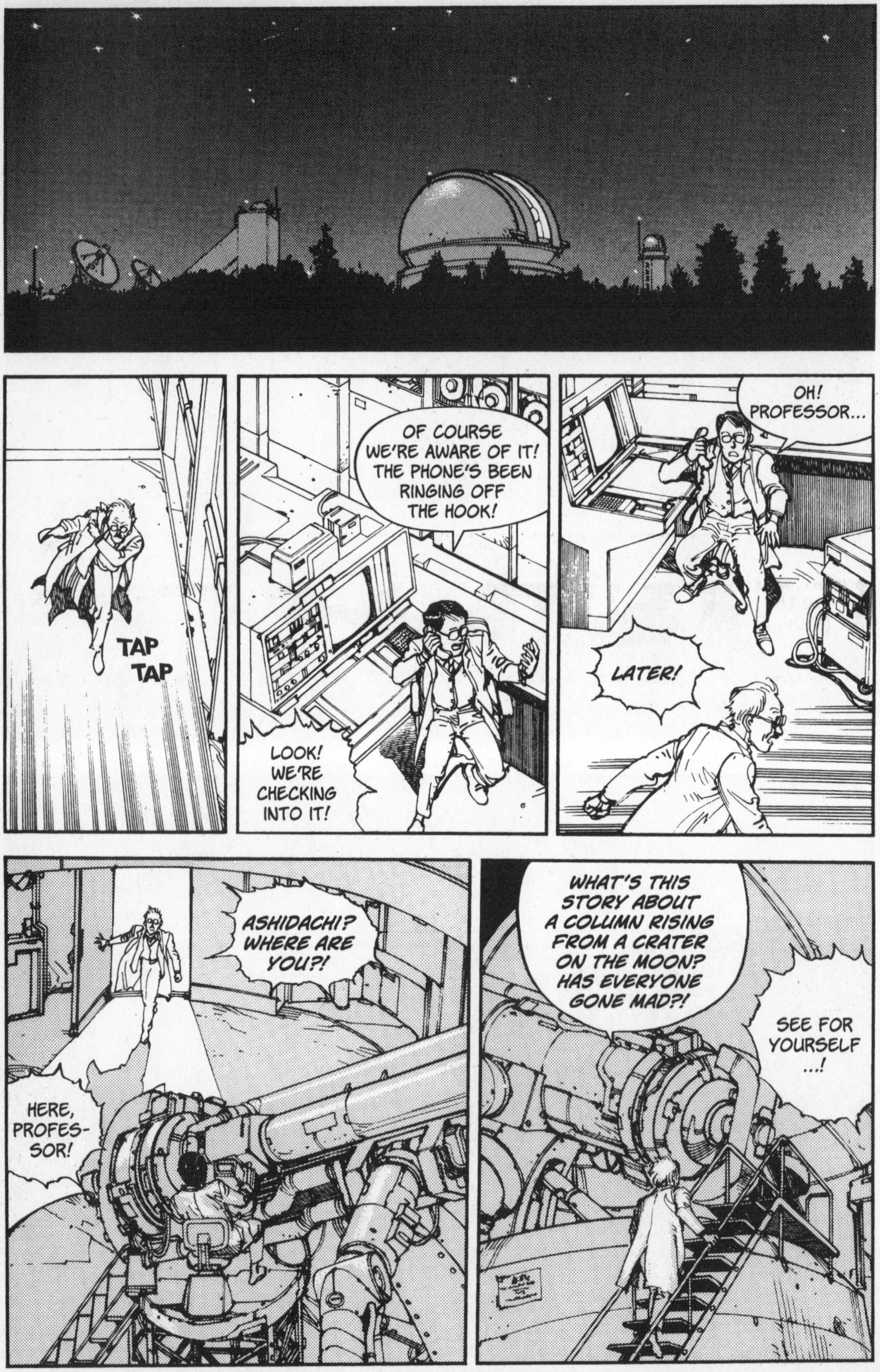
TAP
TAP
OF COURSE WE'RE AWARE OF IT! THE PHONE'S BEEN RINGING OFF THE HOOK!
LOOK! WE'RE CHECKING INTO IT!
OH! PROFESSOR...
LATER!
ASHIDACHI? WHERE ARE YOU?!
HERE, PROFES-SOR!
WHAT'S THIS STORY ABOUT A COLUMN RISING FROM A CRATER ON THE MOON? HAS EVERYONE GONE MAD?!
SEE FOR YOURSELF ...!

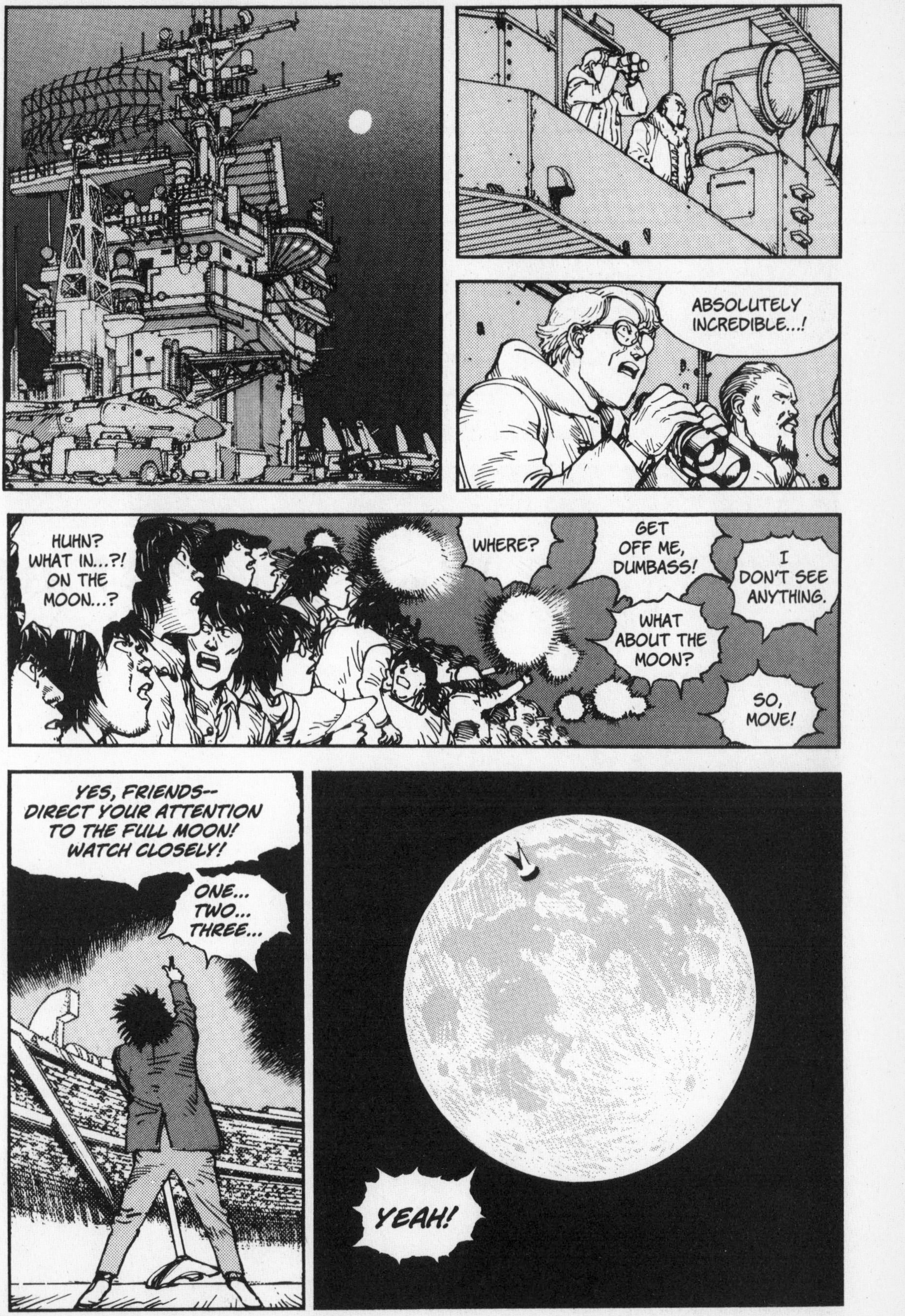
ABSOLUTELY INCREDIBLE...!
HUHN? WHAT IN...?! ON THE MOON...?
WHERE?
GET OFF ME, DUMBASS!
I DON'T SEE ANYTHING.
WHAT ABOUT THE MOON?
SO, MOVE!
YES, FRIENDS-- DIRECT YOUR ATTENTION TO THE FULL MOON! WATCH CLOSELY!
ONE... TWO... THREE...
YEAH!

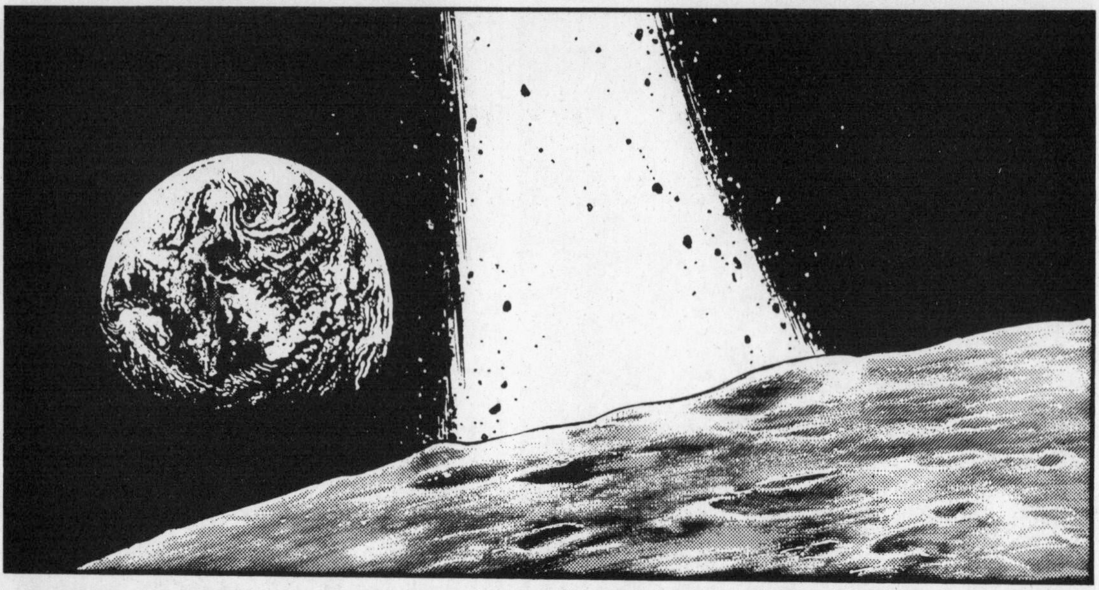

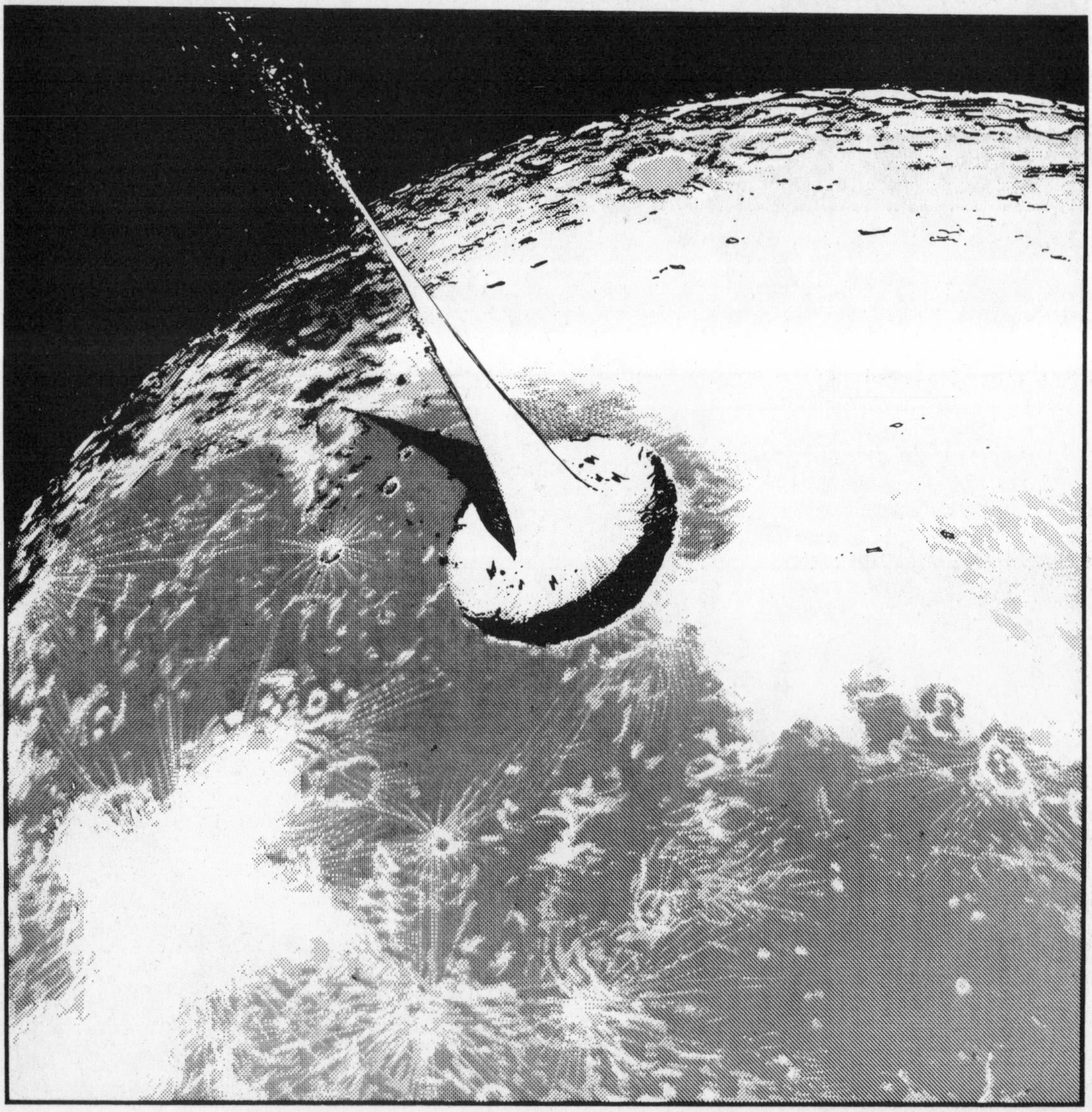

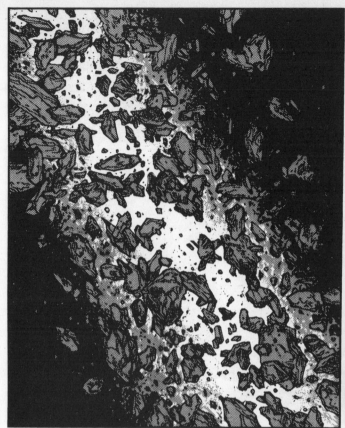
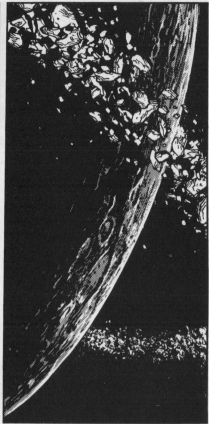
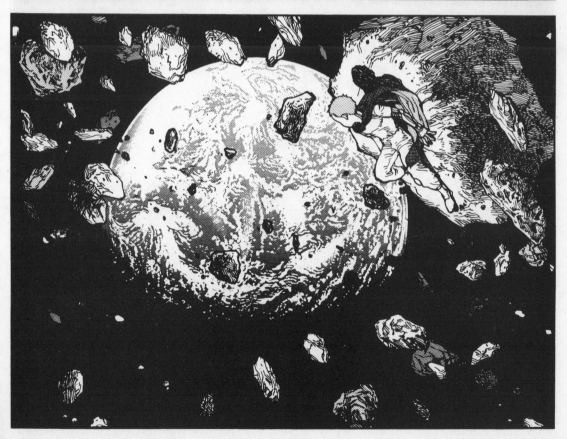

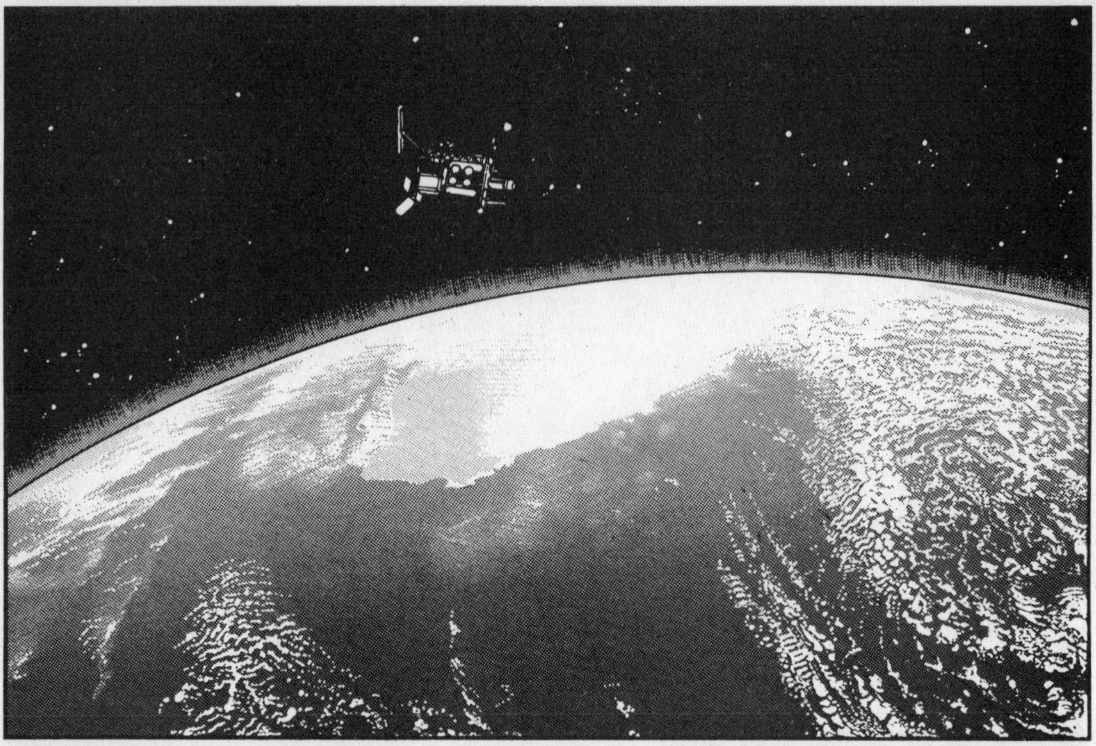
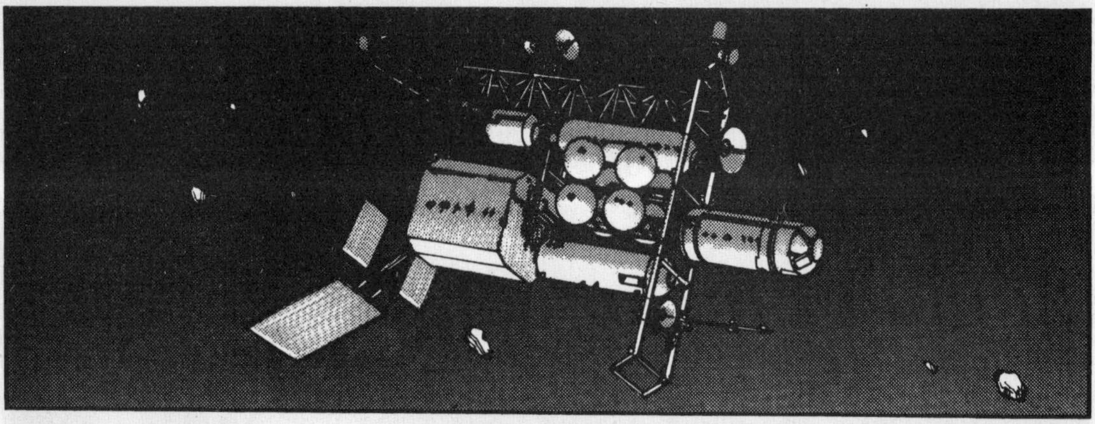
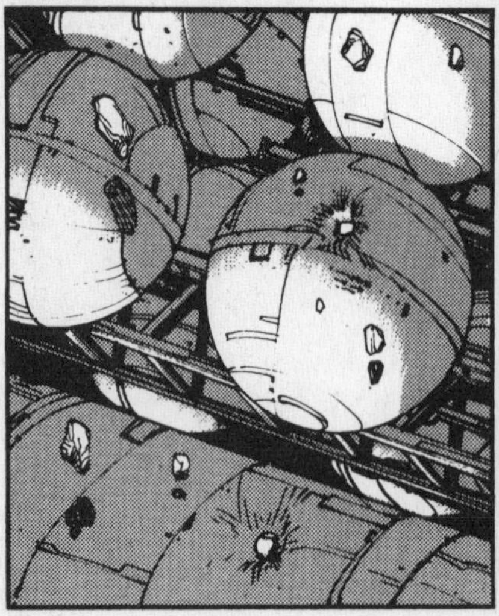
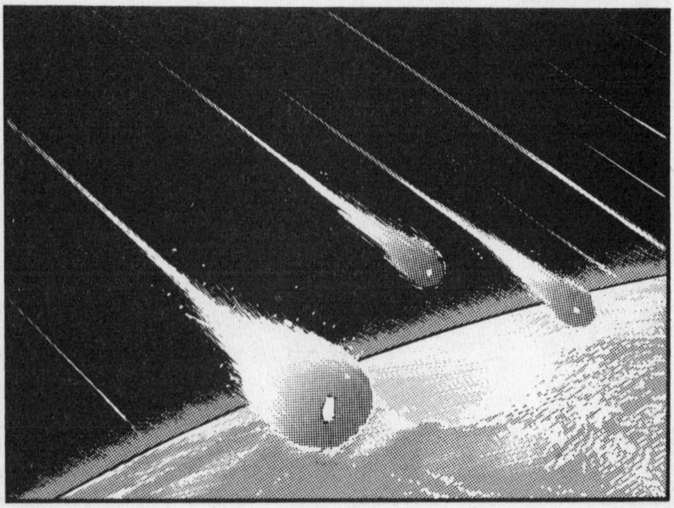

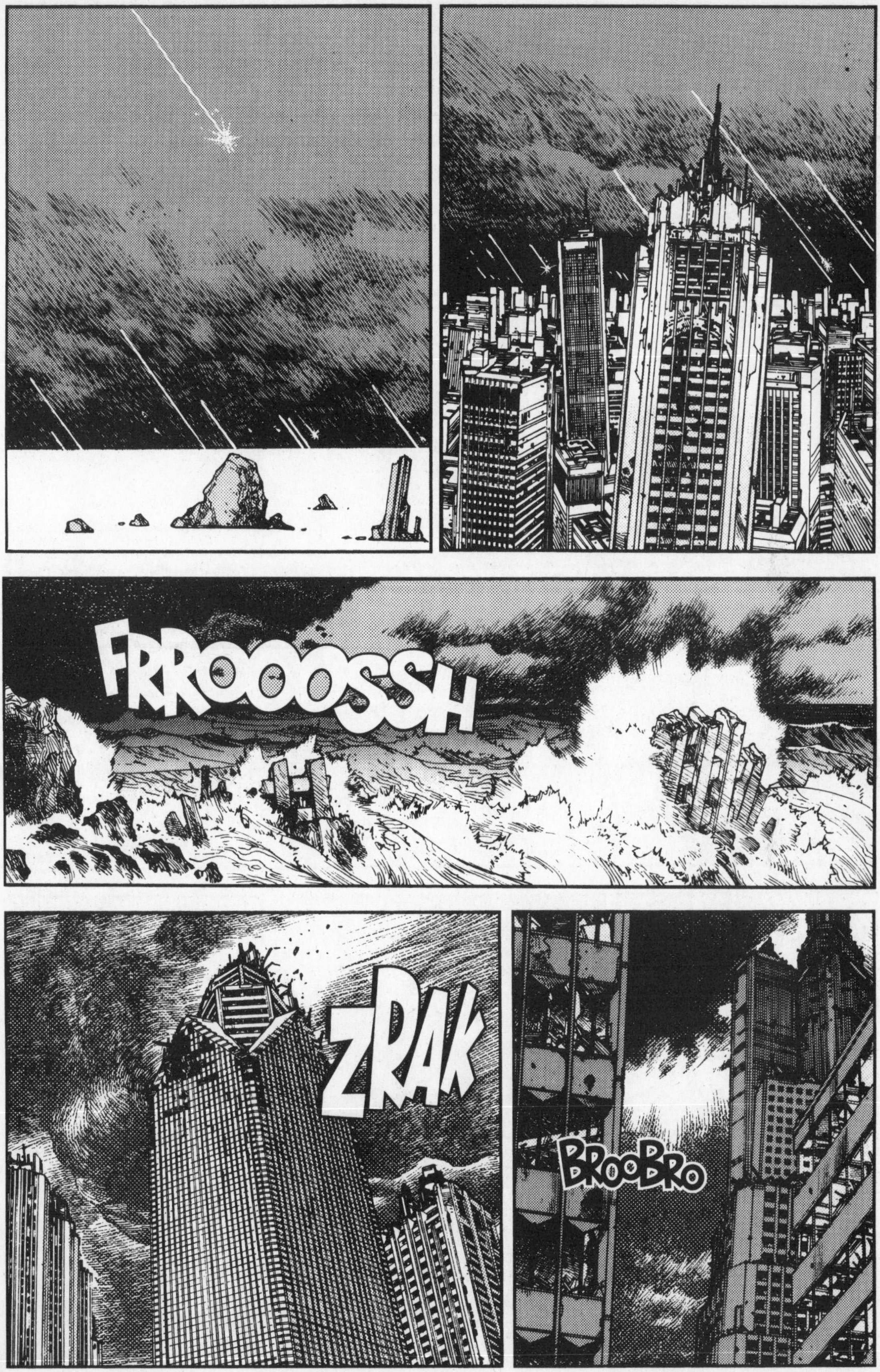
FRROOOSSH
ZRAK
BROOBRO

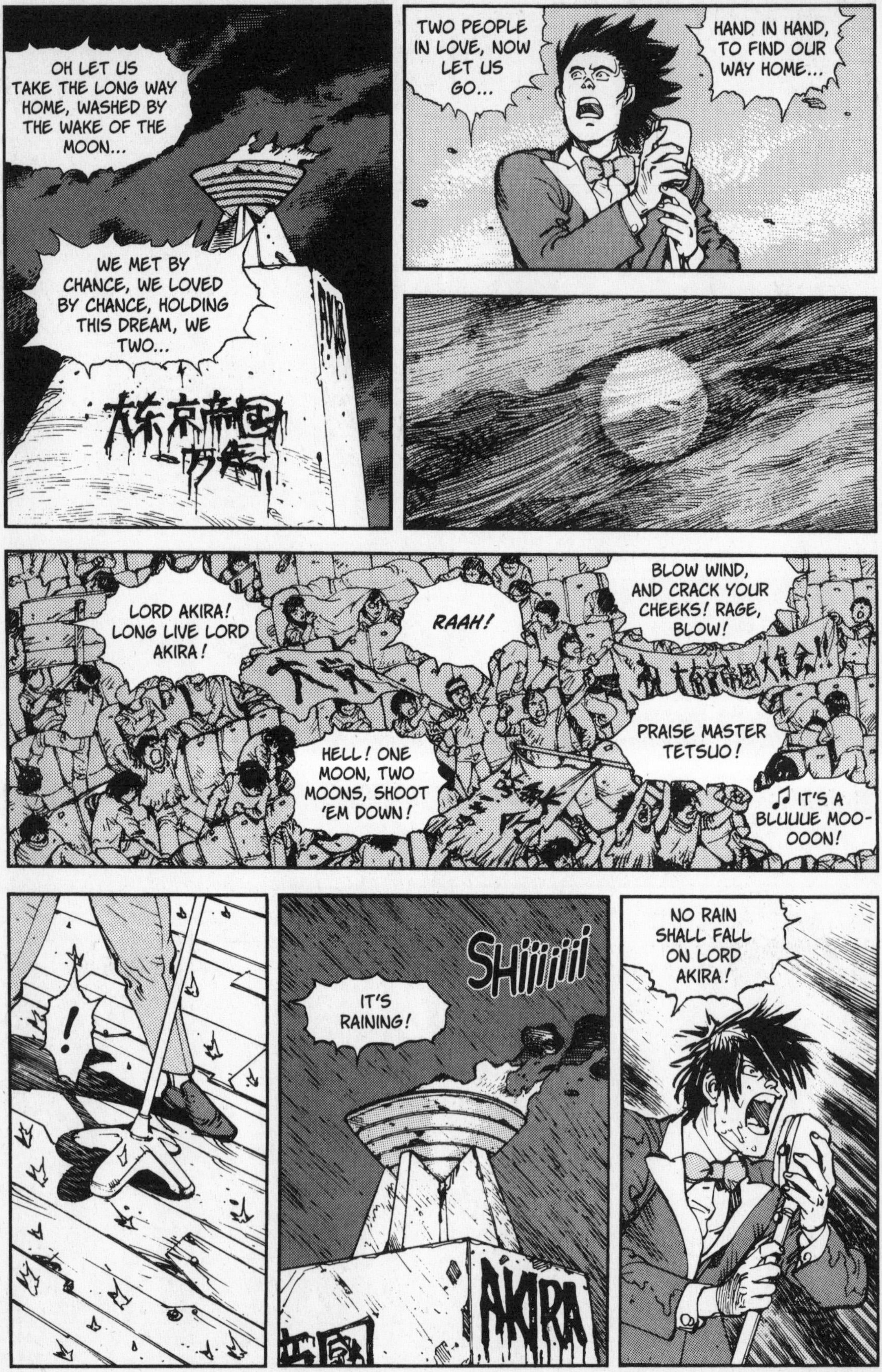
OH LET US TAKE THE LONG WAY HOME, WASHED BY THE WAKE OF THE MOON...
WE MET BY CHANCE, WE LOVED BY CHANCE, HOLDING THIS DREAM, WE TWO...
TWO PEOPLE IN LOVE, NOW LET US GO...
HAND IN HAND, TO FIND OUR WAY HOME...
LORD AKIRA! LONG LIVE LORD AKIRA!
RAAH!
BLOW WIND, AND CRACK YOUR CHEEKS! RAGE, BLOW!
HELL! ONE MOON, TWO MOONS, SHOOT 'EM DOWN!
PRAISE MASTER TETSUO!
♪ IT'S A BLUUUE MOO-OOON!
!
SHiiiiiii
IT'S RAINING!
AKIRA
NO RAIN SHALL FALL ON LORD AKIRA!

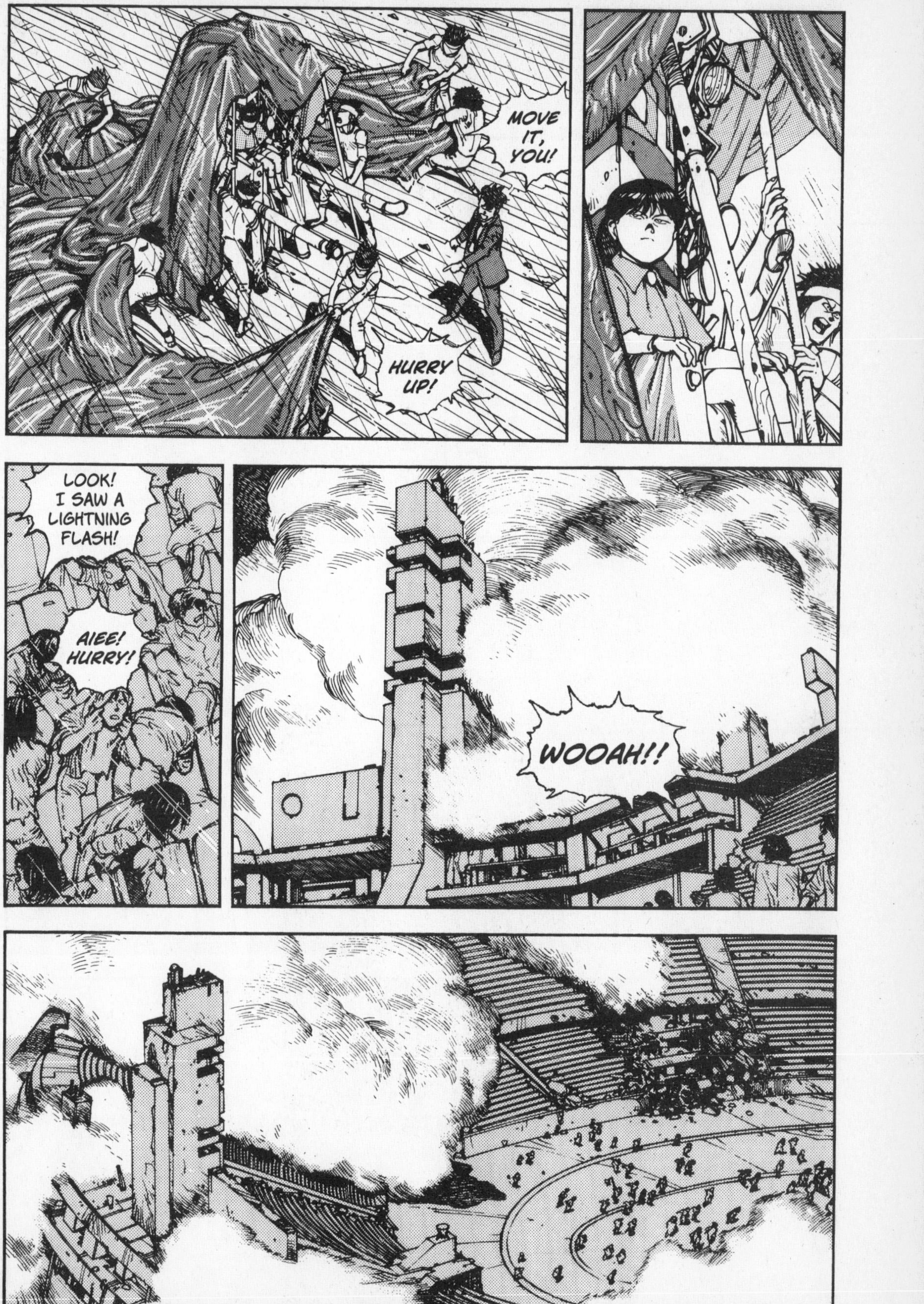
MOVE IT, YOU!
HURRY UP!
LOOK! I SAW A LIGHTNING FLASH!
AIEE! HURRY!
WOOAH!!

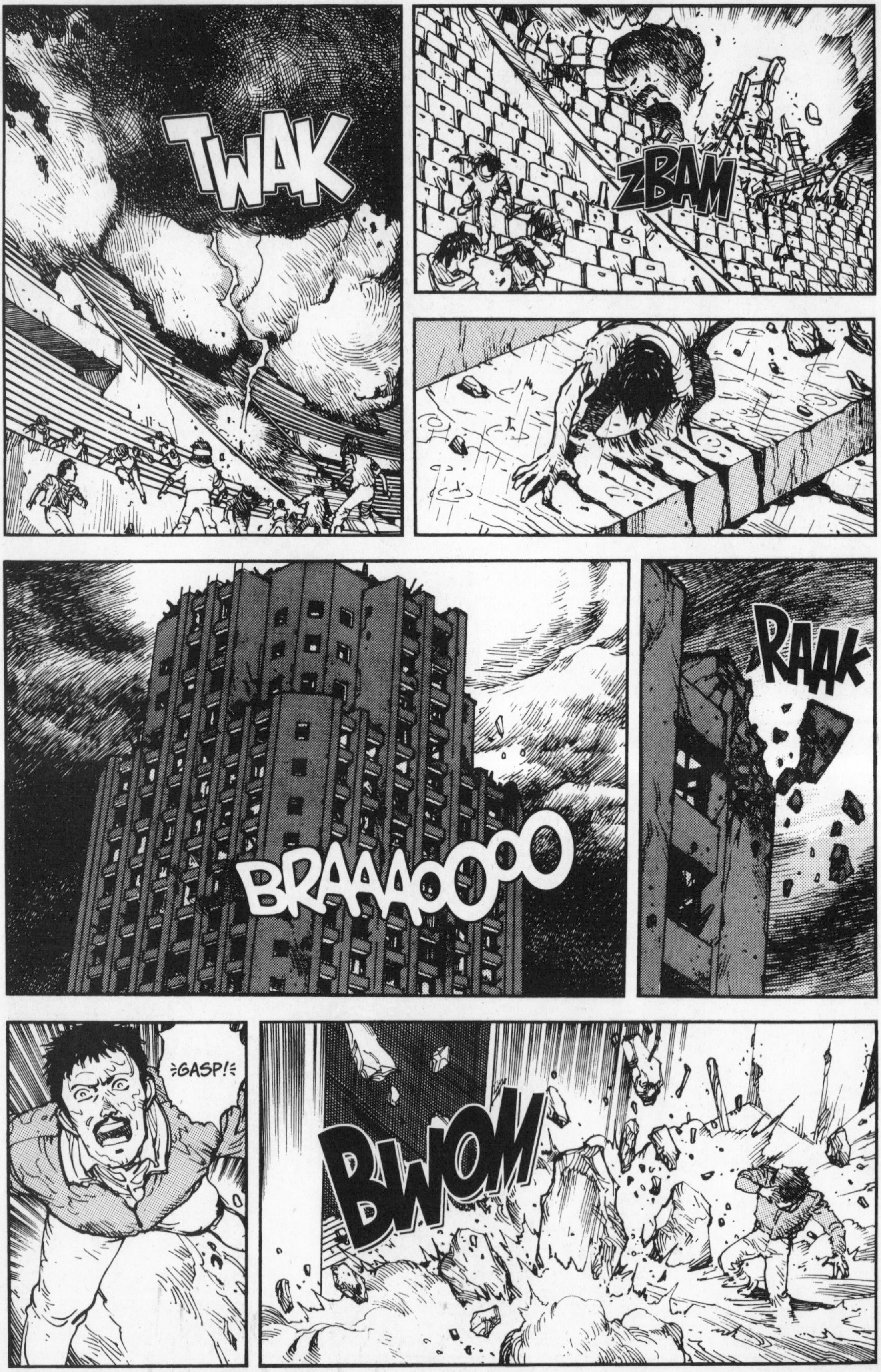

TWAK
ZBAM
BRAAAOOOO
RAAK
GASP!
BWOM

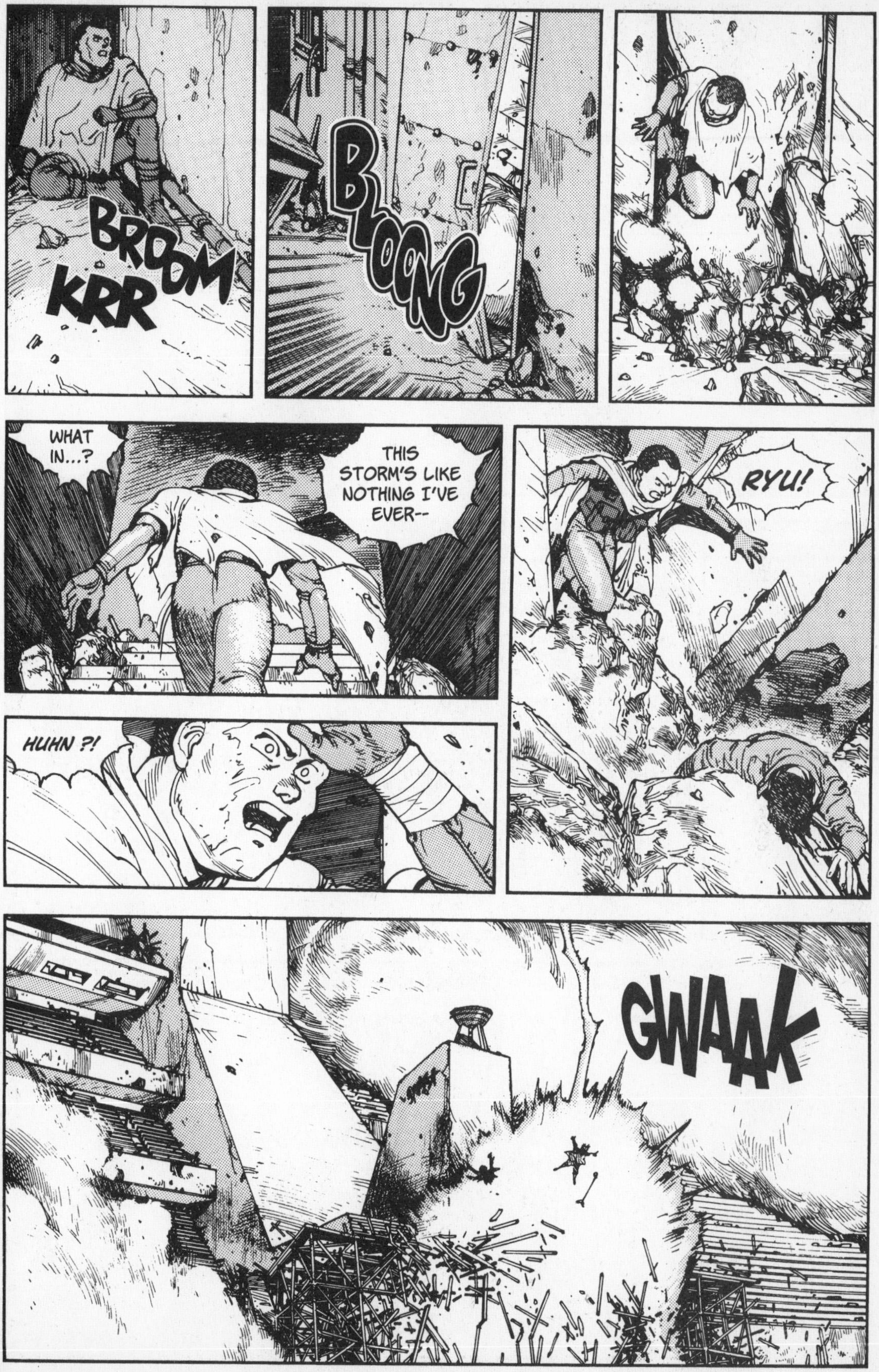
BROOM
KRR
BLOONG
WHAT IN...?
THIS STORM'S LIKE NOTHING I'VE EVER--
RYU!
HUHN ?!
GWAAK

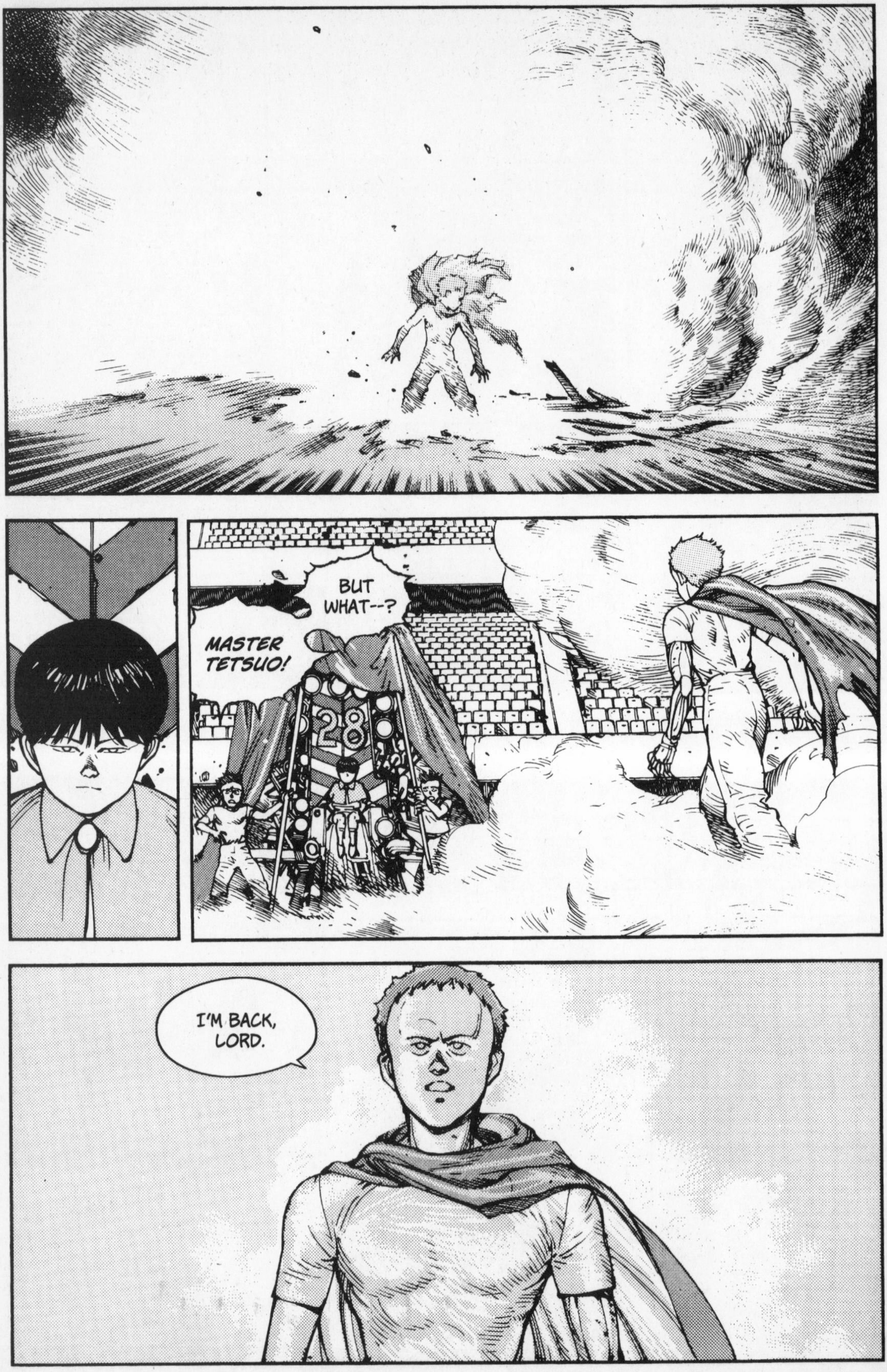
MASTER TETSUO!
BUT WHAT--?
28
I'M BACK, LORD.

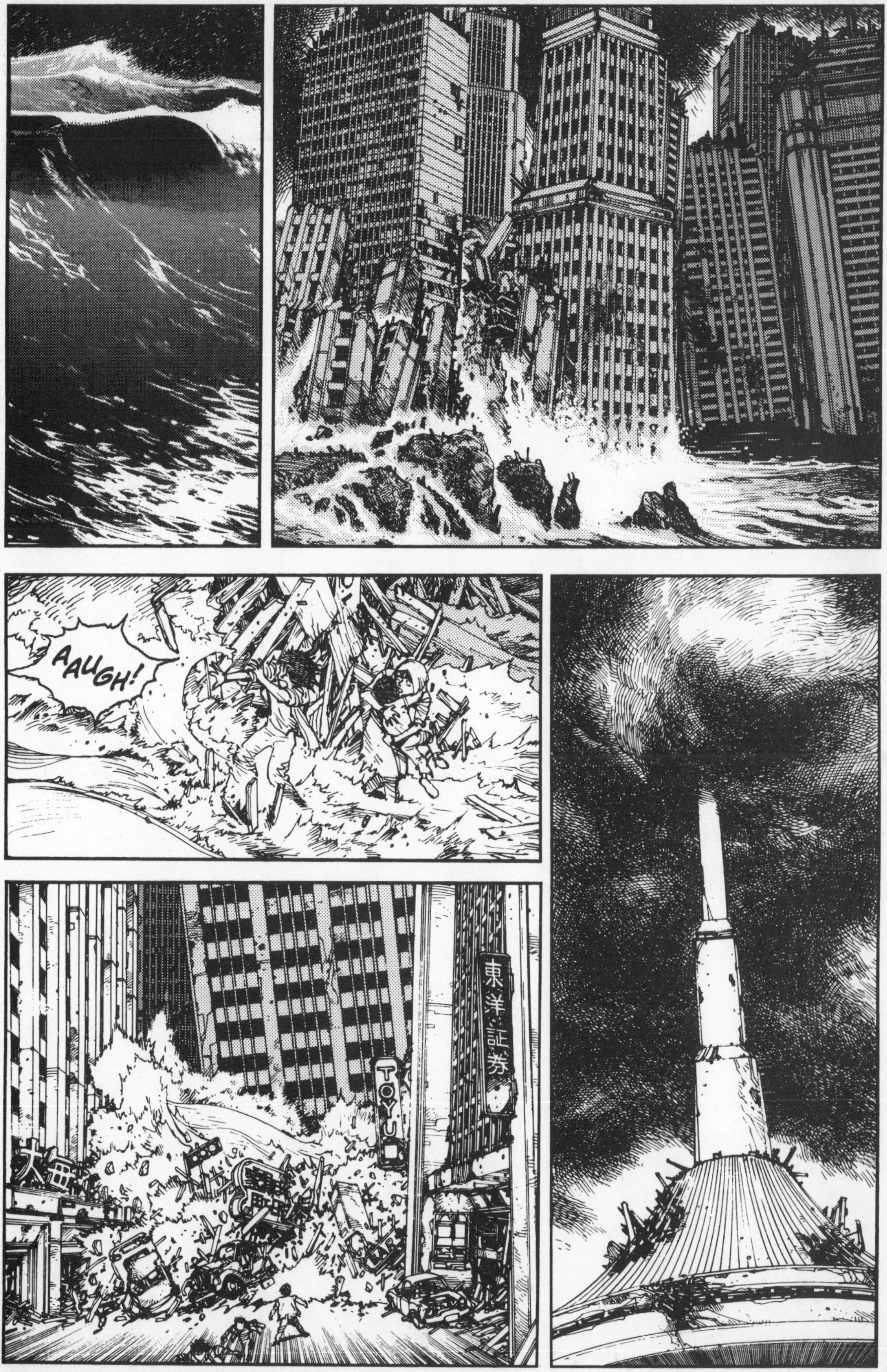
AAUGH!
TOYU
東洋証券

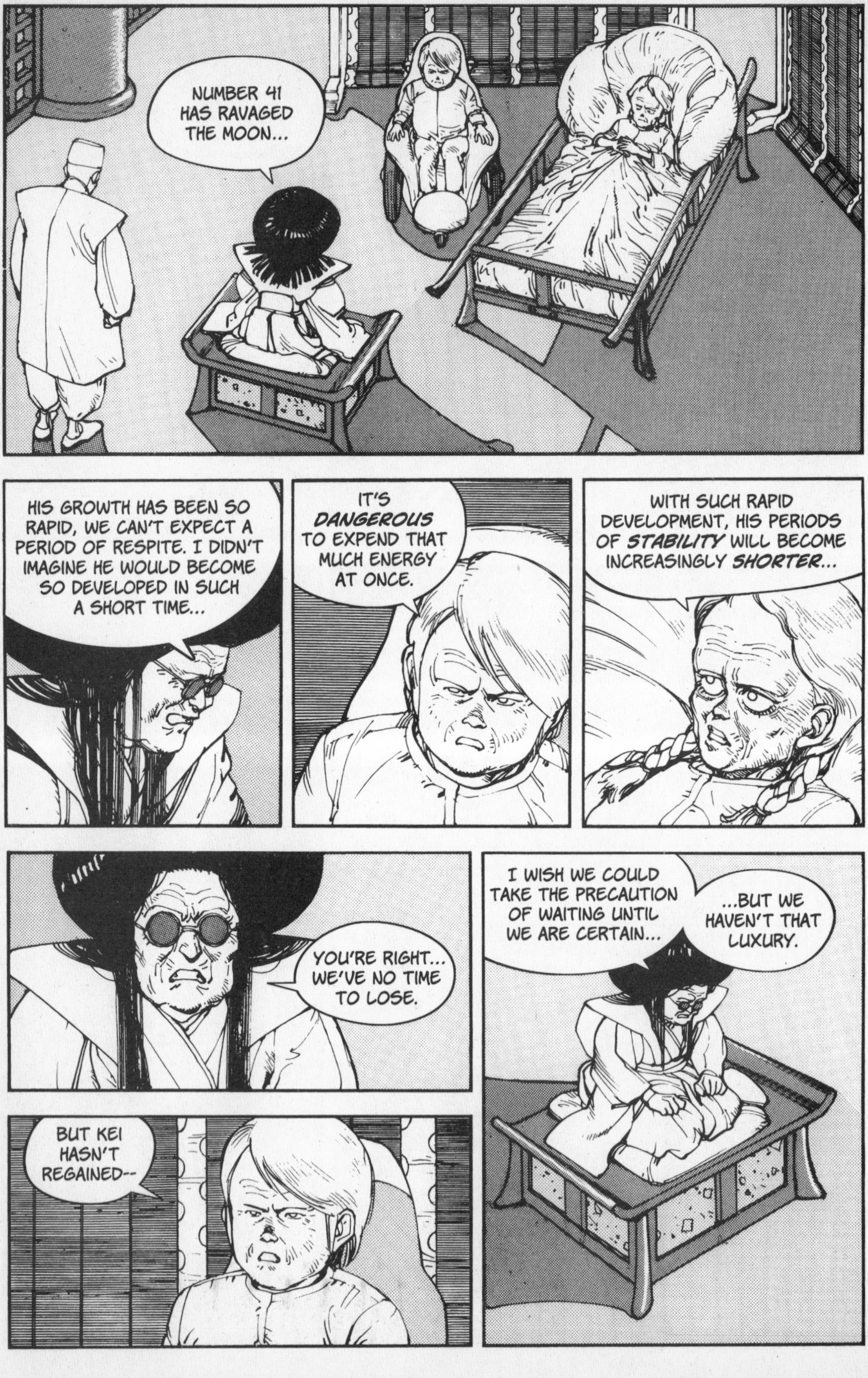
NUMBER 41 HAS RAVAGED THE MOON...
HIS GROWTH HAS BEEN SO RAPID, WE CAN'T EXPECT A PERIOD OF RESPITE. I DIDN'T IMAGINE HE WOULD BECOME SO DEVELOPED IN SUCH A SHORT TIME...
IT'S DANGEROUS TO EXPEND THAT MUCH ENERGY AT ONCE.
WITH SUCH RAPID DEVELOPMENT, HIS PERIODS OF STABILITY WILL BECOME INCREASINGLY SHORTER...
YOU'RE RIGHT... WE'VE NO TIME TO LOSE.
BUT KEI HASN'T REGAINED--
I WISH WE COULD TAKE THE PRECAUTION OF WAITING UNTIL WE ARE CERTAIN...
...BUT WE HAVEN'T THAT LUXURY.

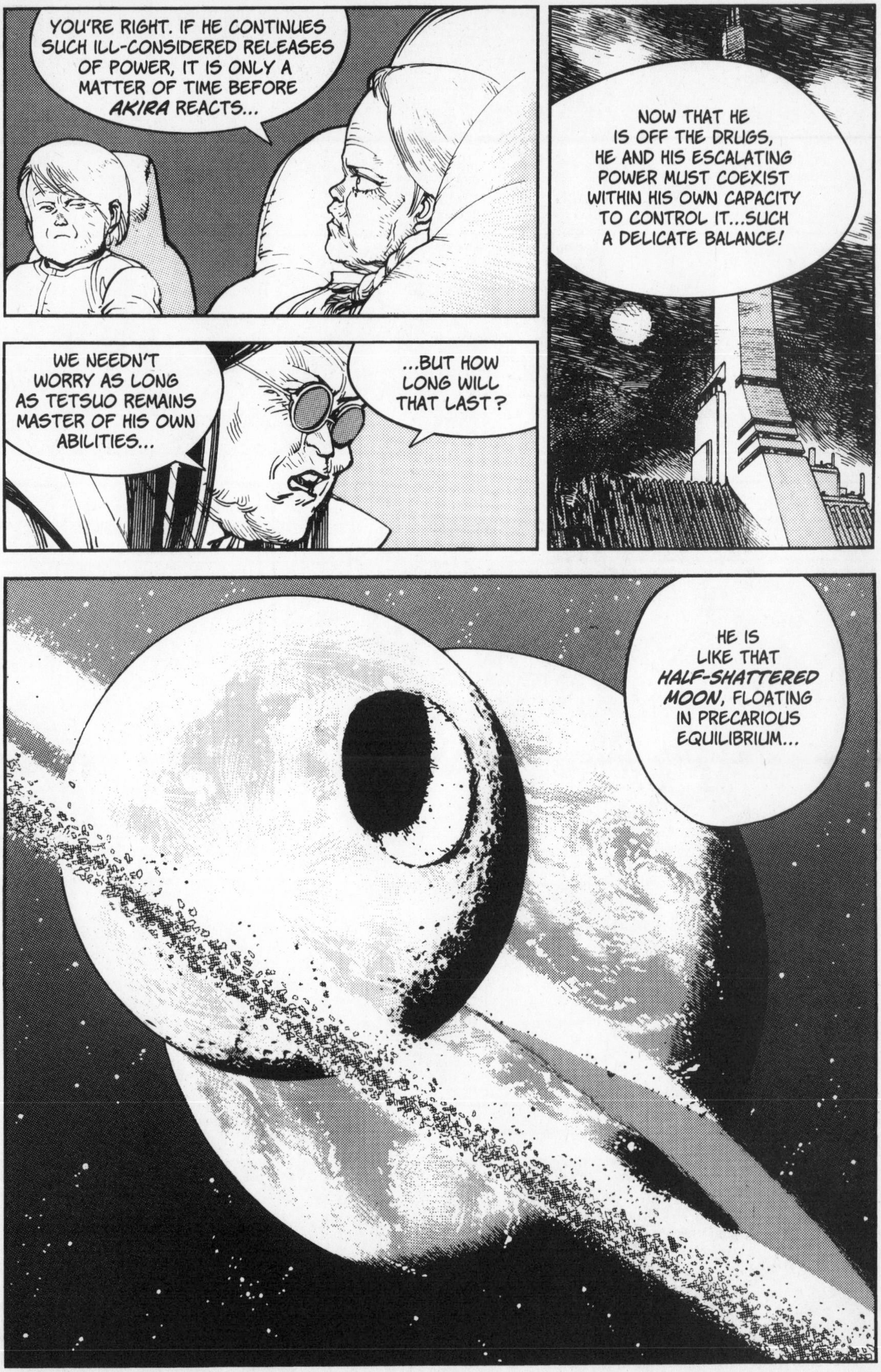
YOU'RE RIGHT. IF HE CONTINUES SUCH ILL-CONSIDERED RELEASES OF POWER, IT IS ONLY A MATTER OF TIME BEFORE *AKIRA* REACTS...
WE NEEDN'T WORRY AS LONG AS TETSUO REMAINS MASTER OF HIS OWN ABILITIES...
...BUT HOW LONG WILL THAT LAST?
NOW THAT HE IS OFF THE DRUGS, HE AND HIS ESCALATING POWER MUST COEXIST WITHIN HIS OWN CAPACITY TO CONTROL IT...SUCH A DELICATE BALANCE!
HE IS LIKE THAT *HALF-SHATTERED MOON*, FLOATING IN PRECARIOUS EQUILIBRIUM...

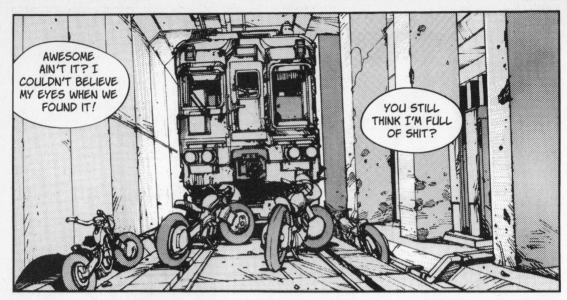

AWESOME AIN'T IT? I COULDN'T BELIEVE MY EYES WHEN WE FOUND IT!
YOU STILL THINK I'M FULL OF SHIT?
NOW WE'RE EVEN FOR THOSE BUSTED BIKES.
NOT YET, PAL.
I'M STILL COSTING OUT THE USABLE PARTS.
DON'T GIMME THAT CRAP! YOU'RE FREAKIN' *LOADED!!*
?
"COSTING OUT"...?! I'M *BROKE*, YOU CHEAP-ASS MISER!
...
I'VE HAD ENOUGH'A YOUR *SHIT*, KANEDA!
SO?! SCREW YOU, YA FAT BASTARD!

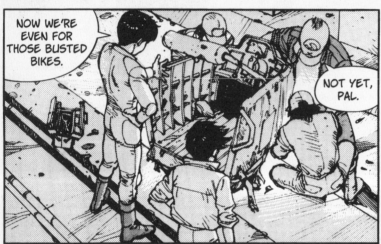

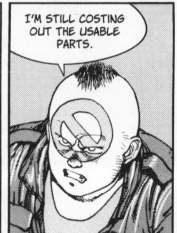

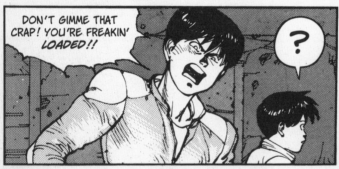

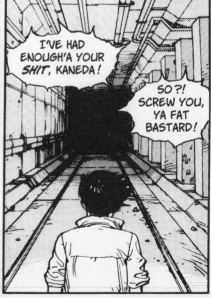

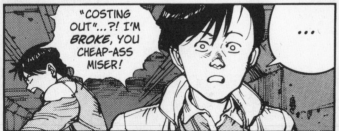

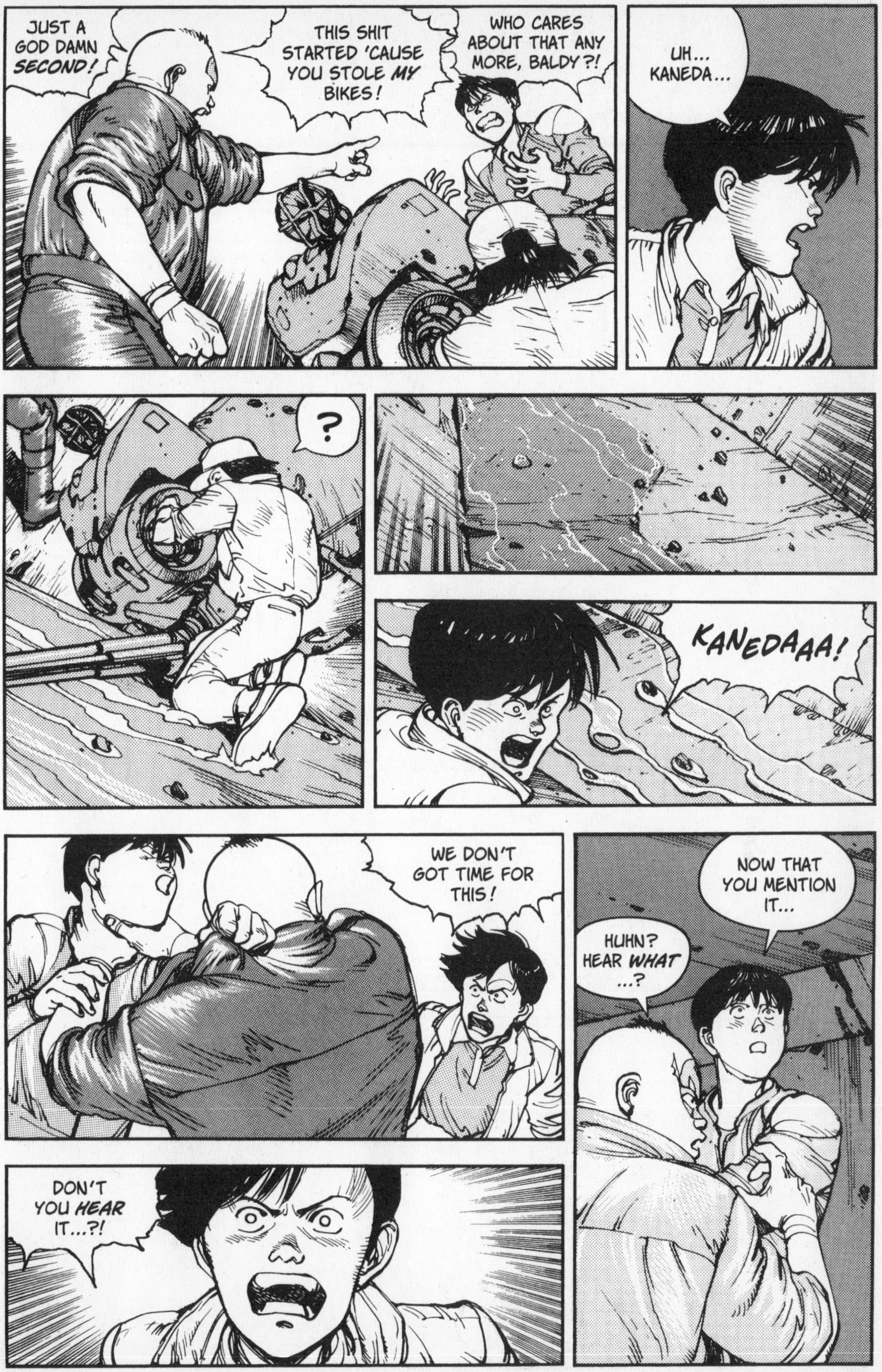
JUST A GOD DAMN SECOND!
THIS SHIT STARTED 'CAUSE YOU STOLE MY BIKES!
WHO CARES ABOUT THAT ANY MORE, BALDY?!
UH... KANEDA...
?
KANEDAAA!
WE DON'T GOT TIME FOR THIS!
DON'T YOU HEAR IT...?!
NOW THAT YOU MENTION IT...
HUHN? HEAR WHAT ...?

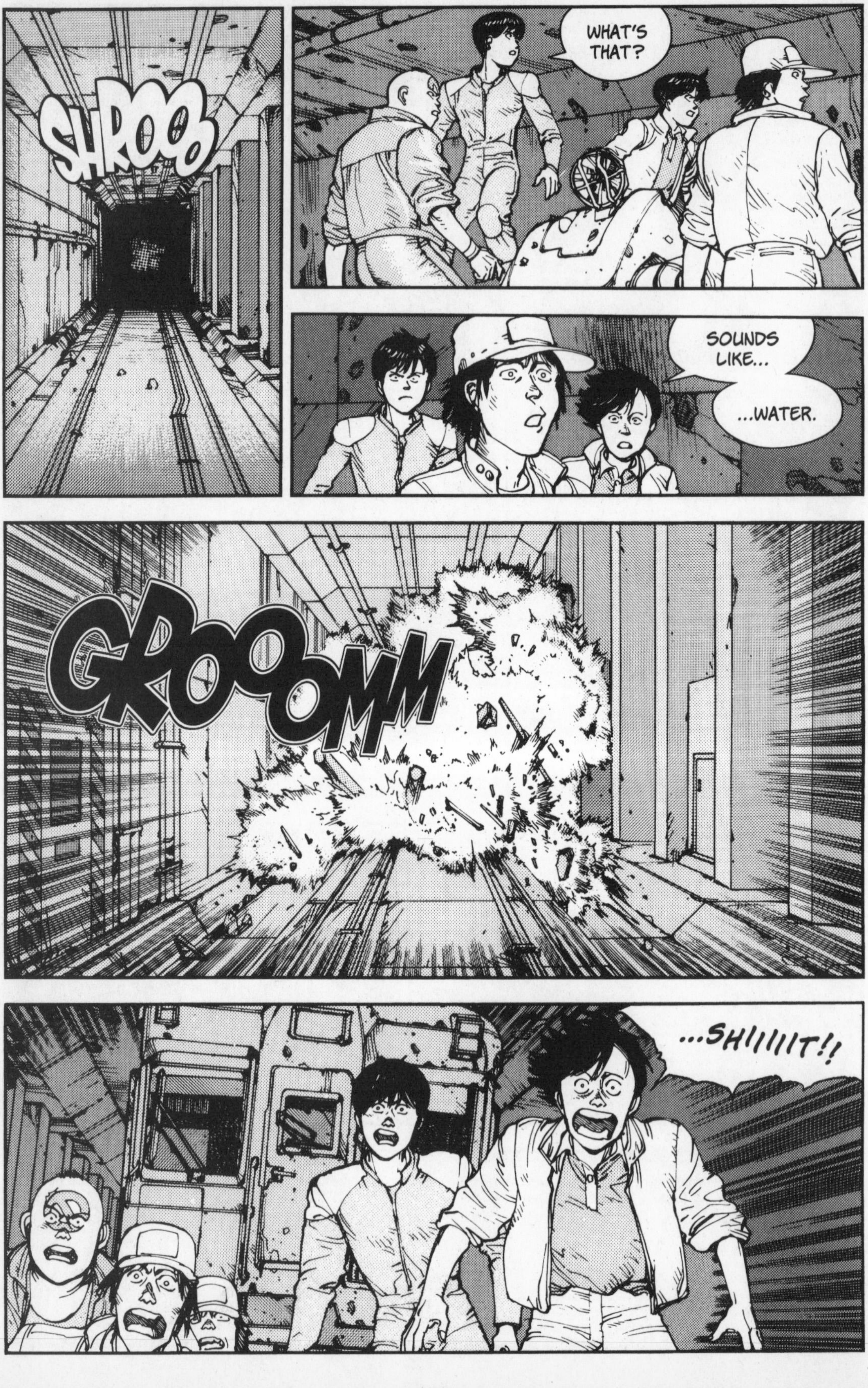
SHROOO
WHAT'S THAT?
SOUNDS LIKE...
...WATER.
GROOOMM
...SHIIIIIT!!

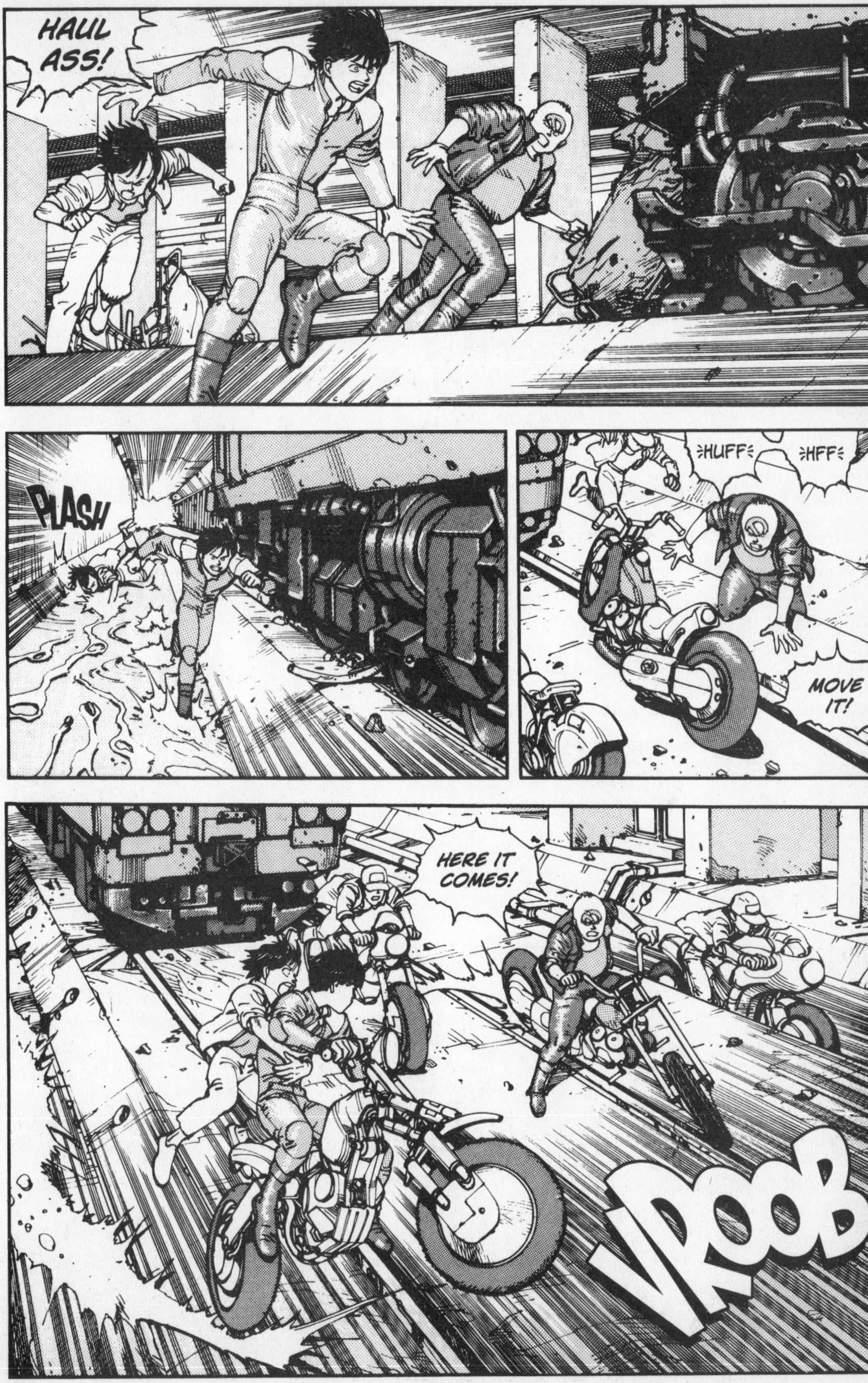
HAUL ASS!
PLASH
HUFF
HFF
MOVE IT!
HERE IT COMES!
VROOB

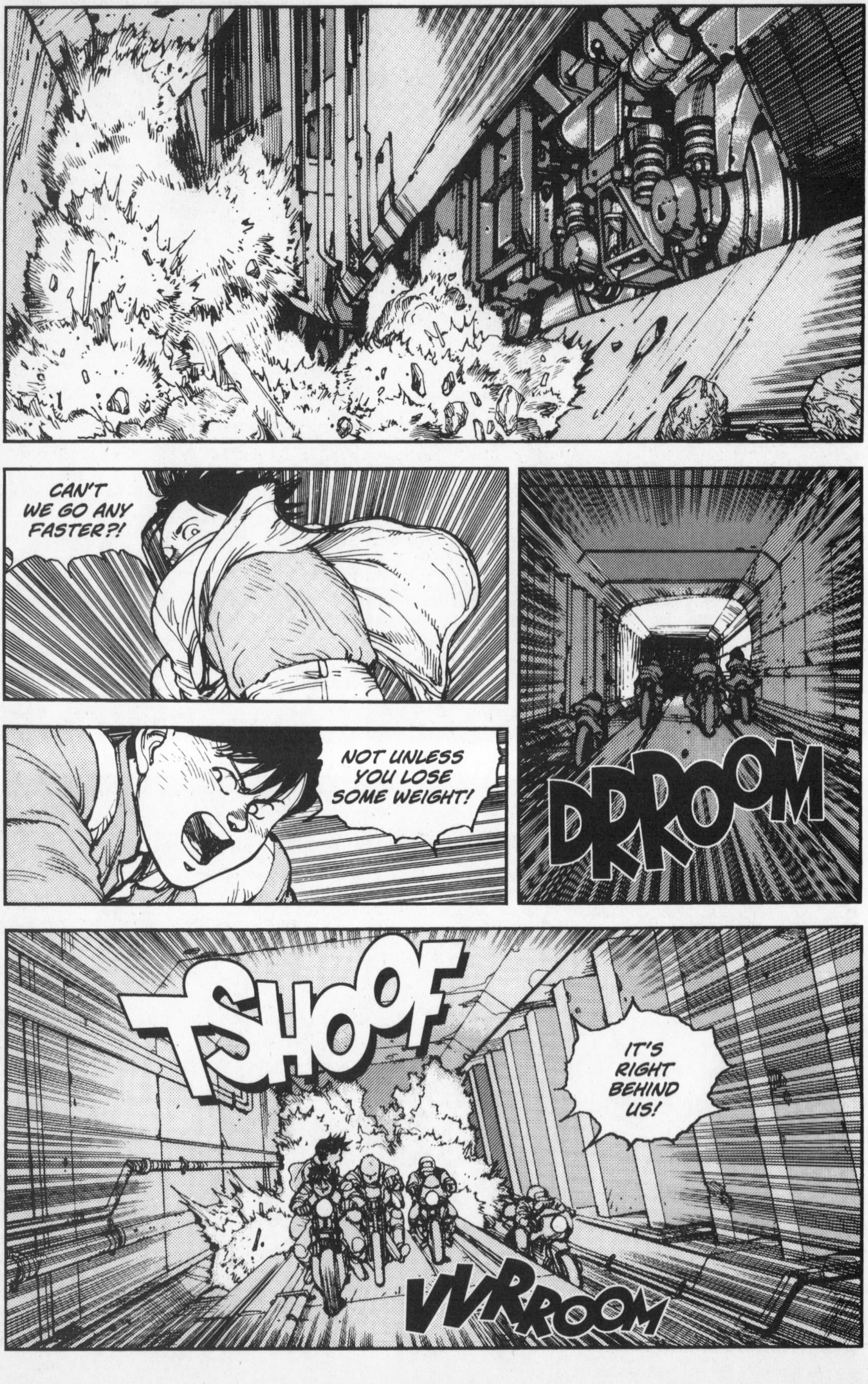
CAN'T WE GO ANY FASTER?!
DRROOM
NOT UNLESS YOU LOSE SOME WEIGHT!
TSHOOF
IT'S RIGHT BEHIND US!
VVRROOM

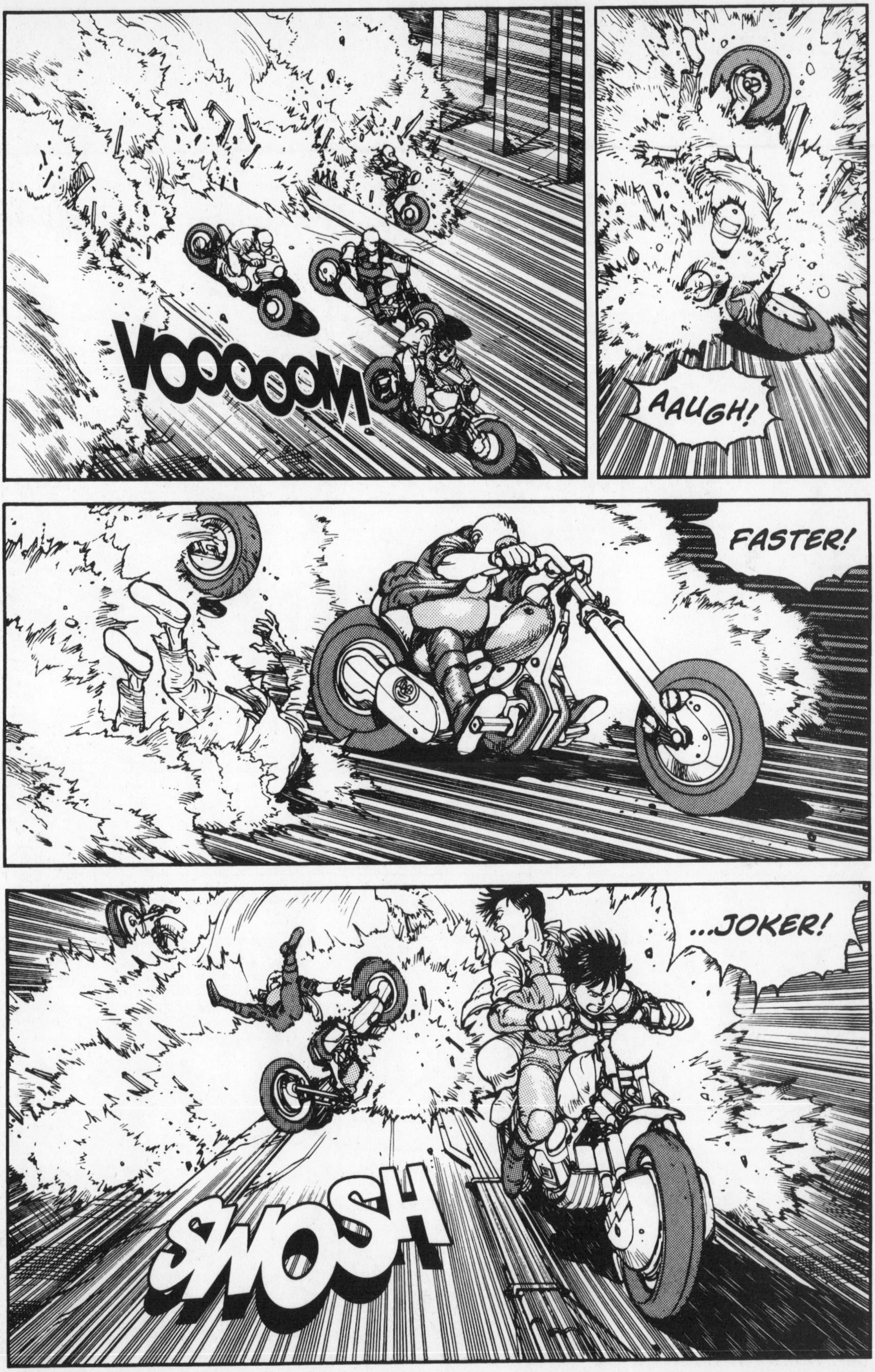
VOOOOOM
AAUGH!
FASTER!
...JOKER!
SWOSH

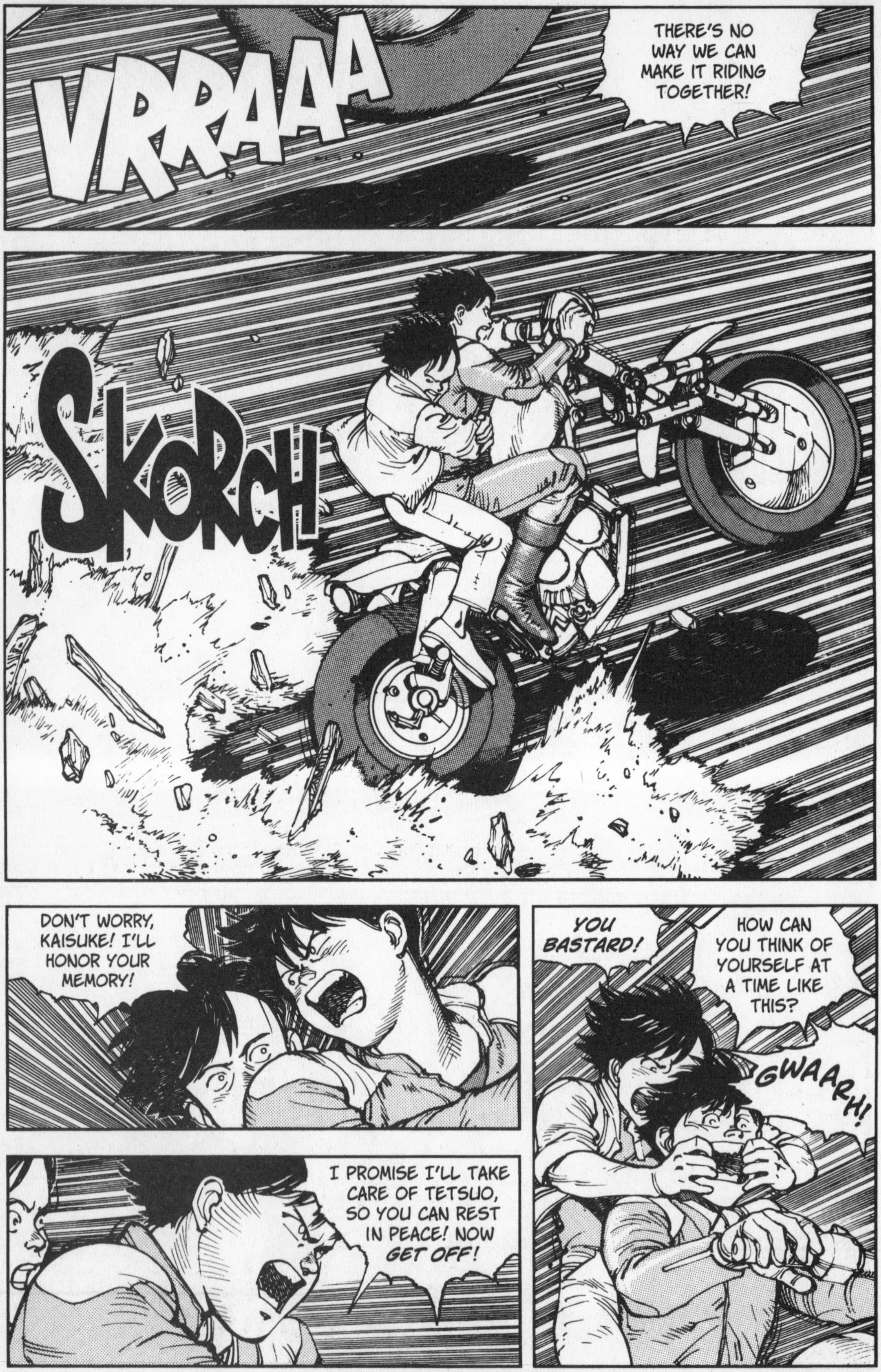
VRRAAA
THERE'S NO WAY WE CAN MAKE IT RIDING TOGETHER!
SKORCH
DON'T WORRY, KAISUKE! I'LL HONOR YOUR MEMORY!
YOU BASTARD!
HOW CAN YOU THINK OF YOURSELF AT A TIME LIKE THIS?
GWAARH!
I PROMISE I'LL TAKE CARE OF TETSUO, SO YOU CAN REST IN PEACE! NOW GET OFF!

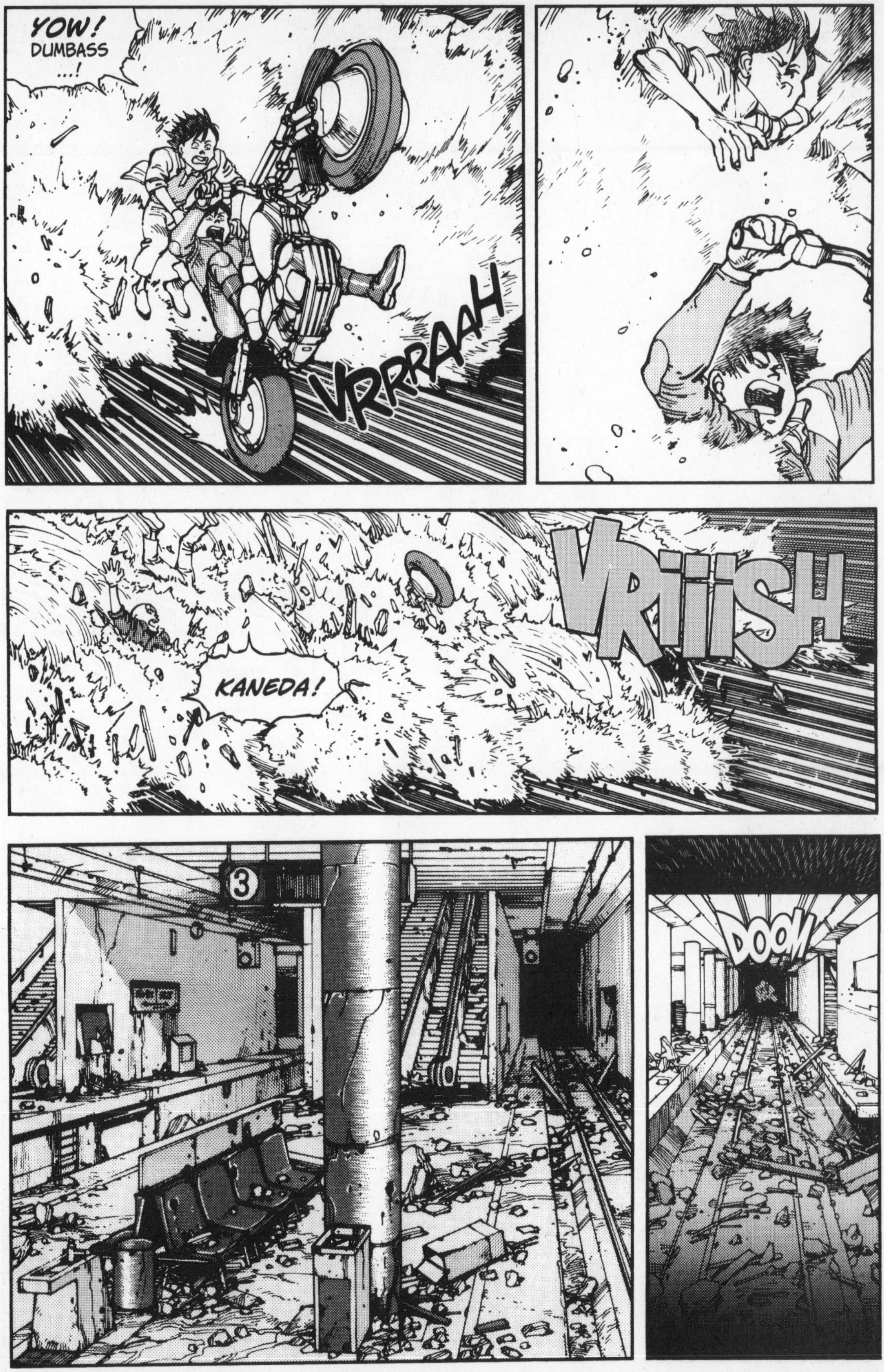
YOW! DUMBASS ...!
VRRRAAH
VRIIISH
KANEDA!
DOOM

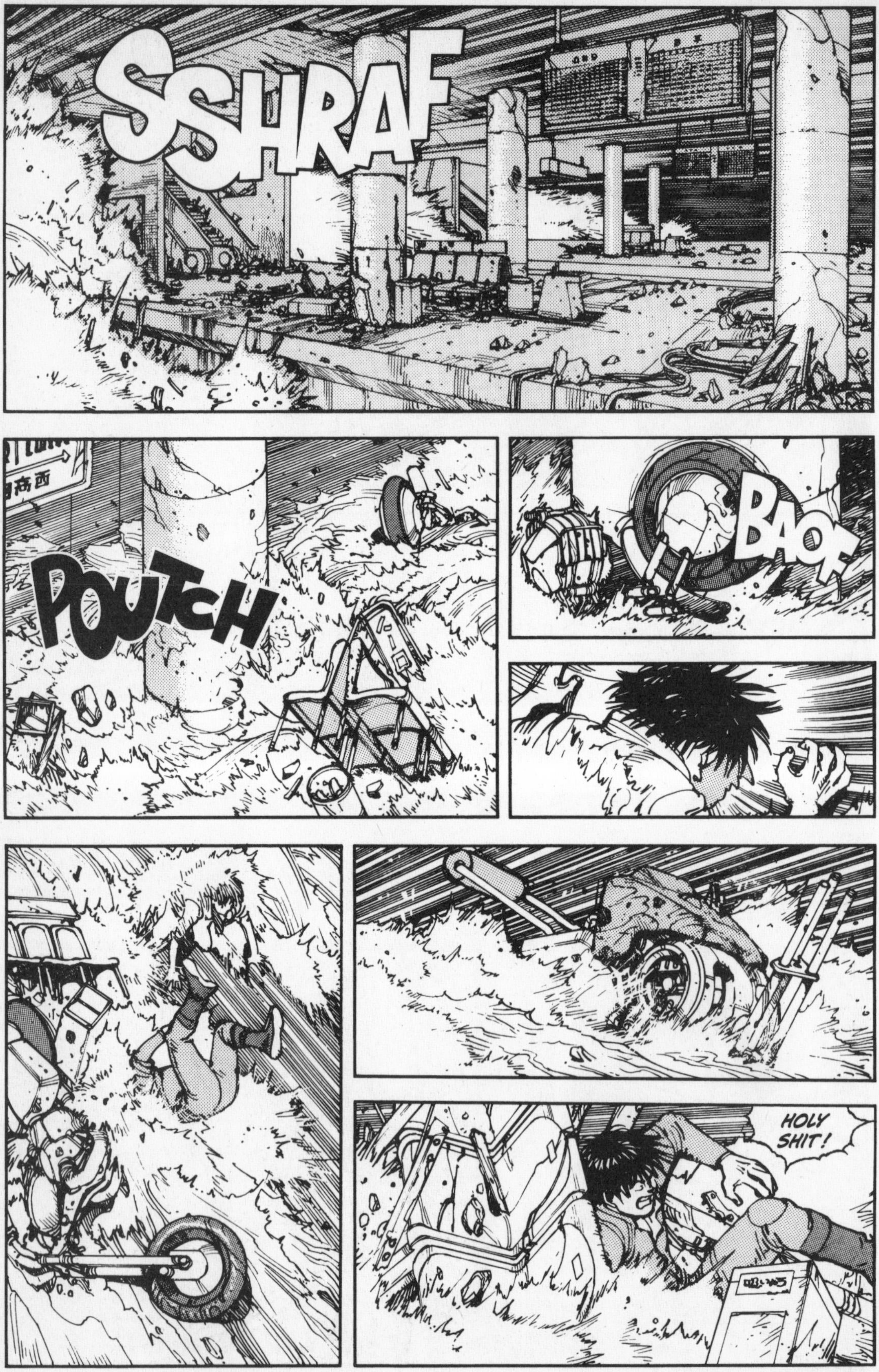
SSHRAF
POUTCH
BAOF
HOLY SHIT!

AW, *MAN!!* MY BIKE!!

≶KOFF≶
≶KOFF≶

≶BLAARGH≶
≶KOFF≶
≶KOFF≶

QUIT YER *BITCHIN'!* AT LEAST YOU STILL GOT IT!

DON'T YOU THINK SOMETHING'S *WEIRD...?* THAT WAS *SEAWATER!*

YEAH...IT WAS *SALTY,* ALL RIGHT.

AND A BIT TOO *FAST* AND A BIT TOO *MUCH* JUST FOR HIGH TIDE...

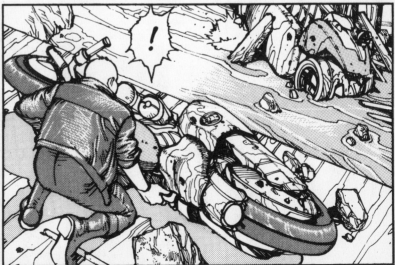

!

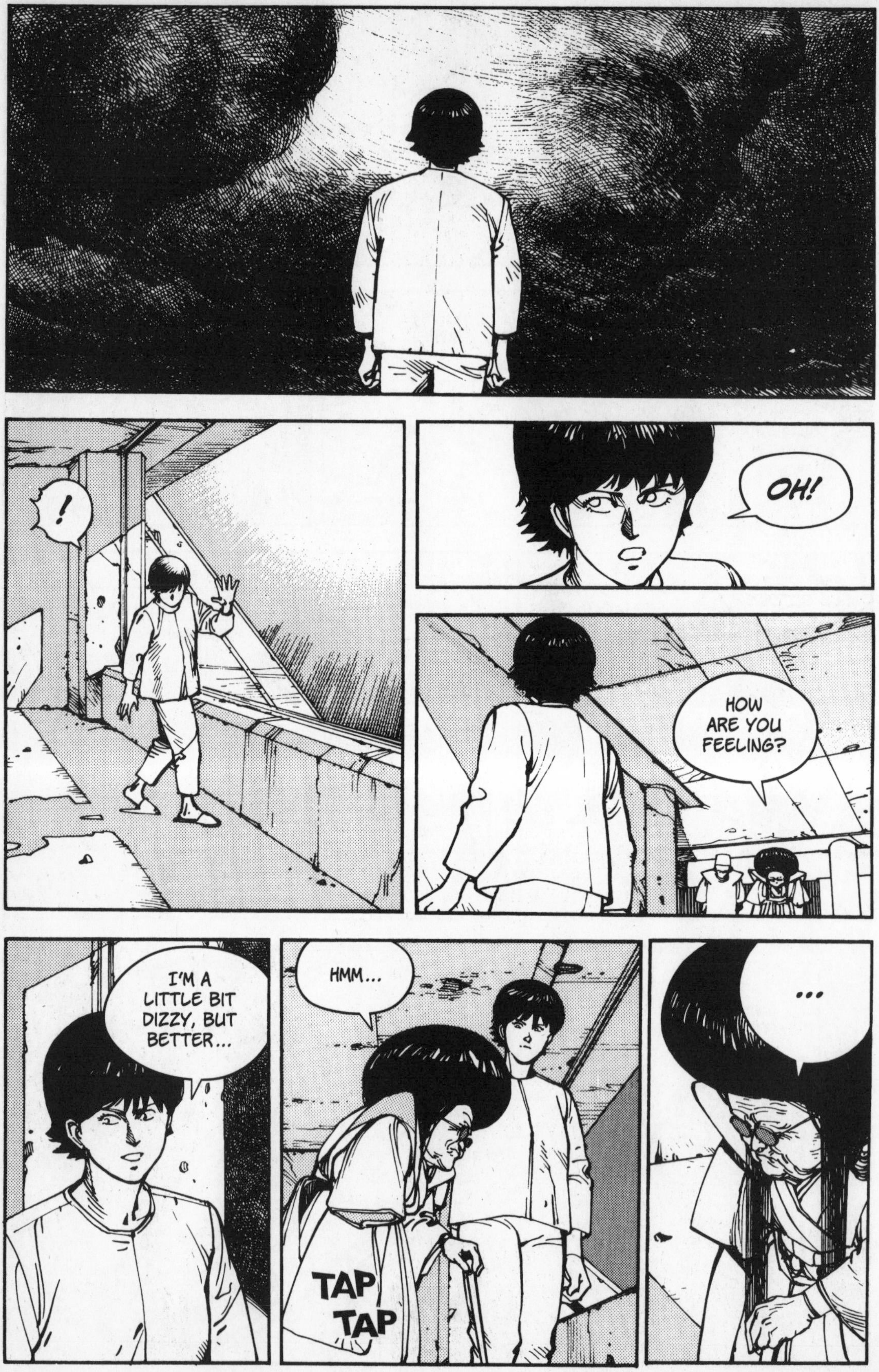
!
OH!
HOW ARE YOU FEELING?
I'M A LITTLE BIT DIZZY, BUT BETTER...
HMM...
TAP TAP
...

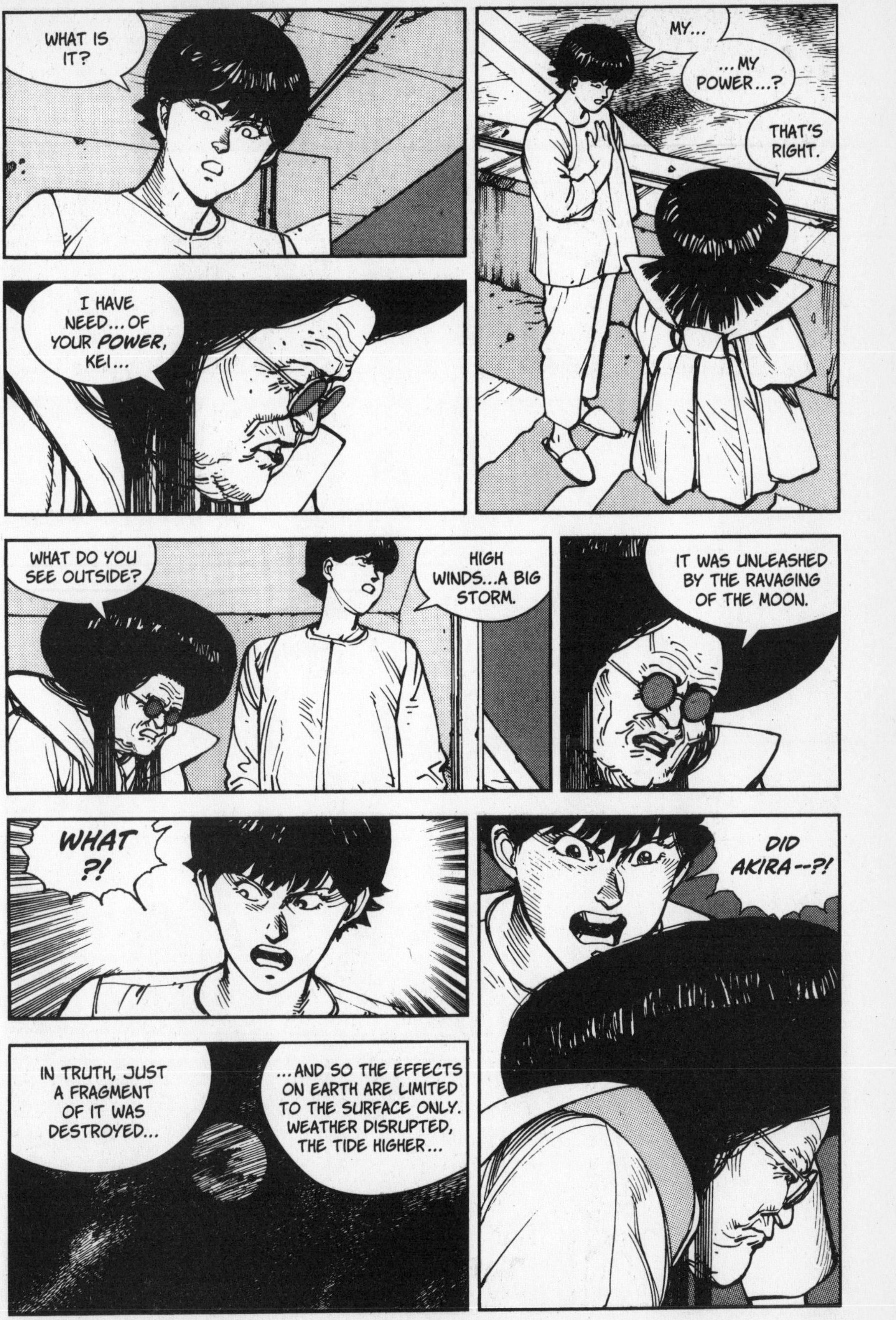
WHAT IS IT?
MY...
...MY POWER...?
THAT'S RIGHT.
I HAVE NEED... OF YOUR POWER, KEI...
WHAT DO YOU SEE OUTSIDE?
HIGH WINDS...A BIG STORM.
IT WAS UNLEASHED BY THE RAVAGING OF THE MOON.
WHAT ?!
DID AKIRA--?!
IN TRUTH, JUST A FRAGMENT OF IT WAS DESTROYED...
...AND SO THE EFFECTS ON EARTH ARE LIMITED TO THE SURFACE ONLY. WEATHER DISRUPTED, THE TIDE HIGHER...

NO. IT WAS NUMBER 41.

TETSUO?!

THE TIME WE'VE AWAITED HAS COME...

"WE"...?

AH...!

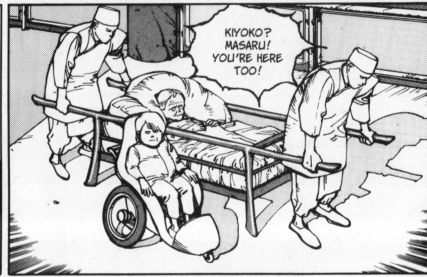

KIYOKO? MASARU! YOU'RE HERE TOO!

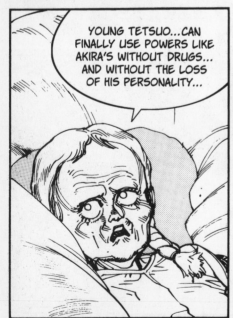

YOUNG TETSUO...CAN FINALLY USE POWERS LIKE AKIRA'S WITHOUT DRUGS... AND WITHOUT THE LOSS OF HIS PERSONALITY...

POWERS...

...LIKE AKIRA'S?!

WE'LL USE THAT POWER TO BURY AKIRA.

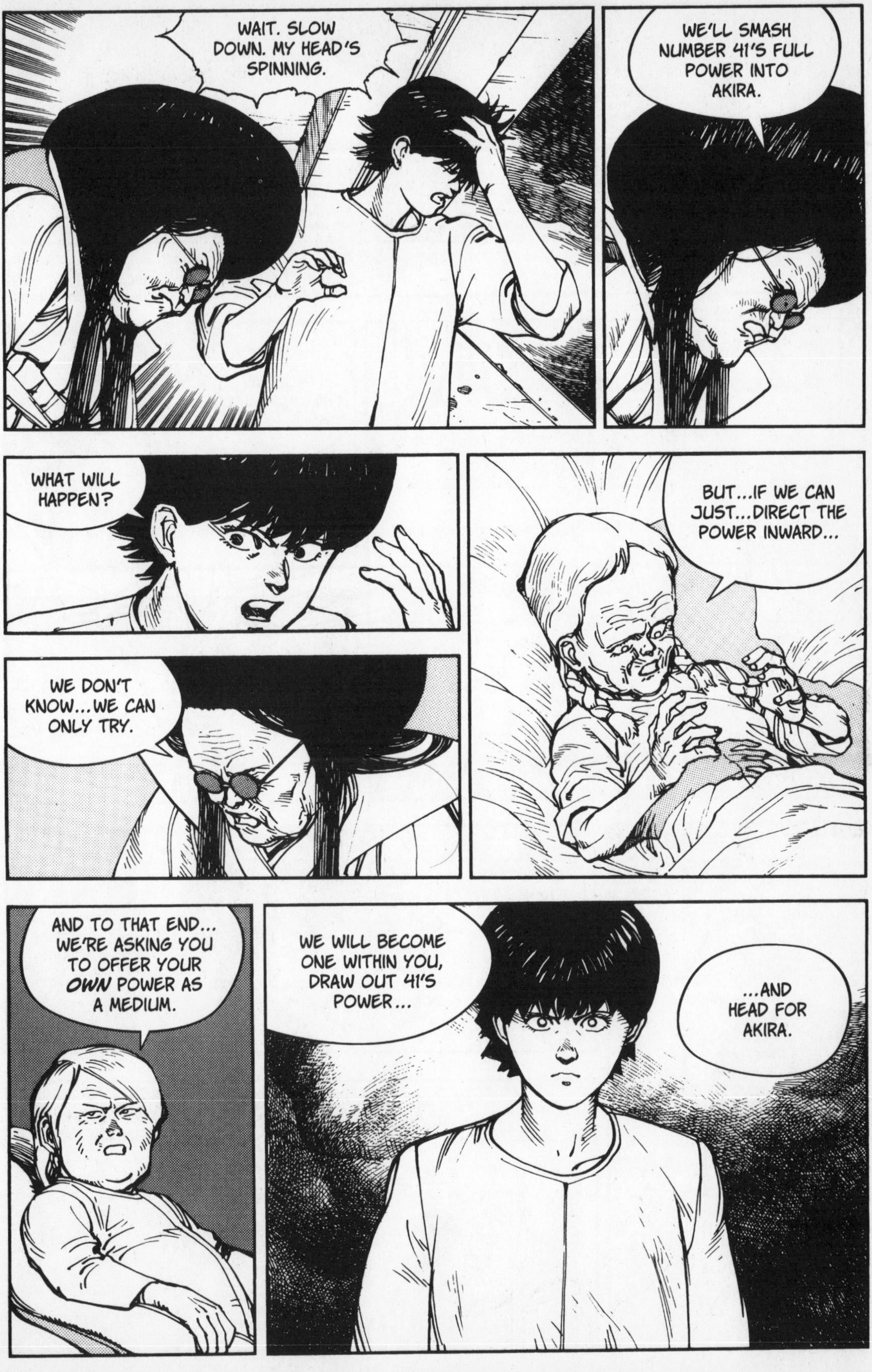
WAIT. SLOW DOWN. MY HEAD'S SPINNING.
WE'LL SMASH NUMBER 41'S FULL POWER INTO AKIRA.
WHAT WILL HAPPEN?
WE DON'T KNOW...WE CAN ONLY TRY.
BUT...IF WE CAN JUST...DIRECT THE POWER INWARD...
AND TO THAT END... WE'RE ASKING YOU TO OFFER YOUR *OWN* POWER AS A MEDIUM.
WE WILL BECOME ONE WITHIN YOU, DRAW OUT 41'S POWER...
...AND HEAD FOR AKIRA.

YOU WANT TO USE ME... LIKE YOU DID BEFORE.

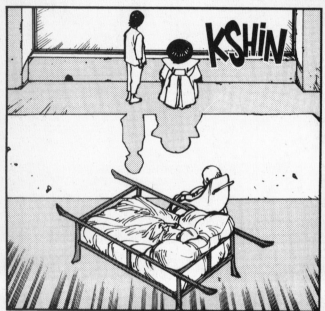

KSHIN

YOU'RE THINKING ABOUT YOUR LOVE...

HUHN?!

FORGIVE ME. I DID NOT INTEND TO PRY INTO YOUR THOUGHTS.

YOU'RE MISTAKEN. KANEDA AND I AREN'T--

KEI, WE HAVEN'T MUCH TIME.

TETSUO'S POWER WILL SOON BE BEYOND HIS CONTROL.

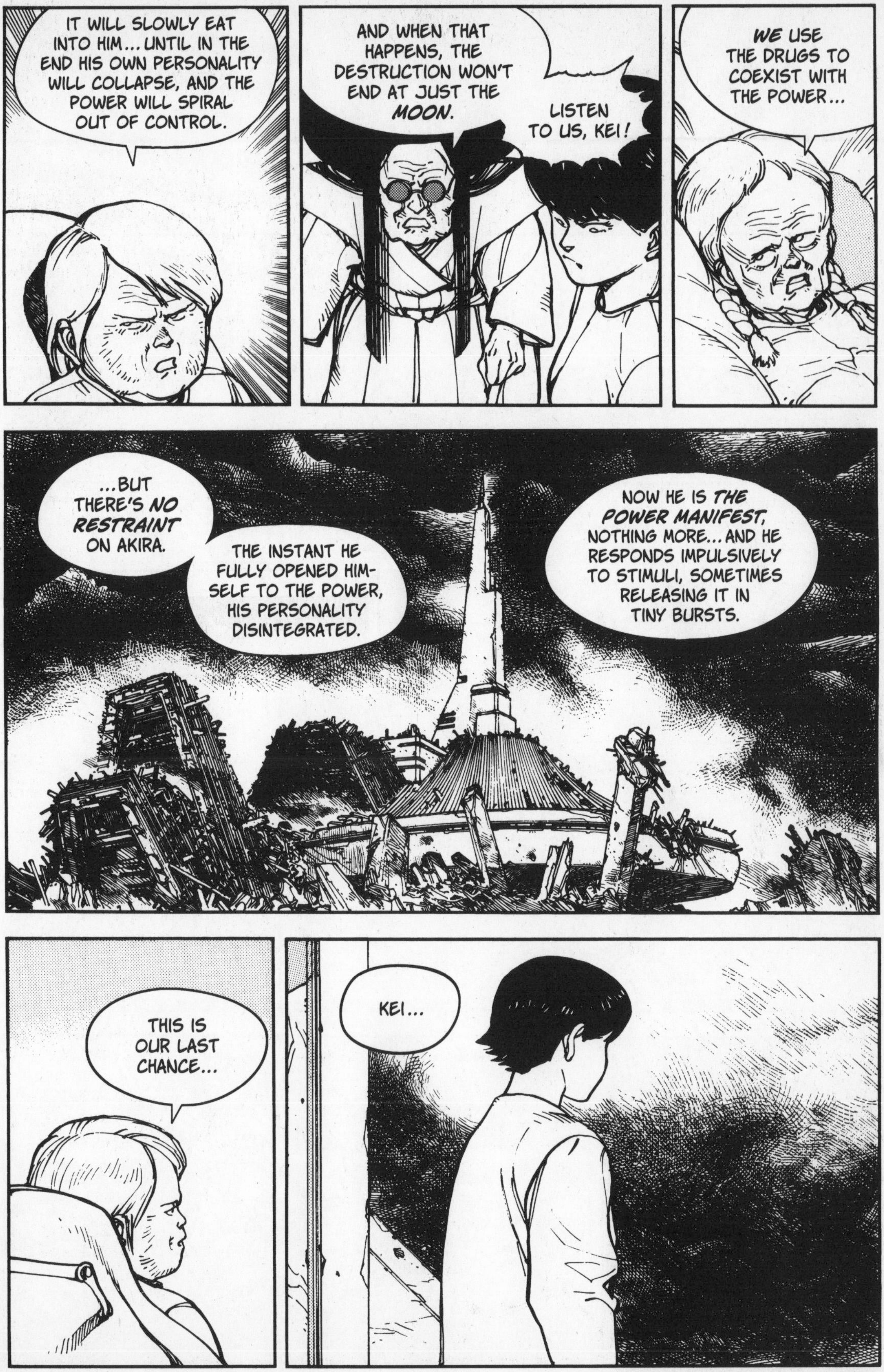
IT WILL SLOWLY EAT INTO HIM... UNTIL IN THE END HIS OWN PERSONALITY WILL COLLAPSE, AND THE POWER WILL SPIRAL OUT OF CONTROL.
AND WHEN THAT HAPPENS, THE DESTRUCTION WON'T END AT JUST THE *MOON*.
LISTEN TO US, KEI!
WE USE THE DRUGS TO COEXIST WITH THE POWER...
...BUT THERE'S *NO RESTRAINT* ON AKIRA.
THE INSTANT HE FULLY OPENED HIM-SELF TO THE POWER, HIS PERSONALITY DISINTEGRATED.
NOW HE IS *THE POWER MANIFEST*, NOTHING MORE... AND HE RESPONDS IMPULSIVELY TO STIMULI, SOMETIMES RELEASING IT IN TINY BURSTS.
THIS IS OUR LAST CHANCE...
KEI...

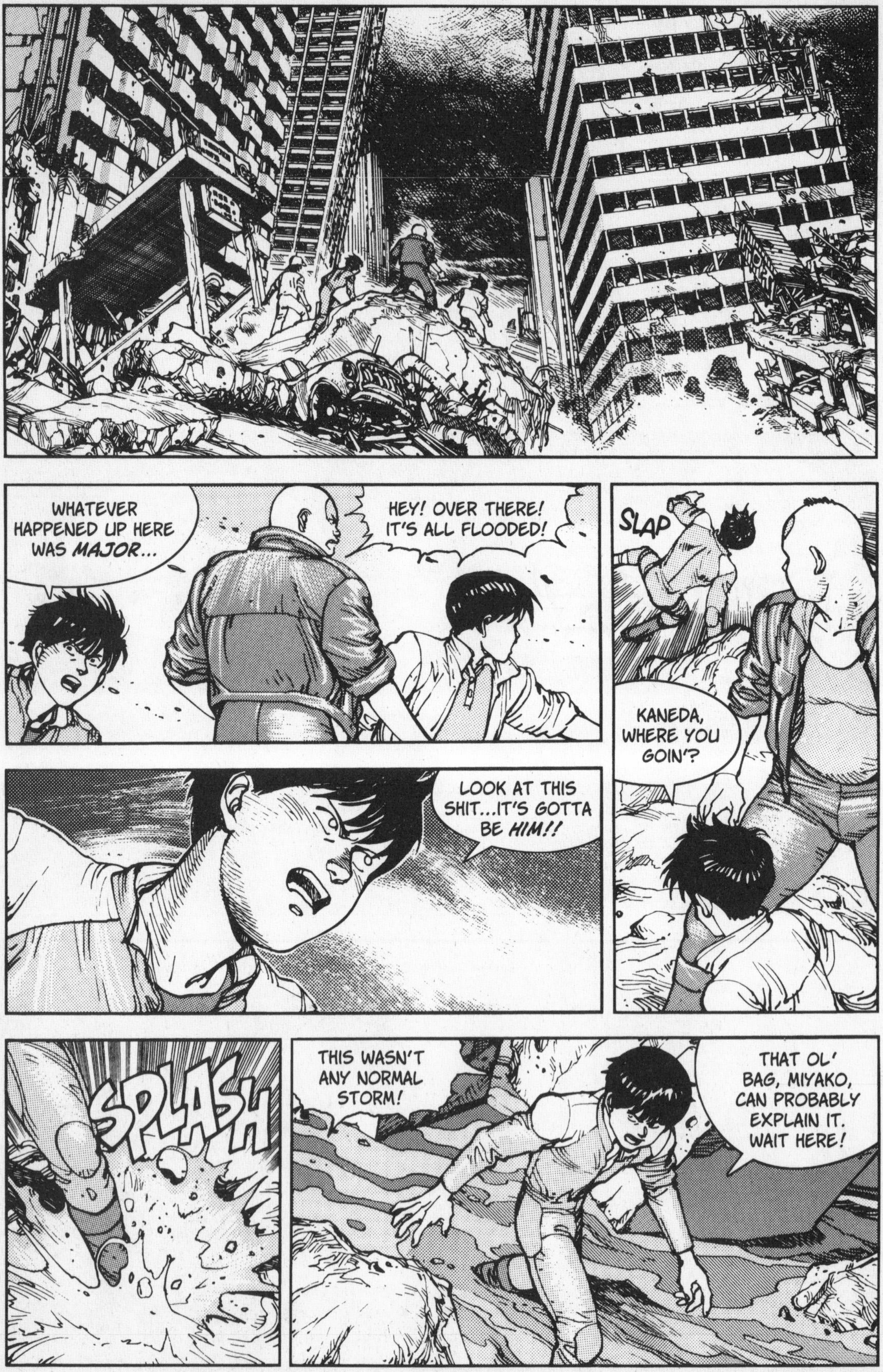
WHATEVER HAPPENED UP HERE WAS *MAJOR*...
HEY! OVER THERE! IT'S ALL FLOODED!
SLAP
KANEDA, WHERE YOU GOIN'?
LOOK AT THIS SHIT...IT'S GOTTA BE *HIM!!*
SPLASH
THIS WASN'T ANY NORMAL STORM!
THAT OL' BAG, MIYAKO, CAN PROBABLY EXPLAIN IT. WAIT HERE!

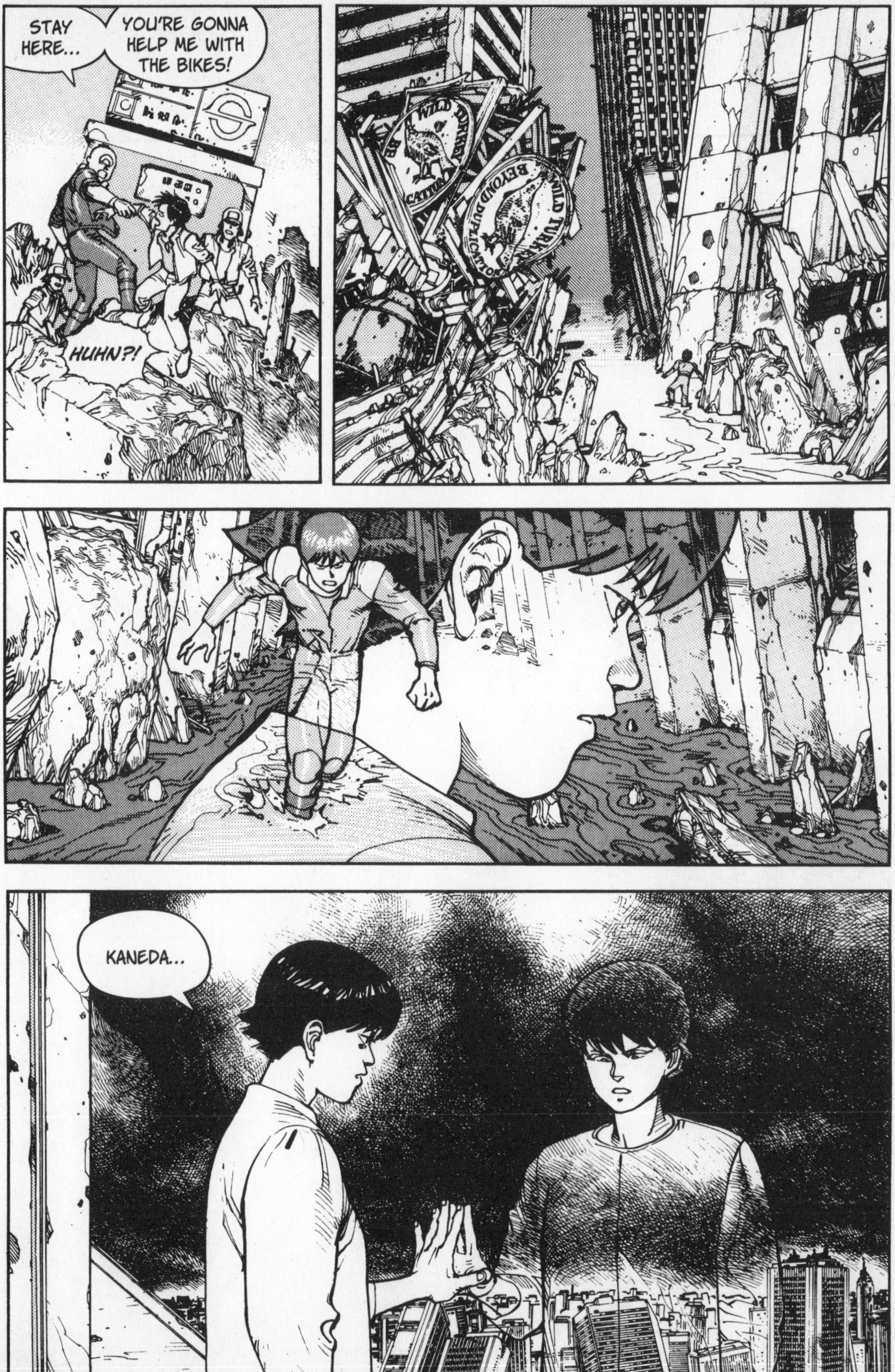
STAY HERE...
YOU'RE GONNA HELP ME WITH THE BIKES!
HUHN?!
WILD TURKEY
BEYOND DUPLICATION
KANEDA...

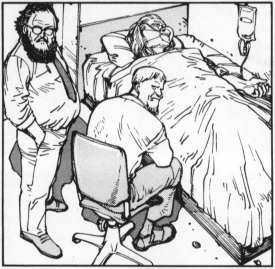

ATTENTION SPECIAL FORCES PERSONNEL! REPORT IMMEDIATELY TO THE OPERATIONS ROOM DRESSED FOR LEVEL FIVE COMBAT!

REPEAT, SPECIAL FORCES PERSONNEL...

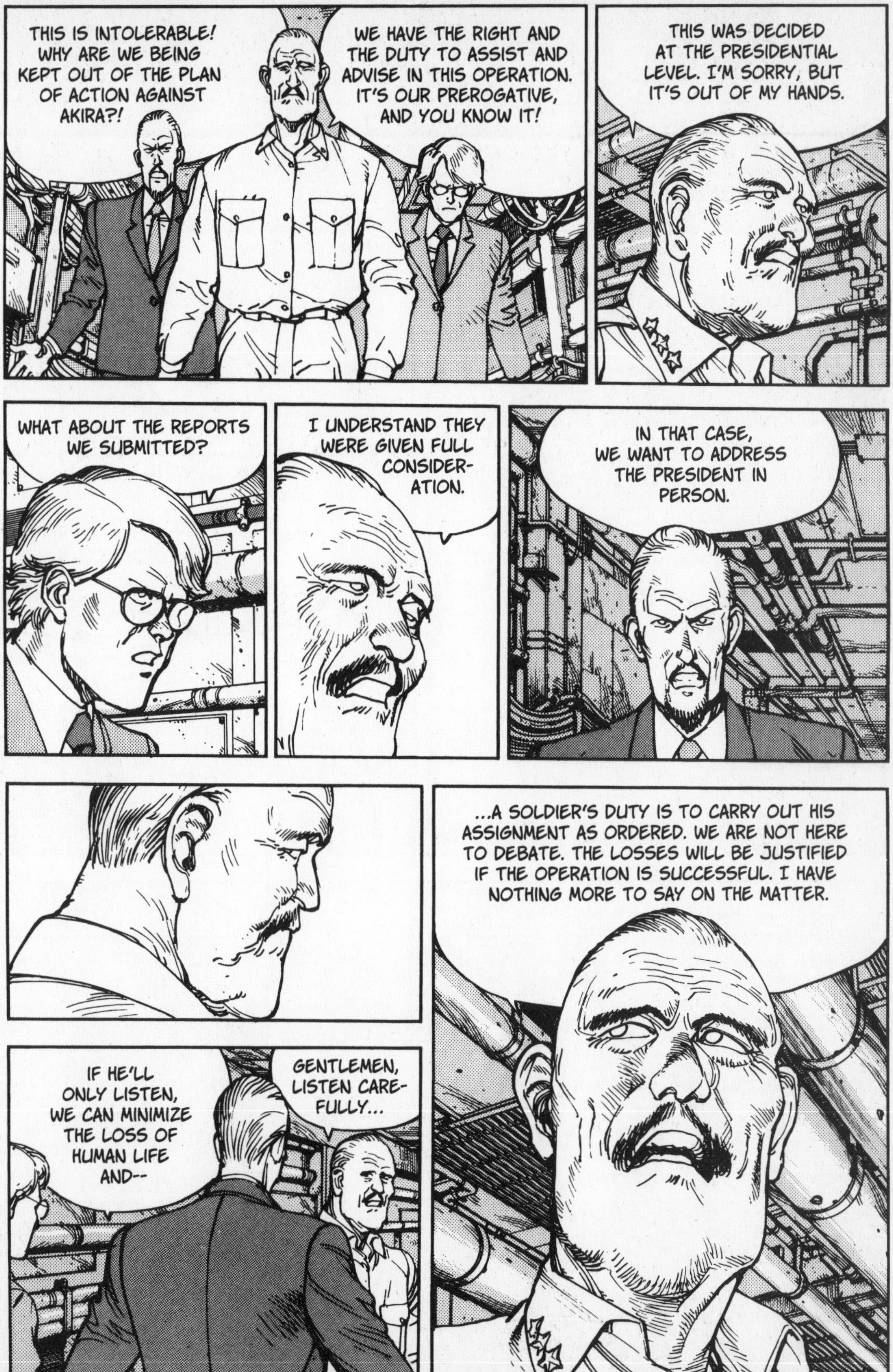
THIS IS INTOLERABLE! WHY ARE WE BEING KEPT OUT OF THE PLAN OF ACTION AGAINST AKIRA?!
WE HAVE THE RIGHT AND THE DUTY TO ASSIST AND ADVISE IN THIS OPERATION. IT'S OUR PREROGATIVE, AND YOU KNOW IT!
THIS WAS DECIDED AT THE PRESIDENTIAL LEVEL. I'M SORRY, BUT IT'S OUT OF MY HANDS.
WHAT ABOUT THE REPORTS WE SUBMITTED?
I UNDERSTAND THEY WERE GIVEN FULL CONSIDER-ATION.
IN THAT CASE, WE WANT TO ADDRESS THE PRESIDENT IN PERSON.
IF HE'LL ONLY LISTEN, WE CAN MINIMIZE THE LOSS OF HUMAN LIFE AND--
GENTLEMEN, LISTEN CARE-FULLY...
...A SOLDIER'S DUTY IS TO CARRY OUT HIS ASSIGNMENT AS ORDERED. WE ARE NOT HERE TO DEBATE. THE LOSSES WILL BE JUSTIFIED IF THE OPERATION IS SUCCESSFUL. I HAVE NOTHING MORE TO SAY ON THE MATTER.

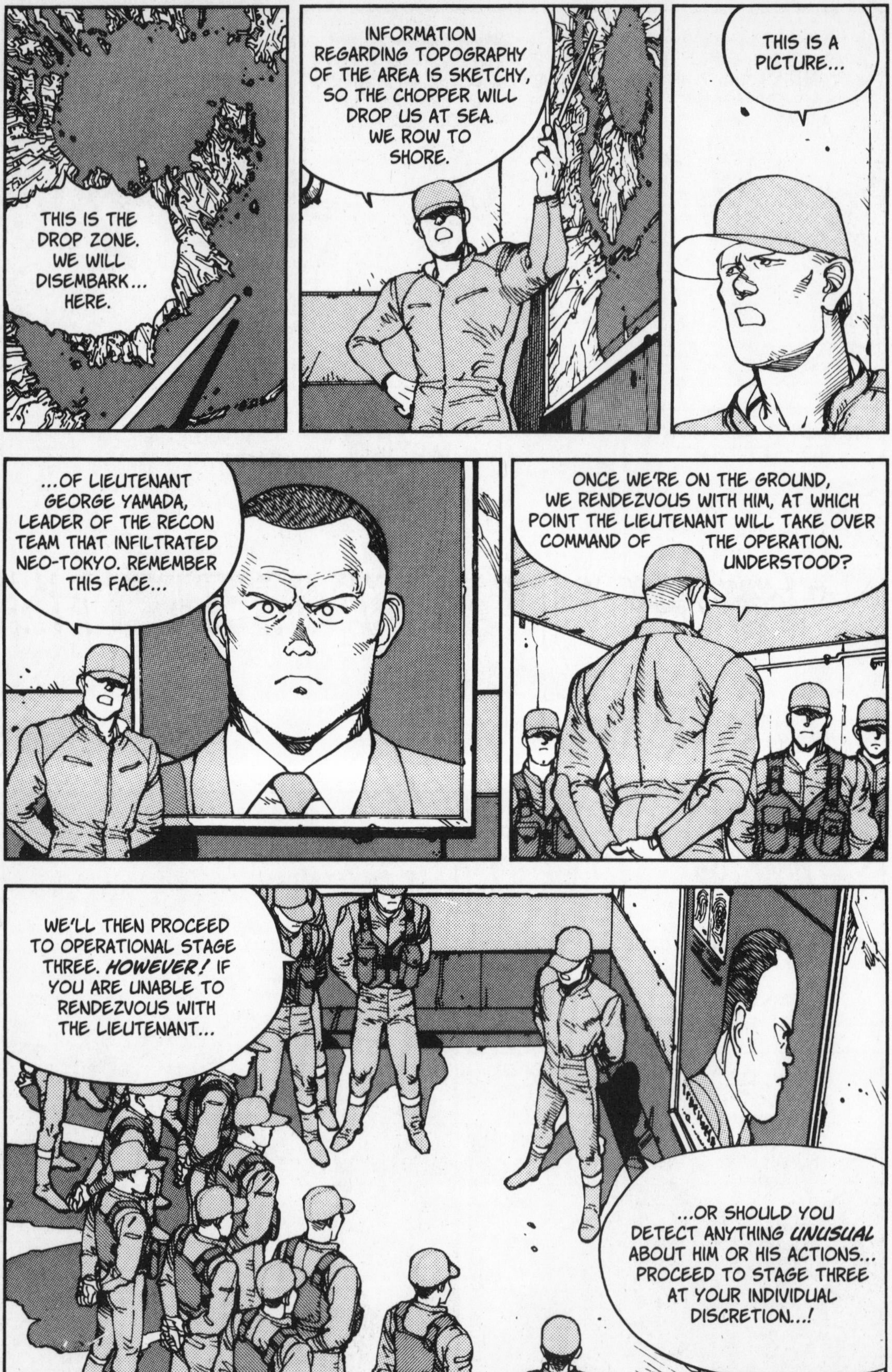
THIS IS THE DROP ZONE. WE WILL DISEMBARK... HERE.
INFORMATION REGARDING TOPOGRAPHY OF THE AREA IS SKETCHY, SO THE CHOPPER WILL DROP US AT SEA. WE ROW TO SHORE.
THIS IS A PICTURE...
...OF LIEUTENANT GEORGE YAMADA, LEADER OF THE RECON TEAM THAT INFILTRATED NEO-TOKYO. REMEMBER THIS FACE...
ONCE WE'RE ON THE GROUND, WE RENDEZVOUS WITH HIM, AT WHICH POINT THE LIEUTENANT WILL TAKE OVER COMMAND OF THE OPERATION. UNDERSTOOD?
WE'LL THEN PROCEED TO OPERATIONAL STAGE THREE. ***HOWEVER!*** IF YOU ARE UNABLE TO RENDEZVOUS WITH THE LIEUTENANT...
...OR SHOULD YOU DETECT ANYTHING *UNUSUAL* ABOUT HIM OR HIS ACTIONS... PROCEED TO STAGE THREE AT YOUR INDIVIDUAL DISCRETION...!

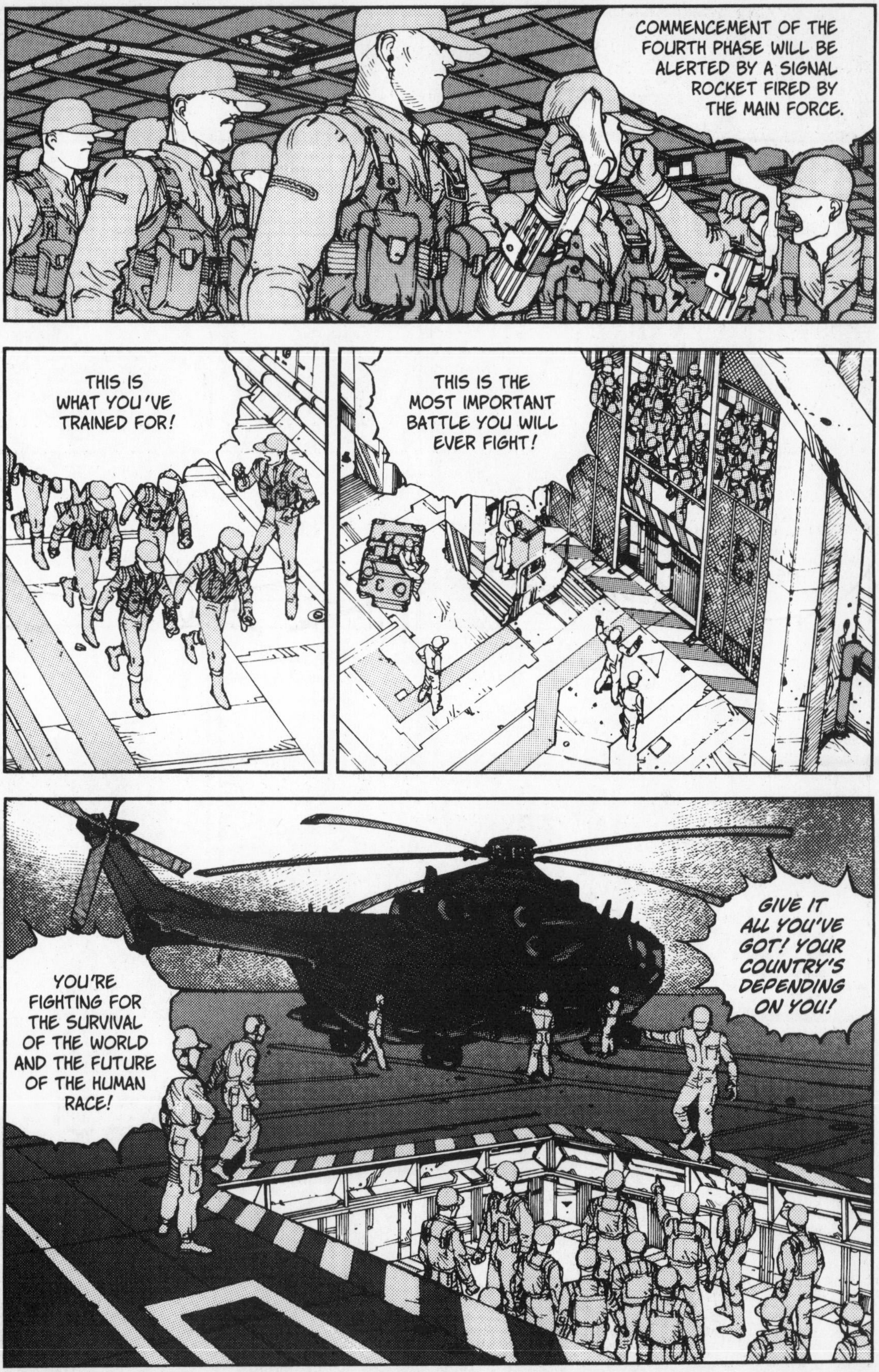
COMMENCEMENT OF THE FOURTH PHASE WILL BE ALERTED BY A SIGNAL ROCKET FIRED BY THE MAIN FORCE.
THIS IS WHAT YOU'VE TRAINED FOR!
THIS IS THE MOST IMPORTANT BATTLE YOU WILL EVER FIGHT!
YOU'RE FIGHTING FOR THE SURVIVAL OF THE WORLD AND THE FUTURE OF THE HUMAN RACE!
GIVE IT ALL YOU'VE GOT! YOUR COUNTRY'S DEPENDING ON YOU!

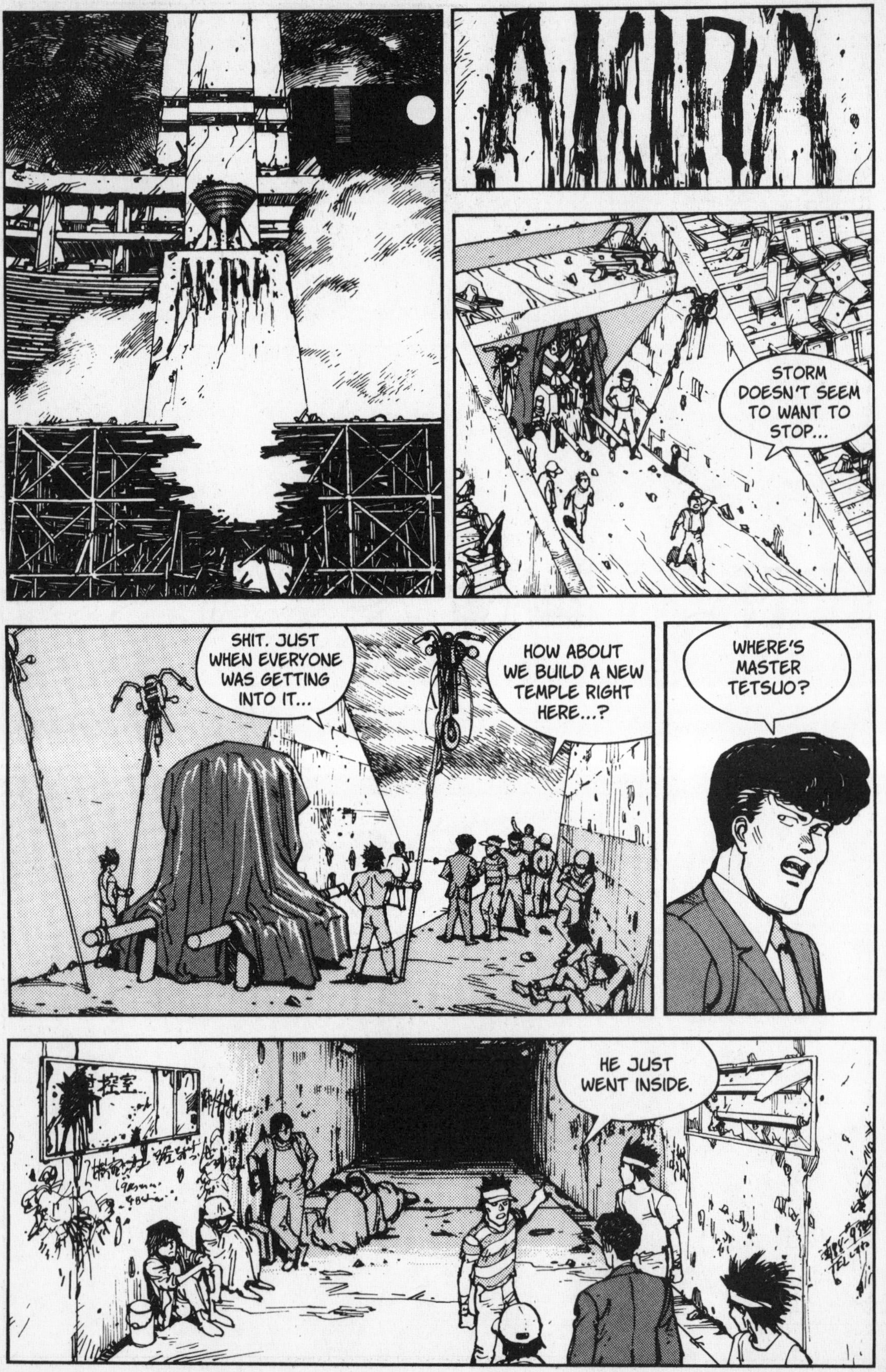
AKIRA
AKIRA
STORM DOESN'T SEEM TO WANT TO STOP...
SHIT. JUST WHEN EVERYONE WAS GETTING INTO IT...
HOW ABOUT WE BUILD A NEW TEMPLE RIGHT HERE...?
WHERE'S MASTER TETSUO?
HE JUST WENT INSIDE.

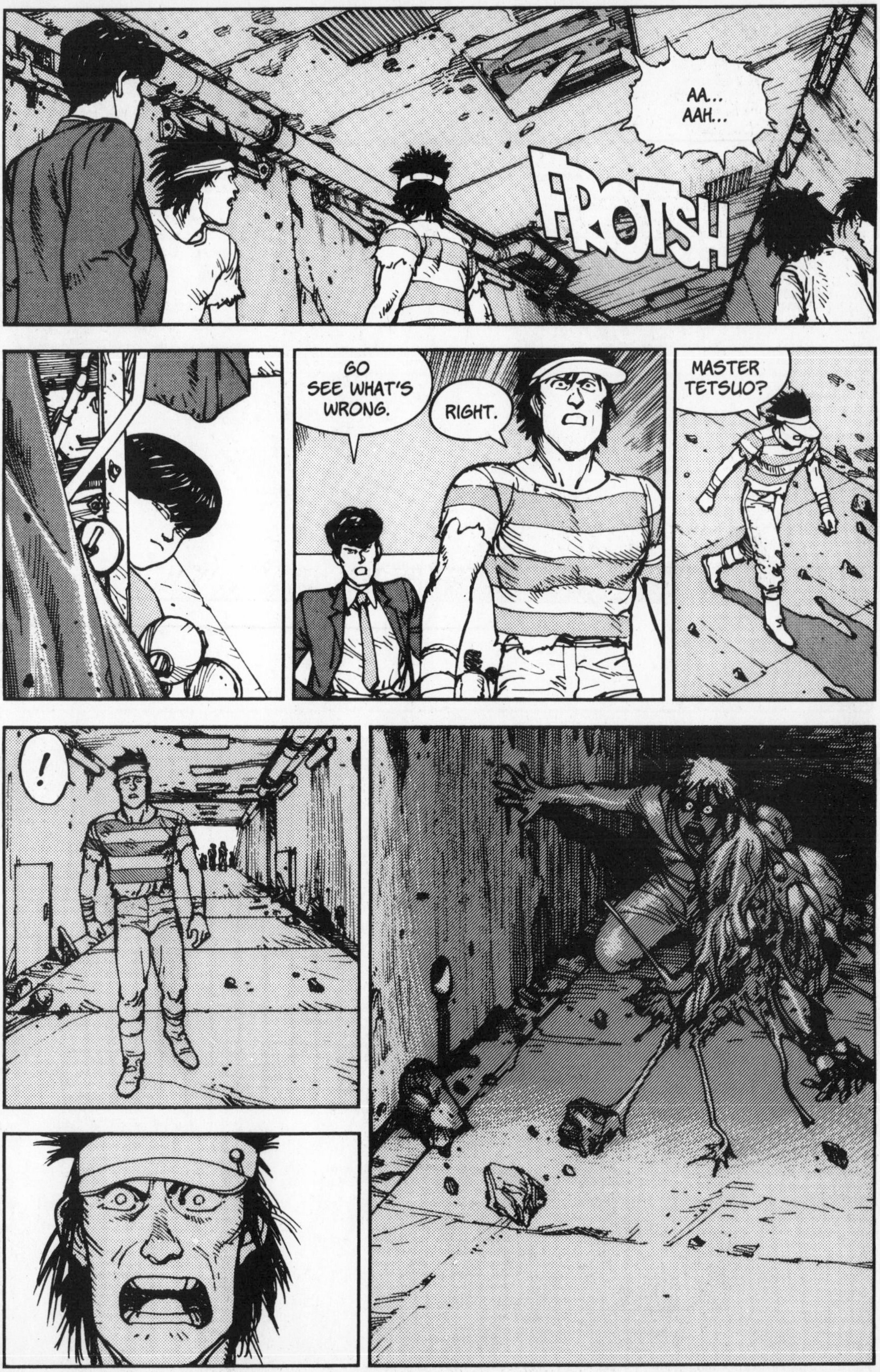
AA... AAH...
FROTSH
GO SEE WHAT'S WRONG.
RIGHT.
MASTER TETSUO?
!

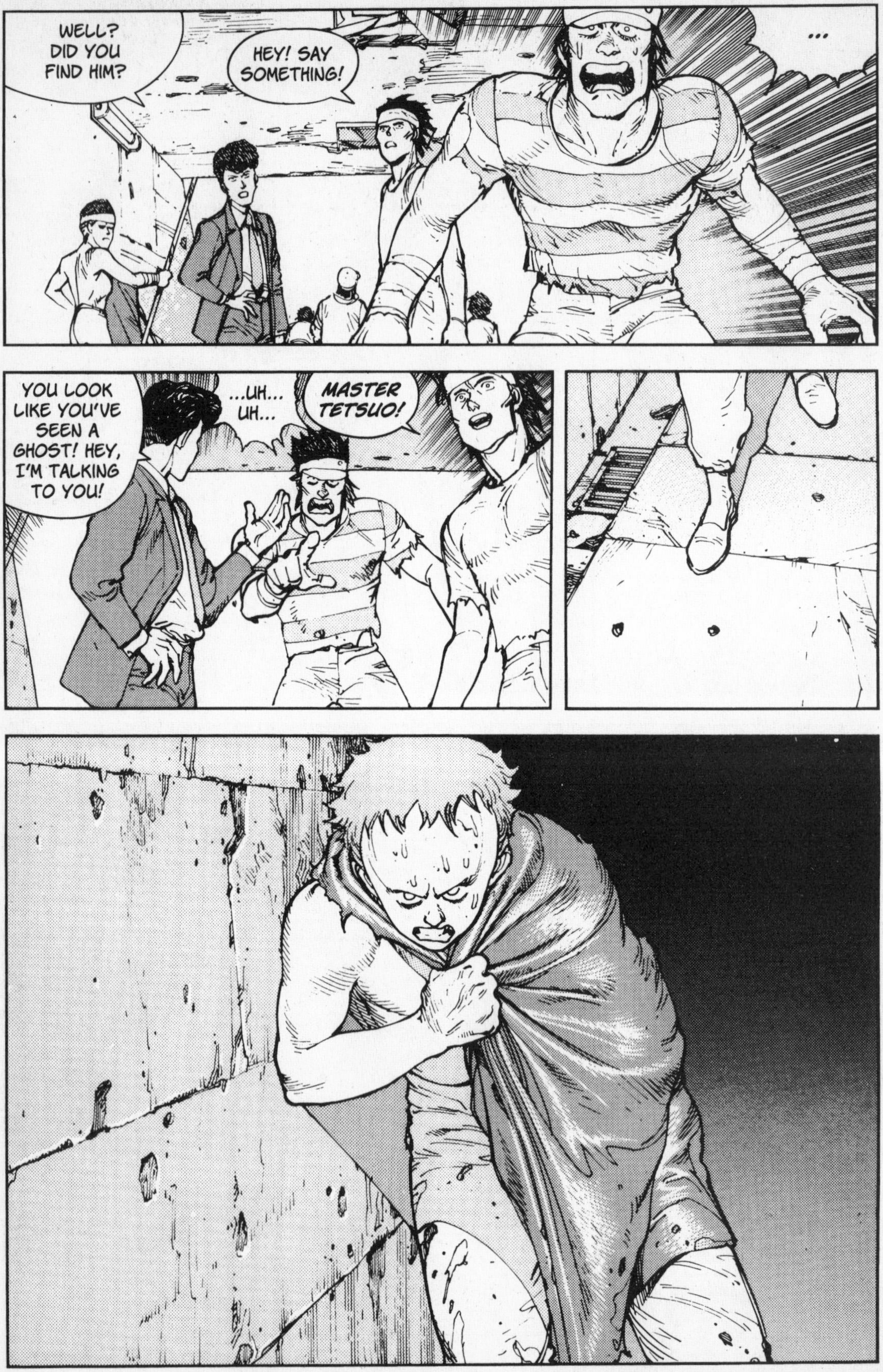
WELL? DID YOU FIND HIM?
HEY! SAY SOMETHING!
...
YOU LOOK LIKE YOU'VE SEEN A GHOST! HEY, I'M TALKING TO YOU!
...UH... UH...
MASTER TETSUO!

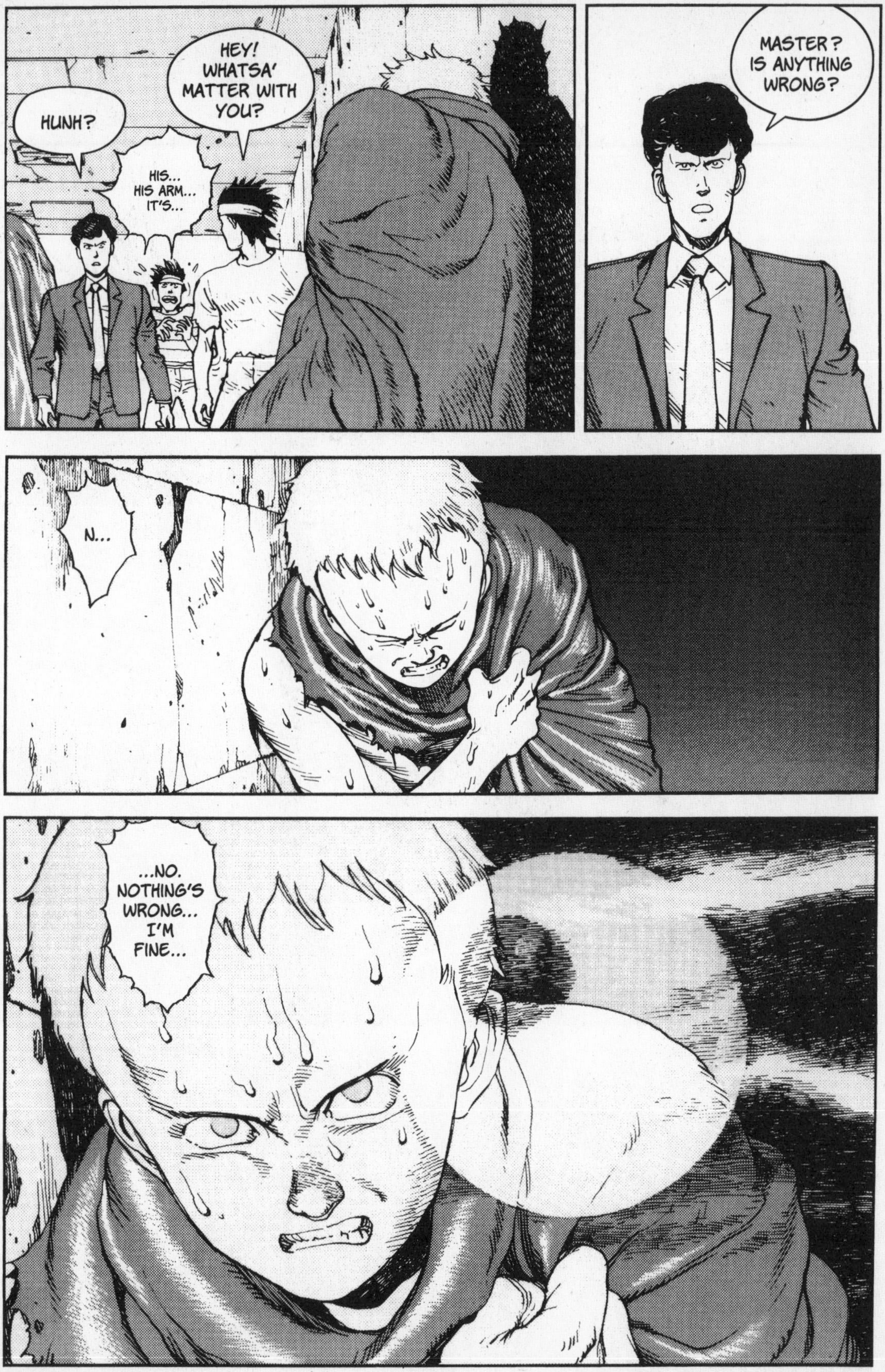
HUNH?
HEY! WHATSA' MATTER WITH YOU?
HIS... HIS ARM... IT'S...
MASTER? IS ANYTHING WRONG?
N...
...NO. NOTHING'S WRONG... I'M FINE...

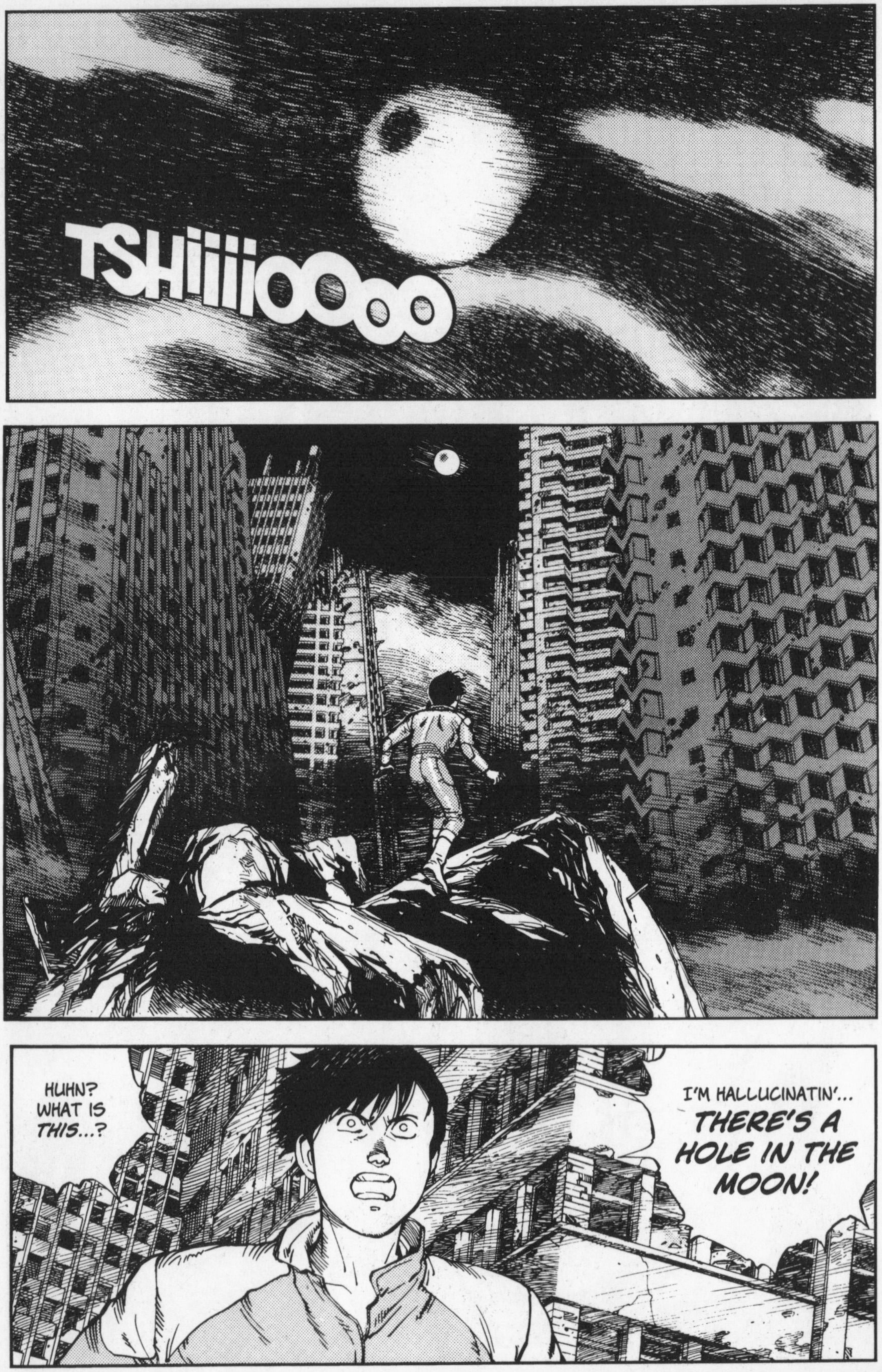
TSHiiiiOOooo
HUHN? WHAT IS THIS...?
I'M HALLUCINATIN'... THERE'S A HOLE IN THE MOON!

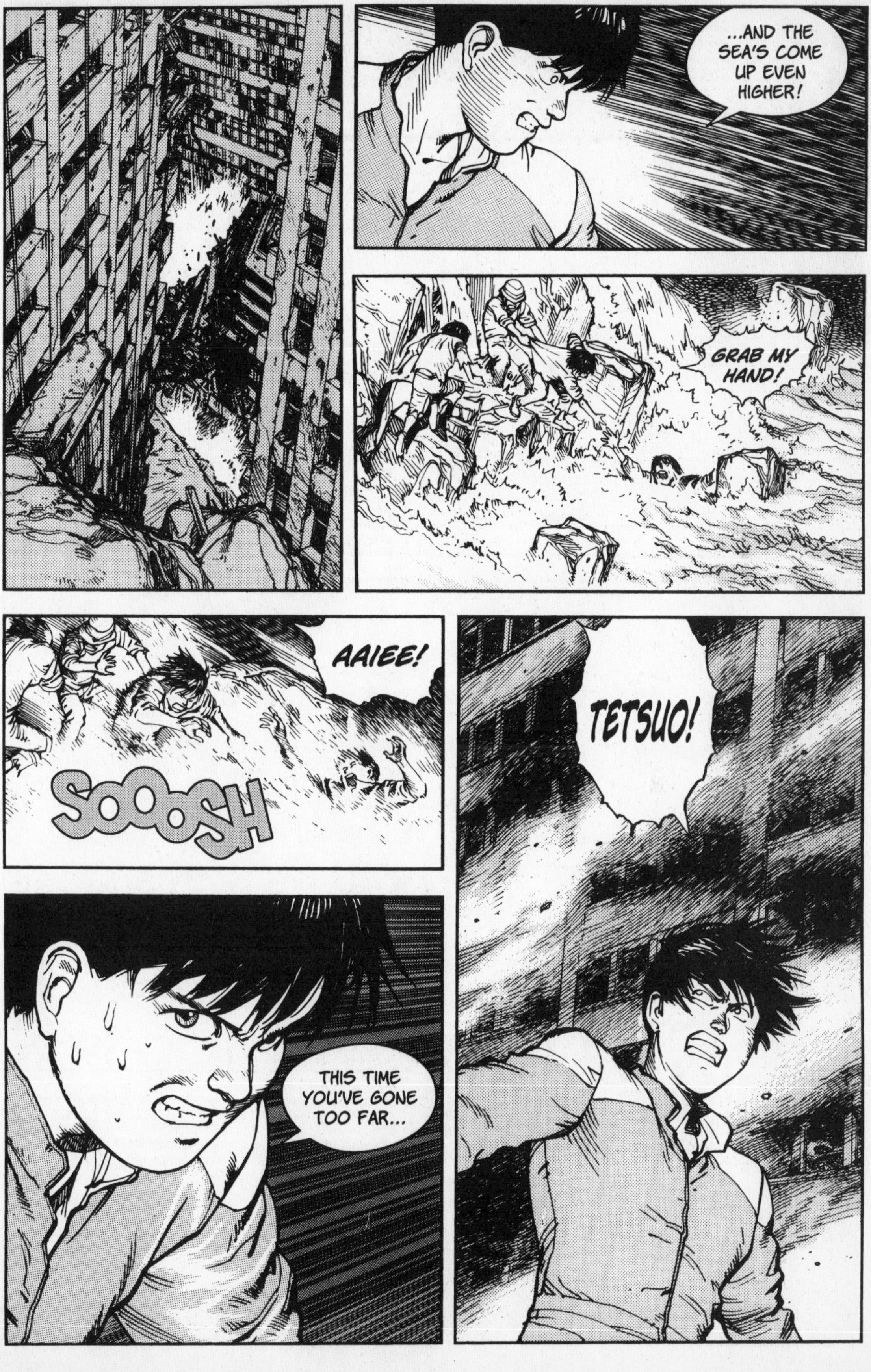
...AND THE SEA'S COME UP EVEN HIGHER!
GRAB MY HAND!
AAIEE!
SOOOOSH
TETSUO!
THIS TIME YOU'VE GONE TOO FAR...

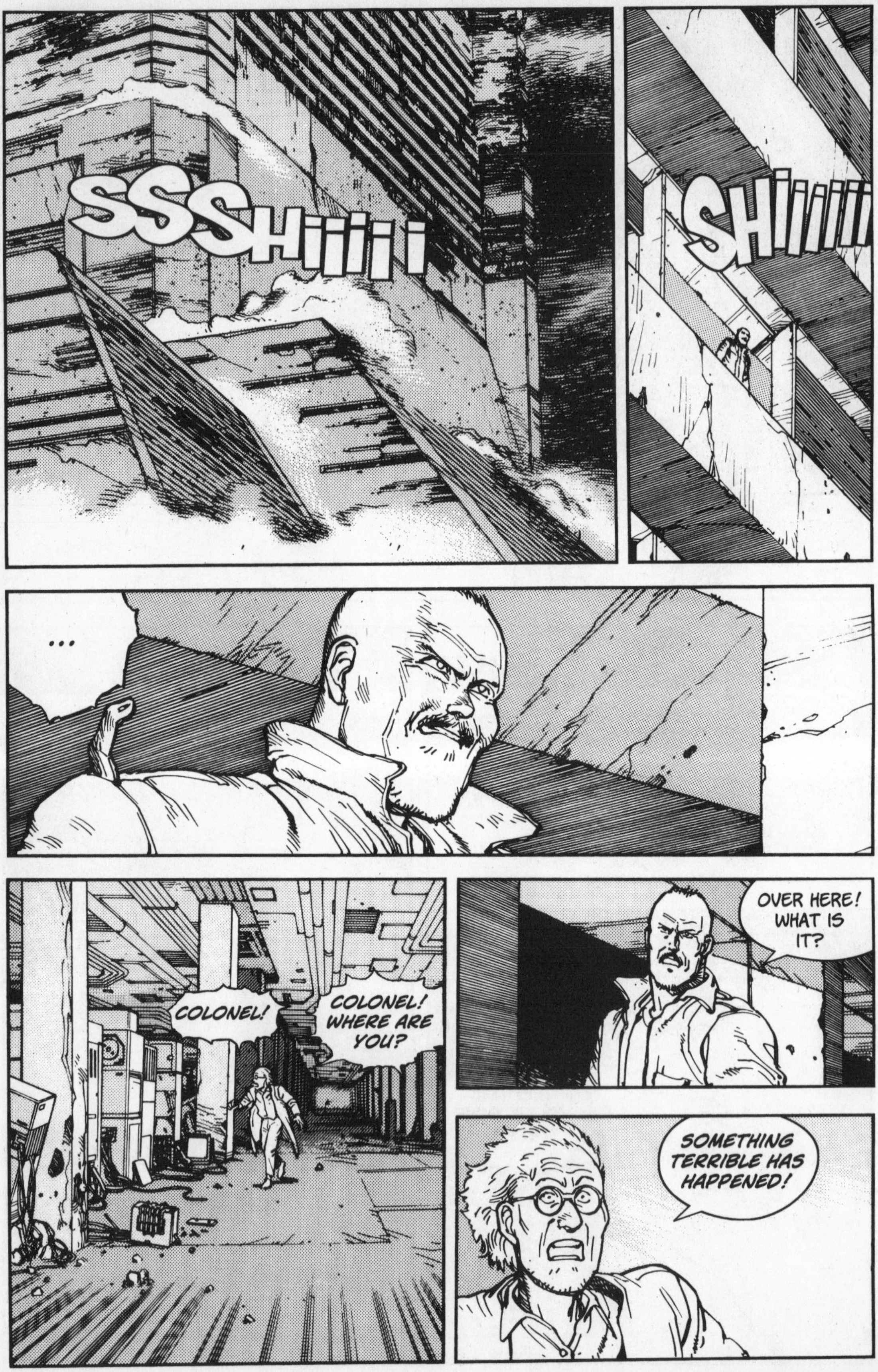
SSSHiiiii i
SHiiiiii
...
COLONEL!
COLONEL! WHERE ARE YOU?
OVER HERE! WHAT IS IT?
SOMETHING TERRIBLE HAS HAPPENED!

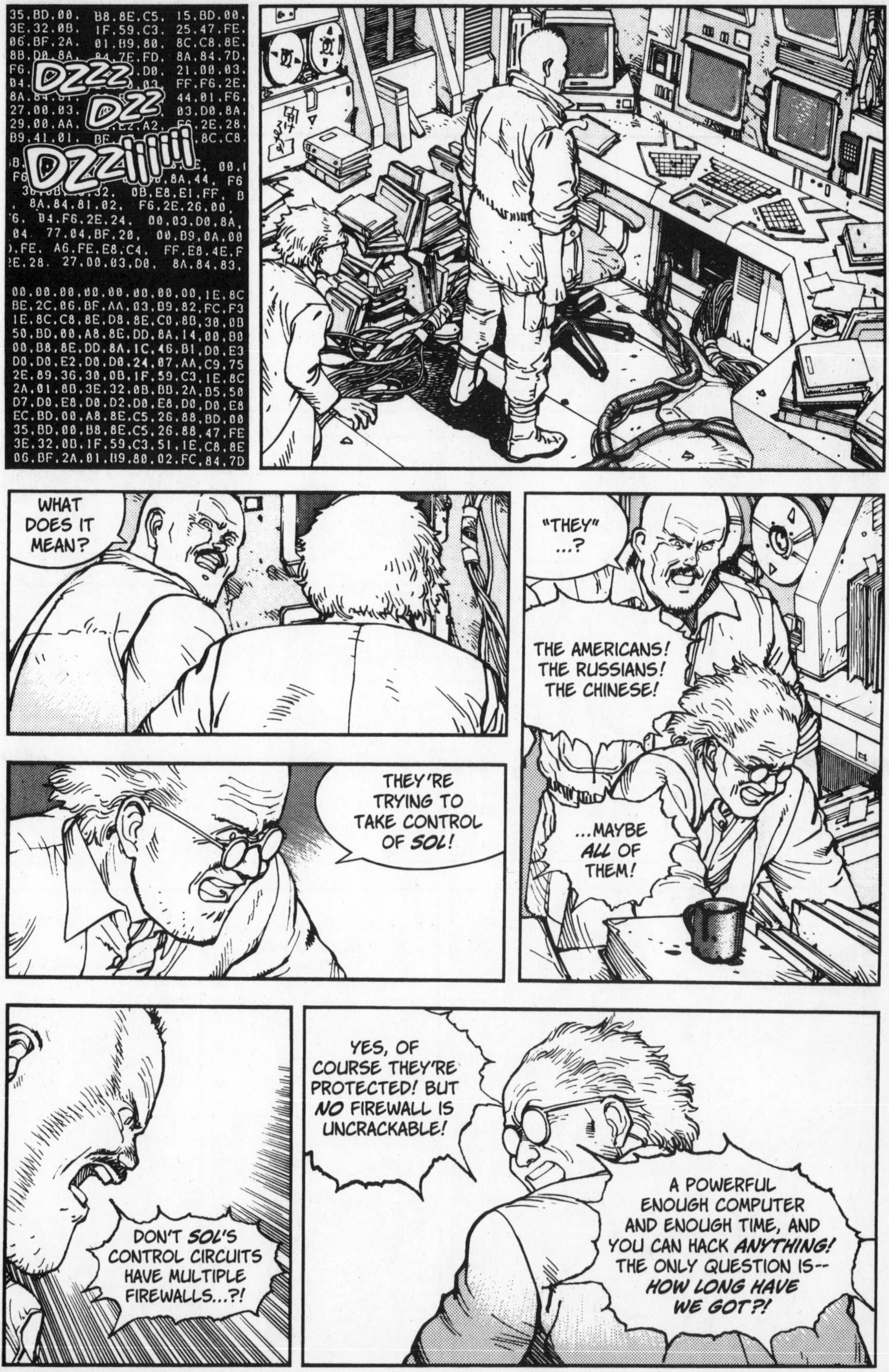

DZZZ
DZZ
DZZiiiiii
WHAT DOES IT MEAN?
THEY'RE TRYING TO TAKE CONTROL OF SOL!
"THEY" ...?
THE AMERICANS! THE RUSSIANS! THE CHINESE!
...MAYBE ALL OF THEM!
DON'T SOL'S CONTROL CIRCUITS HAVE MULTIPLE FIREWALLS...?!
YES, OF COURSE THEY'RE PROTECTED! BUT NO FIREWALL IS UNCRACKABLE!
A POWERFUL ENOUGH COMPUTER AND ENOUGH TIME, AND YOU CAN HACK ANYTHING! THE ONLY QUESTION IS-- HOW LONG HAVE WE GOT?!

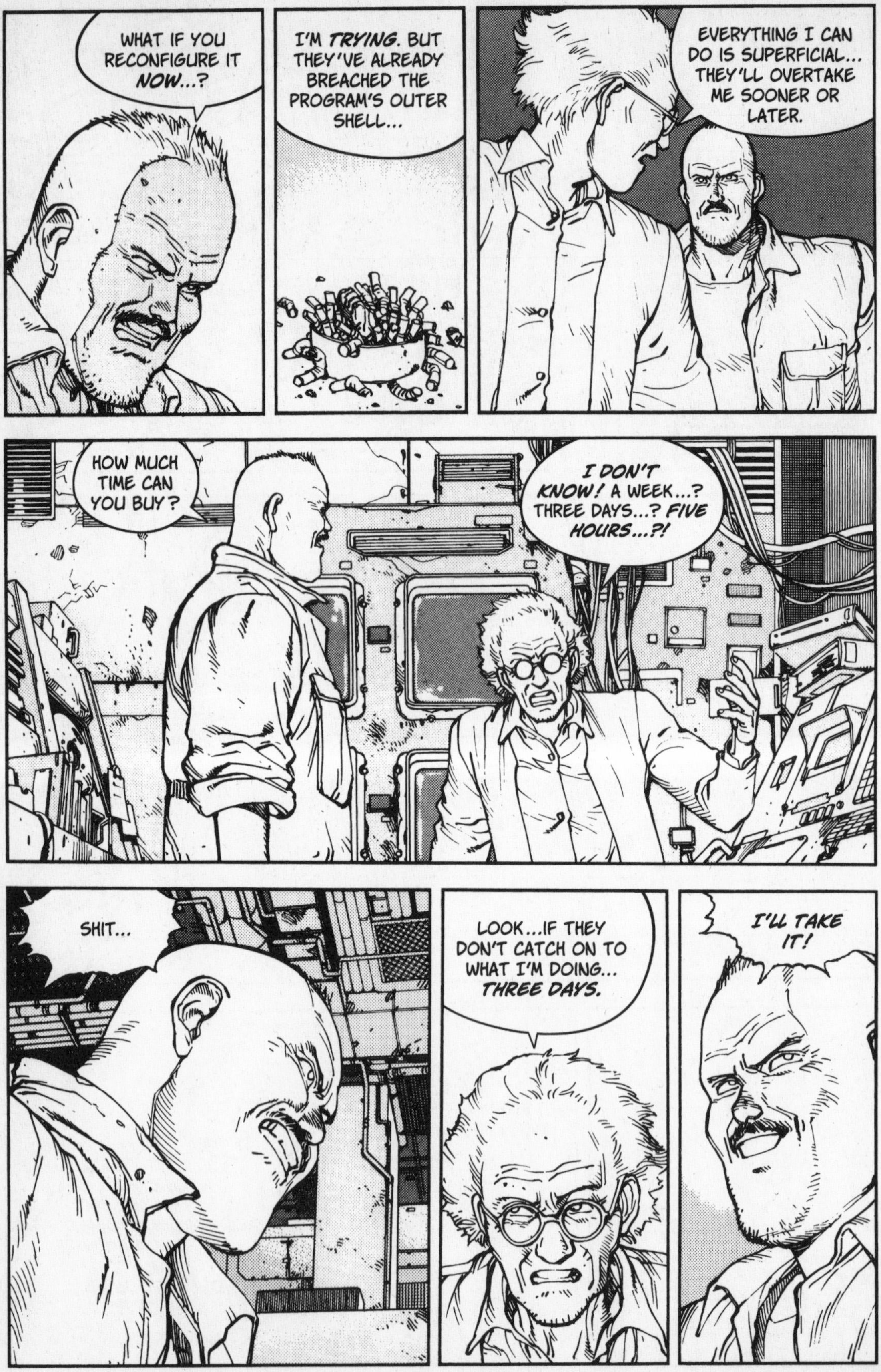
WHAT IF YOU RECONFIGURE IT NOW...?
I'M TRYING. BUT THEY'VE ALREADY BREACHED THE PROGRAM'S OUTER SHELL...
EVERYTHING I CAN DO IS SUPERFICIAL... THEY'LL OVERTAKE ME SOONER OR LATER.
HOW MUCH TIME CAN YOU BUY?
I DON'T KNOW! A WEEK...? THREE DAYS...? FIVE HOURS...?!
SHIT...
LOOK...IF THEY DON'T CATCH ON TO WHAT I'M DOING... THREE DAYS.
I'LL TAKE IT!

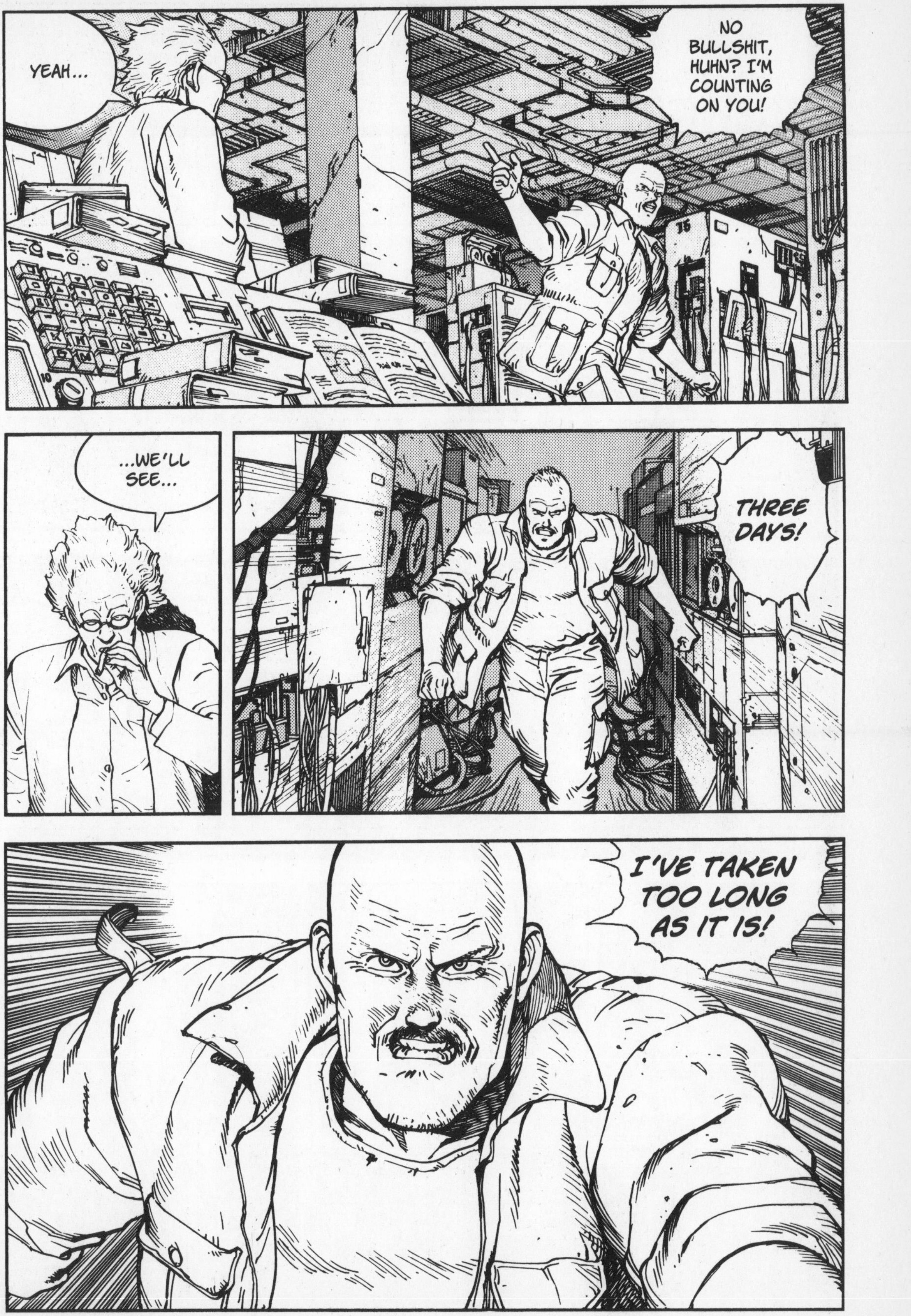
YEAH...
NO BULLSHIT, HUHN? I'M COUNTING ON YOU!
...WE'LL SEE...
THREE DAYS!
I'VE TAKEN TOO LONG AS IT IS!

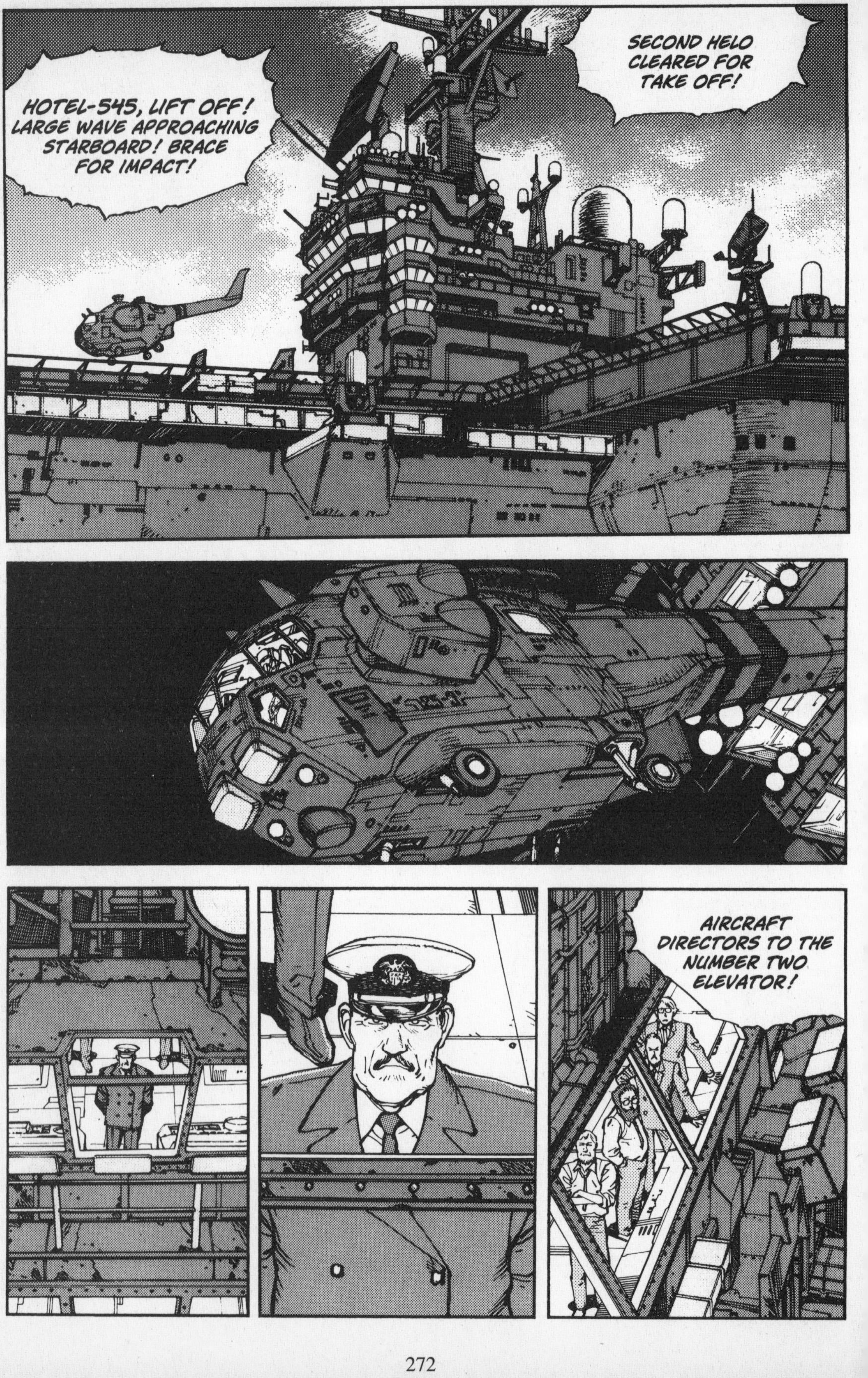
HOTEL-545, LIFT OFF! LARGE WAVE APPROACHING STARBOARD! BRACE FOR IMPACT!
SECOND HELO CLEARED FOR TAKE OFF!
AIRCRAFT DIRECTORS TO THE NUMBER TWO ELEVATOR!

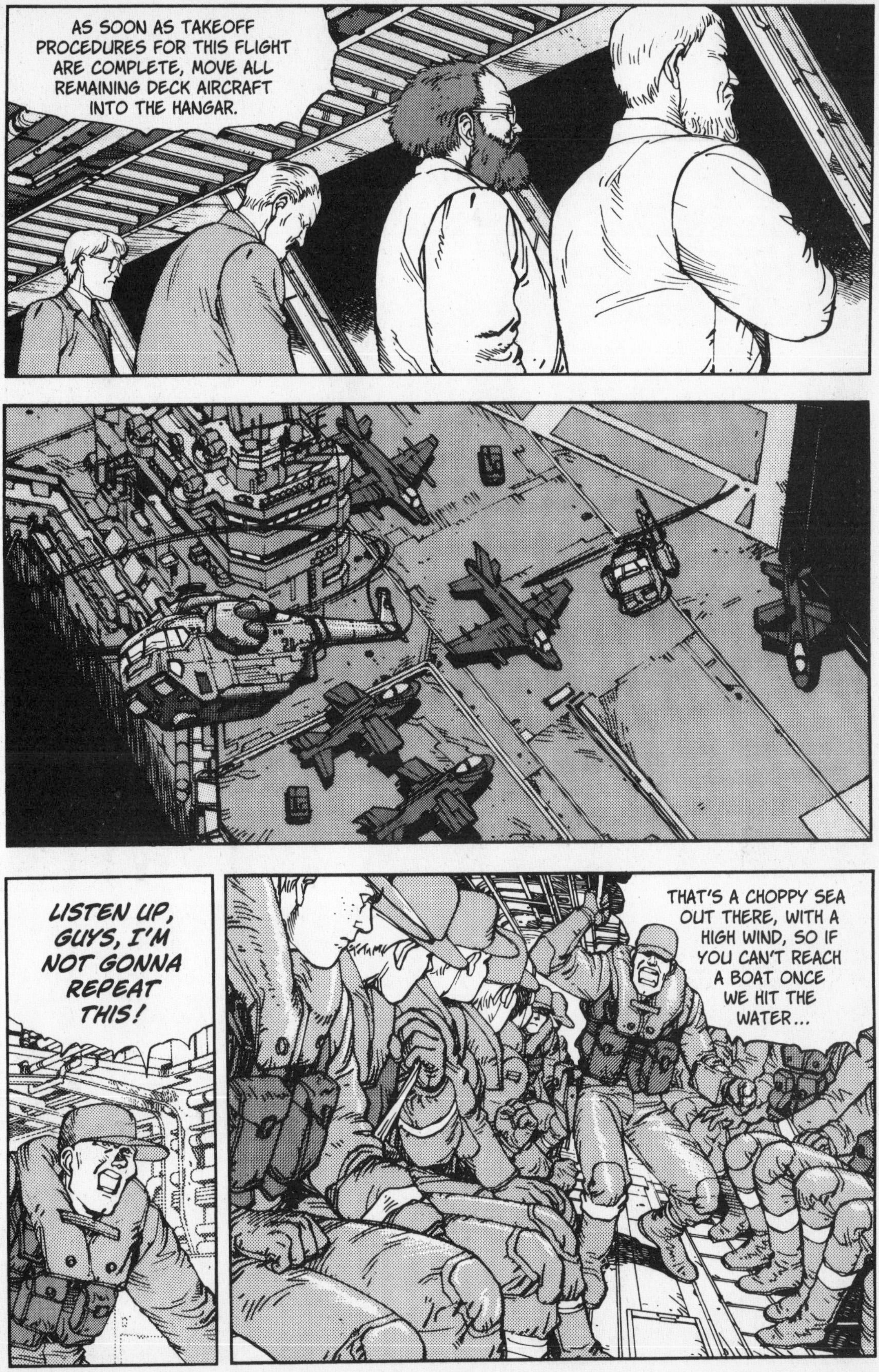
AS SOON AS TAKEOFF PROCEDURES FOR THIS FLIGHT ARE COMPLETE, MOVE ALL REMAINING DECK AIRCRAFT INTO THE HANGAR.
LISTEN UP, GUYS, I'M NOT GONNA REPEAT THIS!
THAT'S A CHOPPY SEA OUT THERE, WITH A HIGH WIND, SO IF YOU CAN'T REACH A BOAT ONCE WE HIT THE WATER...

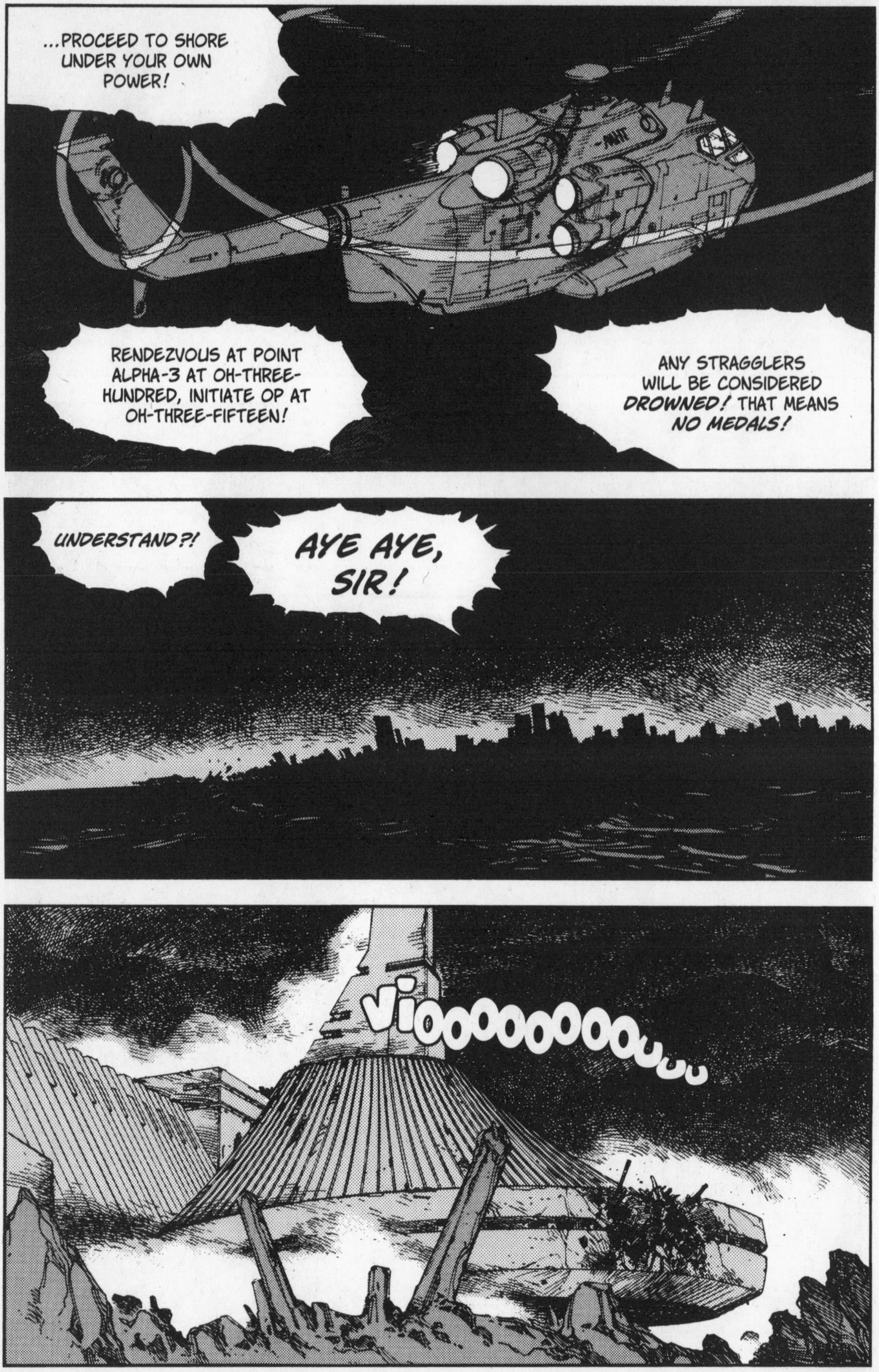
...PROCEED TO SHORE UNDER YOUR OWN POWER!
RENDEZVOUS AT POINT ALPHA-3 AT OH-THREE-HUNDRED, INITIATE OP AT OH-THREE-FIFTEEN!
ANY STRAGGLERS WILL BE CONSIDERED *DROWNED!* THAT MEANS *NO MEDALS!*
UNDERSTAND?!
AYE AYE, SIR!
VIOOOOOOOOUUU

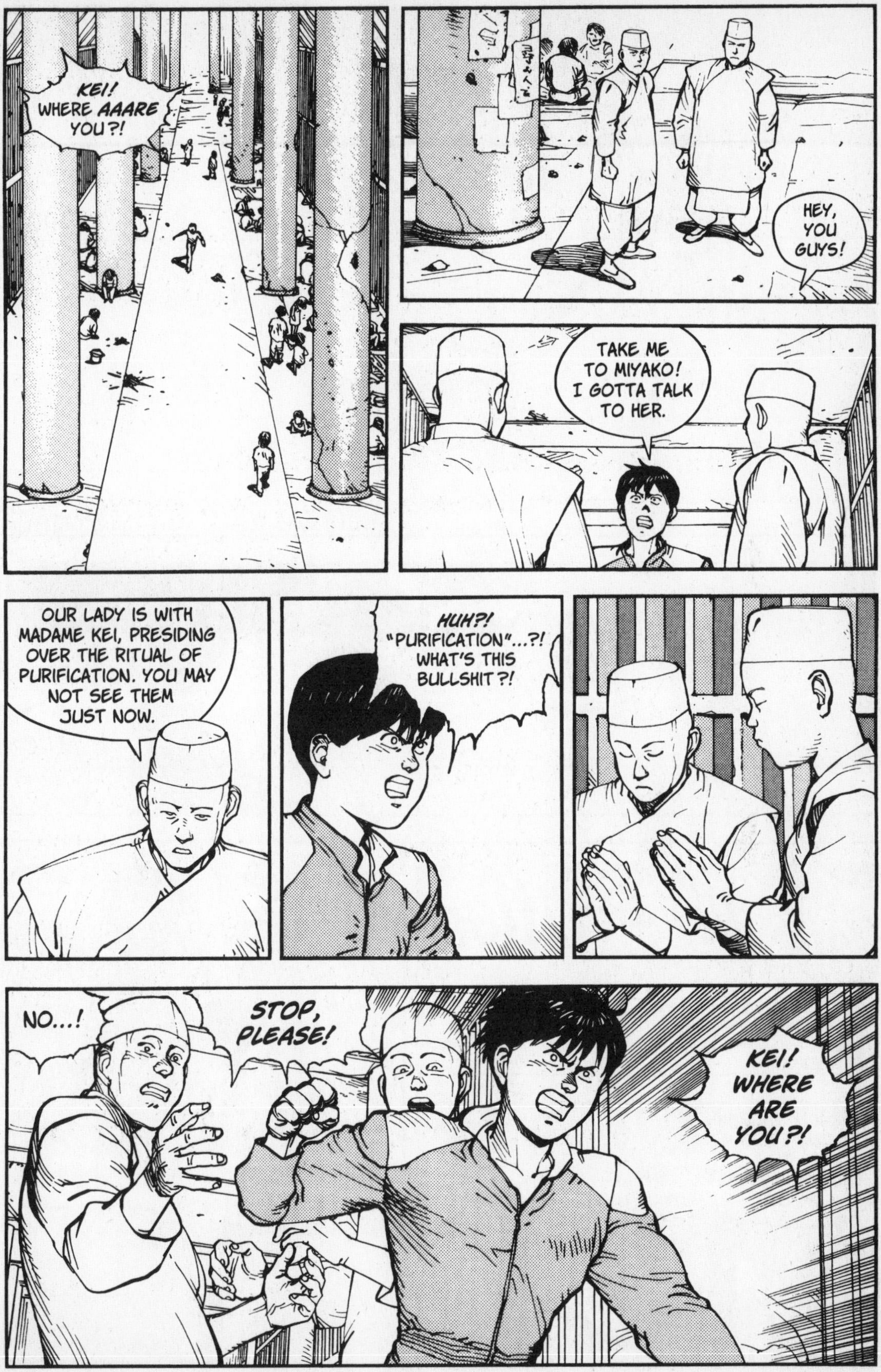
KEI! WHERE AAARE YOU?!
HEY, YOU GUYS!
TAKE ME TO MIYAKO! I GOTTA TALK TO HER.
OUR LADY IS WITH MADAME KEI, PRESIDING OVER THE RITUAL OF PURIFICATION. YOU MAY NOT SEE THEM JUST NOW.
HUH?! "PURIFICATION"...?! WHAT'S THIS BULLSHIT?!
NO...!
STOP, PLEASE!
KEI! WHERE ARE YOU?!

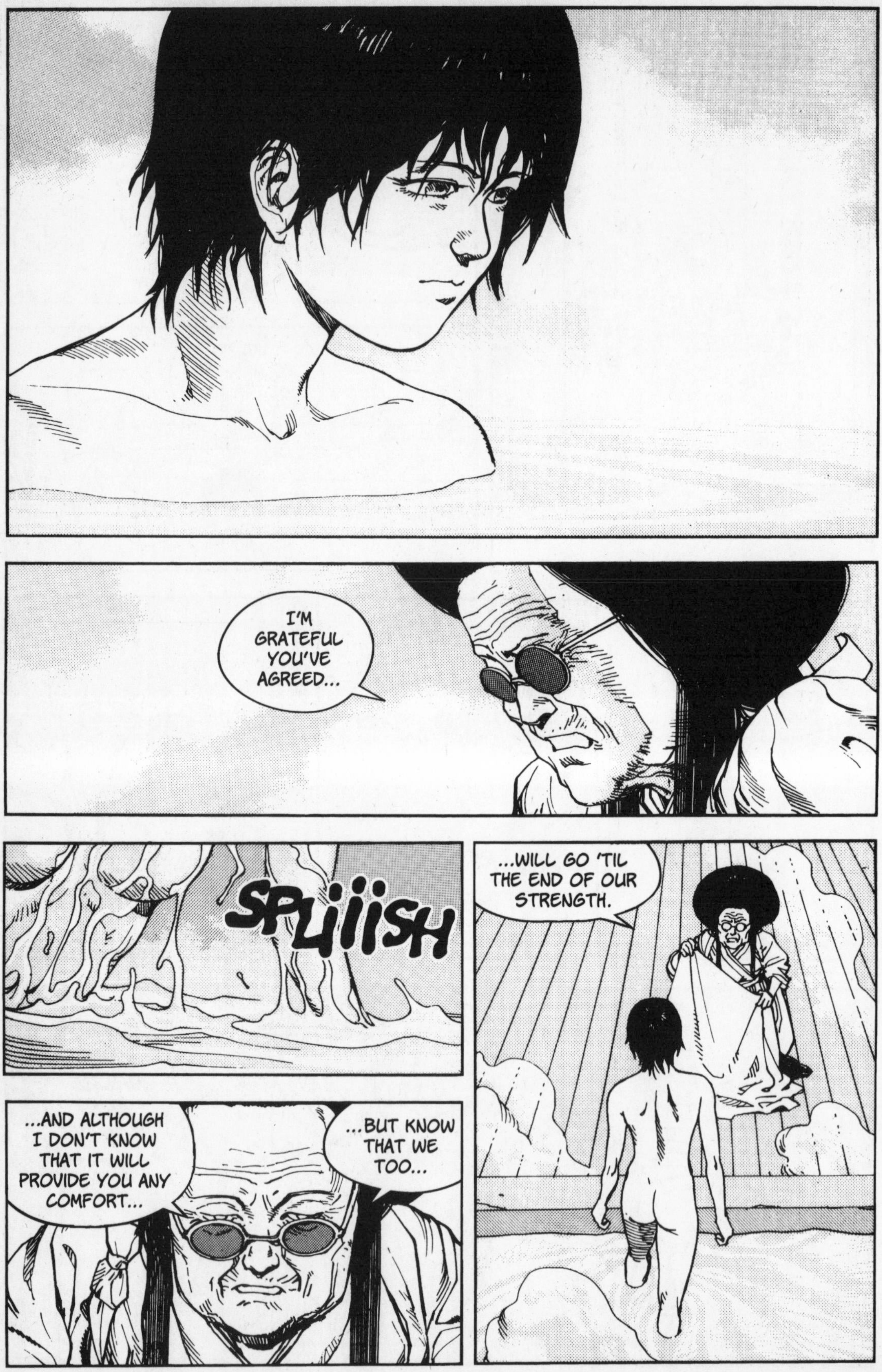
I'M GRATEFUL YOU'VE AGREED...
SPLIIISH
...AND ALTHOUGH I DON'T KNOW THAT IT WILL PROVIDE YOU ANY COMFORT...
...BUT KNOW THAT WE TOO...
...WILL GO 'TIL THE END OF OUR STRENGTH.

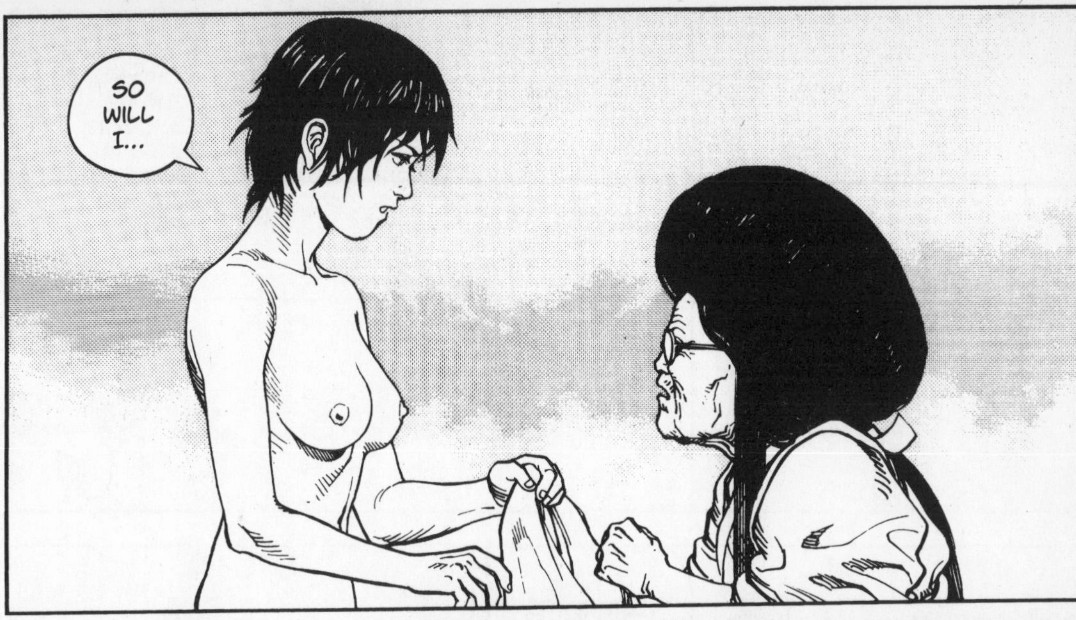
SO WILL I...

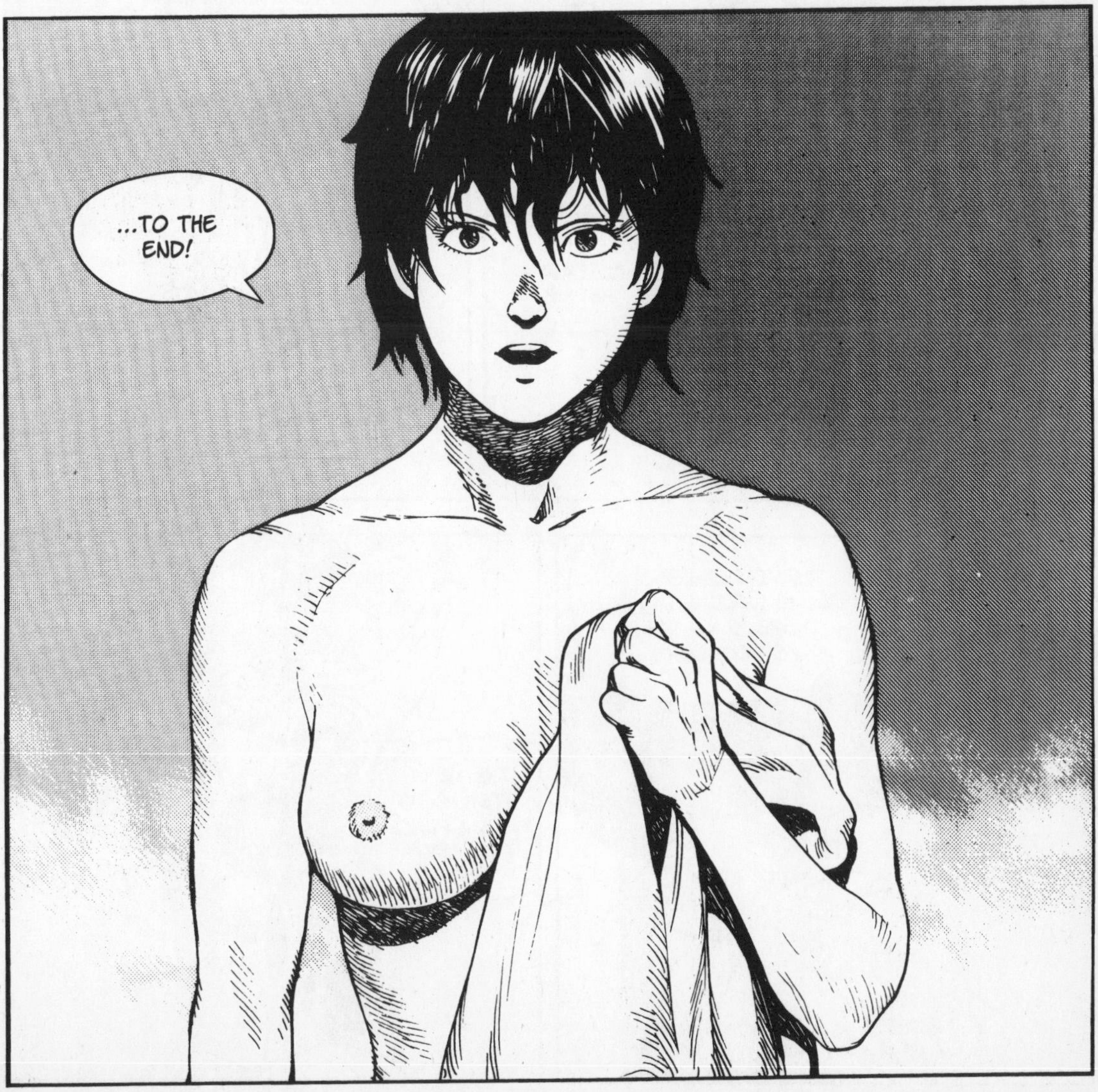
...TO THE END!

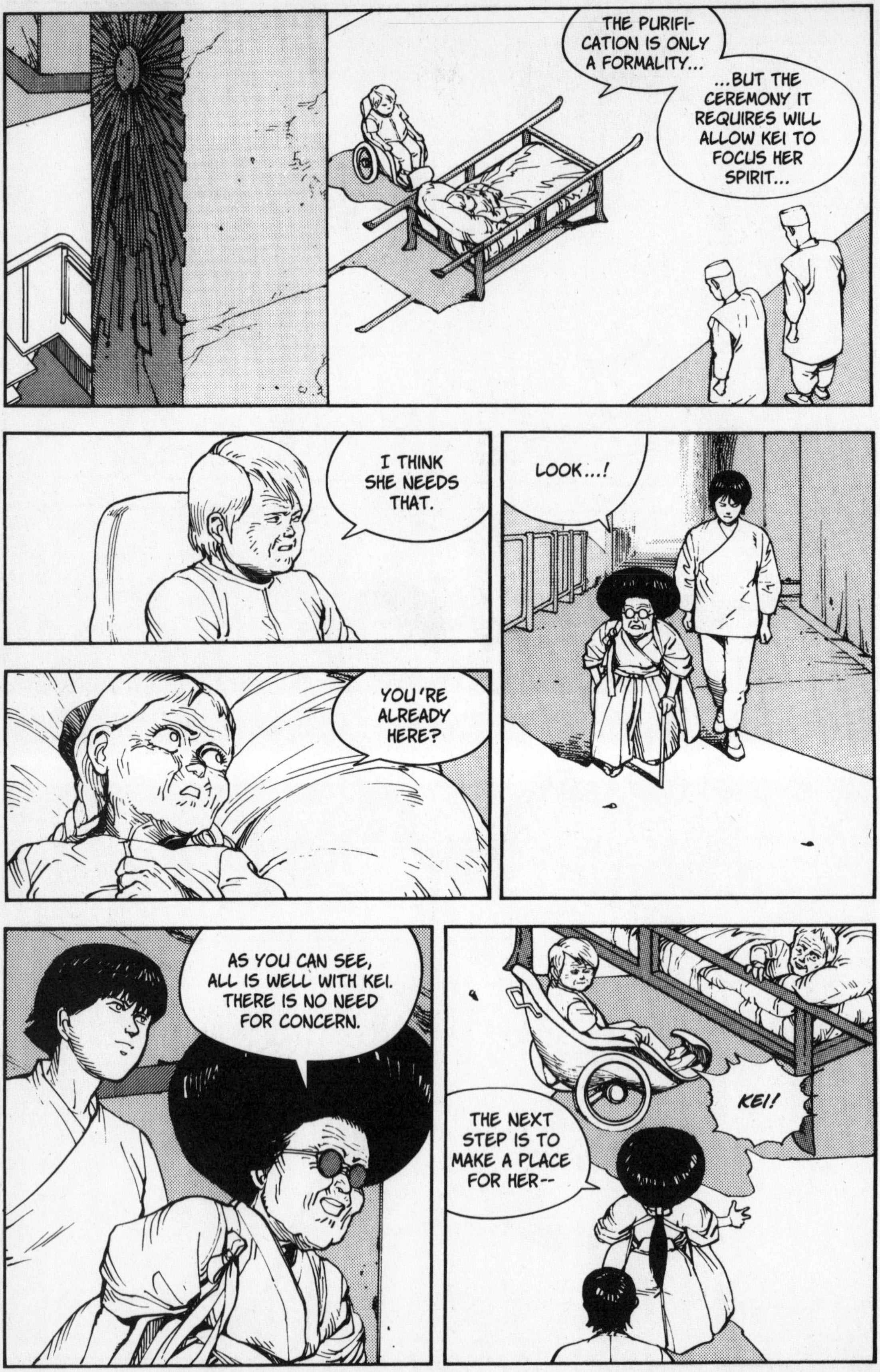
THE PURIFI-CATION IS ONLY A FORMALITY...
...BUT THE CEREMONY IT REQUIRES WILL ALLOW KEI TO FOCUS HER SPIRIT...
I THINK SHE NEEDS THAT.
LOOK...!
YOU'RE ALREADY HERE?
AS YOU CAN SEE, ALL IS WELL WITH KEI. THERE IS NO NEED FOR CONCERN.
KEI!
THE NEXT STEP IS TO MAKE A PLACE FOR HER--

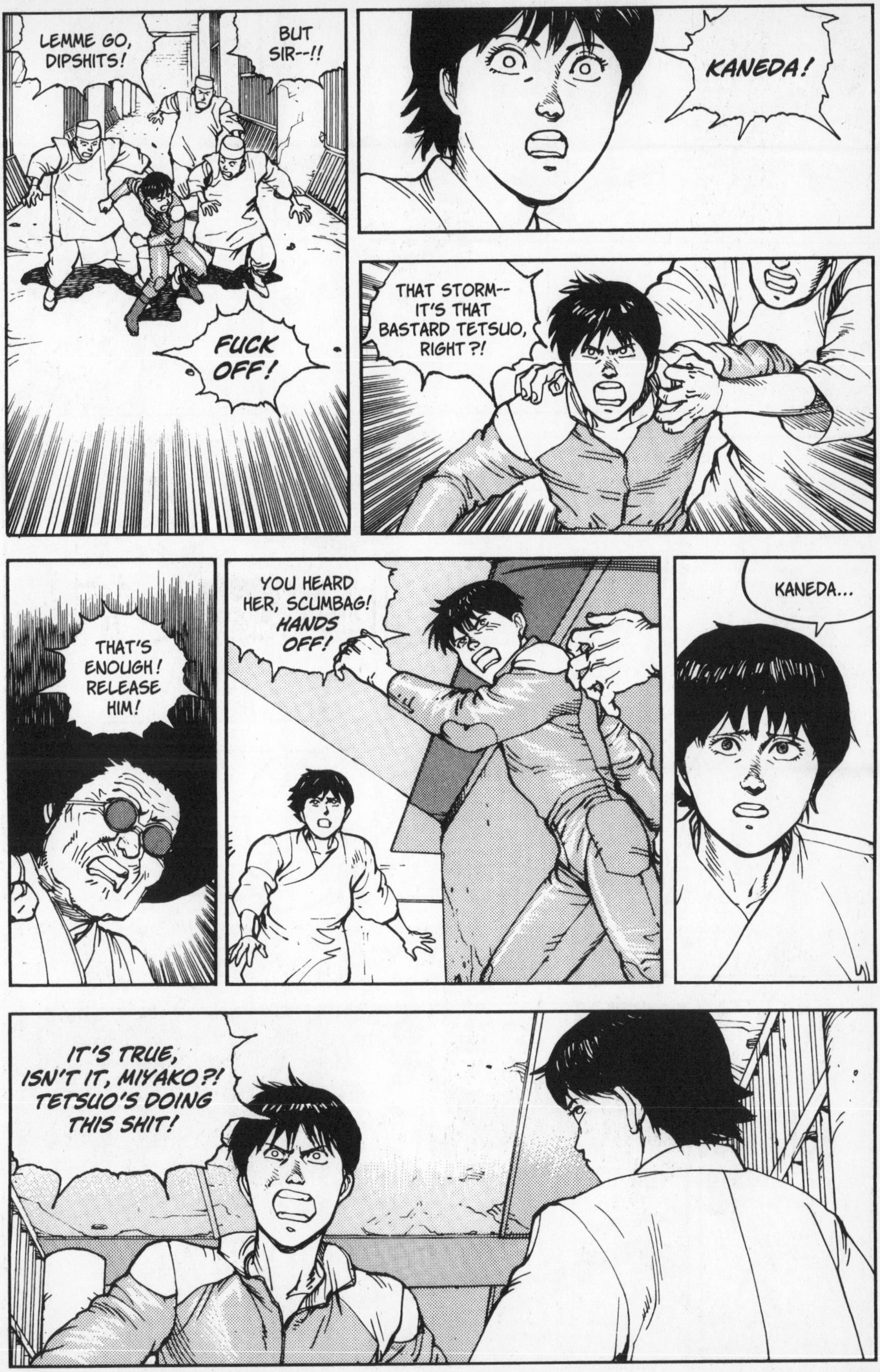

LEMME GO, DIPSHITS!
BUT SIR--!!
FUCK OFF!
KANEDA!
THAT STORM-- IT'S THAT BASTARD TETSUO, RIGHT?!
THAT'S ENOUGH! RELEASE HIM!
YOU HEARD HER, SCUMBAG! HANDS OFF!
KANEDA...
IT'S TRUE, ISN'T IT, MIYAKO?! TETSUO'S DOING THIS SHIT!

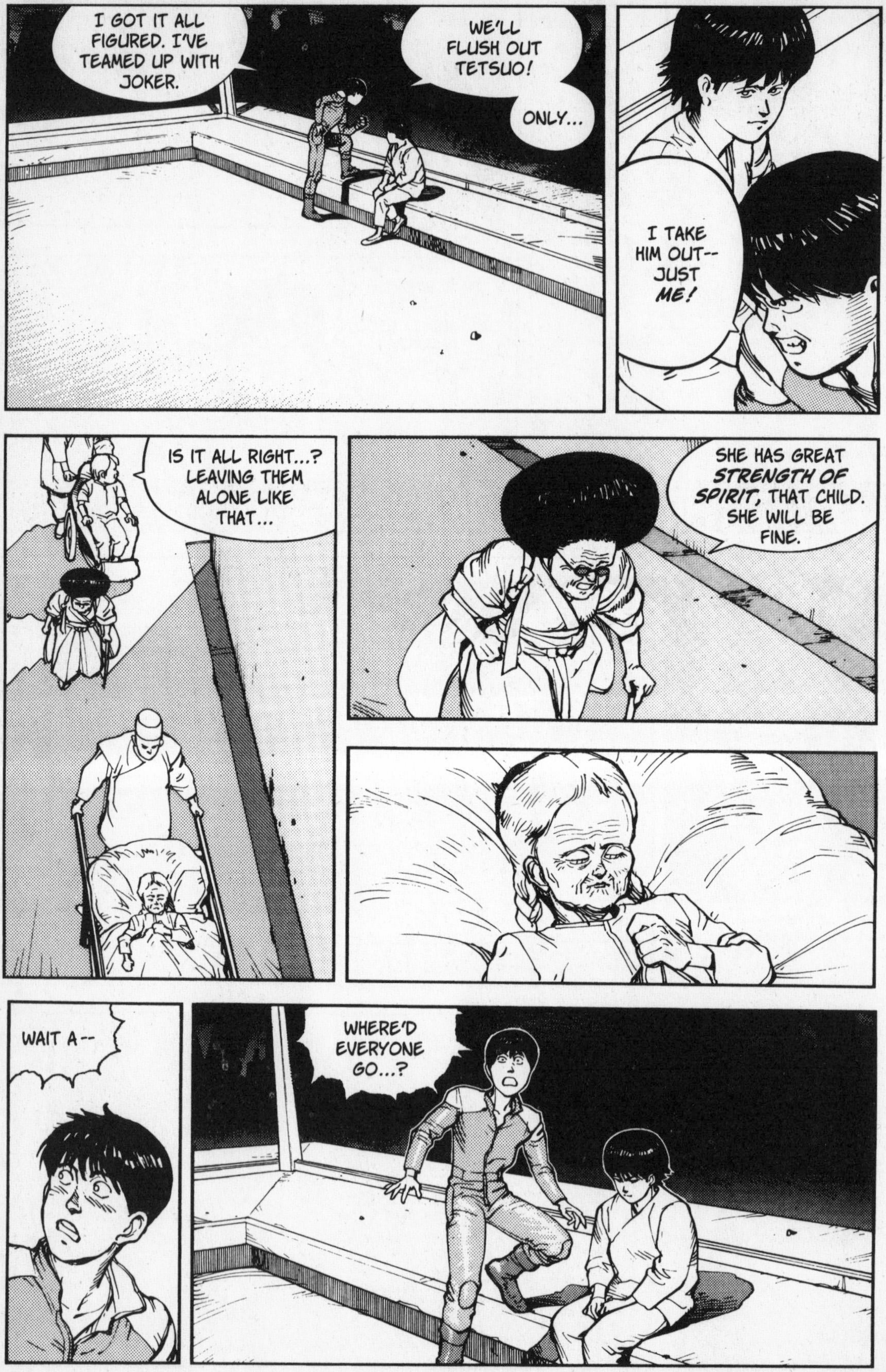
I GOT IT ALL FIGURED. I'VE TEAMED UP WITH JOKER.
WE'LL FLUSH OUT TETSUO!
ONLY...
I TAKE HIM OUT-- JUST *ME!*
IS IT ALL RIGHT...? LEAVING THEM ALONE LIKE THAT...
SHE HAS GREAT *STRENGTH OF SPIRIT,* THAT CHILD. SHE WILL BE FINE.
WAIT A--
WHERE'D EVERYONE GO...?

LISTEN...

...STAY WITH ME TONIGHT.

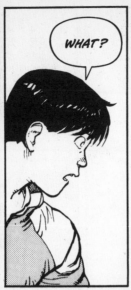

WHAT?

WH...WH...WHAT'D YOU SAY? YOU WANT ME TO...WITH YOU?!

IT WOULD MEAN SO MUCH...

...EVEN IF IT WAS JUST FOR A LITTLE WHILE.

WELL, UH...HA HA... ER...

ARE YOU SERIOUS?! FOR REAL?!

MMHMM...

281

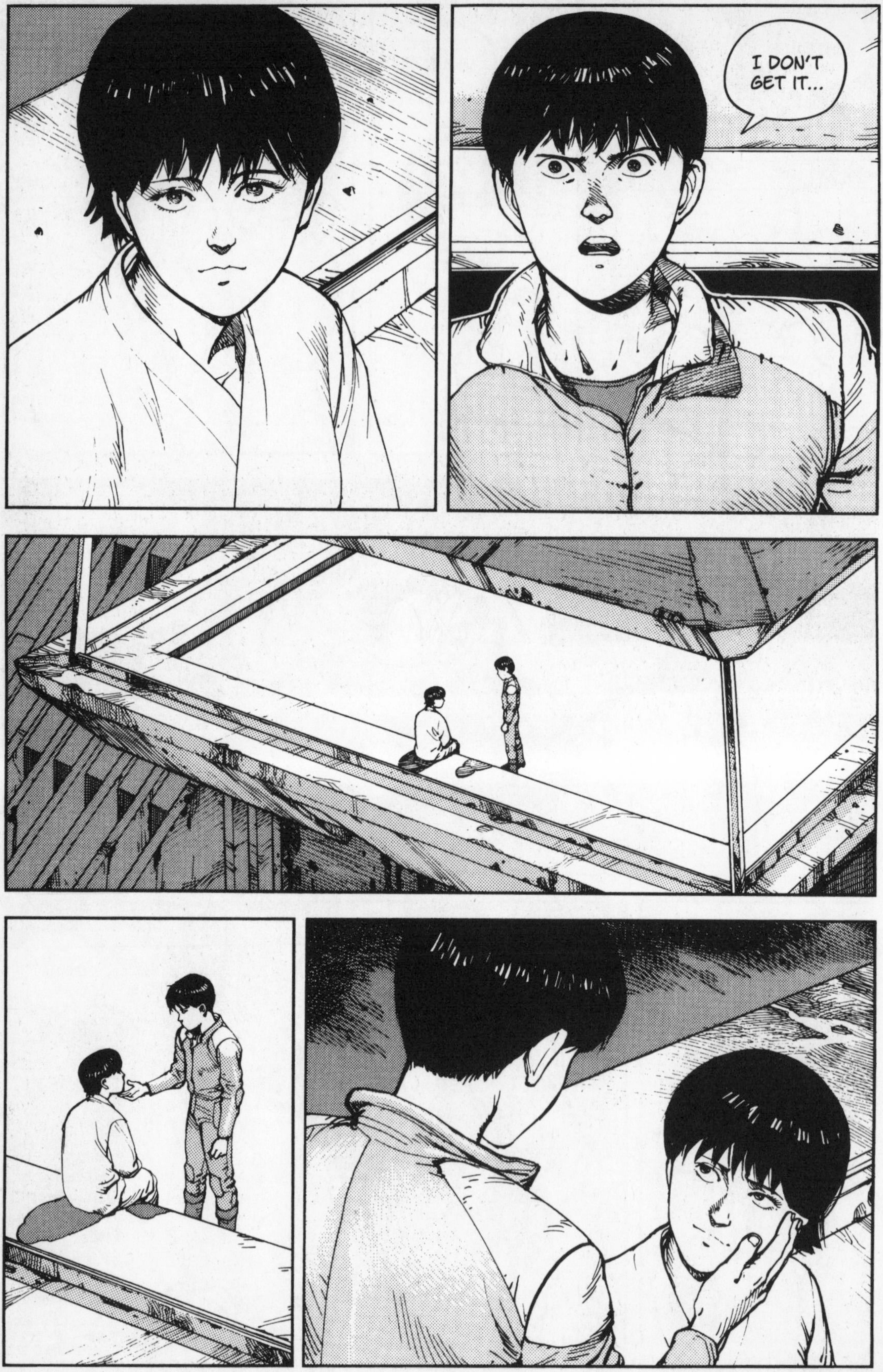
I DON'T GET IT...

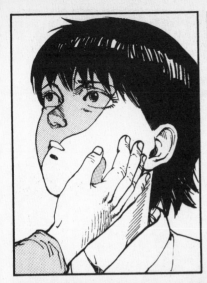
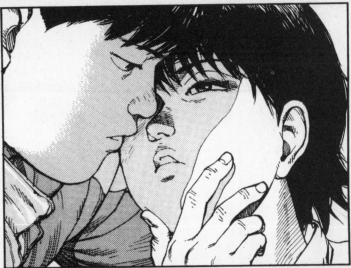

HMM?

....?

HOLD IT!

283

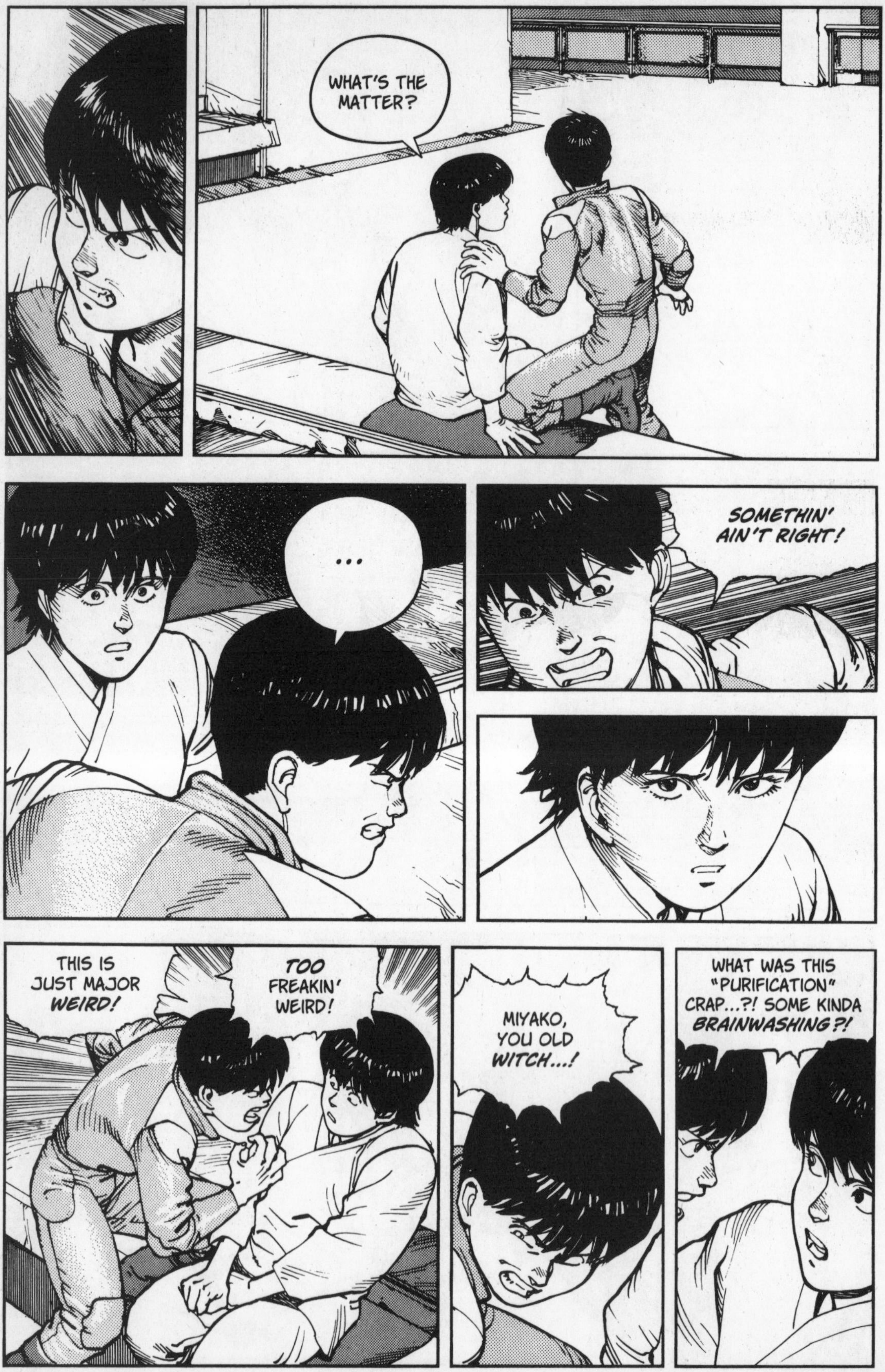
WHAT'S THE MATTER?
...
SOMETHIN' AIN'T RIGHT!
THIS IS JUST MAJOR WEIRD!
TOO FREAKIN' WEIRD!
MIYAKO, YOU OLD WITCH...!
WHAT WAS THIS "PURIFICATION" CRAP...?! SOME KINDA BRAINWASHING?!

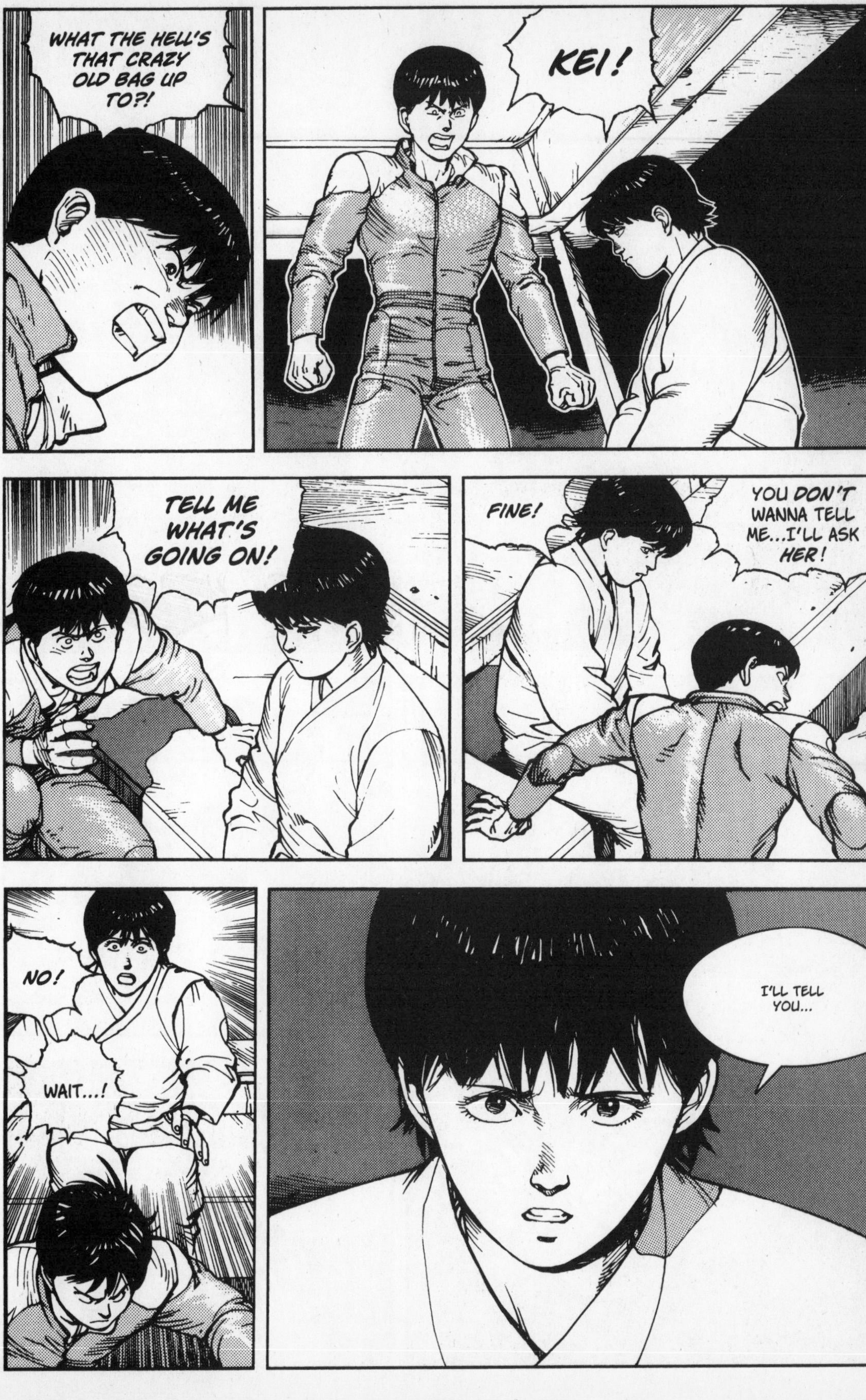
WHAT THE HELL'S THAT CRAZY OLD BAG UP TO?!
KEI!
TELL ME WHAT'S GOING ON!
FINE!
YOU DON'T WANNA TELL ME...I'LL ASK HER!
NO!
WAIT...!
I'LL TELL YOU...

VOOOOO
THIS IS IT, BOYS! SHOW ME THAT YOU GOT A PAIR!
OKAY! JUMP!!
TSSSIF

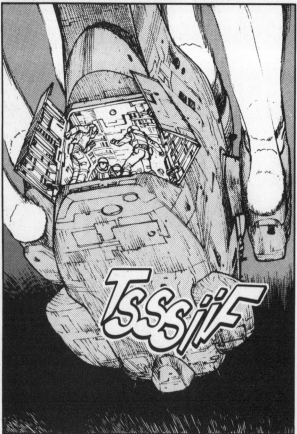

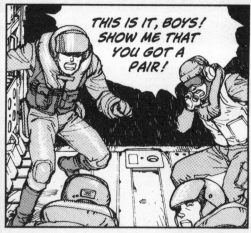

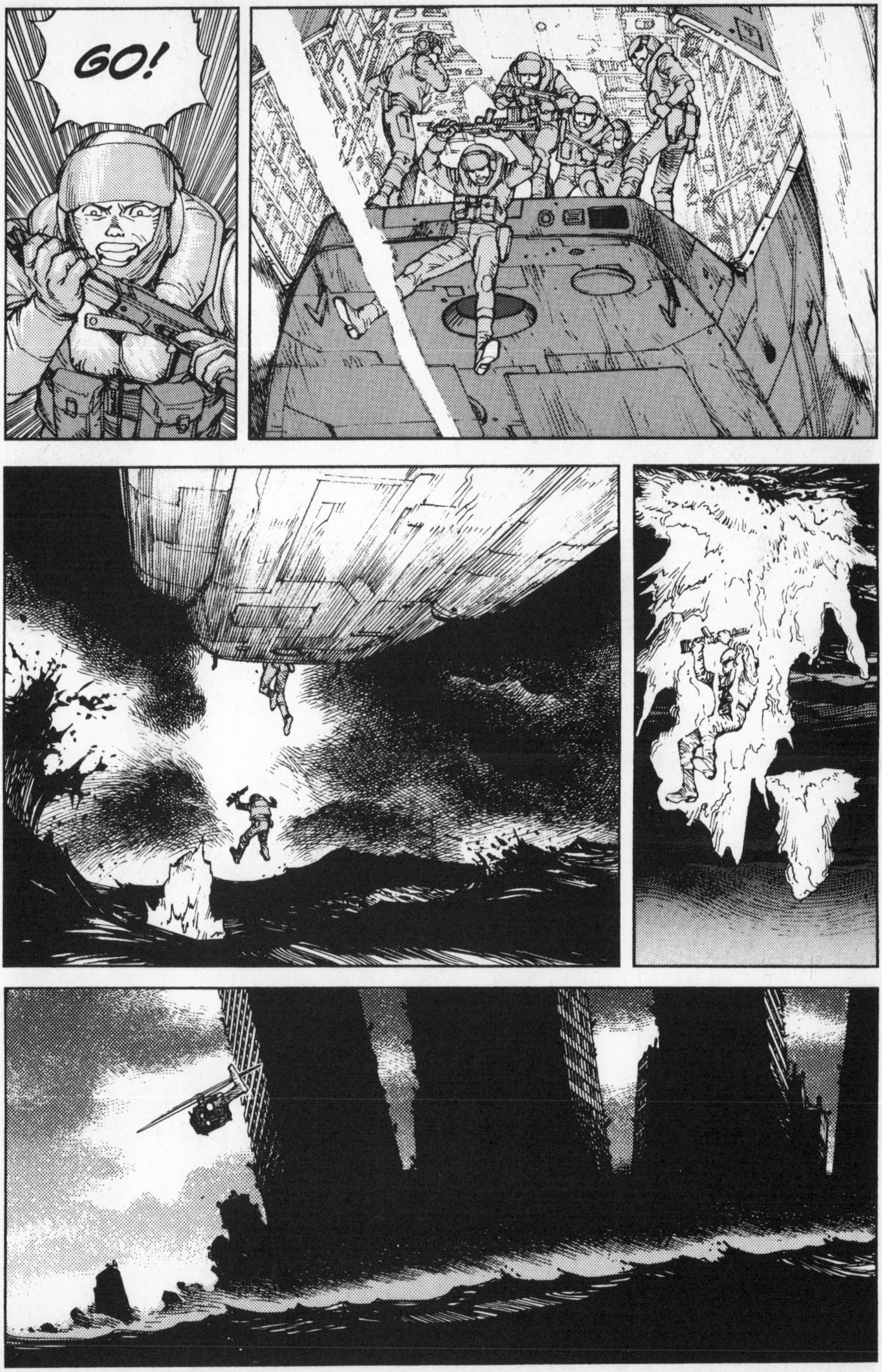
GO!

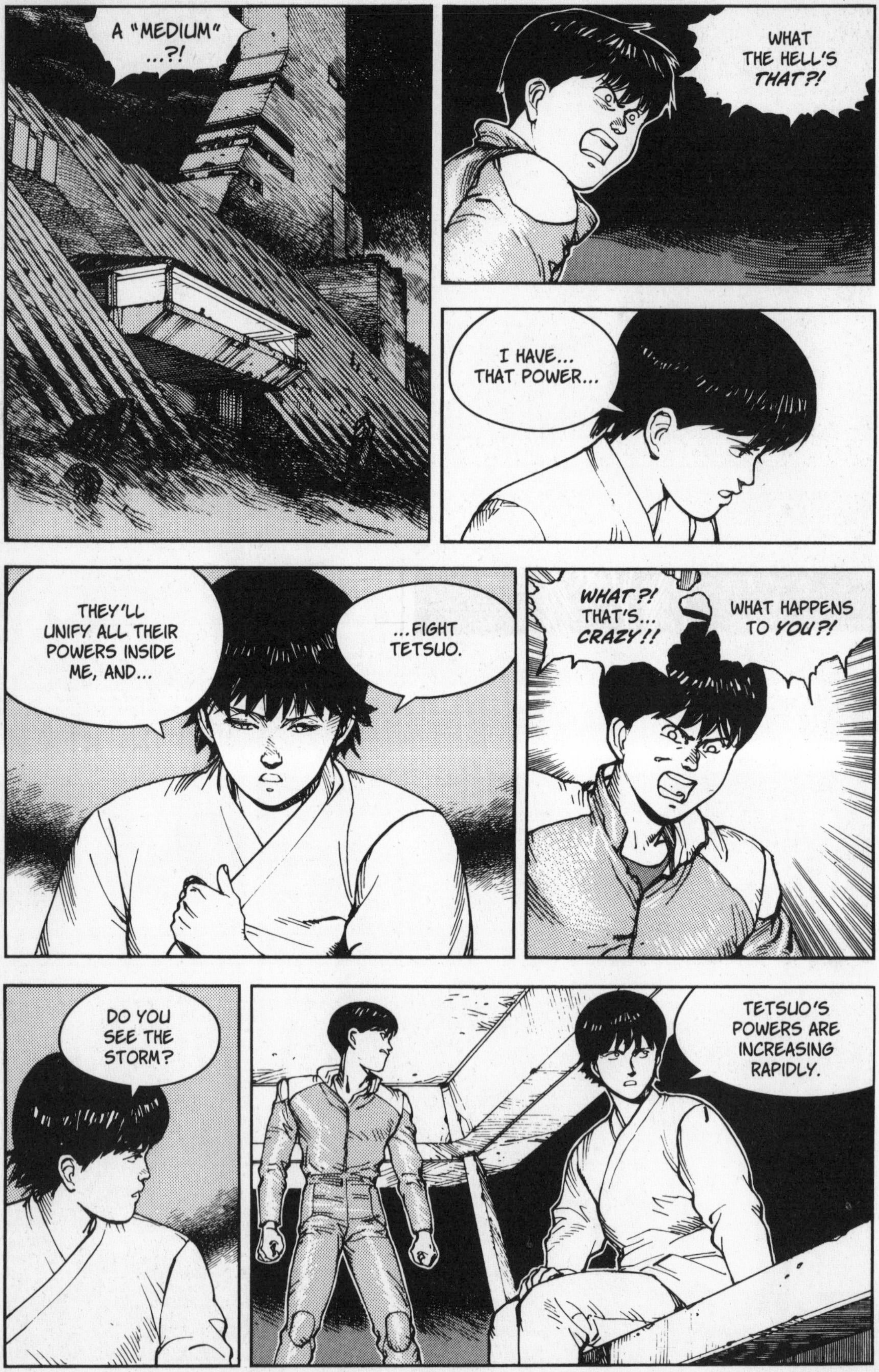
A "MEDIUM" ...?!
WHAT THE HELL'S *THAT?!*
I HAVE... THAT POWER...
THEY'LL UNIFY ALL THEIR POWERS INSIDE ME, AND...
...FIGHT TETSUO.
WHAT?! THAT'S... *CRAZY!!*
WHAT HAPPENS TO *YOU?!*
DO YOU SEE THE STORM?
TETSUO'S POWERS ARE INCREASING RAPIDLY.

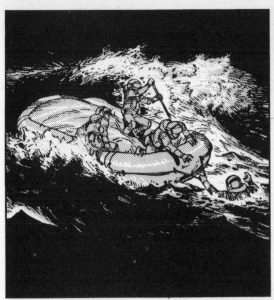

!

!!!

...SOON, TETSUO WILL NO LONGER BE ABLE TO CONTROL THEM.

WE HAVE TO TAKE HIM NOW, BEFORE HE GROWS INTO ANOTHER AKIRA.

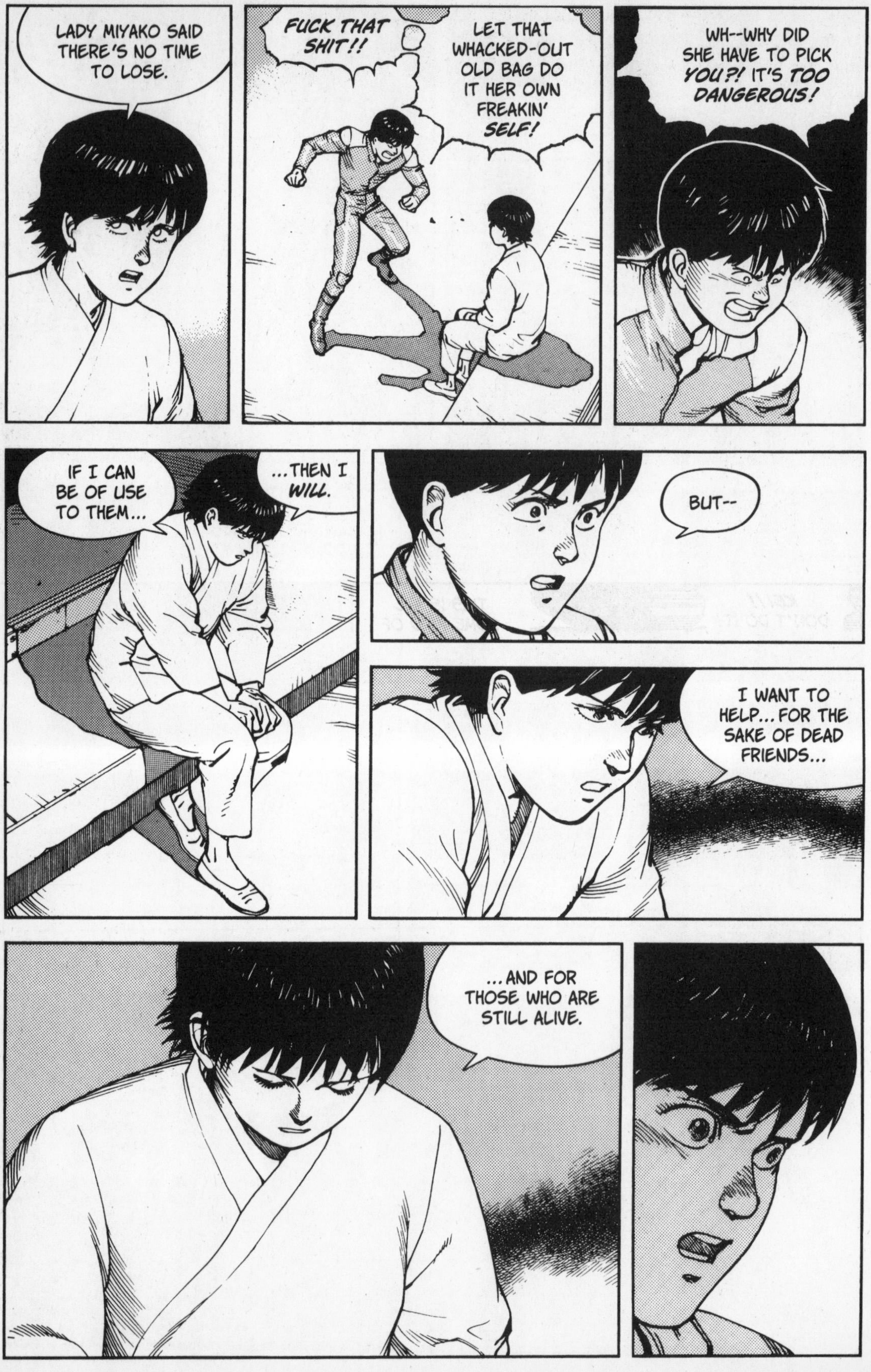
LADY MIYAKO SAID THERE'S NO TIME TO LOSE.
FUCK THAT SHIT!!
LET THAT WHACKED-OUT OLD BAG DO IT HER OWN FREAKIN' SELF!
WH--WHY DID SHE HAVE TO PICK YOU?! IT'S TOO DANGEROUS!
IF I CAN BE OF USE TO THEM...
...THEN I WILL.
BUT--
I WANT TO HELP... FOR THE SAKE OF DEAD FRIENDS...
...AND FOR THOSE WHO ARE STILL ALIVE.

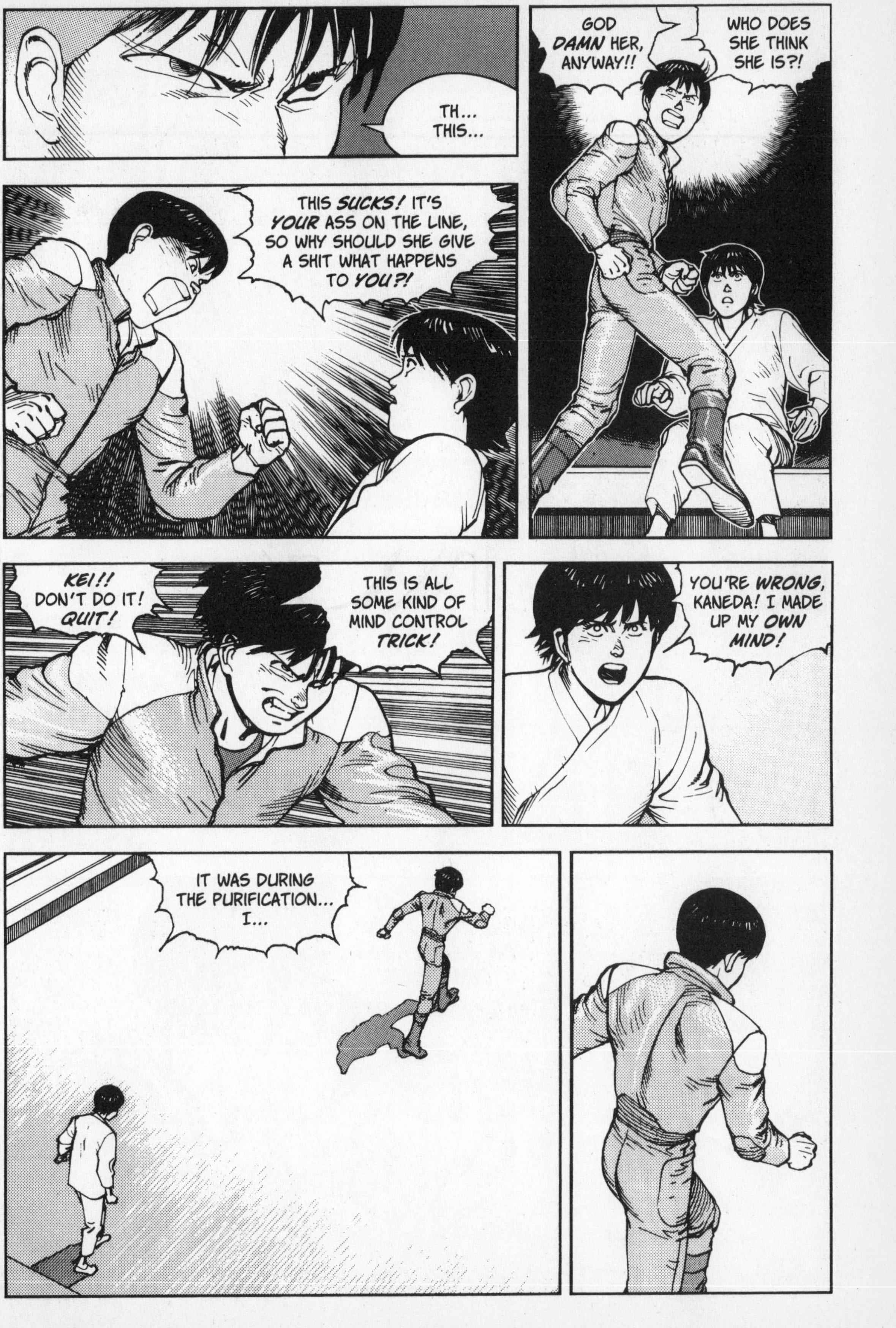
TH... THIS...
GOD DAMN HER, ANYWAY!!
WHO DOES SHE THINK SHE IS?!
THIS SUCKS! IT'S YOUR ASS ON THE LINE, SO WHY SHOULD SHE GIVE A SHIT WHAT HAPPENS TO YOU?!
KEI!! DON'T DO IT! QUIT!
THIS IS ALL SOME KIND OF MIND CONTROL TRICK!
YOU'RE WRONG, KANEDA! I MADE UP MY OWN MIND!
IT WAS DURING THE PURIFICATION... I...

FINE.

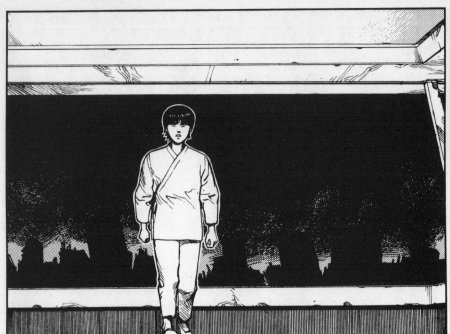

I'LL KILL TETSUO MYSELF!

HE'LL BE DEAD MEAT BEFORE YOU GET ANYWHERE NEAR HIM!

KANEDA...

I WON'T LET YOU RISK YOUR LIFE FOR THESE CREEPS!

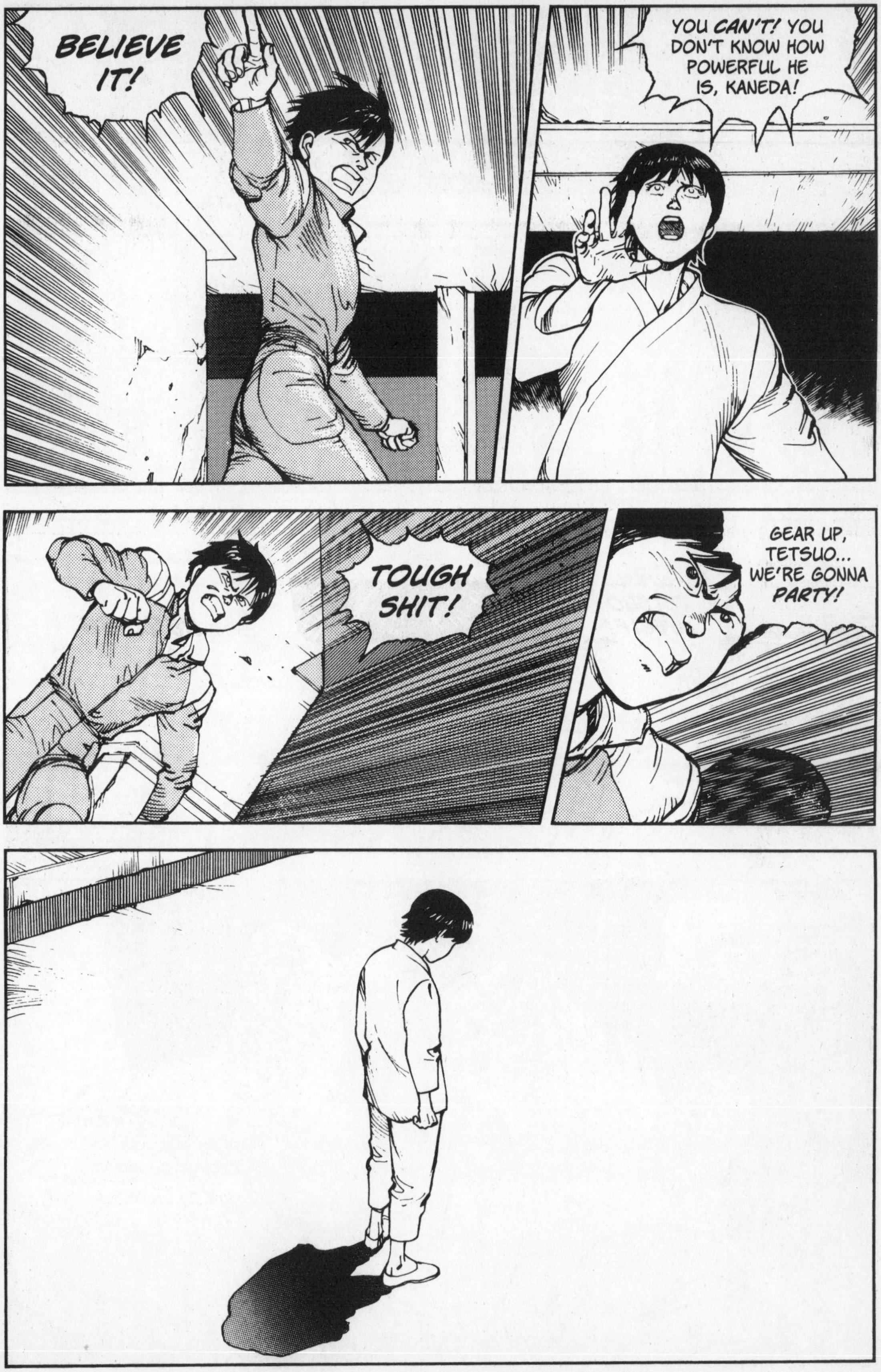
BELIEVE IT!
YOU CAN'T! YOU DON'T KNOW HOW POWERFUL HE IS, KANEDA!
TOUGH SHIT!
GEAR UP, TETSUO... WE'RE GONNA PARTY!

TAP TAP
TAP

KEI...

HUNH?

...KANEDA, WHAT'S--

I FORGOT SOMETHING!

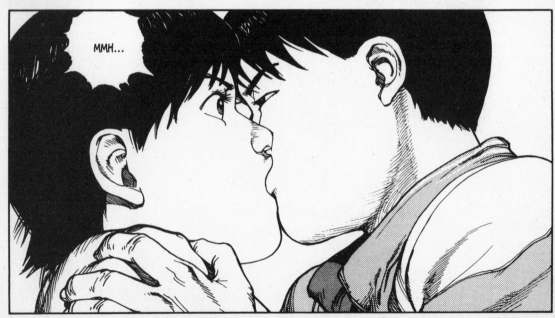

MMH...

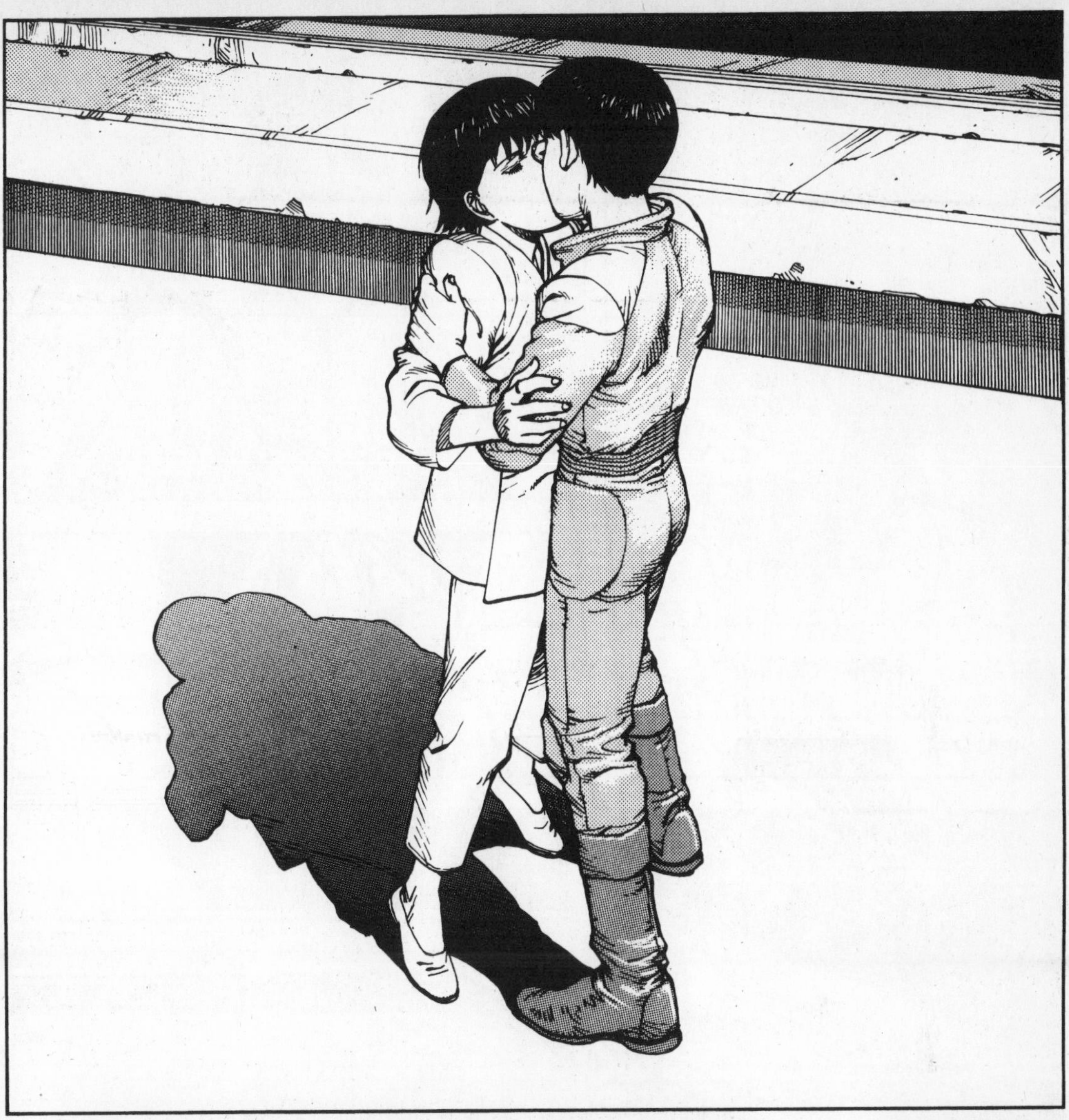

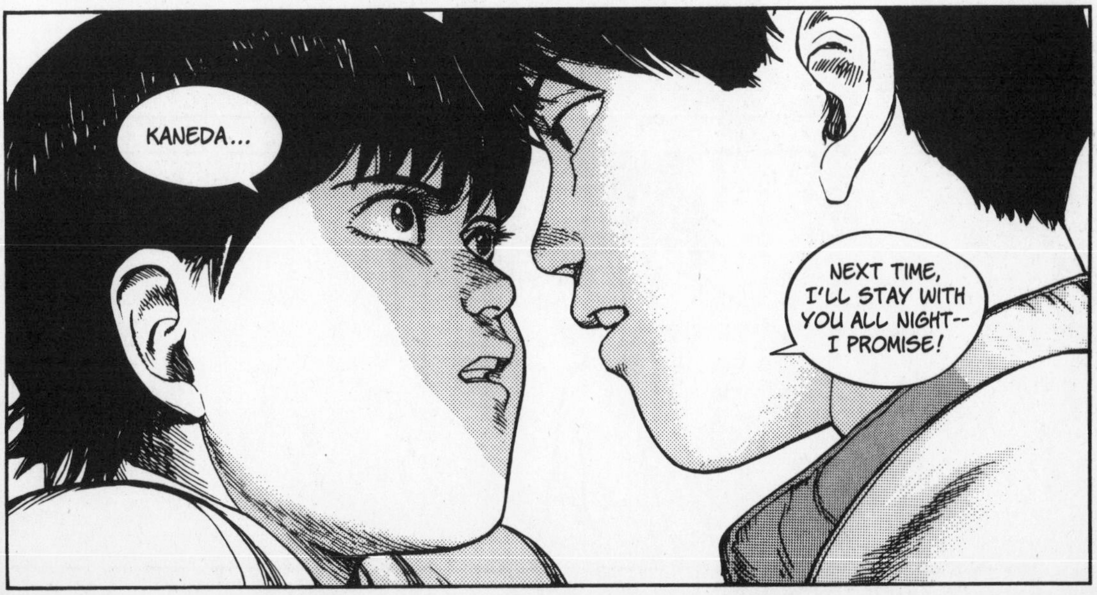

KANEDA...
NEXT TIME, I'LL STAY WITH YOU ALL NIGHT-- I PROMISE!

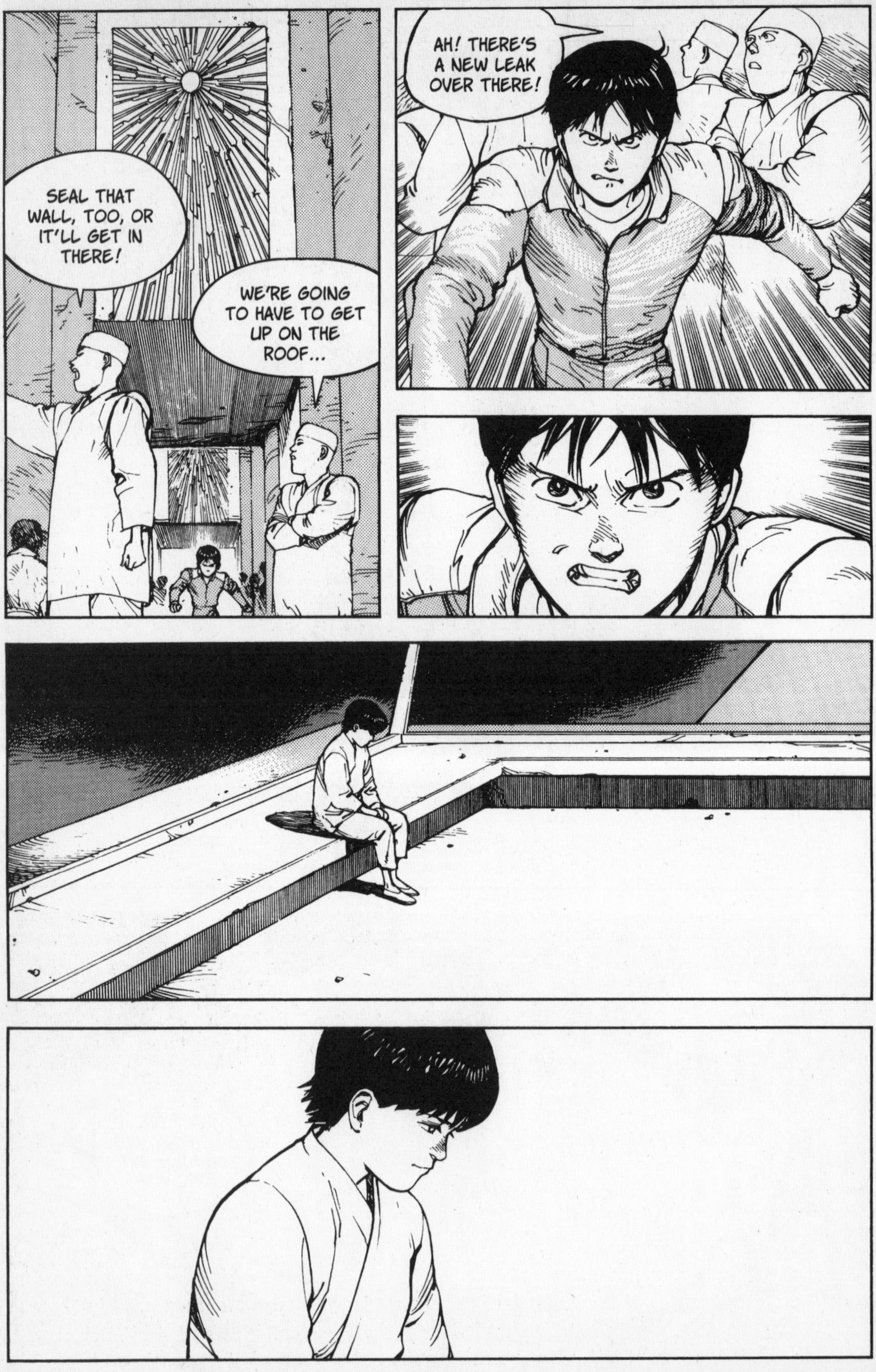
SEAL THAT WALL, TOO, OR IT'LL GET IN THERE!
WE'RE GOING TO HAVE TO GET UP ON THE ROOF...
AH! THERE'S A NEW LEAK OVER THERE!

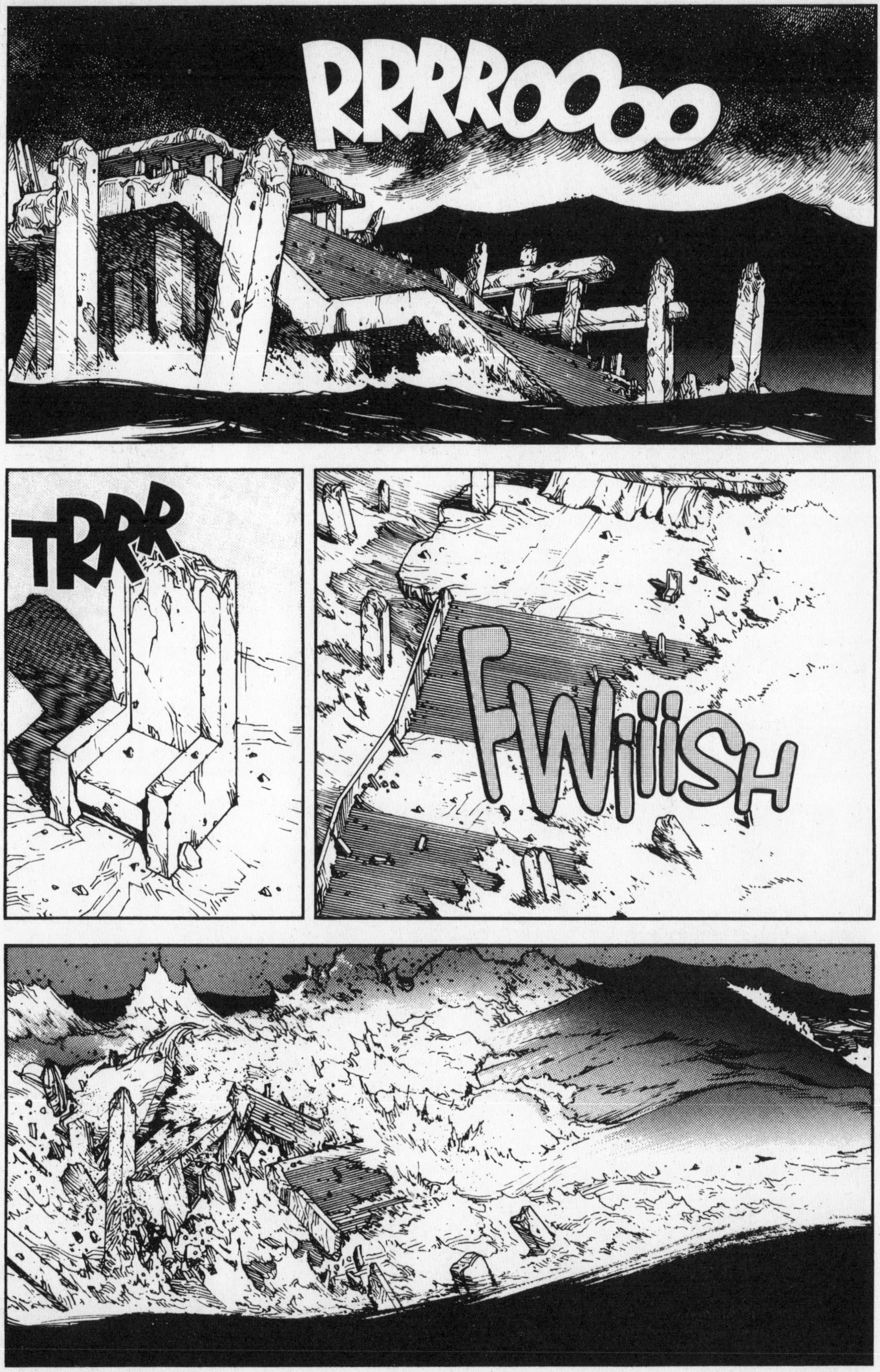
RRRROOooo
TRRR
FWiiiSH

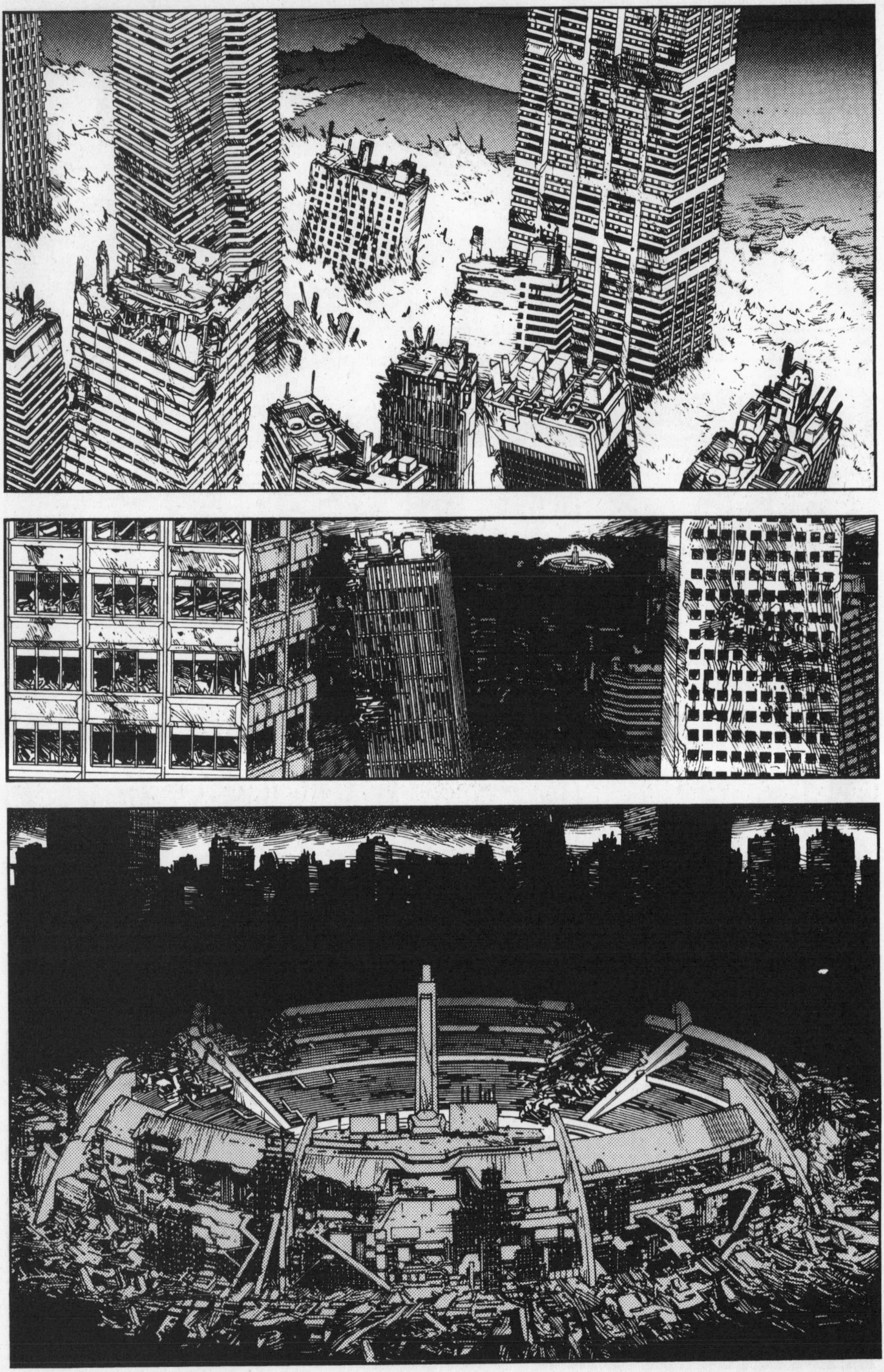

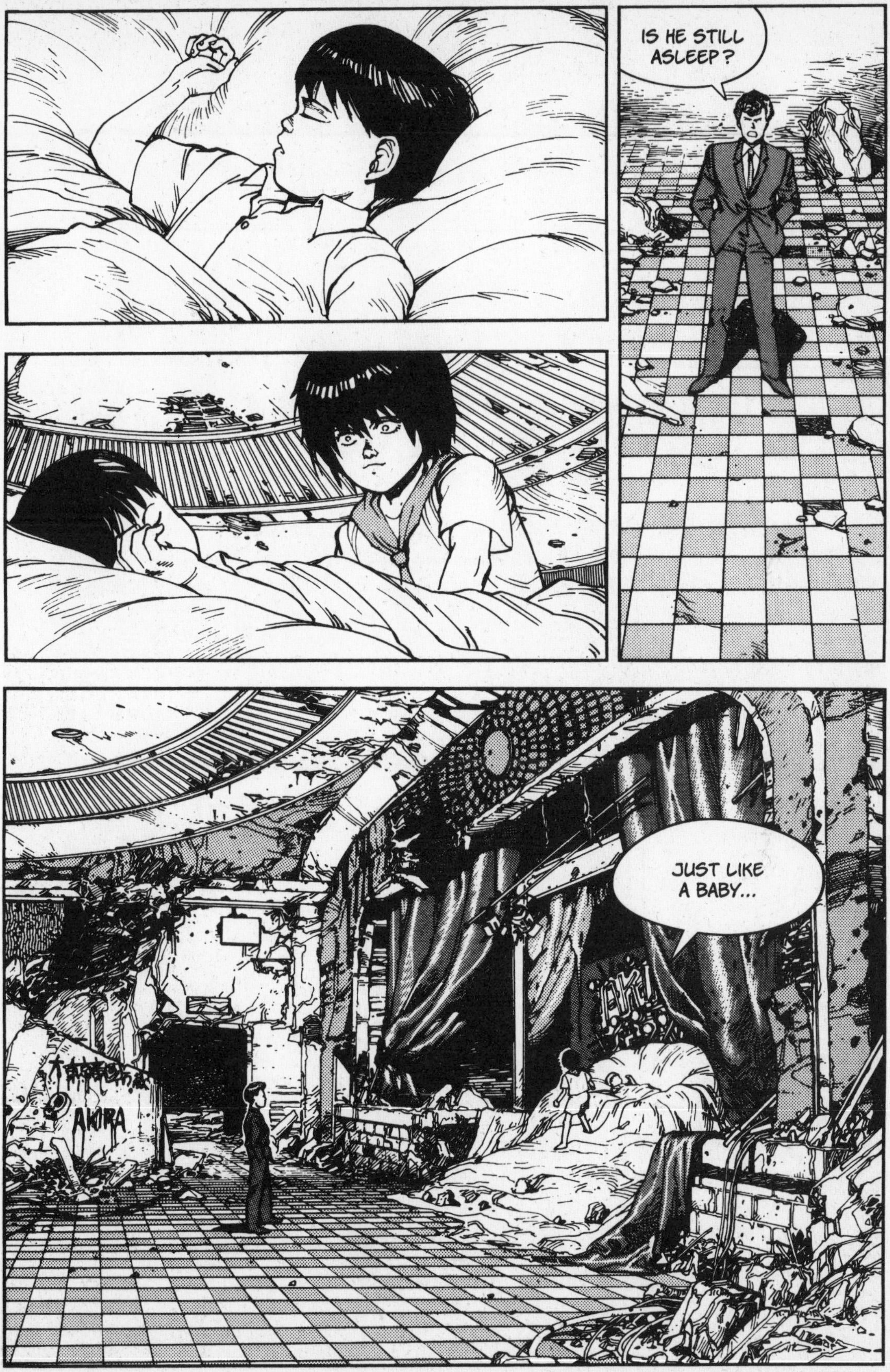
IS HE STILL ASLEEP?
JUST LIKE A BABY...
AKIRA

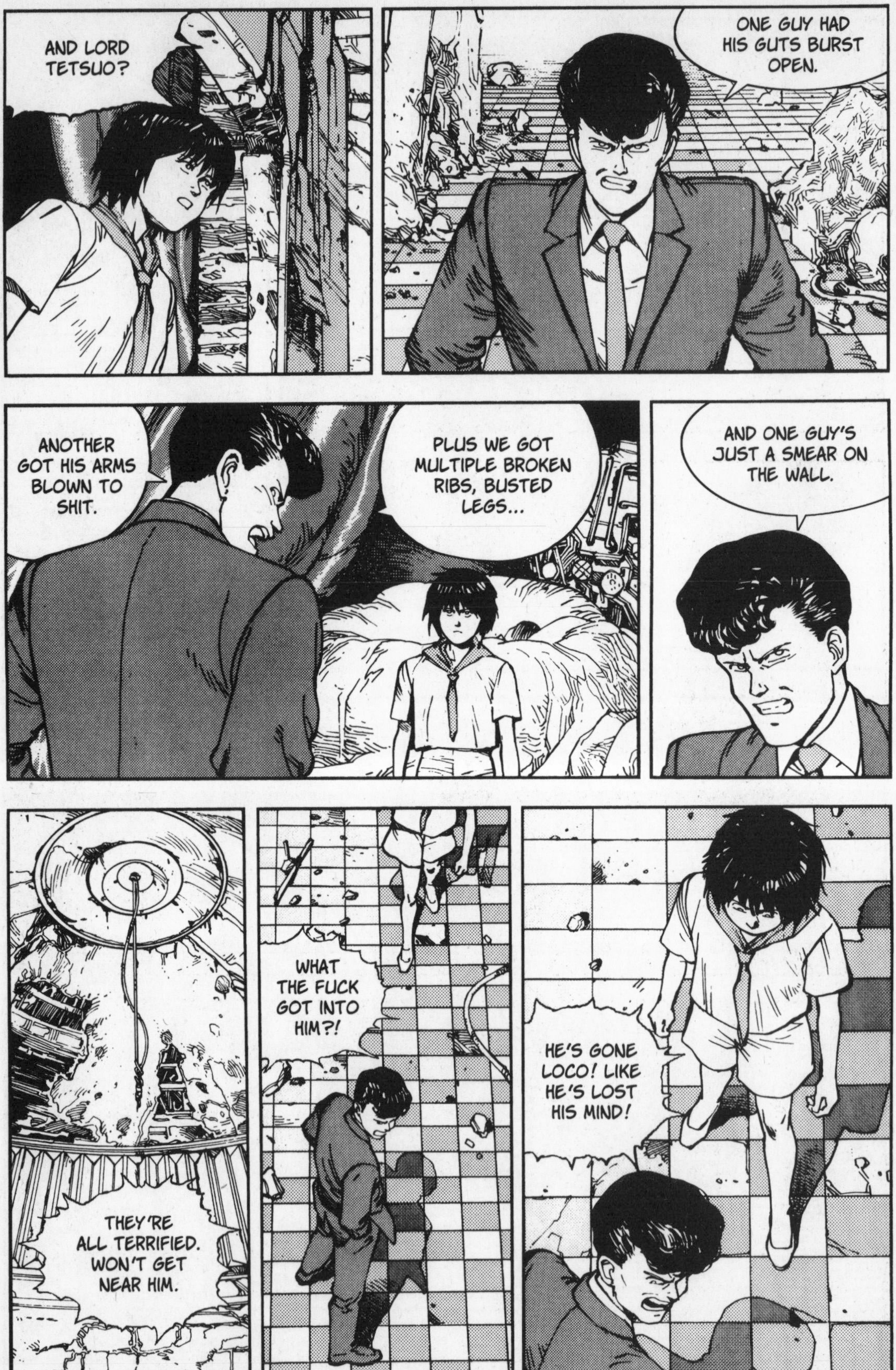
AND LORD TETSUO?
ONE GUY HAD HIS GUTS BURST OPEN.
ANOTHER GOT HIS ARMS BLOWN TO SHIT.
PLUS WE GOT MULTIPLE BROKEN RIBS, BUSTED LEGS...
AND ONE GUY'S JUST A SMEAR ON THE WALL.
THEY'RE ALL TERRIFIED. WON'T GET NEAR HIM.
WHAT THE FUCK GOT INTO HIM?!
HE'S GONE LOCO! LIKE HE'S LOST HIS MIND!

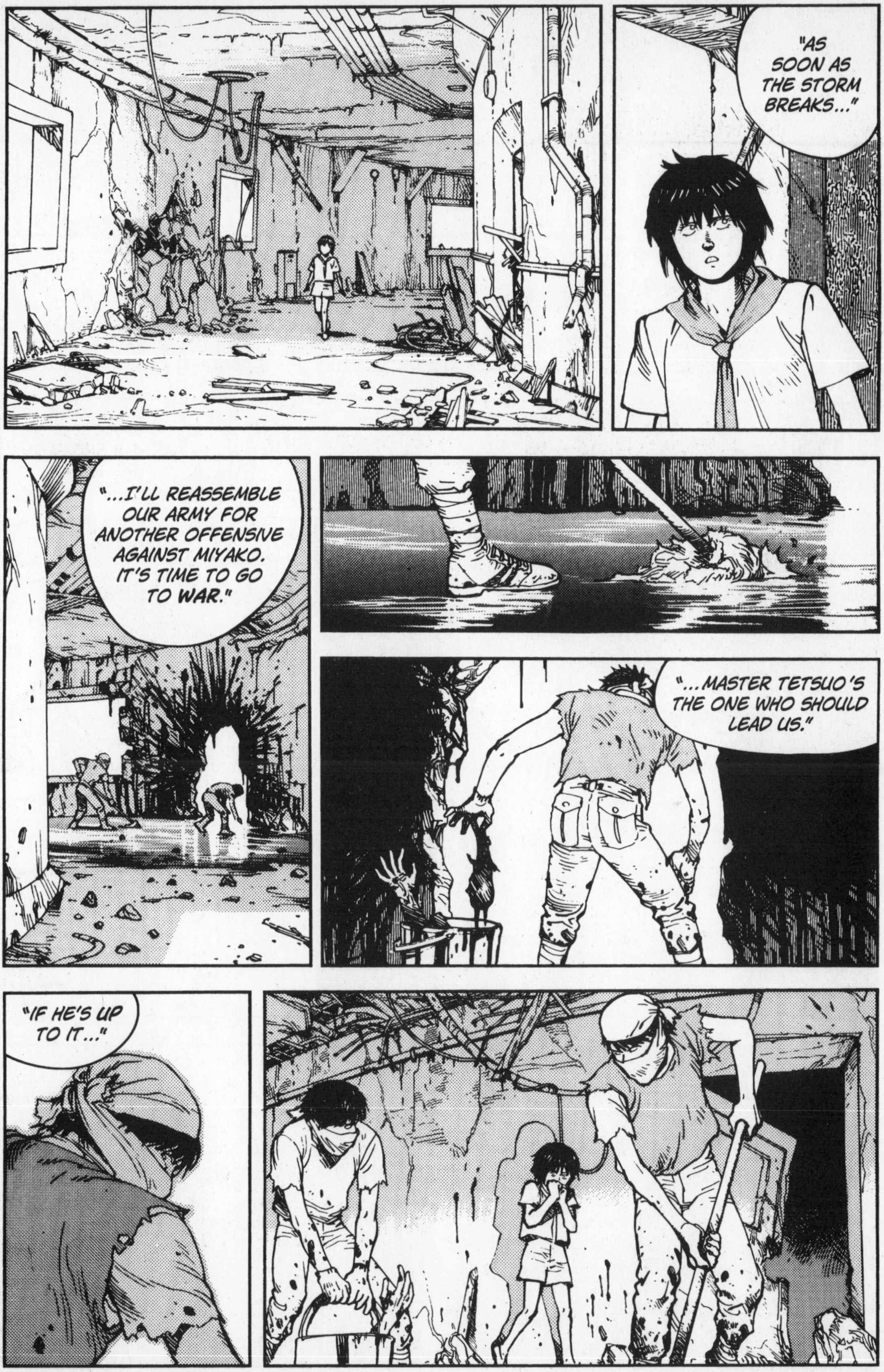
"AS SOON AS THE STORM BREAKS..."
"...I'LL REASSEMBLE OUR ARMY FOR ANOTHER OFFENSIVE AGAINST MIYAKO. IT'S TIME TO GO TO WAR."
"...MASTER TETSUO'S THE ONE WHO SHOULD LEAD US."
"IF HE'S UP TO IT..."

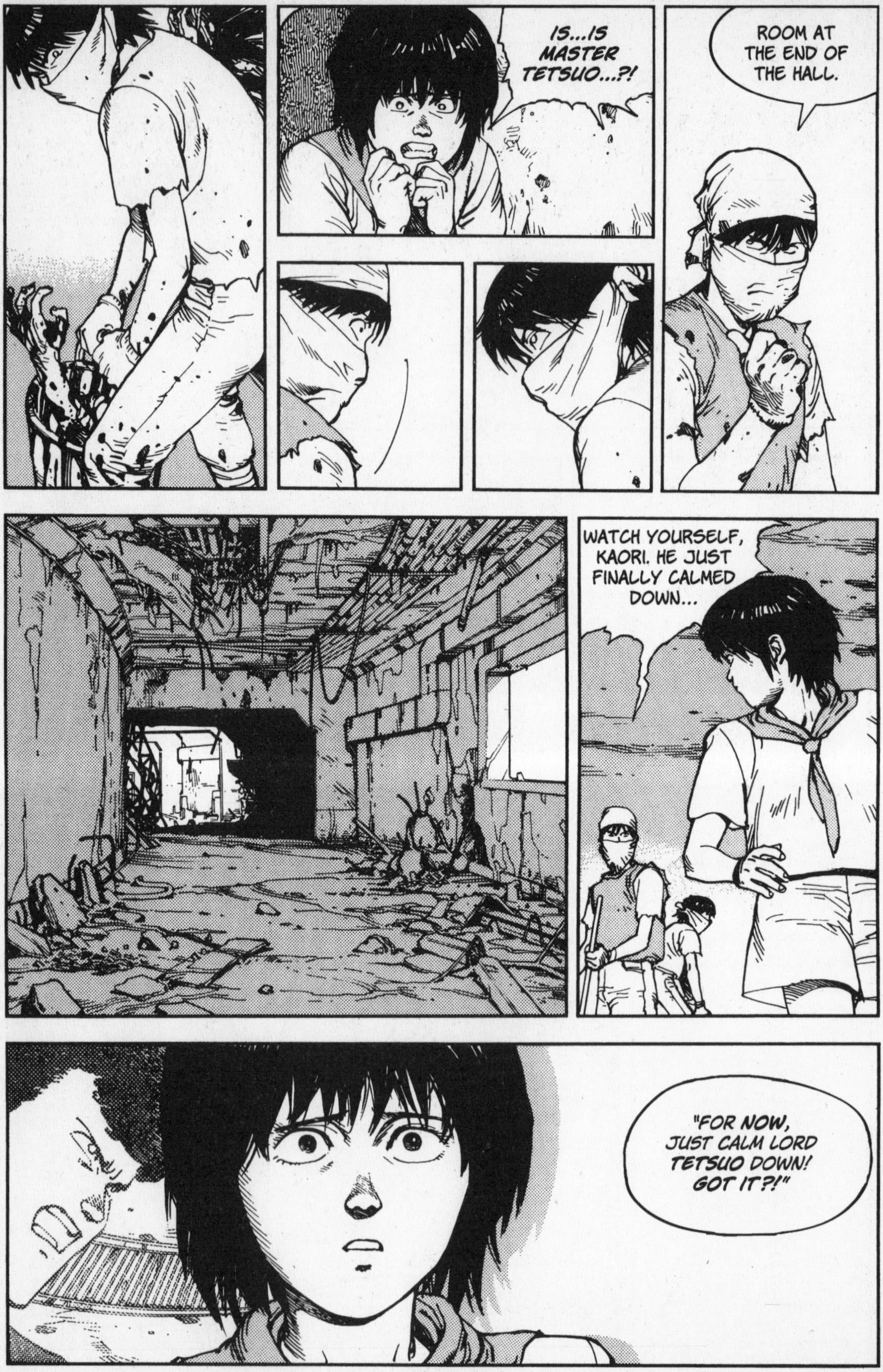
IS...IS MASTER TETSUO...?!
ROOM AT THE END OF THE HALL.
WATCH YOURSELF, KAORI. HE JUST FINALLY CALMED DOWN...
"FOR NOW, JUST CALM LORD TETSUO DOWN! GOT IT?!"

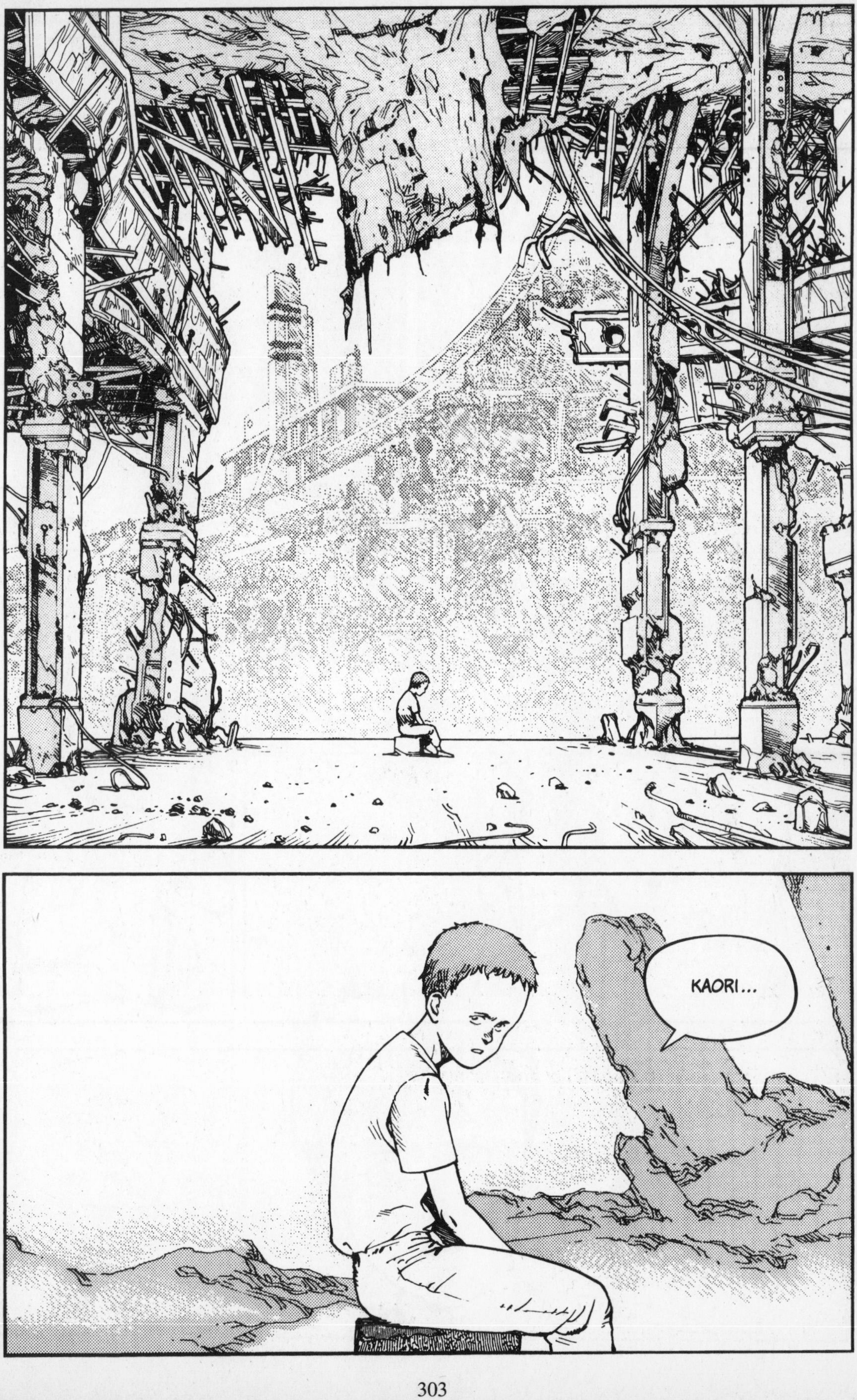
KAORI...

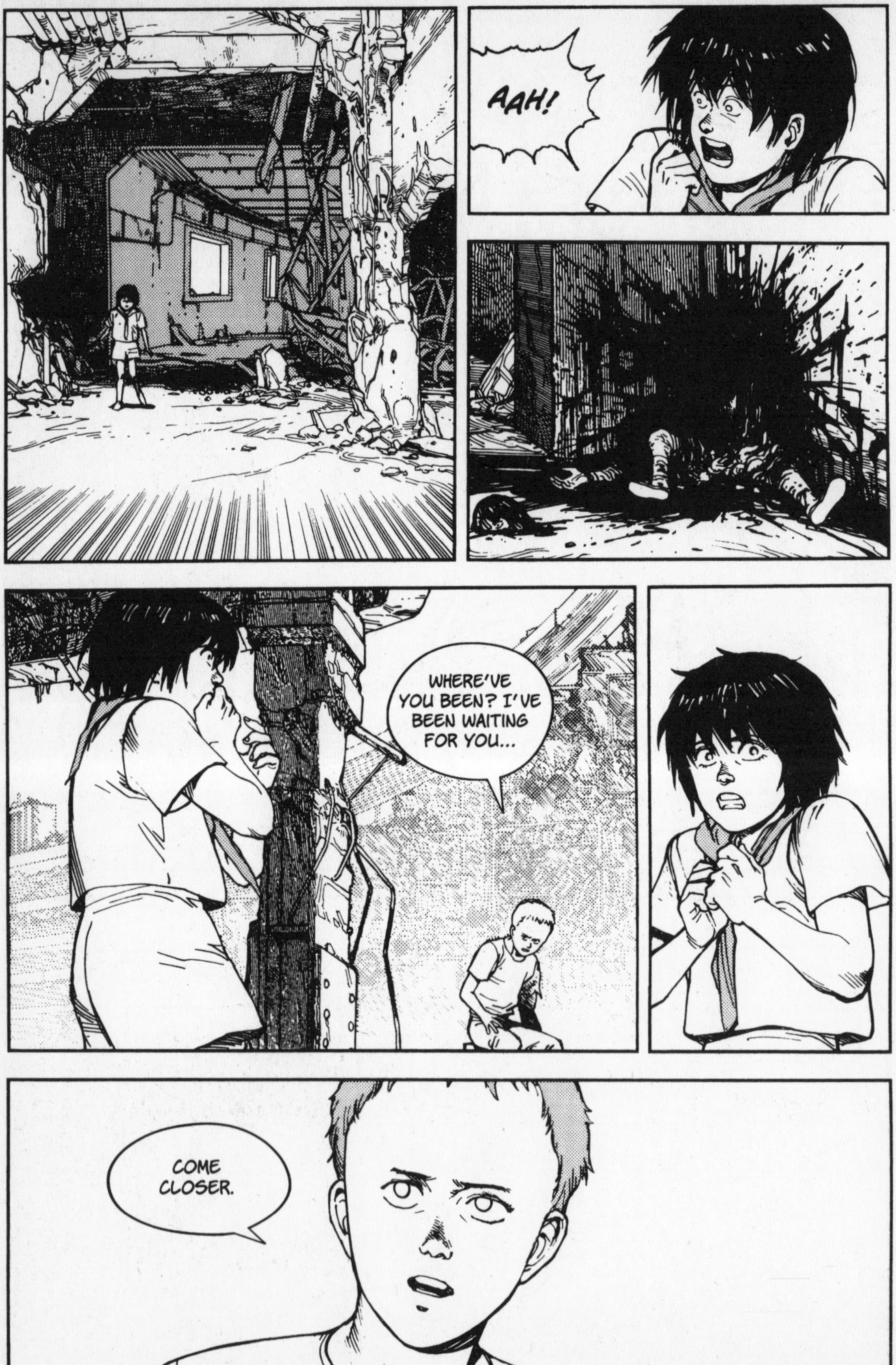
AAH!
WHERE'VE YOU BEEN? I'VE BEEN WAITING FOR YOU...
COME CLOSER.

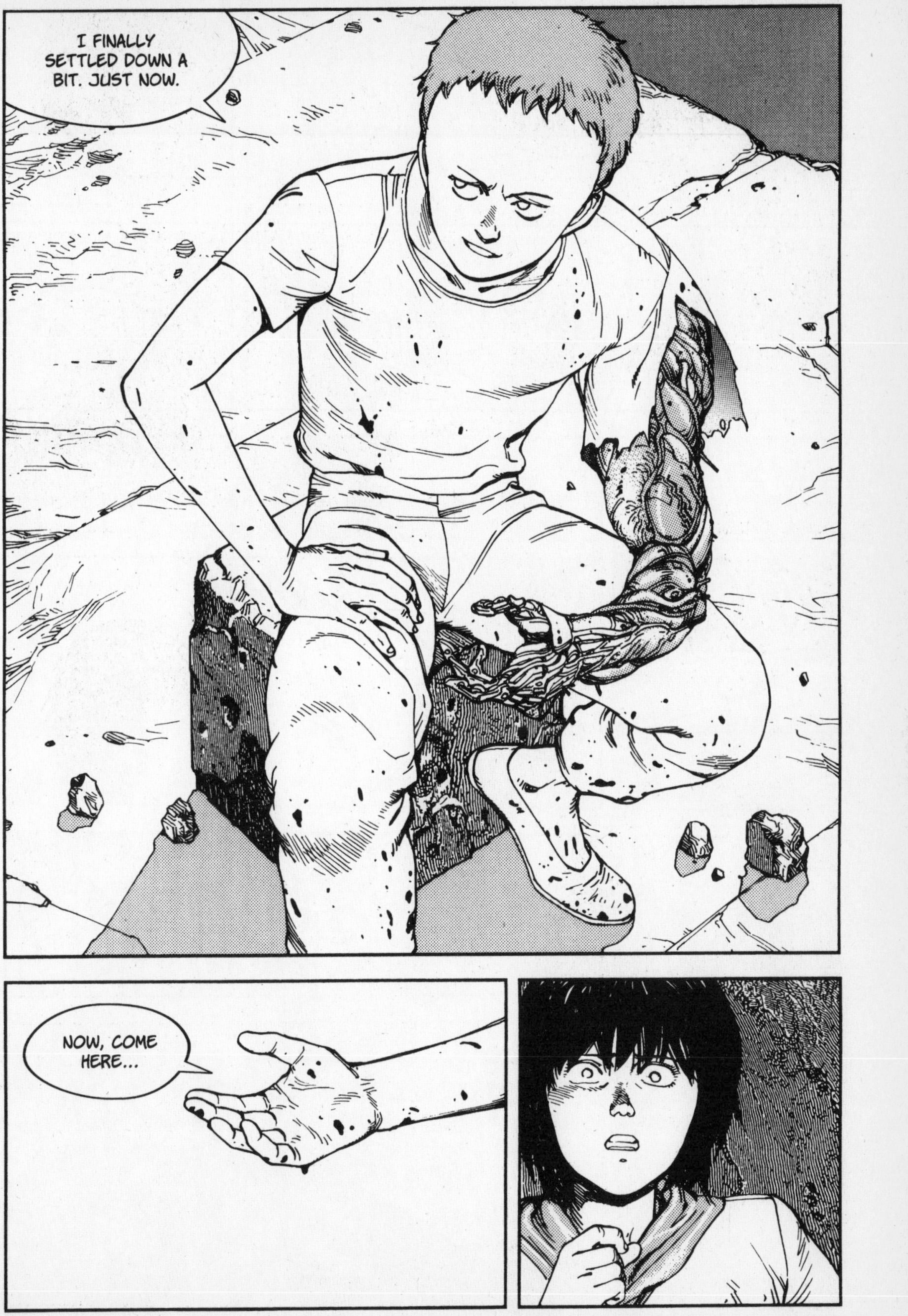
I FINALLY SETTLED DOWN A BIT. JUST NOW.
NOW, COME HERE...

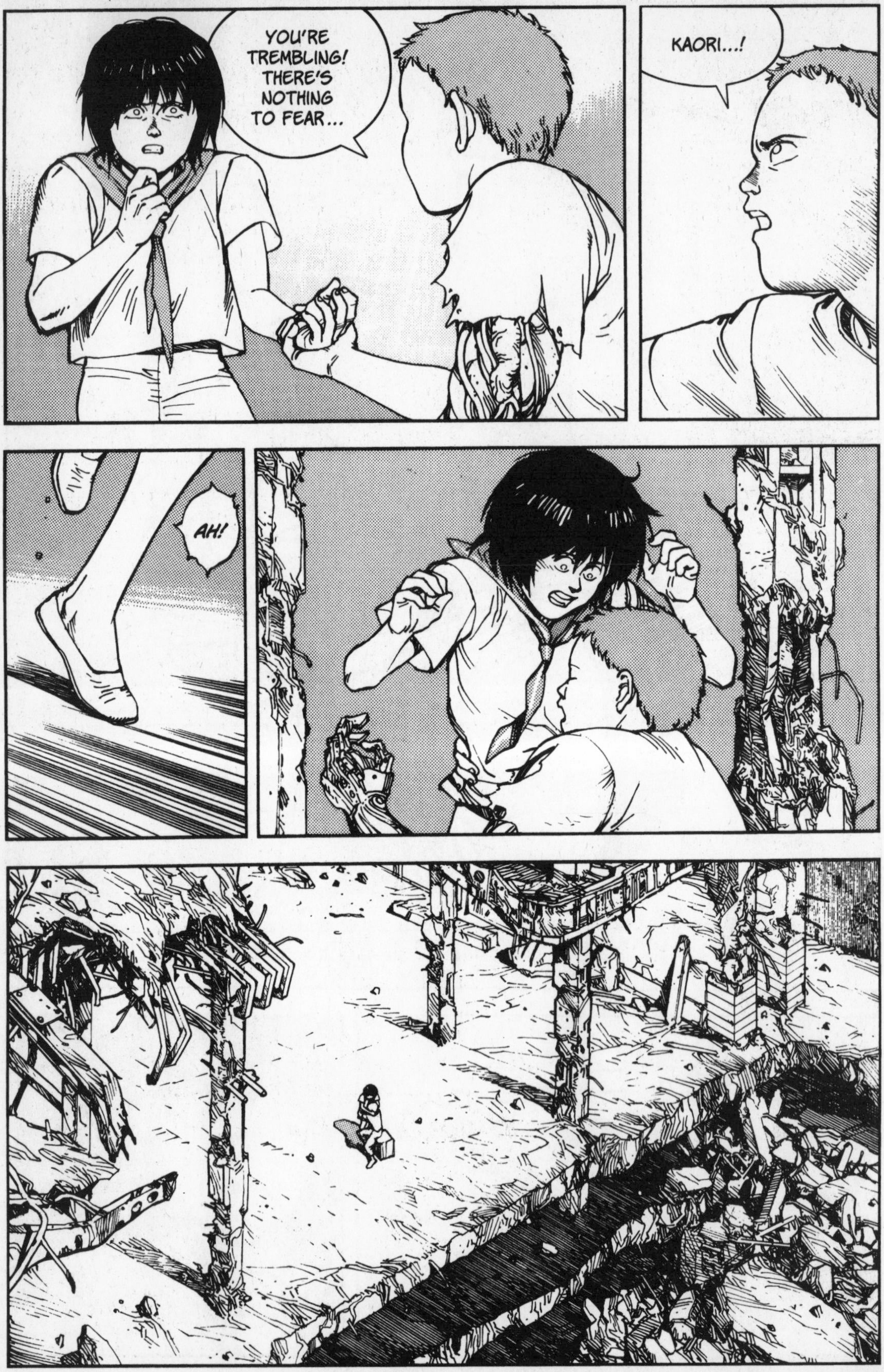
YOU'RE TREMBLING! THERE'S NOTHING TO FEAR...
KAORI...!
AH!

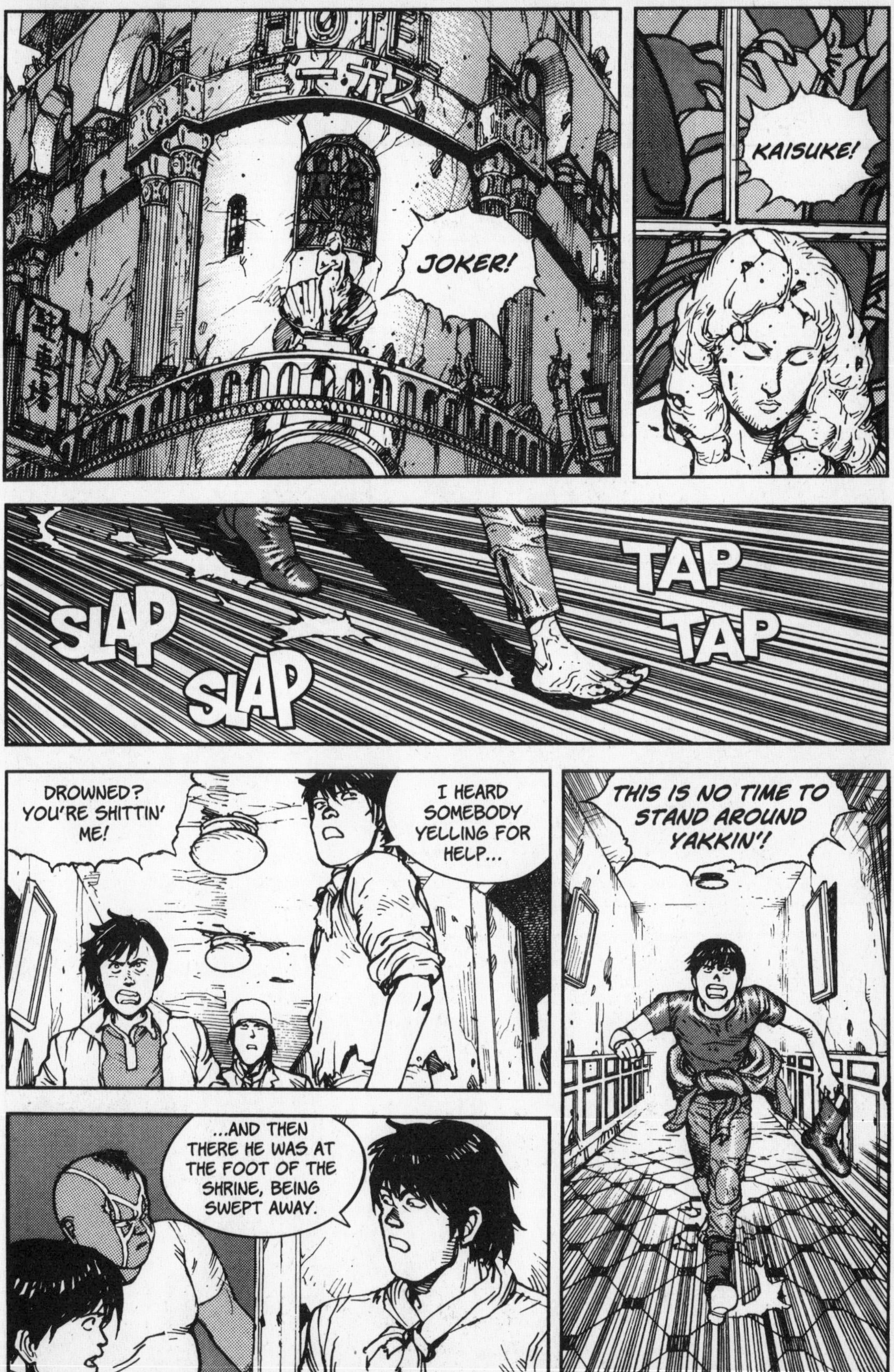
JOKER!
KAISUKE!
SLAP
SLAP
TAP
TAP
DROWNED? YOU'RE SHITTIN' ME!
I HEARD SOMEBODY YELLING FOR HELP...
...AND THEN THERE HE WAS AT THE FOOT OF THE SHRINE, BEING SWEPT AWAY.
THIS IS NO TIME TO STAND AROUND YAKKIN'!

DID YOU HEAR ME?!

I JUST WENT TO MIYAKO'S PLACE! AND GET THIS--

JESUS, KANEDA...CAN'T YOU EVEN SWIM? WHAT A LAME-O...

HUHN?

WHY THE FUCK'D YOU SAVE HIM?

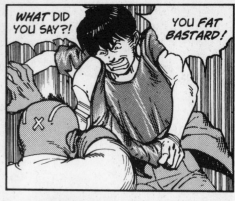

WHAT DID YOU SAY?!

YOU FAT BASTARD!

SO? WHAT IS IT? WHAT'S THE BIG DEAL?

OH?! RIGHT! THE STORY IS--!

AHH?!

PUNCH

BAM

SLiiZ

KANEDA?!

HEY, KANEDA?

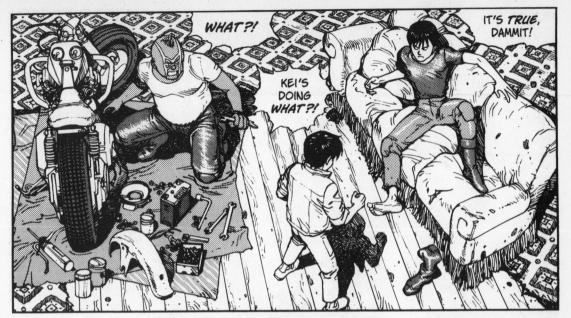

WHAT?!

KEI'S DOING WHAT?!

IT'S TRUE, DAMMIT!

MIYAKO CONVINCED KEI! I COULDN'T TALK HER OUT OF IT!

YOU DOWN WITH US, JOKER?

HOW MUCH TIME DO WE HAVE?

MIYAKO'S READY TO GO RIGHT NOW!

NONE!

BUT...BUT... BUT, KANEDA... WHAT'S THE PLAN?

FUCK PLANS!

STAP

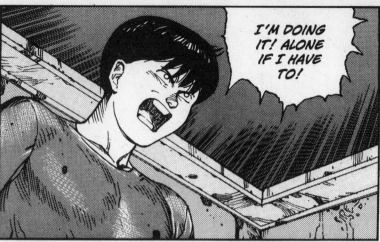

I'M DOING IT! ALONE IF I HAVE TO!

THAT'S CRAZY! WE CAN'T DO NOTHIN' WITHOUT A PLAN! WE DON'T EVEN GOT ANY WEAPONS...!

I'LL FIGHT WITH MY BARE HANDS!

YOU WITH ME, JOKER?

YEAH!!

BUT FIRST, I WANNA SHOW YOU SOMETHING.

THAT'S
NO JOKE!

OH,
SHIT...!

WE GOT
US A REGULAR
ARSENAL!

THAT AIN'T GONNA DO
FOR TETSUO. FOR HIM,
I GOT SOMETHIN'
SPECIAL...

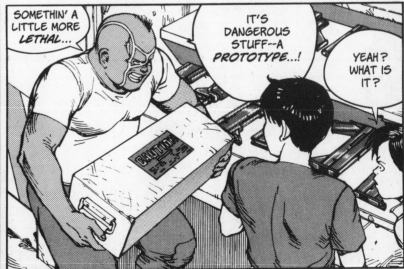

SOMETHIN' A
LITTLE MORE
LETHAL...

IT'S
DANGEROUS
STUFF--A
PROTOTYPE...!

YEAH?
WHAT IS
IT?

A TOP-SECRET MILITARY WEAPON! STATE OF THE ART!

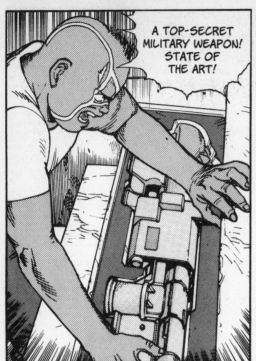

? OH... IT'S A LASER!

HUNH?!

HOW'D *YOU* KNOW THAT?

BEEN THERE, DONE THAT...!

BITCHIN' GAT! SICK! CAN I TRY IT? CAN I, JOKER?

THIS IS THE POWER SWITCH...HERE'S THE TARGETING SIGHT...

GREAT.

HEY! I GOT SOMETHIN' ELSE TO SHOW YOU!

HEY, AREN'T THESE--?

YEAH. THOSE JUNKERS WE FOUND DOWN IN THE SUBWAY!

THEY'RE MOSTLY SHIT. SHAPE THEY'RE IN, IT'D TAKE TWO WEEKS JUST TO GET THE ELECTRICAL SYSTEMS WORKING.

TOO BAD...I COULD USE ONE.

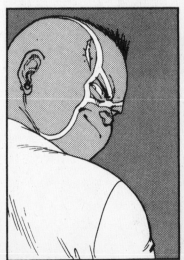

CHECK IT OUT, KANEDA.

SWIIIP

THIS IS WHAT I BUILT FROM THAT SCRAP.

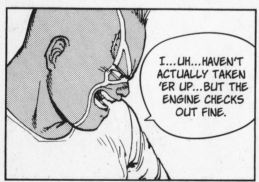

I...UH...HAVEN'T ACTUALLY TAKEN 'ER UP...BUT THE ENGINE CHECKS OUT FINE.

YOU RIDE IT...

UH-UH. THE GUY WHO *BUILT* IT GETS FIRST HONORS...

314

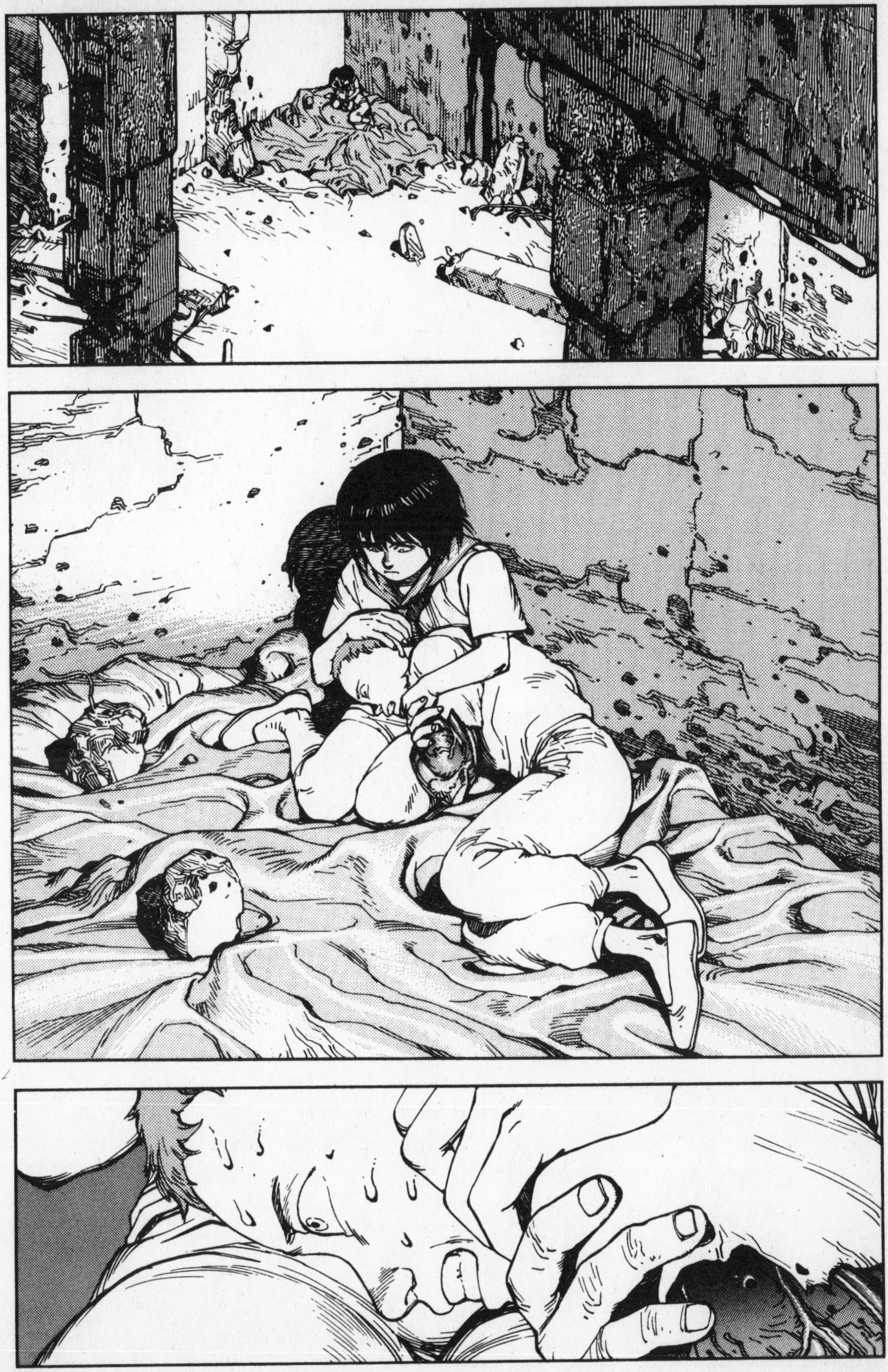

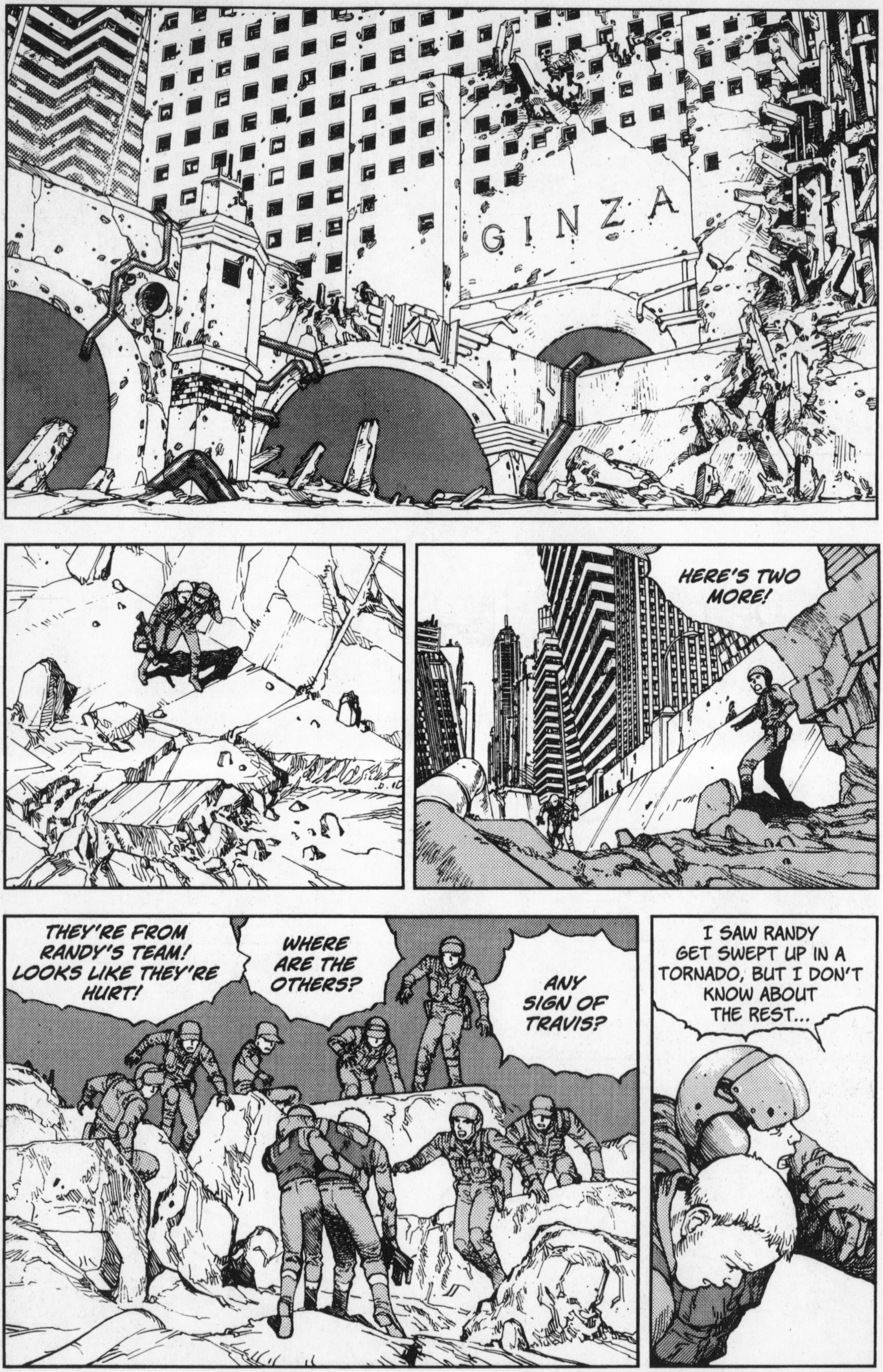

GINZA
HERE'S TWO MORE!
THEY'RE FROM RANDY'S TEAM! LOOKS LIKE THEY'RE HURT!
WHERE ARE THE OTHERS?
ANY SIGN OF TRAVIS?
I SAW RANDY GET SWEPT UP IN A TORNADO, BUT I DON'T KNOW ABOUT THE REST...

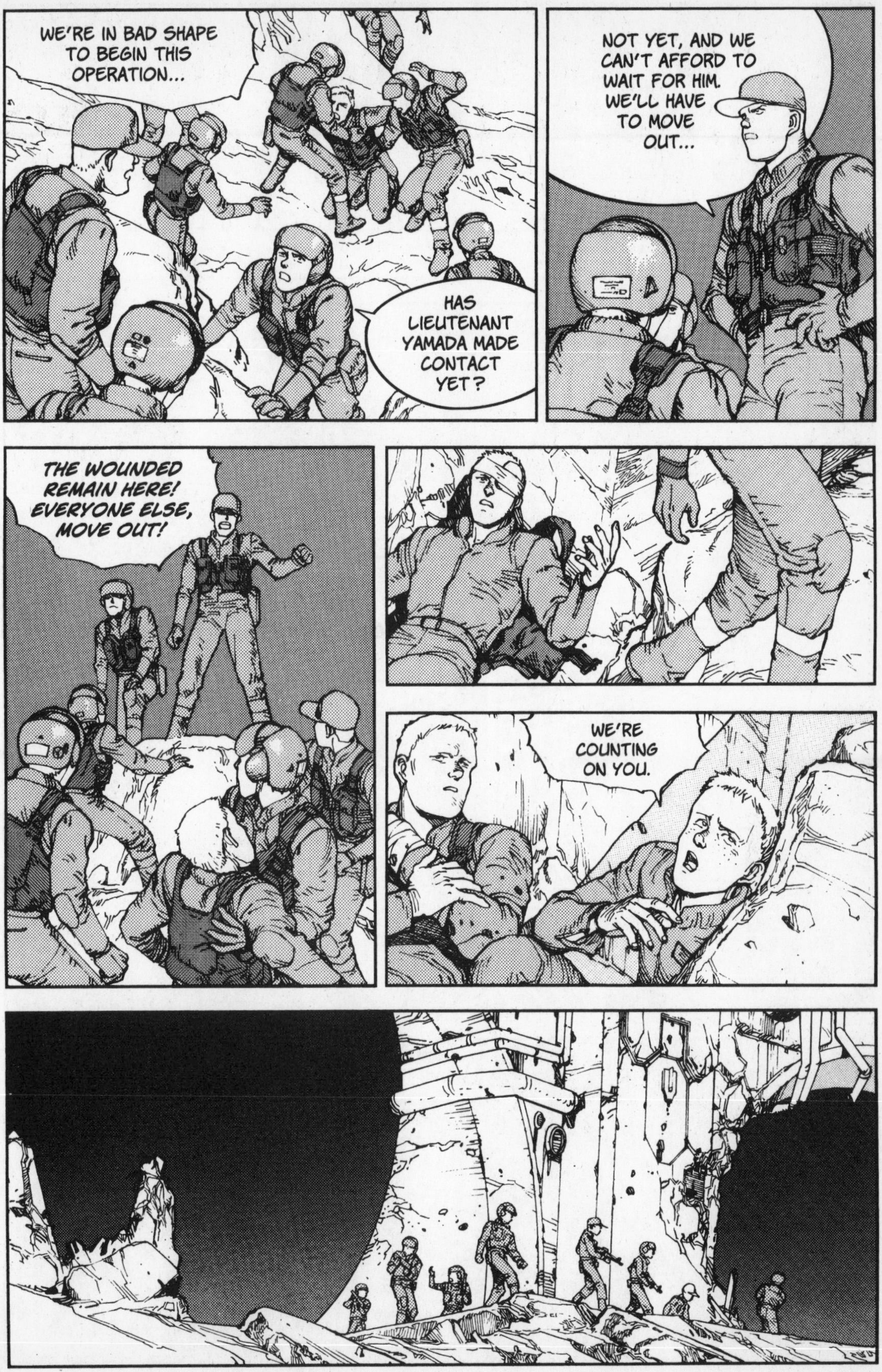
WE'RE IN BAD SHAPE TO BEGIN THIS OPERATION...
HAS LIEUTENANT YAMADA MADE CONTACT YET?
NOT YET, AND WE CAN'T AFFORD TO WAIT FOR HIM. WE'LL HAVE TO MOVE OUT...
THE WOUNDED REMAIN HERE! EVERYONE ELSE, MOVE OUT!
WE'RE COUNTING ON YOU.

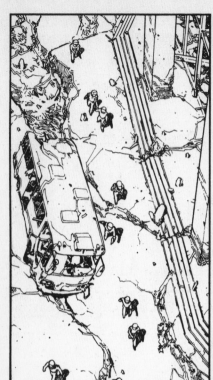

ATTENTION!

I SEE A GROUP OF ARMED MEN!...

!

WH...WHAT'S THAT? WHERE'S THAT COMING FROM?

THEY HAVE INFILTRATED OUR EMPIRE!

GENERAL ALERT!

IT'S LIKE A VOICE IN MY HEAD!

UP THERE!

?!

THEY ARE ENEMIES, COME TO END THE REIGN OF LORD AKIRA!

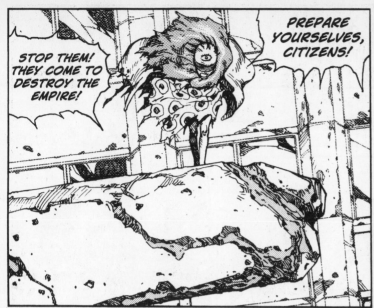

STOP THEM! THEY COME TO DESTROY THE EMPIRE!

PREPARE YOURSELVES, CITIZENS!

HE'S OUT OF RANGE! USE YOUR RIFLE! FIRE!

TAKA TAKATA

HA HA HA HA HAA!

WHAT THE--?! THE BULLETS ARE DEFLECTING?!

HA HA HA! YOU ARE NOTHING! MASTER TETSUO WILL BE DISAPPOINTED BY SUCH WEAK OPPONENTS!

EH...?!

WHO... WHO'S THAT?! STAY BACK...!

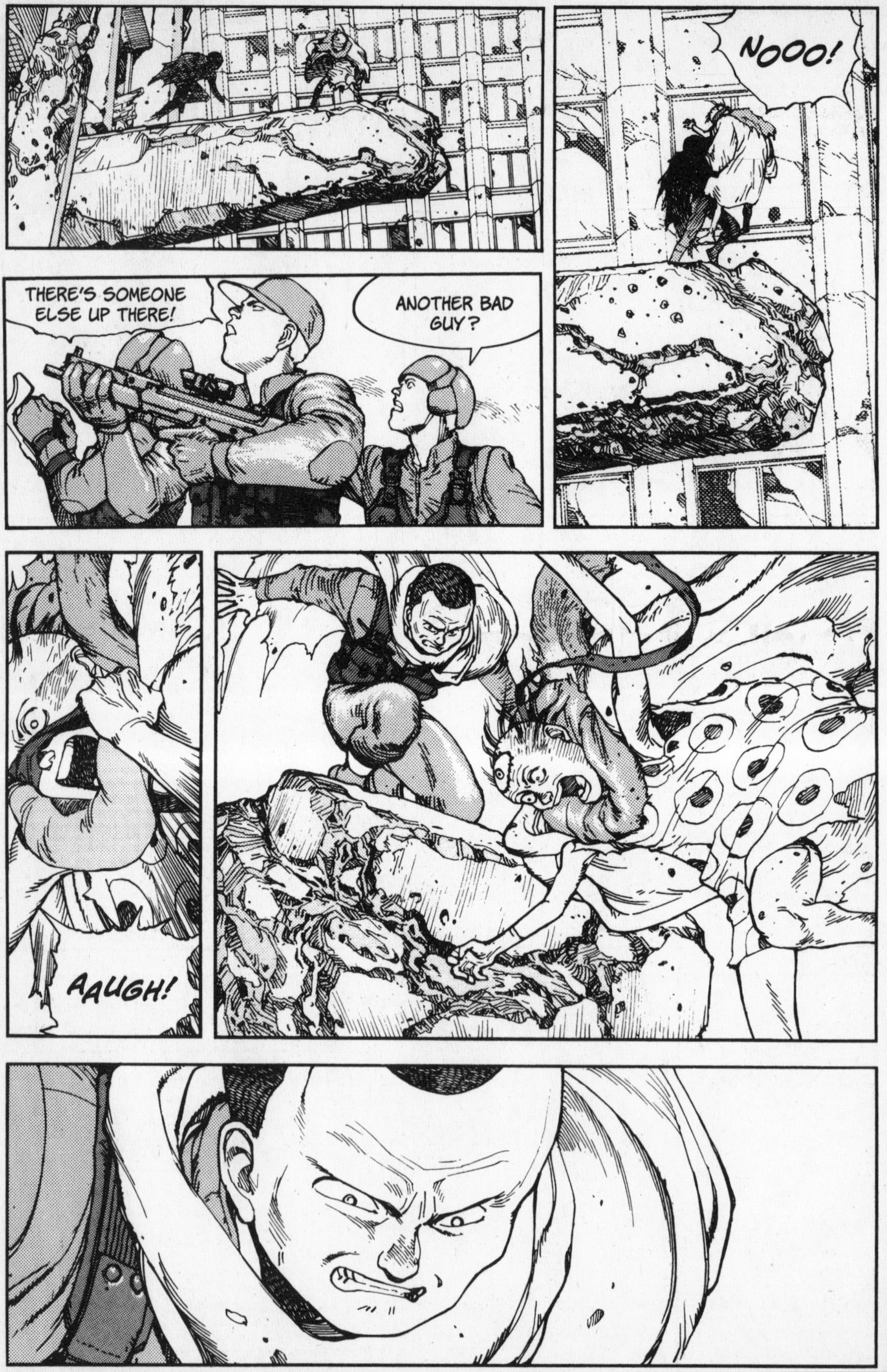
NOOO!
THERE'S SOMEONE ELSE UP THERE!
ANOTHER BAD GUY?
AAUGH!

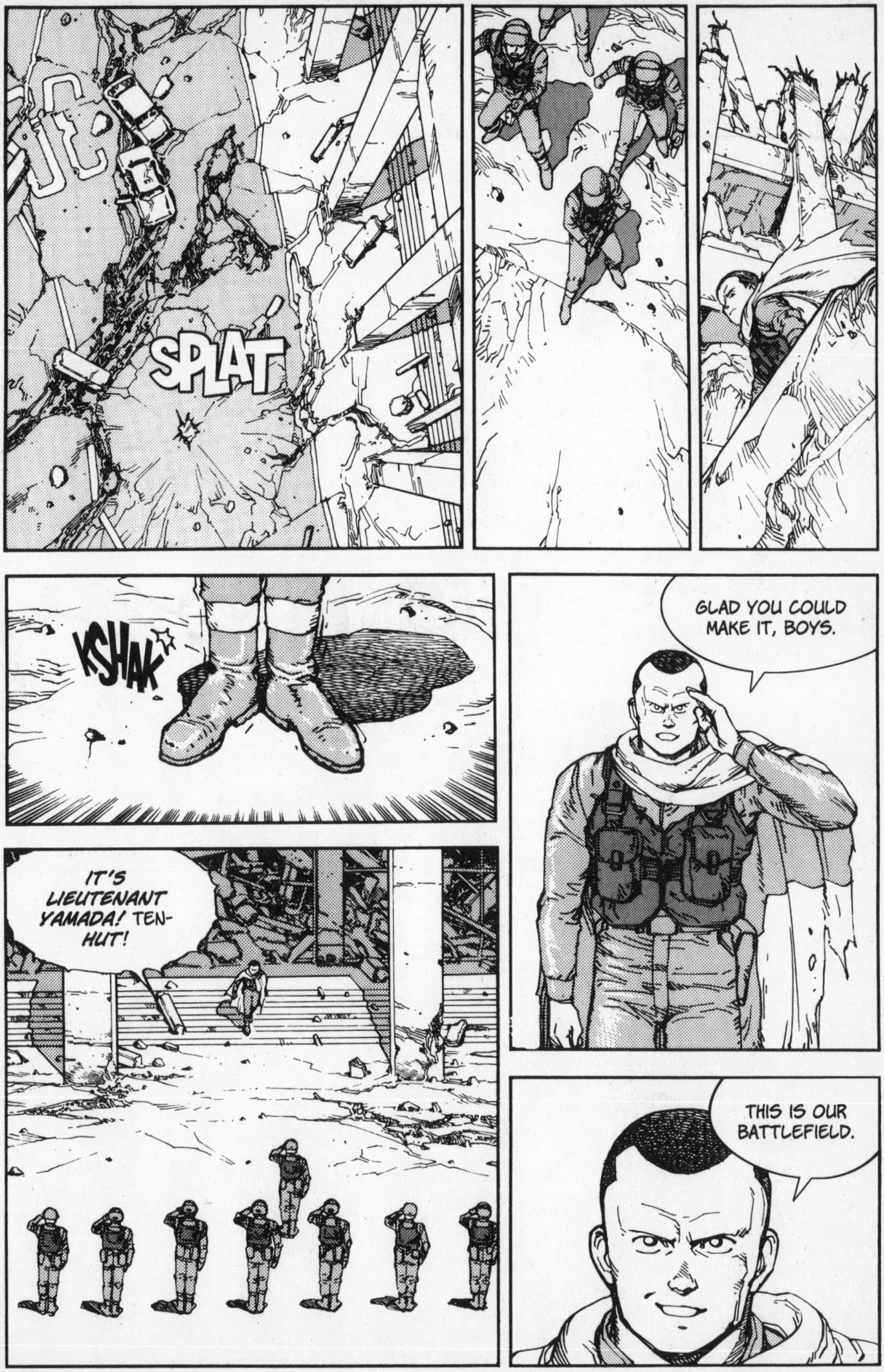
SPLAT
KSHAK
GLAD YOU COULD MAKE IT, BOYS.
IT'S LIEUTENANT YAMADA! TEN-HUT!
THIS IS OUR BATTLEFIELD.

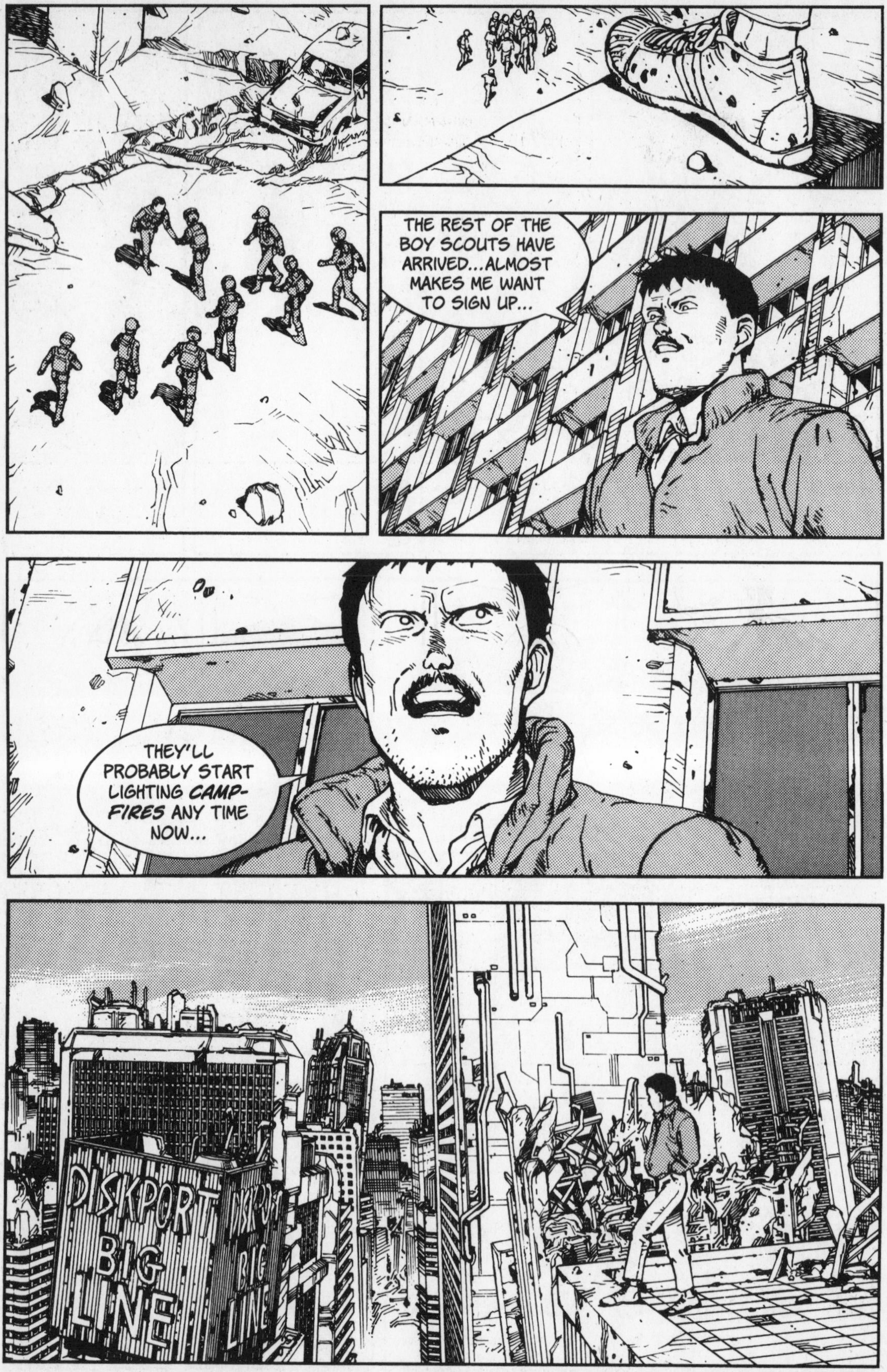
THE REST OF THE BOY SCOUTS HAVE ARRIVED...ALMOST MAKES ME WANT TO SIGN UP...
THEY'LL PROBABLY START LIGHTING CAMP-FIRES ANY TIME NOW...
DISKPORT BIG LINE
BIG LINE

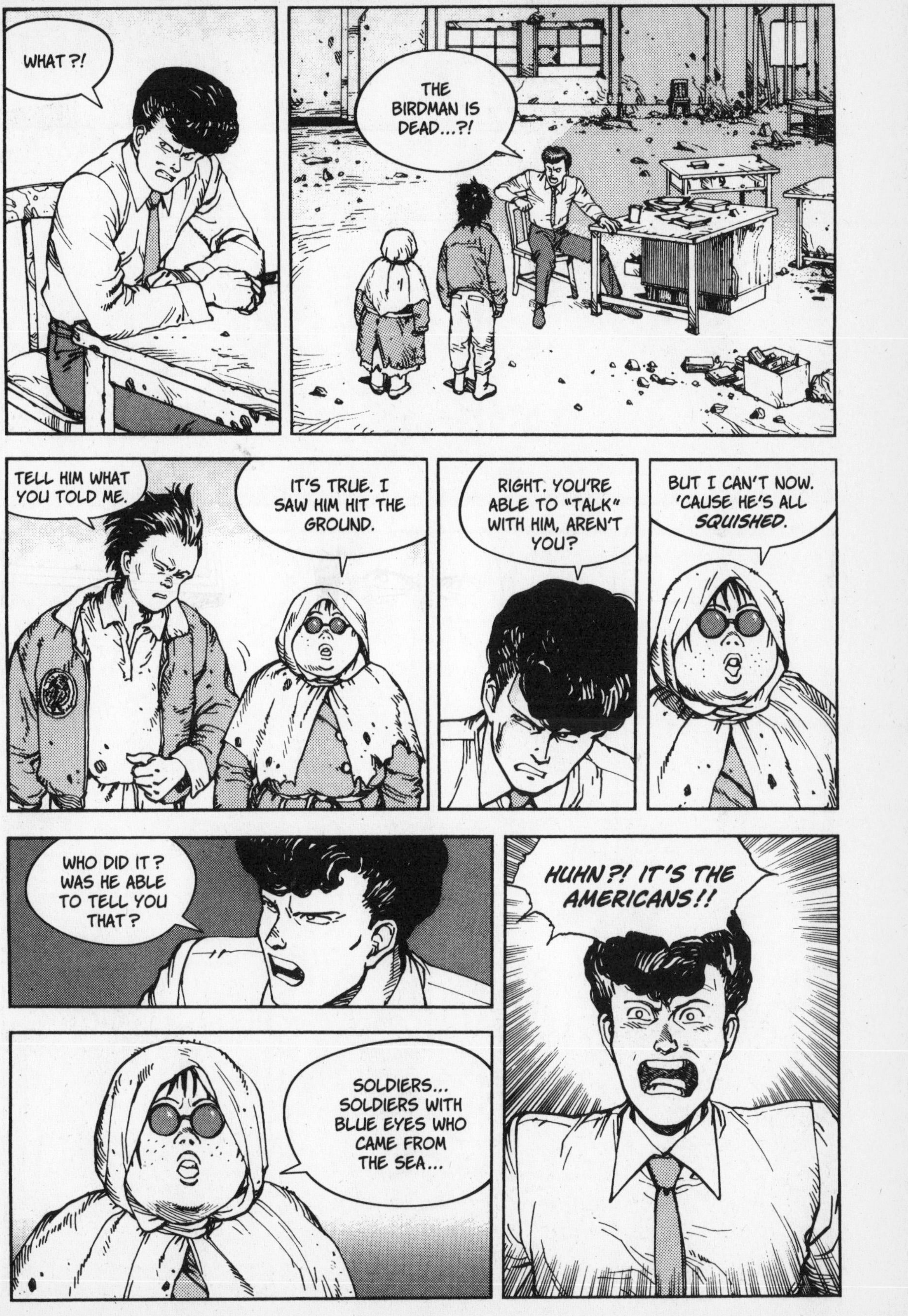
WHAT?!
THE BIRDMAN IS DEAD...?!
TELL HIM WHAT YOU TOLD ME.
IT'S TRUE. I SAW HIM HIT THE GROUND.
RIGHT. YOU'RE ABLE TO "TALK" WITH HIM, AREN'T YOU?
BUT I CAN'T NOW. 'CAUSE HE'S ALL *SQUISHED*.
WHO DID IT? WAS HE ABLE TO TELL YOU THAT?
HUHN?! IT'S THE AMERICANS!!
SOLDIERS... SOLDIERS WITH BLUE EYES WHO CAME FROM THE SEA...

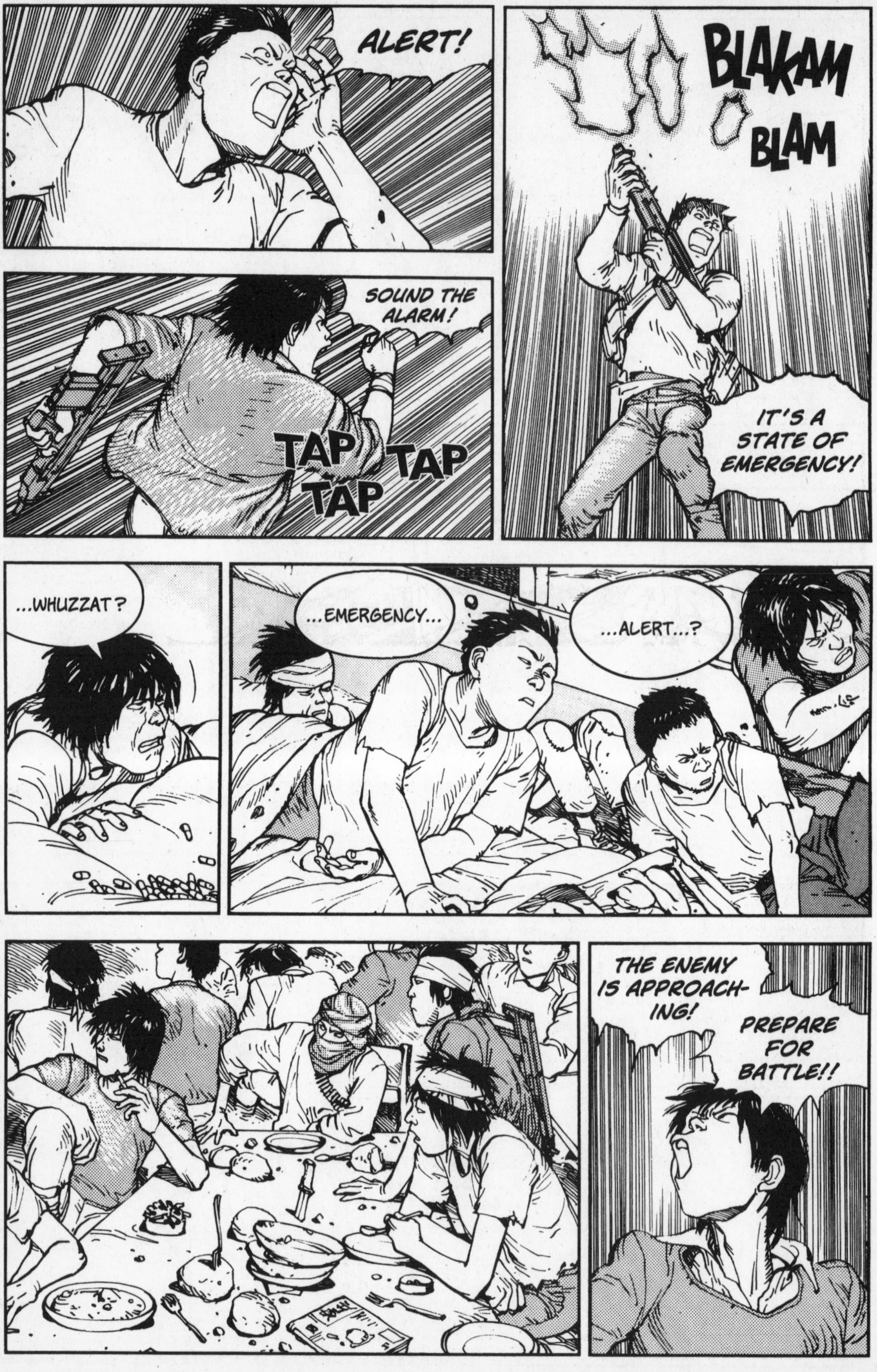
ALERT!
SOUND THE ALARM!
TAP TAP TAP
BLAKAM
BLAM
IT'S A STATE OF EMERGENCY!
...WHUZZAT?
...EMERGENCY...
...ALERT...?
THE ENEMY IS APPROACH-ING!
PREPARE FOR BATTLE!!

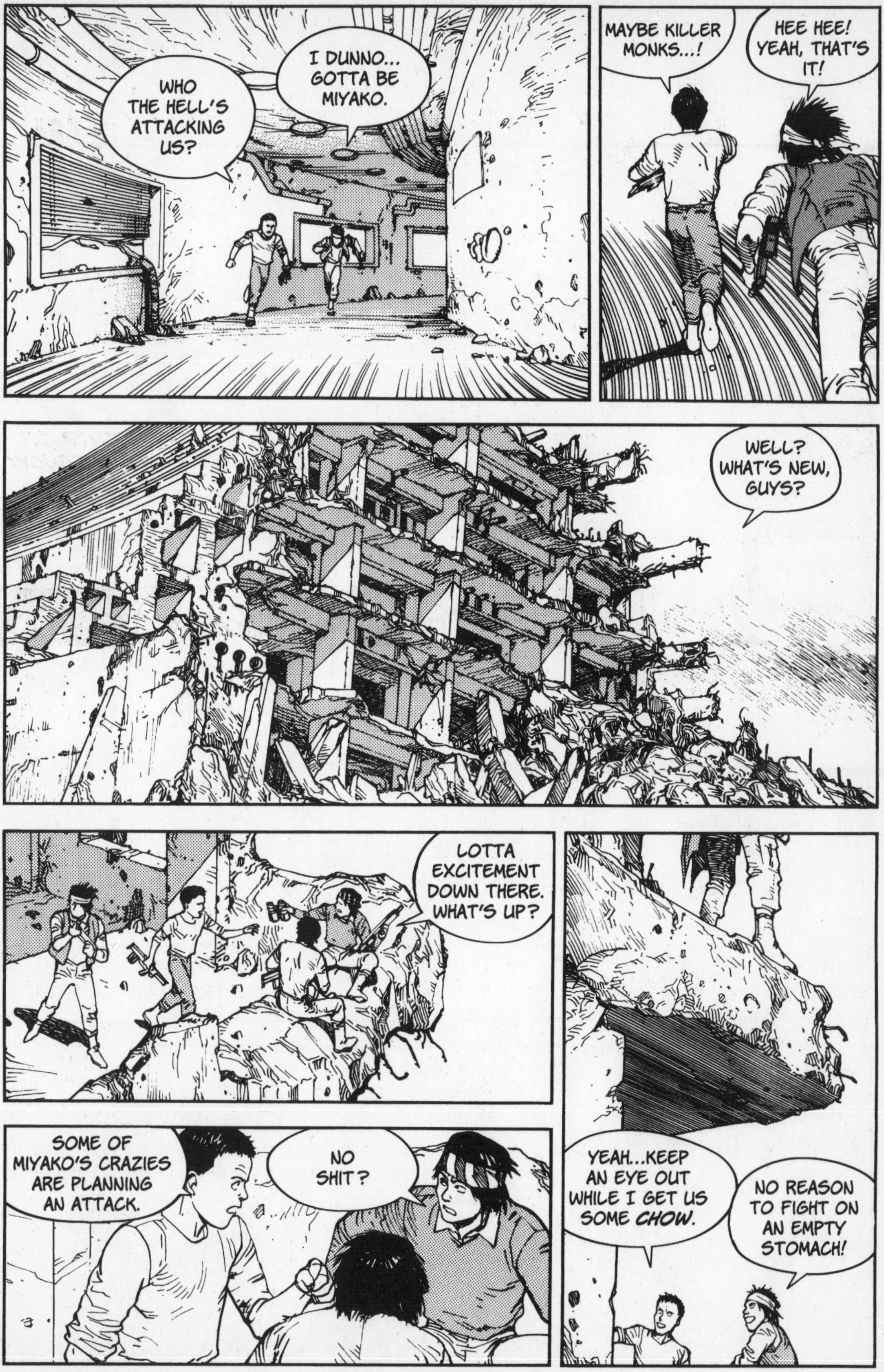
WHO THE HELL'S ATTACKING US?
I DUNNO... GOTTA BE MIYAKO.
MAYBE KILLER MONKS...!
HEE HEE! YEAH, THAT'S IT!
WELL? WHAT'S NEW, GUYS?
LOTTA EXCITEMENT DOWN THERE. WHAT'S UP?
SOME OF MIYAKO'S CRAZIES ARE PLANNING AN ATTACK.
NO SHIT?
YEAH...KEEP AN EYE OUT WHILE I GET US SOME *CHOW*.
NO REASON TO FIGHT ON AN EMPTY STOMACH!

THINK IT'LL BE A BIG ONE?

WE'LL SEE...

BUT THEY AIN'T COMIN' HERE TO PLAY AROUND...

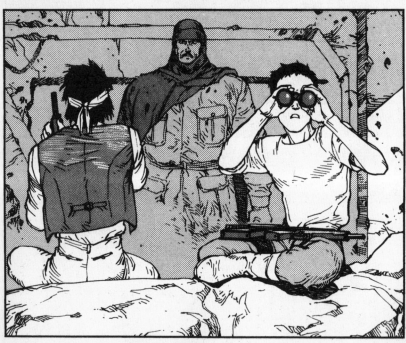

DO YOU KNOW WHERE I CAN FIND *TETSUO*?

HUNH?

326

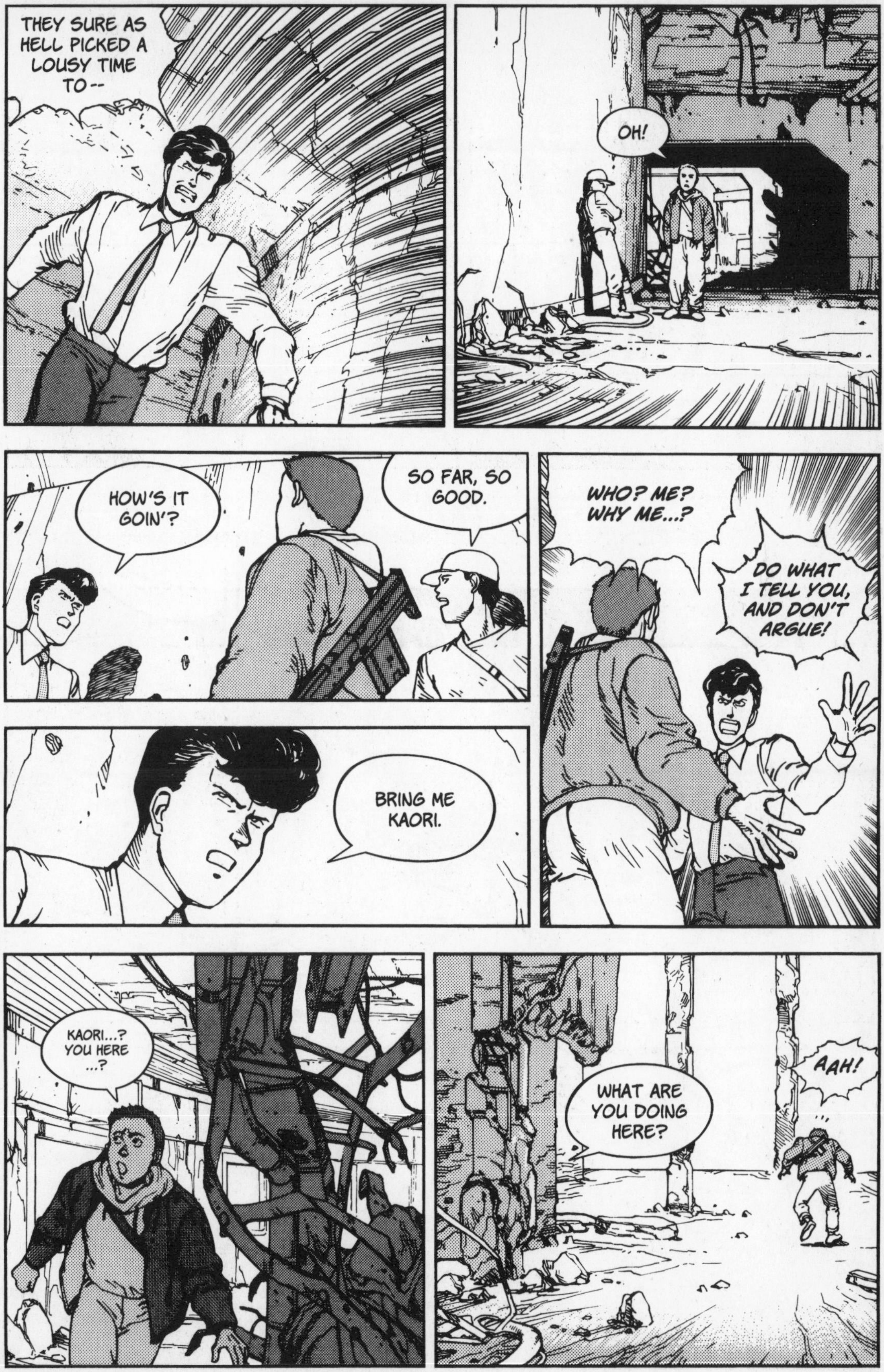
THEY SURE AS HELL PICKED A LOUSY TIME TO--
OH!
HOW'S IT GOIN'?
SO FAR, SO GOOD.
WHO? ME? WHY ME...?
DO WHAT I TELL YOU, AND DON'T ARGUE!
BRING ME KAORI.
KAORI...? YOU HERE ...?
AAH!
WHAT ARE YOU DOING HERE?

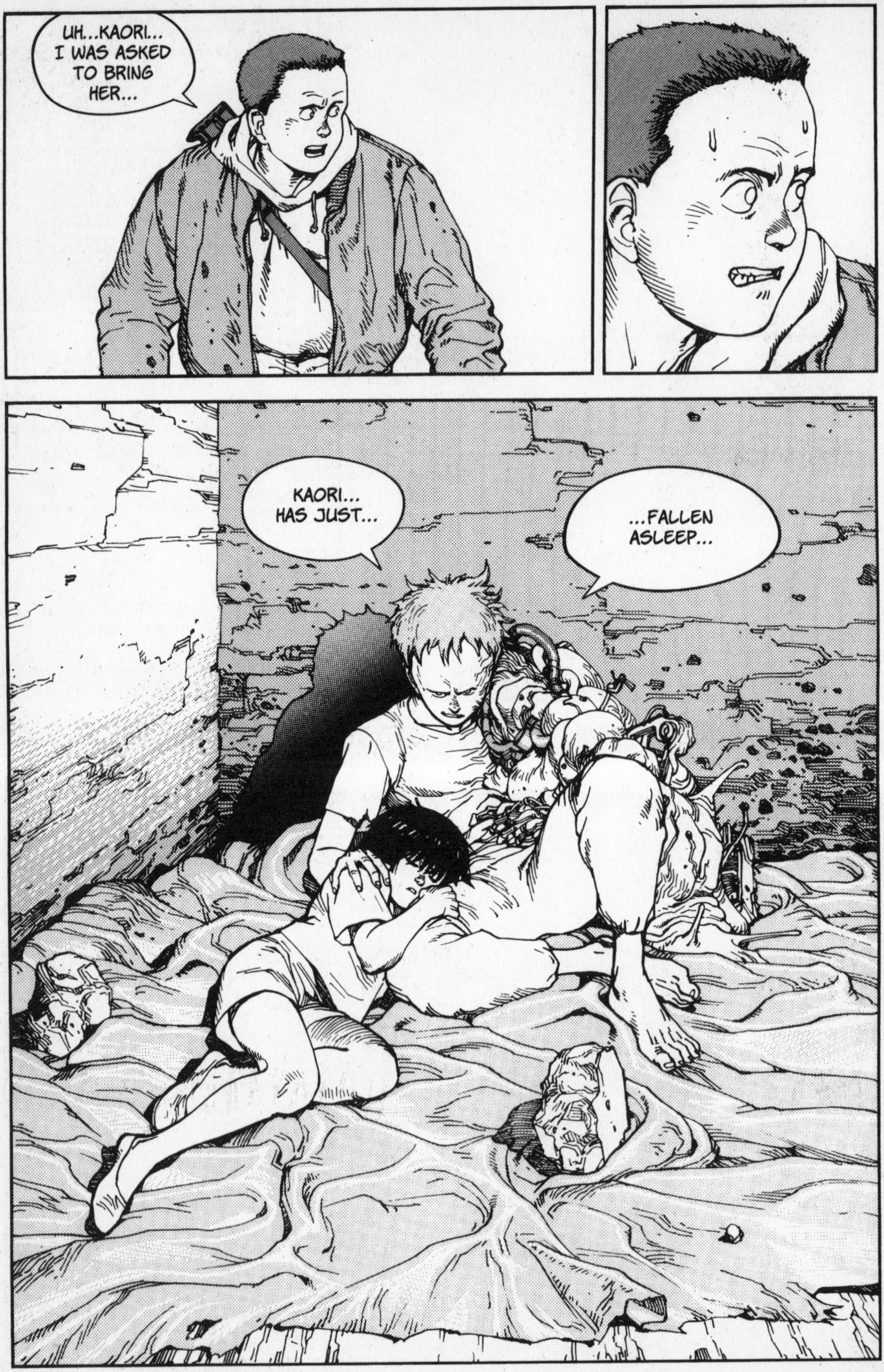
UH...KAORI... I WAS ASKED TO BRING HER...
KAORI... HAS JUST...
...FALLEN ASLEEP...

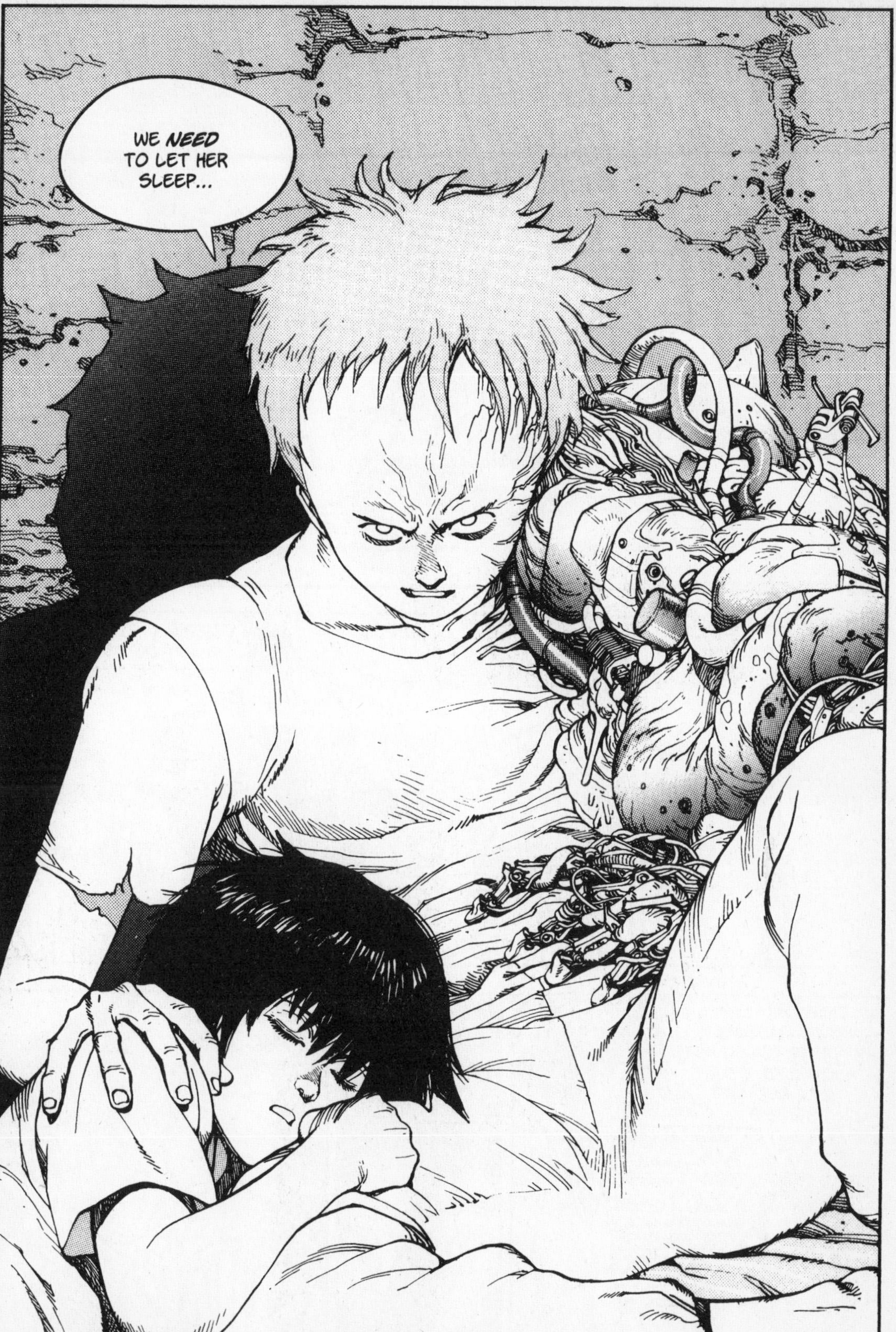
WE NEED TO LET HER SLEEP...

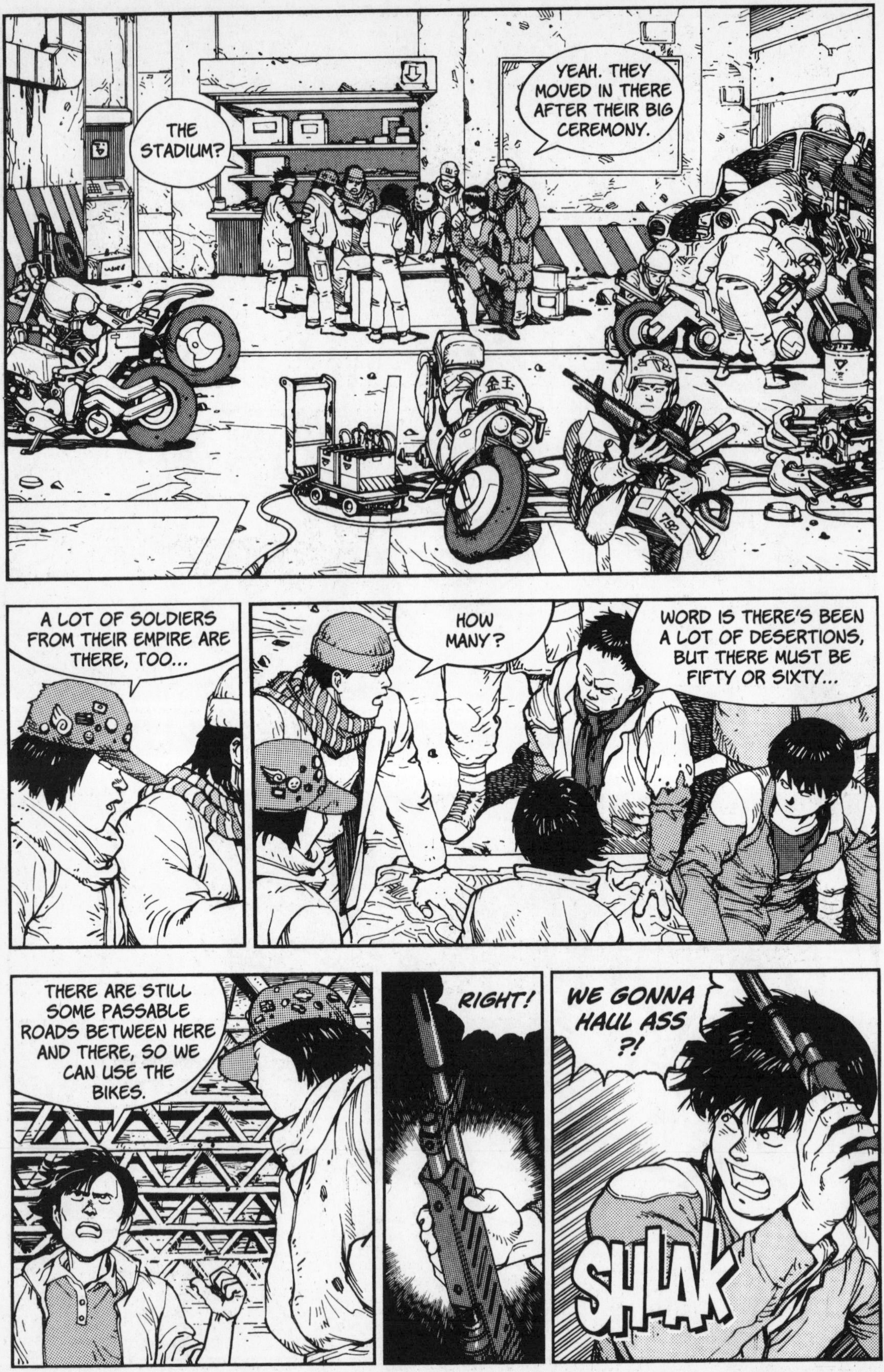
THE STADIUM?
YEAH. THEY MOVED IN THERE AFTER THEIR BIG CEREMONY.
A LOT OF SOLDIERS FROM THEIR EMPIRE ARE THERE, TOO...
HOW MANY?
WORD IS THERE'S BEEN A LOT OF DESERTIONS, BUT THERE MUST BE FIFTY OR SIXTY...
THERE ARE STILL SOME PASSABLE ROADS BETWEEN HERE AND THERE, SO WE CAN USE THE BIKES.
RIGHT!
WE GONNA HAUL ASS ?!
SHLAK

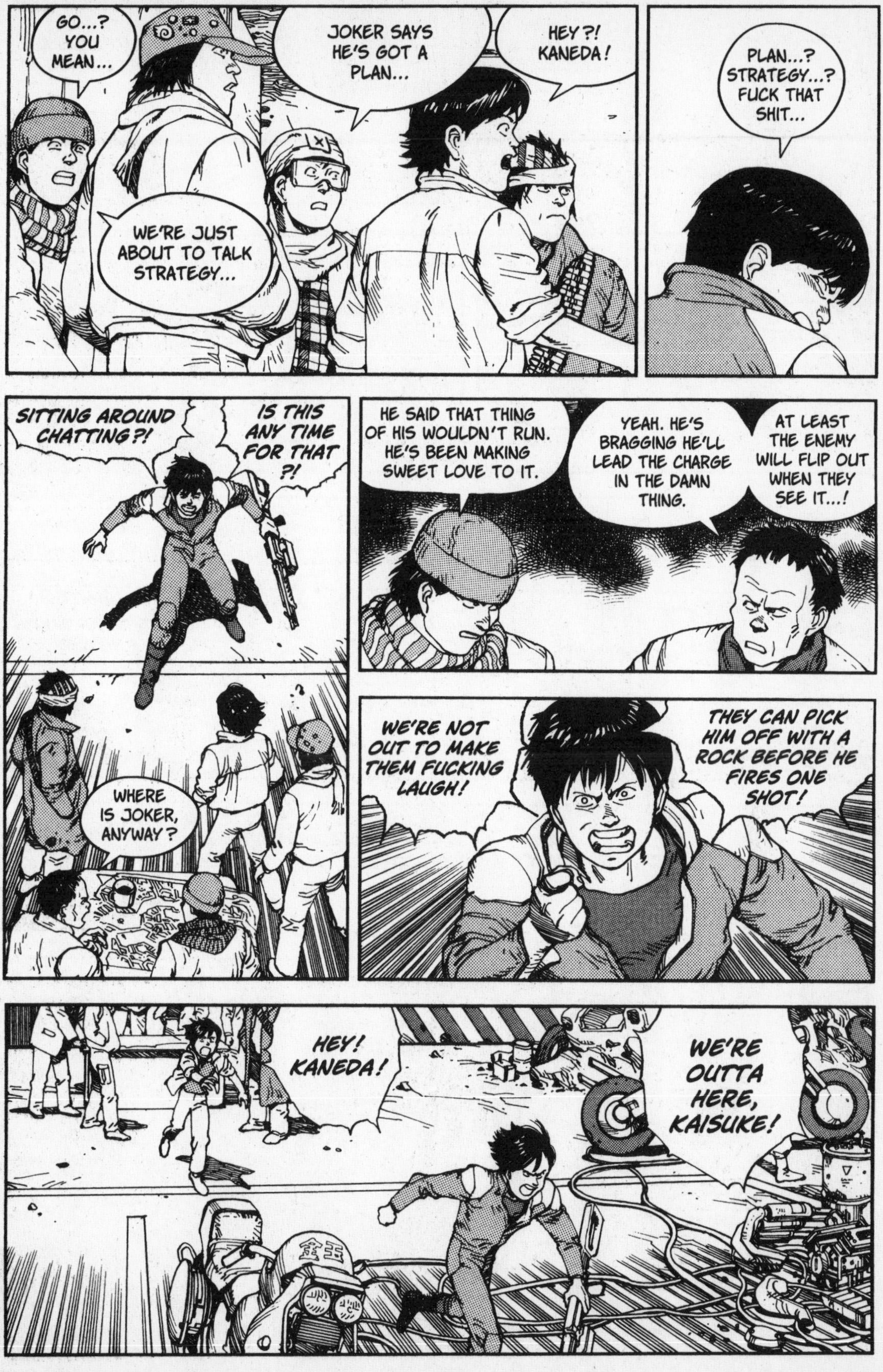
GO...? YOU MEAN...
JOKER SAYS HE'S GOT A PLAN...
HEY?! KANEDA!
WE'RE JUST ABOUT TO TALK STRATEGY...
PLAN...? STRATEGY...? FUCK THAT SHIT...
SITTING AROUND CHATTING?!
IS THIS ANY TIME FOR THAT ?!
WHERE IS JOKER, ANYWAY?
HE SAID THAT THING OF HIS WOULDN'T RUN. HE'S BEEN MAKING SWEET LOVE TO IT.
YEAH. HE'S BRAGGING HE'LL LEAD THE CHARGE IN THE DAMN THING.
AT LEAST THE ENEMY WILL FLIP OUT WHEN THEY SEE IT...!
WE'RE NOT OUT TO MAKE THEM FUCKING LAUGH!
THEY CAN PICK HIM OFF WITH A ROCK BEFORE HE FIRES ONE SHOT!
HEY! KANEDA!
WE'RE OUTTA HERE, KAISUKE!

YOU REALLY GOING BY YOURSELF?

...JUST WHEN I GOT THEM ALL ON BOARD?

WE'RE GOING TOGETHER!

REALLY?

THAT CRAZY GIZMO'LL BE THE PERFECT DECOY!

HUHN?!

SO HURRY UP AND GET THAT FACE-PAINTED PORKER OVER HERE!

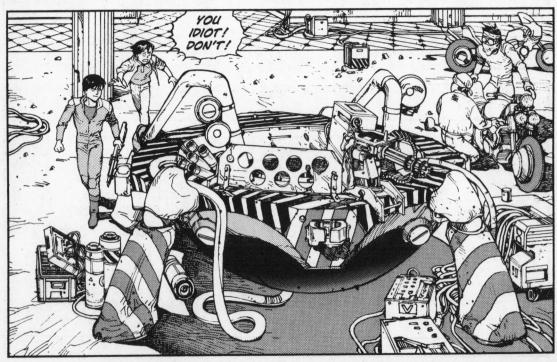

YOU IDIOT! DON'T!

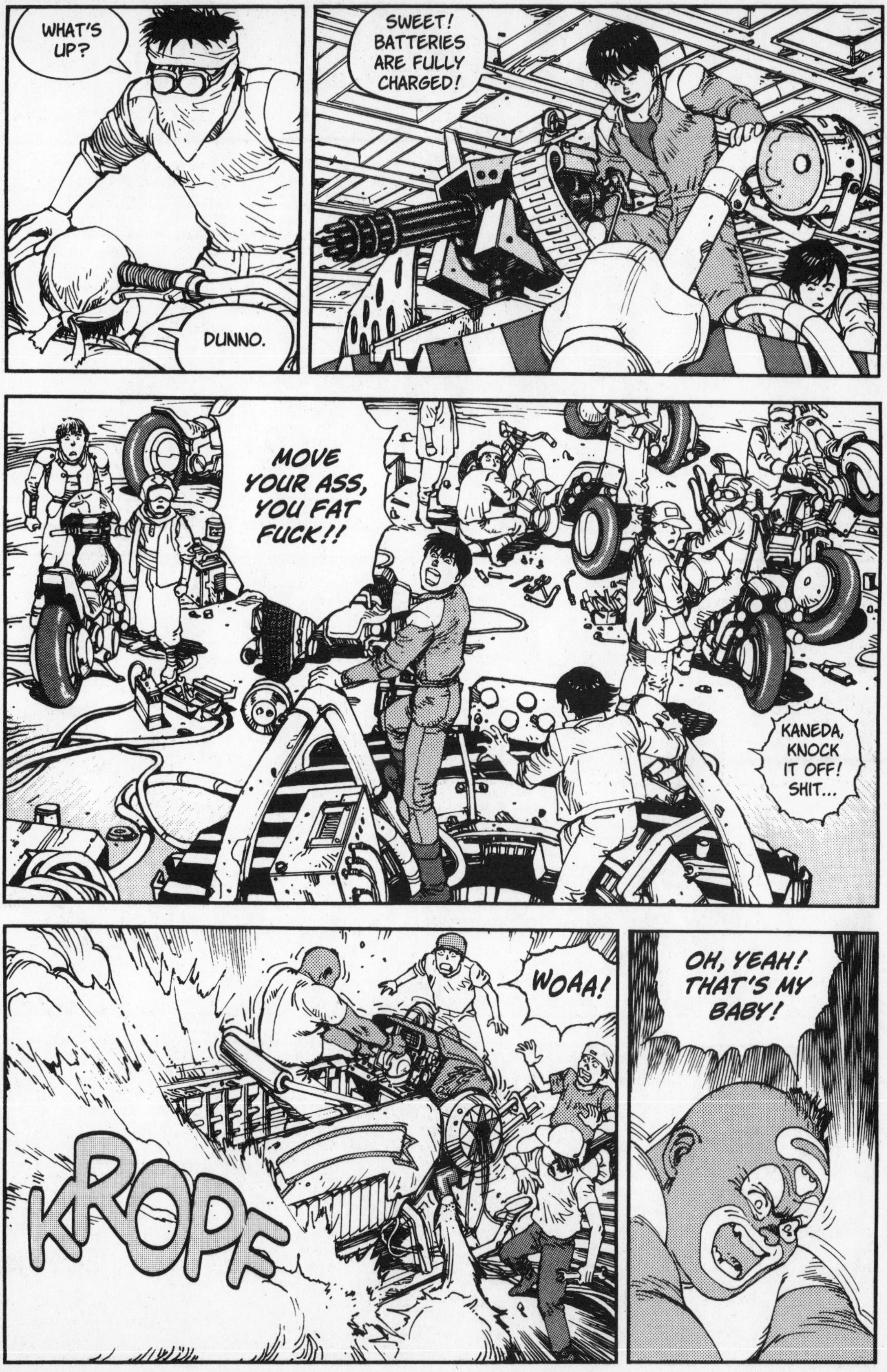
WHAT'S UP?
DUNNO.
SWEET! BATTERIES ARE FULLY CHARGED!
MOVE YOUR ASS, YOU FAT FUCK!!
KANEDA, KNOCK IT OFF! SHIT...
WOAA!
KROPF
OH, YEAH! THAT'S MY BABY!

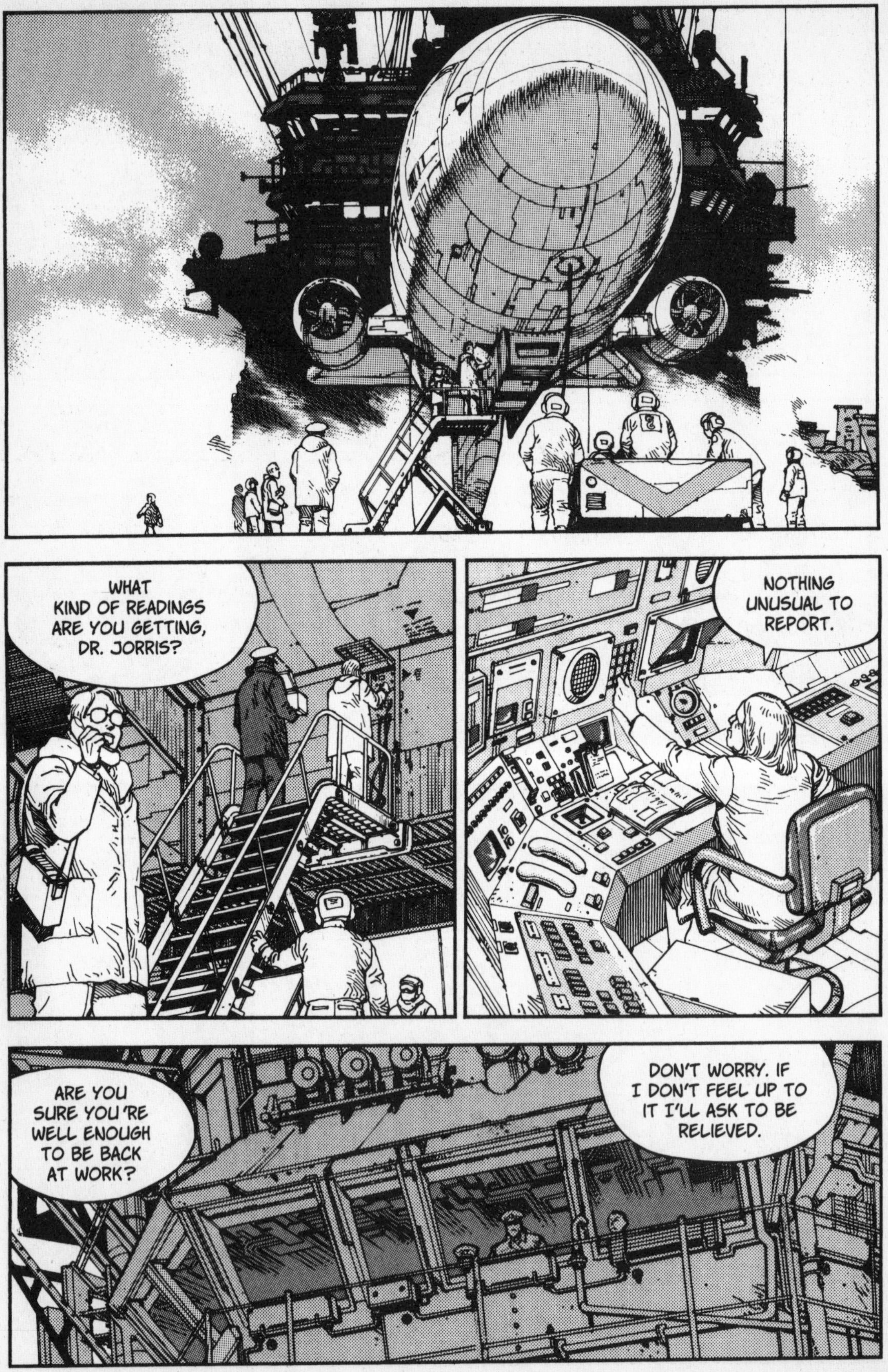
WHAT KIND OF READINGS ARE YOU GETTING, DR. JORRIS?
NOTHING UNUSUAL TO REPORT.
ARE YOU SURE YOU'RE WELL ENOUGH TO BE BACK AT WORK?
DON'T WORRY. IF I DON'T FEEL UP TO IT I'LL ASK TO BE RELIEVED.

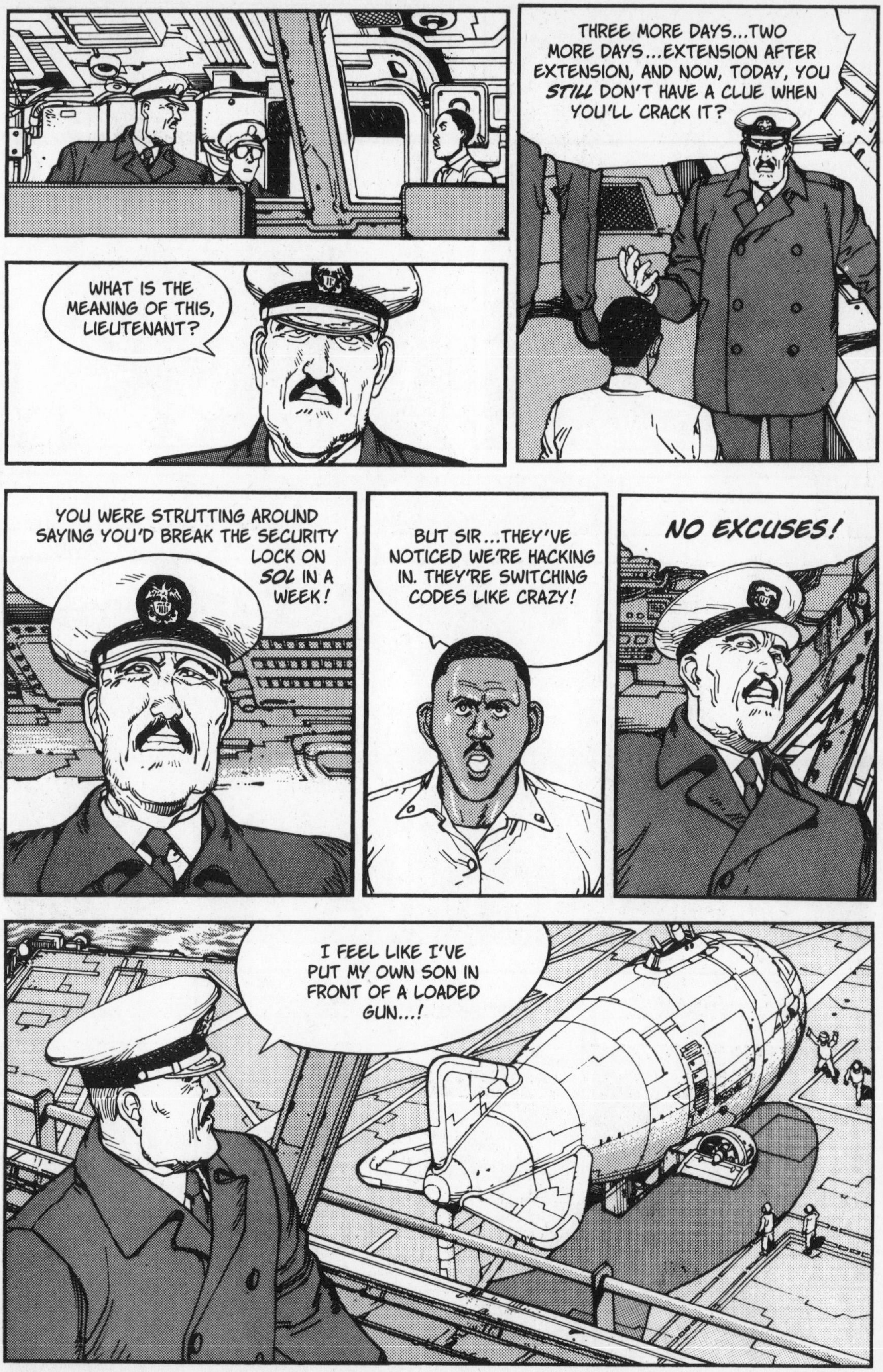
THREE MORE DAYS...TWO MORE DAYS...EXTENSION AFTER EXTENSION, AND NOW, TODAY, YOU *STILL* DON'T HAVE A CLUE WHEN YOU'LL CRACK IT?
WHAT IS THE MEANING OF THIS, LIEUTENANT?
YOU WERE STRUTTING AROUND SAYING YOU'D BREAK THE SECURITY LOCK ON *SOL* IN A WEEK!
BUT SIR...THEY'VE NOTICED WE'RE HACKING IN. THEY'RE SWITCHING CODES LIKE CRAZY!
NO EXCUSES!
I FEEL LIKE I'VE PUT MY OWN SON IN FRONT OF A LOADED GUN...!

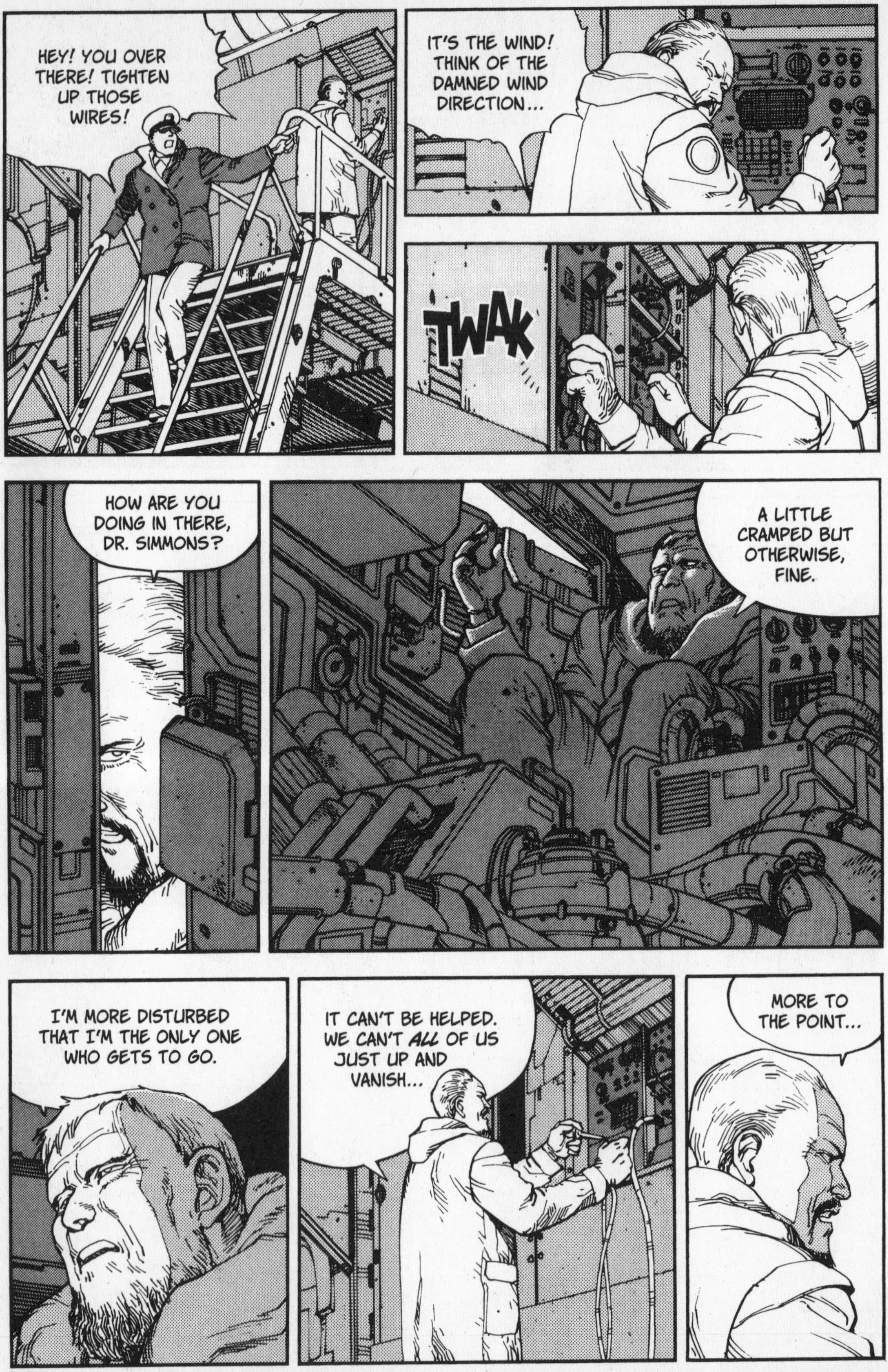
HEY! YOU OVER THERE! TIGHTEN UP THOSE WIRES!
IT'S THE WIND! THINK OF THE DAMNED WIND DIRECTION...
TWAK
HOW ARE YOU DOING IN THERE, DR. SIMMONS?
A LITTLE CRAMPED BUT OTHERWISE, FINE.
I'M MORE DISTURBED THAT I'M THE ONLY ONE WHO GETS TO GO.
IT CAN'T BE HELPED. WE CAN'T ALL OF US JUST UP AND VANISH...
MORE TO THE POINT...

...PLEASE PROCEED WITH THE UTMOST CAUTION.

I UNDERSTAND, DOCTOR BERNANDI. I PROMISE TO COME BACK ALIVE.

BE CAREFUL...

BLINK

ALL CLEAR! RELEASE THE WIRES!

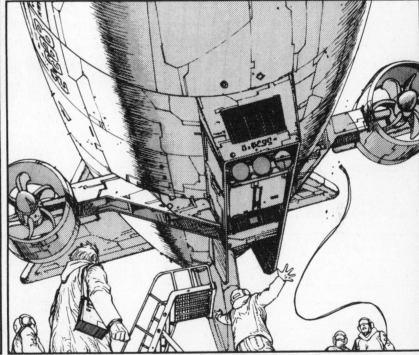

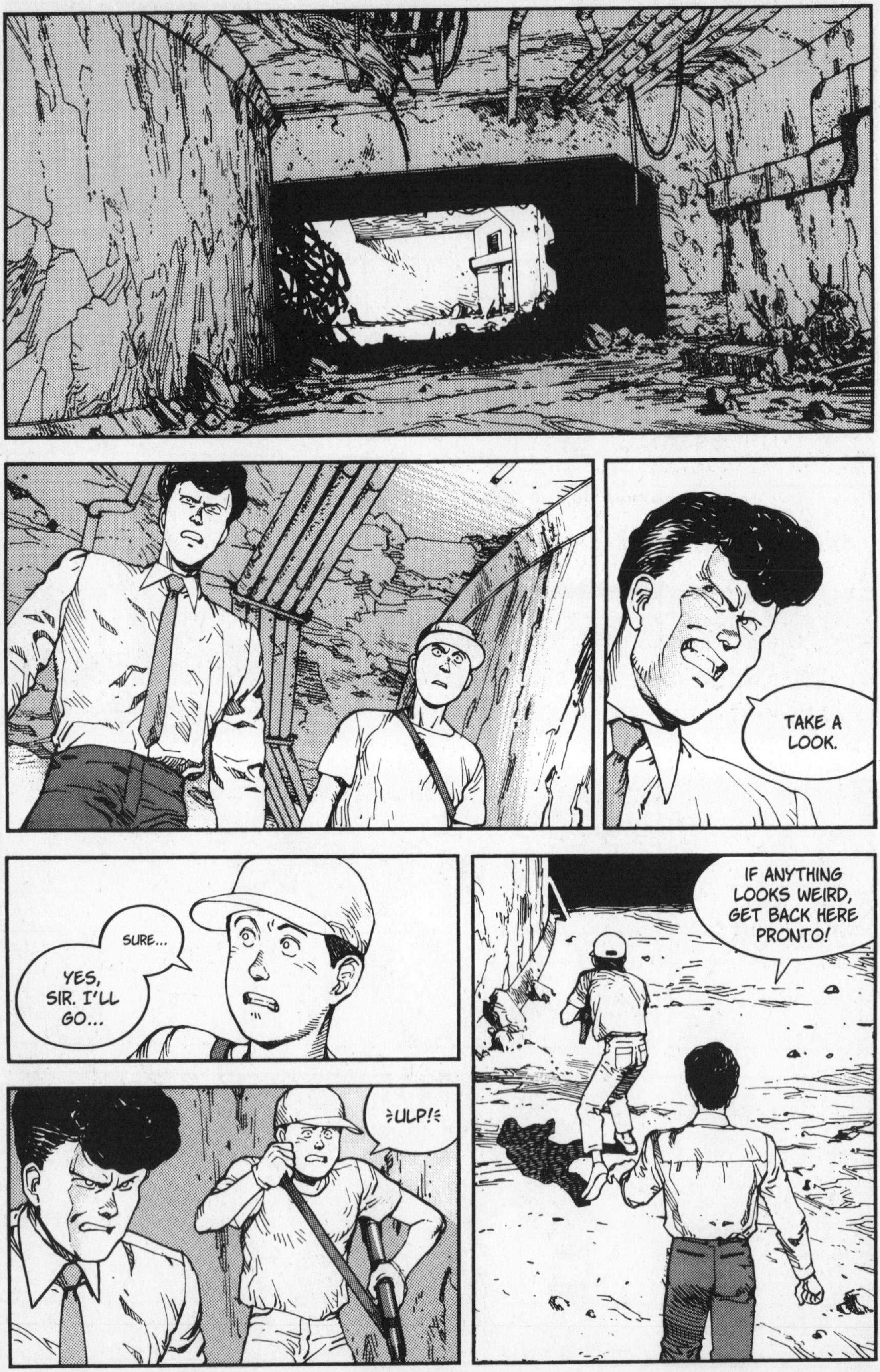
TAKE A LOOK.
SURE...
YES, SIR. I'LL GO...
IF ANYTHING LOOKS WEIRD, GET BACK HERE PRONTO!
≷ULP!≷

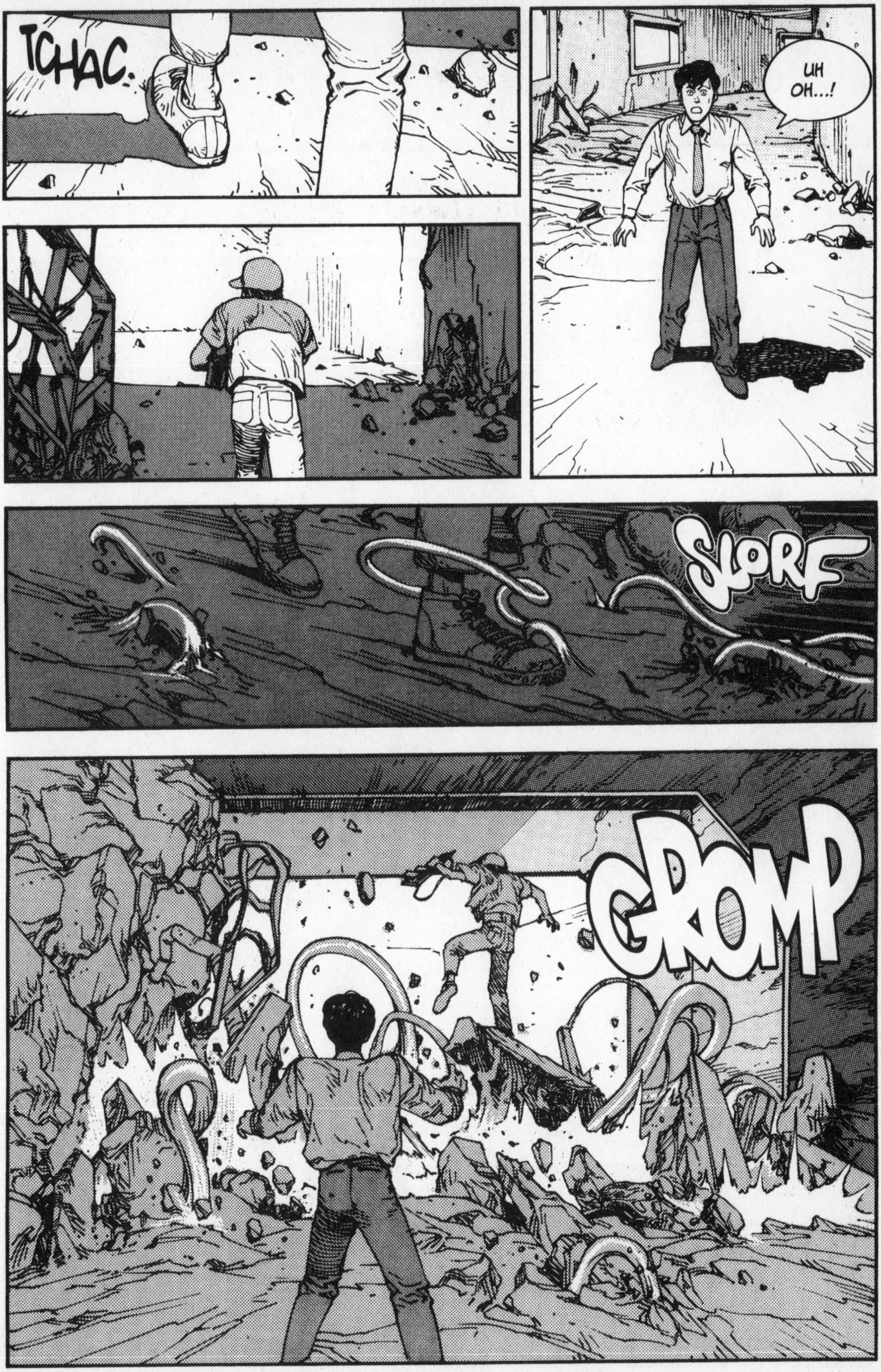
TCHAC.
UH OH...!
SLORF
GROMP

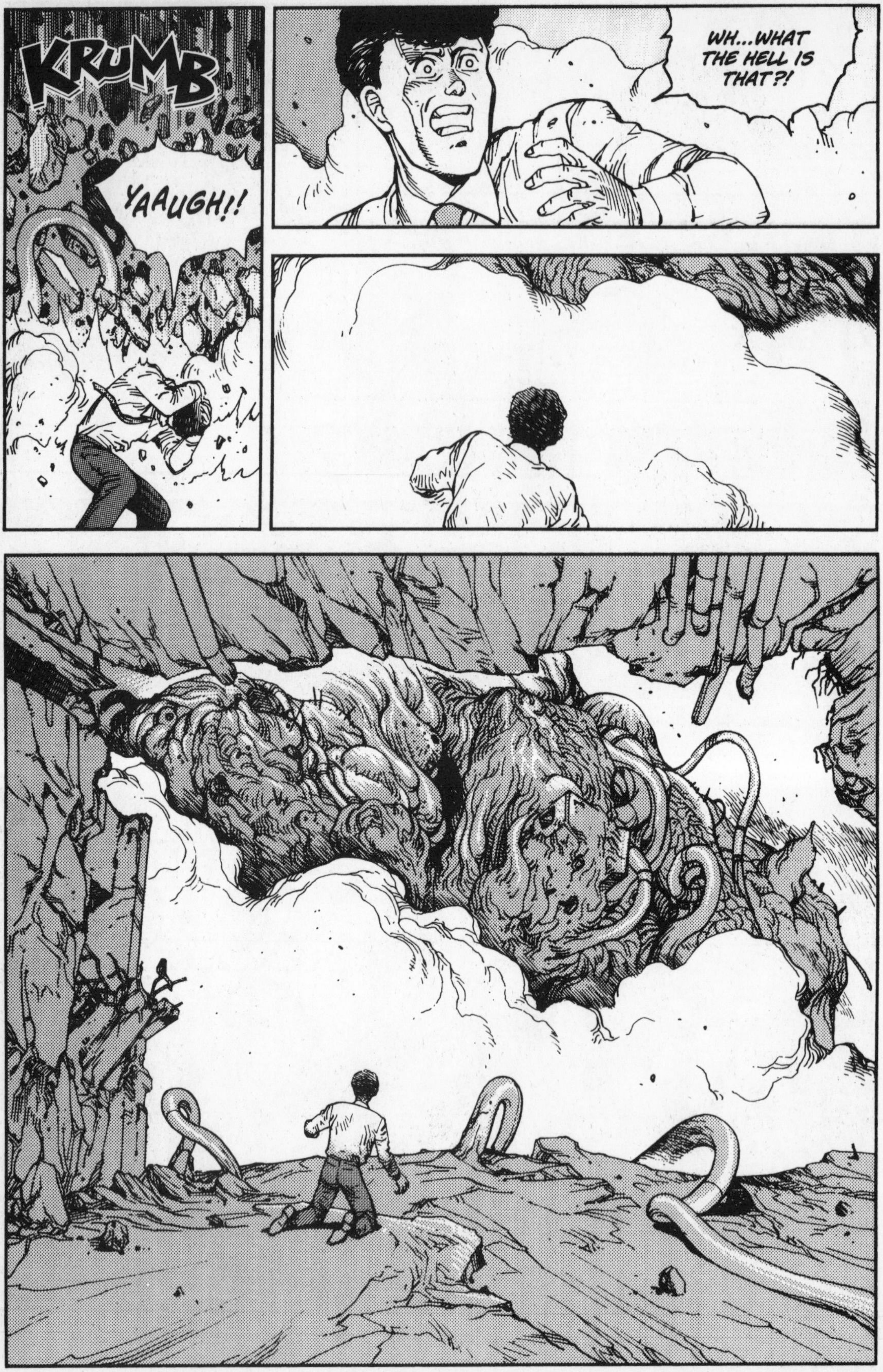
KRUMB
YAAUGH!!
WH...WHAT THE HELL IS THAT?!

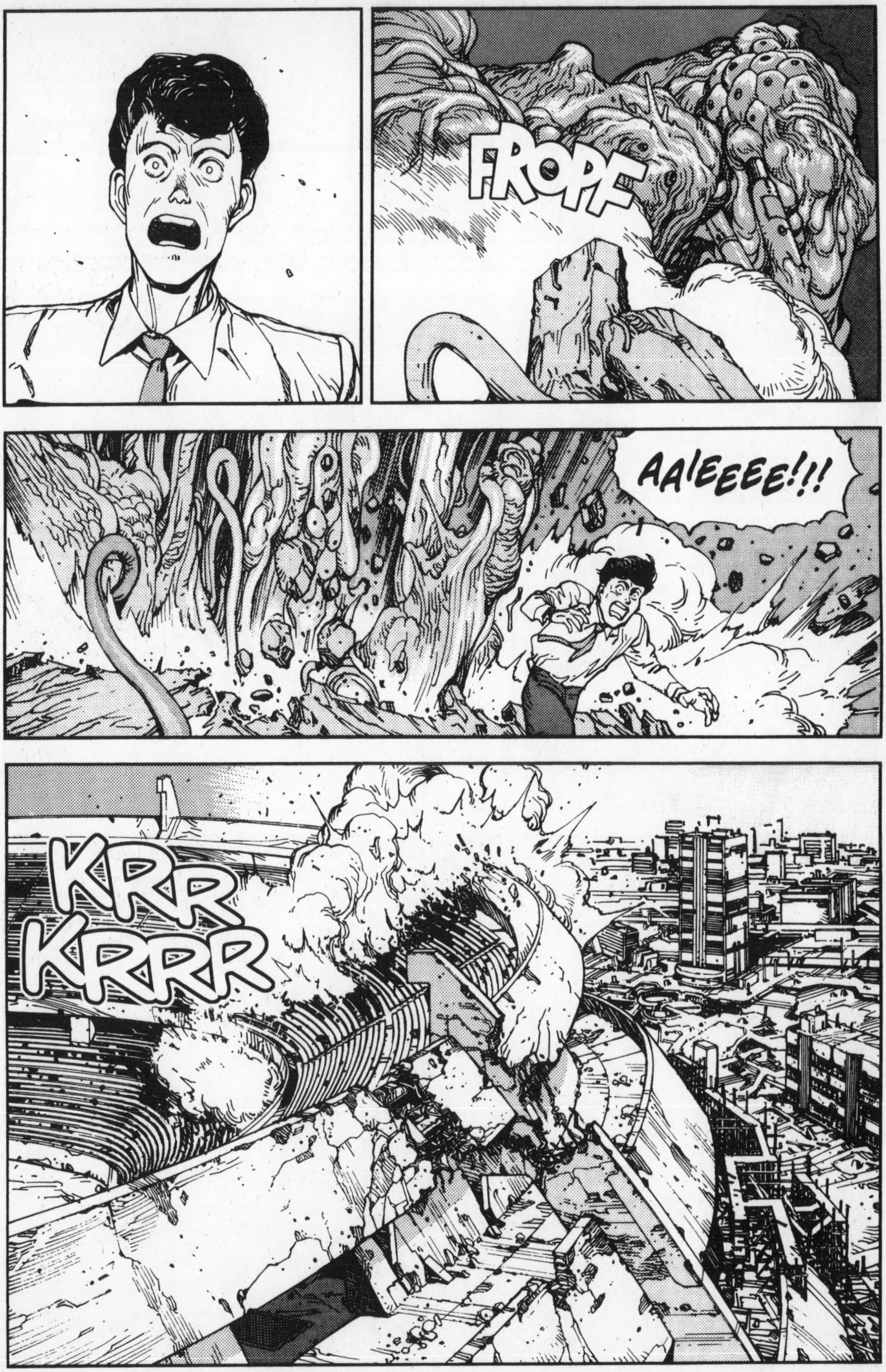
FROPF
AAIEEEE!!!
KRR
KRRR

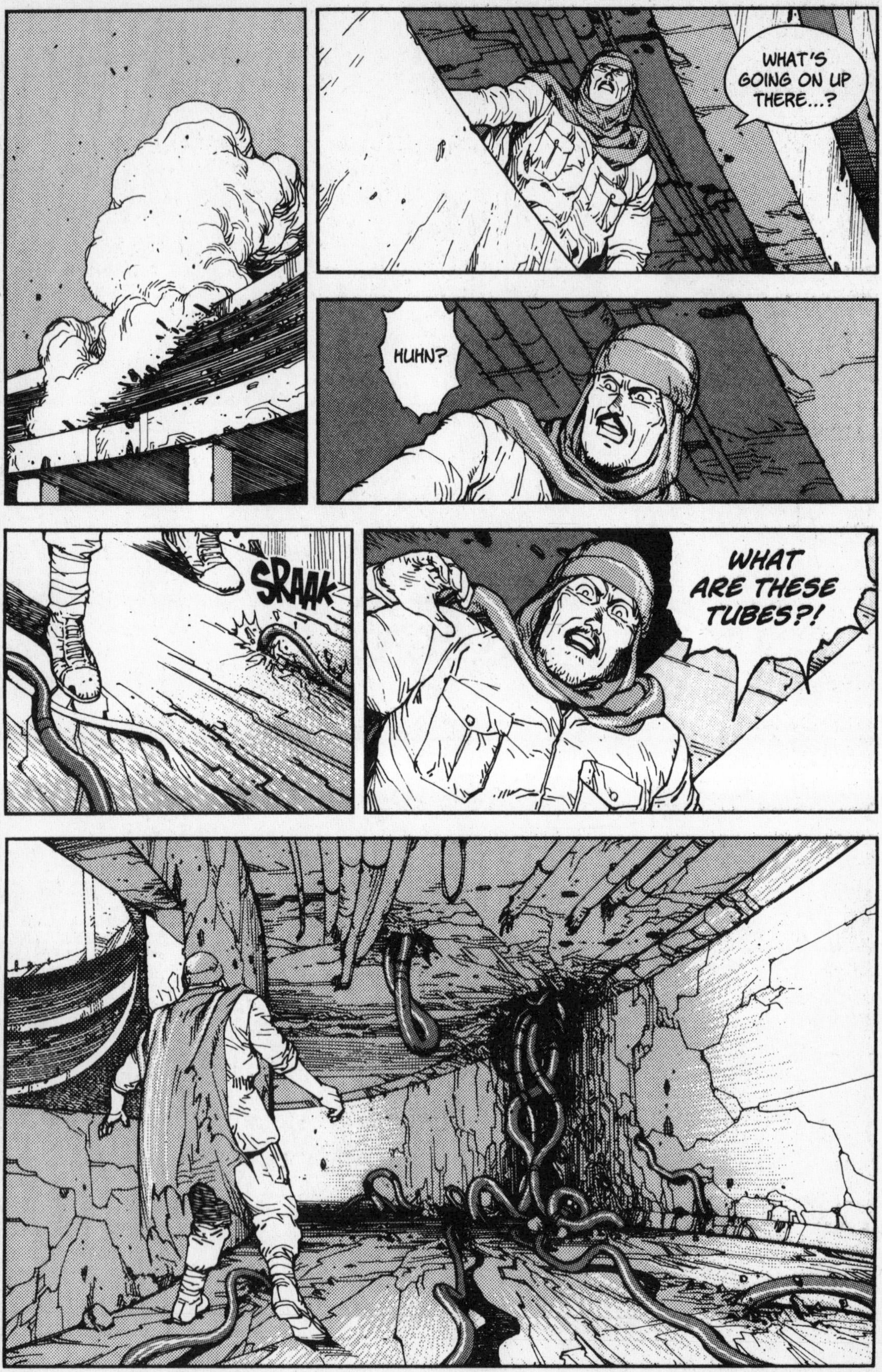
WHAT'S GOING ON UP THERE...?
HUHN?
SRAAK
WHAT ARE THESE TUBES?!

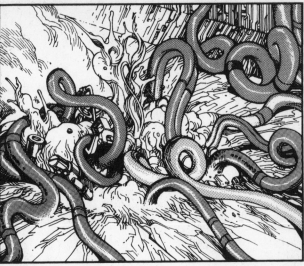

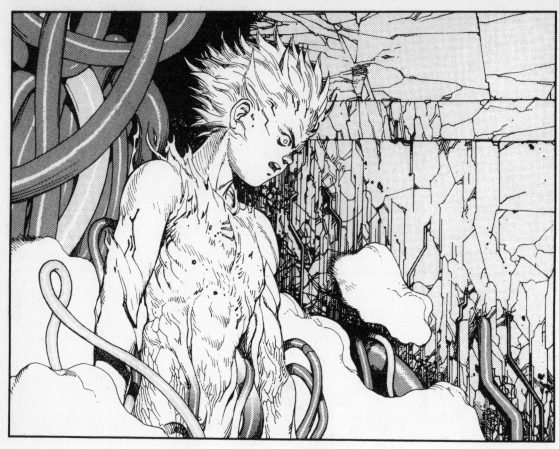

TETSUO!

OOAAGH!

WHERE... AM I...?

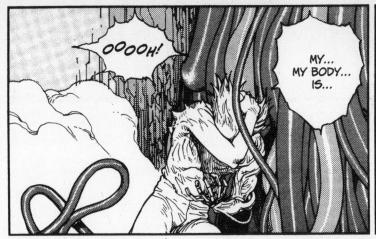

OOOOH!

MY... MY BODY... IS...

NO!

THEY'LL KNOW...

SKROF

WAIT!

AAH!

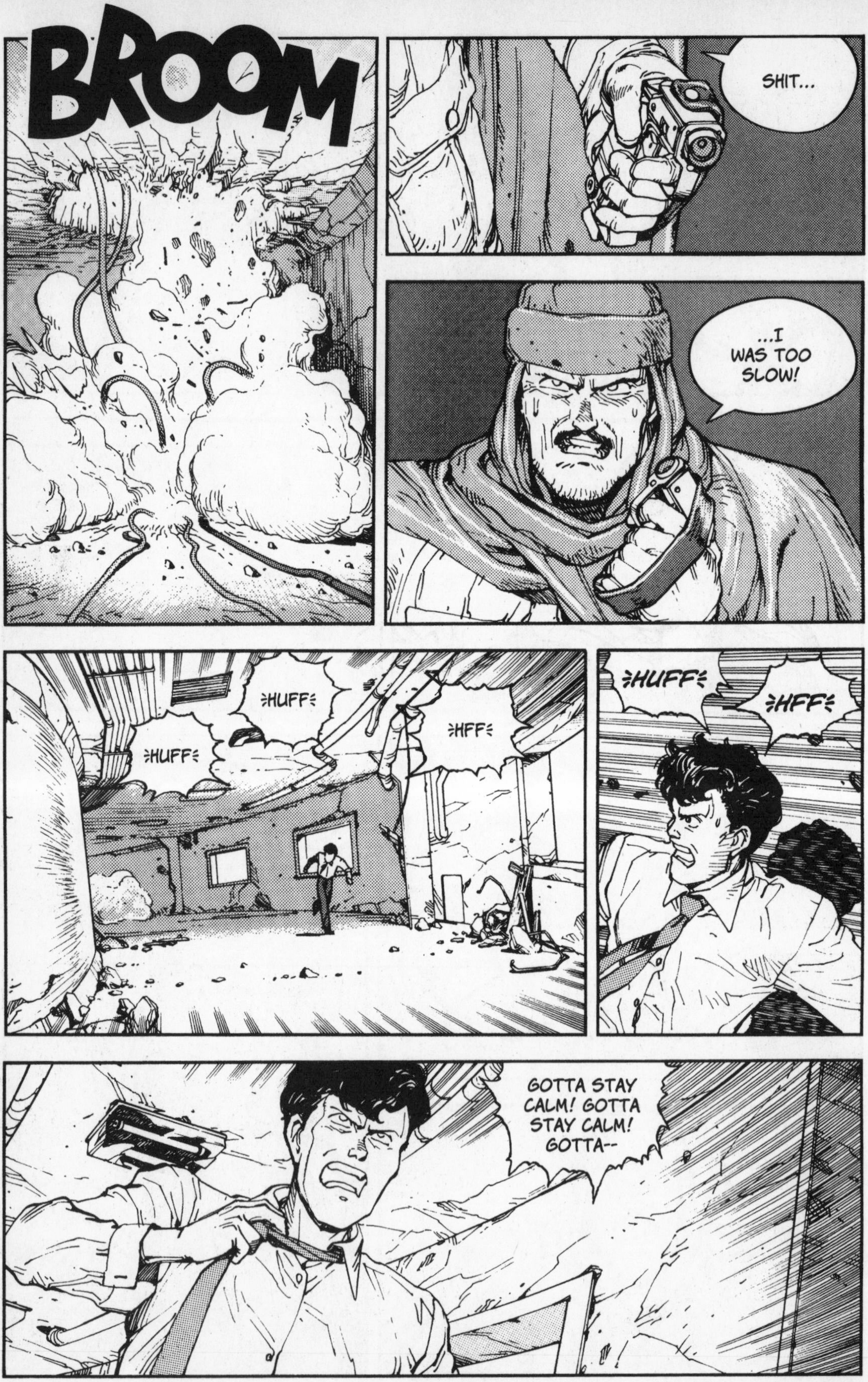
BROOM
SHIT...
...I WAS TOO SLOW!
HUFF
HUFF
HFF
HUFF
HFF
GOTTA STAY CALM! GOTTA STAY CALM! GOTTA--

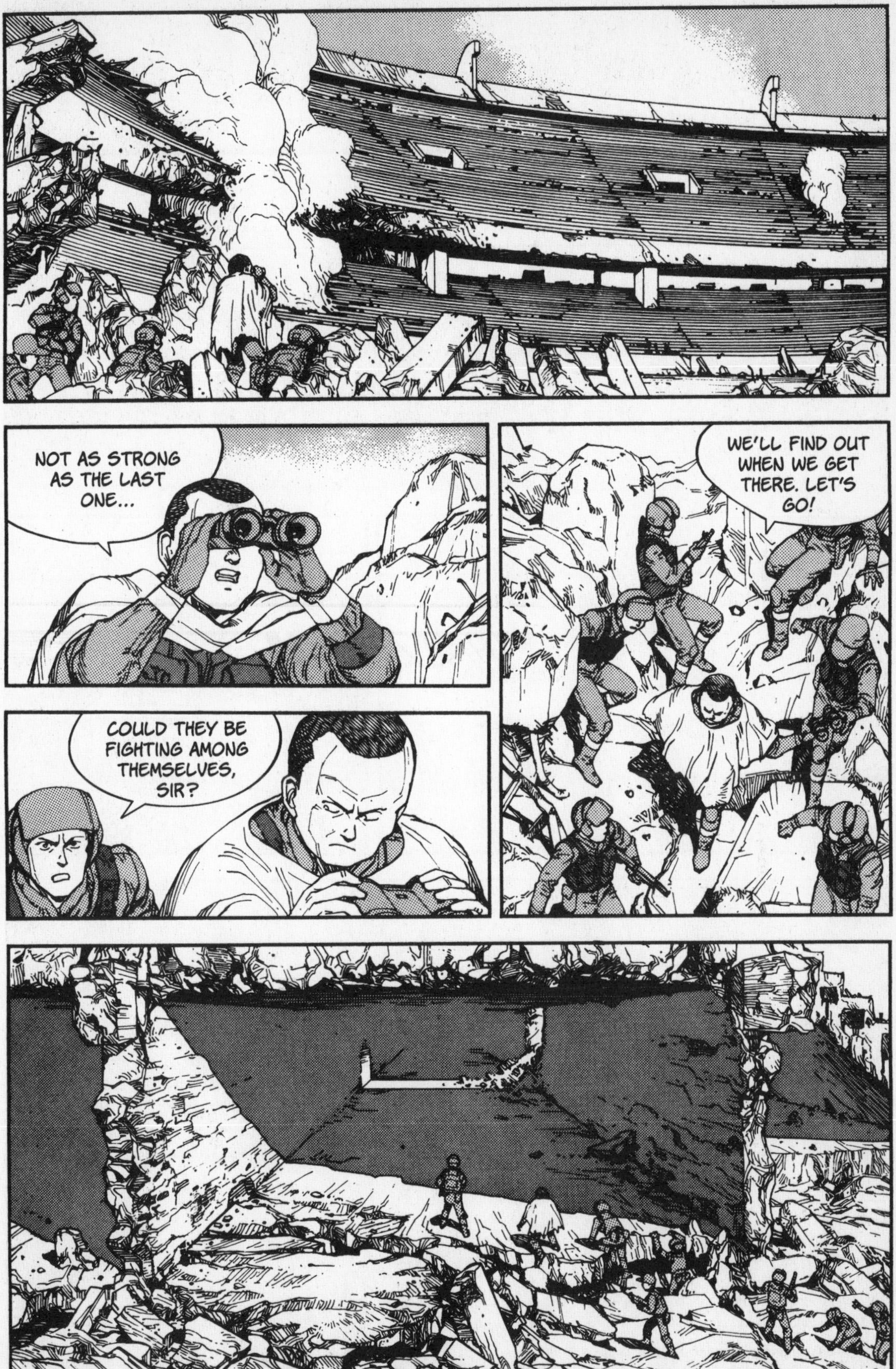

NOT AS STRONG AS THE LAST ONE...
COULD THEY BE FIGHTING AMONG THEMSELVES, SIR?
WE'LL FIND OUT WHEN WE GET THERE. LET'S GO!

FOXTROT VICTOR-25 RETURNING FROM MANEUVERS! TRAINING SEQUENCE COMPLETE!

DECK CREW, REPORT TO STATIONS!

PREPARE FOR LANDING!

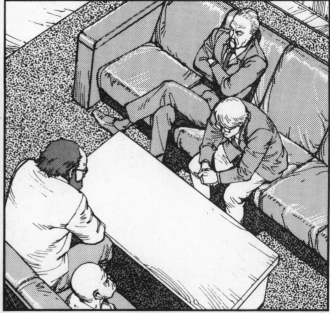

348

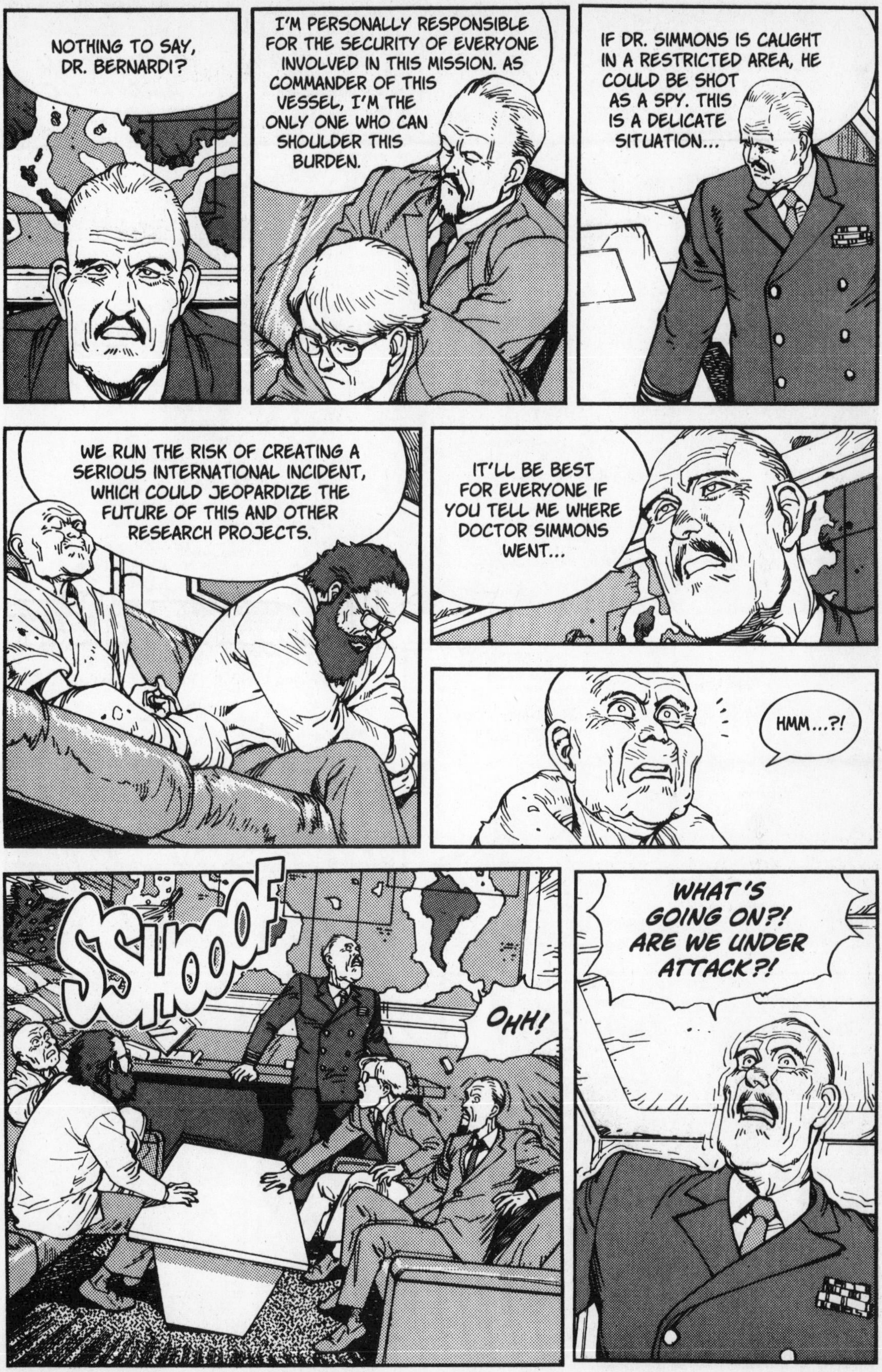
NOTHING TO SAY, DR. BERNARDI?
I'M PERSONALLY RESPONSIBLE FOR THE SECURITY OF EVERYONE INVOLVED IN THIS MISSION. AS COMMANDER OF THIS VESSEL, I'M THE ONLY ONE WHO CAN SHOULDER THIS BURDEN.
IF DR. SIMMONS IS CAUGHT IN A RESTRICTED AREA, HE COULD BE SHOT AS A SPY. THIS IS A DELICATE SITUATION...
WE RUN THE RISK OF CREATING A SERIOUS INTERNATIONAL INCIDENT, WHICH COULD JEOPARDIZE THE FUTURE OF THIS AND OTHER RESEARCH PROJECTS.
IT'LL BE BEST FOR EVERYONE IF YOU TELL ME WHERE DOCTOR SIMMONS WENT...
HMM...?!
SSHOOF
OHH!
WHAT'S GOING ON?! ARE WE UNDER ATTACK?!
...

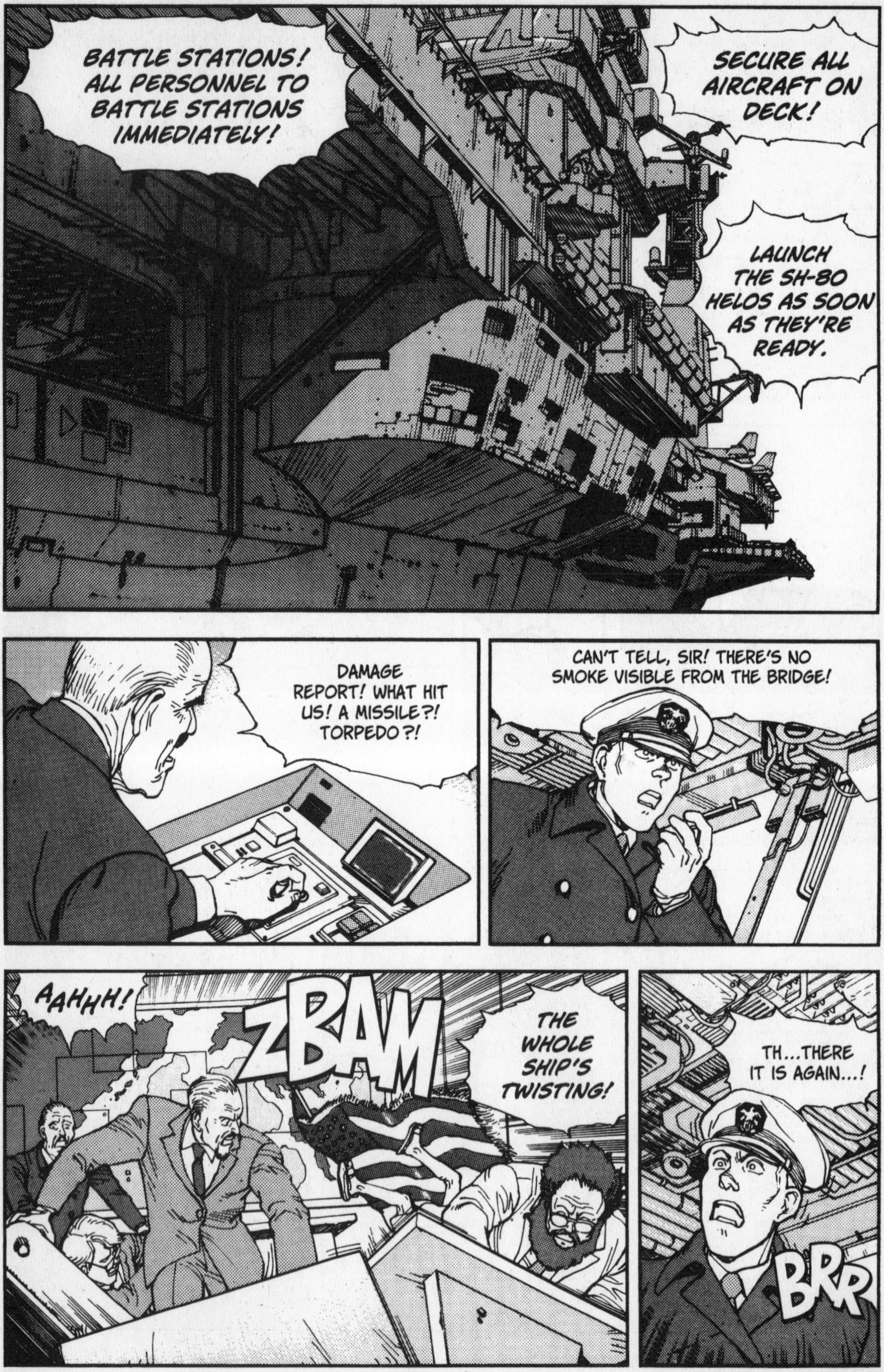
BATTLE STATIONS! ALL PERSONNEL TO BATTLE STATIONS IMMEDIATELY!
SECURE ALL AIRCRAFT ON DECK!
LAUNCH THE SH-80 HELOS AS SOON AS THEY'RE READY.
DAMAGE REPORT! WHAT HIT US! A MISSILE?! TORPEDO?!
CAN'T TELL, SIR! THERE'S NO SMOKE VISIBLE FROM THE BRIDGE!
AAHHHH!
ZBAM
THE WHOLE SHIP'S TWISTING!
TH...THERE IT IS AGAIN...!
BRRR

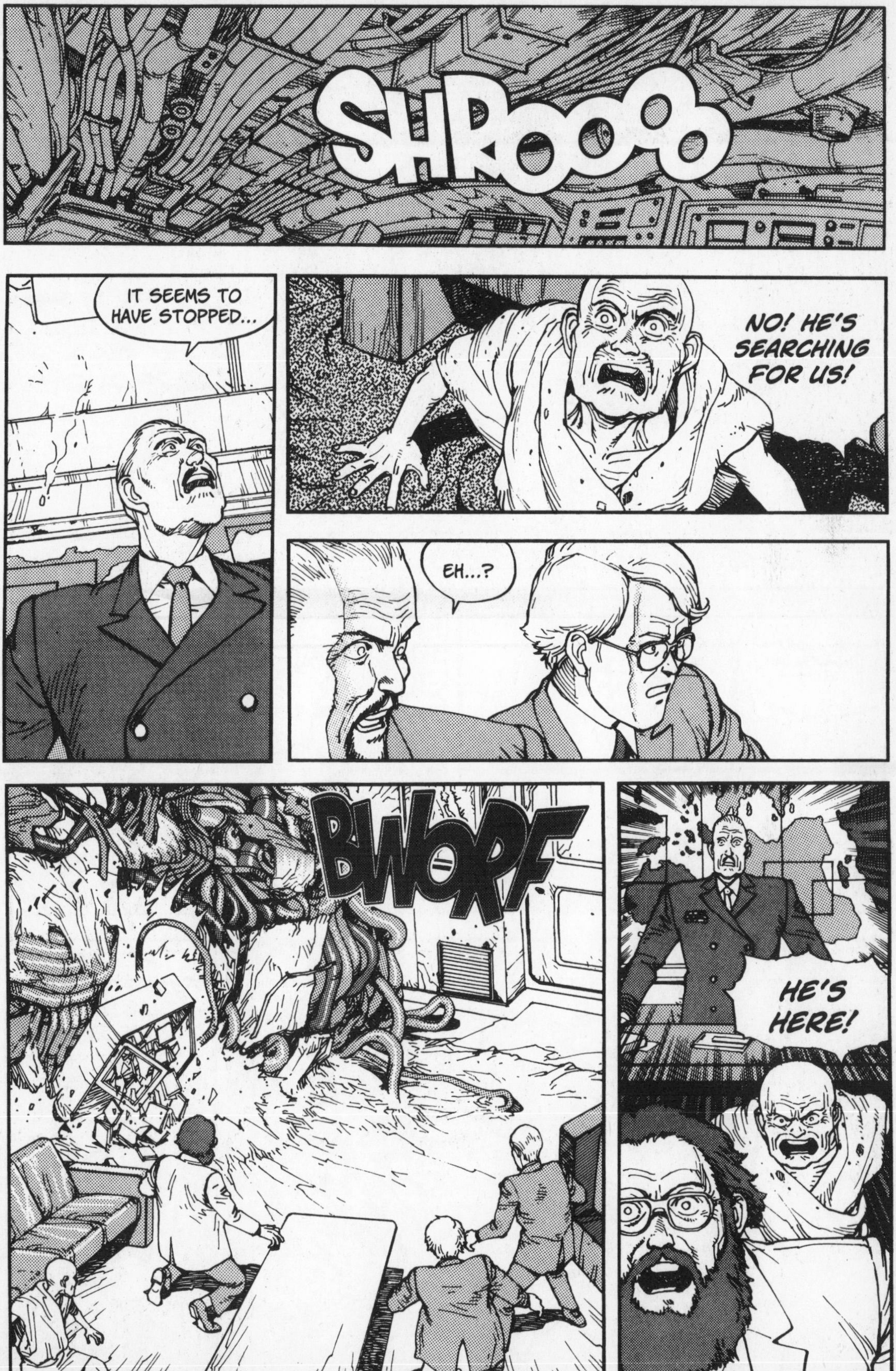
SHROOOO
IT SEEMS TO HAVE STOPPED...
NO! HE'S SEARCHING FOR US!
EH...?
BWORF
HE'S HERE!

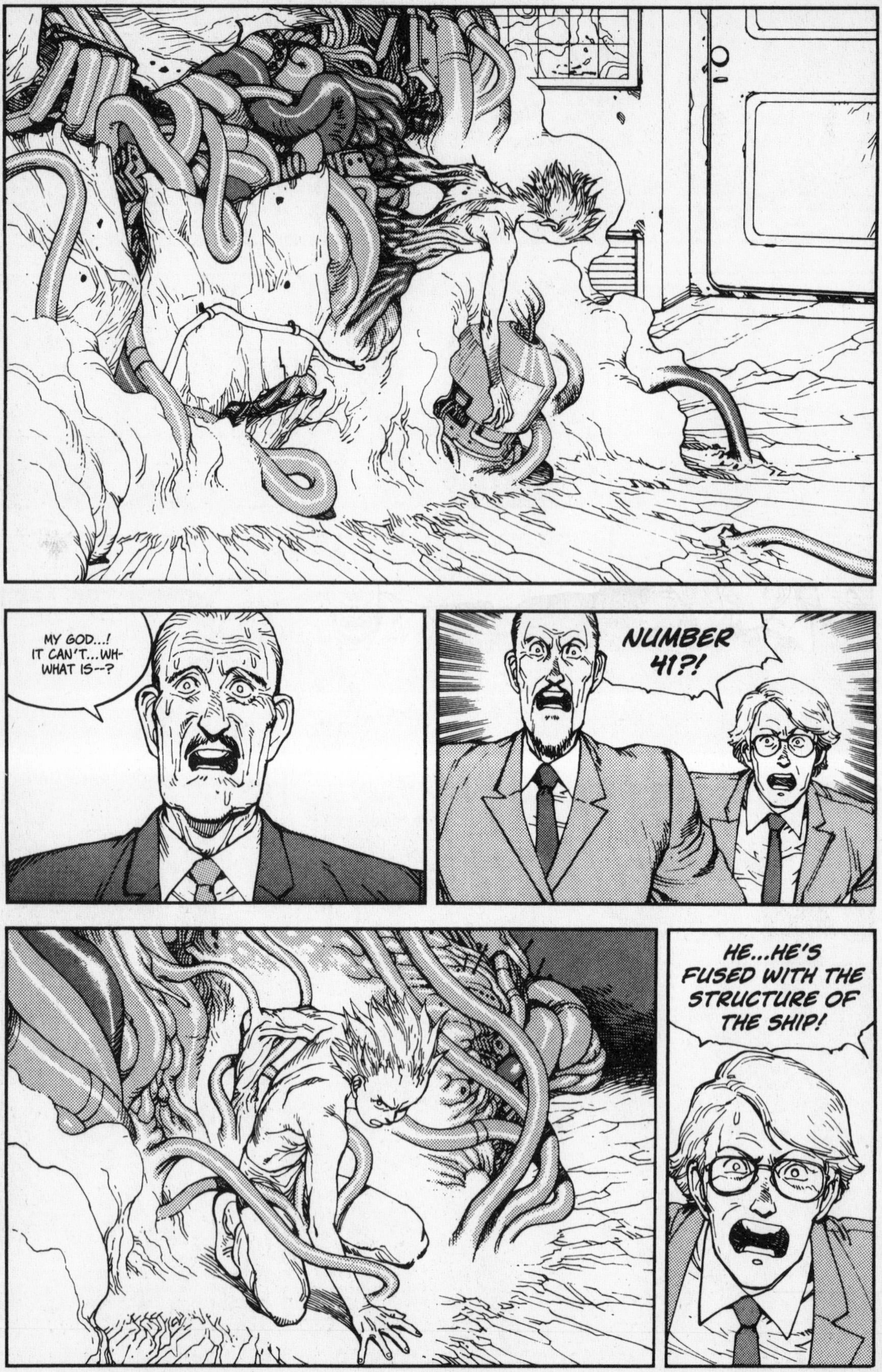
MY GOD...! IT CAN'T...WH-WHAT IS--?
NUMBER 41?!
HE...HE'S FUSED WITH THE STRUCTURE OF THE SHIP!

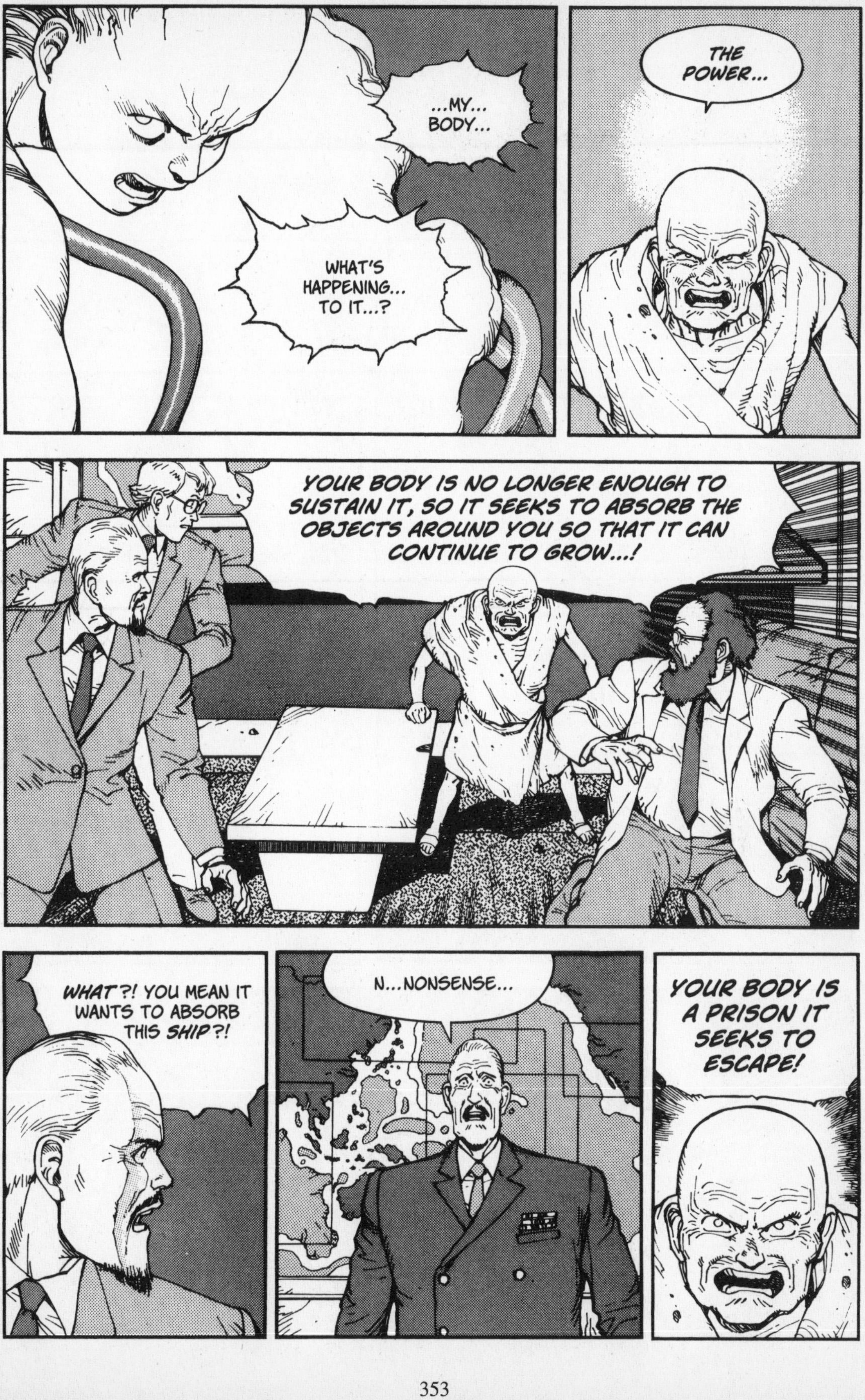
...MY... BODY...
WHAT'S HAPPENING... TO IT...?
THE POWER...
YOUR BODY IS NO LONGER ENOUGH TO SUSTAIN IT, SO IT SEEKS TO ABSORB THE OBJECTS AROUND YOU SO THAT IT CAN CONTINUE TO GROW...!
WHAT?! YOU MEAN IT WANTS TO ABSORB THIS SHIP?!
N...NONSENSE...
YOUR BODY IS A PRISON IT SEEKS TO ESCAPE!

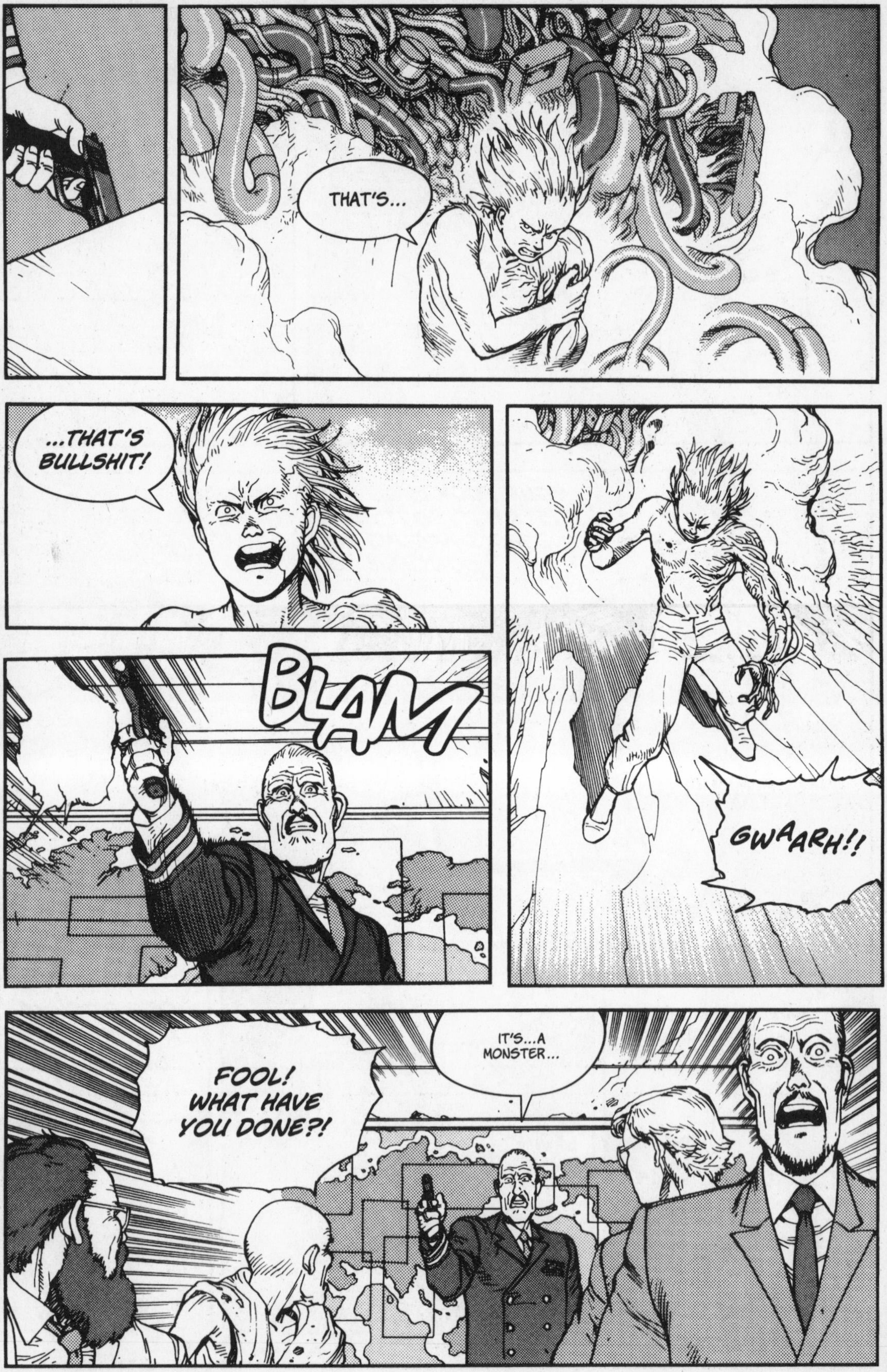
THAT'S...
...THAT'S BULLSHIT!
BLAM
GWAARH!!
FOOL! WHAT HAVE YOU DONE?!
IT'S...A MONSTER...

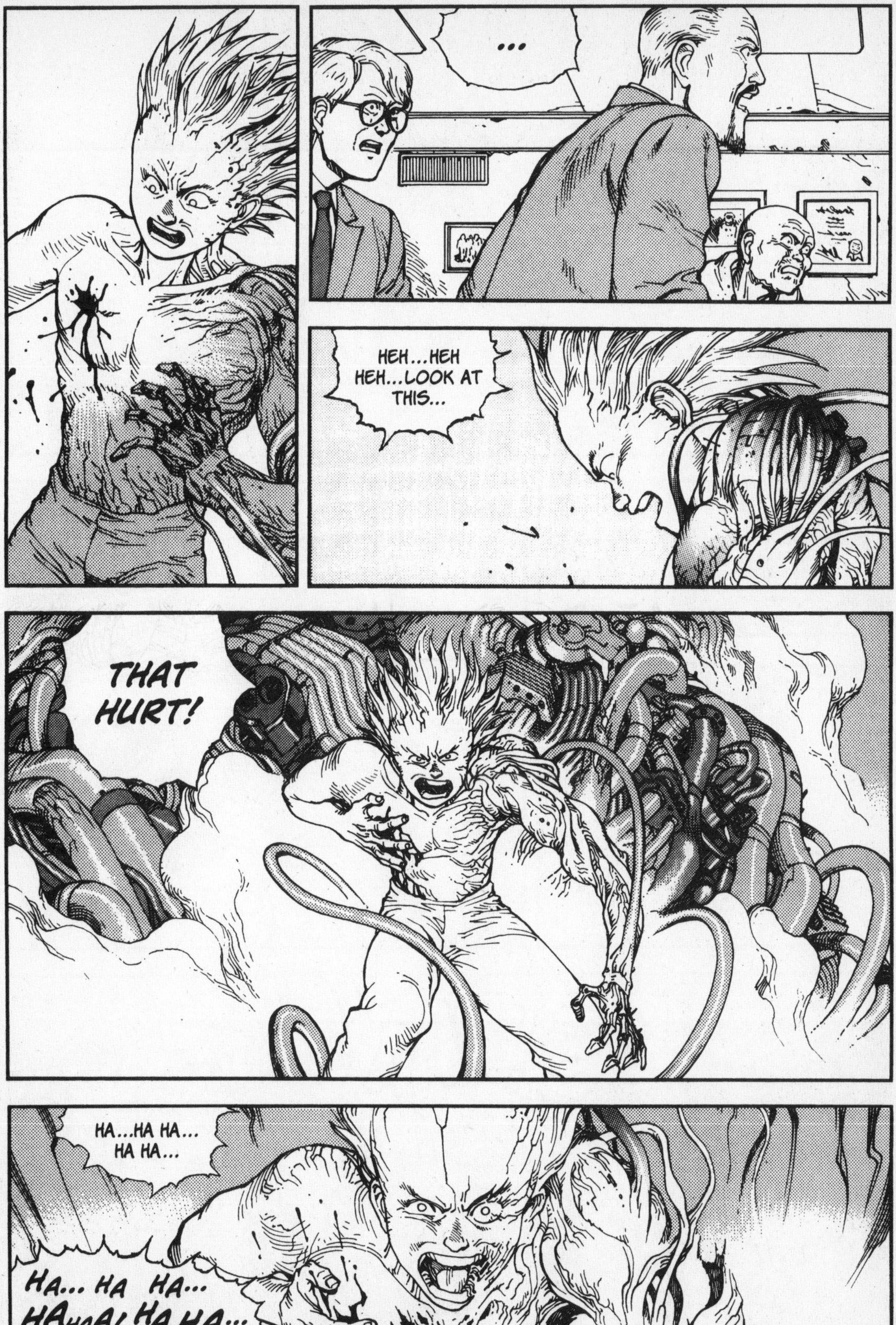
...
HEH...HEH HEH...LOOK AT THIS...
THAT HURT!
HA...HA HA... HA HA...
HA... HA HA...
HAHAA! HA HA...
HAHAHAA!!

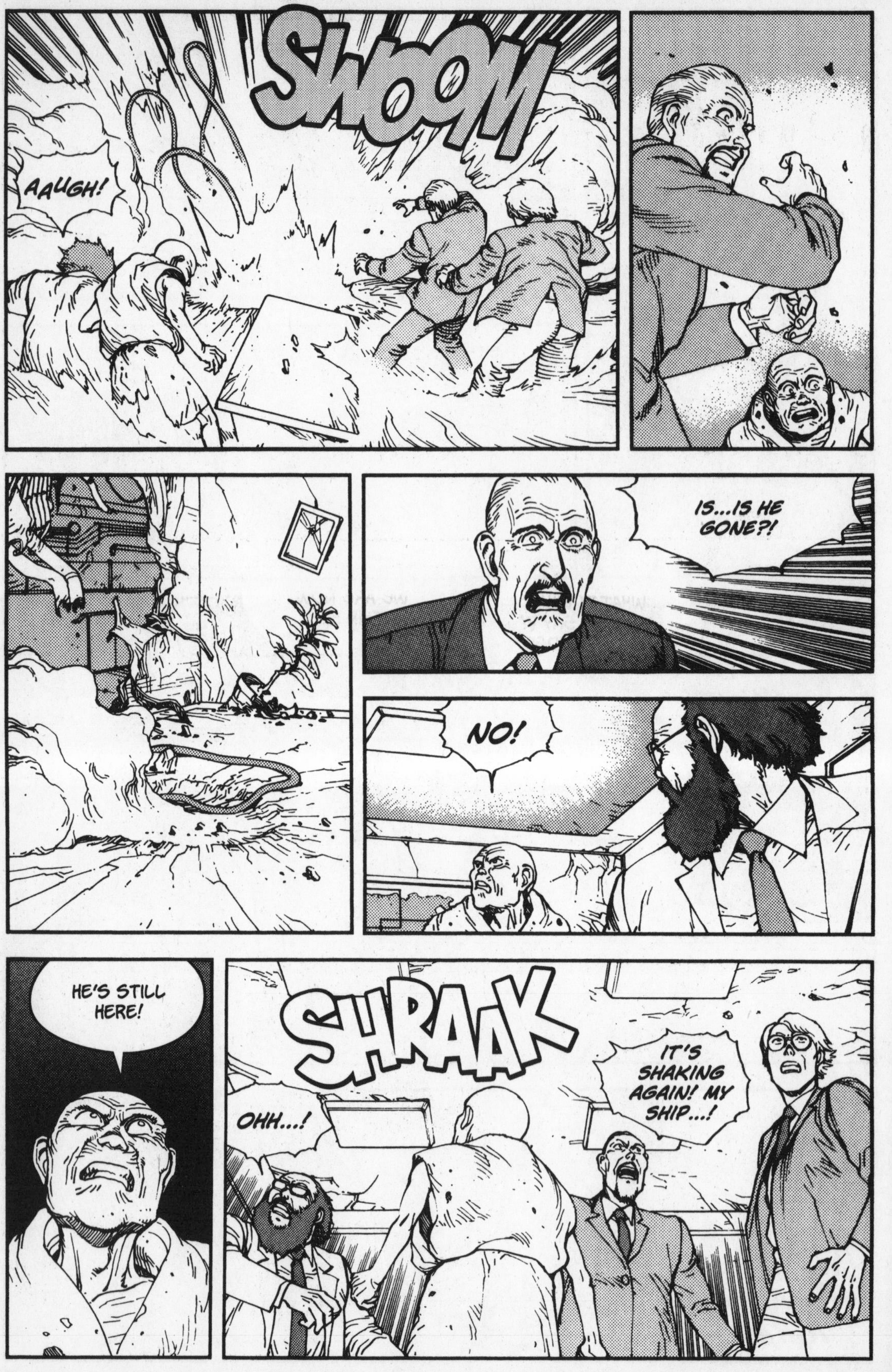
SHOOM
AAUGH!
IS...IS HE GONE?!
NO!
HE'S STILL HERE!
SHRAAK
OHH...!
IT'S SHAKING AGAIN! MY SHIP...!

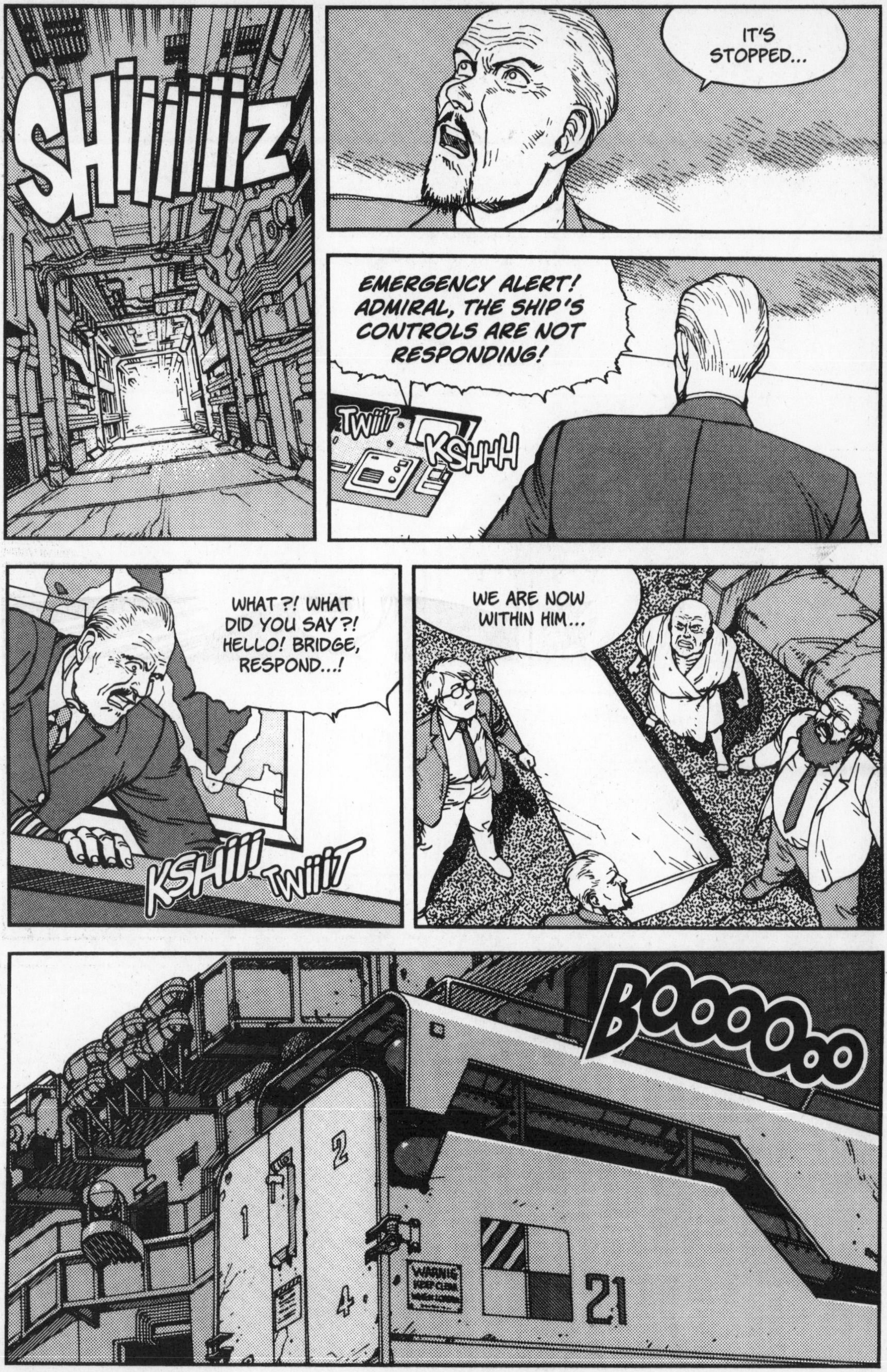
SHIIIIIIZ
IT'S STOPPED...
EMERGENCY ALERT! ADMIRAL, THE SHIP'S CONTROLS ARE NOT RESPONDING!
TWIIIT
KSHHH
WHAT?! WHAT DID YOU SAY?! HELLO! BRIDGE, RESPOND...!
KSHIII
TWIIIT
WE ARE NOW WITHIN HIM...
BOOOOOoo

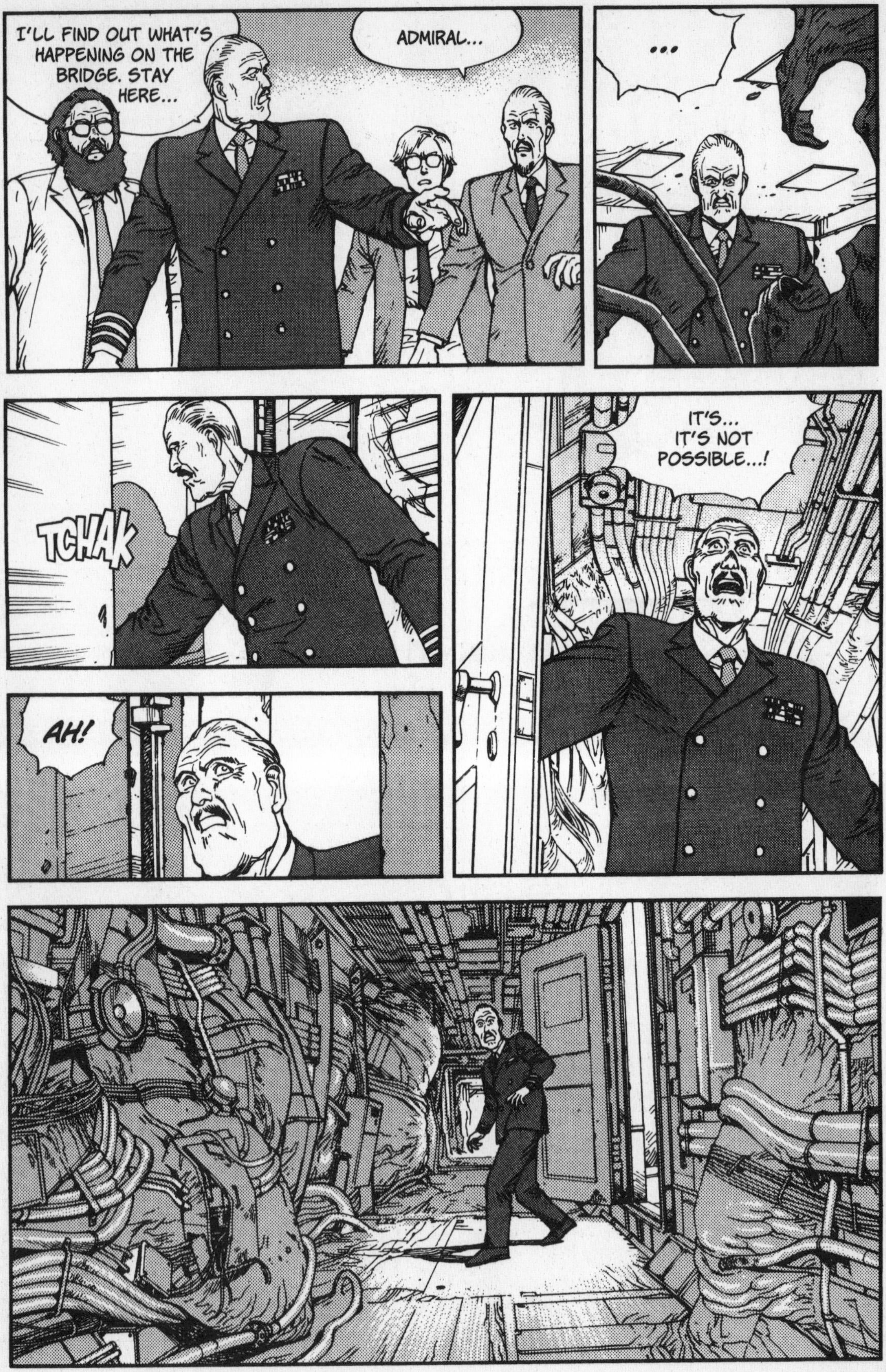

I'LL FIND OUT WHAT'S HAPPENING ON THE BRIDGE. STAY HERE...
ADMIRAL...
...
TCHAK
IT'S... IT'S NOT POSSIBLE...!
AH!

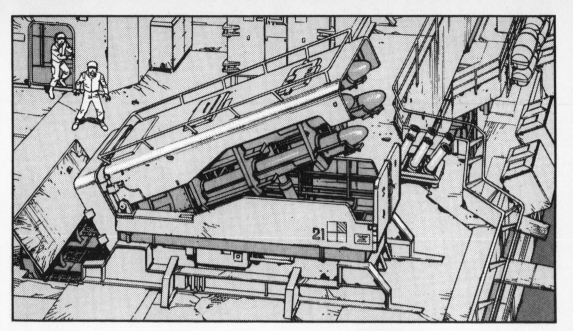

THE NUCLEAR MISSILE LAUNCHERS HAVE ACTIVATED!

THAT CAN'T BE, CAPTAIN... CONTROLS ARE DEAD...! NOTHING'S WORKING...

PSHUU

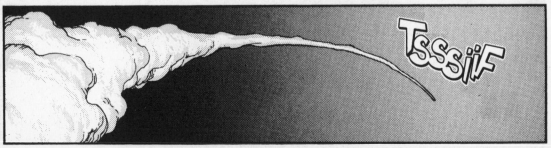TSSSïF

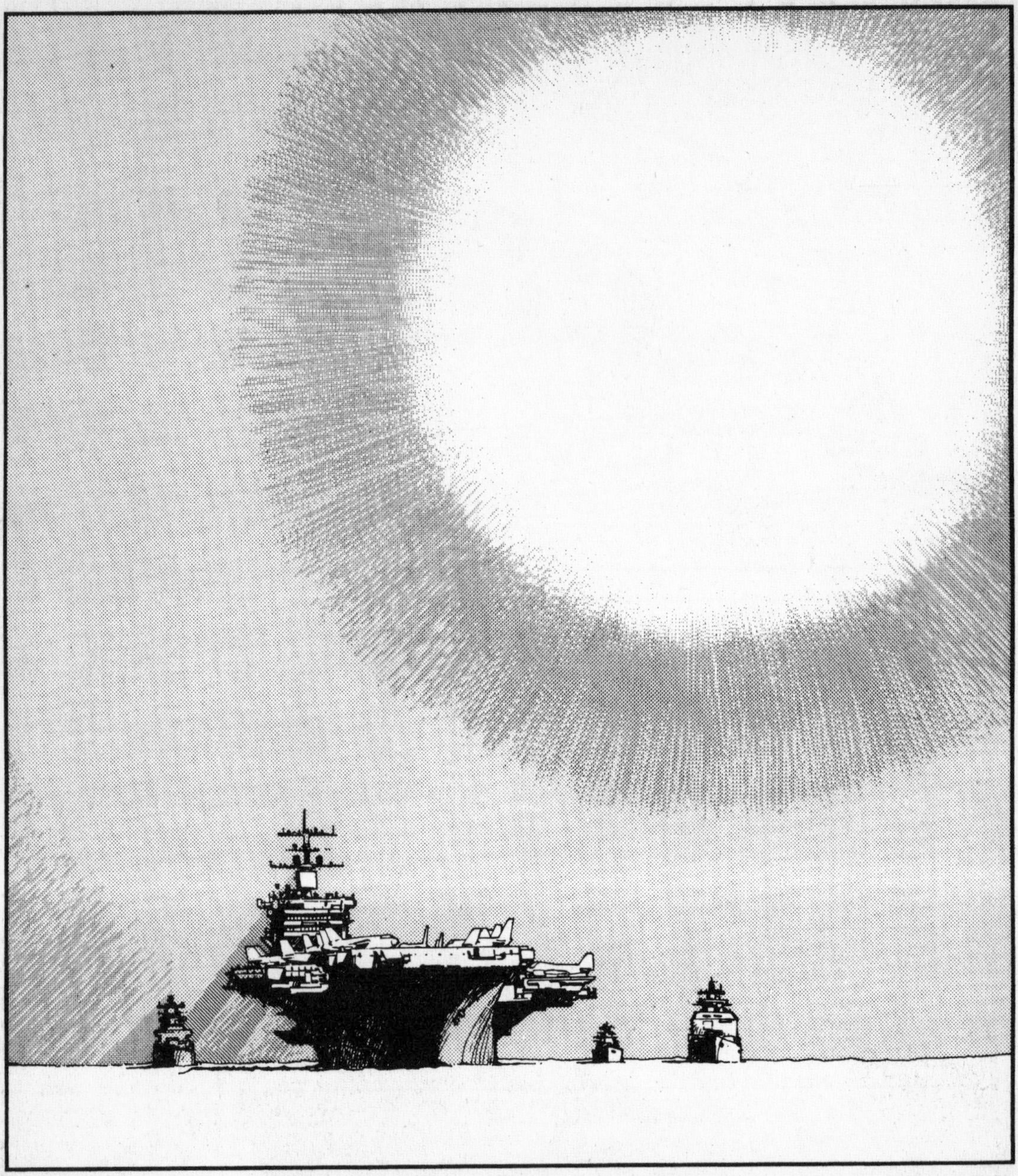

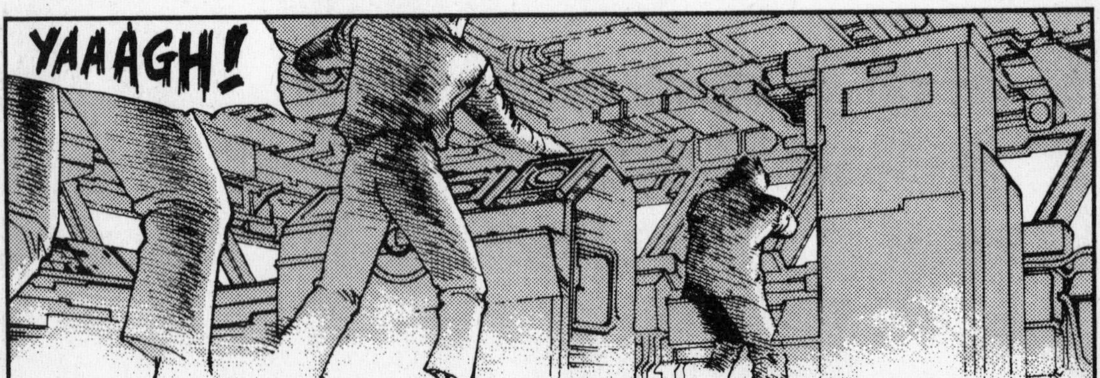
YAAAGH!

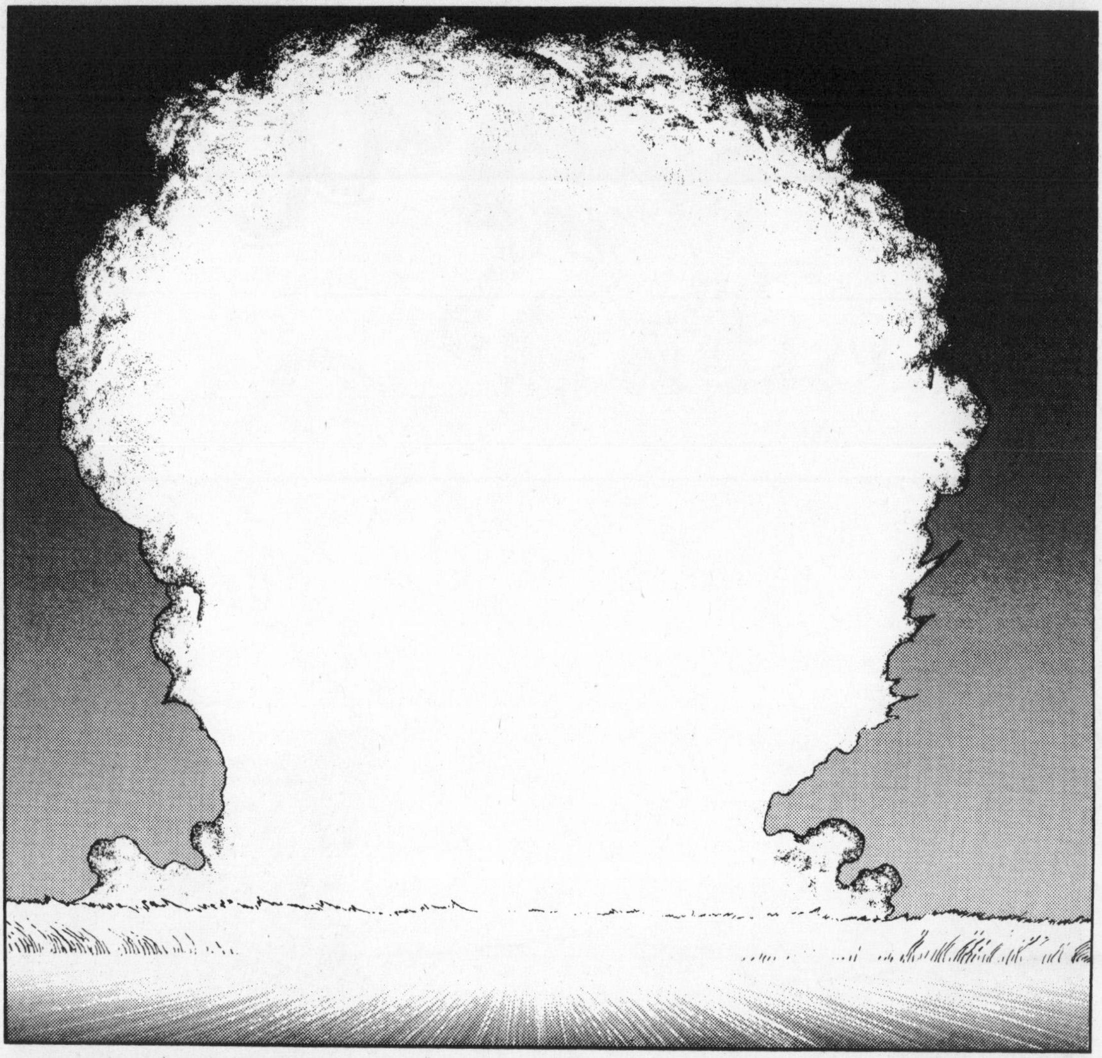
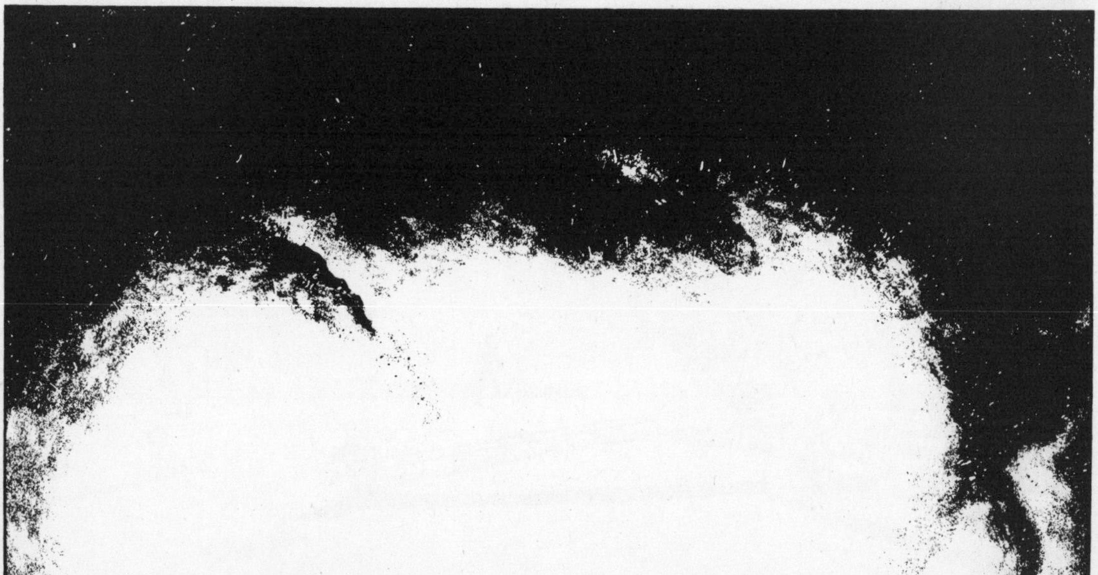

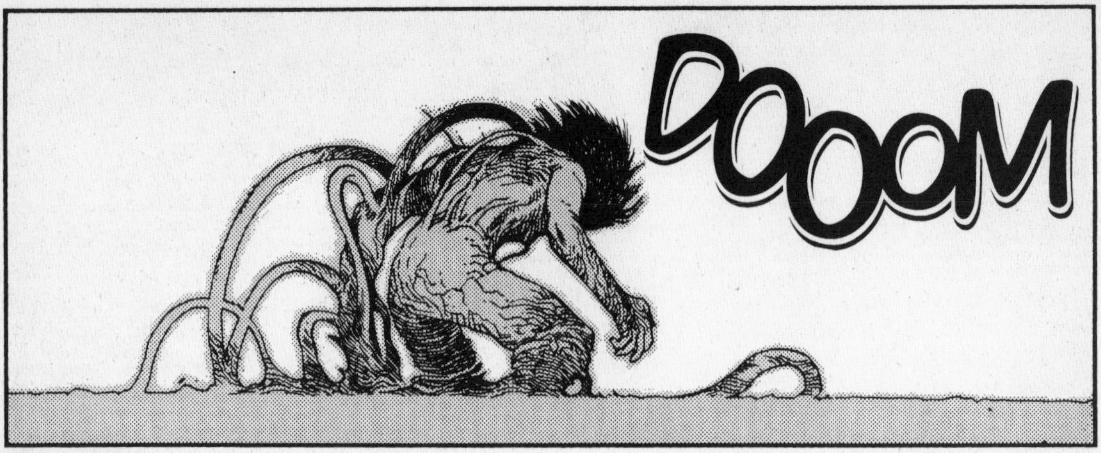
DOOOM
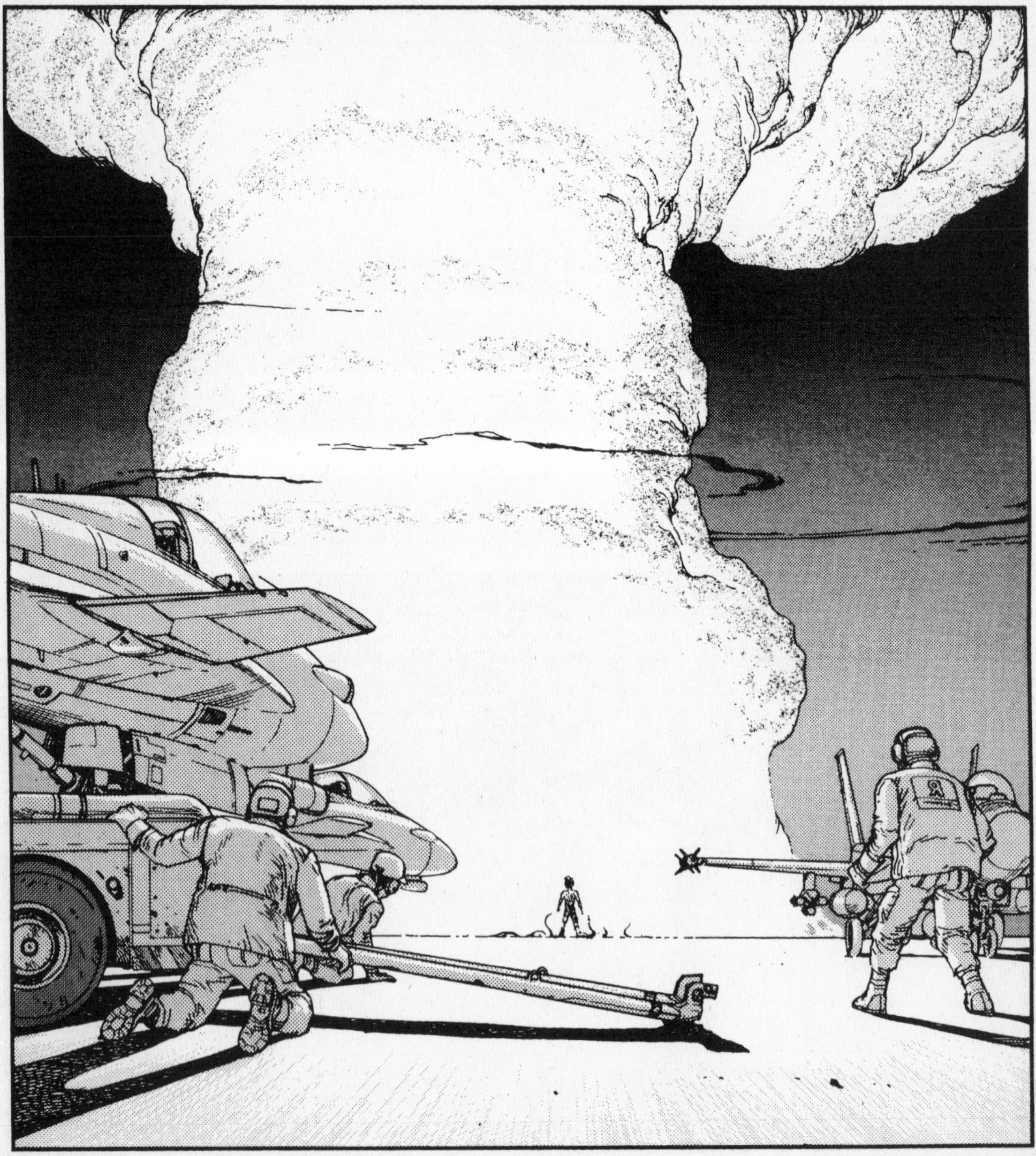

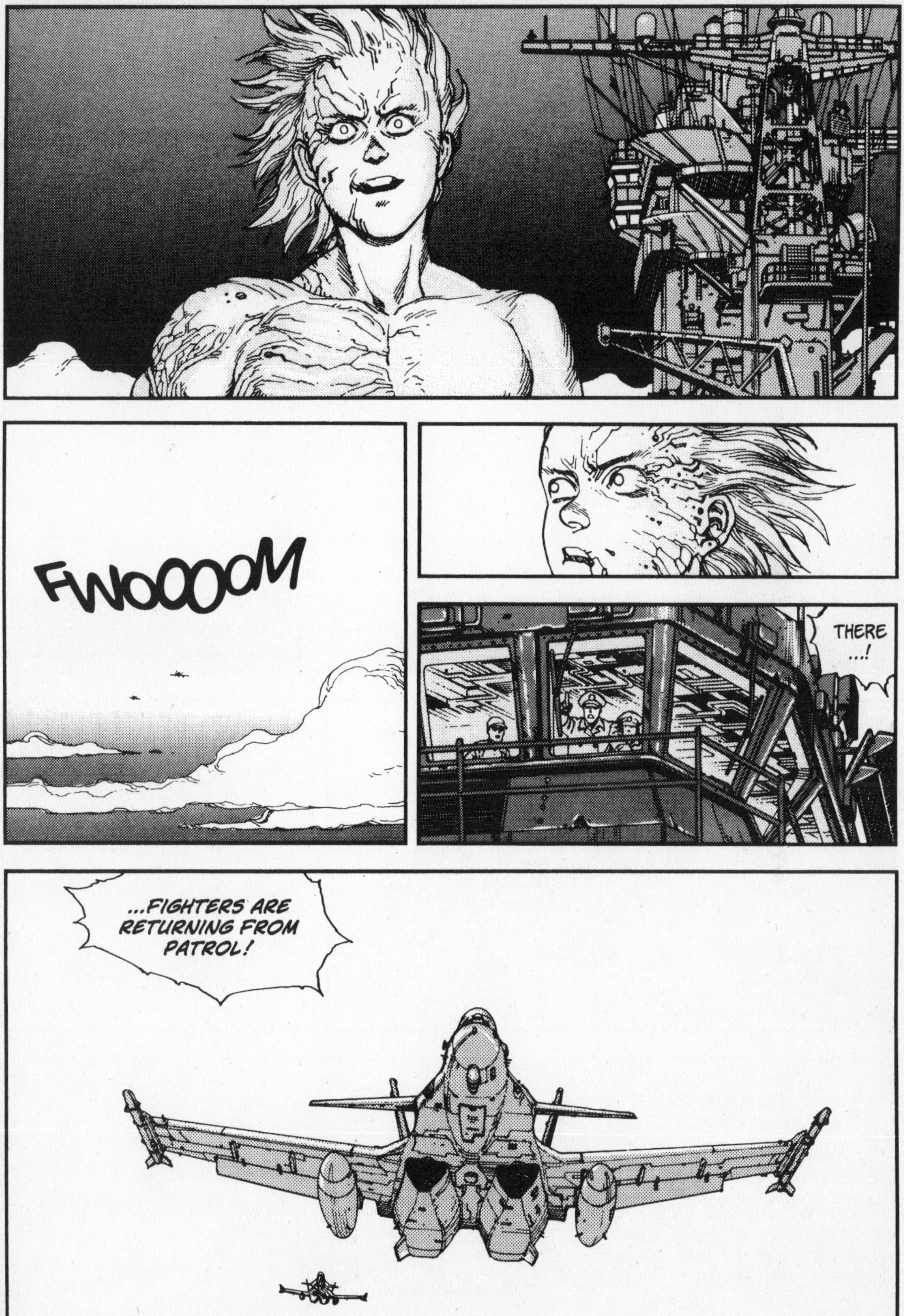
FWOOOOM
THERE ...!
...FIGHTERS ARE RETURNING FROM PATROL!

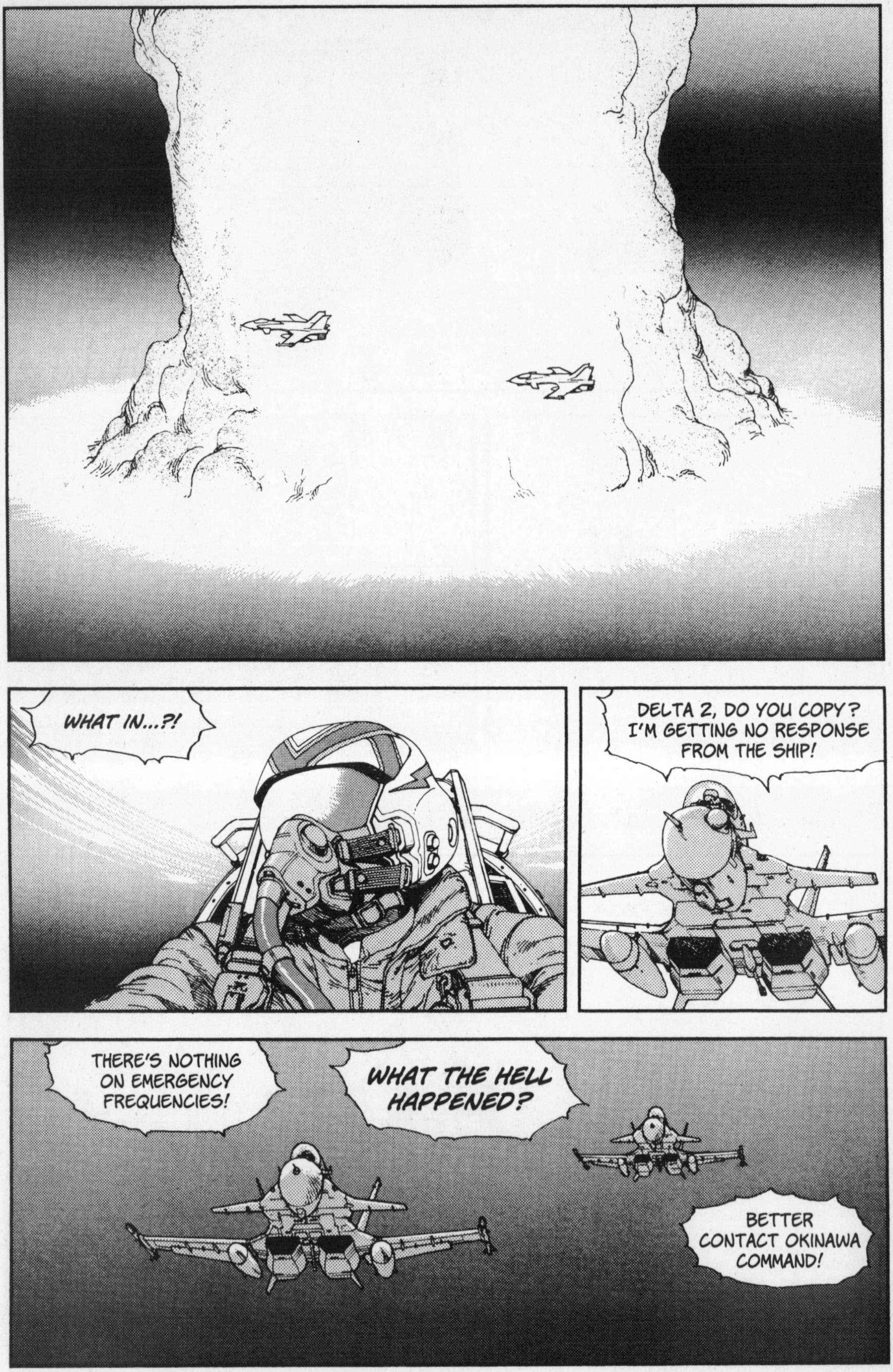
WHAT IN...?!
DELTA 2, DO YOU COPY? I'M GETTING NO RESPONSE FROM THE SHIP!
THERE'S NOTHING ON EMERGENCY FREQUENCIES!
WHAT THE HELL HAPPENED?
BETTER CONTACT OKINAWA COMMAND!

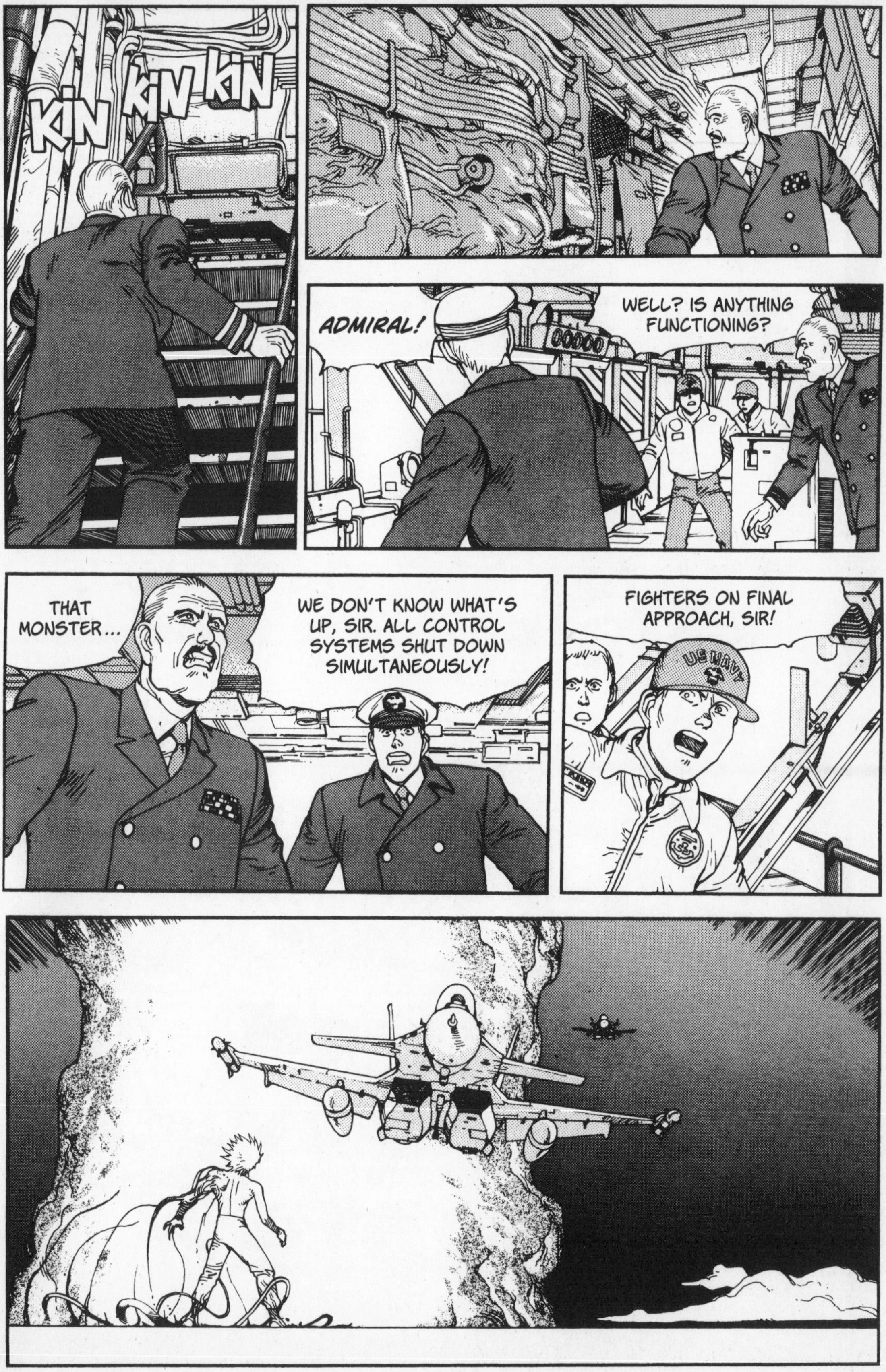
KIN KIN KIN
ADMIRAL!
WELL? IS ANYTHING FUNCTIONING?
THAT MONSTER...
WE DON'T KNOW WHAT'S UP, SIR. ALL CONTROL SYSTEMS SHUT DOWN SIMULTANEOUSLY!
FIGHTERS ON FINAL APPROACH, SIR!
US NAVY

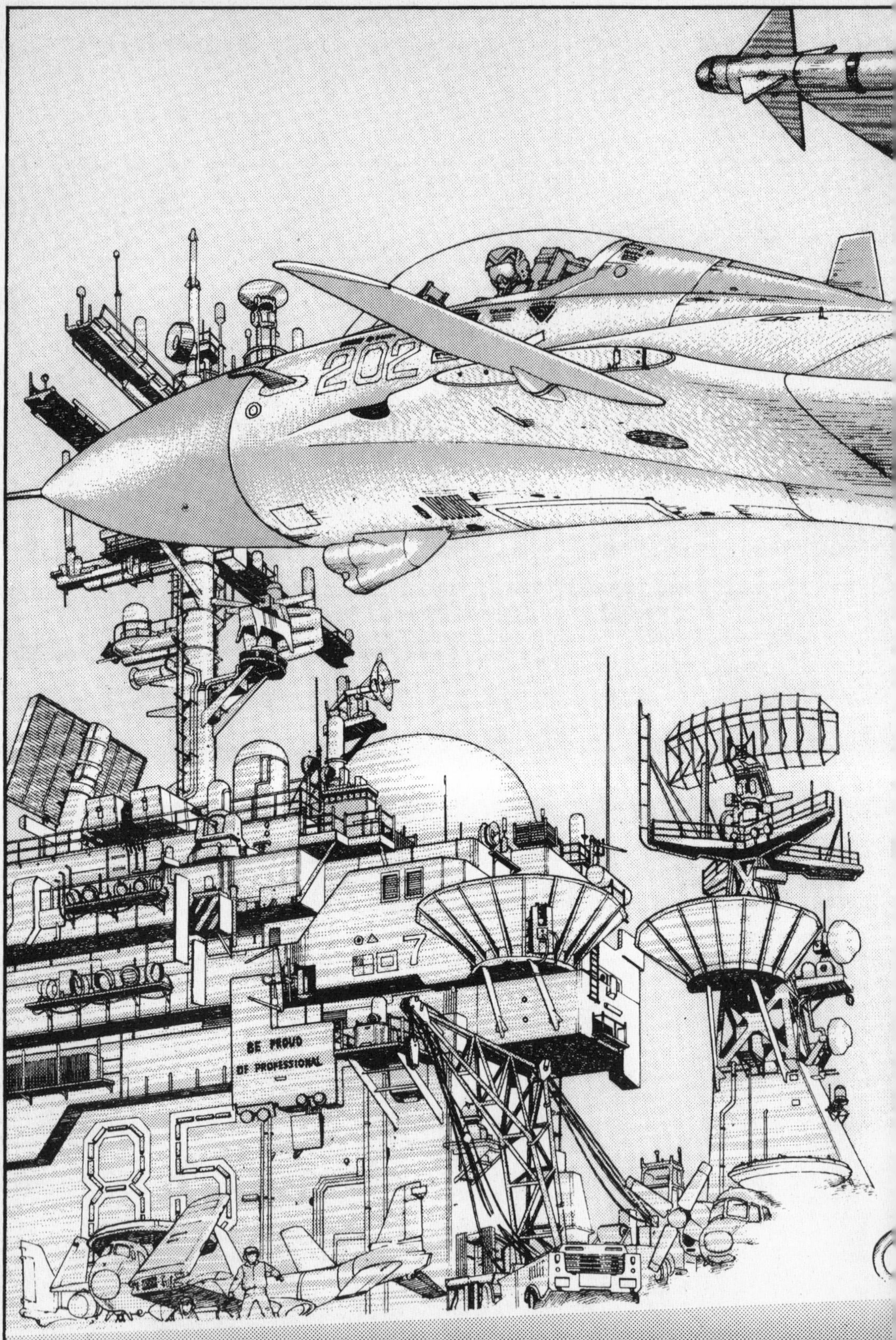
202
7
BE PROUD
OF PROFESSIONAL
85

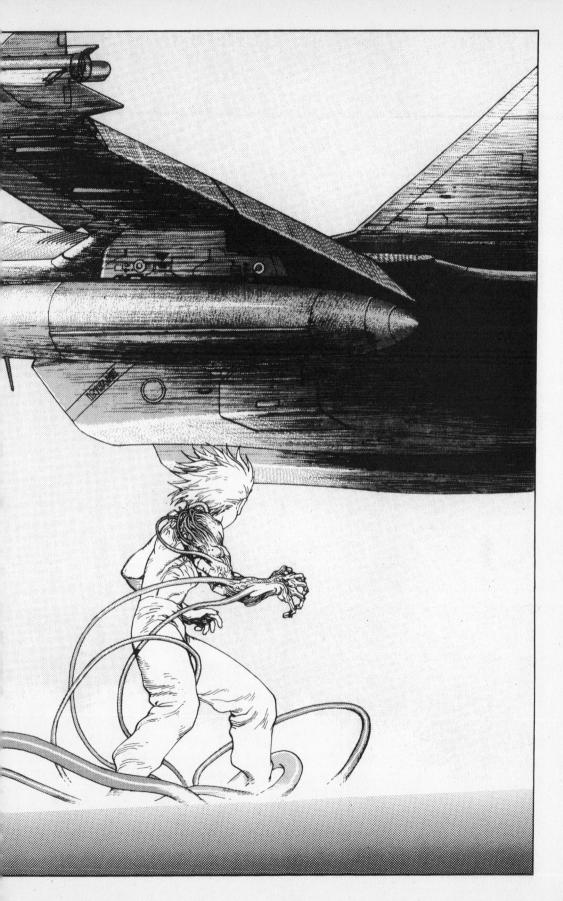

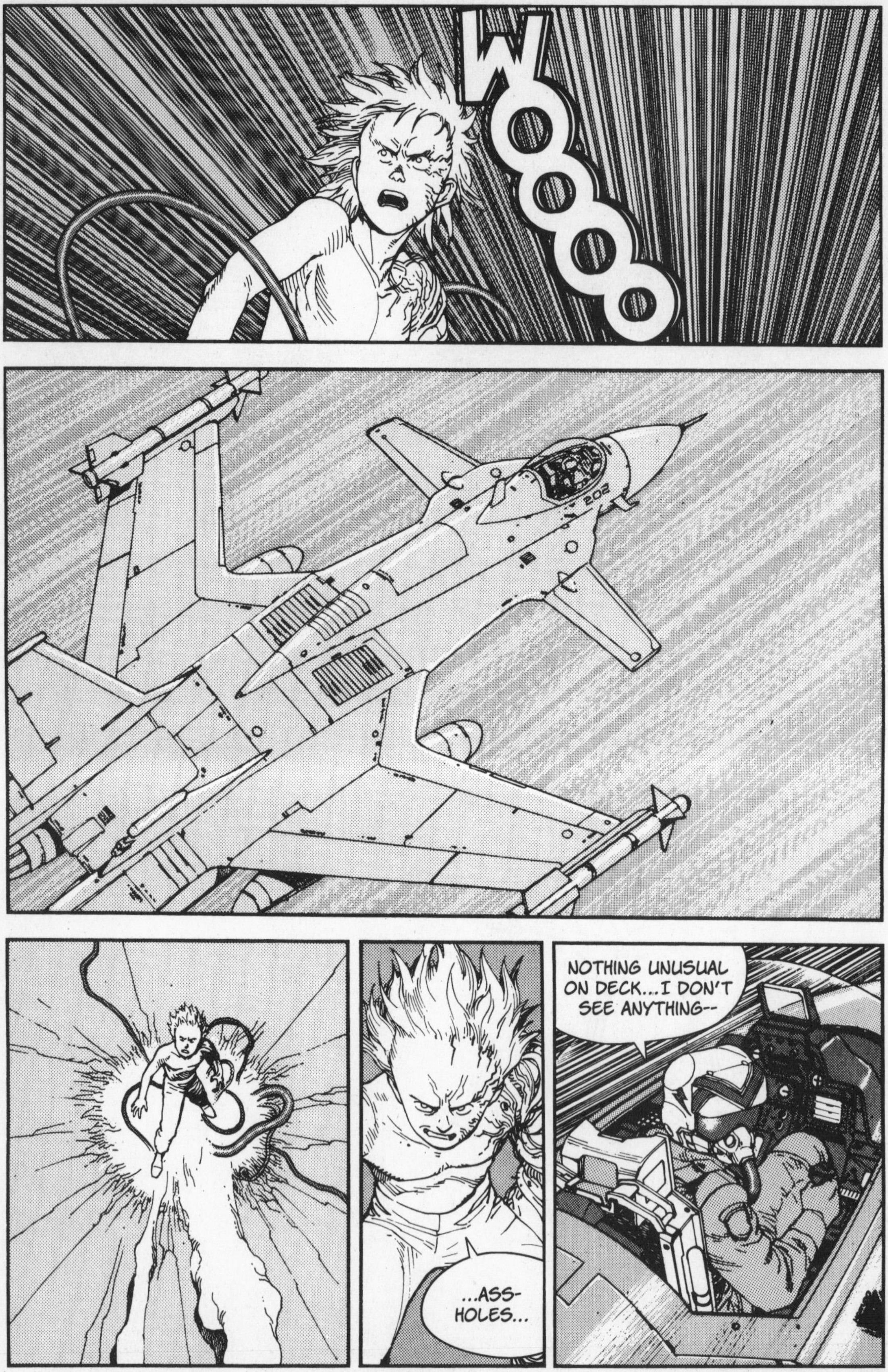
WOOOO
...ASS-
HOLES...
NOTHING UNUSUAL ON DECK...I DON'T SEE ANYTHING--

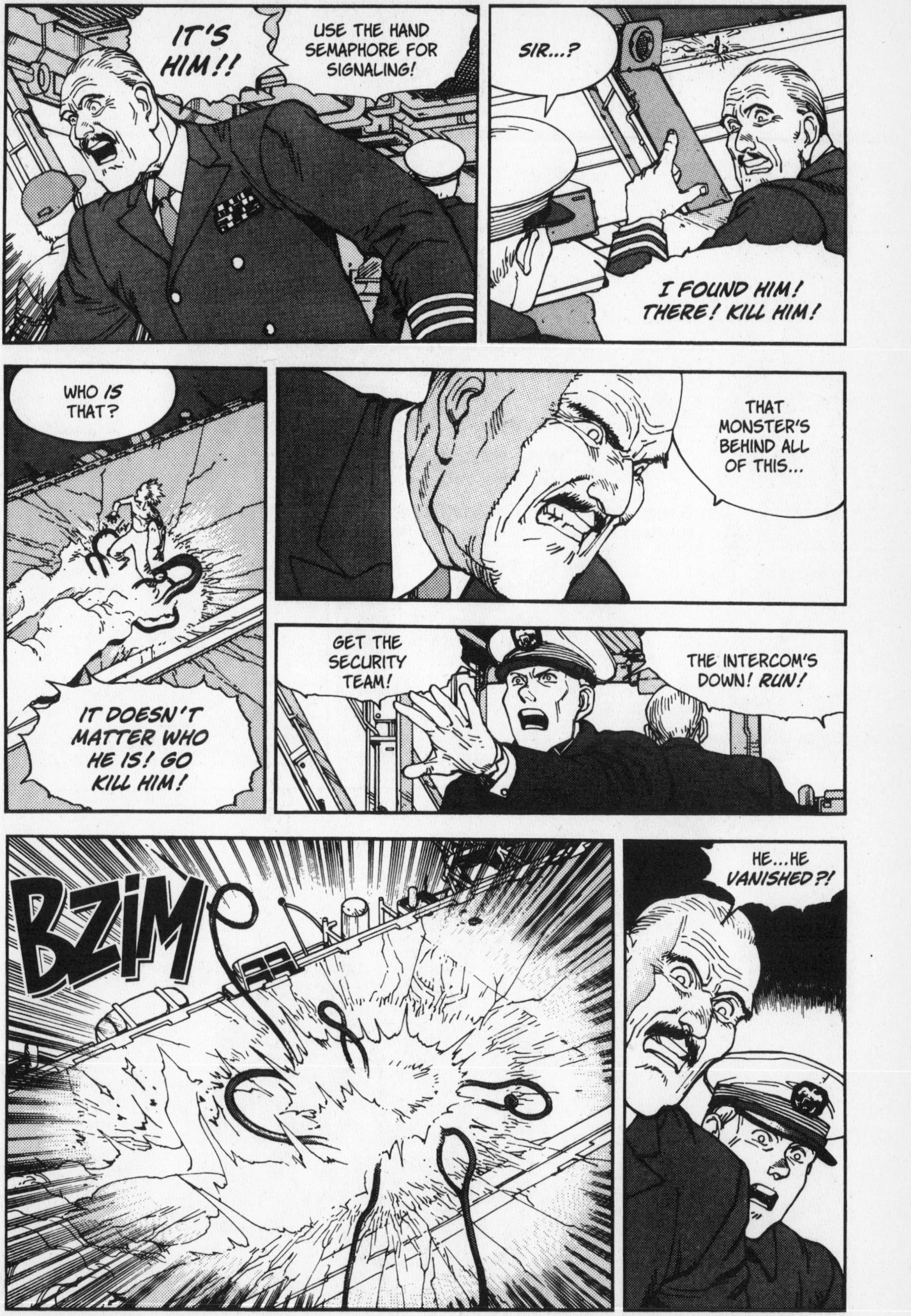
IT'S HIM!!
USE THE HAND SEMAPHORE FOR SIGNALING!
SIR...?
I FOUND HIM! THERE! KILL HIM!
WHO IS THAT?
IT DOESN'T MATTER WHO HE IS! GO KILL HIM!
THAT MONSTER'S BEHIND ALL OF THIS...
GET THE SECURITY TEAM!
THE INTERCOM'S DOWN! RUN!
BZIM
HE...HE VANISHED?!

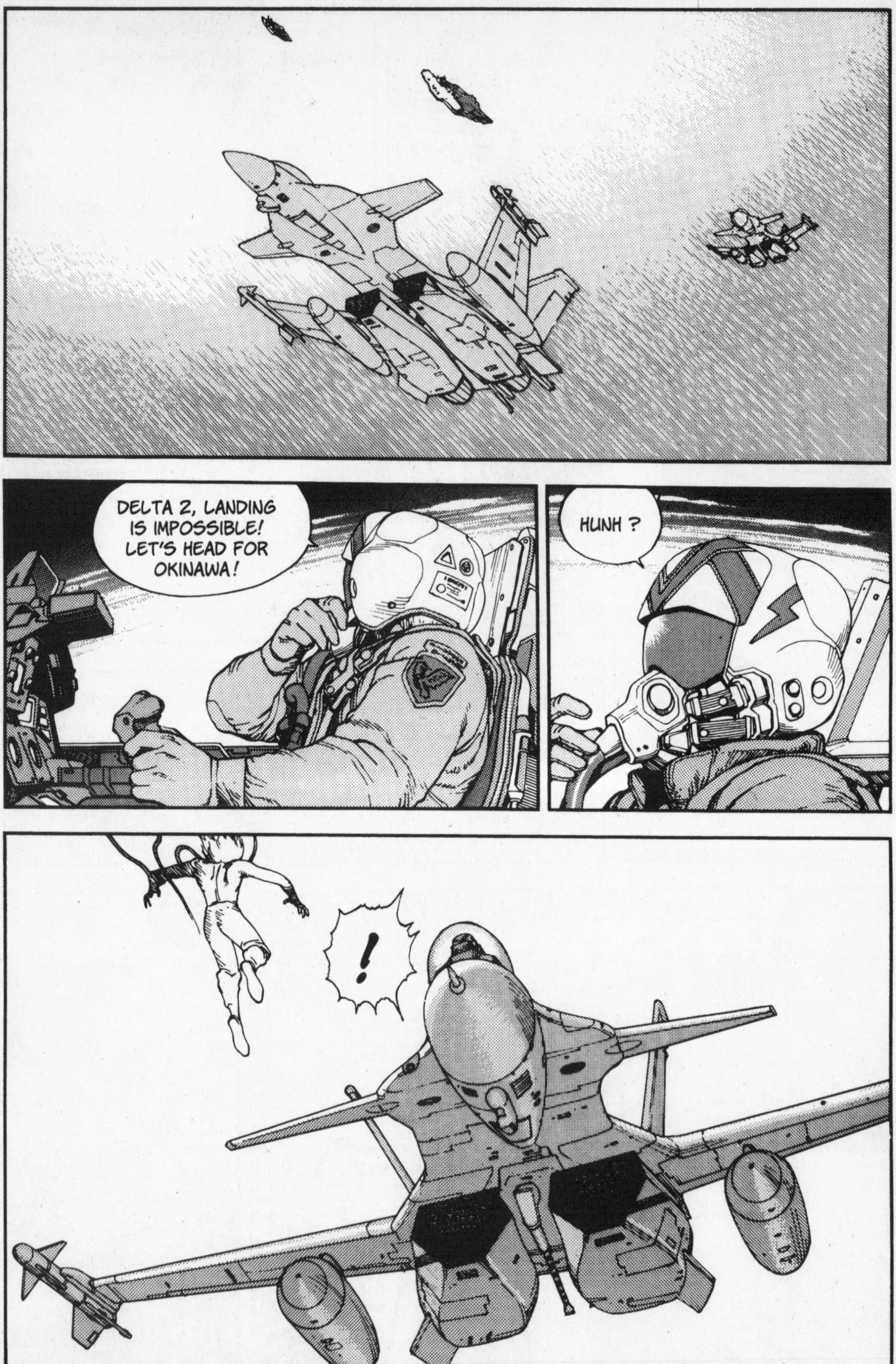
DELTA 2, LANDING IS IMPOSSIBLE! LET'S HEAD FOR OKINAWA!
HUNH ?
!

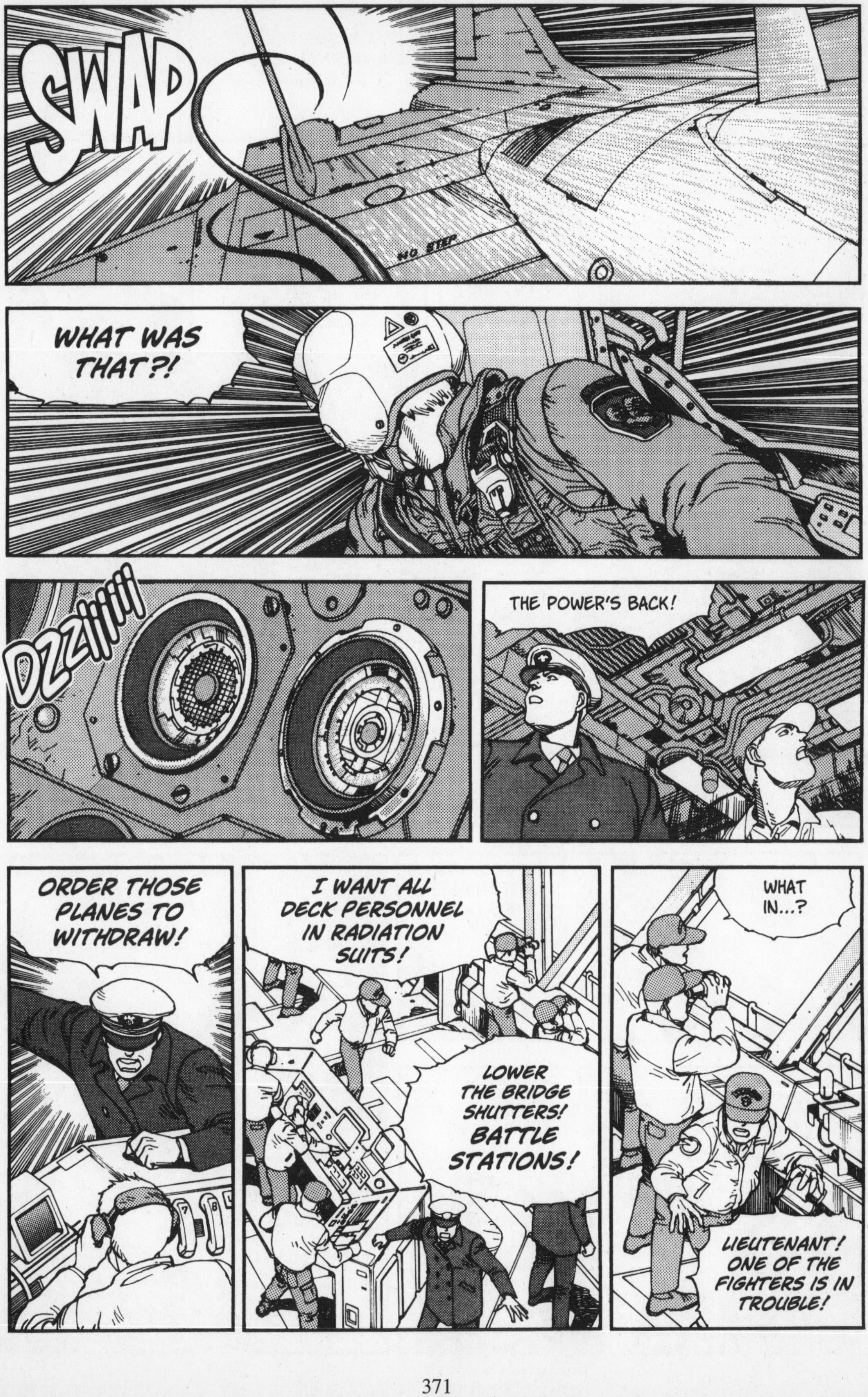
SWAP
NO STEP
WHAT WAS THAT?!
DZZIIIIIII
THE POWER'S BACK!
ORDER THOSE PLANES TO WITHDRAW!
I WANT ALL DECK PERSONNEL IN RADIATION SUITS!
LOWER THE BRIDGE SHUTTERS! BATTLE STATIONS!
WHAT IN...?
LIEUTENANT! ONE OF THE FIGHTERS IS IN TROUBLE!

WHAT IS IT? WHAT'S WRONG?

THE FUSELAGE IS UNDERGOING SOME KIND OF *DEFORMATION*...

WHAT?!

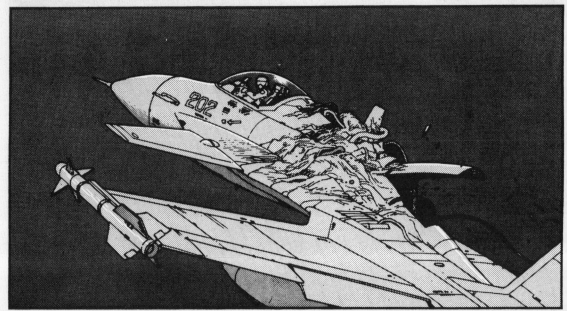

MY GOD, WHAT'S HAPPENING?!... IT'S *IMPOSSIBLE!*

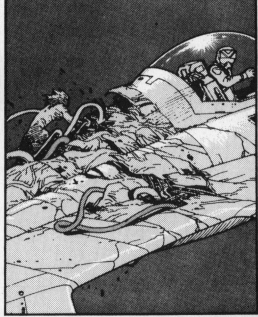

LET ME SEE.

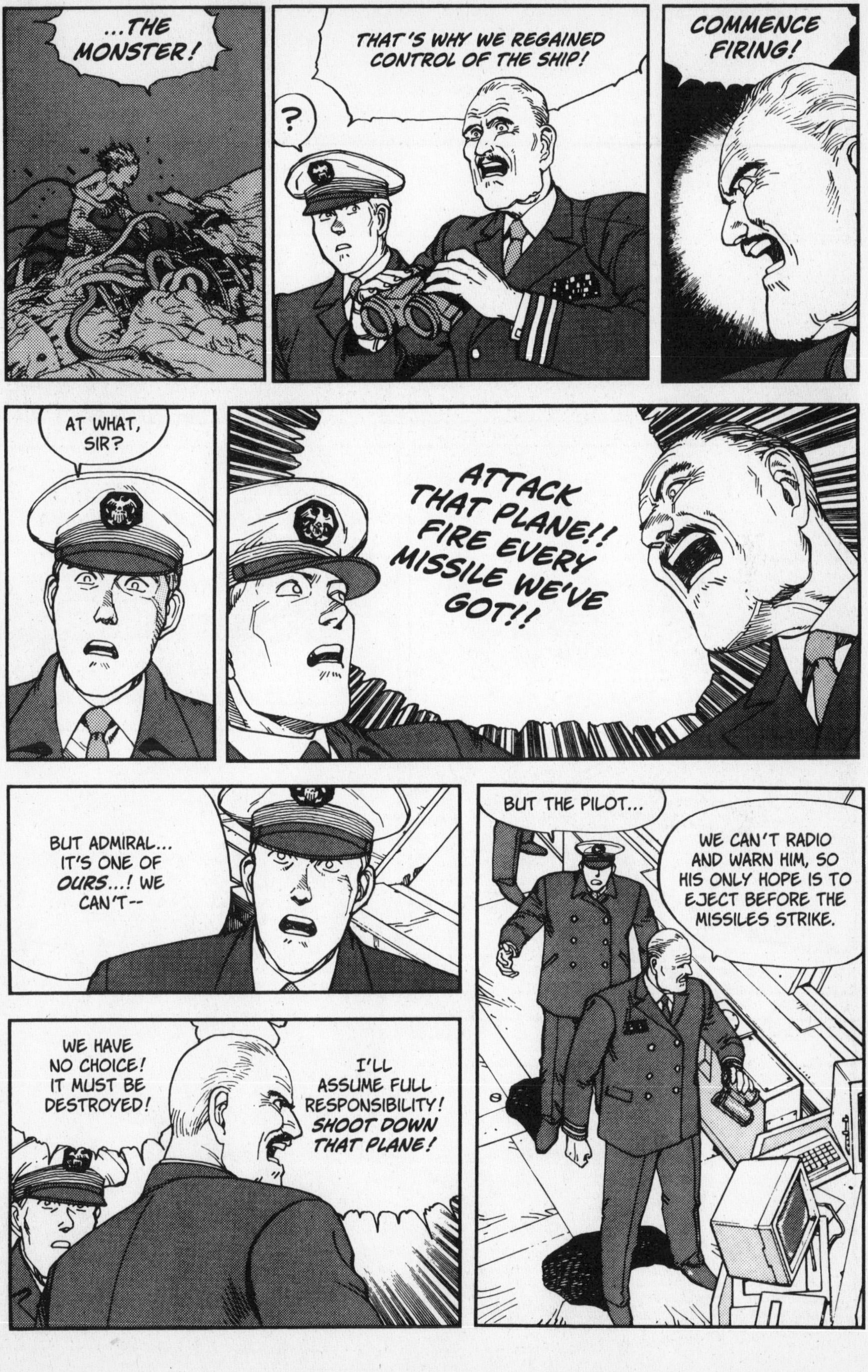
...THE MONSTER!
?
THAT'S WHY WE REGAINED CONTROL OF THE SHIP!
COMMENCE FIRING!
AT WHAT, SIR?
ATTACK THAT PLANE!! FIRE EVERY MISSILE WE'VE GOT!!
BUT ADMIRAL... IT'S ONE OF OURS...! WE CAN'T--
WE HAVE NO CHOICE! IT MUST BE DESTROYED!
I'LL ASSUME FULL RESPONSIBILITY! SHOOT DOWN THAT PLANE!
BUT THE PILOT...
WE CAN'T RADIO AND WARN HIM, SO HIS ONLY HOPE IS TO EJECT BEFORE THE MISSILES STRIKE.

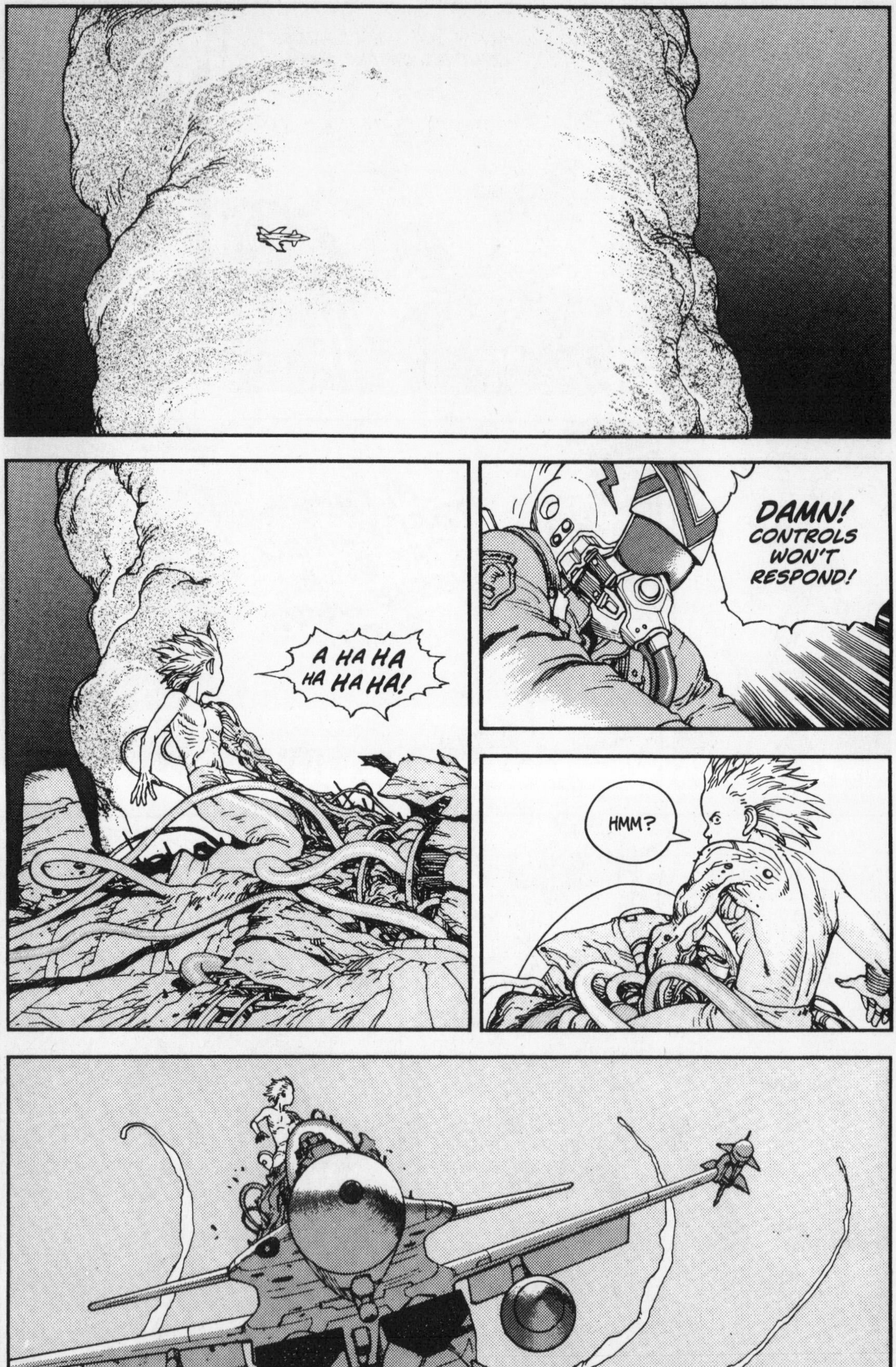
A HA HA
HA HA HA!
DAMN! CONTROLS WON'T RESPOND!
HMM?

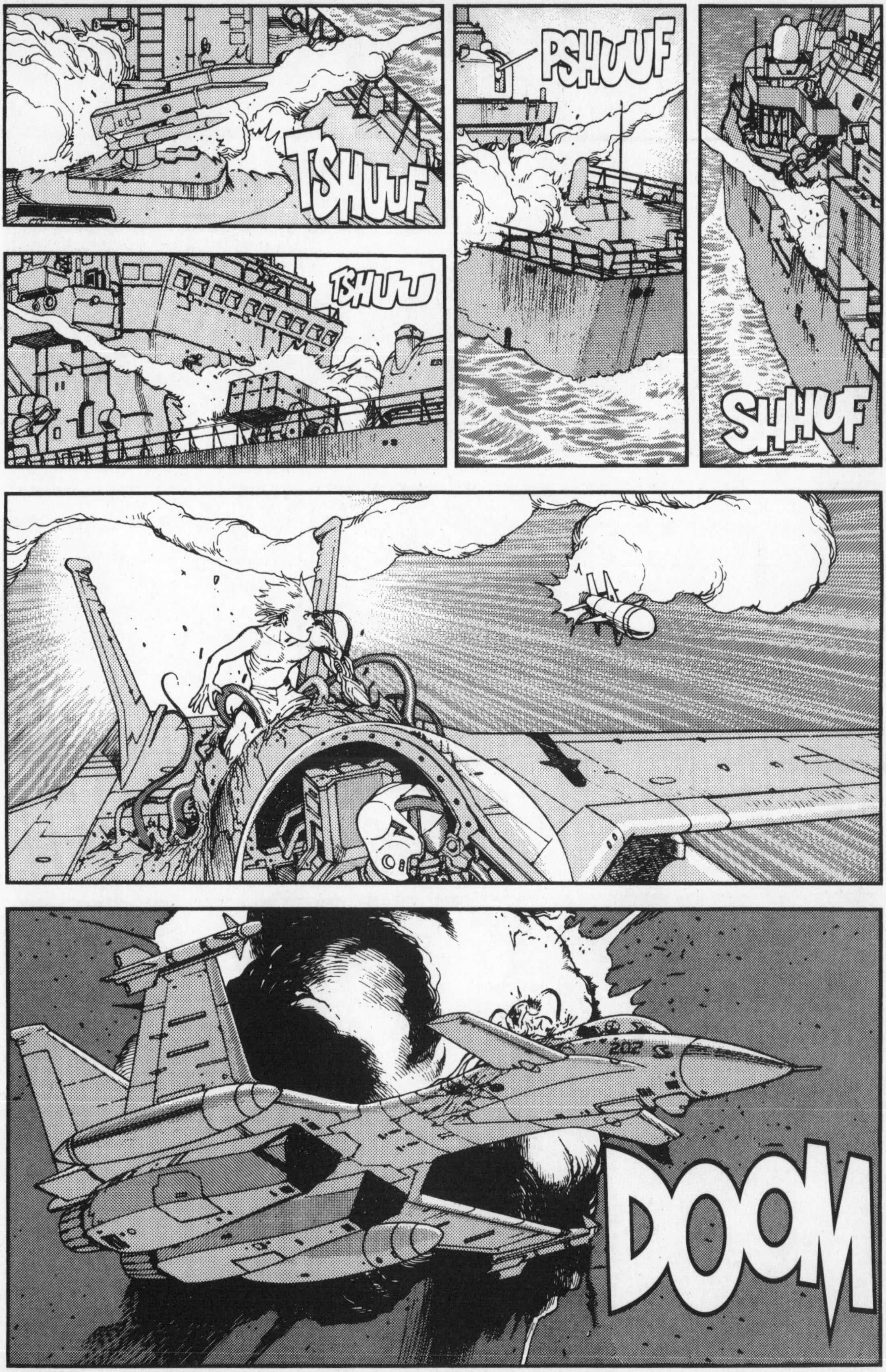
TSHUUF
PSHUUF
TSHUU
SHHUF
DOOM

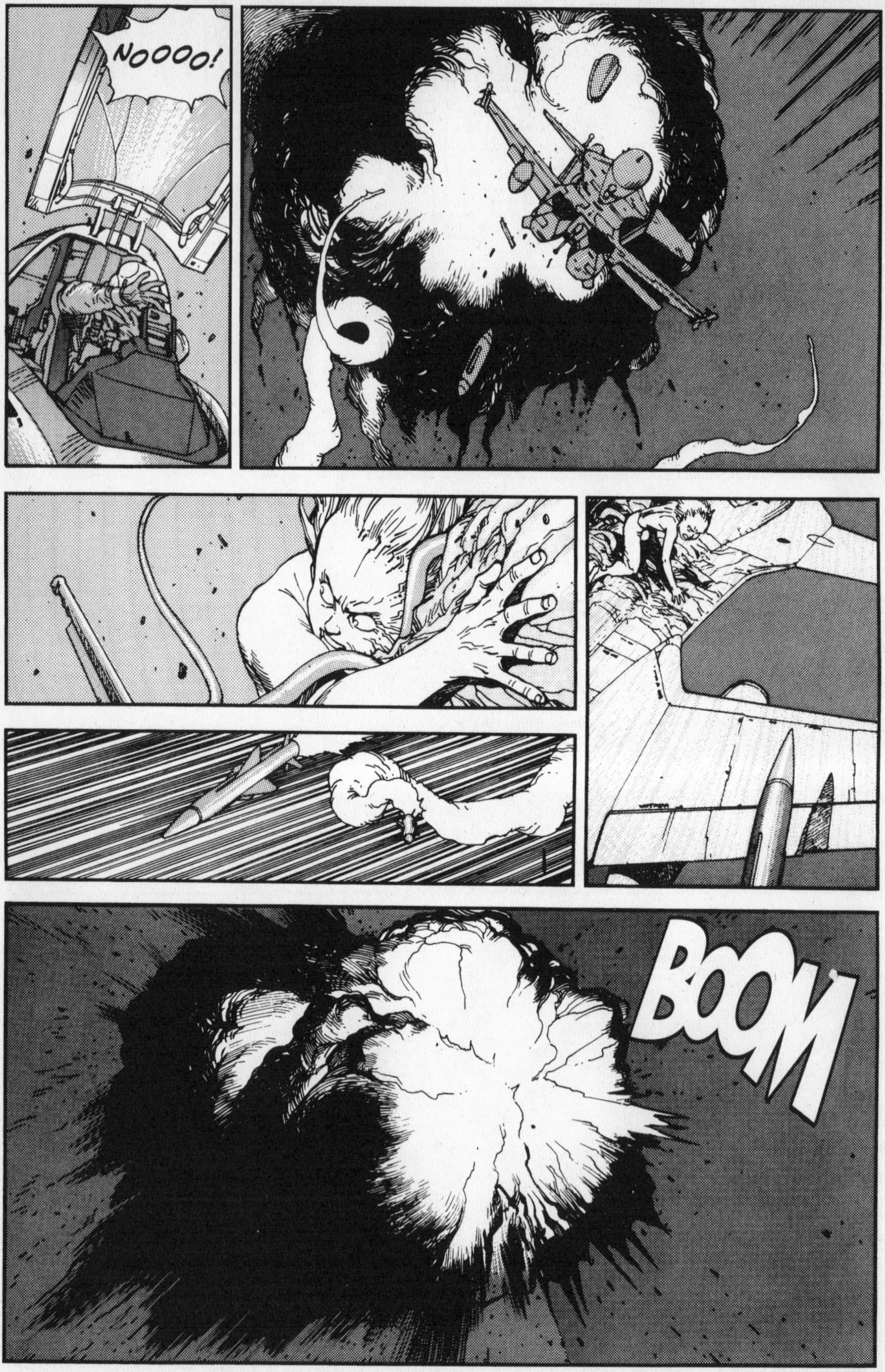
NOOOO!
BOOM

NOW IT'S MY TURN!

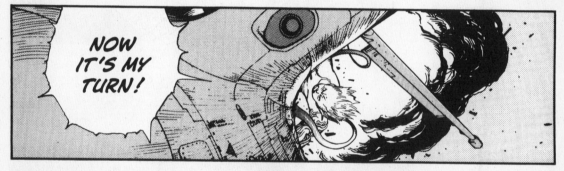

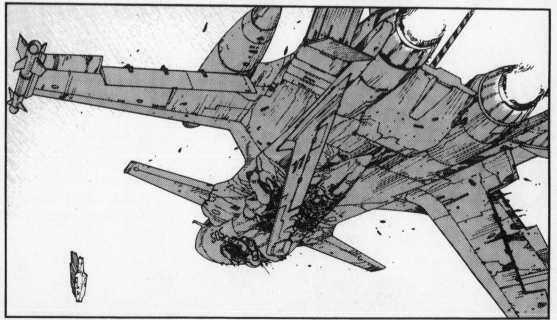

LIEUTENANT! THE PLANE IS DIVING ON US!

IMPOSSIBLE! WE BLEW IT TO HELL!

FSHOK

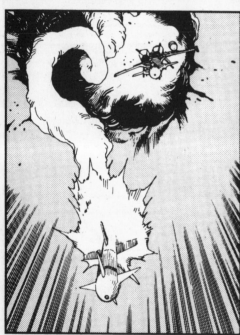

CHBAOF POUM

MISSILE LAUNCH! INCOMING ON OUR POSITION!

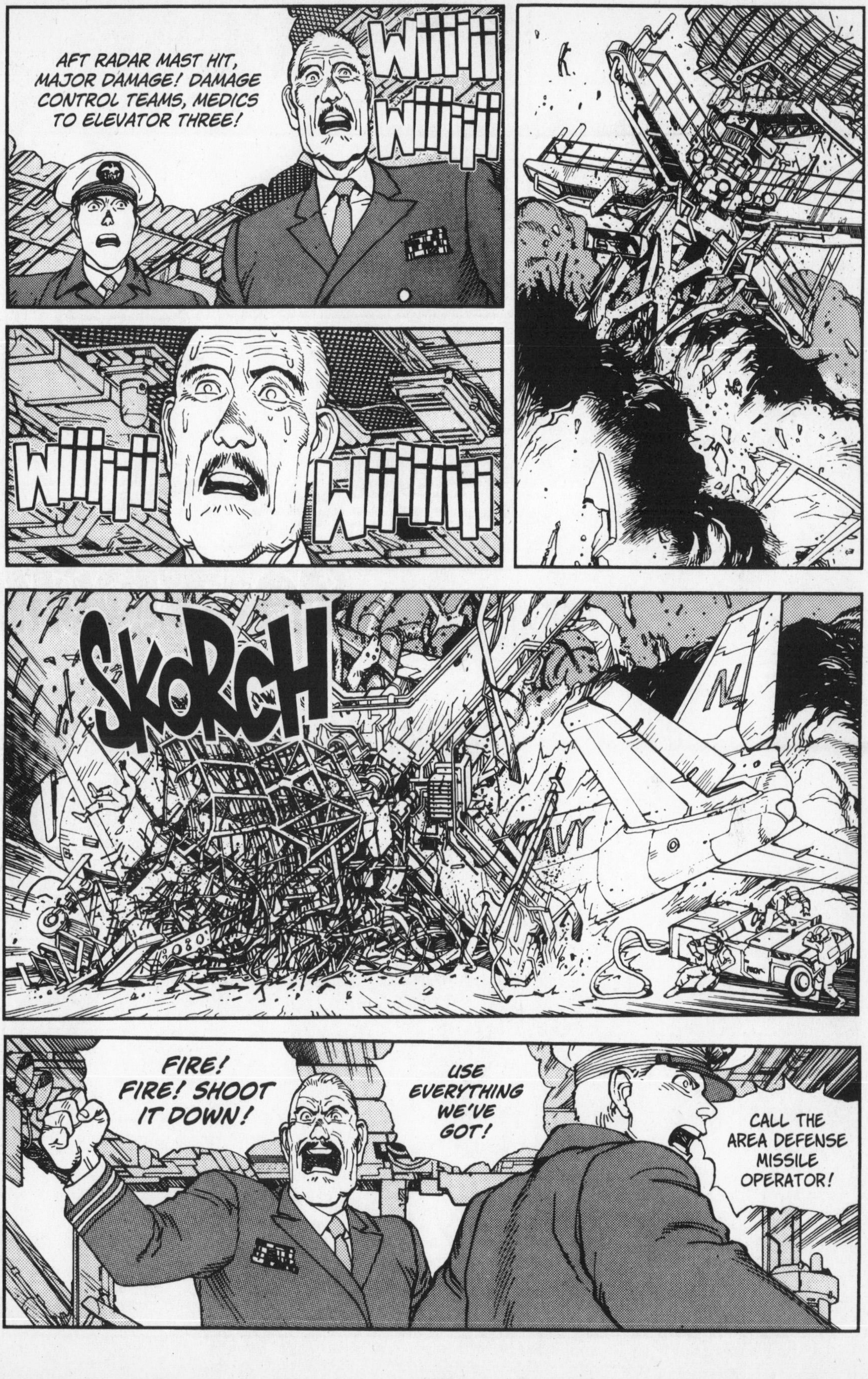
AFT RADAR MAST HIT, MAJOR DAMAGE! DAMAGE CONTROL TEAMS, MEDICS TO ELEVATOR THREE!
WIIIII WIIIIII
WIIIIII WIIIIIII
SKORCH
FIRE! FIRE! SHOOT IT DOWN!
USE EVERYTHING WE'VE GOT!
CALL THE AREA DEFENSE MISSILE OPERATOR!

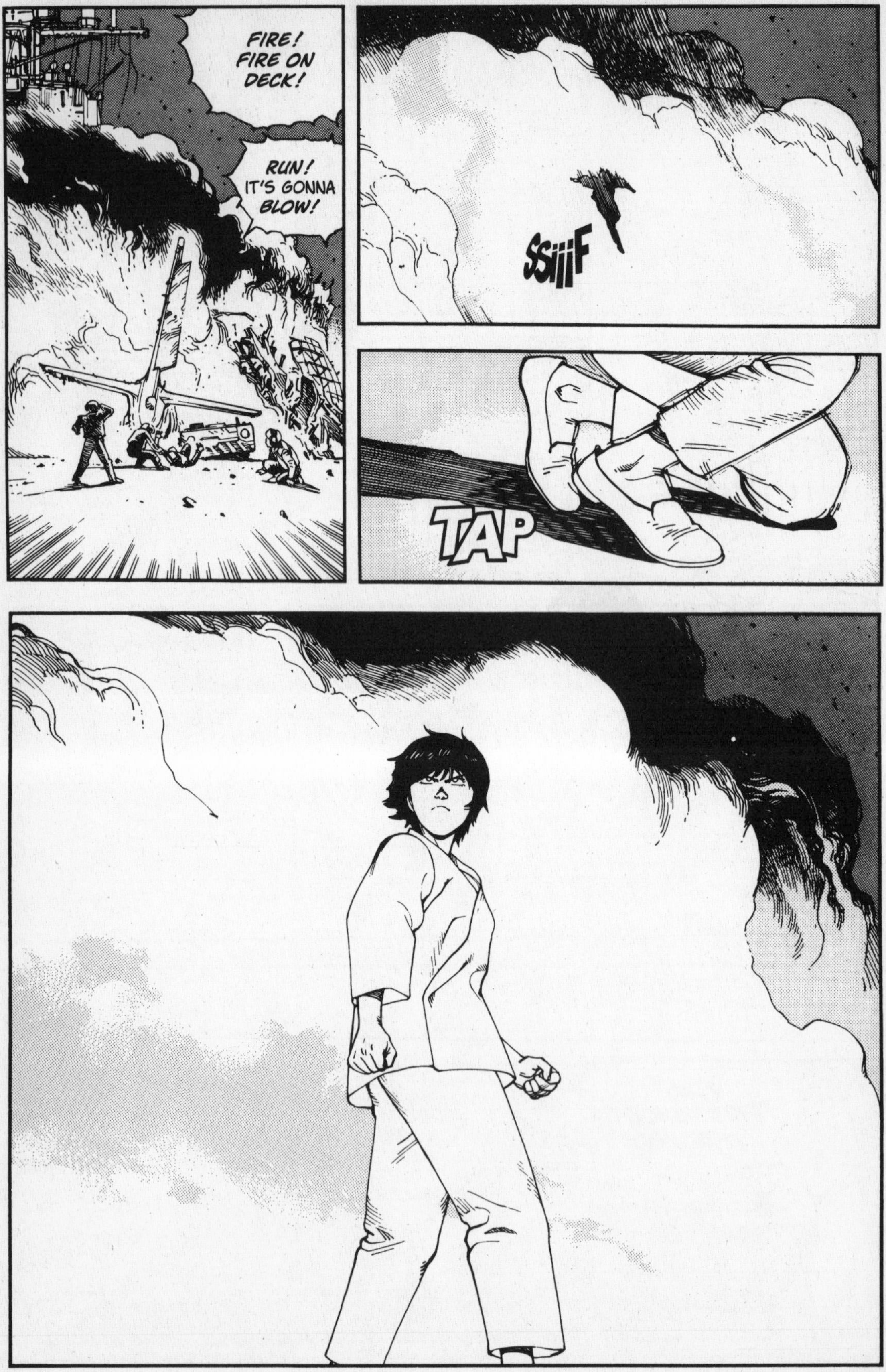
FIRE! FIRE ON DECK!
RUN! IT'S GONNA BLOW!
SSiiiiF
TAP

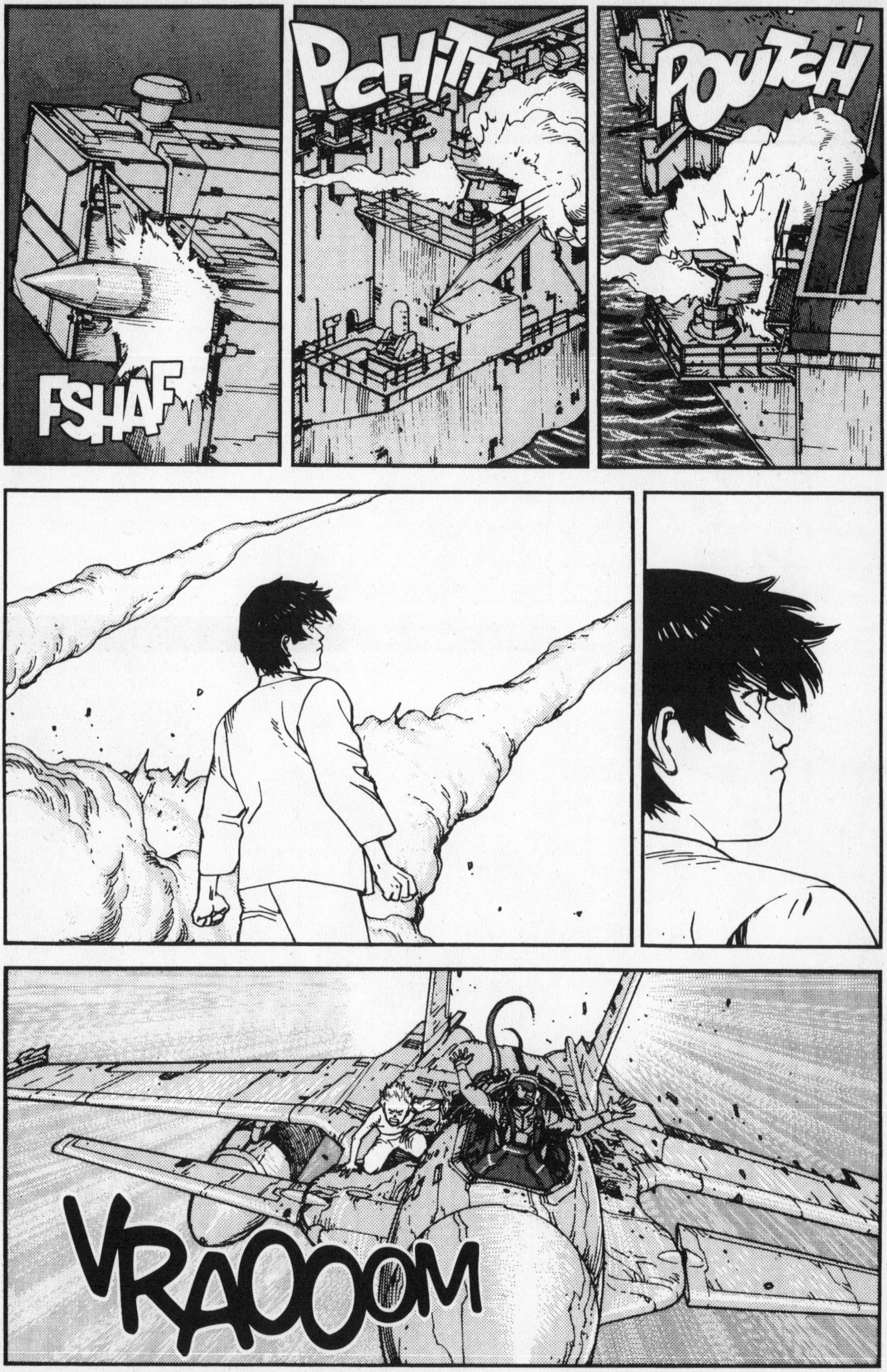
FSHAF
PCHITT
POUTCH
VRAOOOM

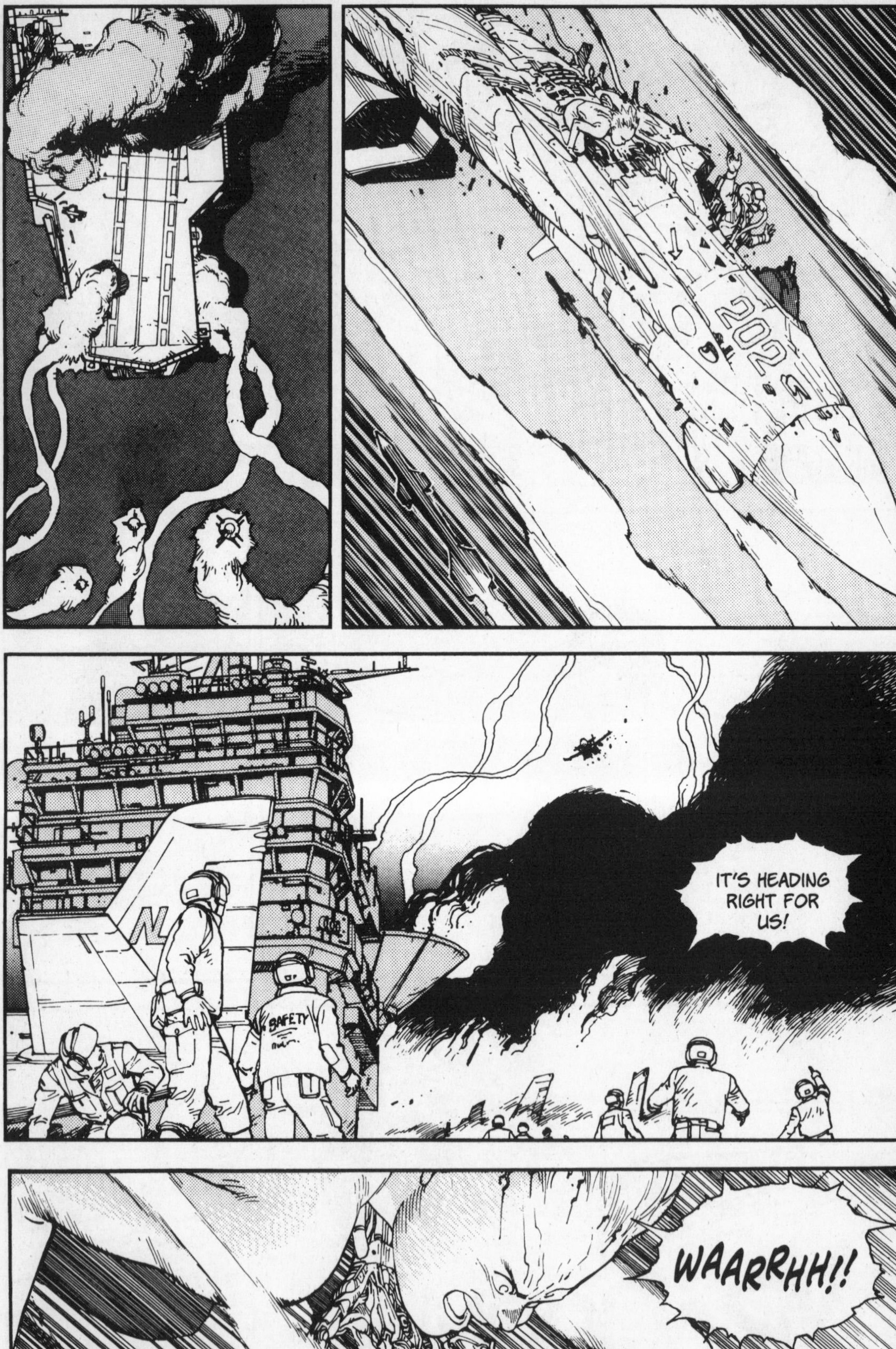
IT'S HEADING RIGHT FOR US!
WAARRHH!!

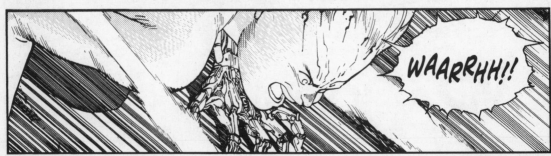

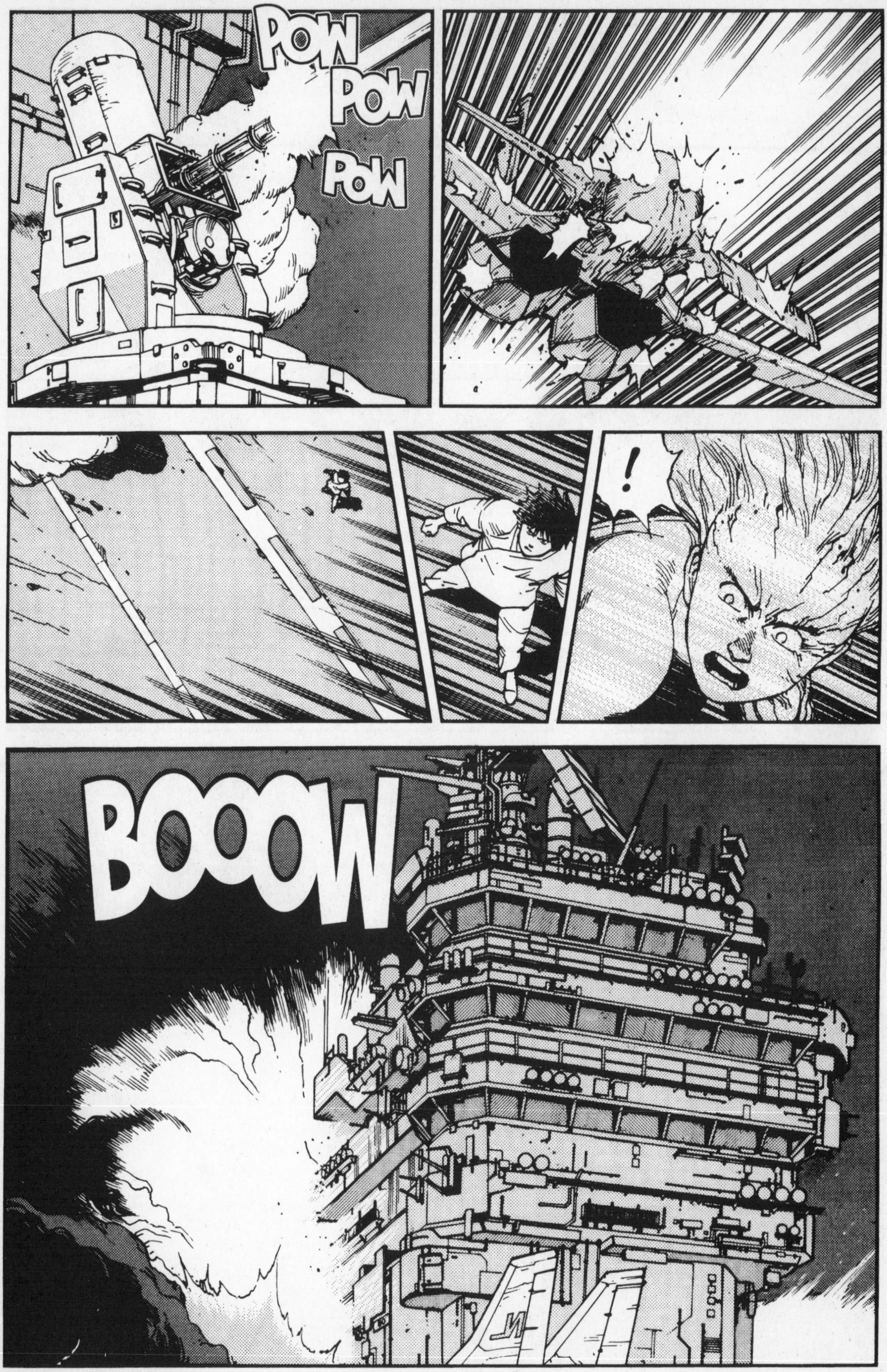
POW
POW
POW
!
BOOOW

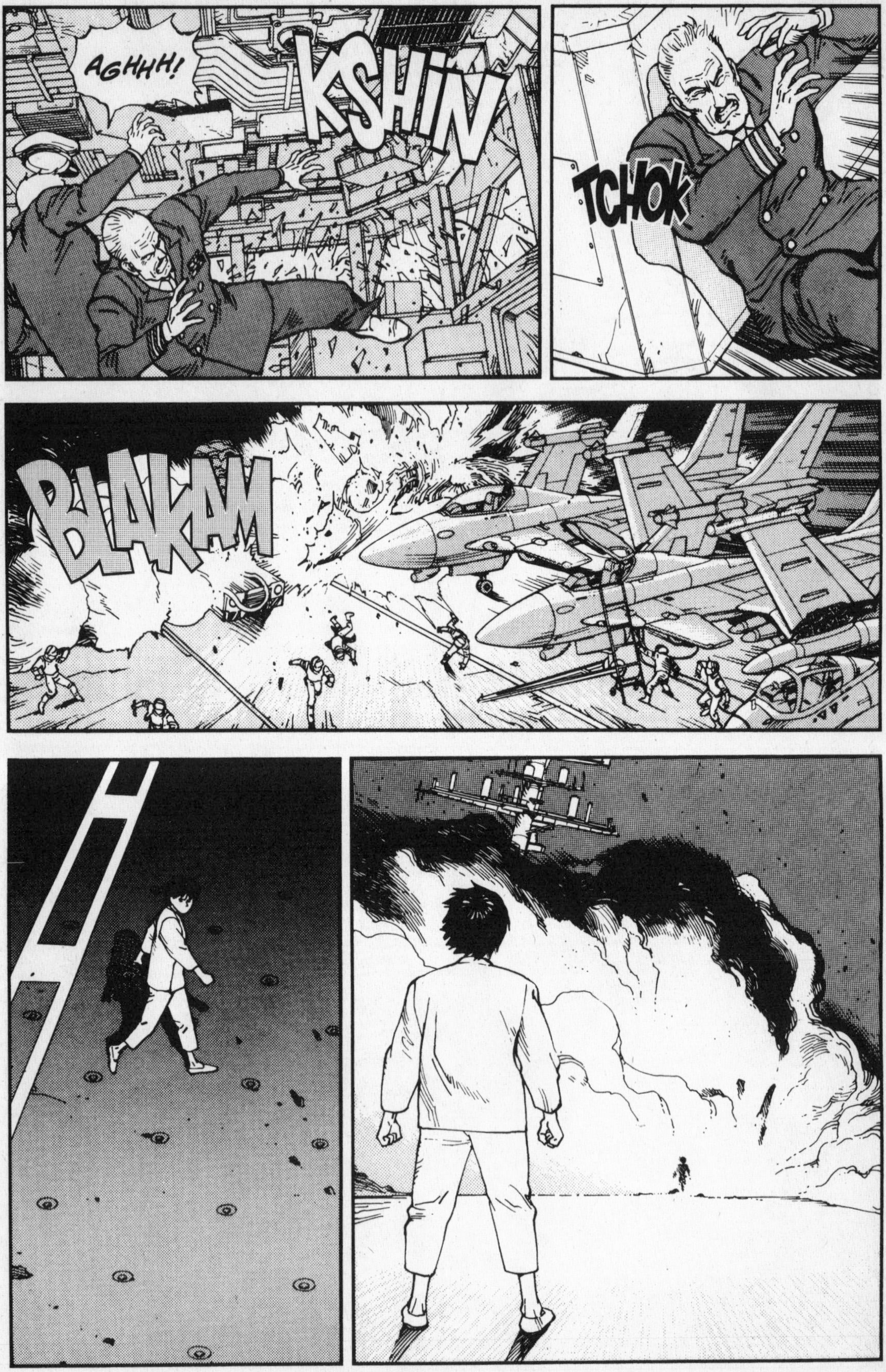
AGHHH!
KSHIN
TCHOK
BLAKAM

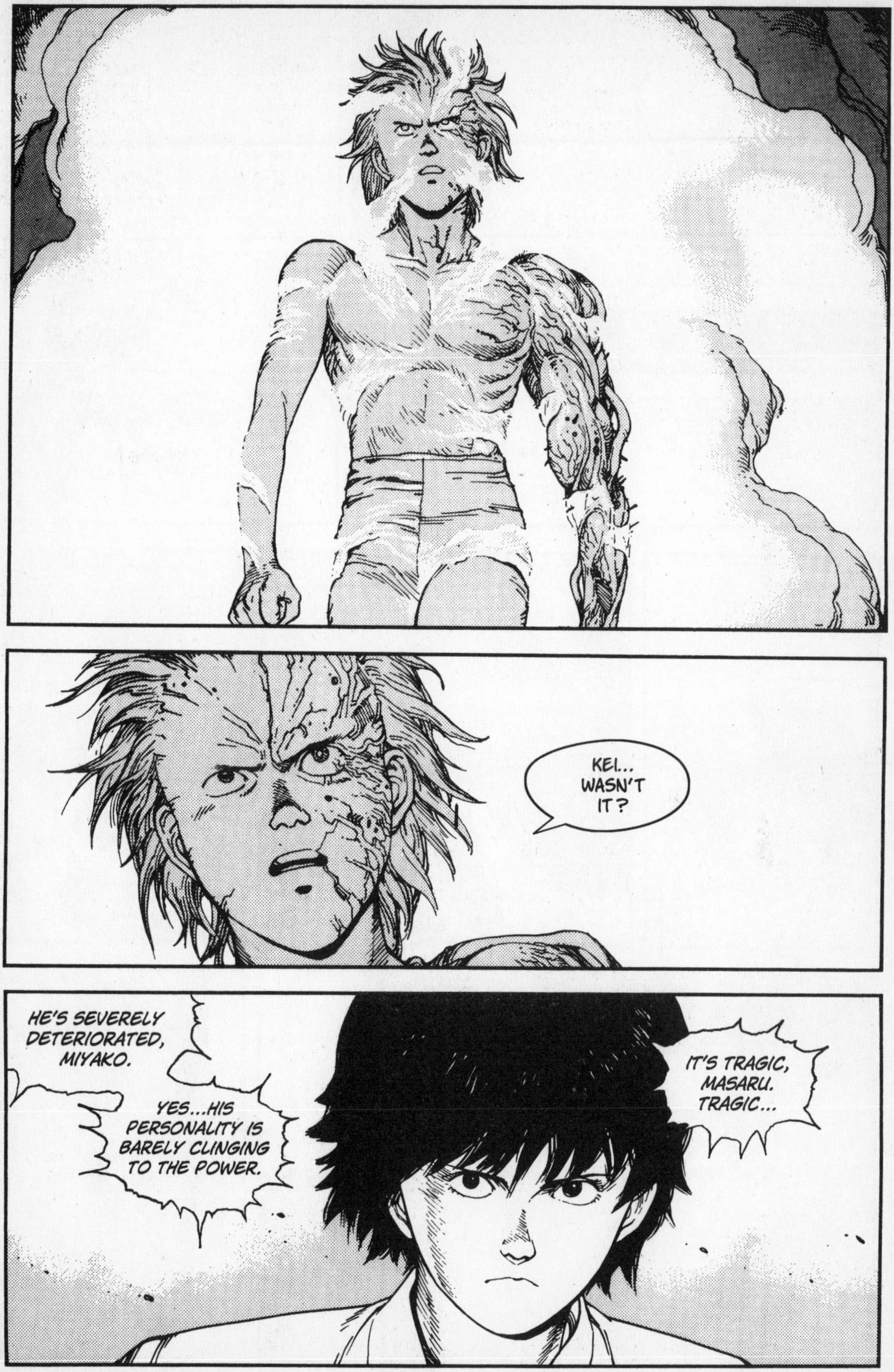
KEI... WASN'T IT?
HE'S SEVERELY DETERIORATED, MIYAKO.
YES...HIS PERSONALITY IS BARELY CLINGING TO THE POWER.
IT'S TRAGIC, MASARU. TRAGIC...

HRRG...!

SO EVEN GRANNY MIYAKO'S ONBOARD, HUH?

NICE PARTY YOU GOT THERE.

WATCH OUT, KEI! HE'S TARGETING YOU!

EH?!

HERE'S A LITTLE PRESENT... FOR OUR LOVELY REUNION.

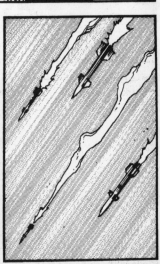

THIS WON'T WORK HERE. TOO MANY PEOPLE COULD GET HURT.

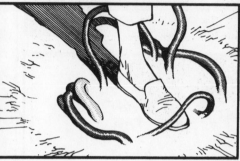

EEEK!

KEEP YOUR SPIRIT CALM, MY DEAR!

CENTER YOUR ENERGY!

COME ON, COME ON... MISSILES COMIN' TO GETCHA!

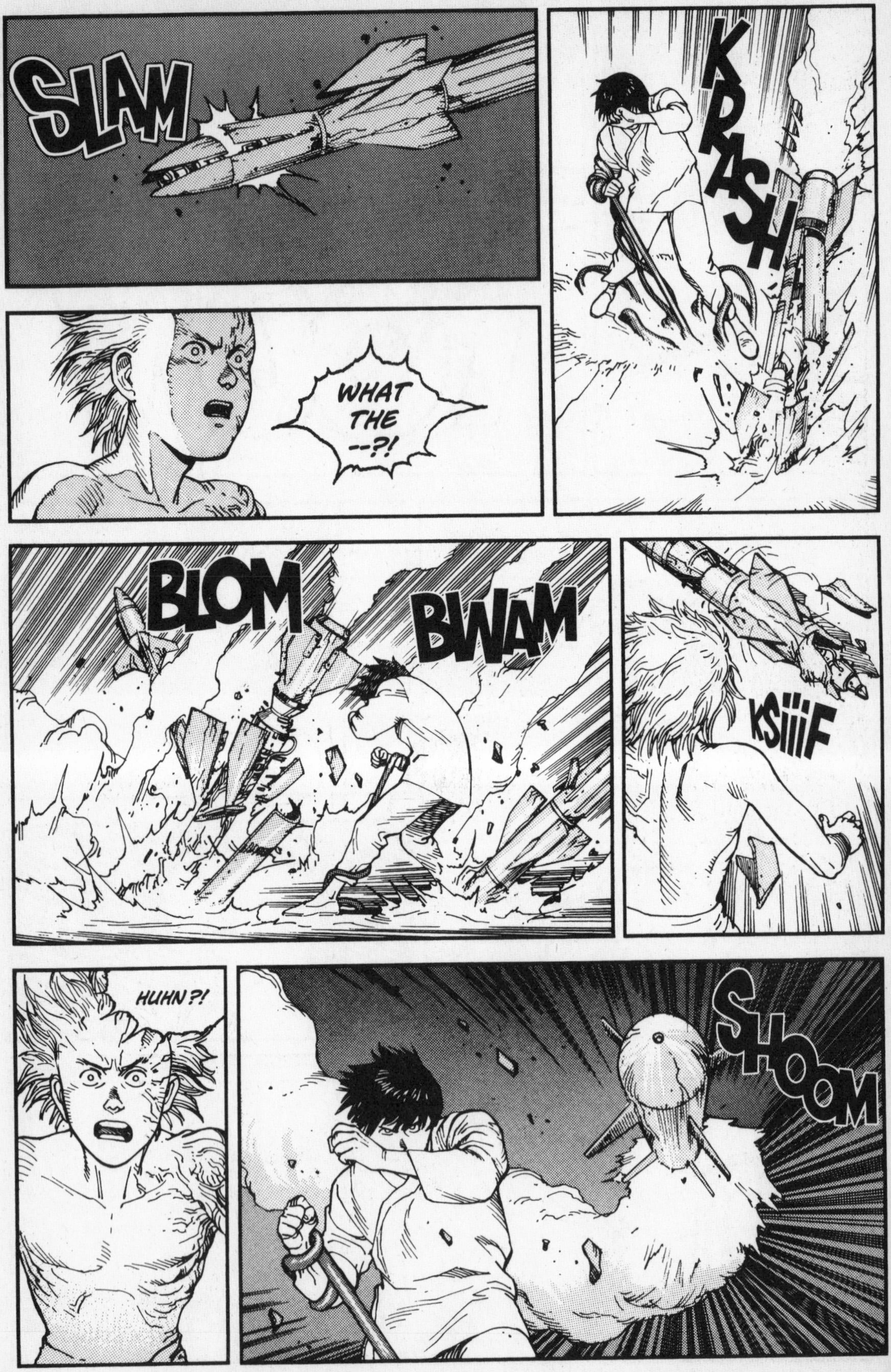
SLAM
KRASH
WHAT THE --?!
BLOM
BWAM
KSIIIIF
HUHN?!
SHOOM

POUM

TETSUO ?!

DON'T PANIC!

THAT LITTLE THING WON'T KILL HIM.

BUT--!

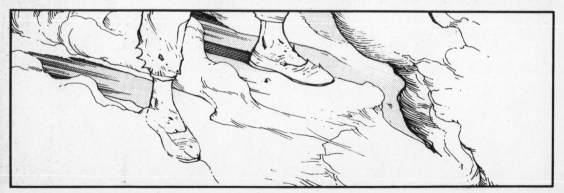

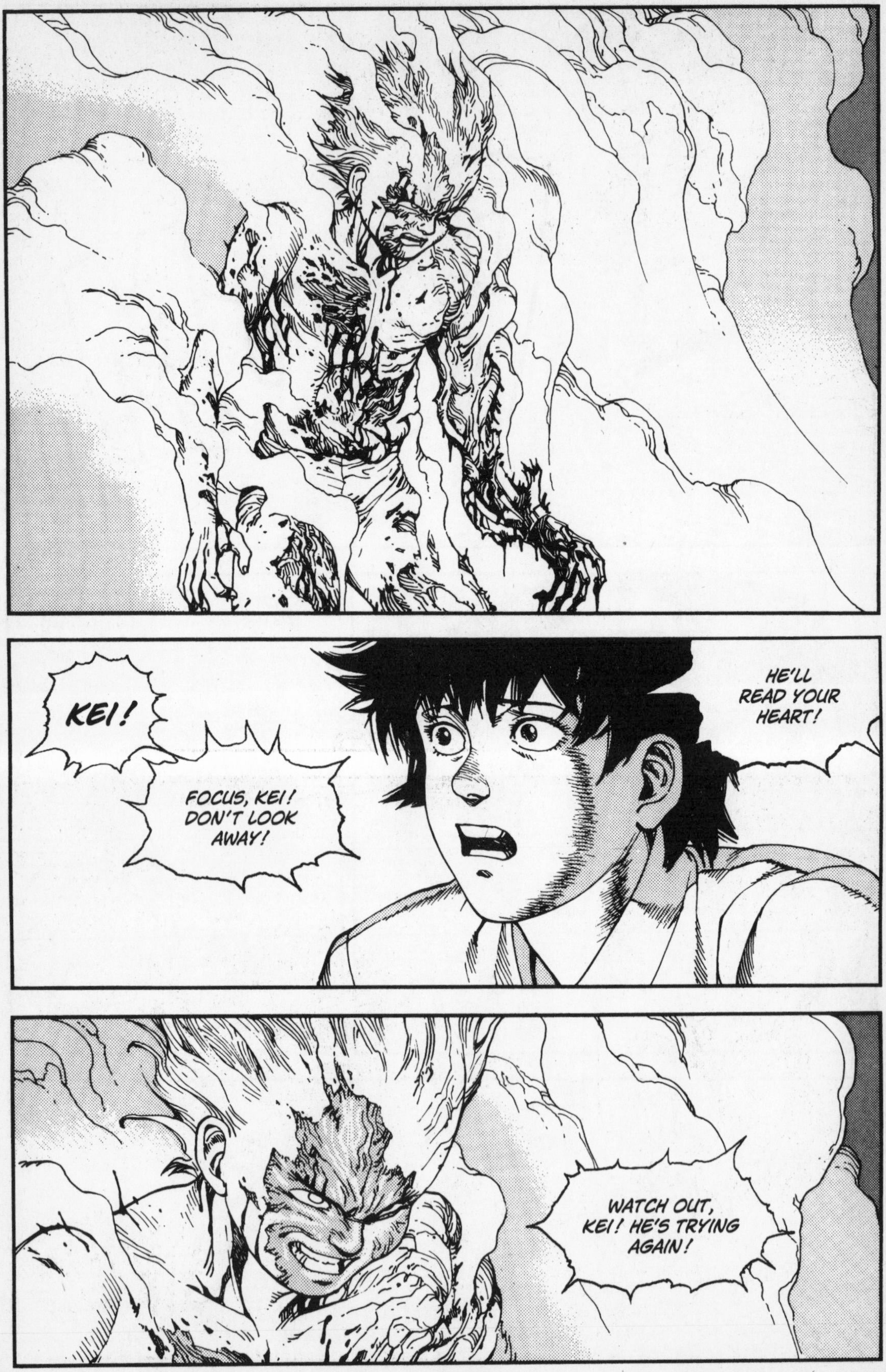
KEI!
FOCUS, KEI! DON'T LOOK AWAY!
HE'LL READ YOUR HEART!
WATCH OUT, KEI! HE'S TRYING AGAIN!

AHH!

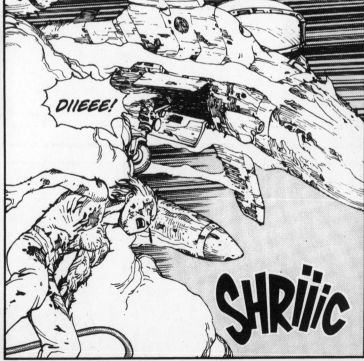

DIIEEE!

SHRiiic

YAAAAH!
NO STEP
SWIIIIF
NO STEP
HUHN ?

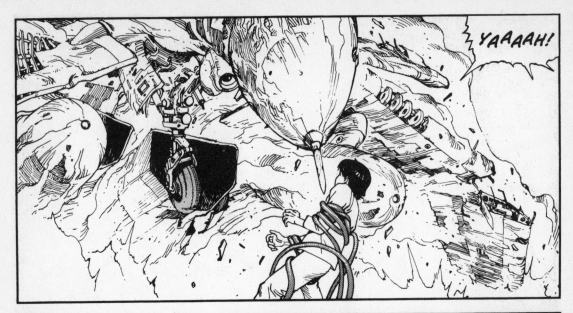

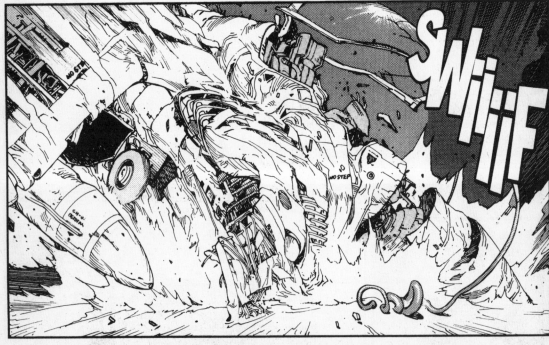

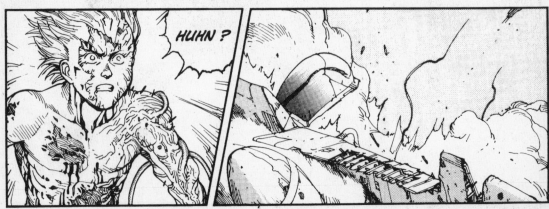

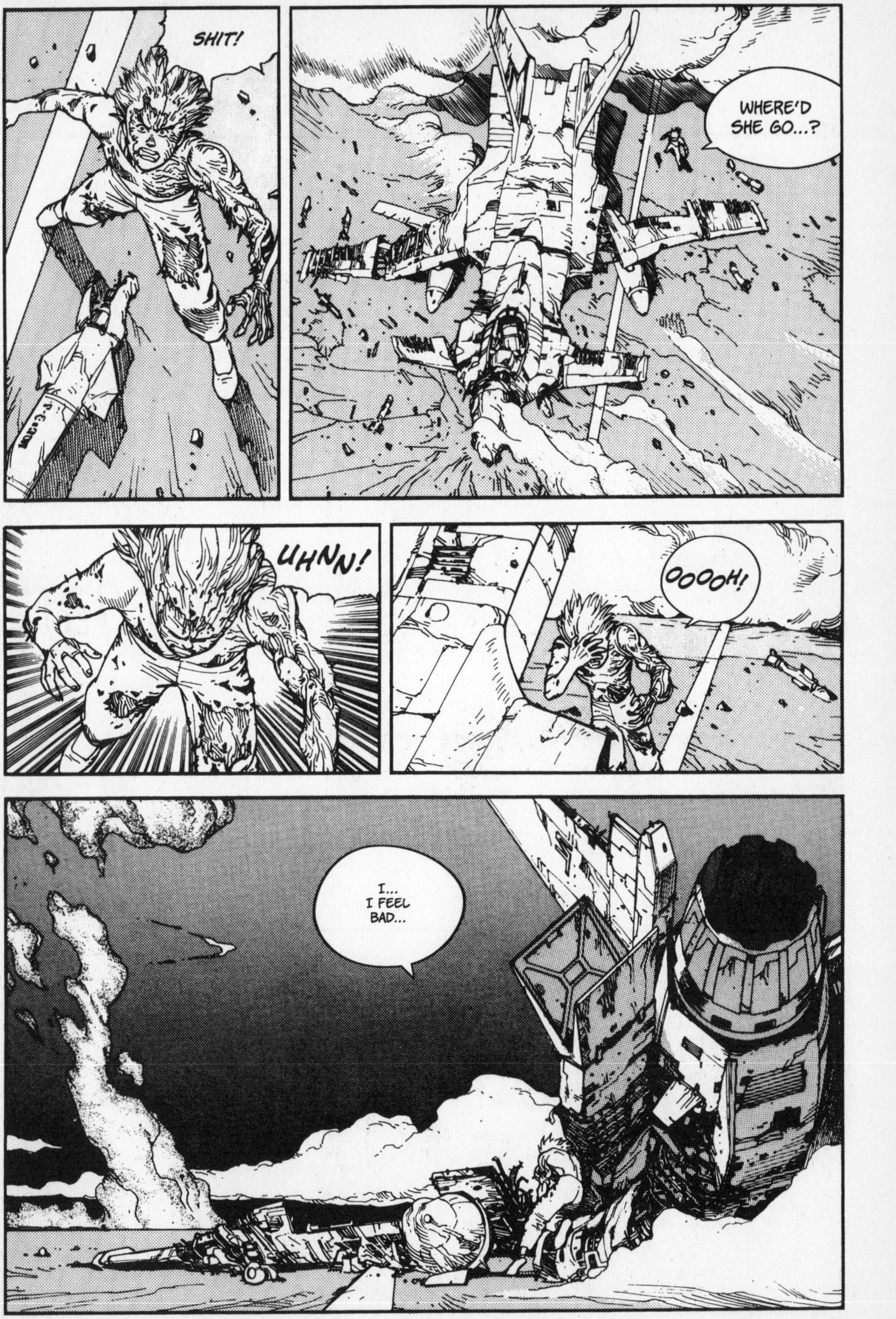
SHIT!
WHERE'D SHE GO...?
UHNN!
OOOOH!
I... I FEEL BAD...

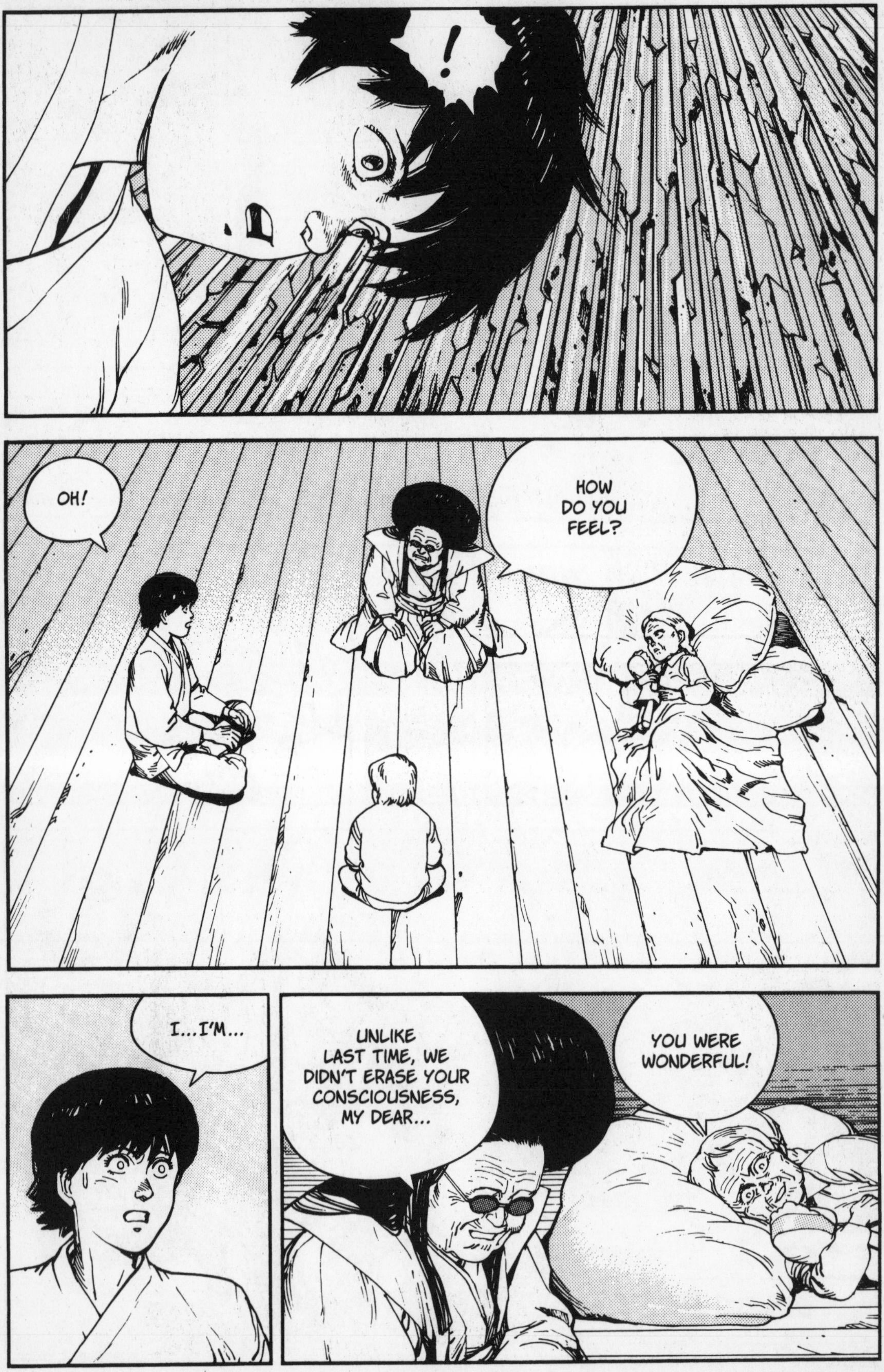
!
OH!
HOW DO YOU FEEL?
I...I'M...
UNLIKE LAST TIME, WE DIDN'T ERASE YOUR CONSCIOUSNESS, MY DEAR...
YOU WERE WONDERFUL!

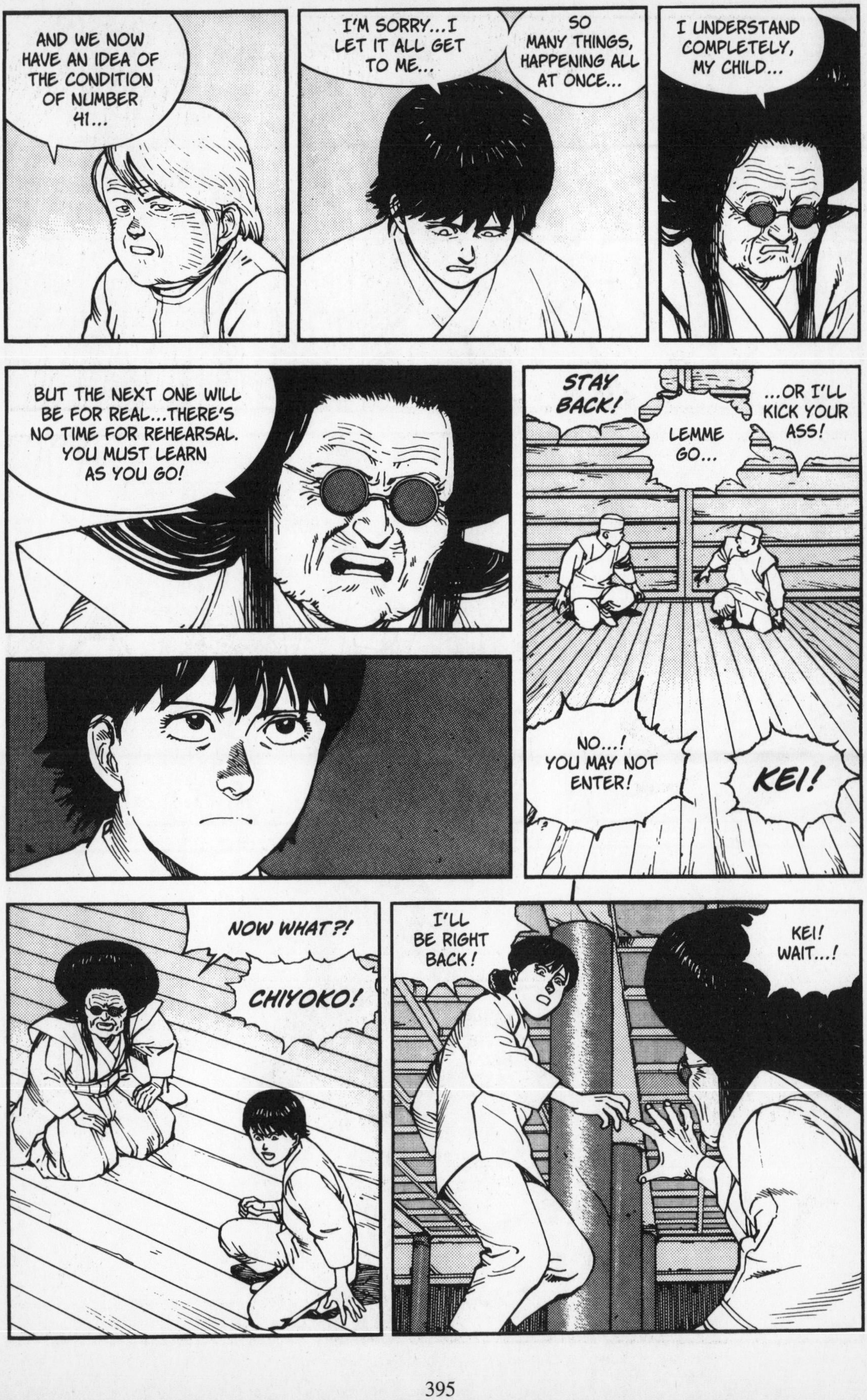
AND WE NOW HAVE AN IDEA OF THE CONDITION OF NUMBER 41...
I'M SORRY...I LET IT ALL GET TO ME...
SO MANY THINGS, HAPPENING ALL AT ONCE...
I UNDERSTAND COMPLETELY, MY CHILD...
BUT THE NEXT ONE WILL BE FOR REAL...THERE'S NO TIME FOR REHEARSAL. YOU MUST LEARN AS YOU GO!
STAY BACK!
LEMME GO...
...OR I'LL KICK YOUR ASS!
NO...! YOU MAY NOT ENTER!
KEI!
NOW WHAT?!
CHIYOKO!
I'LL BE RIGHT BACK!
KEI! WAIT...!

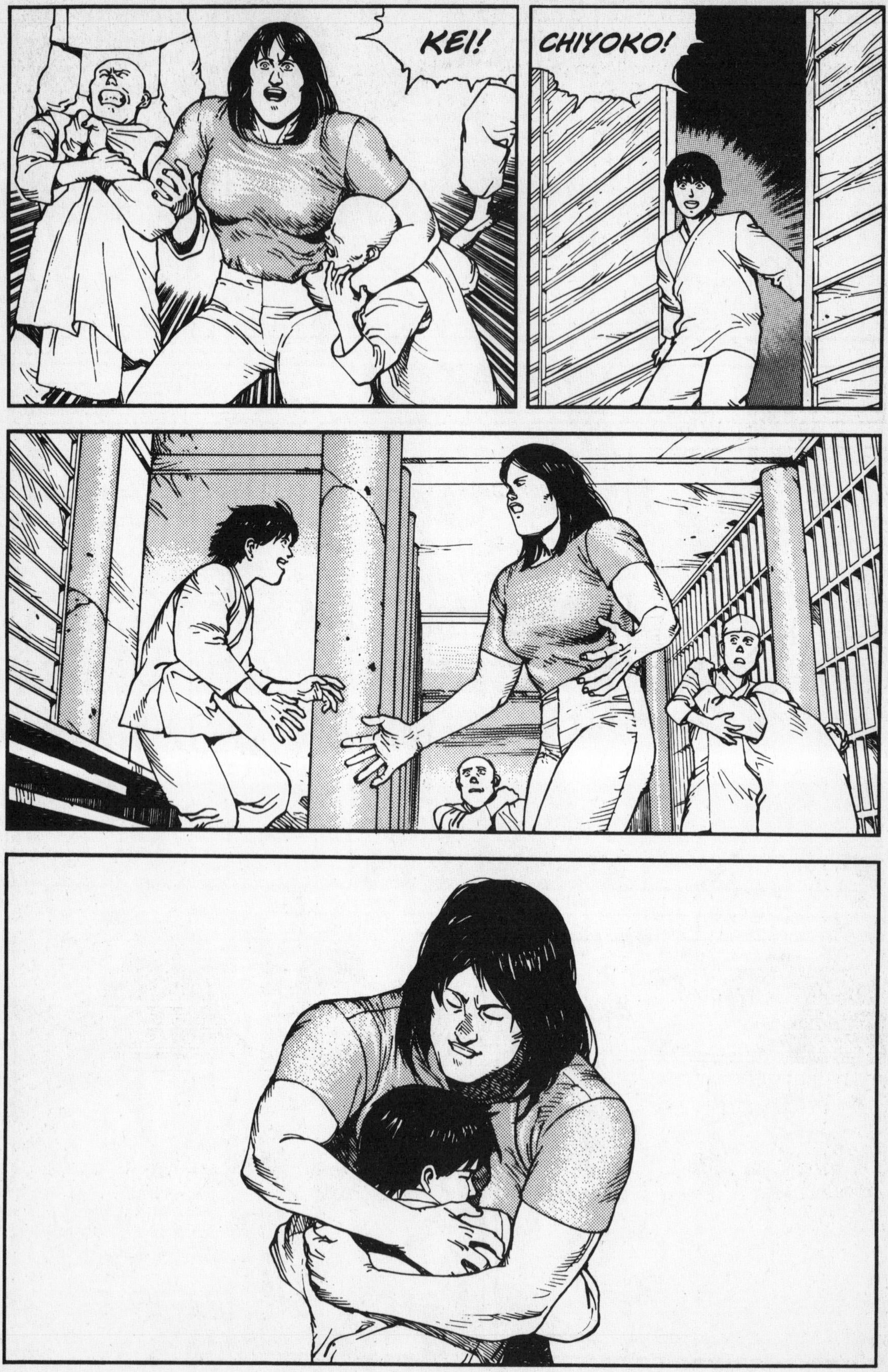
KEI!
CHIYOKO!

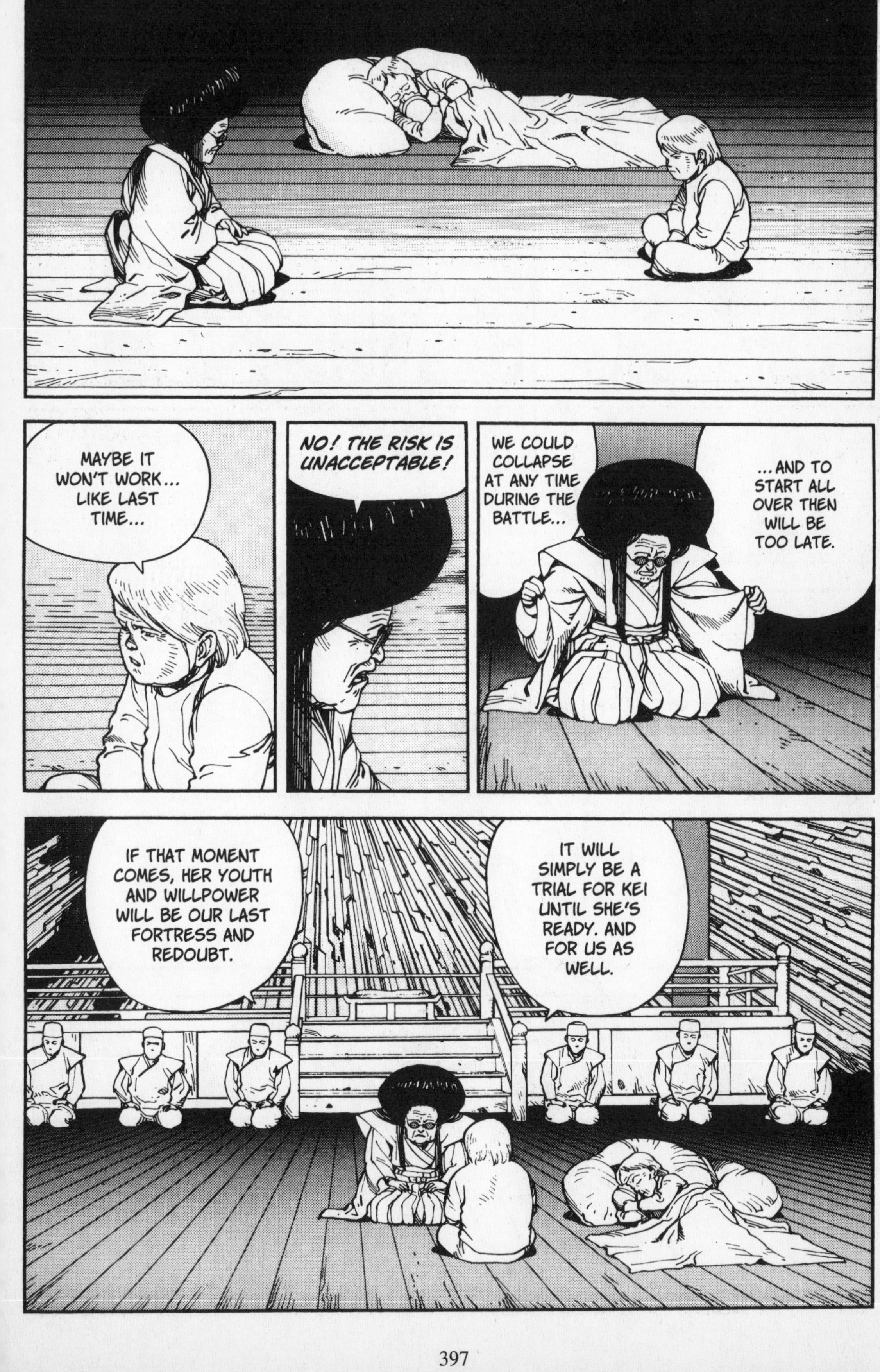
MAYBE IT WON'T WORK... LIKE LAST TIME...
NO! THE RISK IS UNACCEPTABLE!
WE COULD COLLAPSE AT ANY TIME DURING THE BATTLE...
...AND TO START ALL OVER THEN WILL BE TOO LATE.
IF THAT MOMENT COMES, HER YOUTH AND WILLPOWER WILL BE OUR LAST FORTRESS AND REDOUBT.
IT WILL SIMPLY BE A TRIAL FOR KEI UNTIL SHE'S READY. AND FOR US AS WELL.

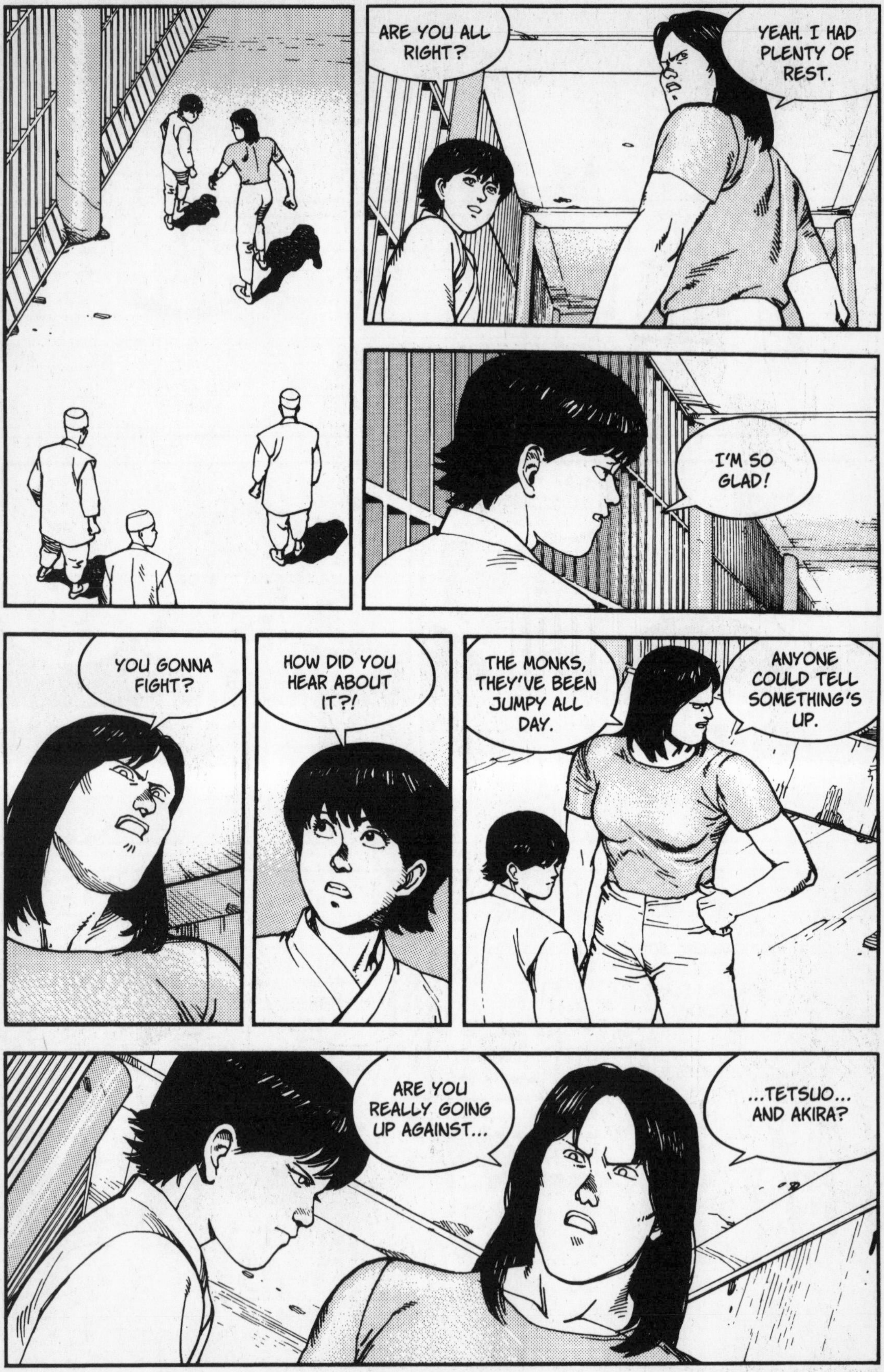
ARE YOU ALL RIGHT?
YEAH. I HAD PLENTY OF REST.
I'M SO GLAD!
YOU GONNA FIGHT?
HOW DID YOU HEAR ABOUT IT?!
THE MONKS, THEY'VE BEEN JUMPY ALL DAY.
ANYONE COULD TELL SOMETHING'S UP.
ARE YOU REALLY GOING UP AGAINST...
...TETSUO... AND AKIRA?

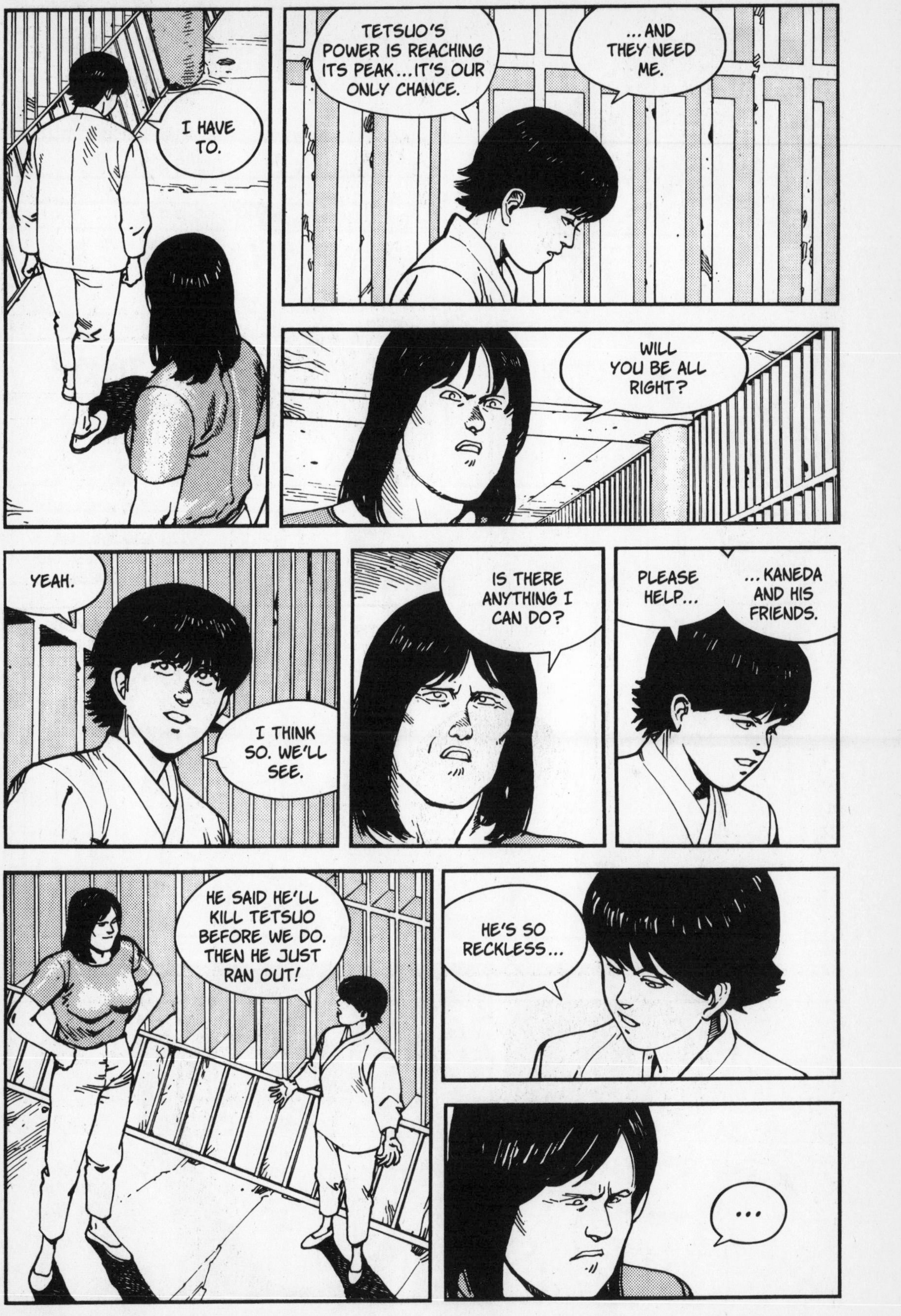
I HAVE TO.
TETSUO'S POWER IS REACHING ITS PEAK...IT'S OUR ONLY CHANCE.
...AND THEY NEED ME.
WILL YOU BE ALL RIGHT?
YEAH.
I THINK SO. WE'LL SEE.
IS THERE ANYTHING I CAN DO?
PLEASE HELP...
...KANEDA AND HIS FRIENDS.
HE SAID HE'LL KILL TETSUO BEFORE WE DO. THEN HE JUST RAN OUT!
HE'S SO RECKLESS...
...

STAY ALIVE.

HUH?

TCHOP

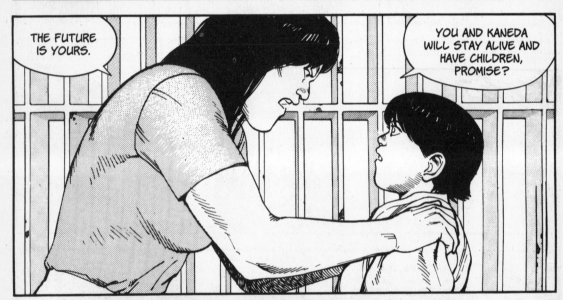

THE FUTURE IS YOURS.

YOU AND KANEDA WILL STAY ALIVE AND HAVE CHILDREN, PROMISE?

O-OKAY...

I'M COUNTING ON YOU.

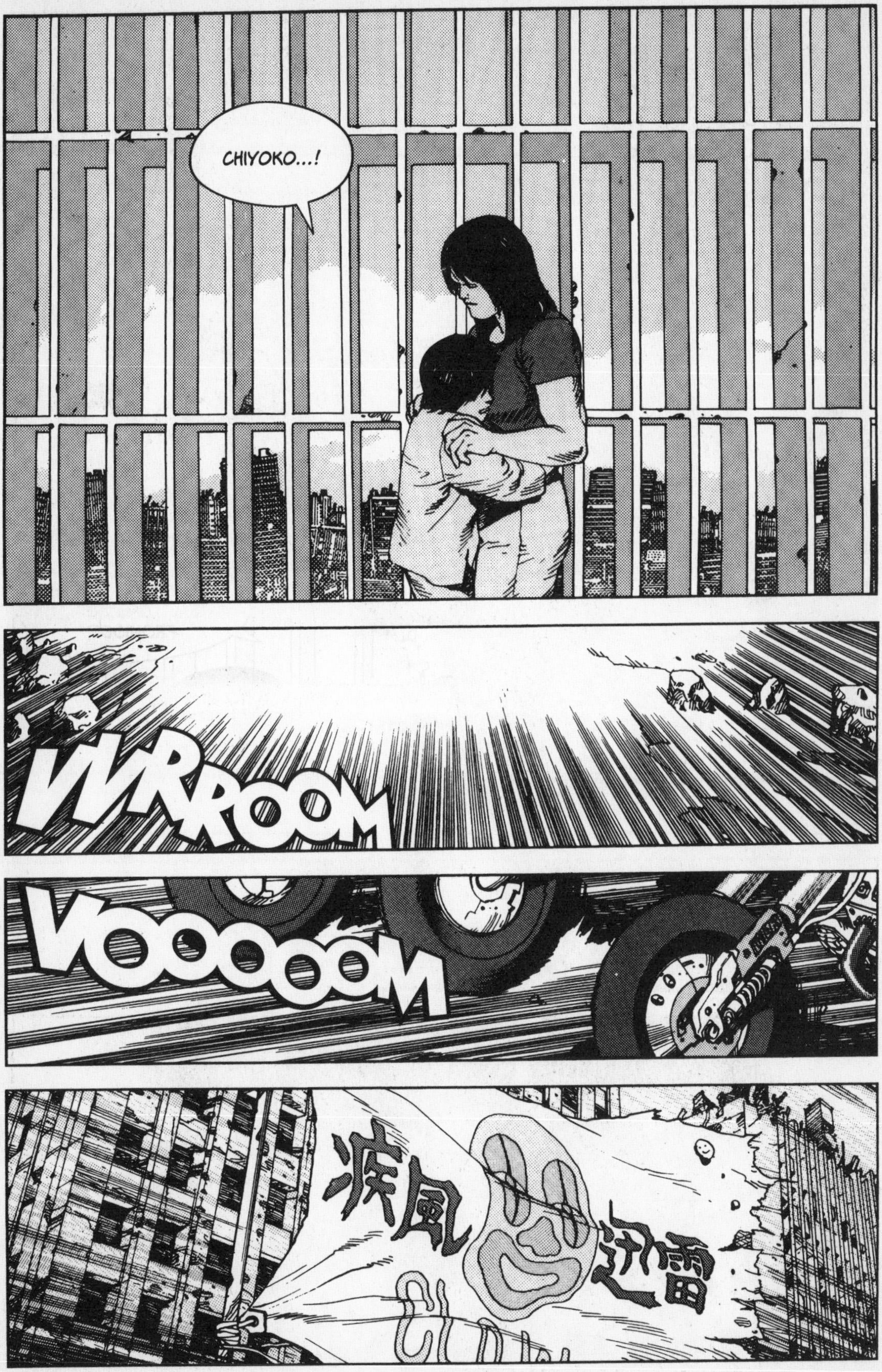
CHIYOKO...!
VVRROOM
VOOOOOM
疾風
迅雷

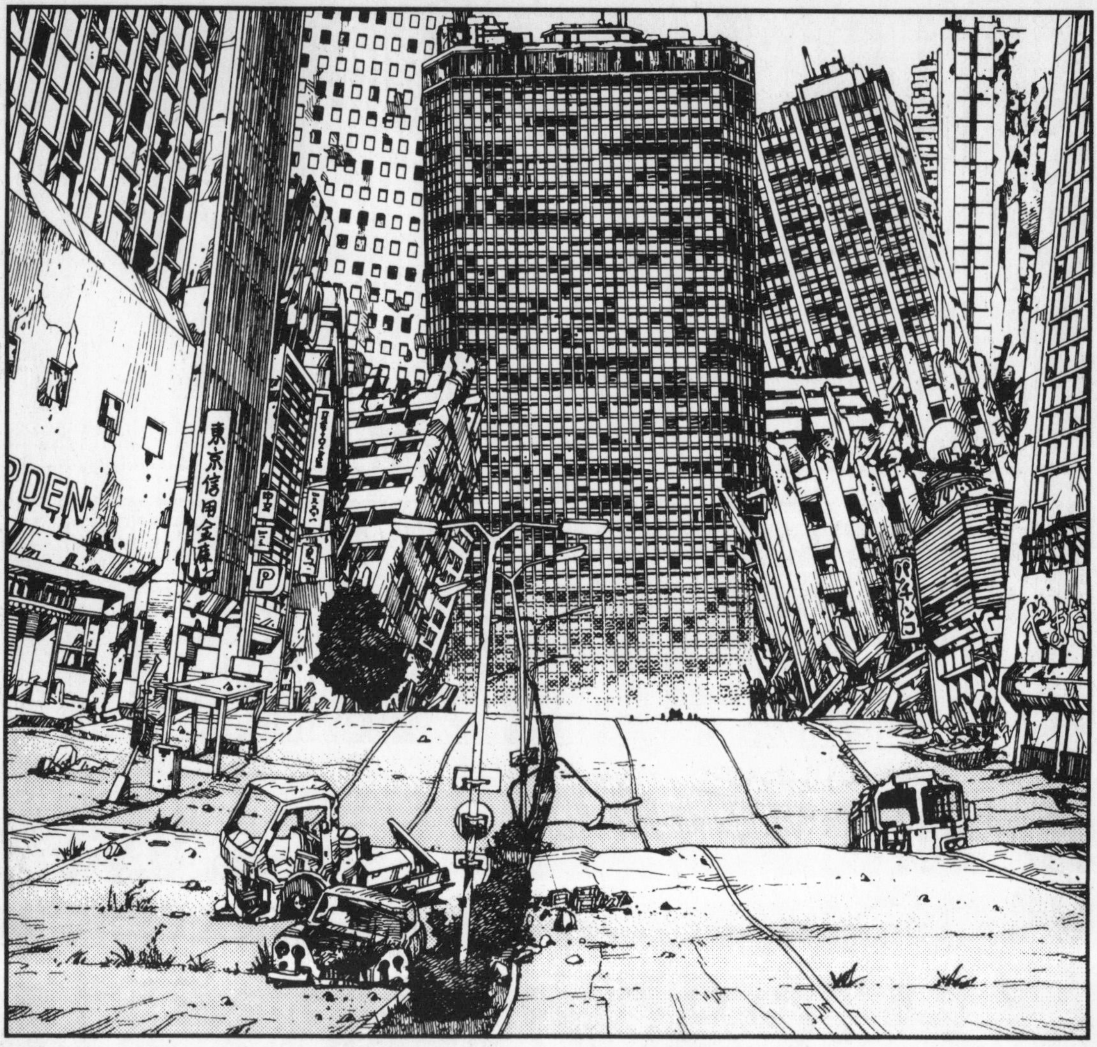
東京信用金庫

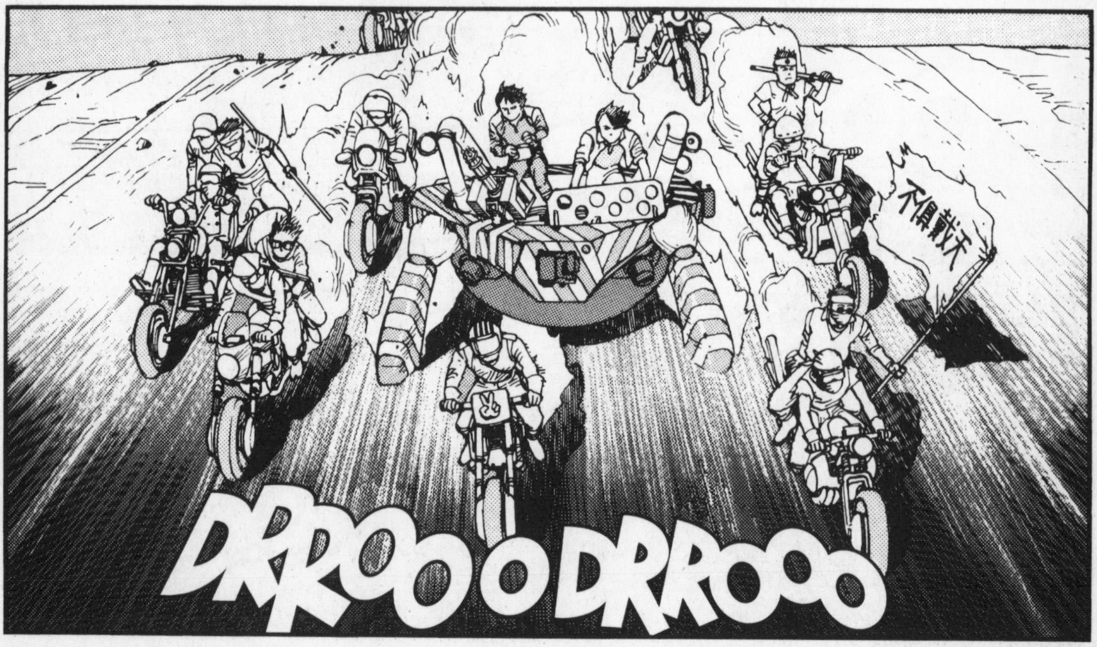
不倶戴天
DRROOO DRROOO

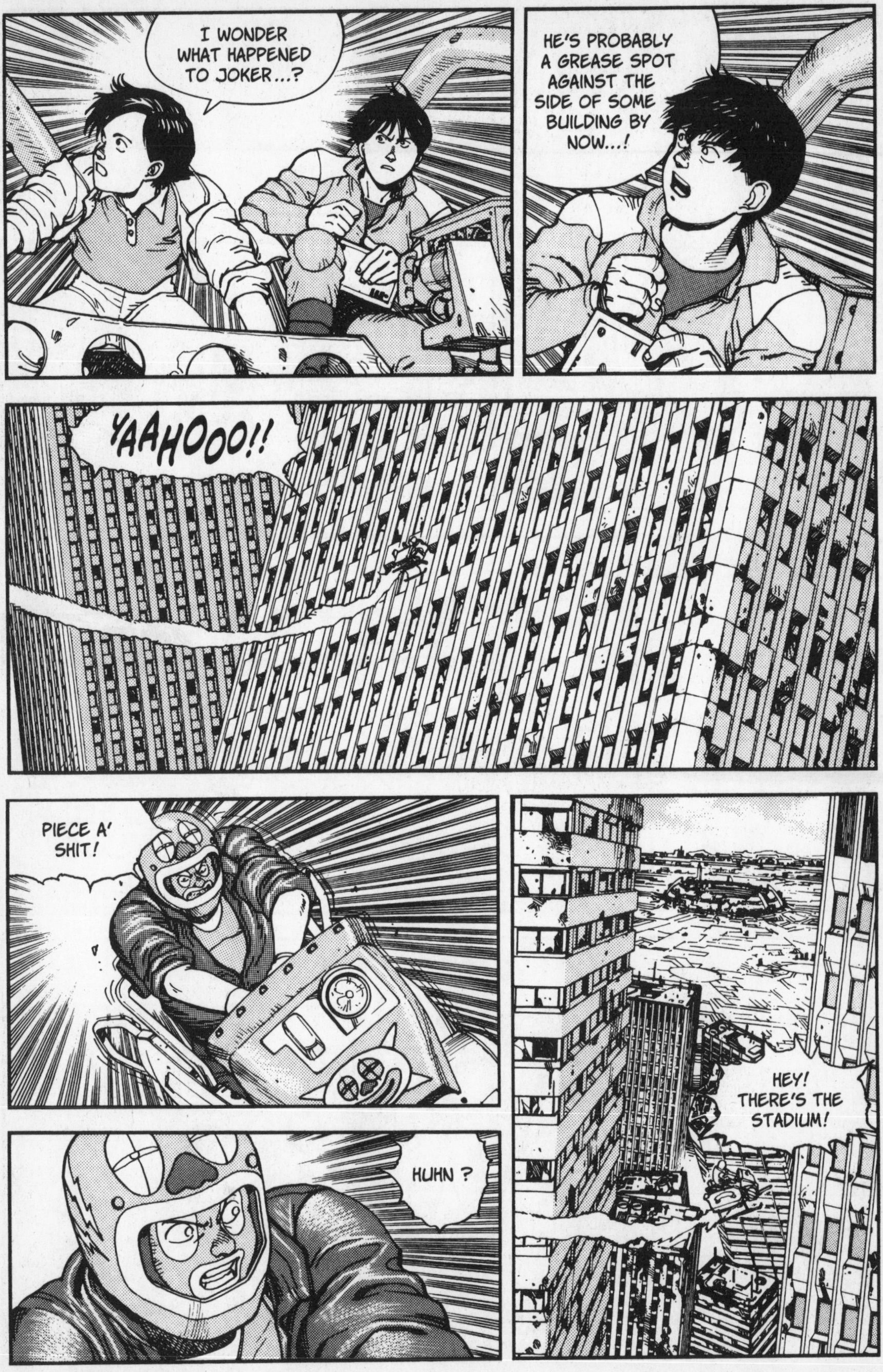
I WONDER WHAT HAPPENED TO JOKER...?
HE'S PROBABLY A GREASE SPOT AGAINST THE SIDE OF SOME BUILDING BY NOW...!
YAAHOOO!!
PIECE A' SHIT!
HUHN ?
HEY! THERE'S THE STADIUM!

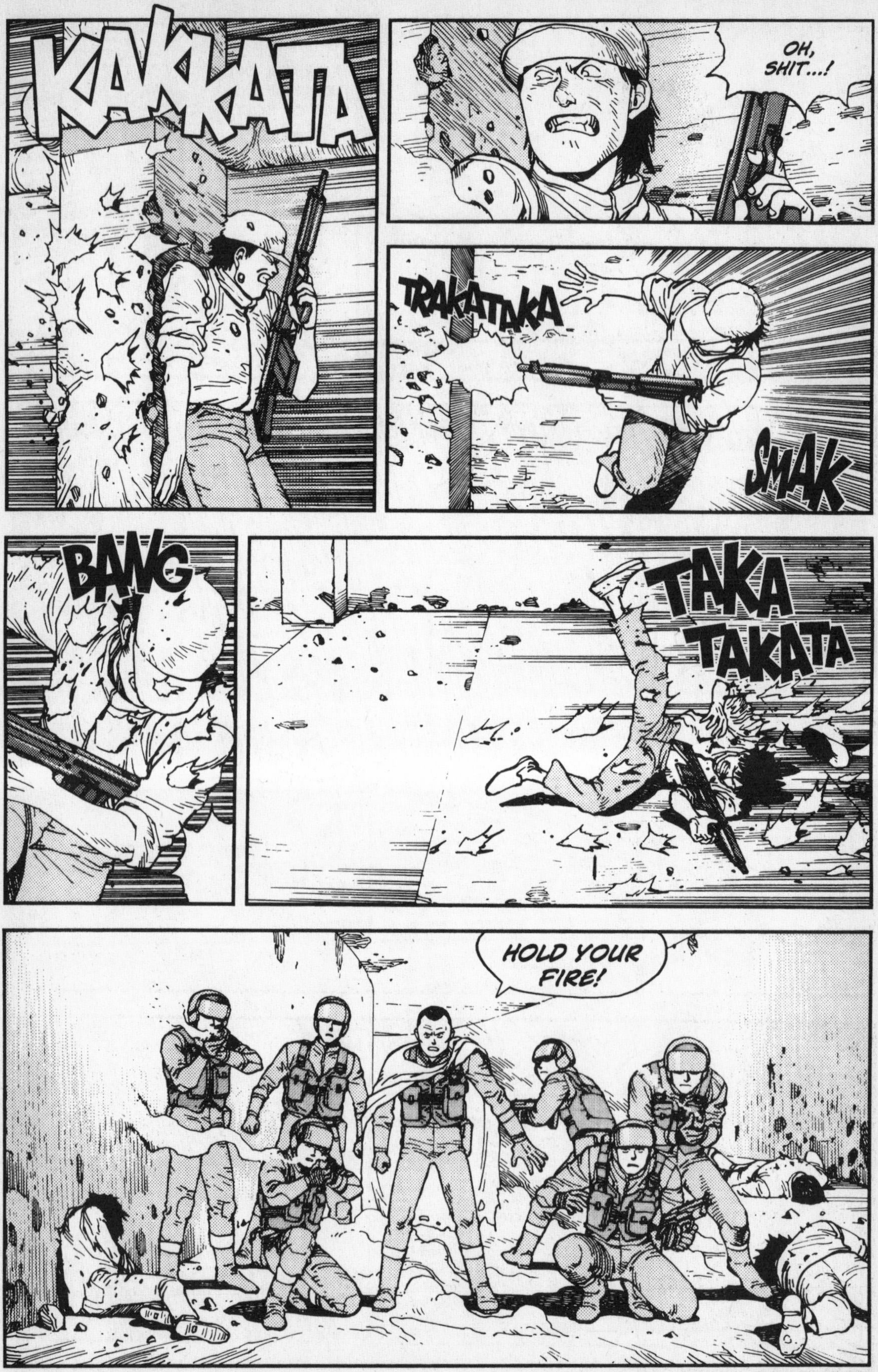
KAKKATA
OH, SHIT...!
TRAKATAKA
SMAK
BANG
TAKA TAKATA
HOLD YOUR FIRE!

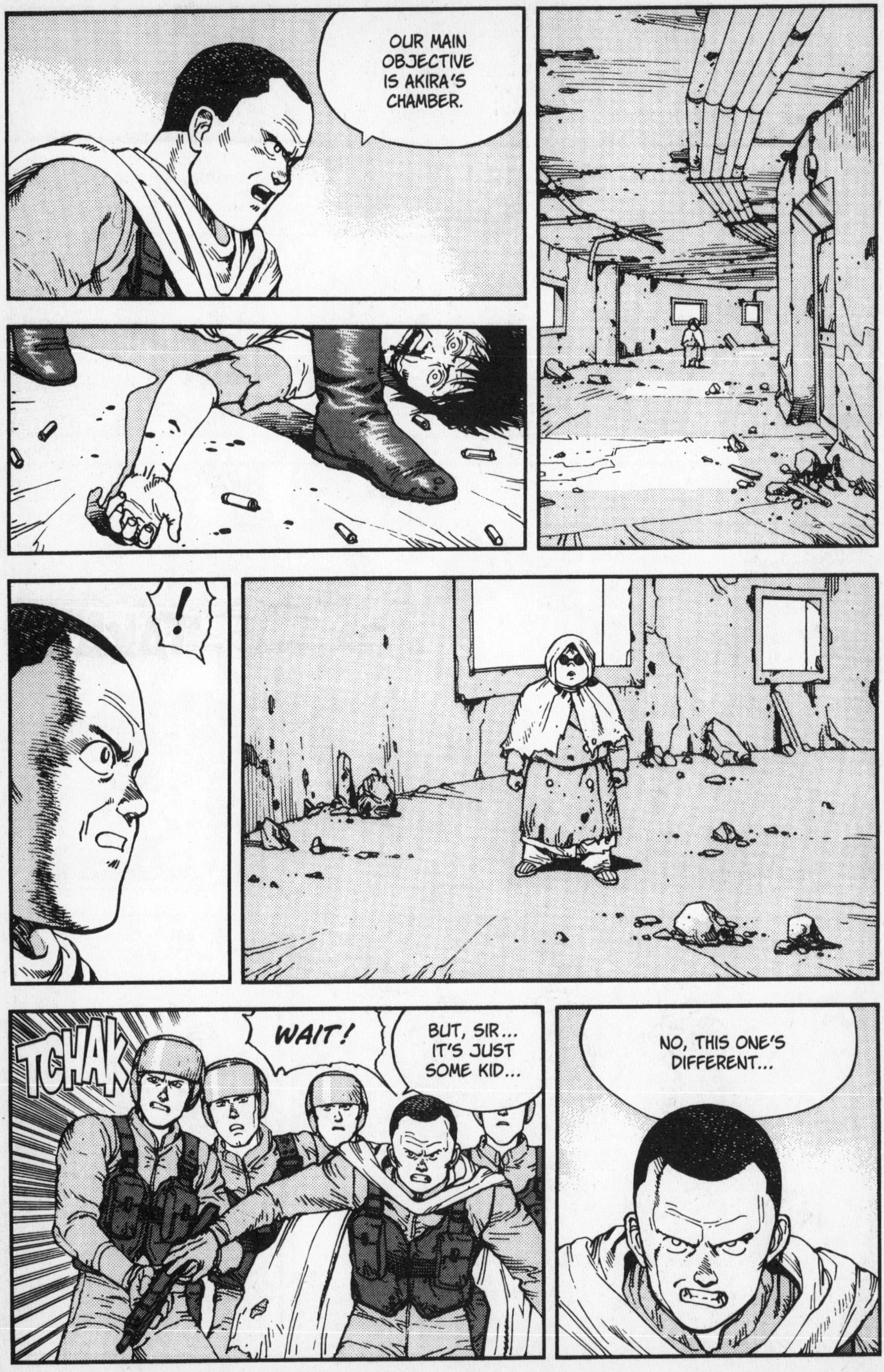
OUR MAIN OBJECTIVE IS AKIRA'S CHAMBER.
!
TCHAK
WAIT!
BUT, SIR... IT'S JUST SOME KID...
NO, THIS ONE'S DIFFERENT...

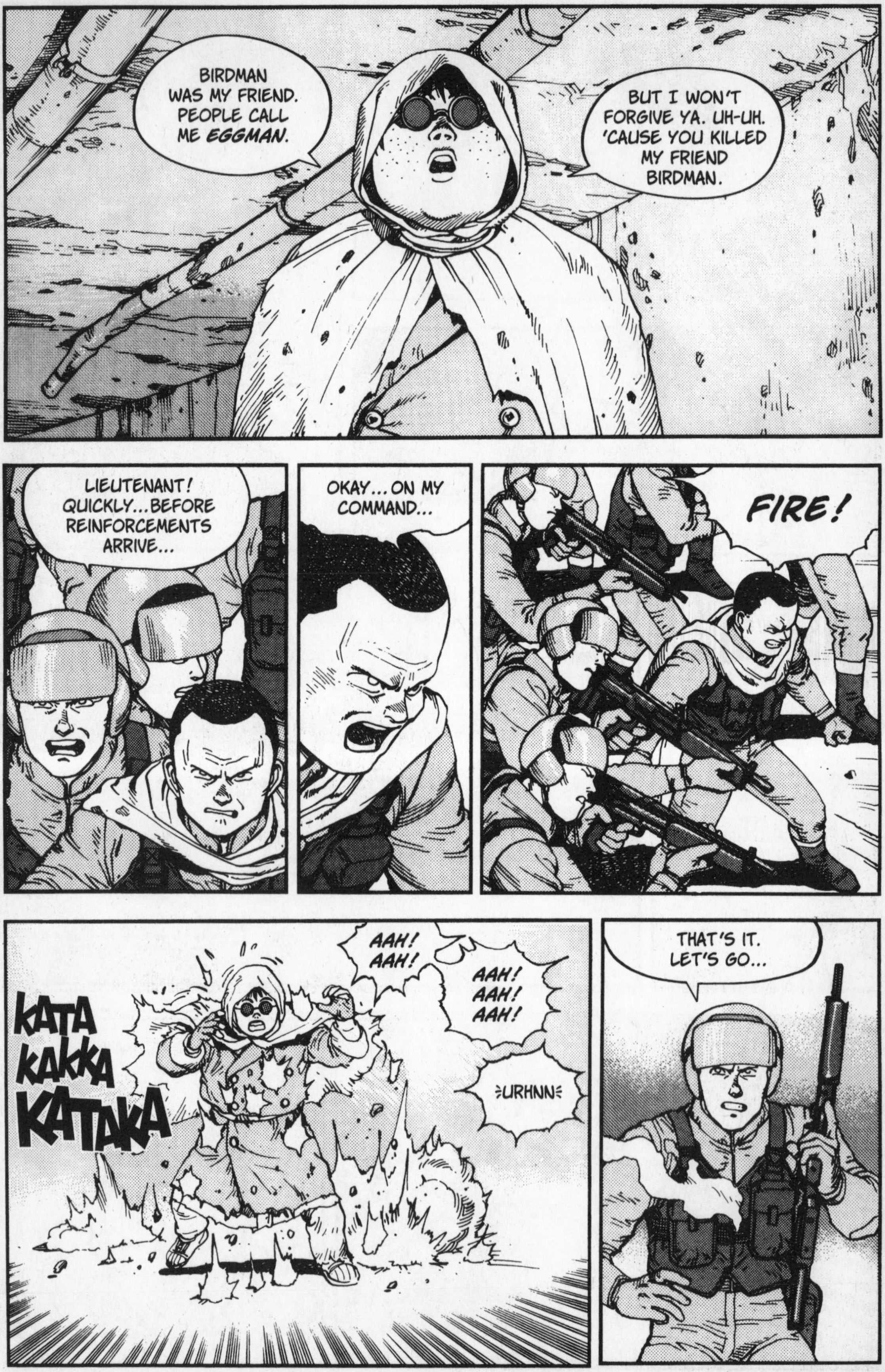
BIRDMAN WAS MY FRIEND. PEOPLE CALL ME EGGMAN.
BUT I WON'T FORGIVE YA. UH-UH. 'CAUSE YOU KILLED MY FRIEND BIRDMAN.
LIEUTENANT! QUICKLY...BEFORE REINFORCEMENTS ARRIVE...
OKAY...ON MY COMMAND...
FIRE!
KATA KAKKA KATAKA
AAH! AAH!
AAH! AAH! AAH!
URHNN
THAT'S IT. LET'S GO...

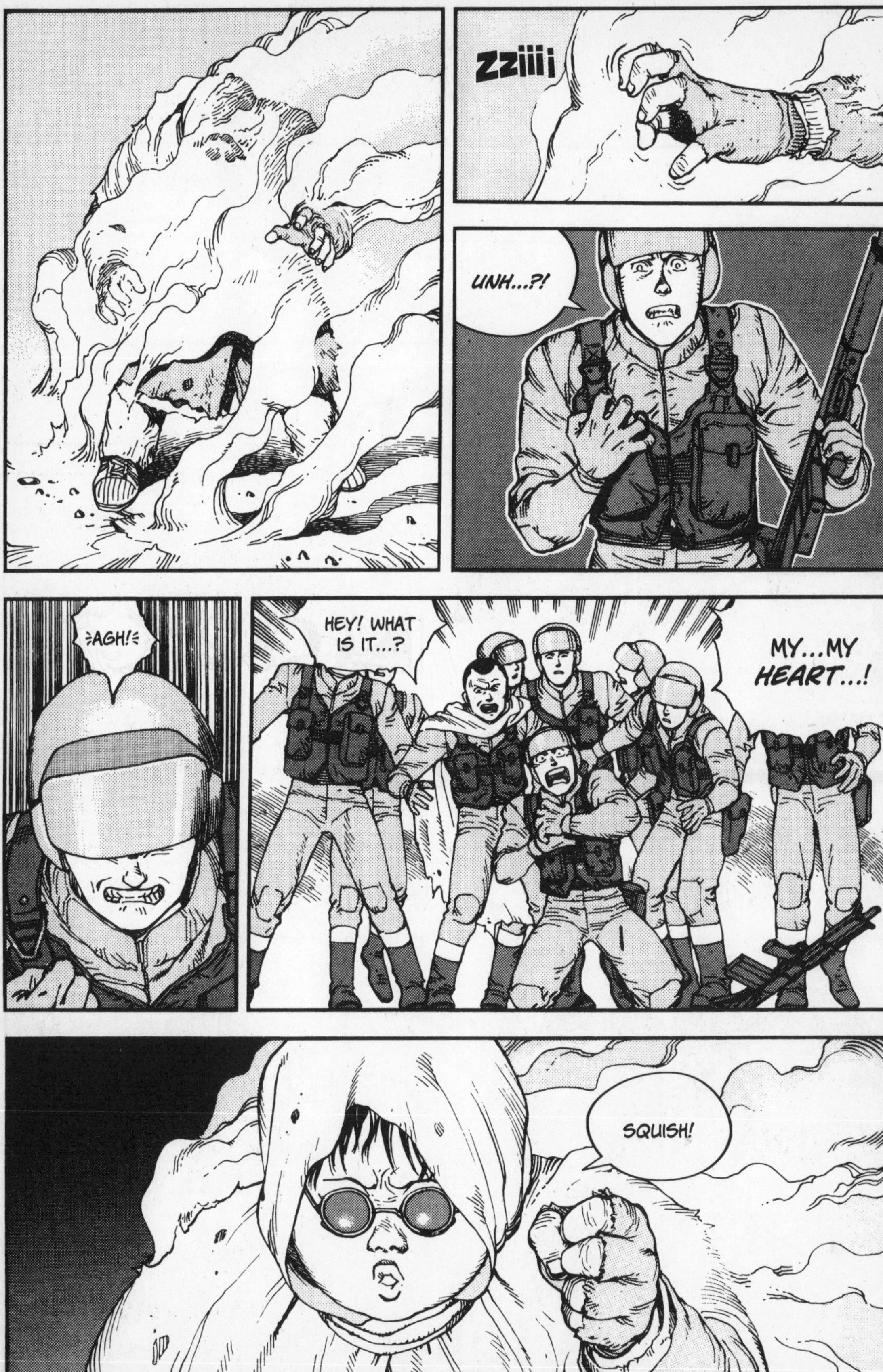
ZZIIII
UNH...?!
AGH!
HEY! WHAT IS IT...?
MY...MY HEART...!
SQUISH!

I TAMED THIS KID WHEN HE WAS STILL PLAYING IN THE RUBBLE...

HAS THE DESTINY I BUILT FOR MYSELF...RUN OUT?

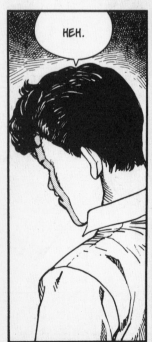

HEH.

THE HELL IT HAS!

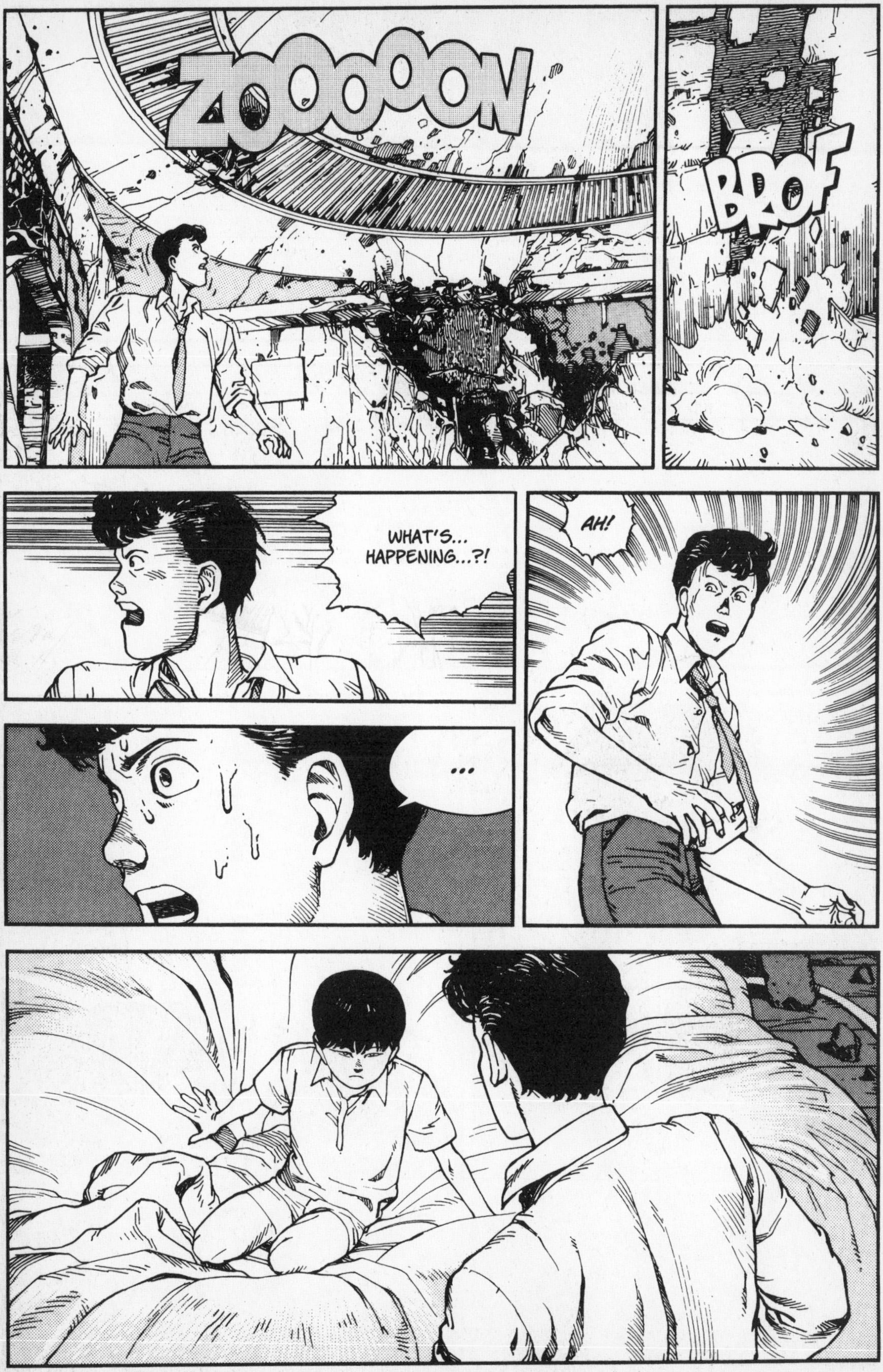

ZOOOOOON
BROF
WHAT'S... HAPPENING...?!
AH!
...

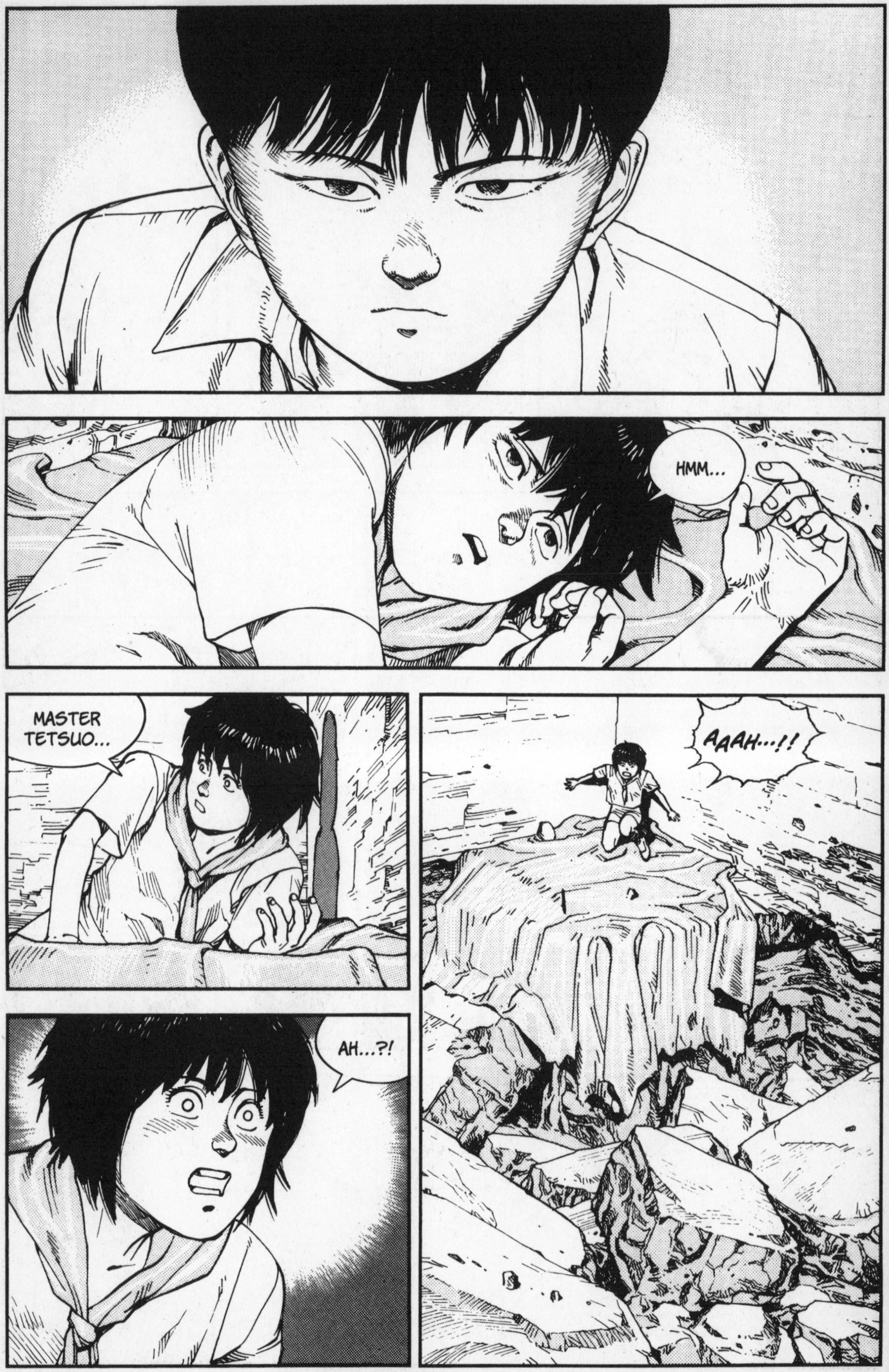
HMM...
MASTER TETSUO...
AAAH...!!
AH...?!

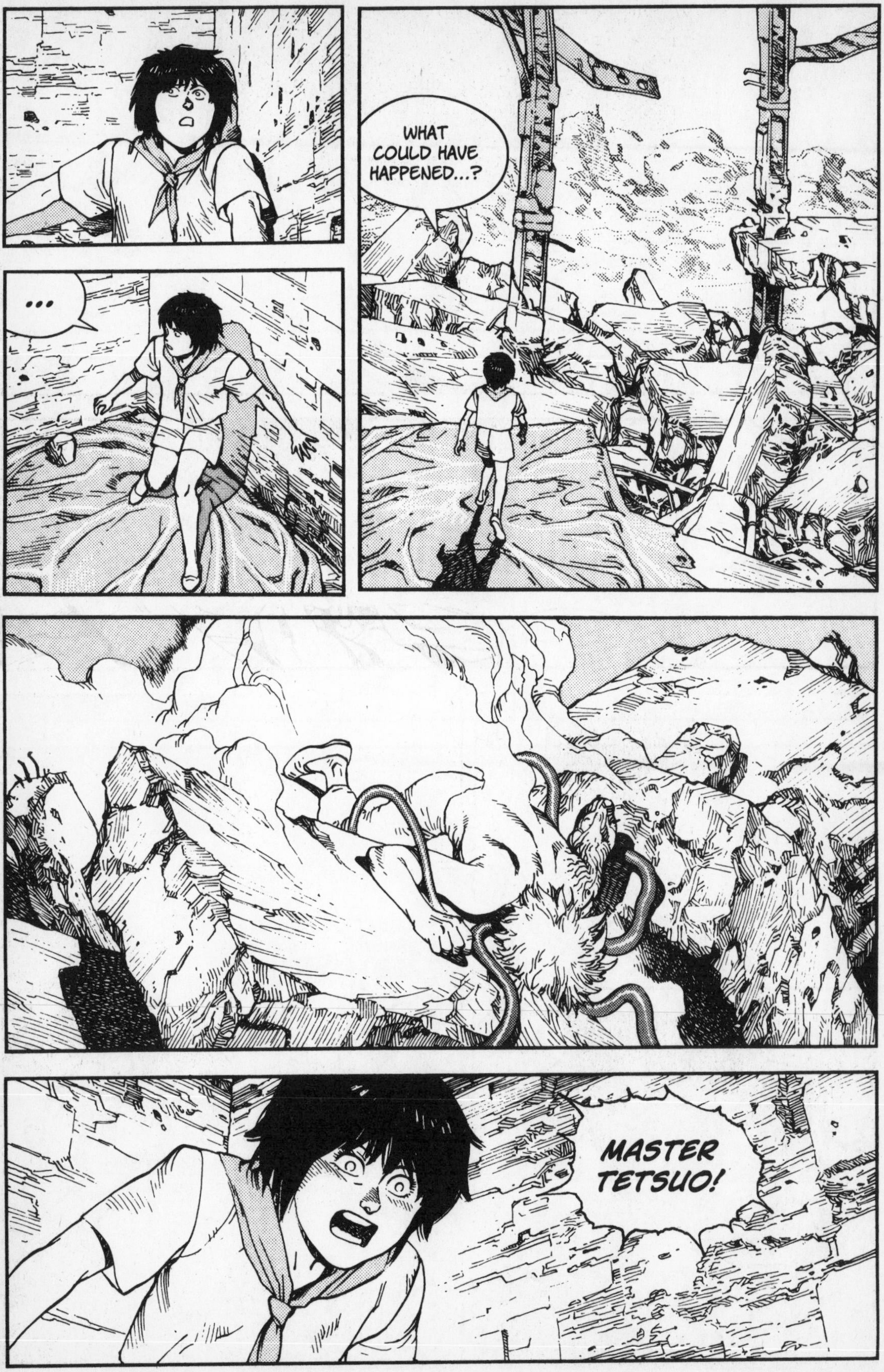
WHAT COULD HAVE HAPPENED...?
...
MASTER TETSUO!

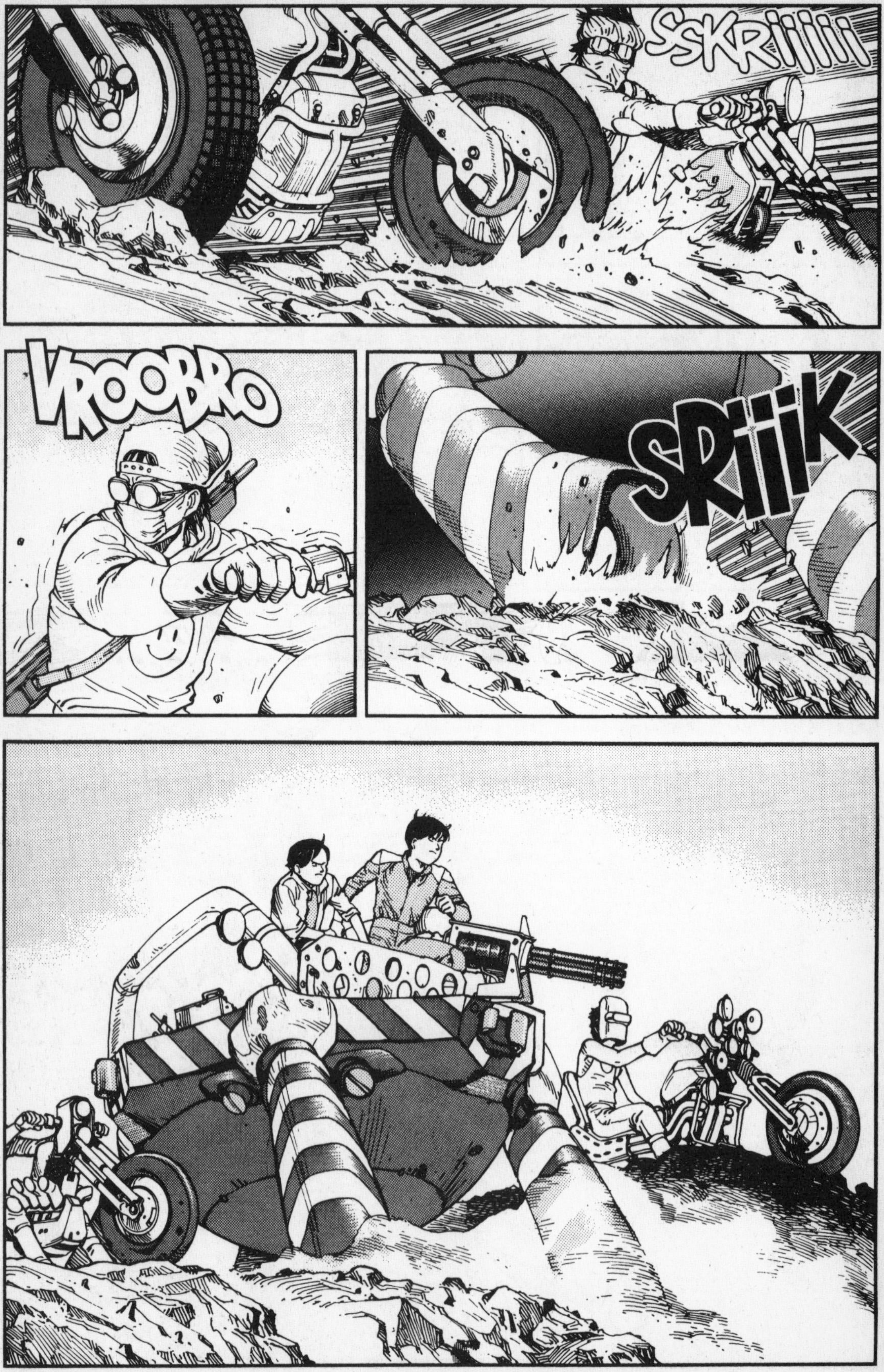
SSKRIIIII
VROOBRO
SRIIIK

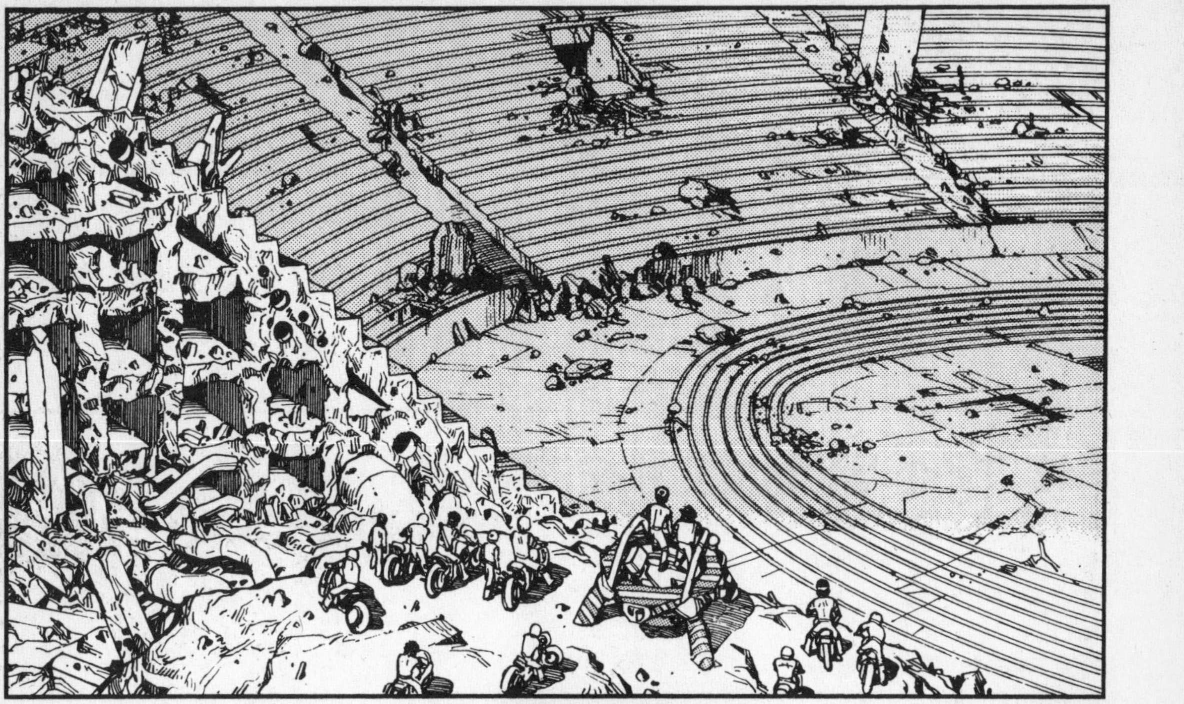

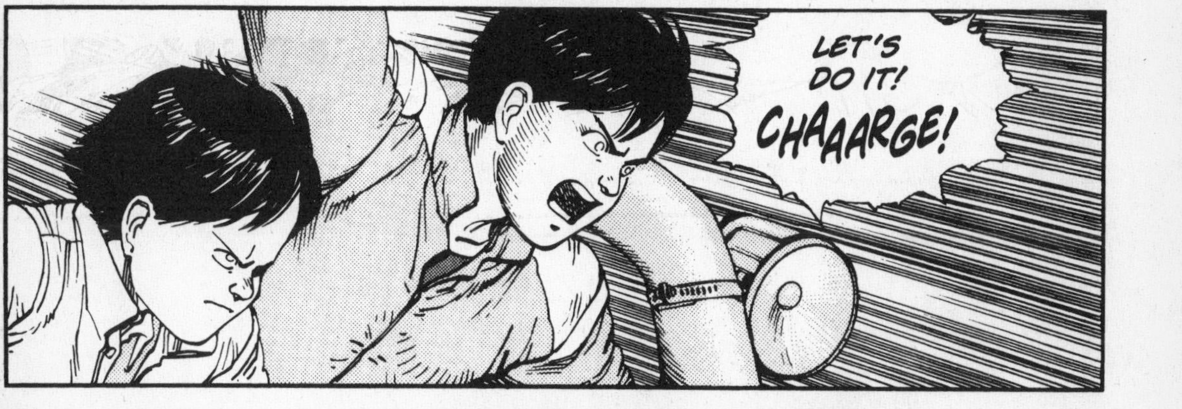
LET'S DO IT! CHAAARGE!

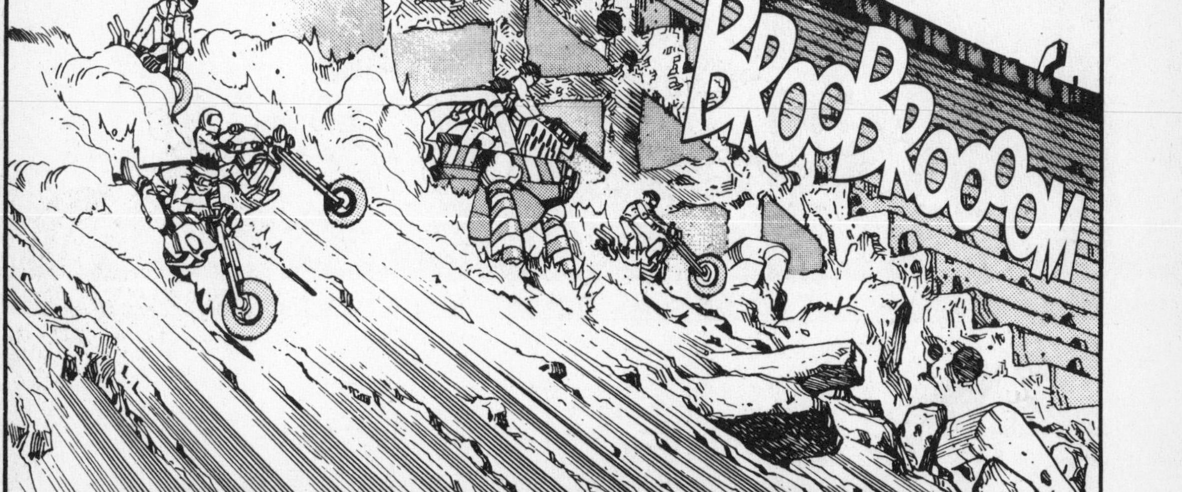
BROOBROOOOM

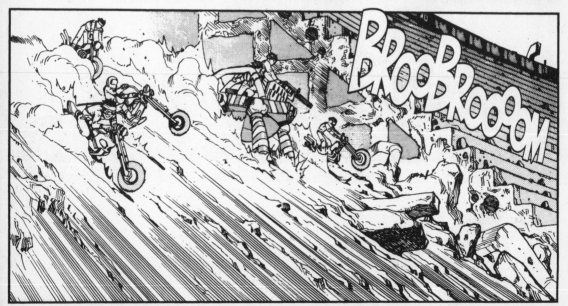

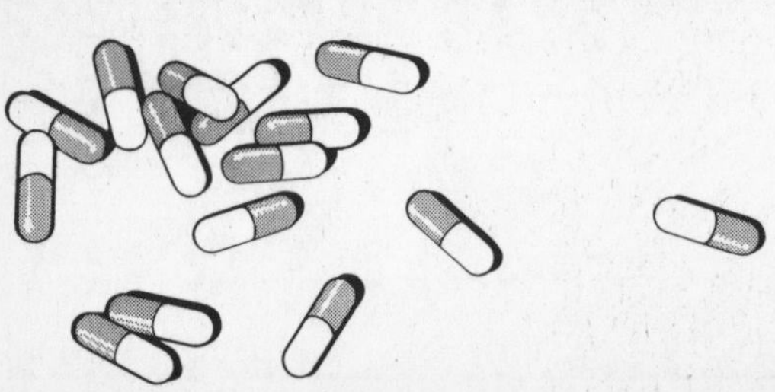

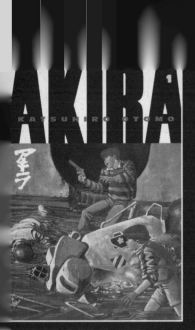
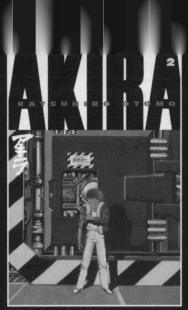
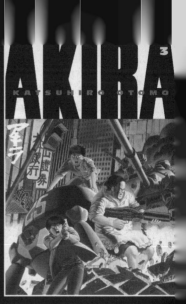

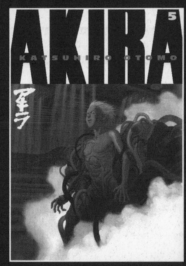
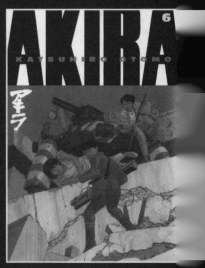

Dark Horse Comics: **Mike Richardson** *publisher* • **Neil Hankerson** *executive vice president* • **Andy Karabatsos** *vice president of finance* • **Randy Stradley** *vice president of publishing* • **Chris Warner** *senior books editor* • **Michael Martens** *vice president of marketing* • **Anita Nelson** *vice president of sales & licensing* • **David Scroggy** *vice president of product development* • **Mark Cox** *art director* • **Dale LaFountain** *vice president of information technology* • **Darlene Vogel** *director of purchasing* • **Ken Lizzi** *general counsel* • **Tom Weddle** *controller*